The Earth and Its Peoples

A GLOBAL HISTORY

EDITION

6

The Earth and Its Peoples

A GLOBAL HISTORY

Volume I: To 1550

Richard W. Bulliet
Columbia University

Pamela Kyle Crossley
Dartmouth College

Daniel R. Headrick
Roosevelt University

Steven W. Hirsch
Tufts University

Lyman L. Johnson
University of North Carolina—Charlotte

David Northrup
Boston College

CENGAGE
Learning

Australia • Brazil • Japan • Korea • Mexico • Singapore • Spain • United Kingdom • United States

CENGAGE
Learning·

**The Earth and Its Peoples: A Global History,
Sixth Edition Volume I: To 1550**
Richard W. Bulliet, Pamela Kyle Crossley,
Daniel R. Headrick, Steven W. Hirsch,
Lyman L. Johnson, David Northrup

Product Director: Suzanne Jeans

Product Manager: Brooke Barbier

Senior Content Developer: Tonya Lobato

Product Assistant: Katie Coaster

Media Developer: Kate MacLean

Marketing Development Manager:
  Kyle Zimmerman

Senior Content Project Manager:
  Carol Newman

Associate Art Director: Hannah Wellman

Manufacturing Planner: Sandee Milewski

Senior Rights Acquisition Specialist:
  Jennifer Meyer Dare

Production Service/Compositor:
  Lachina Publishing Services

Text Designer: Diane Beasley

Cover Designer: Wing Ngan, Ink Design, Inc.

Cover Image: Nok sculpture from Nigeria,
  probably a terracotta base for a large
  statue. Scenes of daily life, harvest, mothers
  with children. The larger figures carry a
  serpent on their raised arms. Terracotta,
  H:50 cm. Inv.70.1998.11.2. Image #
  ART209814/ Musee du Quai Branly, Paris,
  France / Erich Lessing / Art Resource, NY

For product information and technology assistance, contact us at
Cengage Learning Customer & Sales Support, 1-800-354-9706

For permission to use material from this text or product,
submit all requests online at **www.cengage.com/permissions**.
Further permissions questions can be emailed to
permissionrequest@cengage.com.

Library of Congress Control Number: 2013932724

Student Edition:

ISBN-13: 978-1-285-43691-3

ISBN-10: 1-285-43691-1

Cengage Learning
200 First Stamford Place, 4th Floor
Stamford, CT 06902
USA

Cengage Learning is a leading provider of customized learning solutions with office locations around the globe, including Singapore, the United Kingdom, Australia, Mexico, Brazil, and Japan. Locate your local office at **international.cengage.com/region**

Cengage Learning products are represented in Canada by Nelson Education, Ltd.

For your course and learning solutions, visit **www.cengage.com**.

Purchase any of our products at your local college store or at our preferred online store **www.cengagebrain.com**.

Instructors: Please visit **login.cengage.com** and log in to access instructor-specific resources.

Printed in the United States of America
1 2 3 4 5 6 7 17 16 15 14 13

Brief Contents

PART I **The Emergence of Human Communities, to 500 B.C.E.** 2

1 Nature, Humanity, and History, to 3500 B.C.E. 4
2 The First River-Valley Civilizations, 3500–1500 B.C.E. 26
3 The Mediterranean and Middle East, 2000–500 B.C.E. 52
4 New Civilizations Outside the West Asian Core Area, 2300 B.C.E.–350 C.E. 82

PART II **The Formation of New Cultural Communities, 1000 B.C.E.–400 C.E.** 110

5 Greece and Iran, 1000–30 B.C.E. 112
6 An Age of Empires: Rome and Han China, 753 B.C.E.–330 C.E. 142
7 India and Southeast Asia, 1500 B.C.E.–1025 C.E. 168
8 Peoples and Civilizations of the Americas, from 1200 B.C.E. 192

PART III **Growth and Interaction of Cultural Communities, 300 B.C.E.–1200 C.E.** 220

9 Networks of Communication and Exchange, 300 B.C.E.–1100 C.E. 222
10 The Sasanid Empire and the Rise of Islam, 200–1200 242
11 Christian Societies Emerge in Europe, 600–1200 266
12 Inner and East Asia, 400–1200 290

PART IV **Interregional Patterns of Culture and Contact, 1200–1550** 310

13 Mongol Eurasia and Its Aftermath, 1200–1550 312
14 Latin Europe, 1200–1500 338
15 Southern Empires, Southern Seas, 1200–1500 360
16 The Maritime Revolution, to 1550 386

Contents

MAPS xvii

ENVIRONMENT + TECHNOLOGY xix

DIVERSITY + DOMINANCE xix

MATERIAL CULTURE xx

ISSUES IN WORLD HISTORY xx

PREFACE xxi

ABOUT THE AUTHORS xxx

NOTE ON SPELLING AND USAGE xxxi

PART I   The Emergence of Human Communities, to 500 B.C.E.   2

1   Nature, Humanity, and History, to 3500 B.C.E.   4

AFRICAN GENESIS 5

Interpreting the Evidence 5 • Human Evolution 6 • Migrations from Africa 8

TECHNOLOGY AND CULTURE IN THE ICE AGE 11

Food Gathering and Stone Tools 11 • Gender Roles and Social Life 14 • Hearths and Cultural Expressions 15

THE AGRICULTURAL REVOLUTIONS 16

The Transition to Plant Cultivation 16 • Domesticated Animals and Pastoralism 19 • Agriculture and Ecological Crisis 20

LIFE IN NEOLITHIC COMMUNITIES 20

The Triumph of Food Producers 21 • Cultural Expressions 21 • Early Towns and Specialists 22

CONCLUSION 24

KEY TERMS 24 • SUGGESTED READING 25 • SUGGESTED VIEWING 25

● DIVERSITY + DOMINANCE: *Cave Art* 12

● ENVIRONMENT + TECHNOLOGY: *The Iceman* 16

2   The First River-Valley Civilizations, 3500–1500 B.C.E.   26

MESOPOTAMIA 29

Settled Agriculture in an Unstable Landscape 29 • Sumerians and Semites 30 • Cities, Kings, and Trade 31 • Mesopotamian Society 33 • Gods, Priests, and Temples 34 • Technology and Science 35

EGYPT 39

The Land of Egypt: "Gift of the Nile" 39 • Divine Kingship 41 • Administration and Communication 42 The People of Egypt 43 • Belief and Knowledge 44

THE INDUS VALLEY CIVILIZATION 46
Natural Environment 46 • Material Culture 47 • Transformation of the Indus Valley Civilization 49
CONCLUSION 49
KEY TERMS 50 • SUGGESTED READING 51

● **DIVERSITY + DOMINANCE:** *Violence and Order in the Babylonian New Year's Festival* 36
● **MATERIAL CULTURE:** *Lamps and Candles* 38
● **ENVIRONMENT + TECHNOLOGY:** *Environmental Stress in the Indus Valley* 48

3 The Mediterranean and Middle East, 2000–500 B.C.E.

52

THE COSMOPOLITAN MIDDLE EAST, 1700–1100 B.C.E. 54
Western Asia 54 • New Kingdom Egypt 56 • Commerce and Communication 58
THE AEGEAN WORLD, 2000–1100 B.C.E. 60
Minoan Crete 60 • Mycenaean Greece 60 • The Fall of Late Bronze Age Civilizations 62
THE ASSYRIAN EMPIRE, 911–612 B.C.E. 64
God and King 64 • Conquest and Control 64 • Assyrian Society and Culture 65
ISRAEL, 2000–500 B.C.E. 67
Origins, Exodus, and Settlement 67 • Rise of the Monarchy 69 • Fragmentation and Dispersal 70
PHOENICIA AND THE MEDITERRANEAN, 1200–500 B.C.E. 71
The Phoenician City-States 71 • Expansion into the Mediterranean 76 • Carthage's Commercial Empire 77
• War and Religion 78
FAILURE AND TRANSFORMATION, 750–550 B.C.E. 79
CONCLUSION 80
KEY TERMS 81 • SUGGESTED READING 81

● **DIVERSITY + DOMINANCE:** *Protests Against the Ruling Class in Israel and Babylonia* 72
● **ENVIRONMENT + TECHNOLOGY:** *Ancient Textiles and Dyes* 75

4 New Civilizations Outside the West Asian Core Area, 2300 B.C.E.–350 C.E.

82

EARLY CHINA, 2000–221 B.C.E. 84
Geography and Resources 84 • The Late Neolithic: Artifacts and Legends 85 • The Shang Period, 1766–1045 B.C.E. 85
• The Zhou Period, 1045–221 B.C.E. 88 • Confucianism, Daoism, and Chinese Society 91
• The Warring States Period, 481–221 B.C.E. 95
NUBIA, 2300 B.C.E.–350 C.E. 95
Early Cultures and Egyptian Domination 2300–1100 B.C.E. 96 • The Kingdom of Meroë, 800 B.C.E.–350 C.E. 97

PASTORAL NOMADS OF THE EURASIAN STEPPES, 1000–100 B.C.E. 98
Early Nomadism 98 • Steppe Nomads 99 • The Scythians 100 • China and the Nomads 101

CELTIC EUROPE, 1000–50 B.C.E. 102
The Spread of the Celts 102 • Celtic Society 103 • Belief and Knowledge 104

CONCLUSION 105
Environment and Organization 105 • Religion and Power 106 • A Tale of Two Hemispheres 106

KEY TERMS 107 • SUGGESTED READING 107

● **ENVIRONMENT + TECHNOLOGY:** *Divination in Ancient Societies* 88

● **DIVERSITY + DOMINANCE:** *Human Nature and Good Government in the* Analects *of Confucius and the Legalist Writings of Han Fei* 92

● **ISSUES IN WORLD HISTORY:** *Animal Domestication* 108

PART II The Formation of New Cultural Communities, 1000 B.C.E.–400 C.E. 110

5 Greece and Iran, 1000–30 B.C.E. 112

ANCIENT IRAN, 1000–500 B.C.E. 113
Geography and Resources 114 • The Rise of the Persian Empire 115 • Imperial Organization 117 • Ideology and Religion 118

THE RISE OF THE GREEKS, 1000–500 B.C.E. 120
Geography and Resources 121 • The Emergence of the Polis 122 • New Intellectual Currents 126 • Athens and Sparta 128

THE STRUGGLE OF PERSIA AND GREECE, 546–323 B.C.E. 129
Early Encounters 129 • The Height of Athenian Power 130 • Inequality in Classical Greece 132 • Failure of the City-State and Triumph of the Macedonians 133

THE HELLENISTIC SYNTHESIS, 323–30 B.C.E. 136

CONCLUSION 140

KEY TERMS 141 • SUGGESTED READING 141

● **DIVERSITY + DOMINANCE:** *Persian and Greek Perceptions of Kingship* 120

● **MATERIAL CULTURE:** *Wine and Beer in the Ancient World* 134

● **ENVIRONMENT + TECHNOLOGY:** *Ancient Astronomy* 138

6　An Age of Empires: Rome and Han China, 753 B.C.E.–330 C.E.　142

ROME'S CREATION OF A MEDITERRANEAN EMPIRE, 753 B.C.E.–330 C.E. 144
A Republic of Farmers, 753–31 B.C.E. 144 • Expansion in Italy and the Mediterranean 147
• The Failure of the Republic 148 • The Roman Principate, 31 B.C.E.–330 C.E. 149 • An Urban Empire 150
• The Rise of Christianity 153 • Technology and Transformation 154

THE ORIGINS OF IMPERIAL CHINA, 221 B.C.E.–220 C.E. 158
The Qin Unification of China, 221–206 B.C.E. 158 • The Long Reign of the Han, 202 B.C.E.–220 C.E. 159
• Chinese Society 162 • New Forms of Thought and Belief 163 • Decline of the Han 164

CONCLUSION 165

KEY TERMS 167 • SUGGESTED READING 167

● **DIVERSITY + DOMINANCE:** *Socioeconomic Mobility, Winners and Losers in Imperial Rome and Han China* 150

● **ENVIRONMENT + TECHNOLOGY:** *Ancient Glass* 156

7　India and Southeast Asia, 1500 B.C.E.–1025 C.E.　168

FOUNDATIONS OF INDIAN CIVILIZATION, 1500 B.C.E.–300 C.E. 170
The Indian Subcontinent 170 • The Vedic Age 171 • Challenges to the Old Order: Jainism and Buddhism 173
• The Evolution of Hinduism 175

IMPERIAL EXPANSION AND COLLAPSE, 324 B.C.E.–650 C.E. 178
• The Mauryan Empire, 324–184 B.C.E. 178 • Commerce and Culture in an Era of Political Fragmentation 179
• The Gupta Empire, 320–550 C.E. 181

SOUTHEAST ASIA, 50–1025 C.E. 186
Early Civilization 186 • The Srivijayan Kingdom 188

CONCLUSION 190

KEY TERMS 191 • SUGGESTED READING 191 • SUGGESTED VIEWING 191

● **ENVIRONMENT + TECHNOLOGY:** *Indian Mathematics* 182

● **DIVERSITY + DOMINANCE:** *Relations Between Women and Men in the* Kama Sutra *and the* Arthashastra 184

8 Peoples and Civilizations of the Americas, from 1200 B.C.E.   192

FORMATIVE CIVILIZATIONS OF THE OLMEC AND CHAVÍN, 1200–200 B.C.E. 194
The Mesoamerican Olmec, 1200–400 B.C.E. 194 • Early South American Civilization: Chavín, 900–200 B.C.E. 197

CLASSIC-ERA CULTURE AND SOCIETY IN MESOAMERICA, 200–900 199 • Teotihuacan 199
The Maya 200

THE POSTCLASSIC PERIOD IN MESOAMERICA, 900–1300 203
The Toltecs 203 • Cholula 205

NORTHERN PEOPLES 206
Southwestern Desert Cultures 206 • Mound Builders: The Hopewell and Mississippian Cultures 207

ANDEAN CIVILIZATIONS, 200–1400 209
Cultural Response to Environmental Challenge 209 • The Early Intermediate Period Moche 210
• Tiwanaku and Wari 211 • Chimú 215

CONCLUSION 216
KEY TERMS 217 • SUGGESTED READING 217

● **DIVERSITY + DOMINANCE:** *Burials as Historical Texts* 212

● **ENVIRONMENT + TECHNOLOGY:** *The Maya Writing System* 214

● **ISSUES IN WORLD HISTORY:** *Oral Societies and the Consequences of Literacy* 218

PART III   **Growth and Interaction of Cultural Communities, 300 B.C.E.–1200 C.E.**   220

9 Networks of Communication and Exchange, 300 B.C.E.–1100 C.E.   222

THE SILK ROAD 224
Origins and Operations 224 • Nomadism in Central and Inner Asia 225 • The Impact of the Silk Road 226

THE INDIAN OCEAN MARITIME SYSTEM 227
Origins of Contact and Trade 230 • The Impact of Indian Ocean Trade 230

ROUTES ACROSS THE SAHARA 231
Early Saharan Cultures 231 • Trade Across the Sahara 234

SUB-SAHARAN AFRICA 235
A Challenging Geography 235 • The Development of Cultural Unity 235 • African Cultural Characteristics 236
• The Advent of Iron and the Bantu Migrations 236

THE SPREAD OF IDEAS 237
Ideas and Material Evidence 237 • The Spread of Buddhism 238 • The Spread of Christianity 239

CONCLUSION 240

KEY TERMS 241 • SUGGESTED READING 241

● **DIVERSITY + DOMINANCE:** *Travel Accounts of Africa and India* 228
● **ENVIRONMENT + TECHNOLOGY:** *Camel Saddles* 234

10   The Sasanid Empire and the Rise of Islam, 200–1200   242

THE SASANID EMPIRE, 224–651 244
Politics and Society 244 • Religion and Empire 245

THE ORIGINS OF ISLAM 246
The Arabian Peninsula Before Muhammad 246 • Muhammad in Mecca and Medina 247
• Formation of the Umma 248 • Succession to Muhammad 249

THE RISE AND FALL OF THE CALIPHATE, 632–1258 250
The Islamic Conquests, 634–711 250 • The Umayyad and Early Abbasid Caliphates, 661–850 251
• Political Fragmentation, 850–1050 251 • Assault from Within and Without, 1050–1258 254

ISLAMIC CIVILIZATION 256
Law and Dogma 257 • Converts and Cities 257 • Women and Islam 259 • The Recentering of Islam 261

CONCLUSION 264

KEY TERMS 265 • SUGGESTED READING 265

● **DIVERSITY + DOMINANCE:** *Secretaries, Turks, and Beggars* 260
● **ENVIRONMENT + TECHNOLOGY:** *Chemistry* 262
● **MATERIAL CULTURE:** *Head Coverings* 263

11   Christian Societies Emerge in Europe, 600–1200   266

THE BYZANTINE EMPIRE, 600–1200 268
An Empire Beleaguered 268 • Society and Urban Life 269 • Cultural Achievements 270

EARLY MEDIEVAL EUROPE, 600–1000 271
The Time of Insecurity 271 • A Self-Sufficient Economy 273 • Early Medieval Society in the West 274

THE WESTERN CHURCH 275
Politics and the Church 276 • Monasticism 278

KIEVAN RUSSIA, 900–1200 281
The Rise of the Kievan Empire 281 • Society and Culture 283

WESTERN EUROPE REVIVES, 1000–1200 283
The Role of Technology 283 • Cities and the Rebirth of the Trade 284

THE CRUSADES, 1095–1204 285
The Roots of the Crusades 285 • The Impact of the Crusades 286

CONCLUSION 287

KEY TERMS 288 • SUGGESTED READING 288

● **ENVIRONMENT + TECHNOLOGY:** *Iron Production* 276

● **DIVERSITY + DOMINANCE:** *The Struggle for Christian Morality* 278

12 Inner and East Asia, 400–1200   290

THE SUI AND TANG EMPIRES, 581–755 291

Chang'an: Metropolis at the Center of East Asia 292 • Buddhism and the Tang Empire 292 • Upheavals and Repression, 750-879 293 • The End of the Tang Empire, 879-907 297

CHINA AND ITS RIVALS 298

The Liao and Jin Challenge 298 • Song Industries 299 • Economy and Society in Song China 300

NEW KINGDOMS IN EAST ASIA 304

Chinese Influences 304 • Korea 304 • Japan 305 • Vietnam 307

CONCLUSION 308

KEY TERMS 309 • SUGGESTED READING 309

● **DIVERSITY + DOMINANCE:** *Law and Society in China and Japan* 296

● **ENVIRONMENT + TECHNOLOGY:** *Writing in East Asia, 400–1200* 306

PART IV   Interregional Patterns of Culture and Contact, 1200–1550   310

13 Mongol Eurasia and Its Aftermath, 1200–1550   312

THE RISE OF THE MONGOLS, 1200–1260 314

Nomadism in Central and Inner Asia 314 • The Mongol Conquests, 1215-1283 314 • Overland Trade and Disease 318

THE MONGOLS AND ISLAM, 1260–1500 320

Mongol Rivalry 320 • Islam and the State 321 • Culture and Science in Islamic Eurasia 321

REGIONAL RESPONSES IN WESTERN EURASIA 324

Russia and Rule from Afar 324 • New States in Eastern Europe and Anatolia 325

MONGOL DOMINATION IN CHINA, 1271–1368 326

The Yuan Empire, 1271–1368 327 • The Fall of the Yuan Empire 328

THE EARLY MING EMPIRE, 1368–1500 329

Ming China on a Mongol Foundation 329 • Technology and Population 330 • The Ming Achievement 331

CENTRALIZATION AND MILITARISM IN EAST ASIA, 1200–1500 333

Korea from the Mongols to the Choson Dynasty, 1231–1500 333 • Political Transformation in Japan, 1274–1500 334
• The Emergence of Vietnam, 1200–1500 336

CONCLUSION 336

KEY TERMS 337 • SUGGESTED READING 337

● **DIVERSITY + DOMINANCE:** *Observations of Mongol Life* 318

● **ENVIRONMENT + TECHNOLOGY:** *From Gunpowder to Guns* 332

14 Latin Europe, 1200–1500

RURAL GROWTH AND CRISIS 339

Peasants, Population, and Plague 339 • Social Rebellion 341 • Mills and Mines 342

URBAN REVIVAL 343

Trading Cities 343 • Civic Life 346 • Gothic Cathedrals 347

LEARNING, LITERATURE, AND THE RENAISSANCE 350

The Renaissance 350 • Humanists and Printers 352 • Renaissance Artists 353

POLITICAL AND MILITARY TRANSFORMATIONS 354

Monarchs, Nobles, and the Church 354 • The Hundred Years' War 355 • New Monarchies in France and England 357
• Iberian Unification 357 • The Ottoman Frontier 358

CONCLUSION 359

KEY TERMS 359 • SUGGESTED READING 359

● **DIVERSITY + DOMINANCE:** *Persecution and Protection of Jews, 1272–1349* 348

● **ENVIRONMENT + TECHNOLOGY:** *The Clock* 350

15 Southern Empires, Southern Seas, 1200–1500   360

TROPICAL AFRICA AND ASIA 361
The Tropical Environment in Africa and Asia 362 • Human Ecosystems 362 • Water Systems and Irrigation 363 • Mineral Resources 364

NEW ISLAMIC EMPIRES 366
Mali in the Western Sudan 366 • The Delhi Sultanate in India 368

INDIAN OCEAN TRADE 372
Monsoon Mariners 372 • Africa: The Swahili Coast and Zimbabwe 374 • Arabia: Aden and the Red Sea 375 • India: Gujarat and the Malabar Coast 375 • Southeast Asia 376

SOCIAL AND CULTURAL CHANGE 377
Architecture, Learning, and Religion 377 • Social and Gender Distinctions 378

THE WESTERN HEMISPHERE 379
Mesoamerica: The Aztecs 379 • The Andes: The Inka 382

CONCLUSION 383

KEY TERMS 384 • SUGGESTED READING 384

● **MATERIAL CULTURE:** *Salt* 365

● **DIVERSITY + DOMINANCE:** *Personal Styles of Rule in India and Mali* 370

● **ENVIRONMENT + TECHNOLOGY:** *The Indian Ocean Dhow* 373

16 The Maritime Revolution, to 1550   386

GLOBAL MARITIME EXPANSION BEFORE 1450 388
The Indian Ocean 388 • The Pacific Ocean 391 • The Atlantic Ocean 392

EUROPEAN EXPANSION, 1400–1550 394
Motives for Exploration 394 • Portuguese Voyages 394 • Spanish Voyages 396

ENCOUNTERS WITH EUROPE, 1450–1550 399
Western Africa 399 • Eastern Africa 401 • Indian Ocean States 402 • The Americas 406

CONCLUSION 409

KEY TERMS 410 • SUGGESTED READING 411

● **ENVIRONMENT + TECHNOLOGY:** *Vasco da Gama's Fleet* 398

● **DIVERSITY + DOMINANCE:** *Kongo's Christian King* 402

● **ISSUES IN WORLD HISTORY:** *Climate and Population to 1500* 412

INDEX   I-1

Maps

1.1 Human Dispersal to 10,000 Years Ago 9
1.2 Early Centers of Plant and Animal Domestication 18
2.1 River-Valley Civilizations, 3500–1500 B.C.E. 28
2.2 Mesopotamia 30
2.3 Ancient Egypt 40
3.1 The Middle East in the Second Millennium B.C.E. 54
3.2 Minoan and Mycenaean Civilizations of the Aegean 61
3.3 The Assyrian Empire 65
3.4 Phoenicia and Israel 68
3.5 Colonization of the Mediterranean 76
4.1 China in the Shang and Zhou Periods, 1750–221 B.C.E. 87
4.2 Ancient Nubia 96
4.3 Pastoral Nomads of the Eurasian Steppes 99
4.4 The Celtic Peoples 103
5.1 The Persian Empire Between 550 and 522 B.C.E. 114
5.2 Ancient Greece 123
5.3 Hellenistic Civilization 137
6.1 The Roman Empire 146
6.2 Han China 160
7.1 Ancient India 172
7.2 Southeast Asia 187
8.1 Olmec and Chavín Civilizations 196
8.2 Maya Civilization, 250–1400 C.E. 200
8.3 Postclassic Mesoamerica 204
8.4 Culture Areas of North America 207
8.5 Andean Civilizations, 200 B.C.E.–1532 C.E. 210
9.1 Asian Trade and Communication Routes 226
9.2 Africa and the Trans-Saharan Trade Routes 233

10.1 Early Expansion of Muslim Rule 247
10.2 Rise and Fall of the Abbasid Caliphate 253
11.1 The Spread of Christianity 271
11.2 Germanic Kingdoms 272
11.3 Kievan Russia and the Byzantine Empire in the Eleventh Century 282
11.4 The Crusades 286
12.1 The Tang Empire in Inner and Eastern Asia, 750 294
12.2 Liao and Song Empires, ca. 1100 300
12.3 Jin and Southern Song Empires, ca. 1200 300
13.1 The Mongol Domains in Eurasia in 1300 317
13.2 Western Eurasia in the 1300s 322
13.3 The Ming Empire and Its Allies, 1368–1500 330
13.4 Korea and Japan, 1200–1500 334
14.1 The Black Death in Fourteenth-Century Europe 342
14.2 Trade and Manufacturing in Later Medieval Europe 344
14.3 Europe in 1453 356
15.1 Africa and the Indian Ocean Basin: Physical Characteristics 364
15.2 Africa, 1200–1500 367
15.3 South and Southeast Asia, 1200–1500 369
15.4 Arteries of Trade and Travel in the Islamic World, to 1500 374
15.5 Major Mesoamerican Civilizations, 1000 B.C.E.–1519 C.E. 380
16.1 Exploration and Settlement in the Indian and Pacific Oceans Before 1500 392
16.2 Middle America to 1533 393
16.3 European Exploration, 1420–1542 397

Features

ENVIRONMENT + TECHNOLOGY

The Iceman 16
Environmental Stress in the Indus Valley 48
Ancient Textiles and Dyes 75
Divination in Ancient Societies 88
Ancient Astronomy 138
Ancient Glass 156
Indian Mathematics 182
The Maya Writing System 214
Camel Saddles 234
Chemistry 262
Iron Production 276
Writing in East Asia, 400–1200 306
From Gunpowder to Guns 332
The Clock 350
The Indian Ocean Dhow 373
Vasco da Gama's Fleet 398

DIVERSITY + DOMINANCE

Cave Art 12
Violence and Order in the Babylonian New Year's Festival 36
Protests Against the Ruling Class in Israel and Babylonia 72
Human Nature and Good Government in the *Analects* of Confucius and the Legalist Writings of Han Fei 92
Persian and Greek Perceptions of Kingship 120
Socioeconomic Mobility, Winners and Losers in Imperial Rome and Han China 150
Relations Between Women and Men in the *Kama Sutra* and the *Arthashastra* 184
Burials as Historical Texts 212
Travel Accounts of Africa and India 228
Secretaries, Turks, and Beggars 260
The Struggle for Christian Morality 278
Law and Society in China and Japan 296
Observations of Mongol Life 318
Persecution and Protection of Jews, 1272–1349 348
Personal Styles of Rule in India and Mali 370
Kongo's Christian King 402

MATERIAL CULTURE

Lamps and Candles 38
Wine and Beer in the Ancient World 134
Head Coverings 263
Salt 365

ISSUES IN WORLD HISTORY

Animal Domestication 108
Oral Societies and the Consequences of Literacy 218
Climate and Population to 1500 412

Preface

In preparing the sixth edition of this book, we examined the flow of topics from chapter to chapter and decided that certain rearrangements within chapters and in the order of chapters would accommodate the needs of instructors and students better than the template they had followed since the first edition. The first change was reversing the order of the third and fourth chapters to have early Mediterranean and Middle Eastern history directly follow the discussion of the origins of civilization in the Nile Valley and Mesopotamia.

The second change addressed the problem of when and how to discuss the history of pre-Columbian America. The time span to be covered, ranging from roughly 1500 B.C.E. to 1500 C.E., was too long to fit easily into the book's division into eight parts. The new structure we have adopted relocates the long pre-Aztec and pre-Inka narrative from Part III, Growth and Interaction of Cultural Communities, to the end of Part II, The Formation of New Cultural Communities. This change puts the status of the earliest civilizations in the Western Hemisphere on the same footing as the civilizations of early Greece, China, and South and Southeast Asia. It has the added benefit of making the history of East Asia in the Tang and Song periods directly precede the history of the Mongol empire, which allows instructors to have an uninterrupted focus on East Asia. The histories of the Aztecs and Inkas have been shifted to the chapter on tropical history located in Part IV, Interregional Patterns of Culture and Contact. This allows for a discussion of the overall influence of tropical environments and places them in close proximity to our treatment of the coming of Europeans to the New World.

A third structural change has shortened the length of the book from 34 to 33 chapters. To lessen the impression that Europe's domination of the world should always be the primary focus of student attention between the eighteenth and mid-twentieth centuries we have combined the two separate chapters on European imperialism, Chapters 26 and 28 in previous editions, into one. We feel that this change provides a better balance between the saga of European imperialism, accounts of resistance to imperialism, and the rise of independence movements in different parts of the world.

In a related change, we have relocated the chapter dealing with the histories of India, Latin America, and Africa in the first half of the twentieth century from after World War II, the old Chapter 31, to a position between the world wars. The aim of this chapter, titled "Revolutions in Living," is to portray that period not only as a time of political change in parts of the world subjected to European imperialism, but also as one of transformation of daily lives of people in both the industrialized and nonindustrialized worlds. The added focus of the chapter fills a gap between discussion of the Industrial Revolution in the eighteenth and nineteenth centuries and the advent of major technological changes in the post-World War II era.

Finally in this new edition, contributor and East Asian specialist Michael Wert of Marquette University brought a fresh perspective to many of our chapters dealing with East Asia, helping ensure that our coverage is at the forefront of emerging scholarship.

The authors believe that these changes, along with myriad smaller changes detailed below, significantly enhance the overall goal of *The Earth and Its Peoples*, namely, to be a textbook that speaks not only for the past but also to today's student and teacher. Students and instructors alike should take away from this text a broad, and due to the changes, more flowing impression of human societies beginning as sparse and disconnected communities reacting creatively to local circumstances; experiencing ever more intensive stages of contact, interpenetration, and cultural expansion and amalgamation; and arriving at a twenty-first-century world in which people increasingly visualize a single global community.

Process, not progress, is the keynote of this book: a steady process of change over time, at first experienced differently in various regions, but eventually connecting peoples and traditions from all parts of the globe. Students should come away from this book with a sense that the problems and promises of their world are rooted in a past in which people of every sort, in every part of the world, confronted problems of a similar character and coped with them as best they could. We believe that our efforts will help students see where their world has come from and learn thereby something useful for their own lives.

CENTRAL THEMES AND GOALS

We subtitled *The Earth and Its Peoples* "A Global History" because the book explores the common challenges and experiences that unite the human past. Although the dispersal of early humans to every livable environment resulted in a myriad of different economic, social, political, and cultural systems, all societies displayed analogous patterns in meeting their needs and exploiting their environments. Our challenge was to select the particular data and episodes that would best illuminate these global patterns of human experience.

To meet this challenge, we adopted two themes for our history: "technology and the environment" and "diversity and dominance." The first theme represents the commonplace material bases of all human societies at all times. It grants no special favor to any cultural group even as it embraces subjects of the broadest topical, chronological, and geographical range. The second theme expresses the reality that every human society has constructed or inherited structures of domination. We examine practices and institutions of many sorts: military, economic, social, political, religious, and cultural, as well as those based on kinship, gender, and literacy. Simultaneously we recognize that alternative ways of life and visions of societal organization continually manifest themselves both within and in dialogue with every structure of domination.

With respect to the first theme, it is vital for students to understand that technology, in the broad sense of experience-based knowledge of the physical world, underlies all human activity. Writing is a technology, but so is oral transmission from generation to generation of lore about medicinal or poisonous plants. The magnetic compass is a navigational technology, but so is Polynesian mariners' hard-won knowledge of winds, currents, and tides that made possible the settlement of the Pacific islands.

All technological development has come about in interaction with environments, both physical and human, and has, in turn, affected those environments. The story of how humanity has changed the face of the globe is an integral part of our first theme. Yet technology and the environment do not explain or underlie all important episodes of human experience. The theme of "diversity and dominance" informs all our discussions of politics, culture, and society. Thus when narrating the histories of empires, we describe a range of human experiences within and beyond the imperial frontiers without assuming that imperial institutions are a more fit topic for discussion than the economic and social organization of pastoral nomads or the lives of peasant women. When religion and culture occupy our narrative, we focus not only on the dominant tradition but also on the diversity of alternative beliefs and practices.

ORGANIZATION

The *Earth and Its Peoples* uses eight broad chronological divisions to define its conceptual scheme of global historical development.

In **Part One: The Emergence of Human Communities, to 500 B.C.E.,** we examine important patterns of human communal organization primarily in the Eastern Hemisphere. Small, dispersed human communities living by foraging spread to most parts of the world over tens of thousands of years. They responded to enormously diverse environmental conditions, at different times in different ways, discovering how to cultivate plants and utilize the products of domestic animals. On the basis of these new modes of sustenance, population grew, permanent towns appeared, and political and religious authority, based on collection and control of agricultural surpluses, spread over extensive areas.

Part Two: The Formation of New Cultural Communities, 1000 B.C.E.–400 C.E., introduces the concept of a "cultural community," in the sense of a coherent pattern of activities and symbols pertaining to a specific human community. While all human communities develop distinctive cultures, including those discussed in Part One, historical development in this stage of global history prolonged and magnified the impact of some cultures more than others. In the geographically contiguous African-Eurasian landmass, as well as in the Western Hemisphere, the cultures that proved to have the most enduring influence traced their roots to the second and first millennia B.C.E.

Part Three: Growth and Interaction of Cultural Communities, 300 B.C.E.–1200 C.E., deals with early episodes of technological, social, and cultural exchange and interaction on a continental scale both within and beyond the framework of imperial expansion. These are so different from earlier interactions arising from more limited conquests or extensions of political boundaries that they constitute a distinct era in world history, an era that set the world on the path of increasing global interaction and interdependence that it has been following ever since.

In **Part Four: Interregional Patterns of Culture and Contact, 1200–1550**, we look at the world during the three and a half centuries that saw both intensified cultural and commercial contact and increasingly confident self-definition of cultural communities in Europe, Asia, Africa, and the Americas. The Mongol conquest of a vast empire extending from the Pacific Ocean to eastern Europe greatly stimulated trade and interaction. In the West, strengthened European kingdoms began maritime expansion in the Atlantic, forging direct ties with sub-Saharan Africa and entering into conflict with the civilizations of the Western Hemisphere.

Part Five: The Globe Encompassed, 1500–1750, treats a period dominated by the global effects of European expansion and continued economic growth. European ships took over, expanded, and extended the maritime trade of the Indian Ocean, coastal Africa, and the Asian rim of the Pacific Ocean. This maritime commercial enterprise had its counterpart in European colonial empires in the Americas and a new Atlantic trading system. The contrasting capacities and fortunes of traditional land empires and new maritime empires, along with the exchange of domestic plants and animals between the hemispheres, underline the technological and environmental dimensions of this first era of complete global interaction.

In **Part Six: Revolutions Reshape the World, 1750–1870**, the word *revolution* is used in several senses: in the political sense of governmental overthrow, as in France and the Americas; in the metaphorical sense of radical transformative change, as in the Industrial Revolution; and in the broadest sense of a perception of a profound change in circumstances and worldview. Technology and environment lie at the core of these developments. With the rapid ascendancy of the Western belief that science and technology could overcome all challenges—environmental or otherwise—technology became an instrument not only of transformation but also of domination, to the point of threatening the integrity and autonomy of cultural traditions in nonindustrial lands and provoking strong movements of resistance.

Part Seven: Global Diversity and Dominance, 1750–1945, examines the development of a world arena in which people conceived of events on a global scale. Imperialism, international economic connections, and world-encompassing ideological tendencies, such as nationalism and socialism, present the picture of a globe becoming increasingly involved with European political and ideological concerns. Two world wars arising from European rivalries provide a climax to these developments, and European exhaustion affords other parts of the world new opportunities for independence and self-expression.

For **Part Eight: Perils and Promises of a Global Community, 1945 to the Present**, we divide the period since World War II into three time periods: 1945–1975, 1975–2000, and 2000 to the present. The challenges of the Cold War and postcolonial nation building dominate much of the period and unleash global economic, technological, and political forces that become increasingly important in all aspects of human life. With the end of the Cold War, however, new forces come to the fore. Technology is a key topic in Part Eight because of its integral role in both the growth and the problems of a global community. However, its many benefits in improving the quality of life become clouded by negative impacts on the environment.

FEATURES AND NEW PEDAGOGICAL AIDS

As with previous editions, the sixth edition offers a number of valuable features and pedagogical aids designed to pique student interest in specific world history topics and help them process and retain key information. Historical essays for each of the eight parts called Issues in World History are specifically designed to alert students to broad and recurring conceptual issues that are of great interest to contemporary historians; this feature has proved to be an instructor and student favorite. Six in-chapter essays on Material Culture call particular attention to the many ways in which objects and processes of everyday life can play a role in understanding human history on a broad scale. Thus essays like "Bells, Gongs, and Drums" and "Lamps and Candles" are not only interesting in and of themselves but also suggestive of how today's world historians find meaning in the ordinary dimensions of human life. The Environment and Technology feature, which has been a valuable resource in all prior editions of *The Earth and Its Peoples*, serves to illuminate the major theme of the text by demonstrating the shared material bases of all human societies across time. Finally, Diversity and Dominance, also core to the theme of the text, is the primary source feature that brings a myriad of real historical voices to life in a common struggle for power and autonomy.

Pedagogical aids include the following:

- **Chapter Opening Focus Questions** These questions are keyed to every major subdivision of the chapter and serve to help students focus on the core chapter concepts.
- **Section Reviews** Short bullet-point reviews summarize each major section in every chapter and remind students of key information.
- **Chapter Conclusions** Every chapter ends with a comparative conclusion that helps students better synthesize chapter material and understand how it fits into the larger picture.
- **Marginal Key Term with Definitions** Students can handily find key term definitions on the same page where the term first appears.
- **Pronunciation Guide** Hard-to-pronounce words are spelled phonetically for students throughout the text.

CHANGES IN THIS EDITION

In addition to the pedagogical aids outlined above, numerous chapter-by-chapter changes have been made, including new illustrations, new maps, streamlining of the textual discussion, and updates to many of the boxed feature essays. Here are a few highlights:

- In Chapter 1 the feature on "Cave Art" has been expanded.
- Chapter 4 descriptions of early civilizations in the Western Hemisphere have been shifted to Chapter 8 in order to facilitate a more unified discussion of Pre-Columbian America.
- Chapter 4 also contains a substantial new section on pastoral nomadism in the Eurasian steppe. Chapter 6 has a new Diversity and Dominance feature, "Socioeconomic Mobility: Winners and Losers in Imperial Rome and Han China," and a new Environment and Technology feature, "Ancient Glass." A Material Culture essay, "Lamps and Candles," has also been added.
- Chapter 8 has been extensively revised. Discussion of the Olmec and Chavín have been moved from Chapter 3 and the discussion of the Toltec, Tiwanaku, Wari, and Chimú civilizations expanded. Discussion of the Aztec and Inka civilizations appears in Chapter 15.
- Chapter 9 includes discussion of early Egyptian archaeological site of Nabta Playa.
- Chapter 12 contains expanded coverage of Korea.
- Chapter 13 contains expanded coverage of Vietnam and Yunnan province in southwest China.
- Chapter 14 has expanded coverage of eastern Europe and the Ottoman empire.
- Chapter 15 bears a new title, "Southern Empires, Southern Seas," and includes treatment of the Aztec and Inka empires that were previously covered much earlier in the book.
- Chapter 16 reflects new research on South Asian and Polynesian maritime cultures.
- Chapter 17 includes a new feature devoted to the first joint stock company and foreign trade. Coverage of early capitalism is expanded to include a discussion of stock markets and speculative bubbles like the Tulip, South Sea, and Mississippi Company frenzies.
- Chapter 19 includes a new feature, "Hurricanes and the Caribbean Plantation Economy."
- Chapter 20 has expanded to include the history of Russia, hence a new opening that features a Russian popular hero and the change of title to "Territorial Empires Between Europe and China."
- Chapter 21 has a new discussion of Korean history and the Imjin War.
- Chapters 22–23 have been reversed in sequence to provide better continuity to discussions of revolutions in Europe and parallel changes in the Americas.
- Chapter 22 includes a new discussion of proto-industrialization as well as augmented discussions of the spread of industrialization to continental Europe and North America and the early career of Karl Marx. The section "Protest and Reform" has been broadly revised to include machine breaking in the textile sector and rural resistance to mechanization in the Captain Swing riots.
- Chapter 25 has a new feature: "Industrializing Sugar Agriculture in Cuba."
- Chapter 26 combines accounts of European imperialism that were previously contained in this chapter and in Chapter 28.
- Chapter 27 features a revised discussion of early Japanese industrialization as well as an expanded treatment of Marx and Marxism and a new discussion of Mikhail Bakunin and anarchism. The chapter also includes a new feature: "Giuseppe Mazzini on Revolutionary Nationalism."
- Chapter 29 combines in a new chapter a discussion of technology and lifestyle changes that occurred between 1900 and 1945 with accounts of political movements in India, Latin Amer-

ica, and Africa that were previously located in Chapter 31. Highlights include a Diversity and Dominance feature, "Gandhi and the Media," an Environment and Technology feature, "New Materials," and a Material Culture essay, "Bells, Gongs, and Drums."

- Chapter 30 includes a new Environment and Technology feature, "The Magnetophon."
- Chapter 31 includes an updated discussion about the Cold War confrontation between West and East plus a revised discussion of apartheid and South Africa's struggle for independence.
- Chapter 32 contains a thoroughly updated feature, "Connected" to include discussion and pictures of the latest technology. The best current data are included in the demographic tables and discussion.
- Chapter 33 updates world affairs through the first half of 2013 and incorporates new statistical information on maps.

FORMATS

To accommodate different academic calendars and approaches to the course, *The Earth and Its Peoples* is available in three formats. There is a one-volume hardcover version containing all 33 chapters, along with a two-volume paperback edition: Volume I: To 1550 (Chapters 1–16) and Volume II: Since 1500 (Chapters 16–33). For readers at institutions with the quarter system, we offer a three-volume paperback version: Volume A: To 1200 (Chapters 1–12), Volume B: From 1200 to 1870 (Chapters 12–25), and Volume C: Since 1750 (Chapters 22–33). Volume II includes an Introduction that surveys the main developments set out in Volume I and provides a groundwork for students studying only the period since 1500.

ANCILLARIES

A wide array of supplements accompany this text to assist students with different learning needs and to help instructors master today's various classroom challenges.

Instructor Resources

Aplia™ [ISBN: 9781285768113]   is an online interactive learning solution that improves comprehension and outcomes by increasing student effort and engagement. Founded by a professor to enhance his own courses, Aplia provides automatically graded assignments with detailed, immediate explanations on every question. The interactive assignments have been developed to address the major concepts covered in *The Earth and Its Peoples* and are designed to promote critical thinking and engage students more fully in learning. Question types include questions built around animated maps, primary sources such as newspaper extracts, or imagined scenarios, like engaging in a conversation with a historical figure or finding a diary and being asked to fill in some blanks; more in-depth primary source question sets address a major topic with a number of related primary sources and questions that promote deeper analysis of historical evidence. Many of the questions incorporate images, video clips, or audio clips. Students get immediate feedback on their work (not only what they got right or wrong, but why), and they can choose to see another set of related questions if they want more practice. A searchable eBook is available inside the course as well so that students can easily reference it as they work. Map-reading and writing tutorials are also available to get students off to a good start.

Aplia's simple-to-use course management interface allows instructors to post announcements, upload course materials, host student discussions, e-mail students, and manage the gradebook; a knowledgeable and friendly support team offers assistance and personalized support in customizing assignments to the instructor's course schedule. To learn more and view a demo for this book, visit www.aplia.com.

MindTap Reader for *The Earth and Its Peoples* is an eBook specifically designed to address the ways students assimilate content and media assets. MindTap Reader combines thoughtful navigation ergonomics, advanced student annotation, note-taking, and search tools, and embedded media assets such as video and MP3 chapter summaries, primary source documents with critical thinking questions, and interactive (zoomable) maps. Students can use the eBook as their primary text or as a multimedia companion to their printed book. The MindTap Reader eBook is available within the MindTap and Aplia online offerings found at www.cengagebrain.com.

Online PowerLecture with Cognero® [ISBN: 9781285455013]   This PowerLecture is an all-in-one online multimedia resource for class preparation, presentation, and testing. Accessible through Cengage.com/login with your faculty account, you will find available for download: book-specific Microsoft® PowerPoint® presentations; a Test Bank in both Microsoft® Word® and Cognero® formats; an Instructor Manual; Microsoft® PowerPoint® Image Slides; and a JPEG Image Library.

The **Test Bank**, offered in Microsoft® Word® and Cognero® formats, contains multiple-choice and essay questions for each chapter. Cognero® is a flexible, online system that allows you to author, edit, and manage test bank content for *The Earth and Its People*, sixth edition. Create multiple test versions instantly and deliver through your LMS from your classroom, or wherever you may be, with no special installs or downloads required.

The **Instructor's Manual** contains for each chapter: an outline and summary; critical thinking questions; in-class activities; lecture launching suggestions; a list of key terms with definitions; and suggested readings and Web resources. The *Microsoft® PowerPoint® presentations* are ready-to-use, visual outlines of each chapter. These presentations are easily customized for your lectures and offered along with chapter-specific Microsoft® PowerPoint® Image Slides and JPEG Image Libraries. Access your Online PowerLecture at **www.cengage.com/login**.

History CourseMate   Cengage Learning's History CourseMate brings course concepts to life with interactive learning, study tools, and exam preparation tools that support the printed textbook. Use Engagement Tracker to monitor student engagement in the course and watch student comprehension soar as your class works with the printed textbook and the textbook-specific website. An interactive eBook allows students to take notes, highlight, search, and interact with embedded media (such as quizzes, flashcards, primary sources, and videos). Learn more at **www.cengage.com/coursemate**.

CourseReader   CourseReader is an online collection of primary and secondary sources that lets you create a customized electronic reader in minutes. With an easy-to-use interface and assessment tool, you can choose exactly what your students will be assigned—simply search or browse Cengage Learning's extensive document database to preview and select your customized collection of readings. In addition to print sources of all types (letters, diary entries, speeches, newspaper accounts, etc.), their collection includes a growing number of images and video and audio clips.

Each primary source document includes a descriptive headnote that puts the reading into context and is further supported by both critical thinking and multiple-choice questions designed to reinforce key points. For more information visit **www.cengage.com/coursereader**.

Cengagebrain.com   Save your students time and money. Direct them to **www.cengagebrain .com** for choice in formats and savings and a better chance to succeed in your class. Cengagebrain.com, Cengage Learning's online store, is a single destination for more than 10,000 new textbooks, eTextbooks, eChapters, study tools, and audio supplements. Students have the freedom to purchase a-la-carte exactly what they need when they need it. Students can save 50% on the electronic textbook, and can pay as little as $1.99 for an individual eChapter.

Reader Program   Cengage Learning publishes a number of readers, some containing exclusively primary sources, others a combination of primary and secondary sources, and some designed to guide students through the process of historical inquiry. Visit Cengage.com/history for a complete list of readers.

Custom Options   Nobody knows your students like you, so why not give them a text that is tailor-fit to their needs? Cengage Learning offers custom solutions for your course—whether it's making a small modification to The Earth and Its Peoples to match your syllabus or combining multiple sources to create something truly unique. You can pick and choose chapters, include your own material, and add additional map exercises along with the Rand McNally Atlas to create a text that fits the way you teach. Ensure that your students get the most out of their textbook dollar by giving them exactly what they need. Contact your Cengage Learning representative to explore custom solutions for your course.

Student Resources

Writing for College History, **first edition [ISBN: 9780618306039]**   Prepared by Robert M. Frakes, Clarion University. This brief handbook for survey courses in American history, Western Civilization/European history, and world civilization guides students through the various types of writing assignments they encounter in a history class. Providing examples of student writing and candid assessments of student work, this text focuses on the rules and conventions of writing for the college history course.

The History Handbook, **second edition [ISBN: 9780495906766]**   Prepared by Carol Berkin of Baruch College, City University of New York and Betty Anderson of Boston University. This book teaches students both basic and history-specific study skills such as how to read primary sources, research historical topics, and correctly cite sources. Substantially less expensive than comparable skill-building texts, ***The History Handbook*** also offers tips for Internet research and evaluating online sources.

Doing History: Research and Writing in the Digital Age, **second edition [ISBN: 9781133587880]** Prepared by Michael J. Galgano, J. Chris Arndt, and Raymond M. Hyser of James Madison University. Whether you're starting down the path as a history major, or simply looking for a straightforward and systematic guide to writing a successful paper, you'll find this text to be an indispensible handbook to historical research. This text's "soup to nuts" approach to researching and writing about history addresses every step of the process, from locating your sources and gathering information, to writing clearly and making proper use of various citation styles to avoid plagiarism. You'll also learn how to make the most of every tool available to you—especially the technology that helps you conduct the process efficiently and effectively.

The Modern Researcher, **sixth edition [ISBN: 9780495318705]**   Prepared by Jacques Barzun and Henry F. Graff of Columbia University. This classic introduction to the techniques of research and the art of expression is used widely in history courses, but is also appropriate for writing and research methods courses in other departments. Barzun and Graff thoroughly cover every aspect of research, from the selection of a topic through the gathering, analysis, writing, revision, and publication of findings, presenting the process not as a set of rules but through actual cases that put the subtleties of research in a useful context. Part One covers the principles and methods of research; Part Two covers writing, speaking, and getting one's work published.

Rand McNally Historical Atlas of the World, **second edition [ISBN: 9780618841912]**   This valuable resource features over 70 maps that portray the rich panoply of the world's history from preliterate times to the present. They show how cultures and civilization were linked and how they interacted. The maps make it clear that history is not static. Rather, it is about change and movement across time. The maps show change by presenting the dynamics of expansion, cooperation, and conflict. This atlas includes maps that display the world from the beginning of civilization; the political development of all major areas of the world; expanded coverage of Africa, Latin America, and the Middle East; the current Islamic World; and the world population change in 1900 and 2000.

ACKNOWLEDGMENTS

In preparing the sixth edition, we benefited from the critical readings of many colleagues. Our sincere thanks go in particular to contributor Michael Wert of Marquette University who lent his fresh perspective to our coverage of East Asia. We thank Beatrice Manz of the History Department at Tufts University who provided guidance on the new Pastoral Nomads section in Part I. We are also indebted to the following instructors who lent their insight over various editions: Hedrick Alixopuilos, Santa Rosa Junior College; Hayden Bellenoit, U.S. Naval Academy; Dusty Bender, Central Baptist College; Cory Crawford, Ohio University; Adrian De Gifis, Loyola

University New Orleans; Peter de Rosa, Bridgewater State University; Aaron Gulyas, Mott Community College; Darlene Hall, Lake Erie College; Vic Jagos, Scottsdale Community College; Adrien Ivan, Vernon College; Andrew Muldoon, Metropolitan State College of Denver; Percy Murray, Shaw University; Dave Price, Santa Fe College; Anthony Steinhoff, University of Tennessee-Chattanooga; Anara Tabyshalieva, Marshal University; Susan Autry, Central Piedmont Community College; Anna Collins, Arkansas Tech University; William Connell, Christopher Newport University; Christopher Cameron, University of North Carolina at Charlotte; Gregory Crider, Winthrop University; Shawn Dry, Oakland Community College; Nancy Fitch, California State University, Fullerton; Christine Haynes, University of North Carolina at Charlotte; Mark Herman, Edison College; Ellen J. Jenkins, Arkansas Tech University; Frank Karpiel, The Citadel; Ken Koons, Virginia Military Institute; David Longfellow, Baylor University; Heather Lucas, Georgia Perimeter College; Jeff Pardue, Gainesville State College; Craig Patton, Alabama A & M University; Amanda Pipkin, University of North Carolina at Charlotte; Linda Scherr, Mercer County Community College; Robert Sherwood, Georgia Military College; Brett Shufelt, Copiah-Lincoln Community College; Peter Thorsheim, University of North Carolina at Charlotte; Kristen Walton, Salisbury University; Christopher Ward, Clayton State University; William Wood, Point Loma Nazarene University.

When textbook authors set out on a project, they are inclined to believe that 90 percent of the effort will be theirs and 10 percent that of various editors and production specialists employed by their publisher. How very naïve. This book would never have seen the light of day had it not been for the unstinting labors of the great team of professionals who turned the authors' words into beautifully presented print. Our debt to the staff of Cengage Learning remains undiminished in the sixth edition. Brooke Barbier, product manager, has offered us firm but sympathetic guidance throughout the revision process. Tonya Lobato, senior content developer, offered astute and sympathetic assistance as the authors worked to incorporate many new ideas and subjects into the text. Carol Newman, senior content project manager, moved the work through the production stages to meet a challenging schedule. Abbey Stebing did an outstanding job of photo research.

We thank also the many students whose questions and concerns, expressed directly or through their instructors, shaped much of this revision. We continue to welcome all readers' suggestions, queries, and criticisms. Please contact us at our respective institutions.

About the Authors

RICHARD W. BULLIET   Professor of Middle Eastern History at Columbia University, Richard W. Bulliet received his Ph.D. from Harvard University. He has written scholarly works on a number of topics: the social and economic history of medieval Iran (The Patricians of Nishapur and Cotton, Climate, and Camels in Early Islamic Iran), the history of human-animal relations (The Camel and the Wheel and Hunters, Herders, and Hamburgers), the process of conversion to Islam (Conversion to Islam in the Medieval Period), and the overall course of Islamic social history (Islam: The View from the Edge and The Case for Islamo-Christian Civilization). He is the editor of the Columbia History of the Twentieth Century. He has published four novels, coedited The Encyclopedia of the Modern Middle East, and hosted an educational television series on the Middle East. He was awarded a fellowship by the John Simon Guggenheim Memorial Foundation and was named a Carnegie Corporation Scholar.

PAMELA KYLE CROSSLEY   Pamela Kyle Crossley received her Ph.D. in Modern Chinese History from Yale University. She is currently the Robert and Barbara Black Professor of History at Dartmouth College. Her books include The Wobbling Pivot: An Interpretive History of China Since 1800; What Is Global History?; A Translucent Mirror: History and Identity in Qing Imperial Ideology; The Manchus; Orphan Warriors: Three Manchu Generations and the End of the Qing World; and (with Lynn Hollen Lees and John W. Servos) Global Society: The World Since 1900.

DANIEL R. HEADRICK   Daniel R. Headrick received his Ph.D. in History from Princeton University. Professor of History and Social Science, Emeritus, at Roosevelt University in Chicago, he is the author of several books on the history of technology, imperialism, and international relations, including The Tools of Empire: Technology and European Imperialism in the Nineteenth Century; The Tentacles of Progress: Technology Transfer in the Age of Imperialism; The Invisible Weapon: Telecommunications and International Politics; Technology: A World History; Power Over Peoples: Technology, Environments and Western Imperialism, 1400 to the Present; and When Information Came of Age: Technologies of Knowledge in the Age of Reason and Revolution, 1700–1850. His articles have appeared in the Journal of World History and the Journal of Modern History, and he has been awarded fellowships by the National Endowment for the Humanities, the John Simon Guggenheim Memorial Foundation, and the Alfred P. Sloan Foundation.

STEVEN W. HIRSCH   Steven W. Hirsch holds a Ph.D. in Classics from Stanford University and is currently Associate Professor of Classics and History at Tufts University. He has received grants from the National Endowment for the Humanities and the Massachusetts Foundation for Humanities and Public Policy. His research and publications include The Friendship of the Barbarians: Xenophon and the Persian Empire, as well as articles and reviews in the Classical Journal, the American Journal of Philology, and the Journal of Interdisciplinary History. He is currently completing a comparative study of ancient Greco-Roman and Chinese civilizations.

LYMAN L. JOHNSON   Professor Emeritus of History at the University of North Carolina at Charlotte, Lyman L. Johnson earned his Ph.D. in Latin American History from the University of Connecticut. A two-time Senior Fulbright-Hays Lecturer, he also has received fellowships from the Tinker Foundation, the Social Science Research Council, the National Endowment for the Humanities, and the American Philosophical Society. His recent books include Workshop of Revolution: Plebeian Buenos Aires and the Atlantic World, 1776-1810; Death, Dismemberment, and Memory; The Faces of Honor (with Sonya Lipsett-Rivera); Aftershocks: Earthquakes and Popular Politics in Latin America (with Jürgen Buchenau); Essays on the Price History of Eighteenth-Century Latin America (with Enrique Tandeter); and Colonial Latin America (with Mark A. Burkholder). He also has published in journals, including the Hispanic American Historical Review, the Journal of Latin American Studies, the International Review of Social History, Social History, and Desarrollo Económico. He has served as president of the Conference on Latin American History.

DAVID NORTHRUP   David Northrup earned his Ph.D. in African and European History from the University of California, Los Angeles. He has published scholarly works on African, Atlantic, and world history. His most recent books are How English Became the Global Language, the third edition of Africa's Discovery of Europe, 1450–1850, and the Diary of Antera Duke, an Eighteenth-Century African Slave Trader. He taught at a rural secondary school on Nigeria, Tuskegee Institute in Alabama, Boston College, and Venice International University and is a past president of the World History Association.

Note on Spelling and Usage

Where necessary for clarity, dates are followed by the letters C.E. or B.C.E. The abbreviation C.E. stands for "Common Era" and is equivalent to A.D. (anno Domini, Latin for "in the year of the Lord"). The abbreviation B.C.E. stands for "before the Common Era" and means the same as B.C. ("before Christ"). In keeping with our goal of approaching world history without special concentration on one culture or another, we chose these neutral abbreviations as appropriate to our enterprise. Because many readers will be more familiar with English than with metric measurements, however, units of measure are generally given in the English system, with metric equivalents following in parentheses.

In general, Chinese has been Romanized according to the pinyin method. Exceptions include proper names well established in English (e.g., Canton, Chiang Kaishek) and a few English words borrowed from Chinese (e.g., kowtow). Spellings of Arabic, Ottoman Turkish, Persian, Mongolian, Manchu, Japanese, and Korean names and terms avoid special diacritical marks for letters that are pronounced only slightly differently in English. An apostrophe is used to indicate when two Chinese syllables are pronounced separately (e.g., Chang'an).

For words transliterated from languages that use the Arabic script—Arabic, Ottoman Turkish, Persian, Urdu—the apostrophe indicating separately pronounced syllables may represent either of two special consonants, the hamza or the ain. Because most English-speakers do not hear the distinction between these two, they have not been distinguished in transliteration and are not indicated when they occur at the beginning or end of a word. As with Chinese, some words and commonly used place-names from these languages are given familiar English spellings (e.g., Quran instead of Qur'an, Cairo instead of al-Qahira). Arabic romanization has normally been used for terms relating to Islam, even where the context justifies slightly different Turkish or Persian forms, again for ease of comprehension.

Before 1492 the inhabitants of the Western Hemisphere had no single name for themselves. They had neither a racial consciousness nor a racial identity. Identity was derived from kin groups, language, cultural practices, and political structures. There was no sense that physical similarities created a shared identity. America's original inhabitants had racial consciousness and racial identity imposed on them by conquest and the occupation of their lands by Europeans after 1492. All of the collective terms for these first American peoples are tainted by this history. Indians, Native Americans, Amerindians, First Peoples, and Indigenous Peoples are among the terms in common usage. In this book the names of individual cultures and states are used wherever possible. Amerindian and other terms that suggest transcultural identity and experience are used most commonly for the period after 1492.

There is an ongoing debate about how best to render Amerindian words in English. It has been common for authors writing in English to follow Mexican usage for Nahuatl and Yucatec Maya words and place-names. In this style, for example, the capital of the Aztec state is spelled Tenochtitlán, and the important late Maya city-state is spelled Chichén Itzá. Although these forms are still common even in the specialist literature, we have chosen to follow the scholarship that sees these accents as unnecessary. The exceptions are modern place-names, such as Mérida and Yucatán, which are accented. A similar problem exists for the spelling of Quechua and Aymara words from the Andean region of South America. Although there is significant disagreement among scholars, we follow the emerging consensus and use the spellings khipu (not quipu), Tiwanaku (not Tiahuanaco), and Wari (not Huari). In this edition we have introduced the now common spelling Inka (not Inca) but keep Cuzco for the capital city (not Cusco), since this spelling facilitates locating this still-important city on maps.

The Earth and Its Peoples

A GLOBAL HISTORY

CHAPTER 1   Nature, Humanity, and History, to 3500 B.C.E.

CHAPTER 2   The First River-Valley Civilizations, 3500–1500 B.C.E.

CHAPTER 3   The Mediterranean and Middle East, 2000–500 B.C.E.

CHAPTER 4   New Civilizations Outside the West Asian Core Area, 2300 B.C.E.–350 C.E.

British Museum/HIP/Art Resource, NY

Babylonian Map of the World, ca. 600 B.C.E.   This map on a clay tablet, with labels written in Akkadian cuneiform, shows a flat, round world with the city of Babylon at the center. Nearby features of the Mesopotamian landscape include the Euphrates River, mountains, marshes, and cities. Beyond the great encircling salt sea are seven islands. Like many ancient peoples, the Babylonians believed that distant lands were home to legendary beasts, strangely formed peoples, and mysterious natural phenomena.

The Emergence of Human Communities, to 500 B.C.E.

Human beings evolved over several million years from primates in Africa. Able to walk upright and possessing large brains, hands with opposable thumbs, and the capacity for speech, early humans used teamwork and created tools to survive in diverse environments. They spread relatively quickly to almost every habitable area of the world, hunting and gathering wild plant products. Around 10,000 years ago some groups began to cultivate plants, domesticate animals, and make pottery vessels for storage. These developments led to permanent settlements—at first small villages but eventually larger towns.

The earliest complex societies arose in the great river valleys of Mesopotamia, Egypt, Pakistan, and northern China. In these arid regions agriculture depended on river water, and centers of political power arose to organize the labor required to dig and maintain irrigation channels. Kings and priests dominated these early societies from the urban centers, helped by administrators, scribes, soldiers, merchants, craftsmen, and others with specialized skills. Surplus food grown in the countryside by a dependent peasantry sustained the activities of these groups.

As they sought access to raw materials, especially metals, certain centers came to dominate broader expanses of territory. This development also stimulated long-distance trade and diplomatic relations between major powers. Artisans made weapons, tools, and ritual objects from bronze, and culture and technology spread to neighboring regions, such as southern China, Nubia, Syria-Palestine, Anatolia, and the Aegean.

In the Western Hemisphere, different geographical circumstances led to distinctive patterns of technological and cultural response. These early civilizations in southern Mexico and the Andean region of South America are discussed in Part 2.

Chapter Outline

African Genesis
➤ *In light of scientific advances in our understanding of human origins, what have we learned about our relationship to the earth and other living species?*

Technology and Culture in the Ice Age
➤ *How did the physical and mental abilities that gradually evolved in humans enable them to adapt their way of life to new environments during the Great Ice Age?*

The Agricultural Revolutions
➤ *After nearly 2 million years of physical and cultural development, how did human communities in different parts of the world learn to manipulate nature through agriculture and the domestication of animals?*

Life in Neolithic Communities
➤ *What cultural achievements characterized life in the Neolithic period?*

Conclusion

● **DIVERSITY + DOMINANCE** Cave Art
● **ENVIRONMENT + TECHNOLOGY** The Iceman

David Coulson/Robert Estall Photo Agency

Engraving of Two Cattle in the Sahara, ca. 5000 B.C.E. Around 10,000 B.C.E. people settled in the central Sahara and began to engrave rocks with pictures of animals. The engravings display an expert knowledge of animal stance, movement, and anatomy.

Nature, Humanity, and History, to 3500 B.C.E.

Paintings and engravings on stone created tens of thousands of years ago by early humans have been found on every continent. Someone in Central Africa carved this image of cattle around 5000 B.C.E., when the Sahara was not a desert but a verdant savanna supporting numerous species of wildlife. Why the image was carved and what significance it originally held will likely remain a mystery, but for us it is a beautiful work of art that reveals much about our human ancestry.

Long before the invention of writing, societies told themselves stories about how human beings and the natural world were created. Some, like the Yoruba (yoh-roo-bah) people of West Africa, related that the first humans came down from the sky; others, like the Hopi of southwest North America, claimed that they emerged out of a hole in the earth. Although such creation myths typically explain how a people's way of life, social divisions, and cultural system arose, historical accuracy in the modern sense was not their primary purpose. As with the story of Adam and Eve in the Hebrew Bible, their goal was to define the moral principles that people thought should govern their dealings with the supernatural world, with each other, and with the rest of nature.

In the nineteenth century evidence began to accumulate about the actual origins of humanity. Natural scientists were finding remains of early humans who resembled apes. Other discoveries suggested that the familiar ways of life based on farming and herding did not arise within a generation or two of creation, as many myths suggested, but tens of thousands of years after humans first appeared. This evidence provides insights into human identity that are as meaningful as those propounded by the creation myths.

AFRICAN GENESIS

The discovery in the mid-nineteenth century of the remains of ancient creatures that had both humanlike and apelike features generated excitement and controversy. The finds upset many people because they challenged religious beliefs about human origins. Others welcomed the new evidence for what some had long suspected: that the physical characteristics of modern humans had evolved over incredibly long periods of time.

Interpreting the Evidence

In 1856 in the Neander Valley of Germany, laborers discovered fossilized bones of a creature with a body much like that of modern humans but with a face that had heavy brow ridges and a low forehead, like the faces of apes. Although we now know these were Neanderthals, a type of human common in Europe and the Middle East from 135,000 to 25,000 years ago, in the mid-nineteenth century the idea of humans that different from modern people was so novel that some scholars thought they must be deformed individuals from recent times.

Three years after the Neanderthal finds, Charles Darwin, a young English naturalist (student of natural history), published *On the Origin of Species*, in which he argued that the time frame for all biological life was far longer than most people supposed. Darwin based his conclusion on the pioneering research of others and on his own investigations of fossils and living plant and animal species in Latin America. He proposed that the great diversity of living species and the profound changes in them over time could be explained by natural selection, the process by which biological variations that enhance a population's ability to survive become dominant in that species. He theorized that, over long periods of time, the changes brought about by this process could lead to the **evolution** of distinct new species.

Turning to the sensitive subject of human evolution in *The Descent of Man* (1871), Darwin summarized the growing consensus among naturalists that human beings had come into existence through the same process of natural selection. Because humans shared so many physical similarities with African apes, he proposed Africa as the home of the first humans, even though there was no fossil evidence at the time to support his hypothesis.

The next major discoveries pointed to Asia, rather than Africa, as the original human home. On the Indonesian island of Java in 1891, Eugene Dubois uncovered an ancient skullcap of what was soon called Java man. In 1929 near Peking (an old form of Beijing [bay-jeeng]), China, W. C. Pei discovered a similar skullcap of what became known as Peking man.

By then, even older fossils had been found in southern Africa. In 1924 Raymond Dart found the skull of a creature that he named *Australopithecus africanus* (aw-strah-loh-PITH-uh-kuhs ah-frih-KAH-nuhs) (African southern ape), which he argued was transitional between apes and early humans. For many years most specialists disputed Dart's idea because, although *Australopithecus africanus* walked upright like a human, its brain was the size of an ape's.

Since 1950, Louis and Mary Leakey and their son Richard, along with many others, have discovered a wealth of early human fossils in the exposed sediments of the Great Rift Valley of eastern Africa. These finds are strong evidence for Dart's hypothesis and for Darwin's guess that the tropical habitat of the African apes was the cradle of humanity.

The development of modern archaeological techniques has added to our knowledge. Rather than collect isolated bones, researchers sift the neighboring soils to extract the fossilized remains of other creatures, seeds, and even pollen existing at the time, documenting the environment in which early humans lived. They can also measure the age of most finds by the rate of molecular change in potassium, contained in minerals in lava flows, or in carbon from wood and bone.

A major new approach was made possible by the full decipherment of the human genetic code in 2003. Researchers have been able to extrapolate backward from genetic differences among contemporary human populations to answer such questions as: when language first emerged; the approximate size and location in Northeast Africa of the ancestral human population and the date when some of its members moved out of the continent; the paths taken by migrating groups as humans ultimately spread to all habitable parts of the planet; and when the skin color of the various human populations developed.

By combining these forms of evidence with the growing understanding of how other species adapt to their natural environments, researchers can trace the evolutionary changes that produced modern humans over the course of millions of years.

Human Evolution

Biologists classify **australopithecines** (aw-strah-loh-PITH-uh-seen) and humans as members of a family of primates known as **hominids** (HOM-uh-nid). Primates are members of a class of warm-blooded, four-limbed, social animals known as mammals that came to prominence about 65 million years ago. The first hominids are now dated to about 7 million years ago.

Among living primates, modern humans are most closely related to the African apes—chimpanzees and gorillas. Since Darwin's time it has been popular (and controversial) to say that we are descended from apes. In fact, apes and humans share a common ancestor. Over 99 percent of human DNA, the basic genetic blueprint, is identical to that of the great apes. But three traits distinguish humans from apes and other primates. The earliest of these traits to appear was **bipedalism** (walking upright on two legs). Being upright frees the forelimbs from any role in locomotion and enhances an older primate trait: a hand with a long, opposable thumb that can work with the fingers to manipulate objects skillfully. Modern humans' second distinctive trait is a very large brain. Besides enabling humans to think abstractly, experience profound emotions, and construct complex social relationships, this larger brain controls the fine motor

evolution The biological theory that, over time, changes occurring in plants and animals, mainly as a result of natural selection and genetic mutation, result in new species.

australopithecines The several extinct species of humanlike primates that existed from about 4.5 million years ago to 1.4 million years ago (genus *Australopithecus*).

hominid The biological family that includes humans and humanlike primates.

bipedalism The ability to walk upright on two legs, characteristic of hominids.

CHRONOLOGY

	Geological Epochs	Species and Migrations	Technological Advances
7,000,000 B.C.E.		7,000,000 B.C.E. Earliest hominids	
4,000,000 B.C.E.		4,500,000 B.C.E. Australopithecines 2,300,000 B.C.E. Early *Homo habilis*	2,600,000 B.C.E. Earliest stone tools; hunting and gathering (foraging) societies
2,000,000 B.C.E.	2,000,000–9000 B.C.E. Pleistocene (Great Ice Age)	1,800,000–350,000 B.C.E. *Homo erectus*	2,000,000–8000 B.C.E. Paleolithic (Old Stone Age)
1,000,000 B.C.E.		400,000–100,000 B.C.E. Archaic *Homo sapiens*	500,000 B.C.E. Use of fire
100,000 B.C.E.		100,000 B.C.E. Anatomically modern *Homo sapiens* in Africa 50,000 B.C.E. Behaviorally modern *Homo sapiens* possessing language Migrations to Eurasia 46,000 B.C.E. Modern humans in Australia 18,000 B.C.E. Modern humans in Americas	30,000 B.C.E. First cave paintings
10,000 B.C.E.	9000 B.C.E.–present Holocene		8000–2000 B.C.E. Neolithic (New Stone Age); earliest agriculture

movements of the hand and of the tongue, increasing humans' tool-using capacity and facilitating the development of speech. The physical possibility of language, however, depends on a third distinctive human trait: the location of the larynx (voice box). In humans it lies much lower in the neck than in any other primate.

These critical biological traits are due to natural selection, the preservation of genetic changes that enhanced the ability of the ancestors of modern humans to survive and reproduce. Major shifts in the world's climate led to evolutionary changes in human ancestors and other species. Falling temperatures culminated in the **Great Ice Age**, or Pleistocene (PLY-stuh-seen) epoch, extending from about 2 million to about 9000 B.C.E. (see Chronology). These temperature changes and altered rainfall and vegetation imposed great strains on plant and animal species, causing large numbers of new species to evolve.

Beginning approximately 4.5 million years ago, several species of australopithecines evolved in southern and eastern Africa. In northern Ethiopia in 1974, Donald Johanson unearthed a well-preserved skeleton of a twenty-five-year-old female, whom he nicknamed Lucy. Mary Leakey's discovery of fossilized footprints in Tanzania in 1977 provided spectacular visual evidence that australopithecines walked on two legs.

Bipedalism evolved because it provided australopithecines with some advantage for survival. Some studies suggest that walking and running on two legs is very energy efficient. Another theory is that bipeds survived better because they could carry armfuls of food back to their mates and children.

Climate changes between 2 and 3 million years ago led to the evolution of a new species, the first to be classified in the same genus (*Homo*) with modern humans. At Olduvai (ol-DOO-vy) Gorge in northern Tanzania in the early 1960s, Louis Leakey discovered the fossilized remains of a creature that he named **Homo habilis** (HOH-moh HAB-uh-luhs) (handy human). What most distinguished *Homo habilis* from the australopithecines was a brain that was nearly 50 percent larger. Greater intelligence may have enabled *Homo habilis* to locate things to eat throughout the seasons of the year. Seeds and other fossilized remains found in ancient *Homo habilis* camps indicate that the new species ate a greater variety of more nutritious foods than did australopithecines.

By 1 million years ago *Homo habilis* and all the australopithecines had become extinct. In their habitat lived a new hominid, **Homo erectus** (HOH-moh ee-REK-tuhs) (upright human), which first appeared in eastern Africa about 1.8 million years ago. (It is uncertain whether

Great Ice Age Geological era that occurred between about 2 million and 11,000 years ago.

Homo habilis The first human species (now extinct). It evolved in Africa about 2.3 million years ago.

Homo erectus An extinct human species. It evolved in Africa about 1.8 million years ago.

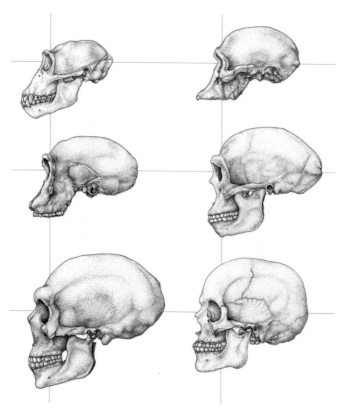

Evolution of the Human Brain   These drawings of skulls show the extensive cranial changes associated with the increase in brain size during 5 million years of evolutionary change. Seen here are the skulls of a chimpanzee, *Australopithecus*, *Homo Habilis*, *Homo Erectus*, *Neanderthal*, and *Homo Sapiens*.

© Copyright Deborah Maizels, 1994

Homo sapiens The current human species. It evolved in Africa sometime between 400,000 and 100,000 years ago.

Homo erectus evolved from *Homo habilis* or both species descended from *Australopithecus*.) These creatures possessed brains a third larger than those of *Homo habilis*, which presumably accounted for their better survivability. A nearly complete skeleton of a twelve-year-old male of the species discovered by Richard Leakey in 1984 on the shores of Lake Turkana in Kenya shows that *Homo erectus* closely resembled modern people from the neck down. *Homo erectus* was very successful in dealing with different environments and underwent hardly any biological changes for over a million years.

Sometime between 400,000 and 100,000 years ago, a new human species emerged: **Homo sapiens** (HOH-moh SAY-pee-enz) (wise human). The brains of *Homo sapiens* were a third larger than those of *Homo erectus*, whom they gradually superseded. Although this species was anatomically similar to people today, archaeological and genetic evidence suggest that a further development around 50,000 years ago produced the first behaviorally modern humans, with the intellectual and social capabilities that we have.

There is no scholarly consensus on when, why, or how humans developed the capacity to speak. In the absence of tangible evidence, this question has even been labeled "the hardest problem in science." Assuming that the shape of the throat and low position of the larynx are essential to vocalizing a wide range of sounds, it ought to be relevant that these features were still evolving in *Homo habilis* and *Homo erectus*. Some scholars link the development of language in the fullest sense to the period around 50,000 years ago when *Homo sapiens* began to migrate out of Africa and employed a larger, more sophisticated set of tools that can be sorted into functional categories.

This slow but remarkable process of physical evolution, which distinguished humans from other primates, was one part of what was happening. Equally remarkable was the way in which humans were extending their habitat.

Migrations from Africa

Early humans first expanded their range in eastern and southern Africa. Then they ventured out of Africa, perhaps following migrating herds of animals or searching for more abundant food supplies in a time of drought. The reasons are uncertain, but the end results are vividly clear: humans successfully colonized diverse environments, including deserts and arctic lands (see Map 1.1). This dispersal demonstrates early humans' talent for adaptation.

Homo erectus was the first human species to inhabit all parts of Africa and to be found outside Africa. Java man and Peking man were members of this species. At that time, Java was not an island but was part of the Southeast Asian mainland. During the Pleistocene, massive glaciers of frozen water spread out from the poles and mountains. At their peak such glaciers covered a third of the earth's surface and contained so much frozen water that ocean levels were lowered by over 450 feet (140 meters), exposing land bridges between many places now isolated by water (see Map 1.1).

DNA and fossil evidence suggest that *Homo sapiens* also first evolved in Africa. The ancestral group from which all modern humans are descended may have comprised as few as 5,000 individuals. From this population, a band of several hundred people initially moved out of Northeast Africa around 50,000 years ago, and their descendants rapidly spread across the planet (although some scientists dispute this "African Genesis" and hold that distinct groups of *Homo sapiens* evolved from *Homo erectus* populations in Africa, Europe, China, and Southeast Asia).

Recent excavations and DNA analysis have shown that early modern humans co-existed and interbred with other species of *Homo* that are now extinct: Neanderthals and Denisovans

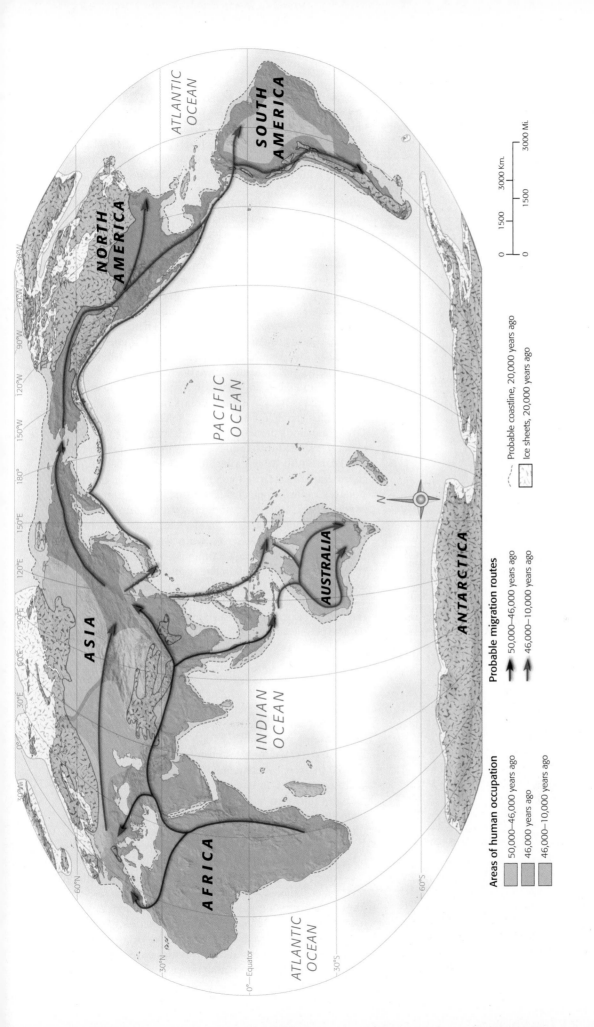

MAP 1.1 **Human Dispersal to 10,000 Years Ago** Early migrations from Africa into southern Eurasia were followed by treks across land bridges during ice ages, when giant ice sheets lowered ocean levels. Boats may also have been employed. © Cengage Learning

Areas of human occupation

50,000–46,000 years ago

46,000 years ago

46,000–10,000 years ago

Probable migration routes

50,000–46,000 years ago

46,000–10,000 years ago

Probable coastline, 20,000 years ago

Ice sheets, 20,000 years ago

John Reader/Science Source

Fossilized Footprints Archaeologist Mary Leakey (shown at top) found these remarkable footprints of a hominid adult and child at Laetoli, Tanzania. The pair had walked through fresh volcanic ash that solidified after being buried by a new volcanic eruption. Dated to 3.5 million years ago, the footprints are the oldest evidence of bipedalism yet found.

(whose bone fragments were recently discovered in Siberia). The small and small-brained *Homo floresiensis*, whose remains were recently excavated in Indonesia, only died out about 12,000 years ago.

Ultimately modern humans displaced older human populations, probably because they were better able to survive environmental conditions in the Ice Age, though some scholars believe the Neanderthals were absorbed into the *Homo sapiens* population through interbreeding.

The Great Ice Age enabled modern humans to penetrate into the Americas and even the Arctic. During glacial periods, people would have been able to cross a land bridge from Siberia to Alaska, perhaps beginning around 18,000 B.C.E., though some scholars believe that the first migrations occurred as early as 35,000 to 25,000 B.C.E. Over thousands of years the population of the Americas grew and spread throughout the hemisphere, penetrating southern South America by 10,500 B.C.E. As they spread, these humans adapted to environments that included polar extremes, tropical rain forests, and high mountain ranges as well as deserts, woodlands, and prairies.

About 46,000 years ago, modern humans, traveling by boat from Java, colonized New Guinea and Australia when both were part of a single landmass, and others crossed the land bridge then existing between the Asian mainland and Japan. When global temperatures rose and the glaciers melted, submerging the land bridges and increasing the extent of ocean between Southeast Asia and Australia, the peoples of the Western Hemisphere and Australia were virtually isolated from the rest of the world for at least 15,000 years.

As populations migrated, they underwent minor evolutionary changes that helped them adapt to extreme environments. One such change was in skin color. The deeply pigmented skin of today's indigenous inhabitants of the tropics (and presumably of all early humans) reduces harmful effects of the harsh tropical sun such as sunburn and skin cancer. At some point between 20,000 and 5,000 years ago, pale skin became characteristic of Europeans living in northern latitudes with far less sunshine, especially during winter months. The loss of pigment enabled their skin to produce more vitamin D from sunshine.

As distinctive as skin color seems, it represents a very minor biological change. What is far more remarkable is that widely dispersed human populations vary so little in their genetic makeup. Whereas other species need to evolve physically to adapt to new environments, modern humans have been able to adapt technologically, changing their eating habits and devising new forms of tools, clothing, and shelter. As a result, human communities have become culturally diverse while remaining physically homogeneous.

SECTION REVIEW

- Nineteenth- and twentieth-century discoveries of hominid fossil remains upset traditional beliefs about human origins.

- In Charles Darwin's theory of evolution, natural selection of traits that promote survival and reproduction accounts for the gradual development of modern humans from primate ancestors.

- Bipedalism, a large brain, and a lower location of the larynx that enables speech are advantages that humans have over other primates.

- Africa is the place of origin of the earliest hominids, about 7 million years ago, and of modern humans 100,000 years ago. About 50,000 years ago they began to migrate to the other continents, using land bridges during glacial periods with low sea levels.

TECHNOLOGY AND CULTURE IN THE ICE AGE

Evidence of early humans' splendid creative abilities came to light in 1940 near Lascaux in southern France. Youths who stumbled onto the entrance to a vast underground cavern found its walls covered with paintings of animals, including many that had been extinct for thousands of years. Other ancient cave paintings have been found in Spain, Africa, Australia, and elsewhere. The artistic quality of ancient cave art is vivid evidence that the biologically modern people who made such art were intellectually modern as well (see Diversity and Dominance: Cave Art).

The production of similar art and specialized tools over wide areas and long periods of time demonstrates that skills and ideas were deliberately passed along within societies. These learned patterns of action and expression constitute **culture**. Culture includes both material objects, such as dwellings, clothing, tools, and crafts, and nonmaterial values, beliefs, and languages. While some animals also learn new ways, their activities are determined primarily by inherited instincts. Among humans, instincts are less important than the cultural traditions that each generation learns from its elders.

culture Socially transmitted patterns of action and expression.

Food Gathering and Stone Tools

When archaeologists examine the remains of ancient human sites, the first thing that jumps out at them is the abundant evidence of human toolmaking. Because the tools that survive are mostly made of stone, the extensive period of history from the appearance of the first fabricated stone tools around 2.6 million years ago until the appearance of metal tools around four thousand years ago has been called the **Stone Age**.

The name can be misleading because not all tools were made of stone. Early humans also made useful objects out of bone, skin, wood, plant fibers, and other materials less likely than stone to survive the ravages of time. Early scholars recognized two phases of the Stone Age: the **Paleolithic (pay-lee-oh-LITH-ik)** (Old Stone Age), down to 8000 B.C.E., and the **Neolithic (NEE-OH-LITH-IK)** (New Stone Age), which is associated with the rise of agriculture. Modern scientists have developed more complex schemes with many subdivisions.

Stone Age The historical period characterized by the production of tools from stone and other nonmetallic substances.

Paleolithic The period of the Stone Age associated with the evolution of humans.

Neolithic The period of the Stone Age associated with the ancient Agricultural Revolution(s).

Most early human activity centered on gathering food. Like the australopithecines, early humans depended heavily on vegetable foods such as leaves, seeds, and grasses, but during the Ice Age the consumption of highly nutritious animal flesh increased. Moreover, unlike australopithecines, humans regularly made tools. These two changes—increased meat eating and toolmaking—appear to be closely linked.

Specimens of crude early tools found in the Great Rift Valley of eastern Africa reveal that *Homo habilis* made tools by chipping flakes off the edges of volcanic stones. The razor-sharp edges of such flakes are highly effective for skinning and butchering wild animals.

Lacking the skill to hunt and kill large animals, small-brained *Homo habilis* probably obtained animal protein by scavenging meat from kills made by animal predators or resulting from accidents. This species probably used large stone "choppers" for cracking open bones to get at the nutritious marrow. The fact that such tools are found far from the volcanic outcrops where they were quarried suggests that people carried them long distances for use at kill sites and camps.

Members of *Homo erectus* were also scavengers, but their larger brains made them more clever. They made more effective tools for butchering large animals, including a hand ax formed by removing chips from both sides of a stone to produce a sharp outer edge. The hand ax was an efficient multipurpose tool, suitable for skinning and butchering animals, for scraping skins clean for use as clothing and mats, for sharpening wooden tools, and for digging up edible roots. Since a hand ax can also be hurled accurately for nearly 100 feet (30 meters), it might also have been used as a projectile to fell animals. *Homo erectus* even hunted elephants by driving them into swamps, where they became trapped and died.

Members of *Homo sapiens* were far more skillful hunters. Using their superior intelligence and an array of finely made tools, they tracked and killed large animals. Sharp stone flakes chipped from carefully prepared rock cores were used in combination with other materials. Attaching a stone point to a wooden shaft made a spear. Embedding several sharp stone flakes in a bone handle produced a sawing tool.

Cave Art

Were the people who lived tens of thousands of years ago different from people today? Biologically, members of *Homo sapiens* have not changed much over time. But what were our ancestors like inside—in their thoughts, imaginations, and emotions? Did their eyes see beauty, their ears hear music, and their minds wonder at the meaning of the world around them and the celestial bodies above them? One way to approach this difficult question is to look at the earliest art.

The oldest recognizable human art, a carefully cross-hatched bone from Blombos Cave east of Cape Town, South Africa, dates from over 70,000 years ago. When the first painted cave was discovered at Altamira in Spain in the later nineteenth century, many people refused to believe that the images were the work of prehistoric people. The quality of the art was too high, the skill of the artists too impressive, to reconcile with conventional conceptions of "cavemen." Scientists calculated that the paintings in Lascaux, the most famous of the caves, discovered in southwestern France in 1940, date to about 15,000 B.C.E. Then in 1994 the discovery of Chauvet (sho-VAY) Cave, in southeastern France, pushed back the evidence

for painting by humans to a much earlier time. Jean-Marie Chauvet and two companions discovered a small cliffside entrance into a vast cave complex. The original entrance to the cave had been closed off long before by a rock slide, thereby sealing and preserving not only the magnificent paintings on the walls of the cave, but also animal bones, human and animal footprints, and other artifacts. The Chauvet Cave paintings are currently dated to between 30,000 and 35,000 years ago. The cave has been put off-limits by the French government to preserve it from human and environmental damage, and even scholars are only allowed in for short periods of time. (However, plans are under way to create a nearby replica of the cave for tourists!)

The prehistoric artists of Chauvet lived during the Ice Age, when glaciers covered much of France. The Ardèche River Gorge, where the cave is located, was teeming with life—modern humans, Neanderthals, and animals of all sorts, both those that humans hunted and dangerous predators. The cave paintings depict the animals of that epoch: cave lions, cave bears, rhinoceroses, wild horses, bison, reindeer, aurochs

Courtesy, Jean Clottes

The Lion Panel in Chauvet Cave, France

Indeed, members of *Homo sapiens* were so successful as hunters that they may have caused a series of ecological crises. Between 40,000 and 13,000 years ago the giant mastodons and mammoths gradually disappeared from Africa, Southeast Asia, and northern Europe. In North America around 11,000 years ago, three-fourths of the large mammals became extinct, including giant bison, camels, ground sloths, stag-moose, giant cats, mastodons, and mammoths. In Australia there was a similar event. However, since these extinctions occurred during severe cold spells at the end of the Ice Age, it is difficult to distinguish the effects of climate change and human predation.

(wild oxen), and mammoths. The only representations of humans are the silhouettes of hands, made by blowing paint around them (experts can identify one particular individual whose handprint is found at several cave locations by a distinctively curling little finger), and a large stalactite projection, near the back of the cave, painted to represent the lower half of a woman. Scholars have noted the similarity of this figure to a multitude of small female statuettes, often called Venuses (after the Roman goddess of sex and love) because of the exaggerated genitalia, found throughout Europe from as early as 35,000 to as late as 11,000 years ago. This similarity suggests a continuity in representation throughout the Paleolithic and, presumably, a continuity in the thoughts behind it, that may have to do with promoting reproduction.

The walls of the cave are not flat, but rather full of projections and indentations, and the artists have skillfully incorporated these natural features into the paintings, as well as etched the outlines of some figures to give them a startling three-dimensional quality. Besides having a rough sense of perspective, they used sophisticated techniques to represent motion and multiplicity, such as a bison with eight legs to indicate rapid motion. Sometimes new figures were painted over earlier figures, suggesting that the activity of painting may have gone on over a long period of time.

No traces of human habitation have been found in the cave, so it evidently had a different purpose. One can only marvel at the effort that must have gone into illuminating the deep recesses of the cave so that the artists could see what they were doing. There are black smudge marks on the walls where torchbearers wiped off excess carbon to keep the torches lit. There is also an altar-like stone platform on which a cave bear's skull had been purposefully set.

The scenes reproduced here, from the large tableau of animal drawings at Chauvet known as the "Lion Panel," show the skill and techniques of the artists and the variety of subject matter. From the right comes a band of female lions on the hunt, approaching a herd of bison, who turn to regard them. Across a cleft in the rock the panel resumes with a herd of rhinoceroses and another group of lions at the far left.

Why did the prehistoric artists of Chauvet and other caves draw what they did? And why in caves? It is a huge challenge for us to understand the meaning and purpose of these cave paintings. Prehistory is, by definition, a time before there were written texts that can tell us about ancient humans' lives and thoughts. For such periods we primarily depend upon archaeology, but while excavated artifacts can tell us about the material culture of a society—their tools, weapons, jewelry, food, burial practices, and the physical spaces in which they operated—it is much harder to infer from physical objects the social institutions, customs, beliefs, and values of the people who made and used them. However, we can regard these paintings as a kind of text because the artists were trying to communicate something to their fellows. Modern scholars, operating across a vast cultural divide between us and the Paleolithic people of Chauvet, can only speculate about the meaning of the paintings to the artists and their contemporaries and the cultural function of the caves.

Commentators often start with the context in which the art was made. Given that humans did not live in Chauvet Cave, what might have been its function? It was no accident that they went to such trouble to work inside dark caves that could be illuminated only with crude torches. However, they probably did not do so with the goal of protecting and preserving their art for tens of thousands of years. Rather, the artists may have gone deep underground "to feel the power of the earth"—they may have believed that the wild animals and the earth itself were full of spiritual energy. (Indeed, many of the archaeologists who have worked in Chauvet and other caves have commented on the mysterious, spiritual feeling induced by being deep inside the earth.) It is thus possible that the artists were the spiritual guides of their communities, and the decorated caverns were holy places where religious ceremonies were performed and where those present would have had powerful religious experiences.

One must also consider the subject matter of the paintings, the preponderance of animals and the absence (with the exceptions already noted) of humans. The animals represented include both those that humans hunted and those they did not, and the artists had a fund of knowledge about the appearance, movement, and behavior of those animals, derived, no doubt, from close observation. It has been suggested that ancient cave art may have expressed the mystical relationship of humans with the animals with whom they shared the world. Perhaps humans could absorb something of the power of the bears, antelope, bison, or other animals depicted in the caves by viewing or touching them.

QUESTIONS FOR ANALYSIS

1. How persuasive are these explanations of the function of the painted caves and the meaning of the paintings? Can you think of alternative explanations?

2. Is there anything in the depiction of the animals that suggests whether the artists were in awe of them, felt superior to them, or felt at one with them? What might be the significance of the fact that not all the animals depicted were ones that people hunted to eat?

3. What comparisons can you make between this cave painting and the rock engraving of cattle that opens this chapter?

---

foragers People who support themselves by hunting wild animals and gathering wild edible plants and insects.

Despite the evidence for hunting, anthropologists do not believe that early humans depended primarily on meat for their food. The few surviving present-day **foragers** (hunting and food-gathering peoples) in Africa derive the bulk of their day-to-day nourishment from wild vegetable foods, with meat reserved for feasts. The same was probably true for Stone Age peoples, even though tools for gathering and processing vegetable foods have left few traces because they were made of perishable materials. Ancient humans would have used skins and mats woven from leaves for collecting fruits, berries, and wild seeds. They would have dug edible roots out of the ground with wooden sticks.

Both meat and vegetables become tastier and easier to digest when they are cooked. The first cooked foods were probably found by accident after wildfires. Humans may have been setting fires deliberately as early as 1.4 million years ago, and maintaining hearths around 500,000 years ago. However, only with the appearance of clay cooking pots some 18,000 years ago in East Asia is there hard evidence of cooking.

Gender Roles and Social Life

Researchers have studied the behavior and organization of nonhuman primates for clues about very early human society. Gorillas and chimpanzees live in groups consisting of several adult males and females and their offspring. Status varies with age and sex, and a dominant male usually heads the group. Sexual unions between males and females generally do not result in long-term pairing. Instead, the strongest ties are those between a female and her children and among siblings. Adult males are often recruited from neighboring bands.

Very early human groups likely shared some of these primate traits, but long before the advent of modern *Homo sapiens* the two-parent family would have been common. We can only guess how this change developed, but it is likely that physical and social evolution were linked. Big-headed humans with large brains have to be born in a less mature state than other mammals so that they can pass through the narrow birth canal. Other large mammals are mature at two or three years of age; humans are not able to care for themselves until the age of twelve to fifteen. The need of human infants and children for much longer nurturing makes care by mothers, fathers, and other family members a biological imperative.

The human reproductive cycle also became unique. In many other species sexual contact is biologically restricted to a special mating season of the year or to the fertile part of the female's menstrual cycle. Moreover, among other primates the choice of mate is usually not a matter for long deliberation. To a female baboon in heat any male will do, and to a male baboon any receptive female is a suitable sexual partner. In contrast, adult humans can mate at any time and are much choosier about their partners. Once they mate, frequent sexual contact promotes deep emotional ties and long-term bonding.

An enduring bond between human parents made it much easier for vulnerable offspring to receive the care they needed during the long period of their childhood. Working together, mothers and fathers could nurture dependent children of different ages at the same time, unlike other large mammals, whose females must raise their offspring nearly to maturity before beginning another reproductive cycle. Spacing births close together also would have enabled humans to multiply more rapidly than other large mammals.

Researchers studying present-day foragers infer that Ice Age women would have done most of the gathering and cooking (which they could do while caring for small children). Older women past childbearing age would have been the most knowledgeable and productive food gatherers. Men, with stronger arms, would have been more suited than women to hunting, particularly for large animals. Since the male hunters will only occasionally have succeeded in bringing down their prey, while the women gatherers provided the bulk of the band's daily diet, it is likely that women held a respected position in early human societies.

All recent foragers have lived in small bands. The community has to have enough members to defend itself from predators and divide responsibility for collection and preparation of foods. However, too

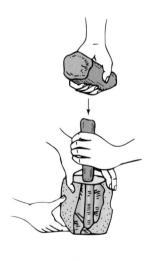

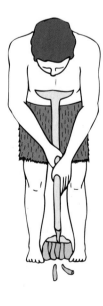

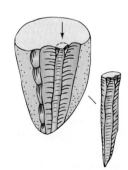

Making Stone Tools   About 35,000 years ago the manufacture of stone tools became highly specialized. Small blades chipped from a rock core were mounted in a bone or wooden handle. Not only were such composite tools more varied than earlier all-purpose hand axes, but the small blades also required fewer rock cores—an important consideration where suitable rocks were scarce.   From Jacques Bordaz, *Tools of the Old and New Stone Age*. Copyright 1970 by Jacques Bordaz. Redrawn by the permission of Addison-Wesley Educational Publishers, Inc.

many members would exhaust the food available in its immediate vicinity. The band has to move at regular intervals to follow migrating animals and take advantage of seasonally ripening plants in different places. Archaeological evidence from Ice Age campsites suggests that early humans, too, lived in highly mobile bands.

Hearths and Cultural Expressions

Because frequent moves were necessary, early hunter-gatherers did not lavish much time on housing. Natural shelters under overhanging rocks or in caves were favorite camping places to which bands returned at regular intervals. Where the climate was severe or where natural shelters did not exist, people erected huts of branches, stones, bones, skins, and leaves. Large, solid structures were common in fishing villages that grew up along riverbanks and lakeshores, where the abundance of fish permitted people to occupy the same site year-round.

Animal skin cloaks were probably an early form of clothing. Although the oldest evidence of fibers woven into cloth dates from about 26,000 years ago, the appearance of the body louse around 70,000 years ago has been linked to people beginning to wear close-fitting garments. An "Iceman" from 5,300 years ago, whose frozen remains were found in the European Alps in 1991, was wearing many different garments made of animal skins sewn together with cord fashioned from vegetable fibers and rawhide (see Environment and Technology: The Iceman).

Although accidents, erratic weather, and disease might take a heavy toll on a foraging band, day-to-day existence was probably not particularly hard or unpleasant. Studies suggest that, in plant- and game-rich areas, obtaining necessary food, clothing, and shelter would have occupied only from three to five hours a day. This would have left a great deal of time for artistic endeavors, toolmaking, and social life.

The foundations of science, art, and religion were built during the Stone Age. Basic to human survival was extensive knowledge about the natural environment. Gatherers learned which local plants were best for food and when they were available, and hunters gained intimate knowledge of the habits of game animals. People learned how to use plant and animal parts for clothing, twine, building materials, and dyes; minerals for paints and stones for tools; as well as natural substances effective for medicine and consciousness altering. It is very likely that the transmission of such knowledge involved verbal communication, even though direct evidence for language appears only in later periods.

Early music and dance have left no traces, but there is abundant evidence of painting and drawing (see Diversity and Dominance: Cave Art). Because many cave paintings feature wild animals that were hunted for food, some believe they were meant to record hunting scenes or formed part of magical and religious rites to ensure successful hunting. However, a newly discovered cave in southern France features rhinoceroses, panthers, bears, and other animals that probably were not hunted. Other drawings include people dressed in animal skins and smeared with paint. In many caves there are stencils of human hands. Are these the signatures of the artists or the world's oldest graffiti? Some scholars suspect that other marks in cave paintings and on bones from this period may represent efforts at counting or writing. Other theories suggest that cave and rock art represent concerns with fertility, efforts to educate the young, or elaborate mechanisms for time reckoning.

Without written texts it is difficult to know about the religious beliefs of early humans. Sites of deliberate human burials from about 100,000 years ago give some hints. The fact that an adult was often buried with stone implements, food, clothing, and red-ochre powder suggests that early people revered their leaders, relatives, and companions enough to honor them after death and may imply a belief in an afterlife where such items would be useful.

Today we recognize that the Old Stone Age, whose existence was scarcely dreamed of two centuries ago, was a formative period. Important in its own right, it also laid the foundation for major changes ahead as human communities passed from being food gatherers to food producers.

SECTION REVIEW

- Unlike other animals, humans have used the learned patterns of culture to adapt to and occupy very diverse environments.

- Early humans made tools, foraged for food, and hunted. They found natural shelters or built temporary shelters, and they provided themselves with clothing.

- In early hunter-gatherer societies, women gathered the plant foods that provided most of the band's diet, while men did the hunting. The two-parent family offered children protection and a long period to mature.

- This lifestyle left them leisure to develop art and religion. Although the remains of their art and religion are difficult to interpret, it is clear that early modern humans had the mental capabilities that we have.

The Iceman

The discovery of the well-preserved remains of a man at the edge of a melting glacier in the European Alps in 1991 provided detailed information about everyday technologies of the fourth millennium B.C.E. Not just the body of this "Iceman" was well preserved. His clothing, his tools, and even the food in his stomach survived in remarkably good condition.

Dressed from head to toe for the cold weather of the mountains, the fifty-year-old man was wearing a fur hat fastened under the chin with a strap, a vest of different colored deerskins, leather leggings and loincloth, and a padded cloak made of grasses. His calfskin shoes also were padded with grass for warmth and comfort. The articles of clothing had been sewn together with fiber and leather cords. He carried a birch-bark drinking cup.

In a leather fanny pack he carried small flint tools for cutting, scraping, and punching holes, as well as some tinder for making a fire. He also carried a leather quiver with flint-tipped arrows, but his 6-foot (1.8-meter) bow was unfinished, lacking a bowstring. In addition, he had a flint knife and a tool for sharpening flints. His most sophisticated tool, indicating the dawning of the age of metals, was a copper-bladed ax with a wooden handle.

His death was violent, caused either by a small arrowhead lodged in his shoulder or a blow to the head. In his stomach, researchers found the remains of the meat-rich meal he had eaten not long before he died.

© Smetek/STERN/Picture Press

The Iceman This is an artist's rendition of what the Iceman might have looked like. Notice his tools, remarkable evidence of the technology of his day.

THE AGRICULTURAL REVOLUTIONS

For most of human existence people ate only wild plants and animals. But around 10,000 years ago global climate changes seem to have induced some societies to enhance their food supplies with domesticated plants and animals. More and more people became food producers over the following millennia. Although hunting and gathering did not disappear, this transition from foraging to food production was one of the great turning points in history because it fostered a rapid increase in population and greatly altered humans' relationship to nature (see Map 1.2).

Because agriculture arose in combination with new kinds of stone tools, archaeologists called this period the Neolithic, or New Stone Age, and the rise of agriculture the Neolithic Revolution. But that name can be misleading: first, stone tools were not its essential component, and second, it was not a single event but a series of separate transformations in different parts of the world. A better term is **Agricultural Revolutions**, which emphasizes that the central change was in food production and that agriculture arose independently in many places. In most cases agriculture included the domestication of animals as well as the cultivation of new food crops.

Agricultural Revolutions The change from food gathering to food production that occurred between about 8000 and 2000 B.C.E. Also known as the Neolithic Revolution.

The Transition to Plant Cultivation

Food gathering gave way to food production in stages spread over hundreds of generations. The process may have begun when forager bands, returning year after year to the same seasonal camps, deliberately scattered the seeds of desirable plants in locations where they would thrive and discouraged the growth of competing plants by clearing them away. Such semicultivation

A Neolithic House This reconstruction of an early permanent human habitation has a single door and no windows. Simple dwellings were constructed of mud-brick over a timber frame or of wattle and daub, a lattice of branches covered with a sticky composite of mud, straw, etc. The roof is thatched, a layering of dried vegetation that sheds water.

Herv Champollion/akg-images/Newscom

could have supplemented food gathering for many generations. Eventually, families choosing to concentrate on food production would have settled permanently near their fields.

The presence of new, specialized tools for agriculture first alerted archaeologists to the beginning of a food production revolution. These included polished stone heads to work the soil, sharp stone chips embedded in bone or wooden handles to cut grain, and stone mortars to pulverize grain. Since stone axes were not very efficient for clearing away shrubs and trees, farmers used fire to get rid of unwanted undergrowth (the ashes were a natural fertilizer).

The transition to agriculture occurred first in the Middle East. By 8000 B.C.E. humans, by selecting the highest-yielding strains, had transformed certain wild grasses into the domesticated grains now known as emmer wheat and barley. They also discovered that alternating the cultivation of grains and pulses (plants yielding edible seeds such as lentils and peas) helped maintain soil fertility. Women, the principal gatherers of wild plant foods, had the expertise to play a major role in this transition to plant cultivation, but the heavy work of clearing the fields would have fallen to men.

Plants domesticated in the Middle East spread to Greece as early as 6000 B.C.E., to the light-soiled plains of central Europe and along the Danube River shortly after 4000 B.C.E., and then to other parts of Europe over the next millennium (see Map 1.2). Early farmers in Europe and elsewhere practiced shifting cultivation, also known as swidden agriculture. After a few growing seasons, the fields were left fallow (abandoned to natural vegetation) for a time to restore their fertility, and new fields were cleared nearby. From around 2600 B.C.E. people in central Europe began using ox-drawn wooden plows to till heavier and richer soils.

Wheat and barley could not spread farther south because the rainfall patterns in most of Africa were unsuited to their growth. Instead, separate Agricultural Revolutions took place in Saharan and sub-Saharan Africa, beginning almost as early as in the Middle East. During a particularly wet period after 8000 B.C.E., people in what is now the eastern Sahara began to cultivate sorghum, a grain derived from wild grasses they had previously gathered. Over the next three thousand years the Saharan farmers domesticated pearl millet, black-eyed peas, a kind of peanut, sesame, and gourds. In the Ethiopian highlands, farmers domesticated finger millet and a grain called tef. The return of drier conditions about 5000 B.C.E. led many Saharan farmers to move to the Nile Valley, where the annual flooding of the river provided moisture for farming. People in the rain forests of equatorial West Africa domesticated rice and yams.

Rice, which thrives in warm and wet conditions, was probably first domesticated in the Yangzi River Valley in central China, possibly as early as 10,000 B.C.E., and by 3000 B.C.E. it had made its way to Southeast Asia and India. In India several pulses domesticated about 2000 B.C.E. (including hyacinth beans, green grams, and black grams) were cultivated along with rice.

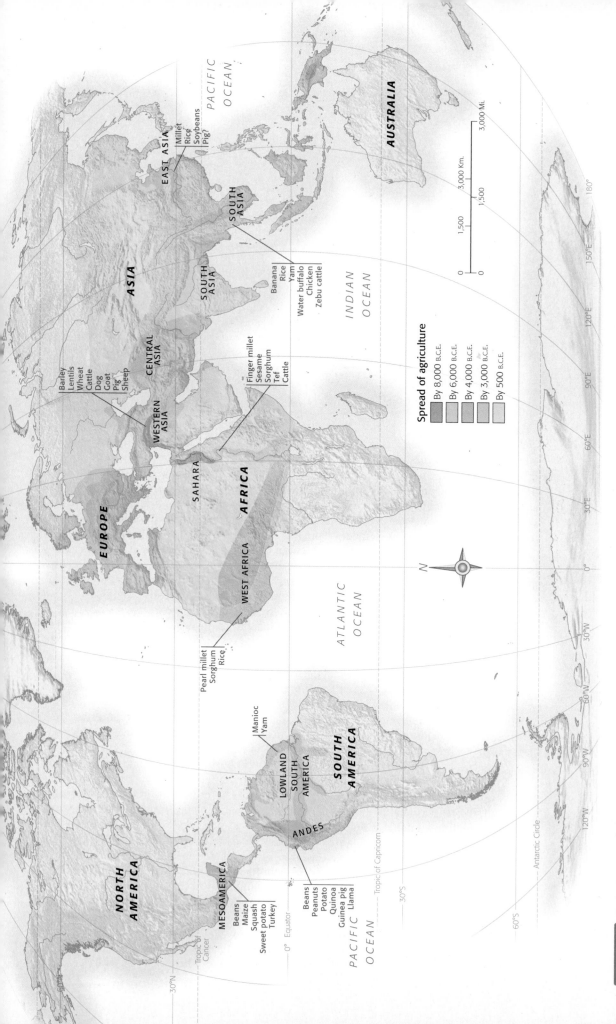

MAP 1.2 **Early Centers of Plant and Animal Domestication** Many different parts of the world made original contributions to domestication during the Agricultural Revolutions that began about 10,000 years ago. Later interactions helped spread these domesticated animals and plants to new locations. In lands less suitable for crop cultivation, pastoralism and hunting remained more important for supplying food. © Cengage Learning

The inhabitants of the American continents were domesticating other crops by about 5000 B.C.E.: maize (mayz), or corn, in Mexico, manioc in Brazil and Panama, and beans and squash in Mesoamerica. By 4000 B.C.E., the inhabitants of Peru were developing potatoes and quinoa (kee-NOH-uh), a protein-rich seed grain. Insofar as their climates and soils permitted, other farming communities throughout the Americas adopted these crops, along with tomatoes and peppers.

Domesticated Animals and Pastoralism

The first domesticated animals were probably dogs descended from wolves that were used initially to help hunters track game and later to herd other domesticated animals as well as provide protection and companionship. There is much debate about the place, date, and process of domestication. Experts have argued for Siberia, the Middle East, and Europe as the site of the first domestication. The time of domestication may go back 30,000 years or more, though the first known burial of a dog with a human—a sure sign of the relationship—is from around 14,000 B.C.E.

The domestication of animals expanded rapidly during the Neolithic period, as other animals were domesticated to provide meat, milk, and energy. Refuse heaps outside some Middle East villages during the centuries after 7000 B.C.E. show that sheep and goat bones gradually replaced gazelle bones. As wild sheep and goats scavenged for food scraps around villages, the tamer animals probably accepted human control and protection in exchange for a ready supply of food. Selective breeding for desirable characteristics such as high milk production and long wooly coats eventually led to distinct breeds of sheep and goats.

Elsewhere, other animal species were domesticated during the centuries before 3000 B.C.E.: wild cattle in northern Africa or the Middle East; donkeys in northern Africa; water buffalo in China; and humped-back Zebu (ZEE-boo) cattle in India. Varieties of domesticated animals spread from one region to another.

Once cattle became tame enough to be yoked to plows, they became essential to grain production. In addition, animal droppings provided valuable fertilizer. In the Americas, however, comparatively few species of wild animals were suitable for domestication, and domesticated animals could not spread from elsewhere because the land bridge to Asia had been submerged by raised sea levels. In the Western Hemisphere, therefore, domesticated llamas provided transport and wool, while guinea pigs and turkeys furnished meat. Hunting remained the most important source of meat for Amerindians.

In the more arid parts of Africa and in some regions of western and Central Asia, pastoralism, a way of life dependent on large herds of small and large stock, predominated. As the Sahara approached its maximum dryness around 2500 B.C.E., pastoralists replaced farmers, who migrated southward (see Chapter 9). Moving their herds to new pastures and watering places throughout the year made pastoralists almost as mobile as foragers and discouraged

Ancient Dog Burial   This husky-like dog, buried 7000 years ago in Siberia, was interred along with, and in the same manner as humans. This, and the fact that he ate the same food as humans, suggests that he was seen as a companion and helper. Skeletal damage has also been interpreted as showing that he carried heavy loads and may have been repeatedly injured on hunts.

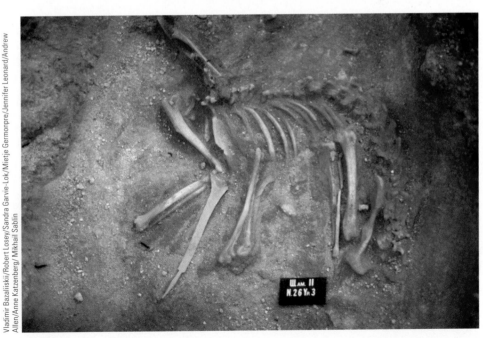

Vladimir Bazaliiskii/Robert Losey/Sandra Garvie-Lok/Mietje Germonpre/Jennifer Leonard/Andrew Allen/Anne Katzenberg/ Mikhail Sablin

accumulation of bulky possessions and construction of substantial dwellings. Early herders probably relied more heavily on milk than on meat, since killing animals reduced their herds. During wet seasons, they may also have done some hasty crop cultivation or bartered meat and skins for plant foods with nearby farming communities.

Agriculture and Ecological Crisis

Why did the Agricultural Revolutions occur? Some theories assume that people were drawn to food production by its obvious advantages, such as the promise of a secure food supply. It has recently been suggested that people in the Middle East might have settled down so they could grow enough grains to ensure themselves a ready supply of beer.

However, most experts believe that climate change drove people to abandon hunting and gathering in favor of agriculture or pastoralism. With the end of the Great Ice Age, the temperate lands became exceptionally warm between 6000 and 2000 B.C.E., the era when people in many parts of the world adopted agriculture. The precise nature of the crisis probably varied. Shortages of wild food in the Middle East caused by a dry spell or population growth may have prodded people to take up food production. Elsewhere, a warmer, wetter climate could turn grasslands into forest, reducing supplies of game and wild grains.

In many drier parts of the world, where wild food remained abundant, people did not take up agriculture. The inhabitants of Australia continued to rely exclusively on foraging until recent centuries. Many Amerindians in the arid grasslands from Alaska to the Gulf of Mexico hunted bison, others in the Pacific Northwest took up salmon-fishing, and east of the Mississippi River food gatherers thrived on abundant supplies of fish, shellfish, and aquatic animals. In Africa, in the equatorial rain forest and in the southern part of the continent, conditions favored retention of the older ways. The reindeer-based societies of northern Eurasia were also unaffected by the spread of farming.

Whatever the causes, the gradual adoption of food production transformed most parts of the world. A hundred thousand years ago there were fewer than 2 million people, and their range was largely confined to the temperate and tropical regions of Africa and Eurasia. The population may have fallen even lower during the last glacial epoch, between 32,000 and 13,000 years ago. Then, as the glaciers retreated and people took up agriculture, their numbers rose. World population may have reached 10 million by 5000 B.C.E. and then mushroomed to between 50 million and 100 million by 1000 B.C.E.[1] This increase led to important changes in social and cultural life.

SECTION REVIEW

- Around 10,000 years ago humans began to cultivate plants, selecting for those with the highest nutritional yield, and to domesticate animals. These Agricultural Revolutions arose in various parts of the world.

- Climate change at the end of the last Ice Age is probably the major reason for the switch from food gathering to food production.

- Agriculturalists gradually spread across much of the planet, but in certain environments pastoralism, the dependence of people on herd animals, prevailed.

- The more secure food supply made possible by agriculture led to a great increase in human population.

LIFE IN NEOLITHIC COMMUNITIES

Evidence that an ecological crisis may have driven people to food production has prompted a reexamination of the assumption that farmers enjoyed better lives than foragers. Modern studies demonstrate that food producers have to work much harder and for much longer periods than do food gatherers, clearing and cultivating land, guiding herds to pastures, and guarding them from predators.

Although early farmers were less likely to starve because they could store food between harvests, their diet was less varied and nutritious than that of foragers. Skeletal remains show that Neolithic farmers were shorter on average than earlier food-gathering peoples. Farmers were also more likely to die at an earlier age because people in permanent settlements were more exposed to diseases. Their water was contaminated by human waste; disease-bearing vermin and insects infested their bodies and homes; and they could catch new diseases from their domesticated animals.

---

[1]Colin McEvedy and Richard Jones, *Atlas of World Population History* (New York: Penguin Books, 1978), 13–15.

The Triumph of Food Producers

So how did farmers displace foragers? Some researchers have envisioned a violent struggle between practitioners of the two ways of life; others have argued for a more peaceful transition. In most cases, farmers seem to have displaced foragers by gradual infiltration rather than by conquest.

The key to the food producers' expansion may have been the fact that their small surpluses gave them a long-term advantage in population growth by ensuring higher survival rates during times of drought or other crisis. Archaeologist Colin Renfrew argues that over a few centuries farming population densities in Europe could have increased by a factor of 50 to 100. As population rose, individuals who had to farm far from their native village would have formed a new settlement close to their fields. A steady, nonviolent expansion of only 12 to 19 miles (20 to 30 kilometers) a generation could have repopulated the whole of Europe between 6500 and 3500 B.C.E.[2] So gradual a process need not have provoked sharp conflicts with existing foragers, who simply could have stayed clear of the agricultural frontier or gradually adopted agriculture themselves. New studies that map genetic changes also attest to a gradual spread of agricultural people across Europe from southeast to northwest.[3]

The expanding farming communities were organized around kinship and marriage. Nuclear families (parents and their children) probably lived in separate households but felt solidarity with all those related to them by descent from common ancestors. These kinship units, known as lineages (LIN-ee-ij) or clans, acted together to defend their common interests and land. Some societies trace descent equally through both parents, but most give greater importance to descent through either the mother (matrilineal [mat-ruh-LIN-ee-uhl] societies) or the father (patrilineal [pat-ruh-LIN-ee-uhl] societies). It is important not to confuse tracing descent through women (matrilineality) with the rule of women (matriarchy [MAY-tree-ahr-key]).

Cultural Expressions

Kinship systems influenced early agricultural people's outlook on the world. Burials of elders might be occasions for elaborate ceremonies expressing their descendants' group solidarity. Plastered skulls found in the ancient city of Jericho (JER-ih-koh) (see Map 2.1) may be evidence of such early ancestor reverence or worship.

A society's religious beliefs tend to reflect its relations to nature. The religion of food gatherers centered on sacred groves, springs, and wild animals, while pastoralists worshiped the sky-god who controlled the rains and guided their migrations. In contrast, the religion of many farming communities centered on the Earth Mother; since women bear children, a female deity was logically believed to be the source of all new life.

The worship of ancestors, gods of the heavens, and earthly nature and fertility deities varied from place to place, and many societies combined the different elements. A recently discovered complex of stone structures in the Egyptian desert that was in use by 5000 B.C.E. includes burial chambers presumably for ancestors, a calendar circle, and pairs of upright stones that frame the rising sun at the summer solstice. The builders must have been deeply concerned with the cycle of the seasons and how they were linked to the movement of heavenly bodies. Other **megaliths** (meaning "big stones") were erected elsewhere. Observation and worship of the sun are evident at the famous Stonehenge site in England, constructed about 2000 B.C.E. Megalithic burial chambers dating from 4000 B.C.E. are evidence of ancestor rituals in western and southern Europe. The early ones appear to have been communal burial chambers, erected by descent groups to mark their claims to farmland. In the Middle East, the Americas, and other parts of the world, giant earth burial mounds may have served similar functions.

Another fundamental contribution of the Neolithic period was the dissemination of the large language families that form the basis of most languages spoken today. The root language of the giant Indo-European language family arose around 5000 B.C.E., probably in the region north of the Black and Caspian Seas. Its spread to the south and west across Europe and south and east into Anatolia (modern Turkey), Iran, and the Indian subcontinent may have been the

megaliths Structures and complexes of very large stones constructed for ceremonial and religious purposes in Neolithic times.

---

[2]Colin Renfrew, *Archaeology and Language: The Puzzle of Indo-European Origins* (New York: Cambridge University Press, 1988), 125, 150.

[3]Cavalli-Sforza, L. Luca, Paolo Menozzi, and Alberto Piazza, *The History and Geography of Human Genes* (Princeton, NJ: Princeton University Press, 1994).

Passage-Tomb at Newgrange, Ireland Dating to around 3200 B.C.E., Newgrange is one of the oldest and most impressive Neolithic structures. A wall of white quartz stones rises above a row of horizontal megaliths on either side of the entrance, from which a passage leads to a spacious interior chamber. For several minutes each year, at sunrise on the winter solstice, the chamber is illuminated by a shaft of light that passes through the "roof-box" above the entrance.

work of pioneering agriculturalists. In the course of this very gradual expansion, Celtic, Germanic, Romance, Slavic, Iranian, and Indian languages developed. Similarly, the Afro-Asiatic language family of the Middle East and northern Africa may have been the result of food producers' expansion, as might the spread of the Sino-Tibetan family in East and Southeast Asia.

Early Towns and Specialists

Most early farmers lived in small villages, but in some parts of the world a few villages grew into more densely populated towns that were centers of trade and specialized crafts. These towns had grander dwellings and ceremonial buildings, as well as large structures for storing surplus food until the next harvest. Farmers could make most of the buildings, tools, and containers they needed in their spare time, but in large communities some craft specialists devoted their full time to making products of unusual complexity or beauty.

Two early towns in the Middle East that have been extensively excavated are Jericho on the west bank of the Jordan River and Çatal Hüyük **(cha-TAHL hoo-YOOK)** in central Turkey (Map 2.1 shows their locations). Jericho, located near a natural spring, was an unusually large and elaborate agricultural settlement around 8000 B.C.E. whose round, mud-brick dwellings may have been modeled on hunters' tents. A millennium later, rectangular buildings with finely plastered walls and floors and wide doorways opened onto central courtyards. A massive stone wall surrounding the 10-acre (4-hectare) settlement defended it against attacks.

The ruins of Çatal Hüyük, an even larger town, date to between 7000 and 5000 B.C.E. and cover 32 acres (13 hectares). Its residents also occupied plastered mud-brick rooms with

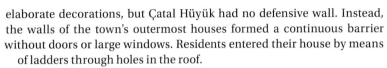

Neolithic Goddess   Many versions of a well-nourished and pregnant female figure were found at Çatal Hüyük. Here she is supported by twin leopards whose tails curve over her shoulders. To those who inhabited the city some 8,000 years ago, the figure likely represented fertility and power over nature.   The Art Archive/Museum of Anatolian Civilisations Ankara/Gianni Dagli Orti

elaborate decorations, but Çatal Hüyük had no defensive wall. Instead, the walls of the town's outermost houses formed a continuous barrier without doors or large windows. Residents entered their house by means of ladders through holes in the roof.

Çatal Hüyük prospered from long-distance trade in obsidian, a hard volcanic rock that craftspeople made into tools, weapons, mirrors, and ornaments. Other residents made fine pottery, wove baskets and woolen cloth, made stone and shell beads, and worked leather and wood. House sizes varied, but there is no evidence of a dominant class or centralized political structure. Fields around the town produced crops of barley and emmer wheat, as well as vegetables. Pigs were kept along with goats and sheep. Yet wild foods—acorns, wild grains, and game animals—still featured prominently in the residents' diet.

Wall paintings, remarkably similar to earlier cave paintings, reveal the continuing importance of hunting. Scenes depict people adorned with the skins of wild leopards, and men were buried with weapons of war and hunting, not the tools of farming.

There is a religious shrine for every two houses. Many rooms contain depictions of horned wild bulls, female breasts, goddesses, leopards, and handprints. Rituals involved burning grains, legumes, and meat as offerings, but there is no evidence of live animal sacrifice. Statues of plump female deities far outnumber statues of male deities, suggesting that the inhabitants primarily venerated a goddess of fertility. According to the site's principal excavator, "it seems extremely likely that the cult of the goddess was administered mainly by women."[4]

Metalworking became an important specialized occupation in the late Neolithic period. At Çatal Hüyük objects of copper and lead—metals that occur naturally in a fairly pure form—date to about 6400 B.C.E. In many parts of the world silver and gold were also worked at an early date. Because of their rarity and softness, those metals did not replace stone tools and weapons but were used primarily to make decorative or ceremonial objects. The discovery of many such objects in graves suggests they were symbols of status and power.

The emergence of towns and individuals engaged in crafts and other specialized occupations added to the workload of agriculturalists. Extra food had to be produced for nonfarmers such as priests and artisans. Added labor was needed to build permanent houses, town walls, and towers, not to mention religious structures and megalithic monuments. It is not known whether these tasks were performed freely or coerced.

SECTION REVIEW

- The lives of farmers are, in many respects, harder and more hazardous than those of hunter-gatherers.

- Agriculturalists, because of their capacity to increase their population, expanded across much of the planet at the expense of hunter-gatherers. The process was gradual and largely peaceful.

- Megaliths and other monumental structures are products of the diverse religious beliefs and practices of Neolithic societies.

- The spread of several large language families, including the Indo-European family, may have been linked to the spread of agriculture.

- In some places small agricultural villages developed into towns that were centers of trade and home to sophisticated craftspeople and people in other specialized professions. Farmers had to produce surpluses to feed nonfarming specialists.

- Jericho and Çatal Hüyük are two excavated sites that give us vivid glimpses of early Neolithic towns.

[4]James Mellaart, *Çatal Hüyük: A Neolithic Town in Anatolia* (New York: McGraw-Hill, 1967), 202.

CONCLUSION

The theory of evolution, supported by an enormous body of evidence, leads to far-reaching conclusions. Every living species evolved from a common ancestor. Humans are descended from earlier hominid species that evolved in Africa beginning about 7 million years ago, and every modern human being is descended from communities that evolved in Africa 50,000 years ago, with some groups then migrating to the other habitable continents. However diverse their cultures became, all human communities are directly related—to each other, to all other living species, and to the earth.

More than 2 million years ago there was a dramatic increase in the variety of tools early humans made—above all from stone, but also from bone, skin, wood, and plant fiber. Paleolithic families enjoyed a primarily vegetarian diet, though their skill at making weapons also made them effective hunters. Work was divided along gender lines, with women responsible for food gathering, cooking, and child rearing, and men for activities such as hunting because of their greater upper-body strength. Humans acquired a profound knowledge of the natural world that helped them create clothing, medicine, and other useful products. Cave and rock art opens a tantalizing window onto their imaginative and spiritual lives.

Research suggests that climate change drove the first human communities to abandon hunting and gathering and adopt the practices of agriculture and pastoralism. In the warmer era following the Great Ice Age around 9000 B.C.E., populations on every major continent except Australia underwent this great transformation, selecting high-yield strains of plants for cultivation and breeding livestock for the consumption of meat and dairy products. By 5000 B.C.E. wheat and barley had been domesticated in the Middle East; sorghum in Africa; rice in India and Southeast Asia; and corn, beans, and squash in Mesoamerica. After the dog, the first animals to be domesticated were sheep, goats, and cattle. Many people living in far northern and southern latitudes never adopted agriculture, but for those who did the consequences were enormous. In less than 10,000 years the global human population increased from 2 to 10 million.

Farming and settled life in the Neolithic period brought plagues of animal-borne diseases and a more labor-intensive way of life, but also the prosperity that gave rise to the first towns, trade, and specialized occupations. Human beings' intimate relationship to their ancestors, the earth, and seasonal cycles of death and rebirth is revealed by archaeological sites with a clearly religious significance—from the megalithic monuments of northern Europe to the household shrines at Çatal Hüyük. However foreign the world of our ancestors may seem, the scientific study of prehistory has brought us much closer to understanding it.

KEY TERMS

evolution p. 6
australopithecines p. 6
hominid p. 6
bipedalism p. 6

Great Ice Age p. 7
Homo habilis p. 7
Homo erectus p. 7
Homo sapiens p. 8

culture p. 11
Stone Age p. 11
Paleolithic p. 11
Neolithic p. 11

foragers p. 13
Agricultural
   Revolutions p. 16
megaliths p. 21

SUGGESTED READING

Anthony, David W. *The Horse, the Wheel, and Language: How Bronze-Age Riders from the Eurasian Steppes Shaped the Modern World*. 2007. A comprehensive overview of contemporary scholarly thinking about the origin and spread of the Indo-European languages.

Bandi, Hans-Georg. *The Art of the Stone Age: Forty Thousand Years of Rock Art*. 1961. A broad, global introduction to the earliest human art.

Cavalli-Sforza, L. Luca, and Francesco Cavalli-Sforza. *The Great Human Diasporas: The History of Diversity and Evolution*. 1995. Groundbreaking study of the genetic evidence for human evolution, though it doesn't take account of discoveries since the decoding of the human genome.

Curtis, Gregory. *The Cave Painters: Probing the Mysteries of the World's First Artists*. 2006. A readable account of both the history of discoveries of cave art and theories about its interpretation.

Ehrenberg, Margaret. *Women in Prehistory*. 1989. Provides interesting, though necessarily speculative, discussions of women's early history.

Fagan, Brian. *People of the Earth: An Introduction to World Prehistory*, 12th ed. 2006. A reliable textbook introduction to human prehistory.

Hodder, Ian. *The Leopard's Tale: Revealing the Mysteries of Catalhoyuk*. 2006. The director of current excavations at one of the earliest cities reveals the latest findings and interpretations.

Johanson, Donald, Leorna Johanson, and Blake Edgar. *In Search of Human Origins*. 1994. An account of the discoveries of early human remains written for nonspecialists by eminent researchers, based on the *Nova* television series of the same name.

Jones, Steve, Robert Martin, and David Pilbeam, eds. *Cambridge Encyclopedia of Human Evolution*. 1992. A highly regarded reference work.

Kuper, Adam. *The Chosen Primate: Human Nature and Cultural Diversity*. 1994. An anthropological analysis of the human species.

Lewin, Roger, and Robert A. Foley. *Principles of Human Evolution*, 3d ed. 2009. Brings together archaeological, genetic, biological, and behavioral evidence inside the broad framework of evolutionary theory.

Mithen, Steven. *After the Ice: A Global Human History, 20,000–5000 BC*. 2006. An entertaining and accessible exploration of the role of climate change in sparking the Agricultural Revolutions.

Mohen, Jean-Pierre. *The World of Megaliths*. 1990. Analyzes early monumental architecture.

Wade, Nicholas. *Before the Dawn: Recovering the Lost History of Our Ancestors*. 2006. A solid account of the exciting new discoveries about human prehistory made possible by the recent decoding of the human genome.

Zimmer, Carl. *Smithsonian Intimate Guide to Human Origins*. 2005. A clear, up-to-date account with many illustrations.

SUGGESTED VIEWING

Herzog, Werner. *Cave of Forgotten Dreams*. 2010. A documentary film about Chauvet Cave, with magnificent images of the cave and its art and expert speculation about the lives and intentions of the ancient artists.

CourseMate Go to the History CourseMate website for primary source links, study tools, and review materials for this chapter. www.cengagebrain.com

Chapter Outline

Mesopotamia
➤ *How did Mesopotamian civilization emerge, and what technologies promoted its advancement?*

Egypt
➤ *What role did the environment and religion play in the evolution of Egyptian civilization?*

The Indus Valley Civilization
➤ *What does the material evidence tell us about the nature of the Indus Valley civilization, and what is the most likely reason for its collapse?*

Conclusion

- **DIVERSITY + DOMINANCE**   Violence and Order in the Babylonian New Year's Festival
- **MATERIAL CULTURE**   Lamps and Candles
- **ENVIRONMENT + TECHNOLOGY**   Environmental Stress in the Indus Valley

The Art Archive/Alamy

Gilgamesh Strangling a Lion   This eighth-century B.C.E. sculpture of a king, possibly Gilgamesh, from the palace of the Assyrian king Sargon II, represents the magical power and omnipotence of kingship. The Gilgamesh story was still popular in Mesopotamia twenty centuries after the king of Uruk's lifetime.

The First River-Valley Civilizations, 3500–1500 B.C.E.

The *Epic of Gilgamesh*, whose roots date to before 2000 B.C.E., defines *civilization* as the people of ancient Mesopotamia (present-day Iraq) understood it. Gilgamesh, an early king (who may be depicted on the sculpture shown here), sends a temple prostitute to tame Enkidu (EN-kee-doo), a wild man who lives like an animal in the grasslands. Using her sexual charms to win Enkidu's trust, the temple prostitute tells him:

> Come with me to the city, to Uruk (OO-rook), to the temple of Anu and the goddess Ishtar . . . to Uruk, where the processions are and music, let us go together through the dancing to the palace hall where Gilgamesh presides.[1]

She clothes Enkidu and teaches him to eat cooked food, drink beer, and bathe and oil his body. Her words and actions signal the principal traits of civilized life in ancient Mesopotamia.

The Mesopotamians, like other peoples throughout history, equated civilization with their own way of life, but *civilization* is an ambiguous concept, and the charge that a particular group is "uncivilized" has been used throughout human history to justify many distressing acts. Thus it is important to explain the common claim that the first advanced civilizations emerged in Mesopotamia and Egypt sometime before 3000 B.C.E.

Scholars agree that certain political, social, economic, and technological traits are indicators of **civilization**: (1) cities as administrative centers, (2) a political system based on control of a defined territory rather than kinship connections, (3) many people engaged in specialized, non-food-producing activities, (4) status distinctions based largely on accumulation of substantial wealth by some groups, (5) monumental building, (6) a system for keeping permanent records, (7) long-distance trade, and (8) major advances in science and the arts. The earliest societies exhibiting these traits developed in the floodplains of great rivers: the Tigris (TIE-gris) and Euphrates (you-FRAY-teez) in Iraq, the Indus in Pakistan, the Yellow (Huang He [hwang huh]) in China, and the Nile in Egypt (see Map 2.1). The periodic flooding of the rivers deposited fertile silt and provided water for agriculture, but it also threatened lives and property. To protect themselves and channel the forces of nature, people living near the rivers created new technologies and forms of political and social organization.

In this chapter we trace the rise of complex societies in Mesopotamia, Egypt, and the Indus River Valley from approximately 3500 to 1500 B.C.E. (China, developing slightly later, is discussed in Chapter 4.) Our starting point roughly coincides with the origins of writing, allowing us to observe aspects of human experience not revealed by archaeological evidence alone.

civilization An ambiguous term often used to denote more complex societies but sometimes used by anthropologists to describe any group of people sharing a set of cultural traits.

---

[1]David Ferry, *Gilgamesh: A New Rendering in English Verse* (New York: Noonday Press, 1992).

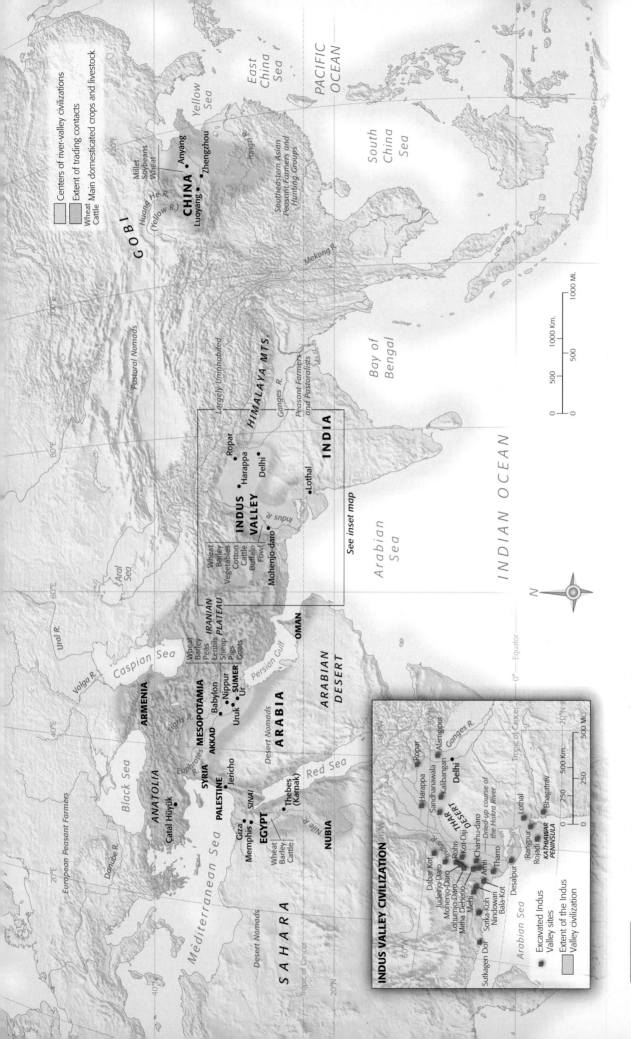

MAP 2.1 **River-Valley Civilizations, 3500–1500 B.C.E.** The earliest complex societies arose in the floodplains of large rivers: in the fourth millennium B.C.E. in the valley of the Tigris and Euphrates Rivers in Mesopotamia and the Nile River in Egypt, in the third millennium B.C.E. in the valley of the Indus River in Pakistan, and in the second millennium B.C.E. in the valley of the Yellow River in China. © Cengage Learning

Map legend:
Centers of river-valley civilizations
Extent of trading contacts
Main domesticated crops and livestock

INDUS VALLEY CIVILIZATION (inset map)
Excavated Indus Valley sites
Extent of the Indus Valley civilization

CHRONOLOGY

	Mesopotamia	Egypt	Indus Valley
3500 B.C.E.		3100–2575 B.C.E. Early Dynastic	
3000 B.C.E.	3000–2350 B.C.E. Early Dynastic (Sumerian)		
2500 B.C.E.		2575–2134 B.C.E. Old Kingdom	2600 B.C.E. Beginning of Indus Valley civilization
	2350–2230 B.C.E. Akkadian (Semitic)	2134–2040 B.C.E. First Intermediate Period	
	2112–2004 B.C.E. Third Dynasty of Ur (Sumerian)	2040–1640 B.C.E. Middle Kingdom	
2000 B.C.E.	1900–1600 B.C.E. Old Babylonian (Semitic)		1900 B.C.E. End of Indus Valley civilization
		1640–1532 B.C.E. Second Intermediate Period	
1500 B.C.E.	1500–1150 B.C.E. Kassite	1532–1070 B.C.E. New Kingdom	

MESOPOTAMIA

Mesopotamia means "land between the rivers" in Greek. The name reflects the centrality of the Euphrates and Tigris Rivers to the way of life in this region (see Map 2.2). Mesopotamian civilization developed in the plain alongside and between the rivers, which originate in the mountains of eastern Anatolia (modern Turkey) and empty into the Persian Gulf. This is an alluvial plain—a flat, fertile expanse built up over many millennia by silt that the rivers deposited.

Mesopotamia lies mostly within modern Iraq. To the north and east, an arc of mountains extends from northern Syria and southeastern Anatolia to the Zagros (ZAG-ruhs) Mountains, which separate the plain from the Iranian Plateau. The Syrian and Arabian deserts lie to the west and southwest, the Persian Gulf to the southeast.

Settled Agriculture in an Unstable Landscape

Although the first domestication of plants and animals took place in the "Fertile Crescent" region of northern Syria and southeastern Anatolia around 8000 B.C.E., agriculture did not come to southern Mesopotamia until approximately 5000 B.C.E. Lacking adequate rainfall (at least 8 inches [20 centimeters] is needed annually), farming in hot, dry southern Mesopotamia depended on irrigation—the artificial provision of water to crops. At first, people probably took advantage of the occasional flooding of the rivers into nearby fields, but the floods could be sudden and violent and tended to come at the wrong time for grain agriculture—in the spring when the crop was ripening in the field. Moreover, the floods sometimes caused the rivers to suddenly change course, cutting off fields and population centers from water and river communication. Shortly after 3000 B.C.E. the Mesopotamians learned to construct canals to carry water to more distant fields.

By 4000 B.C.E. farmers were using ox-drawn plows to turn over the earth. An attached funnel dropped a carefully measured amount of seed into the furrow. Barley was the main cereal crop because of its ability to tolerate hot, dry conditions and withstand the salt drawn to the surface by evaporation. Fields were left fallow (unplanted) every other year to replenish the nutrients in the soil. Date palms provided food, fiber, and wood, while garden plots produced vegetables. Reed plants, which grew on the riverbanks and in the marshy southern delta, could be woven into mats, baskets, huts, and boats. Fish was a dietary staple. Herds of sheep and goats, which

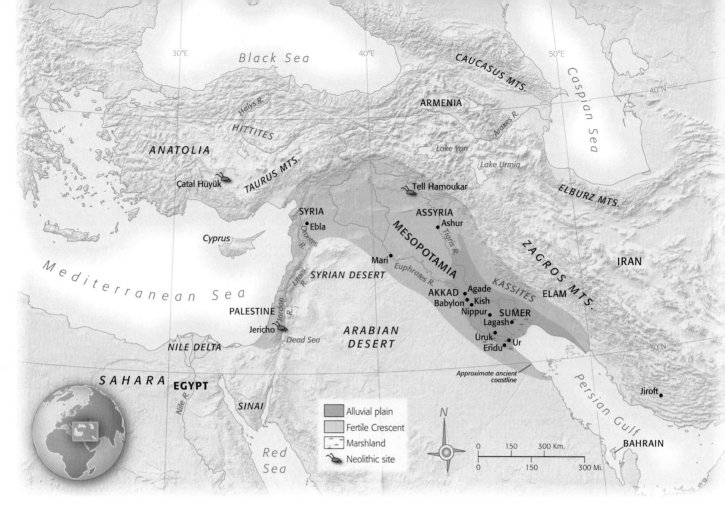

MAP 2.2 **Mesopotamia** In order to organize labor resources to create and maintain an irrigation network in the Tigris-Euphrates Valley, a land of little rain, the Sumerians of southern Mesopotamia developed new technologies, complex political and social institutions, and distinctive cultural practices. © Cengage Learning

grazed on fallow land or beyond the zone of cultivation, provided wool, milk, and meat. Donkeys, originally domesticated in Northeast Africa, and cattle carried or pulled burdens; in the second millennium B.C.E. they were joined by newly introduced camels from Arabia and horses from the mountains.

Sumerians and Semites

Sumerians The people who dominated southern Mesopotamia through the end of the third millennium B.C.E.

Semitic Family of related languages long spoken across parts of western Asia and northern Africa. In antiquity these languages included Hebrew, Aramaic, and Phoenician. The most widespread modern member of the Semitic family is Arabic.

The people living in Mesopotamia at the start of the "historical period"—the period for which we have written evidence—were the **Sumerians**. Archaeological evidence places them in southern Mesopotamia by 5000 B.C.E. and perhaps even earlier. The Sumerians created the framework of civilization in Mesopotamia during a long period of dominance in the fourth and third millennia B.C.E. Other peoples lived in Mesopotamia as well. Personal names recorded in inscriptions from northern cities from as early as 2900 B.C.E. reveal the presence of people who spoke a **Semitic (suh-MIT-ik)** language. (*Semitic* refers to a family of languages spoken in parts of western Asia and northern Africa, including ancient Hebrew, Aramaic [ar-uh-MAY-ik], Phoenician [fi-NEE-shuhn], and modern Arabic.) Possibly the descendants of nomads who had migrated into the Mesopotamian plain from the western desert, these Semites seem to have lived in peace with the Sumerians, adopting their culture and sometimes achieving positions of wealth and power.

By 2000 B.C.E. the Semitic peoples had become politically dominant, and from this time forward the Semitic language Akkadian (uh-KAY-dee-uhn) supplanted Sumerian, although the Sumerian cultural legacy was preserved. Sumerian-Akkadian dictionaries were compiled and Sumerian literature was translated. This cultural synthesis parallels a biological merging of Sumerians and Semites through intermarriage. Other ethnic groups, including mountain peoples such as the Kassites (KAS-ite) as well as Elamites (EE-luh-mite) and Persians from Iran, played a part in Mesopotamian history. But not until the arrival of Greeks in the late fourth century B.C.E. was the Sumerian-Semitic cultural heritage of Mesopotamia fundamentally altered.

Cities, Kings, and Trade

Mesopotamia was a land of villages and cities. Groups of farming families banded together in villages to protect one another; work together at key times in the agricultural cycle; and share tools, barns, and threshing floors. Village society also provided companionship and a pool of potential marriage partners.

Most cities evolved from villages. When a successful village grew, small satellite villages developed nearby and eventually merged with the main village to form an urban center. Historians use the term **city-state** to designate these self-governing urban centers and the agricultural territories they controlled.

Scholars have long believed that the earliest cities and complex societies arose in southern Mesopotamia in the fourth millennium B.C.E., as a result of the need to organize labor to create and maintain irrigation channels. However, recent archaeological discoveries in northern Mesopotamia, where agriculture first developed in this part of the world and was sustained by rainfall, are suggesting a more complicated picture, as a number of sites in northeast Syria appear to have developed urban centers, bureaucracy, and other elements of social complexity at roughly the same time.

Cities needed food, and many Mesopotamian city dwellers went out each day to labor in nearby fields. However, some urban residents did not engage in food production but instead specialized in crafts, manufacturing pottery, artwork, and clothing, as well as weapons, tools, and other objects forged out of metal. Others served the gods or carried out administrative duties. These urban specialists depended on the surplus food production from the villages in their vicinity. In return, the city provided rural districts with military protection against bandits and raiders and a market where villagers could acquire manufactured goods produced by urban specialists.

Stretches of uncultivated land, either desert or swamp, served as buffers between the many small city-states of early Mesopotamia. Nevertheless, disputes over land, water rights, and movable property often sparked hostilities between neighboring cities and prompted most to build protective walls of sun-dried mud bricks.

Southern Mesopotamians opened new land to agriculture by building and maintaining irrigation networks. Canals brought water to fields far from the rivers, and dams raised the level of the river so that water could flow by gravity into the canals. Drainage ditches carried water away from flooded fields before evaporation could draw salt and minerals harmful to crops to the surface. Dikes protected fields near the riverbanks from floods. Because the rivers carried so much silt, clogged channels needed constant dredging.

Successful construction and maintenance of these irrigation systems required leaders who were able to organize large numbers of people to work together. Other projects called for similar coordination: the harvest, sheep shearing, the construction of fortification walls and large

city-state A small independent state consisting of an urban center and the surrounding agricultural territory. A characteristic political form in early Mesopotamia, Archaic and Classical Greece, Phoenicia, and early Italy.

Courtesy, Dominique Collon

Reed Huts in the Marshes of Southern Iraq Reeds growing along the riverbanks or in the swampy lands at the head of the Persian Gulf were used in antiquity—and continue to be used today—for a variety of purposes, including baskets and small watercraft as well as dwellings.

public buildings, and warfare. Little is known about the political institutions of early Mesopotamian city-states, although there are traces of a citizens' assembly that may have evolved from the traditional village council. The two centers of power attested in written records are the temple and the palace of the king.

Each city had one or more centrally located temples that housed the cult (a set of religious practices) of the deity or deities who watched over the community. The temples owned extensive agricultural lands and stored the gifts that worshipers donated. The leading priests, who controlled the shrines and managed their wealth, played prominent political and economic roles in early communities.

In the third millennium B.C.E. the *lugal* (LOO-gahl), or "big man"—we would call him a king—emerged in Sumerian cities. A plausible theory maintains that certain men chosen by the community to lead the armies in time of war extended their authority in peacetime and assumed key judicial and ritual functions. The location of the temple in the city's heart and the less prominent location of the king's palace attest to the later emergence of royalty.

The priests and temples retained influence because of their wealth and religious mystique, but they gradually became dependent on the palace. Normally, the king portrayed himself as the deity's earthly representative and saw to the upkeep and building of temples and the proper performance of ritual. Other royal responsibilities included maintaining city walls and defenses, extending and repairing irrigation channels, guarding property rights, warding off outside attackers, and establishing justice.

Some city-states became powerful enough to dominate others. Sargon (SAHR-gone), ruler of the city of Akkad (AH-kahd) around 2350 B.C.E., was the first to unite many cities under one king and capital. Sargon and the four family members who succeeded him over a period of 120 years secured their power in several ways. They razed the walls of conquered cities and installed governors backed by garrisons of Akkadian troops, and they gave land to soldiers to ensure their loyalty. Being of Semitic stock, they adapted the cuneiform (kyoo-NEE-uh-form) system of writing used for Sumerian (discussed later in the chapter) to express their own language.

For reasons that remain obscure, the Akkadian state fell around 2230 B.C.E. The Sumerian language and culture became dominant again in the cities of the southern plain under the Third Dynasty of Ur (2112–2004 B.C.E.). Through campaigns of conquest and marriage alliances, this dynasty of five kings flourished for a century. Although not controlling territories as extensive as those of the Akkadians, they maintained tight control by means of a rapidly expanding bureaucracy of administrators and obsessive record keeping. Messengers and well-maintained road stations enabled rapid communication, and an official calendar, standardized weights and measures, and uniform writing practices increased the efficiency of the central administration.

In the northwest the kings erected a great wall 125 miles (201 kilometers) in length to keep out the nomadic Amorites (AM-uh-rite), but in the end nomad incursions combined with an Elamite attack from the southeast toppled the Third Dynasty of Ur. The Semitic Amorites founded a new city at **Babylon**, not far from Akkad. Toward the end of a long reign, **Hammurabi** (HAM-uh-rah-bee) (r. 1792–1750 B.C.E.) launched a series of aggressive military campaigns, and Babylon became the capital of what historians call the "Old Babylonian" state, which stretched beyond Sumer and Akkad into the north and northwest from 1900 to 1600 B.C.E. Hammurabi's famous Law Code, inscribed on a polished black stone pillar, provided judges with a lengthy set of examples illustrating principles to use in deciding cases (and thereby left us a fascinating window on the activities of everyday life). Many offenses were met with severe physical punishments and, not infrequently, the death penalty.

The far-reaching conquests of some states were motivated, at least in part, by the need to obtain vital resources. The alternative was to trade for raw materials, and long-distance commerce flourished in most periods. Evidence of boats used in river and sea trade appears as early as the fifth millennium B.C.E. Recent archaeological discoveries outside the core zone in southern Mesopotamia—in Anatolia, northern Mesopotamia, and Iran—are demonstrating that cities and complex societies were evolving across western Asia, probably as a consequence of the long-distance trade networks. Wool, barley, and vegetable oil were exported in exchange for wood from cedar forests in Lebanon and Syria, silver from Anatolia, gold from Egypt, copper from the eastern Mediterranean and Oman (on the Arabian peninsula), and tin from Afghanistan. Precious stones used for jewelry and carved figurines came from Iran, Afghanistan, and Pakistan.

In the third millennium B.C.E. merchants were primarily employed by the palace or temple, the only two institutions with the financial resources and long-distance connections to organize the collection, transport, and protection of goods. Merchants exchanged surplus food from

Babylon The largest and most important city in Mesopotamia. It achieved particular eminence as the capital of the Amorite king Hammurabi in the eighteenth century B.C.E.

Hammurabi Amorite ruler of Babylon (r. 1792–1750 B.C.E.). He conquered many city-states in southern and northern Mesopotamia and is best known for a code of laws, inscribed on a black stone pillar, illustrating the principles to be used in legal cases.

the estates of kings or temples for raw materials and luxury goods. In the second millennium B.C.E. more commerce came into the hands of independent merchants, and guilds (cooperative associations formed by merchants) became powerful forces in Mesopotamian society. Items could be bartered—traded for one another—or valued in relation to fixed weights of precious metal, primarily silver, or measures of grain.

Mesopotamian Society

Urbanized civilizations generate social divisions—variations in the status and legal and political privileges of certain groups of people. The rise of cities, specialization of labor, centralization of power, and the use of written records enabled some groups to amass unprecedented wealth. Temple leaders and kings controlled large agricultural estates, and the palace administration collected taxes from subjects. An elite class acquired large landholdings, and soldiers and religious officials received plots of land in return for their services.

The Law Code of Hammurabi in eighteenth-century B.C.E. Babylonia reflects social divisions that may also have been valid at other times. Society was divided into three classes: (1) the free, landowning class, largely living in the cities, which included royalty, high-ranking officials, warriors, priests, merchants, and some artisans and shopkeepers; (2) the class of dependent farmers and artisans, whose legal attachment to royal, temple, or private estates made them the primary rural workforce; and (3) the class of slaves, primarily employed in domestic service. Penalties for crimes prescribed in the Law Code depended on the class of the offender, with the most severe punishments reserved for the lower orders.

Slavery was not as prevalent and fundamental to the economy as it would be in the later societies of Greece and Rome (see Chapters 5 and 6). Many slaves came from mountain tribes, either captured in war or sold by slave traders. Others were people unable to pay their debts. Normally slaves were not chained, but they were identified by a distinctive hairstyle; if given their freedom, a barber shaved off the telltale mark. In the Old Babylonian period, as the class of people who were not dependent on the temple or palace grew in numbers and importance, the amount of land and other property in private hands increased, and the hiring of free laborers became more common. Slaves, dependent workers, and hired laborers were all compensated with commodities such as food and oil in quantities proportional to their age, gender, and tasks.

Mesopotamian Cylinder Seal   Seals indicated the identity of an individual and were impressed into wet clay or wax to "sign" legal documents or to mark ownership of an object. This seal, produced in the period of the Akkadian Empire, depicts Ea (second from right), the god of underground waters, symbolized by the stream with fish emanating from his shoulders; Ishtar, whose attributes of fertility and war are indicated by the date cluster in her hand and the pointed weapons showing above her wings; and the sun-god Shamash, cutting his way out of the mountains with a jagged knife, an evocation of sunrise.

The daily lives of ordinary Mesopotamians, especially those in villages or on large estates in the countryside, left few archaeological or written remains. Peasants built houses of mud brick and reed, which quickly disintegrate, and they had few metal possessions. Being illiterate, they left no written record of their lives.

It is likewise difficult to discover much about the experiences of women. The written sources were produced by male **scribes**—trained professionals who applied their reading and writing skills to tasks of administration—and for the most part reflect elite male activities. Anthropologists theorize that women lost social standing and freedoms in societies where agriculture superseded hunting and gathering (see Chapter 1). In hunting-and-gathering societies women provided most of the community's food from their gathering activities, and this work was highly valued. But in Mesopotamia food production depended on the heavy physical labor of plowing, harvesting, and digging irrigation channels, jobs usually performed by men. Since food surpluses permitted families to have more children, bearing and rearing children became the primary occupation of many women, preventing them from acquiring the specialized skills of the scribe or artisan. However, women could own property, maintain control of their dowry (a sum of money given by the woman's father to support her in her husband's household), and even engage in trade. Some worked outside the household in textile factories and breweries or as prostitutes, tavern keepers, bakers, or fortunetellers. Non-elite women who stayed at home helped with farming, planted vegetable gardens, cooked, cleaned, fetched water, tended the household fire, and wove baskets and textiles.

The standing of women seems to have declined further in the second millennium B.C.E., perhaps because of the rise of an urbanized middle class and an increase in private wealth. The laws favored the rights of husbands. Although Mesopotamian society was generally monogamous, a man could take a second wife if the first gave him no children, and in later Mesopotamian history kings and wealthy men had several wives. Marriage alliances arranged between families made women into instruments for preserving and increasing family wealth. Alternatively, a family might decide to avoid a daughter's marriage—and the resulting loss of a dowry—by dedicating her to the service of a deity as a "god's bride." Constraints on women's lives that eventually became part of Islamic tradition, such as largely confining themselves to the home and wearing veils in public (see Chapter 9), may have originated in the second millennium B.C.E.

Gods, Priests, and Temples

The Sumerian gods embodied the forces of nature. When the Semitic peoples became dominant, they equated their deities with those of the Sumerians. Myths of the Sumerian gods were transferred to their Semitic counterparts, and many of the same rituals continued to be practiced. People imagined the gods as anthropomorphic (an-thruh-puh-MORE-fik)—like humans in form and conduct. They thought the gods had bodies and senses, sought nourishment from sacrifice, enjoyed the worship and obedience of humanity, and were driven by lust, love, hate, anger, and envy. The Mesopotamians feared their gods, believing them responsible for the natural disasters that occurred without warning in their environment, and sought to appease them.

scribe In the governments of many ancient societies, a professional position reserved for men who had undergone the lengthy training required to be able to read and write using cuneiform, hieroglyphics, or other early, cumbersome writing systems.

Ziggurat of Ur-Nammu, ca. 2100 B.C.E. Built at Ur by King Ur-Nammu for the Sumerian moon-god, Nanna, an exterior made of fine bricks baked in a kiln encloses a sun-dried mud-brick core. Three ramps on the first level converge to form a stairway to the second level. The function of ziggurats is not known.

World Religions Photo Library/The Bridgeman Art Library

The public, state-organized religion is most visible in the archaeological record. Cities built temples and showed devotion to the divinities who protected the community. The temple precinct, encircled by a high wall, contained the shrine of the chief deity; open-air plazas; chapels for lesser gods; housing, dining facilities, and offices for priests and other temple staff; and craft shops, storerooms, and service buildings. The most visible part of the temple compound was the **ziggurat (ZIG-uh-rat)**, a multistory, mud-brick, pyramid-shaped tower approached by ramps and stairs. Scholars are not certain of the ziggurat's function and symbolic meaning.

ziggurat A massive pyramidal stepped tower made of mud bricks. It is associated with religious complexes in ancient Mesopotamian cities, but its function is unknown.

A temple was considered the god's residence, and the statue in its interior shrine was believed to be occupied by the deity's life force. Priests anticipated and met every need of the divine image in a daily cycle of waking, bathing, dressing, feeding, moving around, entertaining, soothing, and revering. These efforts reflected the claim of the Babylonian Creation Myth that humankind had been created from the blood of a vanquished rebel deity in order to serve the gods. Several thousand priests may have staffed a large temple like that of the chief god Marduk at Babylon.

Priests passed their hereditary office and sacred lore to their sons, and their families lived on rations of food from the deity's estates. The amount a priest received depended on his rank within a complicated hierarchy of status and specialized function. The high priest performed the central acts in the great rituals. Certain priests made music to please the gods. Others exorcised evil spirits. Still others interpreted dreams and divined the future by examining the organs of sacrificed animals, reading patterns in the rising incense smoke, or casting dice.

amulet Small charm meant to protect the bearer from evil. Found frequently in archaeological excavations in Mesopotamia and Egypt, amulets reflect the religious practices of the common people.

Harder to determine are the everyday beliefs and religious practices of the common people. Scholars do not know how much access the general public had to the temple buildings, although individuals did place votive statues in the sanctuaries, believing that these miniature replicas of themselves could continually seek the deity's favor. The survival of many **amulets** (small charms meant to protect the bearer from evil) and representations of a host of demons suggests widespread belief in magic—the use of special words and rituals to manipulate and control the forces of nature. For example, people believed that a headache was caused by a demon that could be driven out of the ailing body. In return for a gift or sacrifice, a god or goddess might reveal information about the future. We do know that elite and common folk came together in great festivals such as the twelve-day New Year's Festival held each spring in Babylon to mark the beginning of a new agricultural cycle (see Diversity and Dominance: Violence and Order in the Babylonian New Year's Festival).

Technology and Science

The term *technology*, from the Greek word *techne*, meaning "skill" or "specialized knowledge," normally refers to the tools and machines that humans use to manipulate the physical world. Many scholars now use the term more broadly for any specialized knowledge used to transform the natural environment and human society.

An important example of the broader type of technology is writing, which first appeared in Mesopotamia before 3300 B.C.E. The earliest inscribed tablets, found in the chief temple at Uruk, date from a time when the temple was the most important economic institution in the community. According to a plausible recent theory, writing originated from a system of tokens used to keep track of property—such as sheep, cattle, or wagon wheels—when increases in the amount of accumulated wealth and the complexity of commercial transactions strained people's memories. The tokens, made in the shape of the commodity, were sealed in clay envelopes, and pictures of the tokens were incised on the outside of the envelopes as a reminder of what was inside. Eventually, people realized that the incised pictures were an adequate record, making the tokens inside the envelope redundant. These pictures were the first written symbols. Each symbol represented an object, and it could also stand for the sound of the word for that object if the sound was part of a longer word.

cuneiform A system of writing in which wedge-shaped symbols represented words or syllables. It originated in Mesopotamia and was used initially for Sumerian and Akkadian but later was adapted to represent other languages of western Asia. Literacy was confined to a relatively small group of administrators and scribes.

The usual method of writing involved pressing the point of a sharpened reed into a moist clay tablet. Because the reed made wedge-shaped impressions, the early realistic pictures were increasingly stylized into a combination of strokes and wedges, a system known as **cuneiform** (Latin for "wedge-shaped") writing. Mastering this system required years of training and practice.

Violence and Order in the Babylonian New Year's Festival

The twelve-day Babylonian New Year's Festival was one of the most important religious celebrations in ancient Mesopotamia. Fragmentary documents of the third century B.C.E. (fifteen hundred years after Hammurabi) provide most of our information, but because of the continuity of culture over several millennia, the later Babylonian New Year's Festival preserves many of the beliefs and practices of earlier epochs.

In the first days of the festival, most activities took place in inner chambers of the temple of Marduk, patron deity of Babylon, attended only by high-ranking priests. A key ceremony was a ritualized humiliation of the king, followed by a renewal of the institution of divinely sanctioned kingship:

On the fifth day of the month Nisannu . . . they shall bring water for washing the king's hands and then shall accompany him to the temple Esagil. The *urigallu*-priest shall leave the sanctuary and take away the scepter, the circle, and the sword from the king. He shall bring them before the god Bel [Marduk] and place them on a chair. He shall leave the sanctuary and strike the king's cheek. He shall accompany the king into the presence of the god Bel. He shall drag him by the ears and make him bow to the ground. The king shall speak the following only once: "I did not sin, lord of the countries. I was not neglectful of the requirements of your godship. I did not destroy Babylon. The temple Esagil, I did not forget its rites. I did not rain blows on the cheek of a subordinate." . . . [The *urigallu*-priest responds:] "The god Bel will listen to your prayer. He will exalt your kingship. The god Bel will bless you forever. He will destroy your enemy, fell your adversary." After the *urigallu*-priest says this, the king shall regain his composure. The scepter, circle, and sword shall be restored to the king.

Also in the early days of the festival, a priest recited the entire Babylonian Creation Epic to the image of Marduk. After relating the origins of the gods from the mating of two primordial creatures, Tiamat, the female embodiment of the salt sea, and Apsu, the male embodiment of fresh water, the myth tells how Tiamat gathered an army of older gods and monsters to destroy the younger generation of gods.

All the Anunnaki [the younger gods], the host of gods gathered into that place tongue-tied; they sat with mouths shut for they thought, "What other god can make war on Tiamat? No one else can face her and come back." . . . Lord Marduk exulted, . . . with racing spirits he said to the father of gods, "Creator of the gods who decides their destiny, if I must be your avenger, defeating Tiamat, saving your lives, call the Assembly, give me precedence over all the rest; . . . now and for ever let my word be law; I, not you, will decide the world's nature, the things to come. My decrees shall never be altered, never be annulled, but my creation endures to the ends of the world." . . . He took his route towards the rising sound of Tiamat's rage, and all the gods besides, the fathers of the gods pressed in around him, and the lord approached Tiamat. . . . When Tiamat heard him her wits scattered, she was possessed and shrieked aloud, her legs shook from the crotch down, she gabbled spells, muttered maledictions, while the gods of war sharpened their weapons. . . . The lord shot his net to entangle Tiamat, and the pursuing tumid wind, Imhullu, came from behind and beat in her face. When the mouth gaped open to suck him down he drove Imhullu in, so that the mouth would not shut but wind raged through her belly; her carcass blown up, tumescent. She gaped. And now he shot the arrow that split the belly, that pierced the gut and cut the womb. . . .

He split it apart like a cockle-shell; with the upper half he constructed the arc of sky, he pulled down the bar and set a watch on the waters, so they should never escape. . . . He projected positions for the Great Gods conspicuous in the sky, he gave them a starry aspect as constellations; he measured the year, gave it a beginning and an end, and to each month of the twelve three rising stars. . . . Through her ribs he opened gates in the east and west, and gave them strong bolts on the right and left; and high in the belly of Tiamat he set the zenith. He gave the moon the luster of a jewel, he gave him all the night, to mark off days, to watch by night each month the circle of a waxing waning light. . . . When Marduk had sent out the moon, he took the sun and set him to complete the cycle from this one to the next New Year. . . .

Then Marduk considered Tiamat. He skimmed spume from the bitter sea, heaped up the clouds, spindrift of wet and wind and cooling rain, the spittle of Tiamat. With his own hands

Several hundred signs were in use at any one time, as compared to the twenty-five or so signs in an alphabetic system. The prestige and regular employment that went with their position may have made scribes reluctant to simplify the cuneiform system. In the Old Babylonian period, the growth of private commerce brought an increase in the number of people who could read and write, but only a small percentage of the population was literate.

The earliest Mesopotamian documents are economic, but cuneiform came to have wide-ranging uses. Written documents marked with the seal of the participants became the primary proof of legal actions. Texts were written about political, literary, religious, and scientific topics. Cuneiform is not a language but rather a system of writing. Developed originally for the Sumerian language, it was later adapted to the Akkadian language of the Mesopotamian Semites as well as to other languages of western Asia, such as Hittite, Elamite, and Persian.

from the steaming mist he spread the clouds. He pressed hard down the head of water, heaping mountains over it, opening springs to flow: Euphrates and Tigris rose from her eyes, but he closed the nostrils and held back their springhead. He piled huge mountains on her paps and through them drove water-holes to channel the deep sources; and high overhead he arched her tail, locked-in to the wheel of heaven; the pit was under his feet, between was the crotch, the sky's fulcrum. Now the earth had foundations and the sky its mantle. . . .

Marduk considered and began to speak to the gods assembled in his presence. This is what he said, "In the former time you inhabited the void above the abyss, but I have made Earth as the mirror of Heaven, I have consolidated the soil for the foundations, and there I will build my city, my beloved home. A holy precinct shall be established with sacred halls for the presence of the king. When you come up from the deep to join the Synod you will find lodging and sleep by night. When others from heaven descend to the Assembly, you too will find lodging and sleep by night. It shall be BABYLON the home of the gods. The masters of all crafts shall build it according to my plan." . . . Now that Marduk has heard what it is the gods are saying, he is moved with desire to create a work of consummate art. He told Ea the deep thought in his heart.

> "Blood to blood
> I join,
> blood to bone
> I form
> an original thing,
> its name is MAN,
> aboriginal man
> is mine in making.
> "All his occupations
> are faithful service. . . ."

Ea answered with carefully chosen words, completing the plan for the gods' comfort. He said to Marduk, "Let one of the kindred be taken; only one need die for the new creation. Bring the gods together in the Great Assembly; there let the guilty die, so the rest may live."

Marduk called the Great Gods to the Synod. . . . The king speaks to the rebel gods, "Declare on your oath if ever before you spoke the truth, who instigated rebellion? Who stirred up Tiamat? Who led the battle? Let the instigator of war be

handed over; guilt and retribution are on him, and peace will be yours for ever."

The Great Gods answered the Lord of the Universe, the king and counselor of gods, "It was Kingu who instigated rebellion, he stirred up that sea of bitterness and led the battle for her." They declared him guilty, they bound and held him down in front of Ea, they cut his arteries and from his blood they created man; and Ea imposed his servitude.

Much of the subsequent activity of the festival, which took place in the temple courtyard and streets, was a reenactment of the events of the Creation Myth. The festival occurred at the beginning of spring, when the grain shoots were beginning to emerge, and its essential symbolism concerns the return of natural life to the world. The Babylonians believed that the natural world had an annual life cycle consisting of birth, growth, maturity, and death. In winter the cycle drew to a close, and there was no guarantee that life would return to the world. Babylonians hoped proper performance of the New Year's Festival would encourage the gods to grant a renewal of time and life, in essence to re-create the world.

QUESTIONS FOR ANALYSIS

1. **According to the Creation Epic, how did the present order of the universe come into being? What does the violent nature of this creation tell us about the Mesopotamian view of the physical world and the gods?**

2. **How did the symbolism of the events of the New Year's Festival, with its ritual reading and reenactment of the story of the Creation Myth, validate such concepts as kingship, the primacy of Babylon, and mankind's relationship to the gods?**

3. **What is the significance of the distinction between the "private" ceremonies celebrated in the temple precincts and the "public" ceremonies that took place in the streets of the city? What does the festival tell us about the relationship of different social groups to the gods?**

Source: PRITCHARD, JAMES, ANCIENT NEAR EASTERN TEXTS RELATING TO THE OLD TESTAMENT. © 1969 by Princeton University Press. Reprinted by permission of Princeton University Press.

bronze An alloy of copper with a small amount of tin (or sometimes arsenic), which is harder and more durable than copper alone. The term Bronze Age is applied to the era—the dates of which vary in different parts of the world—when bronze was the primary metal for tools and weapons.

Other technologies enabled the Mesopotamians to meet the challenges of their physical environment. Wheeled carts and sledlike platforms dragged by cattle were used to transport goods in some locations. In the south, where numerous water channels cut up the landscape, boats and barges predominated. In northern Mesopotamia, donkeys were the chief pack animals for overland caravans before the advent of the camel around 1200 B.C.E. (see Chapter 9).

The Mesopotamians had to import metals, but they became skilled in metallurgy, refining ores containing copper and alloying them with arsenic or tin to make **bronze**. Craftsmen poured molten bronze into molds to produce tools and weapons. The cooled and hardened bronze took a sharper edge than stone, was less likely to break, and was more easily repaired. Stone implements remained in use among poor people, who could not afford bronze.

Lamps and Candles

It is hard to imagine today how dark the world was after the sun went down throughout most of human history. The glow of a fire did not extend far. Nor were torches easy to make or long-lasting. A stick wrapped with oil-soaked cloth at one end does make an effective torch, but humans were in need of light long before they figured out how to make cloth. As for flammable oil, vegetable oils extracted from the seeds of olive or palm trees, or from plants like flax, lettuce, and corn, became abundant only with the spread of plant domestication in the Neolithic period. Prior to that, animal fat or tallow could be used, though it had the disadvantage of smelling like meat.

The Neolithic revolutions made available not only vegetable oils but also pottery, and later metal, vessels that could be used as lamps. A fireproof vessel would be filled with oil, and a wick would be placed so that one end was immersed in the oil and the other open to the air. The oil would saturate the wick, and a flame touched to the wick would vaporize a small amount of oil and ignite the resultant gas. A poor wick might sputter, smoke, or go out. The pith or inner porous core of plants of the rush family could be used as wicks in rushlamps, or the oil-soaked pith stiffened by part of the outer skin of the rush could be stood upright and lit like slender candles in rushlights.

Aside from the pith of rushes, wicks were usually made of string or a sliver of wood. Since a wick of greater diameter produces a larger flame, braiding was used to make a thicker string. Of all natural fibers, cotton makes the best wicks because of its absorbency. Different varieties of cotton were native to India and pre-Columbian America, but cotton became a major crop in the Middle East only in the early Islamic period of the eighth century C.E. Christian Europe knew cotton only as an expensive import until the twelfth century, when a cotton industry was founded in northern Italy. Access to superior wicks contributed to an increase in European candle use.

Waxes differ from oils in being solid at room temperature. Molding wax around a wick produces a candle. Beeswax provided an ideal material for odorless candles and was used for lighting as early as ancient Egyptian times. However, beeswax was scarce and expensive. Some premodern trade routes, such as those going south to the Middle East along the rivers of Russia, featured beeswax as a major product. Beeswax candles came to play a prominent and often symbolic role in Christian, Jewish, and Buddhist religious rituals. Mosques, on the other hand, were traditionally lit by oil lamps.

Though whaling was practiced in certain coastal regions in prehistoric times, the extraction of whale oil on an industrial scale began in the sixteenth century and grew rapidly over the next three hundred years. Oil extracted from the whale's fat, or

Ancient Lamp Vessel This 2,500-year-old oil lamp from Megiddo in Israel has grooves for two wicks. It is made of bronze, a valuable metal. Pottery lamps were much cheaper and show up abundantly in ancient archaeological sites. Erich Lessing\Art Resource, NY

blubber, was widely used for lamps. Of even greater value was a wax called spermaceti that was made from an oily substance in the heads of sperm whales. A large whale might yield three tons of spermaceti. It burned without odor in candles and became the standard for candle making until the discovery of paraffin, a wax made from petroleum, in 1830. Paraffin generally replaced spermaceti as the preferred wax for candles.

The small flames of oil lamps and candles did not produce much illumination. *Candela*, the term for a unit of light intensity, became increasingly precise over the course of the nineteenth and twentieth centuries. It is intended to represent the light produced by a single candle, though many technical specifications, such as the color of the light, make it only an approximation. An even rougher approximation equates 120 candelas with the illumination provided by a 100-watt light bulb. This last approximation suggests how little light a single lamp or candle could provide in premodern times for reading, sewing, or doing any kind of fine work after sundown.

QUESTIONS FOR ANALYSIS

1. How would the provision of artificial light affect patterns of life with the change of seasons?

2. What human activities, such as storytelling, might have been enhanced by a lack of light?

3. How did gradual adoption of gaslight (1792) and the electric light bulb (1879) change people's lives?

Widely available clay was used to make dishware and storage vessels. By 4000 B.C.E. the potter's wheel, a revolving platform spun by hands or feet, made possible the rapid production of vessels with precise and complex shapes. Mud bricks, dried in the sun or baked in an oven for greater durability, were the primary building material. Construction of city walls, temples, and palaces required practical knowledge of architecture and engineering. For example, the reed mats that Mesopotamian builders laid between the mud-brick layers of ziggurats served the same stabilizing purpose as girders in modern high-rise construction.

Early military forces were nonprofessional militias of able-bodied men called up for short periods when needed. The powerful states of the later third and second millennia B.C.E. built up armies of well-trained and well-paid full-time soldiers. In the early second millennium B.C.E. horses appeared in western Asia, and the horse-drawn chariot came into vogue. Infantry found themselves at the mercy of swift chariots carrying a driver and an archer who could easily run them down. Mesopotamian soldiers also used increasingly effective siege machinery that enabled them to climb over, undermine, or knock down the walls protecting the cities of their enemies.

Mesopotamians used a base-60 number system in which numbers were expressed as fractions or multiples of 60 (in contrast to our base-10 system; this is the origin of the seconds and minutes we use in calculating time today). Advances in mathematics and careful observation of the skies made the Mesopotamians sophisticated practitioners of astronomy. Priests compiled lists of omens or unusual sightings on earth and in the heavens, together with a record of the events that coincided with them. They consulted these texts at critical times, for they believed that the recurrence of such phenomena could provide clues to future developments. The underlying premise was that the elements of the material universe, from the microscopic to the macrocosmic, were interconnected in mysterious but undeniable ways.

SECTION REVIEW

- Mesopotamia was home to a complex civilization that developed in the plain of the Tigris and Euphrates Rivers, beginning in the fourth millennium B.C.E.

- The elements of civilization initially created by the Sumerians, the earliest known people to live in Mesopotamia, were later taken over and adapted by the Semitic peoples who became dominant in the region.

- City-states, centered on cities that coalesced out of villages and controlled rural territory, were initially independent.

- The temples of the gods, the earliest centers of political and economic power, became subordinate to kings.

- Mesopotamian society was divided into three classes: free landowners and professionals in the cities, dependent peasants and artisans on rural estates, and slaves in domestic service.

- Mesopotamians feared their gods, who embodied the often-violent forces of nature.

- Cuneiform writing evolved from a system of tokens used for economic records, but it came to have a wide range of uses.

- A range of technologies (metallurgy, ceramics, transportation, and engineering) and sciences (mathematics and astronomy) enabled Mesopotamians to meet the challenges of their environment.

EGYPT

No place exhibits the impact of the natural environment on the history and culture of a society better than ancient Egypt. Located at the intersection of Asia and Africa, Egypt was protected by surrounding barriers of desert and a harborless, marshy seacoast. Whereas Mesopotamia was open to migration or invasion and was dependent on imported resources, Egypt's natural isolation and material self-sufficiency fostered a unique culture that for long periods had relatively little to do with other civilizations.

The Land of Egypt: "Gift of the Nile"

The fifth-century B.C.E. Greek traveler Herodotus (he-ROD-uh-tuhs) justifiably called Egypt the "gift of the Nile." The world's longest river, the Nile flows northward from Lake Victoria and several large tributaries in the highlands of tropical Africa, carving a narrow valley between a chain of hills on either side, until it reaches the Mediterranean Sea (see Map 2.3). Though bordered mostly by desert, the banks of the river support lush vegetation. About 100 miles (160 kilometers) from the Mediterranean, the Nile divides into channels to form a triangular delta. Most of the population, then as now, lived on the twisting, green ribbon of land alongside the river or in the Nile Delta. The rest of the country, 90 percent or more, is a bleak and inhospitable desert of mountains, rocks, and dunes. The ancient Egyptians distinguished between the low-lying,

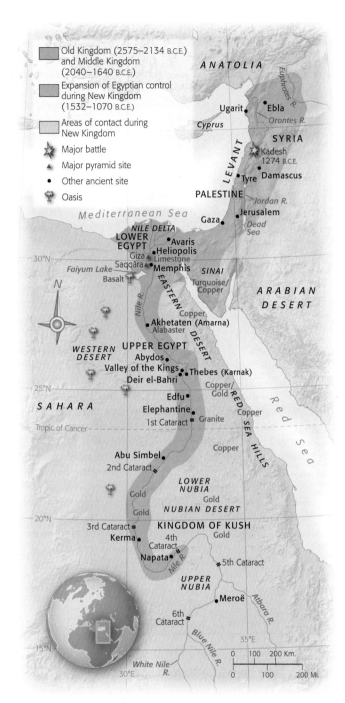

Old Kingdom (2575–2134 B.C.E.) and Middle Kingdom (2040–1640 B.C.E.)

Expansion of Egyptian control during New Kingdom (1532–1070 B.C.E.)

Areas of contact during New Kingdom

✦ Major battle

▲ Major pyramid site

• Other ancient site

🌴 Oasis

MAP 2.3   Ancient Egypt   The Nile River, flowing south to north, carved out of the surrounding desert a narrow green valley that became heavily settled in antiquity.   © Cengage Learning

life-sustaining dark soil of the "Black Land" along the river and the elevated, deadly "Red Land" of the desert.

The river was the main means of travel and communication, with the most important cities located upstream away from the Mediterranean. Because the river flows from south to north, the Egyptians called the southern part of the country "Upper Egypt" and the northern delta "Lower Egypt." In most periods the southern boundary of Egypt was the First Cataract of the Nile, the northernmost of a series of impassable rocks and rapids below Aswan **(AS-wahn)** (about 500 miles [800 kilometers] south of the Mediterranean). At times Egyptians' control extended farther south into what they called "Kush" (later Nubia, today part of southern Egypt and northern Sudan). The Egyptians also settled a chain of large oases west of the river, green and habitable "islands" in the midst of the desert.

While the hot, sunny climate favored agriculture, rain rarely falls south of the delta, and agriculture was entirely dependent on river water. Each September the river overflowed its banks, spreading water into the bordering basins, and irrigation channels carried water farther out into the valley to increase the area suitable for planting. Unlike the Tigris and Euphrates, the Nile flooded at exactly the right time for grain agriculture. When the waters receded, they left behind a moist, fertile layer of mineral-rich silt in which farmers could easily plant their crops. An Egyptian creation myth featured the emergence of a life-supporting mound of earth from a primeval swamp.

The level of the flood's crest determined the abundance of the next harvest. "Nilometers," stone staircases with incised units of measure placed along the river's edge, gauged the flood surge. When the flood was too high, dikes protecting inhabited areas were washed out, and much damage resulted. When the floods were too low for several years, less land could be cultivated, and the country experienced famine and decline. The ebb and flow of successful and failed regimes seems to have been linked to the cycle of floods. Nevertheless, remarkable stability characterized most eras, and Egyptians viewed the universe as an orderly and beneficent place.

Egypt was well endowed with natural resources and far more self-sufficient than Mesopotamia. Egyptians used papyrus reeds growing in marshy areas to make sails, ropes, and a kind of paper. Hunters pursued the abundant wild animals and birds in the marshes and on the edge of the desert, and fishermen netted fish from the river. Building stone was quarried and floated downstream from southern Egypt. Clay for mud bricks and pottery could be found almost everywhere. The state organized armed expeditions and forced labor to exploit copper and turquoise deposits in the Sinai Desert to the east and gold from Nubia to the south.

The farming villages that appeared in Egypt as early as 5500 B.C.E. relied on domesticated plant and animal species that had originated several millennia earlier in western Asia. Egypt's emergence as a focal point of civilization stemmed, at least in part, from a gradual change in climate from the fifth to the third millennium B.C.E. Until then, the Sahara, the vast region that is now the world's largest desert, had a relatively mild and wet climate, and its lakes and grasslands supported a variety of plant and animal species as well as populations of hunter-gatherers (see Chapter 9). As the Sahara became a desert, displaced groups migrated into the Nile Valley, where they developed a sedentary way of life.

Divine Kingship

pharaoh The central figure in the ancient Egyptian state. Believed to be an earthly manifestation of the gods, he used his absolute power to maintain the safety and prosperity of Egypt.

ma'at Egyptian term for the concept of divinely created and maintained order in the universe. The divine ruler was the earthly guarantor of this order.

pyramid A large, triangular stone monument, used in Egypt and Nubia as a burial place for the king. The largest pyramids, erected during the Old Kingdom near Memphis, reflect the Egyptian belief that the proper and spectacular burial of the divine ruler would guarantee the continued prosperity of the land.

The increase in population led to more complex political organization, including a form of local kingship. Later generations of Egyptians saw the conquest of these smaller units and the unification of all Egypt by Menes (MEH-neez), a ruler from the south, as a pivotal event. Kings of Egypt bore the title "Ruler of the Two Lands"—Upper and Lower Egypt—and wore two crowns symbolizing the unification of the country. In contrast to Mesopotamia, Egypt was unified early in its history.

Historians organize Egyptian history using the system of thirty dynasties (sequences of kings from the same family) identified by Manetho, an Egyptian from the third century B.C.E. The rise and fall of dynasties often reflect the dominance of different parts of the country. More generally, scholars refer to the "Old," "Middle," and "New Kingdoms," each a period of centralized political power and brilliant cultural achievement, punctuated by "Intermediate Periods" of political fragmentation and cultural decline. Although experts debate the specific dates for these periods, the chronology on page 29 reflects current opinion.

The Egyptian state centered on the king, often known by the New Kingdom term **pharaoh**, from an Egyptian phrase meaning "palace." From the time of the Old Kingdom, if not earlier, Egyptians considered the king to be a god sent to earth to maintain **ma'at** (muh-AHT), the divinely authorized order of the universe. He was the indispensable link between his people and the gods, and his benevolent rule ensured the welfare and prosperity of the country.

So much depended on the kings that their deaths called forth elaborate efforts to ensure the well-being of their spirits on their perilous journey to rejoin the gods. Massive resources were poured into the construction of royal tombs, the celebration of elaborate funerary rites, and the sustenance of the kings' spirits in the afterlife by perpetual offerings in funerary chapels attached to the royal tombs. Early rulers were buried in flat-topped, rectangular tombs made of mud brick. Around 2630 B.C.E. Djoser (JO-sur), a Third Dynasty king, constructed a stepped **pyramid** consisting of a series of stone platforms laid one on top of the other at Saqqara (suh-KAHR-uh), near Memphis. Rulers in the Fourth Dynasty filled in the steps to create the smooth-sided, limestone pyramids that have become the most memorable symbol of ancient Egypt. Between 2550 and 2490 B.C.E. the pharaohs Khufu (KOO-foo) and Khafre (KAF-ray) erected huge pyramids at Giza, several miles north of Saqqara.

Egyptians accomplished this construction with stone tools (bronze was still expensive and rare) and no machinery other than simple levers, pulleys, and rollers. What made it possible was almost unlimited human muscle power. Calculations of the human resources needed to build a pyramid within the lifetime of the ruler suggest that large numbers of people must have been pressed into service for part of each year, probably during the flood season when no agricultural work could be done. Although this labor was compulsory, the Egyptian masses probably regarded it as a kind of religious service that helped ensure prosperity. The age of the great pyramids lasted only about a century, although pyramids continued to be built on a smaller scale for two millennia.

Andrea Thompson Photography/Getty Images

Solar Ship of King Khufu This full-size ship (143 feet [43.6 meters] long and 19.5 feet [5.9 meters] wide) was buried in a pit at the base of the Great Pyramid ca. 2500 B.C.E. While it was probably intended to carry the resurrected king along with the sun-god Ra across the sky, it may also have been used to transport Khufu's embalmed body to Giza. Ships equipped with sails and oars were well suited for travel on the peaceful Nile and sometimes were used for voyages on the more turbulent Mediterranean and Red Seas.

Michele Burgess/SuperStock

Pyramids of Menkaure, Khafre, and Khufu at Giza, ca. 2500 B.C.E.   With a width of 755 feet (230 meters) and a height of 480 feet (146 meters), the Great Pyramid of Khufu is the largest stone structure ever built. The construction of these massive edifices depended on relatively simple techniques of stonecutting, transport (the stones were floated downriver on boats and rolled to the site on sledges), and lifting (the stones were dragged up the face of the pyramid on mud-brick ramps). However, the surveying and engineering skills required to level the platform, lay out the measurements, and securely position the blocks were very sophisticated and have withstood the test of time.

Administration and Communication

Memphis The capital of Old Kingdom Egypt, near the head of the Nile Delta. Early rulers were interred in the nearby pyramids.

Ruling dynasties usually placed their capitals in the area of their original power base. **Memphis**, near the apex of the delta (close to Cairo, the modern capital), held this central position during the Old Kingdom. **Thebes**, far to the south, supplanted it during the Middle and New Kingdom periods (see Map 2.3).

Thebes Capital city of Egypt and home of the ruling dynasties during the Middle and New Kingdoms. Monarchs were buried across the river in the Valley of the Kings.

The extensive administrative system began at the village level and progressed to the districts into which the country was divided and, finally, to the central government in the capital city. Bureaucrats kept track of land, products, and people, extracting as taxes a substantial portion of the country's annual revenues—at times as much as 50 percent. This income supported the palace, bureaucracy, and army, as well as the construction and maintenance of temples and great monuments celebrating the ruler's reign. The government maintained a monopoly over key sectors of the economy and controlled long-distance trade, unlike in Mesopotamia, where commerce increasingly fell into the hands of an acquisitive urban middle class.

hieroglyphics A system of writing in which pictorial symbols represented sounds, syllables, or concepts. It was used for official and monumental inscriptions in ancient Egypt. Because of the long period of study required to master this system, literacy in hieroglyphics was confined to a relatively small group of scribes and administrators.

The hallmark of the administrative class was literacy. A writing system had been developed by the beginning of the Early Dynastic period. **Hieroglyphics (high-ruh-GLIF-iks)**, the earliest form of this system, were picture symbols standing for words, syllables, or individual sounds. Hieroglyphic writing long continued to be used on monuments and ornamental inscriptions. By 2500 B.C.E., however, a cursive script, in which the original pictorial nature of the symbol was less apparent, had been developed for the everyday needs of administrators and copyists. The Egyptians used writing for many purposes other than administrative record keeping. Their written literature included tales of adventure and magic, love poetry, religious hymns, and instruction manuals on technical subjects. Scribes in workshops attached to the temples made copies of traditional texts. They worked with ink on a writing material made from the **papyrus (puh-PIE-ruhs)** reed. The plant grew only in Egypt but was in demand throughout the ancient world and was exported in large quantities.

papyrus A reed that grows along the banks of the Nile River in Egypt. From it was produced a coarse, paperlike writing medium used by the Egyptians and many other peoples in the ancient Mediterranean and Middle East.

When the monarchy was strong, officials were appointed and promoted on the basis of ability and accomplishment. The king gave them grants of land cultivated by dependent peasants. Low-level officials were assigned to villages and district capitals, while high-ranking officials served in the royal capital. When Old Kingdom officials died, they were buried in tombs around the monumental tomb of the king so that they could serve him in death as they had in life.

Throughout Egyptian history there was an underlying tension between the centralizing power of the monarchy and the decentralizing tendencies of the bureaucracy. One sign of the breakdown of royal power in the late Old Kingdom and First Intermediate Period was the placement of officials' tombs in their home districts, where they spent much of their time and exercised power more or less independently, rather than near the royal tomb. Another sign was the tendency of administrative posts to become hereditary. The early monarchs of the Middle Kingdom restored centralized control by reducing the power and prerogatives of the old elite and creating a new class of loyal administrators.

It has often been said that Egypt lacked real cities because the political capitals were primarily extensions of the palace and central administration. Compared to Mesopotamia, a far larger percentage of Egyptians lived in rural villages and engaged in agriculture, and Egypt's wealth derived to a higher degree from the land and its products. But there were towns and cities in ancient Egypt, although they were less crucial to the economic and cultural dynamism of the country than were Mesopotamian urban centers. Unfortunately, archaeologists have been unable to excavate many ancient urban sites in Egypt because they lie beneath modern communities.

During the Old and Middle Kingdoms, Egypt's foreign policy was essentially isolationist. Technically, all foreigners were considered enemies. When necessary, local militia units backed up a small standing army of professional soldiers. Nomadic groups in the eastern and western deserts and Libyans to the northwest were a nuisance rather than a real danger and were readily handled by the Egyptian military. Egypt's interests abroad focused on maintaining access to valuable resources rather than on acquiring territory. Trade with the coastal towns of the Levant **(luh-VANT)** (modern Israel, the Palestinian territories, Lebanon, and Syria) brought in cedar wood. In return, Egypt exported grain, papyrus, and gold.

In all periods the Egyptians had a particularly strong interest in goods from the south. Nubia had rich sources of gold (Chapter 4 examines the rise of a civilization in Nubia that, though considerably influenced by Egypt, created a vital and original culture that lasted for more than two thousand years), and the southern course of the Nile offered the easiest passage to sub-Saharan Africa. In the Old Kingdom, Egyptian noblemen led donkey caravans south to trade for gold, incense, and products of tropical Africa such as ivory, dark ebony wood, and exotic jungle animals. A line of forts along the southern border protected Egypt from attack. In the early second millennium B.C.E. Egyptian forces struck south into Nubia, extending the border to the Third Cataract of the Nile and taking possession of the gold fields. Still farther to the south, perhaps in the coastal region of present-day Sudan or Eritrea, lay the fabled land of Punt **(poont)**, source of the fragrant myrrh resin burned on the altars of the Egyptian gods.

The People of Egypt

The million to million and a half inhabitants of Egypt included various physical types, ranging from dark-skinned people related to the populations of sub-Saharan Africa to lighter-skinned people akin to the populations of North Africa and western Asia. Although Egypt did not experience the large-scale migrations and invasions common in Mesopotamia, settlers periodically trickled into the Nile Valley and assimilated with the people already living there.

Although some Egyptians had higher status and more wealth and power than others, in contrast to Mesopotamia no formal class structure emerged. At the top of the social hierarchy were the king and high-ranking officials. In the middle were lower-level officials, local leaders, priests and other professionals, artisans, and well-to-do farmers. At the bottom were peasants, who made up the vast majority of the population.

Any account of the lives of ordinary Egyptians is largely conjectural; the villages of ancient Egypt, like those of Mesopotamia, left few traces in the archaeological or literary record. In tomb paintings of the elite, artists indicated status by pictorial conventions, such as obesity for their wealthy and comfortable patrons, baldness and deformity for the working classes. Egyptian poets frequently used metaphors of farming and hunting, and papyrus documents preserved in the hot, dry sands tell of property transactions and legal disputes among ordinary people.

Peasants living in rural villages engaged in the seasonally changing tasks of agriculture: plowing, sowing, tending emerging shoots, reaping, threshing, and storing grain or other products of the soil. They maintained and extended the irrigation network of channels, basins, and dikes. Meat from domesticated animals—cattle, sheep, goats, and poultry—and fish supplemented a diet based on wheat or barley, beer, and vegetables. Villagers shared implements, work animals, and storage facilities and helped one another at peak times in the agricultural cycle and in the construction of houses and other buildings. They prayed and feasted together at festivals to the local gods. Periodically they had to contribute labor to state projects. If taxation or compulsory service was too great a burden, flight into the desert was the only escape.

Some information is available about the lives of women of the upper classes, but it is filtered through the brushes and pens of male artists and scribes. Tomb paintings show women of the royal family and elite classes accompanying their husbands and engaging in typical domestic activities. They are depicted with dignity and affection, though they are clearly subordinate to the men. The artistic convention of depicting men with a dark red and women with a yellow flesh tone implies that the elite woman's proper sphere was indoors, away from the searing sun. In the beautiful love poetry of the New Kingdom, lovers address each other in terms of apparent equality and express emotions of romantic love.

Legal documents show that Egyptian women could own property, inherit property from their parents, and will their property to whomever they wished. Marriage, usually monogamous, was not confirmed by any legal or religious ceremony and essentially constituted a decision by a man and woman to establish a household together. Either party could dissolve the relationship, and the divorced woman retained rights over her dowry. At certain times queens and queen-mothers played significant behind-the-scenes roles in the politics of the court, and priestesses sometimes supervised the cults of female deities. In general, the limited evidence suggests that women in ancient Egypt were treated more respectfully and had more legal rights and social freedom than women in Mesopotamia and other ancient societies.

Belief and Knowledge

Egyptian religion was rooted in the landscape of the Nile Valley and the vision of cosmic order that it evoked. The consistency of their environment—the sun rose every day in a clear and cloudless sky, and the river flooded on schedule every year, ensuring a bounteous harvest—persuaded the Egyptians that the natural world was a place of recurrent cycles and periodic renewal. The sky was imagined to be a great ocean surrounding the inhabited world. The sun-god Re **(ray)** traversed this blue waterway in a boat by day, then returned through the Underworld at night, fighting off the attacks of demonic serpents so that he could be born anew in the morning. In one especially popular story Osiris **(oh-SIGH-ris)**, a god who once ruled Egypt, was slain by his jealous brother Seth, who then scattered the dismembered pieces. Isis, Osiris's devoted sister and wife, found and reconstructed the remnants, and Horus, his son, took revenge on Seth. Osiris was restored to life and installed as king of the Underworld, and his example gave people hope of a new life in a world beyond this one.

The king, who was seen as Horus and as the son of Re, was thus associated with both the return of the dead to life and the life-giving and self-renewing sun-god. He was the chief priest of Egypt, intervening with the gods on behalf of his land and people. Egyptian rulers zealously built new temples, refurbished old ones, and made lavish gifts to the gods. Much of the country's wealth was directed to religious activities in a ceaseless effort to win the gods' favor, maintain the continuity of divine kingship, and ensure the renewal of the life-giving forces that sustained the world.

The many gods of ancient Egypt were diverse in origin and nature. Some were normally depicted with animal heads; others were always given human form. Few myths about the origins and adventures of the gods have survived, but there must have been a rich oral tradition. Many towns had temples for locally prominent deities. When a town became the capital of a ruling dynasty, the chief god of that town became prominent across the land. Thus did Ptah **(puh-TAH)** of Memphis, Re of Heliopolis **(he-lee-OP-uh-lis)**, and Amon **(AH-muhn)** of Thebes become gods of all Egypt, serving to unify the country and strengthen the monarchy. As in Mesopotamia, some temples possessed extensive landholdings worked by dependent peasants, and the priests who administered the deity's wealth were influential locally and sometimes even throughout the land.

Cult activities were carried out in the inner reaches of the temples, off limits to all but the priests who served the needs of the deity by attending to his or her statue. During great festivals,

Scene from the Egyptian Book of the Dead, ca. 1300 B.C.E. The mummy of a royal scribe named Hunefar is approached by members of his household before being placed in the tomb. Behind Hunefar is jackal-headed Anubis, the god who will conduct the spirit of the deceased to the afterlife. The Book of the Dead provided Egyptians with the instructions they needed to complete this arduous journey and gain a blessed existence in the afterlife.

the priests paraded a boat-shaped litter carrying the shrouded statue and cult items of the deity around the town, an event that brought large numbers of people into contact with the deity in an outpouring of devotion and celebration. However, little is known about the day-to-day beliefs and practices of the common people. In the household family members made small offerings to Bes, the grotesque god of marriage and domestic happiness, to local deities, and to the family's ancestors. They relied on amulets and depictions of demonic figures to protect the bearer and ward off evil forces. In later times Greeks and Romans commented that the devotion to magic was especially strong in Egypt.

Egyptians believed in the afterlife and made extensive preparations for safe passage to the next world and a comfortable existence once they arrived there. A common belief was that death was a journey beset with hazards. The Egyptian Book of the Dead, present in many excavated tombs, contained rituals and spells to protect the journeying spirit. The final challenge was the weighing of the deceased's heart in the presence of the judges of the Underworld to determine whether the person had led a good life and deserved to reach the ultimate blessed destination.

Obsession with the afterlife led to great concern about the physical condition of the cadaver, and Egyptians perfected techniques of mummification to preserve the dead body. The idea probably grew out of the early practice of burying the dead in the hot, dry sand on the edge of the desert, where bodies decomposed slowly. The elite classes utilized the most expensive kind of mummification. Vital organs were removed, preserved, and stored in stone jars laid out around the corpse. Body cavities were filled with various packing materials. The cadaver, immersed for long periods in dehydrating and preserving chemicals, eventually was wrapped in linen. The **mummy** was then placed in one or more decorated wooden caskets and deposited in a tomb.

The form of the tomb reflected the wealth and status of the deceased. Common people made do with simple pit graves or small mud-brick chambers. The privileged classes built larger tombs. Kings erected pyramids and other grand edifices, employing subterfuge to hide the sealed chamber containing the body and treasures, as well as curses and other magical precautions to foil tomb

mummy A body preserved by chemical processes or special natural circumstances, often in the belief that the deceased will need it again in the afterlife.

- Most of the population of ancient Egypt lived alongside the river or in the delta.

- Egypt was well endowed with natural resources and largely self-sufficient.

- Because the king was the essential link between the people of Egypt and their gods, lavish resources were poured into the construction of pyramids and other royal tombs.

- Hieroglyphic and other systems of writing were used by administrators, but also for many genres of literature.

- The population of Egypt was physically diverse, and there was no formal system of classes.

- The status and privileges of Egyptian women were superior to those of their Mesopotamian counterparts, and poetry reveals an ideal of romantic love.

- Obsessed with the afterlife, Egyptians used mummification to preserve dead bodies, constructed elaborate tombs, and employed the Book of the Dead to navigate the hazardous journey to a comfortable final destination.

- Egyptians acquired substantial knowledge about medicine, mathematics, astronomy, and engineering.

robbers. Rarely did they succeed, however, and archaeologists have seldom discovered an undisturbed royal tomb. The tombs, usually built at the edge of the desert so as not to tie up valuable farmland, were filled with pictures, food, and the objects of everyday life to provide whatever the deceased might need in the next life. Small figurines called shawabtis (shuh-WAB-tees) were included to play the part of servants and take the place of the deceased in case the afterlife required periodic compulsory labor. The elite classes attached chapels to their tombs and left endowments to subsidize the daily attendance of a priest and offerings of foodstuffs to sustain their spirits for all eternity.

The ancient Egyptians made remarkable advances in many areas of knowledge. The process of mummification taught them about human anatomy, and Egyptian doctors were in demand in the courts of western Asia. They developed mathematics to measure the dimensions of fields and to calculate the quantity of agricultural produce owed to the state. Through careful observation of the stars they constructed the most accurate calendar in the world, and they knew that the appearance of the star Sirius on the horizon shortly before sunrise meant that the Nile flood surge was imminent. Pyramids, temple complexes, and other monumental building projects called for great skill in engineering. Long underground passageways were excavated to connect mortuary temples by the river with tombs near the desert's edge. On several occasions Egyptian kings dredged out a canal more than 50 miles (80 kilometers) long in order to join the Nile Valley to the Red Sea and expedite the transport of goods.

THE INDUS VALLEY CIVILIZATION

Civilization arose almost as early in South Asia as in Mesopotamia and Egypt. In the fertile floodplain of the Indus River, farming created the food surplus essential to urbanized society.

Natural Environment

A plain of more than 1 million acres (400,000 hectares) stretches from the mountains of western Pakistan east to the Thar (tahr) Desert in the Sind (sinned) region of modern Pakistan (see Map 2.1). Over many centuries silt carried downstream and deposited by the Indus River has elevated the riverbed and its banks above the level of the plain. Twice a year the river overflows and inundates surrounding land as far as 10 miles (16 kilometers). In March and April melting snow from the Pamir (pah-MEER) and Himalaya (him-uh-LAY-uh) mountain ranges feeds the floods. In August, the great monsoon (seasonal wind) blowing off the ocean to the southwest brings rains that cause a second flood. Farmers in this region of little rainfall are thus able to plant and harvest two crops a year. In ancient times the Hakra (HAK-ruh) River (sometimes referred to as the Saraswati), which has since dried up, ran parallel to the Indus about 25 miles (40 kilometers) to the east and supplied water to a second cultivable area.

Adjacent regions shared many cultural traits with this core area. To the northeast is the Punjab, where five rivers converge to form the main course of the Indus. Lying beneath the towering Himalaya range, the Punjab receives considerably more rainfall than the central plain but is less prone to flooding. Settlements spread as far east as Delhi (DEL-ee) in northwest India. Settlement also extended south into the great delta where the Indus empties into the Arabian Sea, and southeast into India's hook-shaped Kathiawar (kah-tee-uh-WAHR) Peninsula, an area of alluvial plains and coastal marshes. The Indus Valley civilization covered an area much larger than the zone of Mesopotamian civilization.

Material Culture

The Indus Valley civilization flourished from approximately 2600 to 1900 B.C.E. Although archaeologists have located several hundred sites, the culture is best known from the remains of two great cities first discovered eighty years ago. Since the ancient names of these cities are unknown, they are referred to by modern names: **Harappa** and **Mohenjo-Daro** (moe-hen-joe– DAHR-oh). Unfortunately, the high water table at these sites makes excavation of the earliest levels of settlement nearly impossible.

Settled agriculture in this region dates back to at least 5000 B.C.E. The precise relationship between the Indus Valley civilization and earlier cultural complexes in the Indus Valley and in the hilly lands to the west is unclear. Also unclear are the forces that gave rise to urbanization, population increase, and technological advances in the mid-third millennium B.C.E. Nevertheless, the case for continuity with the earlier cultures seems stronger than the case for a sudden transformation due to the arrival of new peoples.

This society produced major urban centers. Harappa, 3.5 miles (5.6 kilometers) in circumference, may have housed a population of 35,000. Mohenjo-Daro was several times larger. High, thick brick walls surrounded each city, and the streets were laid out in a rectangular grid. Covered drainpipes carried away waste. The consistent width of streets and length of city blocks and the uniformity of the mud bricks used in construction suggest a strong central authority. The seat of this authority may have been the citadel—an elevated, enclosed compound containing large buildings. Scholars think the well-ventilated structures nearby were storehouses of grain for feeding the urban population and for export. The presence of barracks may point to some regimentation of skilled artisans.

Different centers may have had different functions. Mohenjo-Daro dominates the great floodplain of the Indus. Harappa, which is nearly 500 miles (805 kilometers) to the north, is on a frontier between farmland and herding land, and it may have served as a "gateway" for procuring the copper, tin, and precious stones of the northwest. Coastal towns in the south gathered fish and highly prized seashells and engaged in seaborne trade with the Persian Gulf.

Mohenjo-Daro and Harappa have been extensively excavated, and published accounts of the Indus Valley civilization tend to treat them as the norm. Most people, however, lived in smaller settlements, which exhibit the same artifacts and the same standardization of styles and shapes as the large cities. Some scholars attribute this standardization to extensive exchange of goods within the zone of Indus Valley civilization, rather than to the urban centers' control of the smaller settlements.

There is a greater quantity of metal in the Indus Valley than in Mesopotamia and Egypt, and most metal objects are utilitarian tools and other everyday objects. In contrast, more jewelry and other decorative metal objects have been unearthed in Mesopotamia and Egypt. Apparently metals

Harappa Site of one of the great cities of the Indus Valley civilization of the third millennium B.C.E. It was located on the northwest frontier of the zone of cultivation (in modern Pakistan).

Mohenjo-Daro Largest of the cities of the Indus Valley civilization, centrally located in the extensive floodplain of the Indus River in contemporary Pakistan.

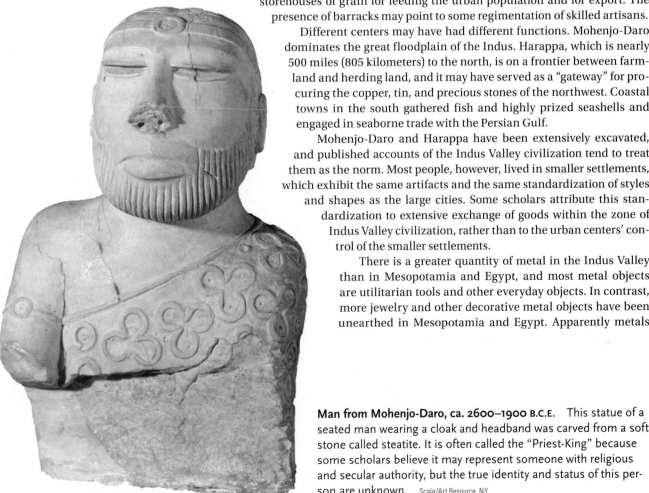

Man from Mohenjo-Daro, ca. 2600–1900 B.C.E. This statue of a seated man wearing a cloak and headband was carved from a soft stone called steatite. It is often called the "Priest-King" because some scholars believe it may represent someone with religious and secular authority, but the true identity and status of this person are unknown. Scala/Art Resource, NY

Environmental Stress in the Indus Valley

The three river-valley civilizations discussed in this chapter were located in arid or semiarid regions. Such regions are particularly vulnerable to changes in the environment. Scholars' debates about the existence and impact of changes in the climate and landscape of the Indus Valley illuminate some of the possible factors at work, as well as the difficulties of verifying and interpreting such long-ago changes.

One of the points at issue is climate change. Earlier scholars believed the climate of the Indus Valley was considerably wetter during the height of that civilization than it is now. They pointed to the enormous quantities of timber needed to bake the millions of mud bricks used to construct the cities (see photo), the distribution of human settlements on land now unfavorable for agriculture, and the representation of jungle and marsh animals on decorated seals. They maintained that the growth of population, prosperity, and complexity in the Indus Valley in the third millennium B.C.E. required wet conditions, and they concluded that the change to a drier climate in the early second millennium B.C.E. pushed this civilization into decline.

Other experts, skeptical about radical climate change, offered alternative calculations of the amount of timber needed and the evidence of plant remains—particularly barley, a grain that is tolerant of dry conditions. However, recent studies of the stabilization of sand dunes, which occurs in periods of heavy rainfall, and analysis of the sediment deposited by rivers and winds have strengthened the view that the Indus Valley used to be wetter and that in the early- to mid-second millennium B.C.E. it entered a period of relatively dry conditions that have persisted to the present.

A clearer case can be made for changes in the landscape caused by shifts in the courses of rivers. These shifts are due, in some cases, to tectonic forces such as earthquakes. Dried-up riverbeds can be detected in satellite photographs or by on-the-ground inspection. It appears that a second major river system, the Hakra, once ran parallel to the Indus some distance to the east. The Hakra, with teeming towns and fertile fields along its banks, appears to have been a second axis of this civilization. Either the Sutlej, which now feeds into the Indus, or the Yamuna, which now pours into the Ganges, may have been the main source of water for the Hakra before undergoing a change of course. The consequences of the drying-up of this major waterway must have been immense—the loss of huge amounts of arable land and the food it produced, the abandonment of cities and villages and migration of their populations, shifts in trade routes, and desperate competition for shrinking resources.

As for the Indus itself, the present-day course of the lower reaches of the river has shifted 100 miles (161 kilometers) to the west since the arrival of the Greek conqueror Alexander the Great in the late fourth century B.C.E., and the deposit of massive volumes of silt has pushed the mouth of the river 50 miles (80 kilometers) farther south. A similar shift of the riverbed and buildup of alluvial deposits may have occurred in the third and second millennia B.C.E. and played a role in the decline of the Indus civilization.

Universal Images Group/DeAgostini/Alamy

Mud-Brick Construction at Mohenjo-Daro   View of the excavated remains of houses in the Lower Town, with the elevated Citadel in the background. Flood-resistant reddish-colored baked bricks were used for the foundations and lower levels, with unbaked bricks above. Construction of fortification walls and buildings required large numbers of bricks and enormous man-hours of labor.

were available to a broad cross-section of the population in the Indus Valley, while primarily reserved for the elite in the Middle East.

Technologically, the Indus Valley people showed skill in irrigation, used the potter's wheel, and laid the foundations of large public buildings with mud bricks fired to rocky hardness in kilns (sun-dried bricks would have dissolved quickly in floodwaters). They had a system of writing with more than four hundred signs. Archaeologists have recovered thousands of inscribed seal stones and copper tablets, but no one has been able to decipher these documents.

The people of the Indus Valley had widespread trading contacts. They had ready access to the metals and precious stones of eastern Iran and Afghanistan, as well as to ore deposits in western India, building stone, and timber. Goods were moved on rivers within the zone of Indus Valley culture. Indus Valley seal stones have been found in the Tigris-Euphrates Valley, indicating that Indus Valley merchants served as middlemen in long-distance trade, obtaining raw materials from the northwest and shipping them to the Persian Gulf. The undeciphered writing on seal stones may represent the names of merchants who stamped their wares.

We know little about the political, social, economic, and religious institutions of Indus Valley society. Attempts to link artifacts and images to cultural features characteristic of later periods of Indian history (see Chapter 7)—including a system of hereditary occupational groups with priests predominating, bathing tanks like those later found in Hindu temples, depictions of gods and sacred animals on seal stones, a cult of the mother-goddess—are highly speculative. Further knowledge about this society awaits additional archaeological finds and the deciphering of the Indus Valley script.

Transformation of the Indus Valley Civilization

The Indus Valley cities were abandoned sometime after 1900 B.C.E. Archaeologists once thought that invaders destroyed them, but they now believe this civilization suffered "systems failure"— a breakdown of the fragile interrelationship of political, social, and economic systems that sustained order and prosperity. The cause may have been one or more natural disasters, such as an earthquake or massive flooding. Gradual ecological changes may also have played a role as the Hakra river system dried up and salinization (an increase in the amount of salt in the soil, inhibiting plant growth) and erosion increased (see Environment and Technology: Environmental Stress in the Indus Valley).

Towns no longer on the river, ports separated from the sea by silt deposits in the deltas, and the loss of fertile soil and water would have necessitated the relocation of populations and a change in the livelihood of those who remained. The causes and pace of change probably varied in different areas. The urban centers eventually succumbed, however, and village-based farming and herding took their place. As the interaction between regions lessened, regional variation replaced the standardization of technology and style of the previous era. It is important to keep in mind that in most cases like this the majority of the population adjusts to the new circumstances. But members of the elite, who depend on the urban centers and complex political and economic structures, lose the source of their authority and are merged with the population as a whole.

SECTION REVIEW

- The Indus Valley civilization occupied a large territory, including the fertile Indus floodplain as well as adjacent regions.

- Both the major urban centers and smaller settlements exhibit a uniformity of techniques and styles that indicates either strong central control or extensive communication between different regions.

- The Indus Valley people were technologically advanced in irrigation, ceramics, and construction. Metals were more widely available than in Mesopotamia and Egypt. The writing system has not been deciphered.

- The Indus Valley had widespread trading contacts, reaching as far as Mesopotamia.

- Cities were abandoned and the civilization declined after 1900 B.C.E., probably as a result of natural disasters or environmental changes.

CONCLUSION

It is no accident that the first civilizations to develop high levels of political centralization, urbanization, and technology were situated in river valleys where rainfall was insufficient for reliable agriculture. Dependent on river water to irrigate the cultivated land that fed their populations, Mesopotamia, Egypt, and the Indus Valley civilization channeled considerable human resources into the construction and maintenance of canals, dams, and dikes. This effort required the formation of political centers that could organize the necessary labor force.

In both Egypt and Mesopotamia, kingship emerged as the dominant political form. The Egyptian king's divine origins and symbolic association with the forces of renewal made him central to the welfare of the entire country and gave him religious authority superseding the temples and priests. Egyptian monarchs lavished much of the country's wealth on their tombs, believing that a proper burial would ensure the continuity of kingship and the attendant blessings that it brought to the land and people. Mesopotamian rulers, who were not normally regarded as divine but still dominated the religious institutions, built new cities, towering walls, splendid palaces, and religious edifices as lasting testaments to their power.

The unpredictable and violent floods in the Tigris-Euphrates Basin were a constant source of alarm for the people of Mesopotamia. In contrast, the predictable, opportune, and gradual Nile floods were eagerly anticipated events in Egypt. The relationship with nature stamped the religious outlooks of both peoples, since their gods embodied the forces of the environment. Mesopotamians nervously tried to appease their harsh deities so as to survive in a dangerous world, whereas Egyptians largely trusted in and nurtured the supernatural powers that, they believed, guaranteed orderliness and prosperity. The Egyptians also believed that, although the journey to the next world was beset with hazards, the righteous spirit that overcame them could look forward to a blessed existence. In contrast, Gilgamesh, the hero of the Mesopotamian epic, is tormented by terrifying visions of the afterlife: disembodied spirits of the dead stumbling around in the darkness of the Underworld for all eternity, eating dust and clay and slaving for the heartless gods of that realm.

Although the populations of Egypt and Mesopotamia were ethnically heterogeneous, both regions experienced a remarkable degree of cultural continuity. New immigrants readily assimilated to the dominant language, belief system, and lifestyles of the civilization. Mesopotamia developed sharp social divisions that were reflected in the class-based penalties set down in the Law Code of Hammurabi, whereas Egyptian society was less urban and less stratified. Mesopotamian women's apparent loss of freedom and legal privilege in the second millennium B.C.E. also may have been related to the higher degree of urbanization and class stratification in this society. In contrast, Egyptian pictorial documents, love poems, and legal records indicate respect and greater equality for women in the valley of the Nile.

Because of the lack of readable texts, we can say very little about the political institutions, social organization, and religious beliefs of the Indus Valley people. However, they clearly possessed technologies on a par with those found in Mesopotamia and Egypt—a writing system, irrigation, bronze-casting, and techniques for producing monumental architecture. The striking uniformity in the planning and construction of cities and towns and in the shapes and styles of artifacts argues for easy communication and some kind of interdependence among the far-flung Indus Valley settlements, as does the relatively rapid collapse of this civilization as a result of ecological changes.

KEY TERMS

civilization p. 27
Sumerians p. 30
Semitic p. 30
city-state p. 31
Babylon p. 32
Hammurabi p. 32

scribe p. 34
ziggurat p. 35
amulet p. 35
cuneiform p. 35
bronze p. 37
pharaoh p. 41

ma'at p. 41
pyramid p. 41
Memphis p. 42
Thebes p. 42
hieroglyphics p. 42
papyrus p. 42

mummy p. 45
Harappa p. 47
Mohenjo-Daro p. 47

SUGGESTED READING

Black, Jeremy, and Anthony Green. *Gods, Demons and Symbols of Ancient Mesopotamia*. 1992. A handy illustrated encyclopedia of myth, religion, and religious symbolism.

Capel, Anne K., and Glenn E. Markoe, eds. *Mistress of the House, Mistress of Heaven: Women in Ancient Egypt*. 1996. Articles by specialists and a museum exhibition catalogue.

Kenoyer, Jonathan Mark. *Ancient Cities of the Indus Valley Civilization*. 1998. Up-to-date treatment by a leading specialist.

Kuhrt, Amelie. *The Ancient Near East, c. 3000–330 B.C.*, 2 vols. 1995. The best introduction to the historical development of western Asia and Egypt.

Lichtheim, Miriam. *Ancient Egyptian Literature: A Book of Readings*, vol. 1, *The Old and Middle Kingdoms*. 1973. Translations of selected original texts and documents.

McIntosh, Jane R. *The Ancient Indus Valley: New Perspectives*. 2007. Another solid treatment of the Indus Valley civilization.

Postgate, J. N. *Early Mesopotamia: Society and Economy at the Dawn of History*. 1992. Presents deep insights into the political, social, and economic dynamics of Mesopotamian society.

Pritchard, James B. *Ancient Near Eastern Texts Relating to the Old Testament*, 3d ed. 1969. An extensive collection of translated documents and texts from the ancient civilizations of western Asia and Egypt.

Redford, Donald B., ed. *The Oxford Encyclopedia of Ancient Egypt*, 3 vols. 2001. A comprehensive resource.

Roaf, Michael. *Cultural Atlas of Mesopotamia and the Ancient Near East*. 1990. An excellent introduction to the geography, chronology, and basic institutions and cultural concepts of ancient western Asia.

Romer, John. *People of the Nile: Everyday Life in Ancient Egypt*. 1982. A highly readable treatment of social history.

Sasson, Jack M., ed. *Civilizations of the Ancient Near East*, 4 vols. 1993. A comprehensive resource, with articles by specialists on a wide range of topics.

Silverman, David P., ed. *Ancient Egypt*. 2003. A lavishly illustrated introduction to the many facets of ancient Egyptian civilization.

Snell, Daniel C. *Life in the Ancient Near East 3100–322 B.C.E.* 1997. A rich account of social and economic matters for those already familiar with the main outlines of ancient Near Eastern history.

Vivante, Bella, ed. *Women's Roles in Ancient Civilizations: A Reference Guide*. 1999. Contains articles by specialists on many ancient societies, including Mesopotamia and Egypt.

CourseMate **Go to the History CourseMate website for primary source links, study tools, and review materials for this chapter.** www.cengagebrain.com

Chapter Outline

The Cosmopolitan Middle East, 1700–1100 B.C.E.
➤ *How did a cosmopolitan civilization develop in the Middle East during the Late Bronze Age, and what forms did it take?*

The Aegean World, 2000–1100 B.C.E.
➤ *What civilizations emerged in the Aegean world, and what relationship did they have to the older civilizations to the east?*

The Assyrian Empire, 911–612 B.C.E.
➤ *How did the Assyrian Empire rise to power and eventually dominate most of the ancient Middle East?*

Israel, 2000–500 B.C.E.
➤ *How did the civilization of Israel develop, following both cultural patterns typical of other societies and its own unique ways?*

Phoenicia and the Mediterranean, 1200–500 B.C.E.
➤ *How did the Phoenicians rise to commercial dominance over much of the Mediterranean world?*

Failure and Transformation, 750–550 B.C.E.
➤ *Between 750 and 550 B.C.E., what factors prompted the transformation of the ancient Middle East?*

Conclusion

● **DIVERSITY + DOMINANCE**   Protests Against the Ruling Class in Israel and Babylonia

● **ENVIRONMENT + TECHNOLOGY**   Ancient Textiles and Dyes

Lebrecht Music and Arts Photo Library/Alamy

Dido Building Carthage   This 1815 C.E. painting by the British artist J. M. W. Turner shows the construction of the newly founded city of Carthage by Dido (seen on the left), a story familiar from the Roman poet Vergil's epic *Aeneid.*

The Mediterranean and Middle East, 2000–500 B.C.E.

Ancient peoples' stories—even when not historically accurate—provide valuable insights into how they thought about their origins and identity. One famous story concerned the founding of the city of Carthage (KAHR-thuhj) in present-day Tunisia, which for centuries dominated the waters and water-borne commerce of the western Mediterranean. Tradition held that Dido and her supporters fled the Phoenician city-state of Tyre (tire) in southern Lebanon after her husband was murdered by her brother, the king. Landing on the North African coast, they made contact with local people, who offered them as much land as a cow's hide could cover. Cleverly cutting the hide into narrow strips, they marked out a substantial territory for Kart Khadasht, the "New City" (called *Carthago* by their Roman enemies). The painting at the beginning of this chapter envisions the construction of the city.

This story highlights the spread of cultural patterns from older centers to new regions, as well as the migration of Late Bronze Age and Early Iron Age peoples in the Mediterranean lands and western Asia. Trade, diplomatic contacts, military conquests, and the relocation of large numbers of people spread knowledge, beliefs, practices, and technologies.

By the early first millennium B.C.E. many societies of the Eastern Hemisphere were entering the **Iron Age**, using iron in addition to bronze for tools and weapons. Iron offered several advantages. It was a single metal rather than an alloy, and there were many sources of iron ore. Once the technology had been mastered—iron has to be heated to a higher temperature than bronze, and its hardness depends on the amount of carbon added during the forging process—iron tools were found to have harder, sharper edges than bronze tools.

The first part of this chapter resumes the story of Mesopotamia and Egypt in the second millennium B.C.E.: their relations with neighboring peoples, the development of a prosperous, "cosmopolitan" network of states in the Middle East, and the period of destruction and decline that set in around 1200 B.C.E. We also look at how the Minoan and Mycenaean civilizations of the Aegean Sea were inspired by the technologies and cultural patterns of the older Middle Eastern centers and prospered from participation in long-distance trade networks. The remainder of the chapter examines the resurgence of this region in the Early Iron Age, from 1000 to 500 B.C.E. The focus is on three societies: the Assyrians of northern Mesopotamia; the Israelites of Israel; and the Phoenicians of Lebanon and their colonies in the western Mediterranean, mainly Carthage. After the decline of the ancient centers dominant throughout the third and second millennia B.C.E., these societies evolved into new political, cultural, and commercial centers.

Iron Age Historians' term for the period during which iron was the primary metal for tools and weapons. The advent of iron technology began at different times in different parts of the world.

THE COSMOPOLITAN MIDDLE EAST, 1700–1100 B.C.E.

Both Mesopotamia and Egypt succumbed to outside invaders in the seventeenth century B.C.E. Eventually the outsiders were either ejected or assimilated, and conditions of stability and prosperity were restored. Between 1500 and 1200 B.C.E. a number of large states dominated the Middle East (see Map 3.1), controlling the smaller states and kinship groups (peoples with simple political structures living in relatively small groups based on perceived descent from common ancestors) as they interacted, competed with, and sometimes fought against one another for control of valuable commodities and trade routes.

The Late Bronze Age in the Middle East was a "cosmopolitan" era of widely shared cultures and lifestyles. Diplomatic relations and commercial contacts between states fostered the flow of goods and ideas, and elite groups shared similar values and enjoyed a relatively high standard of living. The peasants in the countryside, who constituted the majority of the population, saw some improvement in their standard of living but reaped fewer benefits from the increasing contacts and trade.

Western Asia

By 1500 B.C.E. Mesopotamia was divided into two distinct political zones: Babylonia in the south and Assyria in the north (see Map 3.1). The city of Babylon had gained political and cultural ascendancy over the southern plain under the dynasty of Hammurabi in the eighteenth and seventeenth centuries B.C.E. (see Chapter 2). Subsequently Kassites (KAS-ite) from the Zagros (ZAH-groes) Mountains to the east migrated into southern Mesopotamia, and by 1460 B.C.E.

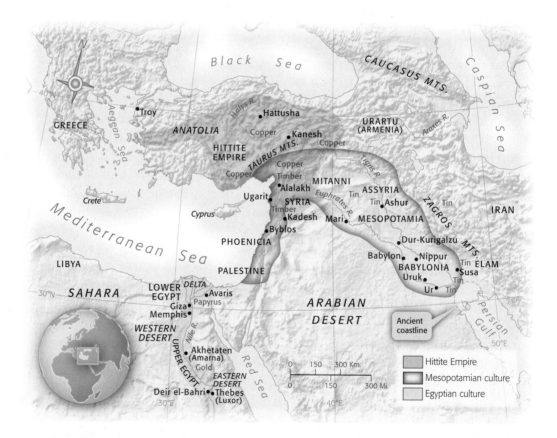

MAP 3.1 The Middle East in the Second Millennium B.C.E. Although warfare was not uncommon, treaties, diplomatic missions, and correspondence in Akkadian cuneiform fostered cooperative relationships between states. All were tied together by extensive networks of exchange centering on the trade in metals, and peripheral regions, such as Nubia and the Aegean Sea, were drawn into the web of commerce. © Cengage Learning

CHRONOLOGY

	Western Asia	Egypt	Syria–Palestine	Mediterranean
2000 B.C.E.	2000 B.C.E. Horses in use 1700–1200 B.C.E. Hittites dominant in Anatolia	2040–1640 B.C.E. Middle Kingdom 1640–1532 B.C.E. Hyksos dominate northern Egypt 1532 B.C.E. Beginning of New Kingdom	1800 B.C.E. Abraham migrates to Canaan	2000 B.C.E. Rise of Minoan civilization on Crete; early Greeks arrive in Greece 1600 B.C.E. Rise of Mycenaean civilization in Greece
1500 B.C.E.	1500 B.C.E. Hittites develop iron metallurgy 1460 B.C.E. Kassites assume control of southern Mesopotamia 1200 B.C.E. Destruction of Hittite kingdom	1470 B.C.E. Queen Hatshepsut dispatches expedition to Punt 1353 B.C.E. Akhenaten launches reforms 1290–1224 B.C.E. Reign of Ramesses the Great 1200–1150 B.C.E. Sea Peoples attack Egypt 1070 B.C.E. End of New Kingdom	1500 B.C.E. Early "alphabetic" script developed at Ugarit 1250–1200 B.C.E. Israelite occupation of Canaan 1150 B.C.E. Philistines settle southern coast of Israel	1450 B.C.E. Destruction of Minoan palaces in Crete 1200–1150 B.C.E. Destruction of Mycenaean centers in Greece
1000 B.C.E.	1000 B.C.E. Iron metallurgy begins 911 B.C.E. Rise of Neo-Assyrian Empire 744–727 B.C.E. Reforms of Tiglathpileser 668–627 B.C.E. Reign of Ashurbanipal 626–539 B.C.E. Neo-Babylonian kingdom 612 B.C.E. Fall of Assyria	750 B.C.E. Kings of Kush control Egypt 671 B.C.E. Assyrian conquest of Egypt	1000 B.C.E. Jerusalem made Israelite capital 969 B.C.E. Hiram of Tyre comes to power 960 B.C.E. Solomon builds First Temple 920 B.C.E. Division into two kingdoms of Israel and Judah 721 B.C.E. Assyrian conquest of northern kingdom 701 B.C.E. Assyrian humiliation of Tyre	1000 B.C.E. Iron metallurgy 814 B.C.E. Foundation of Carthage
600 B.C.E.			587 B.C.E. Capture of Jerusalem 515 B.C.E. Deportees from Babylon return to Jerusalem 450 B.C.E. Completion of Hebrew Bible	550–300 B.C.E. Rivalry of Carthaginians and Greeks in western Mediterranean 450 B.C.E. Hanno the Phoenician explores West Africa

a Kassite dynasty ruled in Babylon. The Kassites retained names in their native language but otherwise embraced Babylonian language and culture and intermarried with the native population. During their 250 years in power, the Kassite rulers of Babylonia defended their core area and traded for raw materials, but they did not pursue territorial conquest.

The Assyrian kingdom in northern Mesopotamia was more ambitious. As early as the twentieth century B.C.E. (the "Old Assyrian" period) the city of Ashur (AH-shoor) on the northern Tigris anchored a busy trade route stretching across the northern plain to the Anatolian Plateau. Assyrian merchant families settled outside the walls of Anatolian cities and exchanged textiles

Remains of a Sunken Cargo Ship from the Late Bronze Age Underwater archaeologists excavate a merchant vessel that went down off the coast of southern Turkey ca. 1300 B.C.E. To the left of the wooden keel and planking is a stone anchor, to the right a row of copper ingots. The vessel was carrying a cargo of copper and tin ingots, as well as Canaanite pots that probably contained incense, fine pottery from Cyprus, sub-Saharan ebony wood and elephant tusks, and some Mycenaean Greek objects, illustrating the wide-ranging seaborne trade in the eastern Mediterranean in that era.

Institute of Nautical Archaeology

and tin (a component of bronze) for Anatolian silver. After 1400 B.C.E. a resurgent "Middle Assyrian" kingdom engaged in campaigns of conquest and expansion of its economic interests.

Other dynamic states emerged on the periphery of the Mesopotamian heartland, including Elam in southwest Iran and Mitanni (mih-TAH-nee) in the broad plain between the upper Euphrates and Tigris Rivers. Most formidable of all were the **Hittites** (HIT-ite), who became the foremost power in Anatolia from around 1700 to 1200 B.C.E. From their capital at Hattusha (haht-tush-SHAH), near present-day Ankara (ANG-kuh-ruh) in central Turkey, they deployed the fearsome new technology of horse-drawn war chariots. The Hittites exploited Anatolia's rich metal deposits to play a key role in international commerce.

The Hittites also first developed a technique for making tools and weapons of iron. Heating the ore until it was soft enough to shape, they pounded it to remove impurities and then plunged it into cold water to harden. They kept knowledge of this process secret because it provided military and economic advantages. In the disrupted period after 1200 B.C.E., blacksmiths from the Hittite core area may have migrated and spread iron technology.

During the second millennium B.C.E. Mesopotamian political and cultural concepts spread across western Asia. Akkadian (uh-KAY-dee-uhn) became the language of diplomacy and correspondence between governments. The Elamites (EE-luh-mite) and Hittites, among others, adapted the cuneiform system to write their own languages. In the Syrian coastal city-state of Ugarit (OO-guh-reet), thirty cuneiform symbols were used to write consonant sounds, an early use of the alphabetic principle and a considerable advance over the hundreds of signs required in conventional cuneiform and hieroglyphic writing. Mesopotamian myths, legends, and styles of art and architecture were widely imitated. Newcomers who had learned and improved on the lessons of Mesopotamian civilization often put pressure on the old core area. The small, fractious city-states of the third millennium B.C.E. had been concerned only with their immediate neighbors in southern Mesopotamia. In contrast, the larger states of the second millennium B.C.E. interacted politically, militarily, and economically in a geopolitical sphere encompassing all of western Asia.

Hittites A people from central Anatolia who established an empire in Anatolia and Syria in the Late Bronze Age. With wealth from the trade in metals and military power based on chariot forces, the Hittites vied with New Kingdom Egypt for control of Syria-Palestine before falling to unidentified attackers ca. 1200 B.C.E.

New Kingdom Egypt

After flourishing for nearly four hundred years (see Chapter 2), the Egyptian Middle Kingdom declined in the seventeenth century B.C.E. As officials in the countryside became increasingly independent and new groups migrated into the Nile Delta, central authority broke down and

Egypt entered a period of political fragmentation and economic decline. Around 1640 B.C.E. northern Egypt came under foreign rule for the first time, at the hands of the Hyksos (HICK-soes), or "Princes of Foreign Lands."

Historians are uncertain who the Hyksos were and how they came to power. Semitic peoples had been migrating from the Syria-Palestine region (present-day Syria, Jordan, Lebanon, Israel, and the Palestinian territories) into the eastern Nile Delta for centuries. In the chaotic conditions of this time, various groups may have cooperated to establish control, first in the delta and then in the middle of the country. The Hyksos possessed advantageous military technologies, such as the horse-drawn war chariot and a composite bow, made of wood and horn that had greater range and velocity than the simple wooden bow. They intermarried with Egyptians, used the Egyptian language, and maintained Egyptian institutions and culture. Nevertheless, in contrast to the easy assimilation of outsiders such as the Kassites in Mesopotamia, the Egyptians, with their strong ethnic identity, continued to regard the Hyksos as "foreigners."

As with the formation of the Middle Kingdom five hundred years earlier, the reunification of Egypt under a native dynasty was accomplished by princes from Thebes. After three decades of warfare, Kamose (KAH-mose) and Ahmose (AH-mose) expelled the Hyksos from Egypt and inaugurated the New Kingdom, which lasted from about 1532 to 1070 B.C.E.

A century of foreign domination had injured Egyptian pride and shattered the isolationist mindset of earlier eras. New Kingdom Egypt was an aggressive and expansionist state. By extending its territorial control north into Syria-Palestine and south into Nubia, Egypt won access to timber, gold, and copper (bronze metallurgy took hold in Egypt around 1500 B.C.E.), as well as taxes and tribute payments from the conquered peoples. The occupied territories provided a buffer zone, protecting Egypt from attack. In Nubia, Egypt imposed direct control and pressed the native population to adopt Egyptian language and culture. In the Syria-Palestine region, in contrast, the Egyptians stationed garrisons at strategically placed forts and supported cooperative local rulers.

In this period of innovation, Egypt fully participated in the diplomatic and commercial networks linking the states of western Asia. Egyptian soldiers, administrators, diplomats, and merchants traveled widely, bringing back new fruits and vegetables, new musical instruments, and new technologies, such as an improved potter's wheel and weaver's loom.

One woman held the throne of New Kingdom Egypt. When her husband died, Queen **Hatshepsut** (hat-SHEP-soot) claimed the royal title for herself (r. 1473–1458 B.C.E.). In inscriptions she often used the male pronoun for herself, and drawings and sculptures show her wearing the long, conical beard of the Egyptian ruler.

Around 1470 B.C.E. Hatshepsut sent a naval expedition down the Red Sea to the fabled land of Punt (poont), probably near the coast of eastern Sudan or Eritrea. Hatshepsut was seeking the source of myrrh (murr), a reddish-brown resin from the hardened sap of a local tree, which the Egyptians burned on the altars of their gods and used in medicines and cosmetics. When the expedition returned with myrrh and sub-Saharan luxury goods—ebony, ivory, cosmetics, live monkeys, panther skins—Hatshepsut celebrated the achievement in a great public display and in words and pictures on the walls of her mortuary temple at Deir el-Bahri (DARE uhl–BAH-ree). She may have used the success of this expedition to bolster her claim to the throne. After her death, her image was defaced and her name blotted out wherever it appeared, presumably by officials opposed to a woman ruler.

A century later another untraditional ruler ascended the throne as Amenhotep (ah-muhn-HOE-tep) IV, but he soon began to refer to himself as **Akhenaten** (ah-ken-AHT-n) (r. 1353–1335 B.C.E.), meaning "beneficial to the Aten" (AHT-n) (the disk of the sun). Changing his name was one way to spread his belief in Aten as the supreme deity. He closed the temples of other gods, challenging the age-old supremacy of the chief god Amon (AH-muhn) and the power and influence of his priests. Some scholars have credited Akhenaten with the invention of monotheism— the belief in one exclusive god. It is likely, however, that Akhenaten was attempting to reassert the superiority of the king over the priests and to renew belief in the king's divinity. Worship of Aten was confined to the royal family: the people of Egypt were pressed to revere the divine ruler.

Akhenaten built a new capital at modern-day Amarna (uh-MAHR-nuh), halfway between Memphis and Thebes (see Map 3.1). He transplanted thousands of Egyptians to construct the site and serve the ruling elite. Akhenaten and his artists created a new style that broke with the conventions of earlier art: the king, his wife Nefertiti (nef-uhr-TEE-tee), and their daughters were depicted in fluid, natural poses with strangely elongated heads and limbs and swelling abdomens.

Hatshepsut Queen of Egypt (r. 1473–1458 B.C.E.). She dispatched a naval expedition to Punt (possibly northeast Sudan or Eritrea), the faraway source of myrrh. There is evidence of opposition to a woman as ruler, and after her death her name and image were frequently defaced.

Akhenaten Egyptian pharaoh (r. 1353–1335 B.C.E.). He built a new capital at Amarna, fostered a new style of naturalistic art, and created a religious revolution by imposing worship of the sun-disk.

The Mortuary Temple of Queen Hatshepsut at Deir el-Bahri, Egypt, ca. 1460 B.C.E. This beautiful complex of terraces, ramps, and colonnades featured relief sculptures and texts commemorating the famous expedition to Punt. Hatshepsut, facing resistance from traditionalists opposed to a woman ruling Egypt, sought to prove her worth by publicizing the opening of direct contact with the source of highly prized myrrh. EugenZ/Shutterstock.com

Akhenaten's reforms were strongly resented by government officials and priests whose privileges and wealth were linked to the traditional system. After his death the temples were reopened; Amon was reinstated as chief god; the capital was returned to Thebes; and the institution of kingship was weakened to the advantage of the priests. The boy-king Tutankhamun **(tuht-uhnk-AH-muhn)** (r. 1333–1323 B.C.E.), famous solely because his was the only royal tomb found by archaeologists that had not been pillaged by robbers, reveals both in his name (meaning "beautiful in life is Amon") and in his insignificant reign the ultimate failure of Akhenaten's revolution.

The rulers of a new dynasty, the Ramessides **(RAM-ih-side)**, returned to the policy of conquest and expansion that Akhenaten had neglected. The greatest of these monarchs, **Ramesses II (RAM-ih-seez)**, ruled for sixty-six years (r. 1290–1224 B.C.E.) and dominated his age. Ramesses undertook monumental building projects all over Egypt. Living into his nineties, he had many wives and may have fathered more than a hundred children. Since 1990 archaeologists have been excavating a network of corridors and chambers carved deep into a hillside near Thebes, where many sons of Ramesses were buried.

Ramesses II A long-lived ruler of New Kingdom Egypt (r. 1290–1224 B.C.E.). He reached an accommodation with the Hittites of Anatolia after a standoff in battle at Kadesh in Syria. He built on a grand scale throughout Egypt.

Commerce and Communication

Early in his reign Ramesses II fought the Hittites to a draw in a major battle at Kadesh in northern Syria (1285 B.C.E.). Subsequently, diplomats negotiated a treaty, which was strengthened by Ramesses's marriage to a Hittite princess. At issue was control of Syria-Palestine, strategically located between the great powers of the Middle East and at the end of the east-west trade route across Asia. Inland cities—such as Mari **(MAH-ree)** on the upper Euphrates and Alalakh **(UH-luh-luhk)** in western Syria—received overland caravans. Coastal towns—particularly Ugarit

Ramesses II in a War Chariot Attacks Nubian Enemies This is a restoration of a 13th century B.C.E. painting on the wall of a temple at Beit el Wali. Other paintings depict the pharaoh attacking Asiatic enemies and making offerings to the high god Amon.

and the Phoenician towns of the Lebanese seaboard—extended commerce to the lands ringing the Mediterranean Sea.

Any state seeking to project its power needed metals for tools, weapons, and ornamentation, and commerce in metals energized the long-distance trade of the time. Assyrians were interested in silver from Anatolia (discussed previously), and the Egyptians had a passion for Nubian gold (see Chapter 4). Copper came from Anatolia and Cyprus, tin from Afghanistan and possibly the British Isles. Both ores had to be carried long distances and pass through a number of hands before reaching their final destinations.

New modes of transportation expedited communications and commerce across great distances and inhospitable landscapes. Horses, domesticated by nomadic peoples in Central Asia, were brought into Mesopotamia through the Zagros Mountains around 2000 B.C.E. and reached Egypt before 1600 B.C.E. The speed of travel and communication made possible by horses contributed to the creation of large states and empires, enabling soldiers and government agents to cover great distances quickly. Swift, maneuverable horse-drawn chariots became the premier instrument of war. The team of driver and archer could run up and unleash a volley of arrows or trample terrified foot-soldiers.

Sometime after 1500 B.C.E. in western Asia, but not for another thousand years in Egypt, people began to make common use of camels, though the animal may have been domesticated a millennium earlier in southern Arabia. Thanks to their strength and ability to go long distances without water, camels were able to travel across barren terrain. Their physical qualities eventually led to the emergence of a new kind of desert nomad and the creation of cross-desert trade routes (see Chapter 9).

SECTION REVIEW

- In the Late Bronze Age trade and diplomatic contacts between states fostered the flow of goods and ideas, and elite groups enjoyed similar lifestyles and a relatively high standard of living.

- Immigrant groups that came to power in Babylonia (Kassites) and Egypt (Hyksos) assimilated to Babylonian and Egyptian language and culture.

- New peoples in western Asia who learned and improved on the technologies and culture of Mesopotamian civilization challenged the old core area.

- The Hittites used the technologies of chariot warfare and iron metallurgy to dominate Anatolia.

- New Kingdom Egypt abandoned traditional isolationism and extended control over Syria-Palestine and Nubia. The era was marked by rulers who challenged tradition—Hatshepsut, Akhenaten, and Ramesses.

- Long-distance trade networks were based on metals and expedited by the advent of horses and camels.

THE AEGEAN WORLD, 2000–1100 B.C.E.

The influence of Mesopotamia, Syria-Palestine, and Egypt was felt as far away as the Aegean Sea, a gulf of the eastern Mediterranean. The emergence of the Minoan (mih-NO-uhn) civilization on the island of Crete and the Mycenaean (my-suh-NEE-uhn) civilization of Greece is another manifestation of the fertilizing influence of older centers on outlying lands and peoples, who then struck out on their own unique paths of cultural evolution. With few deposits of metals and little timber, Aegean peoples had to import these commodities, as well as additional food supplies, from abroad. As a result, the rise, success, and eventual fall of the Minoan and Mycenaean societies were closely tied to their commercial and political relations with other peoples in the region.

Minoan Crete

Minoan Prosperous civilization on the Aegean island of Crete in the second millennium B.C.E. The Minoans engaged in far-flung commerce around the Mediterranean and exerted powerful cultural influences on the early Greeks.

By 2000 B.C.E. the island of Crete (see Map 3.2) was home to the first European civilization to have complex political and social structures and advanced technologies like those found in western Asia and northeastern Africa. Archaeologists named this civilization **Minoan** after King Minos, who, in Greek legend, ruled a naval empire in the Aegean and kept the monstrous Minotaur (MIN-uh-tor) (half-man, half-bull) in a mazelike labyrinth built by the ingenious inventor Daedalus (DED-ih-luhs). Thus later Greeks recollected a time when Crete had been home to many ships and skilled craftsmen.

The ethnicity of the Minoans is uncertain, and their writing has not been deciphered. But the distribution of Cretan pottery and other artifacts around the Mediterranean and Middle East testifies to widespread trading connections. Egyptian, Syrian, and Mesopotamian influences can be seen in the design of the Minoan palaces, centralized government, and system of writing. The absence of identifiable representations of Cretan rulers, however, contrasts sharply with the grandiose depictions of kings in the Middle East and suggests a different conception of authority. Also noteworthy is the absence of fortifications at the palace sites and the presence of high-quality indoor plumbing.

Statuettes of women with elaborate headdresses and serpents coiling around their limbs may represent fertility goddesses. Colorful frescoes (paintings done on the moist plaster surfaces of walls) in the palaces portray groups of women in frilly skirts conversing or watching performances. We do not know whether pictures of young acrobats vaulting over the horns and back of an onrushing bull show a religious activity or mere sport. The stylized depictions of scenes from nature on vases—plants with swaying leaves and playful octopuses winding their tentacles around the surface of the vase—communicate a delight in the beauty and order of the natural world.

All the Cretan palaces except at Cnossus (NOSS-suhs), along with the houses of the elite and peasants in the countryside, were deliberately destroyed around 1450 B.C.E. Because Mycenaean Greeks took over at Cnossus, most historians regard them as the culprits.

Mycenaean Greece

Mycenae Site of a fortified palace complex in southern Greece that controlled a Late Bronze Age kingdom. In Homer's epic poems, Mycenae was the base of King Agamemnon, who commanded the Greeks besieging Troy. Contemporary archaeologists call the complex Greek society of the second millennium B.C.E. "Mycenaean."

shaft graves A term used for the burial sites of elite members of Mycenaean Greek society in the mid-second millennium B.C.E. At the bottom of deep shafts lined with stone slabs, the bodies were laid out along with gold and bronze jewelry, implements, weapons, and masks.

Speakers of an Indo-European language ancestral to Greek migrated into the Greek peninsula around 2000 B.C.E. Through intermarriage, blending of languages, and melding of cultural practices, the indigenous population and the newcomers created the first Greek culture. For centuries this society remained simple and static. Farmers and shepherds lived in Stone Age conditions, wringing a bare living from the land. Then, sometime around 1600 B.C.E., life changed relatively suddenly.

In 1876 a German businessman, Heinrich Schliemann (SHLEE-muhn), discovered a circle of graves at **Mycenae** (my-SEE-nee), in southern Greece. These deep, rectangular **shaft graves** contained the bodies of men, women, and children and were filled with gold jewelry and ornaments, weapons, and utensils. Clearly, some people in this society had acquired wealth, authority, and the capacity to mobilize human labor. Subsequent excavation uncovered a large palace complex, massive walls, more shaft graves, and other evidence of a rich and technologically advanced civilization that lasted from around 1600 to 1150 B.C.E.

How can the sudden rise of Mycenae and other centers in mainland Greece be explained? These early Greeks were clearly influenced by the Minoan palaces, centralized economy, and administrative bureaucracy, as well as the writing system. They adopted Minoan styles of

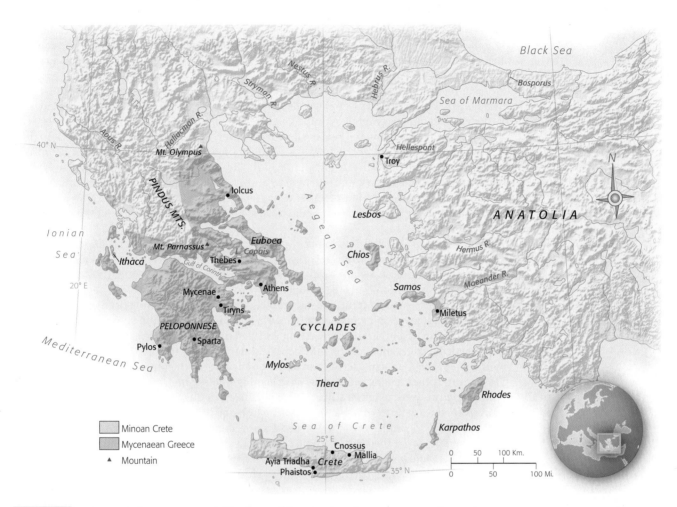

MAP 3.2 **Minoan and Mycenaean Civilizations of the Aegean** The earliest complex civilizations in Europe arose in the Aegean Sea. The Minoan civilization on the island of Crete evolved in the later third millennium B.C.E. and had a major cultural influence on the Mycenaean Greeks. Palaces decorated with fresco paintings, a centrally controlled economy, and the use of writing for record keeping are conspicuous features of these societies. © Cengage Learning

Linear B A set of syllabic symbols, derived from the writing system of Minoan Crete, used in the Mycenaean palaces of the Late Bronze Age to write an early form of Greek. It was used primarily for palace records, and the surviving Linear B tablets provide substantial information about the economic organization of Mycenaean society and tantalizing clues about political, social, and religious institutions.

architecture, pottery, and fresco and vase painting. The sudden accumulation of power and wealth may have resulted from the profits from trade and piracy and perhaps also from pay and booty brought back by mercenaries (soldiers who served for pay in foreign lands).

This first advanced civilization in Greece is called "Mycenaean" because Mycenae was the first site excavated. Other excavated centers reveal similar features: a hilltop location and high, thick fortification walls made of stones so large that later Greeks believed the giant, one-eyed Cyclopes (SIGH-kloe-pees) of legend had lifted them into place. The fortified citadel provided refuge for the entire community in time of danger and contained the palace and administrative complex. A large central hall with an open hearth and columned porch was surrounded by courtyards, living quarters for the royal family and their retainers, offices, storerooms, and workshops. Palace walls were covered with brightly painted frescoes depicting scenes of war, the hunt, and daily life, as well as decorative motifs from nature.

Nearby lay the tombs of the rulers and leading families: shaft graves at first; later, grand beehive-shaped structures made of stone and covered with a mound of earth. Large houses belonging to the aristocracy lay just outside the walls. The peasants lived on the lower slopes and in the plain below, close to the land they worked.

Additional information is provided by over four thousand baked clay tablets written in a script called **Linear B**, which uses pictorial signs to represent syllables and is an early form of Greek. Palace administrators kept track of people, animals, and objects in exhaustive detail, listing the number of chariot wheels in storerooms, the rations paid to workers, and the gifts dedicated to various gods. The government exercised a high degree of control over the economy, organizing grain production and the wool industry from raw material to finished product. The tablets reveal little, however, about the political and legal system, social structure, gender relations, and religious beliefs. They tell nothing about historical figures (not even the name of a single Mycenaean king), particular historical events, or relations with other Mycenaean centers or foreign peoples.

Long-distance contact and trade were made possible by the seafaring skill of Minoans and Mycenaeans. Commercial vessels depended primarily on wind and sail. In general, ancient sailors preferred to sail in daylight hours and keep the land in sight. Their light, wooden vessels with low keels could run up onto the beach, allowing the crew to go ashore to eat and sleep at night.

Cretan and Greek pottery and crafted goods are found not only in the Aegean but also in other parts of the Mediterranean and Middle East. The oldest artifacts are Minoan; then Minoan and Mycenaean objects are found side by side; and eventually Greek wares replace Cretan goods altogether. Such evidence indicates that Cretan merchants pioneered trade routes and established trading posts and were later joined by Mycenaean traders, who supplanted them in the fifteenth century B.C.E.

The numerous Aegean pots found throughout the Mediterranean and Middle East once contained such products as wine and olive oil. Other possible exports include textiles, weapons, and other crafted goods, as well as slaves and mercenary soldiers. Aegean sailors also may have transported the trade goods of other peoples.

As for imports, amber (a translucent, yellowish-brown fossilized tree resin used for jewelry) from northern Europe and ivory carved in Syria have been discovered at Aegean sites, and the large population of southern Greece may have relied on imports of grain. Above all, the Aegean lands needed metals, both gold and the copper and tin needed to make bronze. Several sunken ships carrying copper ingots have been found on the floor of the Mediterranean. Only the elite classes owned metal goods, which may have been symbols of their superior status.

Mycenaeans were tough, warlike, and acquisitive, trading with those who were strong and taking from those who were weak. In the fourteenth and thirteenth centuries B.C.E. these qualities led them into conflict with the Hittite kings of Anatolia. Documents in the archives at the Hittite capital refer to the king and land of Ahhijawa (uh-key-YAW-wuh), most likely a Hittite rendering of *Achaeans* (uh-KEY-uhns), a term used by Homer for the Greeks. They indicate that relations were sometimes friendly, sometimes strained, and that the people of Ahhijawa took advantage of Hittite preoccupation or weakness. The *Iliad*, Homer's tale of the Achaeans' ten-year siege and eventual destruction of Troy, a city on the fringes of Hittite territory controlling the sea route between the Mediterranean and Black Seas, should be seen against this backdrop of Mycenaean belligerence and opportunism. Archaeology has confirmed a destruction at Troy around 1200 B.C.E.

The Fall of Late Bronze Age Civilizations

Hittite difficulties with Ahhijawa and the attack on Troy foreshadowed the troubles that culminated in the destruction of many of the old centers of the Middle East and Mediterranean around 1200 B.C.E. In this period, for reasons not well understood, large numbers of people were on the move. As migrants swarmed into one region, they displaced other peoples, who then joined the tide of refugees.

Around 1200 B.C.E. unidentified invaders destroyed the Hittite capital, Hattusha, and the Hittite kingdom in Anatolia came crashing down. The tide of destruction moved south into Syria, and the great coastal city of Ugarit was swept away. Egypt managed to beat back two attacks: an assault on the Nile Delta around 1220 B.C.E. by "Libyans and Northerners coming from all lands," and a major invasion by the "Sea Peoples" about thirty years later. Although the Egyptian ruler claimed a great victory, the Philistines (FIH-luh-steen) occupied the coast of Palestine (this is the origin of the name subsequently used for this region). Egypt soon surrendered all its territory in Syria-Palestine and lost contact with the rest of western Asia. The Egyptians also lost their foothold in Nubia, opening the way for the emergence of the native kingdom centered on Napata (see Chapter 4).

Among the invaders listed in the Egyptian inscriptions are the Ekwesh (ECK-wesh), who could be Achaeans—that is, Greeks. In these troubled times it is easy to imagine the participation of opportunistic Mycenaeans. The Mycenaean centers also saw trouble coming; at some sites they began to build more extensive fortifications and took steps to guarantee the water supply of the citadels. But their efforts were in vain, and nearly all the palaces were destroyed in the first half of the twelfth century B.C.E.

Fresco from the Aegean Island of Thera, ca. 1650 B.C.E. This picture shows the arrival of a fleet in a harbor as people watch from the walls of the town. The Minoan civilization of Crete was famous in legend for its naval power. The fresco reveals the appearance and design of ships in the Bronze Age Aegean. In the seventeenth century B.C.E., the island of Thera was devastated by a massive volcanic explosion, thought by many to be the origin of the myth of Atlantis sinking beneath the sea. Dea/G Nimatallah/De Agostini Editore/Age Fotostock

How these events came about is unclear. The archaeological record contains no trace of foreign invaders. An attractive explanation combines external and internal factors, since it is likely to be more than coincidence that the demise of Mycenaean civilization occurred at roughly the same time as the fall of other great civilizations in the region. Since the Mycenaean ruling class depended on the import of vital commodities and the profits from trade, the destruction of major trading partners and disruption of trade routes would have weakened their position. Competition for limited resources may have led to internal unrest and, ultimately, political collapse.

The end of Mycenaean civilization illustrates the interdependence of the major centers of the Late Bronze Age. It also highlights the consequences of political and economic collapse. The destruction of the palaces ended the domination of the ruling class. The massive administrative apparatus revealed in the Linear B tablets disappeared. The technique of writing was forgotten, since it had been known only to a few palace officials and was no longer useful. Archaeological studies indicate the depopulation of some regions of Greece and an inflow of people to other regions that had escaped destruction. The Greek language persisted, and a thousand years later people were still worshiping gods mentioned in the Linear B tablets. People also continued to make the vessels and implements that they were familiar with, although with a marked decline in artistic and technical skill in a much poorer society. The cultural uniformity of the Mycenaean Age gave way to regional variations in shapes, styles, and techniques, reflecting increased isolation of different parts of Greece.

SECTION REVIEW

- The Minoan civilization on the island of Crete and the Mycenaean civilization of Greece were strongly influenced by the older centers in Egypt, Syria, and Mesopotamia, yet they followed unique paths of cultural evolution.

- By 2000 B.C.E. Crete was home to the first European civilization with complex political and social structures and advanced technologies.

- The sudden rise to wealth and power of Mycenae and other centers in mainland Greece ca. 1600 was due to the influence of Minoan Crete and the Mycenaeans' insertion into trade networks.

- The Linear B tablets reveal how the Mycenaean palaces exerted centralized control over the economy, and Hittite documents show the Mycenaeans to be aggressive and acquisitive.

- The economic interdependence of Late Bronze Age states increased their vulnerability to attacks by migrating peoples ca. 1200 B.C.E. The region descended into a centuries-long "Dark Age."

Thus perished the cosmopolitan world of the Late Bronze Age in the Mediterranean and Middle East. Societies that had long prospered through complex links of trade, diplomacy, and shared technologies now collapsed in the face of external violence and internal weakness, and the peoples of the region entered a centuries-long "Dark Age" of poverty, isolation, and loss of knowledge.

THE ASSYRIAN EMPIRE, 911–612 B.C.E.

Neo-Assyrian Empire An empire extending from western Iran to Syria-Palestine, conquered by the Assyrians of northern Mesopotamia between the tenth and seventh centuries B.C.E. They used force and terror and exploited the wealth and labor of their subjects. They also preserved and continued the cultural and scientific developments of Mesopotamian civilization.

A number of new centers emerged in western Asia and the eastern Mediterranean in the centuries after 1000 B.C.E. The most powerful and successful was the **Neo-Assyrian Empire** (911–612 B.C.E.). Compared to the flat expanse of Babylonia to the south, the Assyrian homeland in northern Mesopotamia is hillier and has a more temperate climate and greater rainfall.

Peasant farmers, accustomed to defending themselves against raiders from the mountains to the east and north and the arid plain to the west, provided the foot-soldiers for the revival of Assyrian power. The rulers of the Neo-Assyrian Empire led a ceaseless series of campaigns: westward across the plain and desert as far as the Mediterranean, north into mountainous Urartu **(ur-RAHR-too)** (modern Armenia), east across the Zagros range onto the Iranian Plateau, and south along the Tigris River to Babylonia. These campaigns provided immediate booty and the long-term prospect of tribute and taxes. They also secured access to vital resources such as iron and silver and gave the Assyrians control of international commerce. Driven by pride, greed, and religious conviction, the Assyrians defeated the other great kingdoms of the day. At its peak their empire stretched from Anatolia, Syria-Palestine, and Egypt in the west, across Armenia and Mesopotamia, and as far as western Iran. The Assyrians created a new kind of empire, larger in extent than anything seen before (see Map 3.3) and dedicated to the enrichment of the imperial center at the expense of the subjugated periphery.

God and King

The king was literally and symbolically the center of the Assyrian universe. All the land belonged to him, and all the people, even the highest-ranking officials, were his servants. Assyrians believed that the gods chose the king as their earthly representative. Normally the king selected one of his sons to succeed him, then had the choice confirmed by divine oracles and the Assyrian elite. In the revered ancient city of Ashur the high priest anointed the new king's head with oil and gave him the insignia of kingship: a crown and scepter. The kings also were buried in Ashur.

Messengers and spies brought the king information from every corner of the empire. The king appointed officials, heard complaints, dictated correspondence to an army of scribes, and received foreign envoys. He was the military leader, responsible for planning campaigns, and was often away from the capital commanding operations in the field.

The king also devoted much of his time to supervising the state religion, attending elaborate public and private rituals, and overseeing the upkeep of the temples. He made no decisions of state without consulting the gods through rituals of divination, and all actions were carried out in the name of Ashur, the chief god. Military victories were cited as proof of Ashur's superiority over the gods of the conquered peoples.

Relentless government propaganda secured popular support for military campaigns that mostly benefited the king and the nobility. Royal inscriptions posted throughout the empire catalogued recent victories, extolled the unshakeable determination of the king, and promised ruthless punishments to anyone who resisted. Relief sculptures depicting hunts, battles, sieges, executions, and deportations covered the walls of the royal palaces. Looming over most scenes was the king, larger than anyone else, muscular and fierce. Few visitors to the Assyrian court could fail to be awed and intimidated.

Conquest and Control

Superior military organization and technology lay behind Assyria's unprecedented conquests. Early armies consisted of men who served in return for grants of land and peasants and slaves contributed by large landowners. Later, King Tiglathpileser **(TIG-lath-pih-LEE-zuhr)**

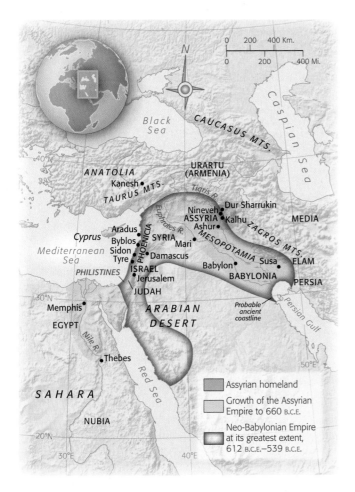

MAP 3.3 **The Assyrian Empire** From the tenth to the seventh century B.C.E. the Assyrians of northern Mesopotamia created the largest empire the world had yet seen, extending from the Iranian Plateau to the eastern shore of the Mediterranean and containing a diverse array of peoples. © Cengage Learning

(r. 744–727 B.C.E.) created a core army of professional soldiers made up of Assyrians and the most formidable subject peoples. At its peak the Assyrian state could mobilize a half-million troops, including light-armed bowmen and slingers who launched stone projectiles, armored spearmen, cavalry equipped with bows or spears, and four-man chariots.

Iron weapons gave Assyrian soldiers an advantage over many opponents, and cavalry provided speed and mobility. Assyrian engineers developed machinery and tactics for besieging fortified towns. They dug tunnels under the walls, built mobile towers for archers, and applied battering rams to weak points. Couriers and signal fires provided long-distance communication, while a network of spies gathered intelligence.

The Assyrians used terror tactics to discourage resistance and rebellion, inflicting harsh punishments and publicizing their brutality: civilians were thrown into fires, prisoners were skinned alive, and the severed heads of defeated rulers hung on city walls. **Mass deportation**—the forced uprooting of entire communities and resettlement elsewhere—broke the spirit of rebellious peoples. Although this tactic had a long history in the ancient Middle East, the Neo-Assyrian monarchs used it on an unprecedented scale, and up to 4 million people may have been relocated. Deportation also shifted human resources from the periphery to the center, where the deportees worked on royal and noble estates, opened new lands for agriculture, and built palaces and cities.

mass deportation The forcible removal and relocation of large numbers of people or entire populations. The mass deportations practiced by the Assyrian and Persian Empires were meant as a terrifying warning of the consequences of rebellion. They also brought skilled and unskilled labor to the imperial center.

The Assyrians never discovered an effective method of governing an empire of such vast distances, varied landscapes, and diverse peoples. Control tended to be tight at the center and in lands closest to the core area, and less so farther away. The Assyrian kings waged many campaigns to reinstate control over territories subdued in previous wars. Provincial officials oversaw the collection of tribute and taxes, maintained law and order, raised troops, undertook public works, and provisioned armies and administrators passing through their territory. Provincial governors were subject to frequent inspections by royal overseers.

The Assyrians ruthlessly exploited the wealth and resources of their subjects. Military campaigns and administration were funded by plunder and tribute. Wealth from the periphery was funneled to the center, where the king and nobility grew rich. Triumphant kings expanded the ancestral capital and religious center at Ashur and built magnificent new royal cities encircled by high walls and containing ornate palaces and temples. Dur Sharrukin **(DOOR SHAH-rookeen)**, the "Fortress of Sargon," was completed in a mere ten years by a massive labor force composed of prisoners of war and Assyrian citizens who owed periodic service to the state.

Nevertheless, the Assyrian Empire was not simply parasitic. There is some evidence of royal investment in provincial infrastructure. The cities and merchant classes thrived on expanded long-distance commerce, and some subject populations were surprisingly loyal to their Assyrian rulers.

Assyrian Society and Culture

The Assyrian elite class was bound to the monarch by oaths of obedience, fear of punishment, and the expectation of rewards, such as land grants or shares of booty and taxes. Skilled professionals—priests, diviners, scribes, doctors, and artisans—were similarly bound.

Wall Relief from the Palace of Sennacherib at Nineveh Against a backdrop of wooded hills representing the landscape of Assyria, workers are hauling a huge stone sculpture from the riverbank to the palace under the watchful eyes of officials and soldiers. They accomplish this task with simple equipment—a lever, a sledge, and thick ropes—and a lot of human muscle power.

SECTION REVIEW

- Tough farmers in northern Mesopotamia provided the foot-soldiers for the rise of the Neo-Assyrian Empire, which dominated western Asia from the late tenth to seventh centuries B.C.E.

- Ceaseless campaigns of conquest brought booty, tribute and taxes, and control of international commerce and valuable resources.

- The all-powerful Assyrian king, claiming the support of the god Ashur, was at the center of government and the state religion.

- The Assyrians employed military might, propaganda, and state terrorism to intimidate their subjects, but they never developed an effective system of political control and frequently had to reconquer territory.

- The Assyrians ruthlessly funneled the wealth and resources of their subjects to the center, where the king and nobility grew rich. Frequent mass deportations provided manpower to build royal cities and work the lands of the elite.

- Assyrian scholars preserved and added to the long intellectual and scientific legacy of Mesopotamian civilization.

Surviving sources primarily shed light on the deeds of kings and elites, and only a little is known about the lives and activities of the millions of Assyrian subjects. The government did not distinguish between native Assyrians and the increasingly large number of immigrants and deportees in the Assyrian homeland. All were referred to as "human beings," entitled to the same legal protections and liable for the same labor and military service. Over time the inflow of outsiders changed the ethnic makeup of the core area.

The vast majority of subjects worked on the land. The agricultural surpluses they produced allowed substantial numbers of people—the standing army, government officials, religious experts, merchants, artisans, and other professionals in the towns and cities—to engage in specialized activities.

Individual artisans and small workshops in the towns manufactured pottery, tools, and clothing, and most trade took place at the local level. The state fostered long-distance trade, since imported luxury goods—metals, fine textiles, dyes, gems, and ivory—brought in substantial customs revenues and found their way to the royal family and elite classes. Silver was the basic medium of exchange, weighed out for each transaction in a time before the invention of coins.

Assyrian scholars preserved and built on the achievements of their Mesopotamian predecessors. When arch-

Library of Ashurbanipal
A large collection of writings drawn from the ancient literary, religious, and scientific traditions of Mesopotamia. It was assembled by the seventh-century B.C.E. Assyrian ruler Ashurbanipal. The many tablets unearthed by archaeologists constitute one of the most important sources of present-day knowledge of the long literary tradition of Mesopotamia.

aeologists excavated the palace of Ashurbanipal (ah-shur-BAH-nee-pahl) (r. 668–627 B.C.E.), one of the last Assyrian kings, at Nineveh (NIN-uh-vuh), they discovered more than twenty-five thousand tablets or fragments. The **Library of Ashurbanipal** contained official documents as well as literary and scientific texts. Some were originals that had been brought to the capital; others were copies made at the king's request. The "House of Knowledge" referred to in some documents may have been an academy that attracted learned men to the imperial center. Much of what we know about Mesopotamian art, literature, science, and earlier history comes from discoveries at Assyrian sites.

ISRAEL, 2000–500 B.C.E.

The small land of Israel probably appeared insignificant to the Assyrian masters of western Asia, but it would play an important role in world history. Two interconnected dramas played out here between around 2000 and 500 B.C.E. First, a loose collection of nomadic groups engaged in herding and caravan traffic became a sedentary, agricultural people, developed complex political and social institutions, and became integrated into the commercial and diplomatic networks of the Middle East. Second, these people transformed the austere cult of a desert god into the concept of a single, all-powerful, and all-knowing deity, in the process creating ethical and intellectual traditions that underlie the beliefs and values of Judaism, Christianity, and Islam.

The land and people at the heart of this story have gone by various names: Canaan, Israel, Palestine; Hebrews, Israelites, Jews. For the sake of consistency, the people are referred to here as *Israelites*, the land they occupied in antiquity as **Israel**.

Israel In antiquity, the land between the eastern shore of the Mediterranean and the Jordan River, occupied by the Israelites from the early second millennium B.C.E. The modern state of Israel was founded in 1948.

Israel is a crossroads, linking Anatolia, Egypt, Arabia, and Mesopotamia (see Map 3.4). Its natural resources are few. The Negev Desert and the vast wasteland of the Sinai (SIE-nie) lie to the south. The Mediterranean coastal plain was usually in the hands of others, particularly the Philistines, throughout much of this period. Galilee to the north, with its sea of the same name, was a relatively fertile land of grassy hills and small plains. The narrow ribbon of the Jordan River runs down the eastern side of the region into the Dead Sea, so named because its high salt content is toxic to life.

Origins, Exodus, and Settlement

Information about ancient Israel comes partly from archaeological excavations and documents such as the royal annals of Egypt and Assyria. Fundamental, but also problematic, are the texts preserved in the **Hebrew Bible** (called the Old Testament by Christians), a compilation of several collections of materials that originated with different groups and advocated particular interpretations of past events. Traditions about the Israelites' early history were long transmitted orally. Not until the tenth century B.C.E. were they written down in a script borrowed from the Phoenicians. The text that we have today dates from the fifth century B.C.E., with a few later additions, and reflects the point of view of the priests who controlled the Temple in Jerusalem. The Hebrew language of the Bible reflects the speech of the Israelites until about 500 B.C.E., when it was supplanted by Aramaic. Although historians disagree about how accurately this document represents Israelite history, it provides a foundation to be used critically and tested against archaeological discoveries.

Hebrew Bible A collection of sacred books containing diverse materials concerning the origins, experiences, beliefs, and practices of the Israelites. Most of the extant text was compiled by members of the priestly class in the fifth century B.C.E. and reflects the concerns and views of this group.

The history of ancient Israel follows a familiar pattern in the ancient Middle East: nomadic pastoralists, occupying marginal land between the inhospitable desert and settled agricultural areas, sometimes engaged in trade and sometimes raided the farms and villages of settled peoples, but eventually they settled down to an agricultural way of life and later developed a unified state.

The Hebrew Bible tells the story of Abraham and his descendants. Born in the city of Ur in southern Mesopotamia, Abraham rejected the idol worship of his homeland and migrated with his family and livestock across the Syrian Desert. Eventually he arrived in the land of Israel, which had been promised to him and his descendants by the Israelite god, Yahweh.

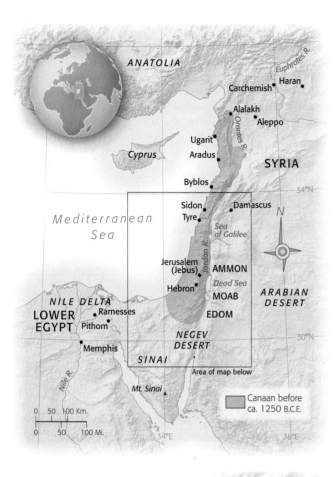

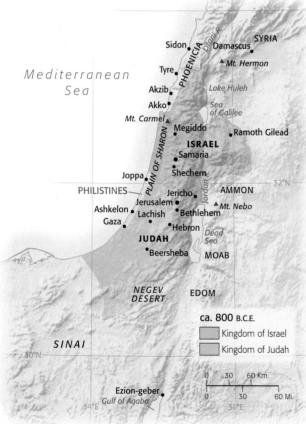

MAP 3.4 **Phoenicia and Israel** The lands along the eastern shore of the Mediterranean Sea—sometimes called the Levant or Syria-Palestine—have always been a crossroads, traversed by migrants, nomads, merchants, and armies moving between Egypt, Arabia, Mesopotamia, and Anatolia.

© Cengage Learning

These "recollections" of the journey of Abraham (who, if he was a real person, probably lived around 1800 B.C.E.) may compress the experiences of generations of pastoralists who migrated from the grazing lands between the upper reaches of the Tigris and Euphrates Rivers to the Mediterranean coastal plain. They camped by a permanent water source in the dry season, then drove herds of sheep, cattle, and donkeys to a well-established sequence of grazing areas during the rest of the year. The animals provided them with milk, cheese, meat, and cloth.

The nomadic Israelites and the settled peoples were suspicious of one another. This friction between herders and farmers permeates the biblical story of the innocent shepherd Abel, who was killed by his farmer brother Cain, and the story of Sodom (SOE-duhm) and Gomorrah (guh-MORE-uh), two cities that Yahweh destroyed because of their wickedness.

In the Hebrew Bible, Abraham's son Isaac and then his grandson Jacob became the leaders of this migratory group of herders. In the next generation the squabbling sons of Jacob's several wives sold their brother Joseph as a slave to passing merchants heading for Egypt. Through luck and ability Joseph became a high official at the pharaoh's court. Thus he was in a position to help his people when drought struck and forced the Israelites to migrate to Egypt. The sophisticated Egyptians looked down on these rough herders and eventually enslaved them and put them to work on royal building projects.

Several points need to be made about this biblical account. First, the Israelite migration to Egypt and later enslavement may have been connected to the rise and fall of the Hyksos. Second, although surviving Egyptian sources do not refer to Israelite slaves, they do complain about Apiru (uh-PEE-roo), a derogatory term applied to caravan drivers, outcasts, bandits, and other marginal groups. Some scholars believe there may be a connection between the similar-sounding terms *Apiru* and *Hebrew*. Third, the period of alleged Israelite slavery coincided with the ambitious building programs launched by several New Kingdom pharaohs. However, there is little archaeological evidence of an Israelite presence in Egypt.

According to the Hebrew Bible, the Israelites were led out of captivity by Moses, an Israelite with connections to the Egyptian royal family. The narrative of their departure, the Exodus, is overlaid with folktale motifs, including the ten plagues that Yahweh inflicted on Egypt to persuade the pharaoh to release the Israelites, and the miraculous parting of the waters of the Red Sea that enabled the refugees to escape. Oral tradition may have embellished memories of a real emigration from Egypt followed by years of wandering in the wilderness of Sinai.

During their forty years in the desert, as reported in the Hebrew Bible, the Israelites entered into a "covenant" or pact with their god, Yahweh: they would be his "Chosen People" if they promised to worship him exclusively. This covenant was confirmed by tablets that Moses brought down from the top of Mount Sinai, inscribed with the Ten Commandments that set out the basic tenets of Jewish belief and practice. The Commandments prohibited murder, adultery, theft, lying, and envy and demanded respect for parents and rest from work on the Sabbath, the seventh day of the week.

The biblical account proceeds to tell how Joshua, Moses's successor, led the Israelites from the east side of the Jordan River into the land of Canaan (KAY-nuhn) (modern Israel and the Palestinian territories), where they attacked and destroyed Canaanite (KAY-nuh-nite) cities. Archaeological evidence confirms the destruction of some Canaanite towns between 1250 and 1200 B.C.E., though not precisely the towns mentioned in the biblical account. Shortly thereafter, lowland sites were resettled and new sites were established in the hills. The material culture of the new settlers was cruder but continued Canaanite patterns. Most scholars doubt that Canaan was conquered by a unified Israelite army. In a time of widespread disruption, movements of peoples, and decline and destruction of cities throughout this region, it is more likely that Israelite migrants took advantage of the disorder and were joined by other groups and even refugees from the Canaanite cities.

The new coalition of peoples invented a common ancestry. The "Children of Israel," as they called themselves, were divided into twelve tribes supposedly descended from the sons of Jacob and Joseph. Each tribe was installed in a different part of the country and led by one or more chiefs. Such leaders usually had limited power and were primarily responsible for mediating disputes and seeing to the welfare and protection of the group. Certain charismatic figures, famed for their daring in war or genius in arbitration, were called "Judges" and enjoyed a special standing that transcended tribal boundaries. The tribes also shared access to a shrine in the hill country at Shiloh (SHIE-loe), which housed the Ark of the Covenant, a sacred chest containing the tablets that Yahweh had given Moses.

Rise of the Monarchy

The troubles afflicting the eastern Mediterranean around 1200 B.C.E. also brought the Philistines to the coastal plain of Israel, where they came into frequent conflict with the Israelites. Their wars were memorialized in Bible stories about the long-haired strongman Samson, who toppled a Philistine temple, and the shepherd boy David, whose slingshot felled the towering warrior Goliath. A religious leader named Samuel recognized the need for a strong central authority and anointed Saul as the first king of Israel around 1020 B.C.E. When Saul perished in battle, the throne passed to David (r. ca. 1000–960 B.C.E.). Many scholars regard the biblical account for the period of the monarchy as more historically reliable than the earlier parts, although some maintain that the archaeological record still does not match up very well with that narrative and that the wealth and power of the early kings have been greatly exaggerated.

A gifted musician, warrior, and politician, David oversaw Israel's transition from tribal confederacy to unified monarchy. He strengthened royal authority by making the captured hill city of Jerusalem his capital. Soon after, David brought the Ark to Jerusalem, making the city the religious as well as political center of the kingdom. A census was taken to facilitate the collection of taxes, and a standing army, with soldiers paid by and loyal to the king, was established. These innovations enabled David to win military victories and expand Israel's borders.

The reign of David's son Solomon (r. ca. 960–920 B.C.E.) marked the high point of the Israelite monarchy. Alliances and trade linked Israel with near and distant lands. Solomon and Hiram, the king of Phoenician Tyre, dispatched a fleet into the Red Sea to bring back gold, ivory, jewels, sandalwood, and exotic animals. The story of the visit to Solomon by the queen of Sheba may be mythical, but it reflects the reality of trade with Saba (SUH-buh) in south Arabia (present-day Yemen) or the Horn of Africa (present-day Somalia). The wealth gained from military and commercial ventures supported a lavish court life, a sizable bureaucracy, and an intimidating chariot army that made Israel a regional power. Solomon undertook an ambitious building program employing slaves and the compulsory labor of citizens. To strengthen the link between religious and secular authority, he built the **First Temple** in Jerusalem. The Israelites now had a central shrine and an impressive set of rituals that could compete with other religions in the area.

First Temple A monumental sanctuary built in Jerusalem by King Solomon in the tenth century B.C.E. to be the religious center for the Israelite god Yahweh. The Temple priesthood conducted sacrifices, received a tithe or percentage of agricultural revenues, and became economically and politically powerful.

The Western Wall in Jerusalem The sole remaining remnant of King Herod's magnificent Second Temple, the religious center of ancient Judaism. It replaced Solomon's Temple, destroyed in the Babylonian conquest of 586 B.C.E., but was destroyed by the Romans in 70 C.E. in the course of suppressing a revolt in Judaea. The site is also sacred to Islam, with the golden Dome of the Rock in the background.

Protasov AN/Shutterstock.com

The Temple priests became a powerful and wealthy class, receiving a share of the annual harvest in return for making animal sacrifices to Yahweh on behalf of the community. The expansion of Jerusalem, new commercial opportunities, and the increasing prestige of the Temple hierarchy changed the social composition of Israelite society. A gap between urban and rural, rich and poor, polarized a people that previously had been relatively homogeneous. Fiery prophets, claiming revelation from Yahweh, accused the monarchs and aristocracy of corruption, impiety, and neglect of the poor (see Diversity and Dominance: Protests Against the Ruling Class in Israel and Babylonia).

The Israelites lived in extended families, several generations residing together under the authority of the eldest male. Male heirs were of paramount importance, and first-born sons received a double share of the inheritance. If a couple had no son, they could adopt one, or the husband could have a child by the wife's slave attendant. If a man died childless, his brother was expected to marry his widow and sire an heir.

In early Israel, because women provided vital goods and services that sustained the family, they were respected and had some influence with their husbands. Unlike men, however, they could not inherit property or initiate divorce, and a woman caught in extramarital relations could be put to death. Peasant women labored with other family members in agriculture or herding in addition to caring for the house and children. As the society became urbanized, some women worked outside the home as cooks, perfumers, wet nurses, prostitutes, and singers of laments at funerals. A few women reached positions of power, such as Deborah the Judge, who led troops in battle against the Canaanites. "Wise women" composed sacred texts in poetry and prose. This reality has been obscured, in part by the male bias of the Hebrew Bible, in part because the status of women declined as Israelite society became more urbanized.

Fragmentation and Dispersal

monotheism Belief in the existence of a single divine entity. Some scholars cite the devotion of the Egyptian pharaoh Akhenaten to Aten (sundisk) and his suppression of traditional gods as the earliest instance. The Israelite worship of Yahweh developed into an exclusive belief in one god, and this concept passed into Christianity and Islam.

After Solomon's death around 920 B.C.E., resentment over royal demands for money and labor and the neglect of tribal prerogatives split the monarchy into two kingdoms: Israel in the north, with its capital at Samaria (suh-MAH-ree-yuh); and Judah (JOO-duh) in the southern territory around Jerusalem (see Map 3.4). The two were sometimes at war, sometimes allied.

This period saw the final formulation of **monotheism**, the belief in Yahweh as the one and only god. Nevertheless, many Israelites were attracted to the ecstatic rituals of the Canaanite storm-god Baal (BAHL) and the fertility goddess Asherah (uh-SHARE-uh). Prophets condemned the adoption of foreign ritual and threatened that Yahweh would punish Israel severely.

The two Israelite kingdoms and other small states in the region laid aside their rivalries to mount a joint resistance to the Neo-Assyrian Empire, but to no avail. In 721 B.C.E. the Assyrians destroyed the northern kingdom of Israel and deported much of its population to the east. New settlers were brought in from Syria, Babylon, and Iran, changing the area's ethnic, cultural, and religious character. The kingdom of Judah survived more than a century longer, sometimes rebelling, sometimes paying tribute to the Assyrians or the Neo-Babylonian kingdom (626–539 B.C.E.) that succeeded them. When the Neo-Babylonian monarch Nebuchadnezzar (NAB-oo-kuhd-nez-uhr) captured Jerusalem in 587 B.C.E., he destroyed the Temple and deported to Babylon the royal family, the aristocracy, and many skilled workers such as blacksmiths and scribes.

The deportees prospered so well in their new home "by the waters of Babylon" that half a century later most of their descendants refused the offer of the Persian monarch Cyrus (see Chapter 5) to return to their homeland. This was the origin of the **Diaspora** (die-ASS-peh-rah)—a Greek word meaning "dispersion" or "scattering." This dispersion outside the homeland of many Jews—as we may now call these people, since an independent Israel no longer existed—continues to this day. To maintain their religion and culture, the Diaspora communities developed institutions like the synagogue (Greek for "bringing together"), a communal meeting place that served religious, educational, and social functions.

Several groups of Babylonian Jews did make the long trek back to Judah in the later sixth and fifth centuries B.C.E. They rebuilt the Temple in modest form and edited the Hebrew Bible into roughly its present form.

The loss of political autonomy and the experience of exile had sharpened Jewish identity. With an unyielding monotheism as their core belief, Jews lived by a rigid set of rules. Dietary restrictions forbade the eating of pork and shellfish and mandated that meat and dairy products not be consumed together. Ritual baths were used to achieve spiritual purity. The Jews venerated the Sabbath (Saturday, the seventh day of the week) by refraining from work and from fighting, following the example of Yahweh, who, according to the Bible, rested on the seventh day after creating the world (this is the origin of the concept of the week and the weekend). These strictures and others, including a ban on marrying non-Jews, tended to isolate the Jews from other peoples, but they also fostered a powerful sense of community and the belief that the Jews were protected by a watchful and beneficent deity.

Diaspora Greek word meaning "dispersal," used to describe the communities of a given ethnic group living outside their homeland. Jews, for example, spread from Israel to western Asia and Mediterranean lands in antiquity and today can be found throughout the world.

SECTION REVIEW

- Because of its strategic location, the small, resource-poor land of Israel has played an important role in world history.

- The history of the ancient Israelites can be reconstructed by critically comparing information in the Hebrew Bible with archaeological discoveries.

- The early Israelites were nomadic pastoralists, but eventually they settled down as farmers and herders in Canaan.

- As a result of their rivalry with the coastal Philistines, the once loosely organized Israelite tribes united under a monarchy, with Jerusalem as the capital.

- Urbanization, wealth from trade, and the status of the Temple priesthood created divisions within Israelite society. Fiery prophets railed against the greed and corruption of the elite.

- Following conquests by the Assyrian Empire and Neo-Babylonian kingdom, many Israelites were taken from their homeland. Diaspora communities created new institutions, a distinctive way of life, and a strong Jewish identity.

PHOENICIA AND THE MEDITERRANEAN, 1200–500 B.C.E.

Phoenicians Semitic-speaking Canaanites living on the coast of modern Lebanon and Syria in the first millennium B.C.E. From major cities such as Tyre and Sidon, Phoenician merchants and sailors explored the Mediterranean, engaged in widespread commerce, and founded Carthage and other colonies in the western Mediterranean.

While the Israelite tribes were forging a united kingdom, the people who occupied the Mediterranean coast to the north were developing their own distinctive civilization. Historians follow the Greeks in calling them **Phoenicians** (fi-NEE-shun), though they referred to themselves as "Can'ani"—Canaanites. Despite few written records and archaeological remains disturbed by frequent migrations and invasions, some of their history can be reconstructed.

The Phoenician City-States

When the eastern Mediterranean was disturbed by violent upheavals and mass migrations around 1200 B.C.E., many Canaanite settlements in the Syria-Palestine region were destroyed. Aramaeans (ah-ruh-MAY-uhn)—nomadic pastoralists similar to the early Israelites—migrated into the interior portions of Syria. Farther south, Israelite herders and farmers settled in the

Protests Against the Ruling Class in Israel and Babylonia

Israelite society underwent profound changes in the period of the monarchy, and the new opportunities for some to acquire considerable wealth led to greater disparities between rich and poor. A series of prophets publicly challenged the behavior of the Israelite ruling elite. They denounced the changes in Israelite society as corrupting people and separating them from the religious devotion and moral rectitude of an earlier, better time. The prophets often spoke out on behalf of the uneducated, illiterate, and powerless lower classes, and they thus provide valuable information about the experiences of different social groups. Theirs was not objective reporting, but rather the angry, anguished visions of unconventional individuals.

The following excerpt from the Hebrew Bible is taken from the book of Amos. A herdsman from the southern kingdom of Judah in the era of the divided monarchy, Amos was active in the northern kingdom of Israel in the mid-eighth century B.C.E., when Assyria threatened the Syria-Palestine region.

1:1 The following is a record of what Amos prophesied. He was one of the herdsmen from Tekoa. These prophecies about Israel were revealed to him during the time of King Uzziah of Judah and King Jeroboam son of Joash of Israel. . . .

3:1 Listen, you Israelites, to this message which the Lord is proclaiming against you. This message is for the entire clan I brought up from the land of Egypt:

3:2 "I have chosen you alone from all the clans of the earth. Therefore I will punish you for all your sins." . . .

3:9 "Gather on the hills around Samaria! [capital of the northern kingdom] Observe the many acts of violence taking place within the city, the oppressive deeds occurring in it." . . .

3:11 "Therefore," says the sovereign Lord, "an enemy will encircle the land. Your power, Samaria, will be taken away; your fortresses will be looted."

3:12 This is what the Lord says: "Just as a shepherd salvages from the lion's mouth a couple of leg bones or a piece of an ear, so the Israelites who live in Samaria will be salvaged. They will be left with just a corner of a bed, and a part of a couch." . . .

4:1 Listen to this message, you "cows of Bashan" who live on Mount Samaria! You oppress the poor; you crush the needy. You say to your husbands, "Bring us more to drink so we can party!"

4:2 The sovereign Lord confirms this oath by his own holy character: "Certainly the time is approaching! You will be carried away in baskets, every last one of you in fishermen's pots.

4:3 Each of you will go straight through the gaps in the walls; you will be thrown out toward Harmon." . . .

5:11 "Therefore, because you make the poor pay taxes on their crops and exact a grain tax from them, you will not live in the houses you built with chiseled stone, nor will you drink the wine from the fine vineyards you planted.

5:12 Certainly I am aware of your many rebellious acts and your numerous sins. You torment the innocent, you take bribes, and you deny justice to the needy at the city gate. . . .

5:21 I absolutely despise your festivals. I get no pleasure from your religious assemblies.

5:22 Even if you offer me burnt and grain offerings, I will not be satisfied; I will not look with favor on the fattened calves you offer in peace.

5:23 Take away from me your noisy songs; I don't want to hear the music of your stringed instruments." . . .

6:4 They lie around on beds decorated with ivory, and sprawl out on their couches. They eat lambs from the flock, and calves from the middle of the pen.

6:5 They sing to the tune of stringed instruments; like David they invent musical instruments.

6:6 They drink wine from sacrificial bowls, and pour the very best oils on themselves.

6:7 Therefore they will now be the first to go into exile, and the religious banquets where they sprawl out on couches will end.

7:10 Amaziah the priest of Bethel sent this message to King Jeroboam of Israel: "Amos is conspiring against you in the very heart of the kingdom of Israel! The land cannot endure all his prophecies.

7:11 As a matter of fact, Amos is saying this: 'Jeroboam will die by the sword and Israel will certainly be carried into exile away from its land.'"

7:12 Amaziah then said to Amos, "Leave, you visionary! Run away to the land of Judah! Earn money and prophesy there!

7:13 Don't prophesy at Bethel any longer, for a royal temple and palace are here!"

7:14 Amos replied to Amaziah, "I was not a prophet by profession. No, I was a herdsman who also took care of sycamore fig trees.

7:15 Then the Lord took me from tending flocks and gave me this commission, 'Go! Prophesy to my people Israel!'" . . .

8:8 "Because of this the earth will quake, and all who live in it will mourn. The whole earth will rise like the River Nile, it will surge upward and then grow calm, like the Nile in Egypt.

8:9 In that day," says the sovereign Lord, "I will make the sun set at noon, and make the earth dark in the middle of the day.

8:10 I will turn your festivals into funerals, and all your songs into funeral dirges. I will make everyone wear funeral clothes and cause every head to be shaved bald. I will make you mourn as if you had lost your only son; when it ends it will indeed have been a bitter day." . . .

9:8 "Look, the sovereign Lord is watching the sinful nation, and I will destroy it from the face of the earth. But I will not completely destroy the family of Jacob," says the Lord. . . .

9:11 "In that day I will rebuild the collapsing hut of David. I will seal its gaps, repair its ruins, and restore it to what it was like in days gone by."

A document from Babylon, which may have been composed around 1000 B.C.E., reveals the prevalence of similar inequities and abuses in that society. It is presented as a dialogue between a man in distress (who, despite his claim of low status, is literate and presumably comes from the urban middle class) and his compassionate friend.

Sufferer

I have looked around in the world, but things are turned
  around.
The god does not impede the way of even a demon.
A father tows a boat along the canal,
While his son lies in bed.
The eldest son makes his way like a lion,
The second son is happy to be a mule driver.
The heir goes about along the streets like a peddler,
The younger son (has enough) that he can give food to the
  destitute.
What has it profited me that I have bowed down to my god?
I must bow even to a person who is lower than I,
The rich and opulent treat me, as a younger brother, with
  contempt. . . .

Friend

O wise one, O savant, who masters knowledge,
Your heart has become hardened and you accuse the god
  wrongly.
The mind of the god, like the center of the heavens, is remote;
Knowledge of it is very difficult; people cannot know it . . .
In the case of a cow, the first calf is a runt,
The later offspring is twice as big.
A first child is born a weakling,
But the second is called a mighty warrior.

Sufferer

. . .People extol the words of a strong man who has learned
  to kill
But bring down the powerless who has done no wrong.
They confirm (the position of) the wicked for whom what
  should be an abomination is considered right
Yet drive off the honest man who heeds the will of his god.
They fill the [storehouse] of the oppressor with gold,
But empty the larder of the beggar of its provisions.

They support the powerful, whose . . . [text uncertain] is guilt,
But destroy the weak and trample the powerless.
And, as for me, an insignificant person, a prominent person
  persecutes me.

Friend

Narru, king of the gods, who created mankind,
And majestic Zulummar, who pinched off the clay for them,
And goddess Mami, the queen who fashioned them,
Gave twisted speech to the human race.
With lies, and not truth, they endowed them forever.
Solemnly they speak favorably of a rich man,
"He is a king," they say, "riches should be his,"
But they treat a poor man like a thief,
They have only bad to say of him and plot his murder,
Making him suffer every evil like a criminal, because he has
  no . . . [text uncertain].
Terrifyingly they bring him to his end, and extinguish him
  like glowing coals.

Sufferer

. . .I have gone about the square of my city unobtrusively,
My voice was not raised, my speech was kept low.
I did not raise my head, but looked at the ground,
I did not worship even as a slave in the company of my
  associates.
May the god who has abandoned me give help,
May the goddess who has [forsaken me] show mercy,
The shepherd, the sun of the people, pastures (his flock) as a
  god should.

QUESTIONS FOR ANALYSIS

1. For whom is Amos's message primarily intended? How does the ruling class react to Amos's prophetic activity, and how does he respond to their tactics?

2. What does Amos see as wrong in Israelite society, and who is at fault? Why are even the religious practices of the elite criticized?

3. What will be the means by which God punishes Israel, and why does God punish it this way? What grounds for hope remain?

4. What are the main complaints of the Babylonian Sufferer, and where does he look for a solution? Do the Babylonian gods seem to be less directly involved in human affairs than the Israelite deity?

Source: Excerpts from the Hebrew Bible quoted by permission. NETS Bible copyright © 1996–2006 by Biblical Studies Press, L.L.C. http://www.bible.org. All rights reserved. Excerpts from Babylonian document: PRITCHARD, JAMES; ANCIENT NEAR EASTERN TEXTS RELATING TO THE OLD TESTAMENT. © 1969 by Princeton University Press. Reprinted by permission of Princeton University Press.

Phoenician Ivory Panel, Ninth to Eighth Century B.C.E.
This panel, originally covered with gold leaf and inlaid with red carnelian and blue lapis lazuli, depicts a lioness devouring a boy. Produced in Phoenicia, perhaps as tribute for the Assyrian king, it was probably part of a wooden throne. It was found in a well in the palace area of the Assyrian capital Nimrud, where it was discarded when the city was destroyed in the late seventh century B.C.E.
The Trustees of the British Museum / Art Resource, NY

interior of present-day Israel. The Philistines occupied the southern coast and introduced iron-based metallurgy to this part of the world.

By 1100 B.C.E. Canaanite territory had shrunk to a narrow strip of present-day Lebanon between the mountains and the sea (see Map 3.4). Rivers and rocky spurs of Mount Lebanon sliced the coastal plain into a series of small city-states, chief among them Byblos (BIB-loss), Berytus (buh-RIE-tuhs), Sidon (SIE-duhn), and Tyre. The inhabitants of this densely populated area adopted new political forms and turned to seaborne commerce and new kinds of manufacture for their survival. A thriving trade in raw materials (cedar and pine, metals, incense, papyrus), foodstuffs (wine, spices, salted fish), and crafted luxury goods (carved ivory, glass, and textiles colored with a highly prized purple dye extracted from the murex snail) brought considerable wealth to the Phoenician city-states and gave them an important role in international politics (see Environment and Technology: Ancient Textiles and Dyes).

The Phoenicians developed earlier Canaanite models into an "alphabetic" system of writing with about two dozen symbols, in which each symbol represented a sound. (The Phoenicians represented only consonants, leaving the vowel sounds to be inferred by the reader. The Greeks later added symbols for vowel sounds, creating the first truly alphabetic system of writing—see Chapter 5.) Little Phoenician writing survives, however, probably because scribes used perishable papyrus.

Before 1000 B.C.E. Byblos was the most important Phoenician city-state. It was a distribution center for cedar timber from the slopes of Mount Lebanon and for papyrus from Egypt. King Hiram, who came to power in 969 B.C.E., was responsible for Tyre's rise to prominence. According to the Hebrew Bible, he formed a close alliance with the Israelite king Solomon and provided skilled Phoenician craftsmen and cedar wood for building the Temple in Jerusalem. In return, Tyre gained access to silver, food, and trade routes to the east and south. In the 800s B.C.E. Tyre took control of nearby Sidon and dominated the Mediterranean coastal trade.

Ancient Textiles and Dyes

Throughout human history the production of textiles—cloth for clothing, blankets, carpets, and coverings of various sorts—required an expenditure of human labor second only to the work necessary to provide food. Nevertheless, textile production in antiquity has left few archaeological traces. The plant fibers and animal hair used for cloth quickly decompose except in rare circumstances. Some textile remains have been found in the hot, dry conditions of Egypt, the cool, arid Andes of South America, and the peat bogs of northern Europe. But most of our knowledge of ancient textiles depends on the discovery of equipment used in textile production—such as spindles, loom weights, and dyeing vats—and on pictorial representations and descriptions in texts.

Cloth production usually has been the work of women for a simple but important reason. Responsibility for child rearing limits women's ability to participate in other activities but does not consume all their time and energy. In many societies textile production has been complementary to child-rearing activities, for it can be done in the home, is relatively safe, does not require great concentration, and can be interrupted without consequence. The growing and harvesting of plants such as cotton or flax (from which linen is made) and the shearing of wool from sheep and, in the Andes, llamas are outdoor activities, but the subsequent stages of production can be carried out inside the home. The basic methods of textile production did not change much from early antiquity until the late eighteenth century C.E., when the fabrication of textiles was transferred to mills and mass production began.

When textile production has been considered "women's work," most of the output has been for household consumption. However, women weavers in Peru developed new raw materials, new techniques, and new decorative motifs around three thousand years ago. They began to use the wool of llamas and alpacas in addition to cotton. Three women worked side by side and passed the weft from hand to hand in order to produce a fabric of greater width. Women weavers also introduced embroidery and decorated garments with new religious motifs, such as the jaguar-god. Their high-quality textiles were given as tribute to the elite and were used to trade for luxury goods.

More typically, men dominated commercial production. In ancient Phoenicia, fine textiles with bright, permanent colors became a major export product. Most prized was the red-purple known as Tyrian purple because Tyre was the major source. Persian and Hellenistic kings wore robes dyed this color, and a white toga with a purple border was the sign of a Roman senator.

Felt decoration depicting a fenix/Hermitage, St. Petersburg, Russia/De Agostini Picture Library/A. Dagli Orti/The Bridgeman Art Library

Scythian Felt Cloth from Pazyryk, ca. 500 B.C.E. Found in a subterranean tomb in Siberia, the textile was preserved by the permafrost. It depicts a winged figure with a human upper body and antlers.

The production of Tyrian purple was an exceedingly laborious process. The spiny dye-murex snail lives on the sandy Mediterranean bottom at depths ranging from 30 to 500 feet (10 to 150 meters). Nine thousand snails were needed to produce 1 gram (0.035 ounce) of dye. The dye was made from a colorless liquid in the snail's hypobranchial gland. The gland sacs were removed, crushed, soaked with salt, and exposed to sunlight and air for some days; then they were subject to controlled boiling and heating.

Huge mounds of broken shells on the Phoenician coast are testimony to the ancient industry. The snail may have been rendered nearly extinct at many locations, and some scholars speculate that Phoenician colonization in the Mediterranean was motivated in part by the search for new sources of snails.

Located on an offshore island, Tyre was practically impregnable. It had two harbors connected by a canal, a large marketplace, a magnificent palace complex with treasury and archives, and temples to the gods Melqart **(MEL-kahrt)** and Astarte **(uh-STAHR-tee)**. Some of its thirty thousand inhabitants lived in suburbs on the mainland. Its one weakness was its dependence on the mainland for food and fresh water.

Little is known about the internal affairs of Tyre and other Phoenician cities. The names of a series of kings are preserved, and the scant evidence suggests that the political arena was dominated by leading merchant families. Between the ninth and seventh centuries B.C.E. the Phoenician city-states contended with Assyrian aggression, followed in the sixth century B.C.E. by the expansion of the Neo-Babylonian kingdom and later the Persian Empire (see Chapter 5). The Phoenician city-states preserved their autonomy by playing the great powers off against one another when possible and by accepting a subordinate relationship to a distant master when necessary.

Expansion into the Mediterranean

After 900 B.C.E. Tyre turned its attention westward, establishing colonies on Cyprus, a copper-rich island 100 miles (161 kilometers) from the Syrian coast (see Map 3.4). By 700 B.C.E. a string of settlements in the western Mediterranean formed a "Phoenician triangle" composed of the North African coast from western Libya to Morocco; the south and southeast coast of Spain, including Gades **(GAH-days)** (modern Cadiz **[kuh-DEEZ]**) on the Strait of Gibraltar, controlling passage between the Mediterranean and the Atlantic Ocean; and the islands of Sardinia, Sicily, and Malta off the coast of Italy (see Map 3.5). Many settlements were situated on promontories or offshore islands in imitation of Tyre. The Phoenician trading network spanned the entire Mediterranean.

MAP 3.5 **Colonization of the Mediterranean** In the ninth century B.C.E., the Phoenicians of Lebanon began to explore and colonize parts of the western Mediterranean, including the coast of North Africa, southern and eastern Spain, and the islands of Sicily and Sardinia. The Phoenicians were primarily interested in access to valuable raw materials and trading opportunities. © Cengage Learning

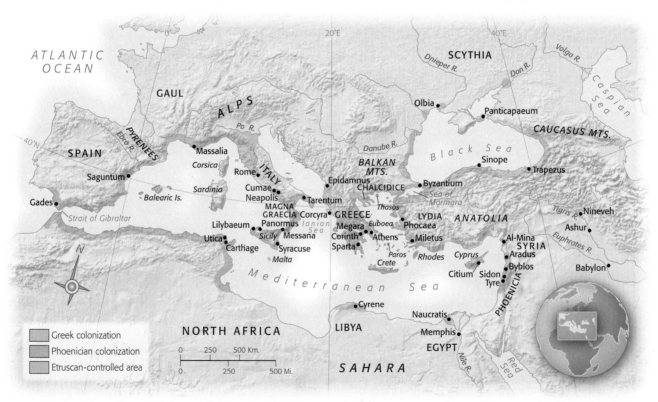

Frequent and destructive Assyrian invasions of Syria-Palestine and the lack of arable land to feed a swelling population probably motivated Tyrian expansion. Overseas settlement provided an outlet for excess population, new sources of trade goods, and new trading partners. Tyre maintained its autonomy until 701 B.C.E. by paying tribute to the Assyrian kings. In that year it finally fell to an Assyrian army that stripped it of much of its territory and population, allowing Sidon to become the leading city in Phoenicia.

Carthage's Commercial Empire

Carthage City located in present-day Tunisia, founded by Phoenicians ca. 800 B.C.E. It became a major commercial center and naval power in the western Mediterranean until defeated by Rome in the third century B.C.E.

Historians know far more about **Carthage** and the other Phoenician colonies in the western Mediterranean than they do about the Phoenician homeland. Much of this comes from Greek and Roman reports of their wars with the western Phoenician communities. For example, the account of the origins of Carthage that begins this chapter comes from Roman sources but probably is based on a Carthaginian original. Archaeological excavation has roughly confirmed the city's traditional foundation date of 814 B.C.E. The new settlement grew rapidly and soon dominated other Phoenician colonies in the west.

Located just outside the present-day city of Tunis in Tunisia, on a promontory jutting into the Mediterranean, Carthage stretched between the original hilltop citadel and a double harbor. The inner harbor could accommodate 220 warships. A watchtower allowed surveillance of the surrounding area, and high walls made it impossible to see in from the outside. The outer commercial harbor was filled with docks for merchant ships and shipyards. In case of attack, the harbor could be closed off by a huge iron chain.

Government offices ringed a large central square where magistrates heard legal cases outdoors. The inner city was a maze of narrow, winding streets, multistory apartment buildings, and sacred enclosures. Farther out was a sprawling suburban district where the wealthy built spacious villas amid fields and vegetable gardens. This entire urban complex was enclosed by a wall 22 miles (35 kilometers) in length. At the most critical point—the 2-½-mile-wide (4-kilometer) isthmus connecting the promontory to the mainland—the wall was over 40 feet (13 meters) high and 30 feet (10 meters) thick and had high watchtowers.

With a population of roughly 400,000, Carthage was one of the largest cities in the world by 500 B.C.E. The population was ethnically diverse, including people of Phoenician stock, indigenous peoples ancestral to modern-day Berbers, and immigrants from other Mediterranean lands as well as sub-Saharan Africa. The Phoenicians readily intermarried with other peoples.

Each year two "judges" were elected from upper-class families to serve as heads of state and carry out administrative and judicial functions. The real seat of power was the Senate, where members of the leading merchant families, who sat for life, directed the affairs of the state. An inner circle of thirty or so senators made the crucial decisions. The leadership occasionally convened an Assembly of the citizens to elect public officials or vote on important issues, particularly when they were divided or wanted to stir up popular enthusiasm for some venture.

There is little evidence at Carthage of the kind of social and political unrest that plagued Greece and Rome. A merchant aristocracy (unlike an aristocracy of birth) was not a closed group, and a climate of economic and social mobility allowed newly successful families and individuals to push their way into the circle of influential citizens. Insofar as everyone benefited from the riches of empire, the masses were usually ready to defer to those who made prosperity possible.

Carthaginian power rested on its navy, which dominated the western Mediterranean for centuries. Phoenician towns provided a network of friendly ports. The Carthaginian fleet consisted of fast, maneuverable galleys (warships propelled by oars). Each bore a sturdy, pointed ram in front that could pierce the hull of an enemy vessel below the water line, while marines (soldiers aboard a ship) fired weapons. Innovations in the placement of benches and oars eventually made room for as many as 170 rowers. The Phoenicians and their Greek rivals set the standard for naval technology in this era.

Carthaginian foreign policy, reflecting the economic interests of the dominant merchant class, focused on protecting the sea lanes, gaining access to raw materials, and fostering trade. Indeed, Carthage claimed the waters of the western Mediterranean as its own. Foreign merchants were free to sail to Carthage to market their goods, but if they tried to operate elsewhere on their own, they risked having their ships sunk by the Carthaginian navy. Treaties between Carthage and other states included formal recognition of this maritime commercial monopoly.

The archaeological record provides few clues about the commodities traded by the Carthaginians. These may have included perishable goods—foodstuffs, textiles, animal skins, slaves—and raw metals whose Carthaginian origin would not be evident. Carthaginian ships carried goods manufactured elsewhere, and products brought to Carthage by foreign traders were re-exported.

There is also evidence for trade with sub-Saharan Africa. Hanno **(HA-noe)**, a Carthaginian captain of the fifth century B.C.E., claimed to have sailed through the Strait of Gibraltar into the Atlantic Ocean and to have explored the West African coast (see Map 3.5). Other Carthaginians explored the Atlantic coast of Spain and France and secured control of an important source of tin in the "Tin Islands," probably Cornwall in southwestern England.

War and Religion

The Carthaginian state did not directly rule a large territory. A belt of fertile land in northeastern Tunisia, owned by Carthaginians but worked by native peasants and imported slaves, provided a secure food supply. Beyond this core area the Carthaginians ruled most of their "empire" indirectly and allowed other Phoenician communities in the western Mediterranean to remain independent. These Phoenician communities looked to Carthage for military protection and followed its lead in foreign policy. Only Sardinia and southern Spain were put under the direct control of a Carthaginian governor and garrison, presumably to safeguard their agricultural, metal, and manpower resources.

Carthage's focus on trade may explain the unusual fact that citizens were not required to serve in the army: they were of more value in other capacities, such as trading activities and the navy. Since the indigenous North African population was not politically or militarily well organized, Carthage had little to fear close to home. When Carthage was drawn into a series of wars with the Greeks and Romans from the fifth through third centuries B.C.E., it relied on mercenaries from the most warlike peoples in its dominions or from neighboring areas. These well-paid mercenaries were under the command of Carthaginian officers; generals were chosen by the Senate and kept in office for as long as they were needed. In contrast to most ancient states, the Carthaginians separated military command from civilian government.

Like the deities of Mesopotamia (see Chapter 2), the gods of the Carthaginians—chief among them Baal Hammon **(BAHL ha-MOHN)**, a male storm-god, and Tanit **(TAH-nit)**, a female fertility figure—were powerful and capricious entities who had to be appeased by anxious worshipers. Roman sources report that members of the Carthaginian elite would sacrifice their own male children in times of crisis. Excavations at Carthage and other western Phoenician towns have turned up *tophets* **(TOE-fet)**—walled enclosures where thousands of small, sealed urns containing the burned bones of children lay buried. Originally practiced by the upper classes, child sacrifice became more common and involved broader elements of the population after 400 B.C.E.

Plutarch **(PLOO-tawrk)**, a Greek who lived around 100 C.E., long after the demise of Carthage, wrote the following on the basis of earlier sources:

> *The Carthaginians are a hard and gloomy people, submissive to their rulers and harsh to their subjects, running to extremes of cowardice in times of fear and of cruelty in times of anger; they keep obstinately to their decisions, are austere, and care little for amusement or the graces of life.*[1]

---

[1]Plutarch, *Moralia*, 799 D, trans. B. H. Warmington, *Carthage* (Harmondsworth, England: Penguin, 1960), 163.

SECTION REVIEW

- Following the upheavals ca. 1200 B.C.E., Canaanite communities on the coast of Lebanon adopted the city-state political form and turned to seaborne commerce and new kinds of manufacture for their survival.

- In the tenth century B.C.E., Tyre, located on a practically impregnable offshore island and led by a king and merchant aristocracy, became the dominant Phoenician state.

- A string of settlements in the western Mediterranean formed a "Phoenician triangle" comprising the coasts of North Africa and Spain and islands off the coast of Italy.

- Carthage, founded in present-day Tunisia a little before 800 B.C.E., led the coalition of Phoenician communities in the western Mediterranean.

- Carthaginian power rested on its navy, which enforced a Carthaginian commercial monopoly in the western Mediterranean. For land warfare, Carthage relied on mercenaries from the most warlike peoples in the region, under the command of Carthaginian officers.

- The religion of the Carthaginians, which included the sacrifice of children in times of crisis, was perceived as different and despicable by their Greek and Roman rivals.

The Tophet of Carthage   Here, from the seventh to second centuries B.C.E., the cremated bodies of sacrificed children were buried. Archaeological excavation has confirmed the claim in ancient sources that the Carthaginians sacrificed children to their gods at times of crisis. Stone markers, decorated with magical signs and symbols of divinities as well as family names, were placed over ceramic urns containing the ashes and charred bones of one or more infants or, occasionally, older children.

We should not take the hostile opinions of Greek and Roman sources at face value. Still, it is clear that the Carthaginians were perceived as different and that cultural barriers, leading to misunderstanding and prejudice, played a significant role in the conflicts among these peoples of the ancient Mediterranean. In Chapter 6 we follow the protracted and bloody struggle between Rome and Carthage for control of the western Mediterranean.

FAILURE AND TRANSFORMATION, 750–550 B.C.E.

The extension of Assyrian power over the entire Middle East had enormous consequences for all the peoples of the region. In 721 B.C.E. the Assyrians destroyed the northern kingdom of Israel and deported a substantial portion of the population, and for over a century the southern kingdom of Judah faced relentless pressure. Assyrian threats and demands for tribute spurred the Phoenicians to explore and colonize the western Mediterranean. Tyre's fall to the Assyrians in 701 B.C.E. accelerated the decline of the Phoenician homeland, but the western colonies, especially Carthage, flourished. Even Egypt, for so long impregnable behind its desert barriers, fell to Assyrian invaders in the mid-seventh century B.C.E. Southern Mesopotamia was reduced to a protectorate, with Babylon alternately razed and rebuilt by Assyrian kings of differing dispositions. Urartu and Elam, Assyria's nearby rivals, were destroyed.

By 650 B.C.E. Assyria stood supreme in western Asia. But the arms race with Urartu, the frequent expensive campaigns, and the protection of lengthy borders had sapped Assyrian resources. Assyrian brutality and exploitation aroused the hatred of conquered peoples. At the same time, changes in the ethnic composition of the army and the population of the homeland had reduced popular support for the Assyrian state.

Two new political entities spearheaded resistance to Assyria. First, Babylonia had been revived by the Neo-Babylonian, or Chaldaean (chal-DEE-uhn), dynasty (the Chaldaeans had infiltrated southern Mesopotamia around 1000 B.C.E.). Second, the Medes (MEED), an Iranian people, were extending their kingdom on the Iranian Plateau in the seventh century B.C.E. The two powers launched a series of attacks on the Assyrian homeland that destroyed the chief cities by 612 B.C.E. The destruction systematically carried out by the victorious attackers led to the depopulation of northern Mesopotamia.

The Medes took over the Assyrian homeland and the northern plain as far as eastern Anatolia, but most of the

SECTION REVIEW

- The extension of Assyrian power over the entire Middle East had enormous consequences for all the peoples of the region.

- The costs of frequent military campaigns, the hatred of conquered peoples aroused by Assyrian brutality, and changes in the ethnic composition of the army and the population of the homeland weakened the Assyrian state.

- The Neo-Babylonians and the Medes of northwest Iran launched a series of attacks on the Assyrian homeland that destroyed the chief cities by 612 B.C.E. and led to the depopulation of northern Mesopotamia.

- The Neo-Babylonian kingdom took over much of the territory of the Assyrian Empire and fostered a cultural renaissance.

Neo-Babylonian kingdom
Under the Chaldaeans (nomadic kinship groups that settled in southern Mesopotamia in the early first millennium B.C.E.), Babylon again became a major political and cultural center in the seventh and sixth centuries B.C.E. After participating in the destruction of Assyrian power, the monarchs Nabopolassar and Nebuchadnezzar took over the southern portion of the Assyrian domains.

territory of the old empire fell to the **Neo-Babylonian kingdom** (626–539 B.C.E.), thanks to the energetic campaigns of kings Nabopolassar **(NAB-oh-poe-lass-uhr)** (r. 625–605 B.C.E.) and Nebuchadnezzar (r. 604–562 B.C.E.). Babylonia underwent a cultural renaissance. The city of Babylon was enlarged and adorned, becoming the greatest metropolis of the world in the sixth century B.C.E. Old cults were revived, temples rebuilt, festivals resurrected. The related pursuits of mathematics, astronomy, and astrology reached new heights.

CONCLUSION

The Late Bronze Age in the Middle East was a "cosmopolitan" era of shared lifestyles and technologies. Patterns of culture that had originated long before in Egypt and Mesopotamia persisted into this era. Peoples such as the Amorites, Kassites, and Chaldaeans, who migrated into the Tigris-Euphrates plain, were largely assimilated into the Sumerian-Semitic cultural tradition, adopting its language, religious beliefs, political and social institutions, and forms of artistic expression. Similarly, the Hyksos, who migrated into the Nile Delta and controlled much of Egypt for a time, adopted the ancient ways of Egypt. When the founders of the New Kingdom finally ended Hyksos domination, they reinstituted the united monarchy and the religious and cultural traditions of earlier eras.

The Late Bronze Age expansion of commerce and communication stimulated the emergence of new civilizations, including those of the Minoans and Mycenaean Greeks in the Aegean Sea. These new civilizations borrowed heavily from the technologies and cultural practices of Mesopotamia and Egypt, creating dynamic syntheses of imported and indigenous elements.

Ultimately, the very interdependence of the societies of the Middle East and eastern Mediterranean made them vulnerable to the destructions and disorder of the decades around 1200 B.C.E. The entire region slipped into a "Dark Age" of isolation, stagnation, and decline that lasted several centuries. The early centuries after 1000 B.C.E. saw a resurgence of political organization and international commerce, as well as the spread of technologies and ideas. The Assyrians created an empire of unprecedented size and diversity through superior organization and military technology, and they maintained it through terror and deportations of subject peoples.

The Israelites began as nomadic pastoralists and then settled permanently in Canaan. Conflict with the Philistines forced them to adopt a more complex political structure, and under the monarchy Israelite society grew more urban and economically stratified. While the long, slow evolution of the Israelites from wandering groups of herders to an agriculturally based monarchy followed a common pattern in ancient western Asia, the religious and ethical concepts that they formulated were unique and have had a powerful impact on world history.

After the upheavals of the Late Bronze Age, the Phoenician city-states along the coast of Lebanon flourished. Under pressure from the Neo-Assyrian Empire, the Phoenicians, with Tyre in the lead, began spreading westward into the Mediterranean. Carthage became the most important city outside the Phoenician homeland. Ruled by leading merchant families, it extended its commercial empire throughout the western Mediterranean, maintaining power through naval superiority.

The far-reaching expansion of the Assyrian Empire was the most important factor in the transformation of the ancient Middle East. The Assyrians destroyed many older states and, directly or indirectly, displaced large numbers of people. Their brutality, as well as the population shifts that resulted from their deportations, undercut support for their state. The Chaldaeans and Medes led resistance to Assyrian rule. After the swift collapse of Assyria, the Chaldaeans expanded the Neo-Babylonian kingdom, enlarged the city of Babylon, and presided over a cultural renaissance.

KEY TERMS

Iron Age p. 53
Hittites p. 56
Hatshepsut p. 57
Akhenaten p. 57
Ramesses II p. 58
Minoan p. 60

Mycenae p. 60
shaft graves p. 60
Linear B p. 61
Neo-Assyrian Empire p. 64
mass deportation p. 65

Library of Ashurbanipal p. 67
Israel p. 67
Hebrew Bible p. 67
First Temple p. 69
monotheism p. 70

Diaspora p. 71
Phoenicians p. 71
Carthage p. 77
Neo-Babylonian kingdom p. 80

SUGGESTED READING

Barber, Elizabeth Wayland. *Women's Work: The First 20,000 Years: Women, Cloth, and Society in Early Times.* 1994. An intriguing account of textile manufacture in antiquity, with emphasis on the primary role of women and its social implications.

Bryce, Trevor. *The Kingdom of the Hittites*, new edition. 2005. The most up-to-date treatment of the history of the Hittites.

Castleden, Rodney. *The Mycenaeans.* 2005. An up-to-date reconstruction of the earliest complex Greek society.

Curtis, J. E., and J. E. Reade, eds. *Art and Empire: Treasures from Assyria in the British Museum.* 1995. The catalogue for a museum exhibition, with chapters relating the art to many facets of Assyrian life.

Hornung, Erik. *Akhenaten and the Religion of Light.* 1999. Focused on religious innovations, but deals more broadly with many facets of the reign of Akhenaten.

Krzyszkowska, O., and L. Nixon. *Minoan Society.* 1983. Examines the archaeological evidence for the Minoan civilization of Crete.

Kuhrt, Amelie. *The Ancient Near East, c. 3000–300 B.C.*, 2 vols. 1995. The best introduction to the historical development of western Asia and Egypt.

Lesko, Barbara, ed. *Women's Earliest Records: From Ancient Egypt and Western Asia.* 1989. A collection of papers on the experiences of women in the ancient Middle East.

Markoe, Glenn. *Phoenicians.* 2000. A general introduction to the Phoenicians in their homeland.

Miles, Richard. *Carthage Must Be Destroyed: The Rise and Fall of an Ancient Civilization.* 2011. A wide-ranging treatment of Carthaginian history and civilization.

Pritchard, James B., ed. *Ancient Near Eastern Texts Relating to the Old Testament*, 3d ed. 1969. A large collection of primary texts in translation from ancient western Asia and Egypt.

Sandars, N. K. *The Sea Peoples: Warriors of the Ancient Mediterranean.* 1978. Explores the disruptions and destructions in the eastern Mediterranean in the Late Bronze Age.

Sasson, Jack M., ed. *Civilizations of the Ancient Near East*, 4 vols. 1995. Fundamental for all periods in the ancient Middle East, with nearly two hundred articles by contemporary experts and a bibliography on a wide range of topics.

Shanks, Hershel, ed. *Ancient Israel: From Abraham to the Roman Destruction of the Temple*, 3d ed. 2010. A general historical introduction to Israel throughout antiquity, with chapters written by leading experts.

Van De Mieroop, Marc. *A History of the Ancient Near East ca. 3000–323 BC*, 2d ed. 2006. Includes extensive coverage of northern and southern Mesopotamia in the second and first millennia B.C.E.

CourseMate Go to the History CourseMate website for primary source links, study tools, and review materials for this chapter. www.cengagebrain.com

Chapter Outline

Early China, 2000–221 B.C.E.
➤ *How did early Chinese rulers use religion to justify and strengthen their power?*

Nubia, 2300 B.C.E.–350 C.E.
➤ *How did the technological and cultural influences of Egypt affect the formation of Nubia?*

Pastoral Nomads of the Eurasian Steppes, 1000–100 B.C.E.
➤ *How was the rise of steppe nomadism dependent on interactions with settled agricultural peoples, and what new challenges did the nomads pose to farming societies?*

Celtic Europe, 1000–50 B.C.E.
➤ *What were the causes behind the spread of Celtic peoples across much of continental Europe, and the later retreat of Celtic cultures to the western edge of the continent?*

Conclusion

- **ENVIRONMENT + TECHNOLOGY**   Divination in Ancient Societies
- **DIVERSITY + DOMINANCE**   Human Nature and Good Government in the *Analects* of Confucius and the Legalist Writings of Han Fei

Erich Lessing / Art Resource, NY

Wall Painting of Nubians Arriving in Egypt with Rings and Bags of Gold, Fourteenth Century B.C.E.
This image decorated the tomb of an Egyptian administrator in Nubia.

New Civilizations Outside the West Asian Core Area, 2300 B.C.E.–350 C.E.

Around 2200 B.C.E. an Egyptian official named Harkhuf (HAHR-koof) set out from Aswan (AS-wahn), on the southern boundary of Egypt, for a place called Yam, far to the south in the land that later came to be called Nubia. He brought gifts from the Egyptian pharaoh for the ruler of Yam, and he returned home with three hundred donkeys loaded with incense, ebony, ivory, and other exotic products from tropical Africa. Despite the diplomatic fiction of exchanging gifts, we should probably regard Harkhuf as a brave and enterprising merchant. He returned with something so special that the eight-year-old boy pharaoh, Pepi II, could not contain his excitement. He wrote:

> Come north to the residence at once! Hurry and bring with you this pygmy whom you brought from the land of the horizon-dwellers live, hale, and healthy, for the dances of the god, to gladden the heart, to delight the heart of king Neferkare [Pepi] who lives forever! When he goes down with you into the ship, get worthy men to be around him on deck, lest he fall into the water! When he lies down at night, get worthy men to lie around him in his tent. Inspect ten times at night! My majesty desires to see this pygmy more than the gifts of the mine-land and of Punt![1]

Scholars identify Yam with Kerma, later the capital of the kingdom of Nubia, on the upper Nile in modern Sudan. For Egyptians, Nubia was a wild and dangerous place. Yet it was developing a more complex political organization, and this illustration demonstrates how vibrant the commerce and cultural interaction between Nubia and Egypt would later become.

In this chapter we discuss other parts of the world outside the core area in western Asia that has been central to this point: East Asia, sub-Saharan Africa, the Eurasian steppes, and continental Europe. These societies emerged later than those in Mesopotamia, Egypt, and the Indus Valley and in more varied ecological conditions— sometimes independently, sometimes under the influence of older centers. Whereas the older river-valley civilizations were largely self-sufficient, many of the new civilizations discussed in the previous chapter and in this chapter were shaped by networks of long-distance trade. In the second millennium B.C.E. a civilization based on irrigation agriculture arose in the valley of the Yellow River and its tributaries in northern China. In the same epoch, in Nubia (southern Egypt and northern Sudan), the first complex society in tropical Africa continued to develop from the roots observed earlier by Harkhuf. The first millennium B.C.E. also witnessed the rise of a new kind of nomadism on the Eurasian steppes and the spread of Celtic peoples across much of continental Europe. These societies represent a variety of responses to different environmental and historical circumstances. However, they have certain features in common and collectively point to a distinct stage in the development of human societies.

---

[1] Quoted in Miriam Lichtheim, ed., *Ancient Egyptian Literature: A Book of Readings* (Berkeley: University of California Press, 1978).

EARLY CHINA, 2000–221 B.C.E.

On the eastern edge of the vast Eurasian landmass, Neolithic cultures developed as early as 8000 B.C.E. A more complex civilization evolved in the second and first millennia B.C.E. Under the Shang and Zhou dynasties, many of the elements of classical Chinese civilization emerged and spread across East Asia. As in Mesopotamia, Egypt, and the Indus Valley, the rise of cities, specialization of labor, bureaucratic government, writing, and other advanced technologies depended on the exploitation of a great river system—the Yellow River (Huang He [hwahng-HUH]) and its tributaries—to support intensive agriculture.

Geography and Resources

China is isolated by formidable natural barriers: the Himalaya (him-uh-LAY-uh) mountain range on the southwest; the Pamir (pah-MEER) and Tian Mountains and the Takla Makan (TAH-kluh muh-KAHN) Desert on the west; and the Gobi (GO-bee) Desert and the treeless, grassy hills and plains of the Mongolian steppe to the northwest and north (see Map 4.1). To the east lies the vast Pacific Ocean. Although China's separation was not total—trade goods, people, and ideas moved back and forth between China, India, and Central Asia—in many respects its development was distinctive.

Most of East Asia is covered with mountains, making overland travel and transport difficult. The great river systems of eastern China, however—the Yellow and the Yangzi (yang-zuh) Rivers and their tributaries—facilitate east-west movement. In the eastern river valleys dense populations practiced intensive agriculture; on the steppe lands of Mongolia, the deserts and oases of Xinjiang (shin-jyahng), and the high plateau of Tibet sparser populations lived largely by herding. The climate zones of East Asia range from the dry, subarctic reaches of Manchuria in the north to the lush, subtropical forests of the south, and a rich variety of plant and animal life are adapted to these zones.

Within the eastern agricultural zone, the north and the south have quite different environments. Each region developed distinctive patterns for land use, the kinds of crops grown, and the organization of agricultural labor. The monsoons that affect India and Southeast Asia (see Chapter 2) drench southern China with heavy rainfall in the summer, the most beneficial time for agriculture. In northern China rainfall is much more erratic. As in Mesopotamia and the Indus Valley, Chinese civilization developed in relatively adverse conditions on the northern plains, a demanding environment that stimulated important technologies and political traditions as well as the philosophical and religious views that became hallmarks of Chinese civilization. By the third century C.E., however, the gradual flow of population toward the warmer southern lands caused the political and intellectual center to move south.

The eastern river valleys and North China Plain contained timber, stone, scattered deposits of metals, and, above all, potentially productive land. Winds blowing from Central Asia deposit a yellowish-brown dust called **loess** (less) (these particles suspended in the water give the Yellow River its distinctive hue and name). Over the ages a thick mantle of soil has accumulated that is extremely fertile and soft enough to be worked with wooden digging sticks.

In this landscape, agriculture required the coordinated efforts of large numbers of people. Forests had to be cleared. Earthen dikes were constructed to protect nearby fields from recurrent floods on the Yellow River. To cope with the periodic droughts, reservoirs were dug to store river water and rainfall. Retaining walls partitioned the hillsides into flat arable terraces.

The staple crops in the northern region were millet, a grain indigenous to China, and wheat, which had spread to East Asia from the Middle East. Rice, which requires a warmer climate, prospered in the Yangzi River Valley. The cultivation of rice required a great outlay of labor. Rice paddies—the fields where rice is grown—must be flat and surrounded by water channels to bring and lead away water according to a precise schedule. Seedlings sprout in a nursery and are transplanted to the paddy, which is then flooded. Flooding eliminates weeds and rival plants and supports microscopic organisms that keep the soil fertile. When the crop is ripe, the paddy is drained; the rice stalks are harvested with a sickle; and the edible kernels are separated out. The reward for this effort is a harvest that can feed more people per cultivated acre than any other grain, which explains why the south eventually became more populous than the north.

loess A fine, light silt deposited by wind and water. It constitutes the fertile soil of the Yellow River Valley in northern China.

CHRONOLOGY

	China	Nubia	Celtic Europe	Eurasian Steppes
2500 B.C.E.	8000–2000 B.C.E. Neolithic cultures	4500 B.C.E. Early agriculture in Nubia		
2000 B.C.E.	2000 B.C.E. Bronze metallurgy 1750–1045 B.C.E. Shang dynasty	2200 B.C.E. Harkhuf's expeditions to Yam 1750 B.C.E. Rise of kingdom of Kush based on Kerma		
1500 B.C.E.		1500 B.C.E. Egyptian conquest of Nubia		
1000 B.C.E.	1045–221 B.C.E. Zhou dynasty 600 B.C.E. Iron metallurgy	1000 B.C.E. Decline of Egyptian control in Nubia 750 B.C.E. Rise of kingdom based on Napata 712–660 B.C.E. Nubian kings rule Egypt	1000 B.C.E. Origin of Celtic culture in Central Europe	1000 B.C.E. Initial development of pastoral nomadism 700 B.C.E. Scythians drive out Cimmerians and settle area north of Black Sea
500 B.C.E.	551–479 B.C.E. Life of Confucius 356–338 B.C.E. Lord Shang brings Legalist reforms to Qin state	300 B.C.E.–350 C.E. Kingdom of Meroë	500 B.C.E. Celtic elites trade for Mediterranean goods 500–300 B.C.E. Migrations across Europe 390 B.C.E. Celts sack Rome	440 B.C.E. Greek historian Herodotus reports on nomadic Scythians 300 B.C.E. Ruler of Chinese state of Zhao equips troops like nomad horsemen 100 B.C.E. Chinese historian Sima Qian describes Xiongnu nomads

The Late Neolithic: Artifacts and Legends

Archaeological evidence shows that the Neolithic population of China grew millet, raised pigs and chickens, and used stone tools. Workers made pottery on a wheel and fired it in high-temperature kilns. Some also pioneered the production of silk cloth, first raising silkworms on the leaves of mulberry trees, then carefully unraveling their cocoons to produce silk thread. They built walls of pounded earth by hammering the soil inside temporary wooden frames until it became hard as cement. By 2000 B.C.E. the Chinese had begun to make bronze (a thousand years after the beginnings of bronze-working in the Middle East).

In later times legends depicted the early rulers of China, starting with the Yellow Emperor, as ideal and benevolent masters in a tranquil Golden Age. They were followed by a dynasty called Xia (shah), who were in turn succeeded by the **Shang** (shahng) dynasty. Since scholars are uncertain about the historical reality of the Xia, Chinese history really begins with the rise of the Shang.

Shang The dominant people in the earliest Chinese dynasty for which we have written records (ca. 1766–1045 B.C.E.).

The Shang Period, 1766–1045 B.C.E.

Little is known about how the Shang rose to dominance around 1766 B.C.E., since written documents only appear toward the end of Shang rule. These documents are the so-called oracle bones, the shoulder bones of cattle and the bottom shells of turtles employed by Shang rulers to obtain information from ancestral spirits and gods (see Environment and Technology: Divination in Ancient Societies). The writing on the oracle bones concerns the king, his court, weather and its impact on agriculture, warfare against enemies, and religious practices, with little about other aspects of Shang society. The same limitations apply to the archaeological record, primarily treasure-filled tombs of the Shang ruling class.

The earliest known oracle bone inscriptions date to the thirteenth century B.C.E., but the system was already so sophisticated that some scholars believe writing in China could be considerably older. In the Shang writing system the several hundred characters (written symbols) were originally pictures of objects that become simplified over time, with each character representing a one-syllable word for an object or idea. It is likely that only a small number of people at court used this system. Nevertheless, the Shang writing system is the ancestor of the systems still used in China and elsewhere in East Asia today. Later Chinese writing developed thousands of more complex characters that provide information about both the meaning of the word and its sound.

Scholars have reconstructed the major features of Shang religion from the oracle bones. The supreme god, Di **(dee)**, who resides in the sky and unleashes the power of storms, is felt to be distant and unconcerned with the fate of humans, and cannot be approached directly. When people die, their spirits survive in the same supernatural sphere as Di and other gods of nature. These ancestral spirits, organized in a heavenly hierarchy that mirrors the social hierarchy on earth, can intervene in human affairs. The Shang ruler has direct access to his more recent ancestors, who have access to earlier generations, who can, in turn, intercede with Di. Thus the ruler is the crucial link between Heaven and earth, using his unrivaled access to higher powers to promote agricultural productivity and protect his people from natural and man-made disasters. This belief, which persisted throughout Chinese history, has been an extremely effective rationale for authoritarian rule.

The king was often on the road, traveling to the courts of his subordinates to reinforce their loyalty, but it is uncertain how much territory in the North China Plain was effectively controlled by the Shang. Excavations at sites elsewhere in China show artistic and technological traditions so different that they are probably the products of independent groups. Both the lack of writing elsewhere in early China and the Han-era conception that China had always been unified obscure from us the probable ethnic, linguistic, and cultural diversity of early China.

The Shang elite were a warrior class reveling in warfare, hunting, exchanging gifts, feasting, and drinking. They fought with bronze weapons and rode into battle on horse-drawn chariots, a technology that originated in western Asia. Frequent military campaigns provided these warriors with a theater for brave achievements and yielded considerable plunder. Many prisoners of war were taken in these campaigns and made into slaves and sacrificial victims.

Shang Period Bronze Vessel Vessels such as this large wine jar were used in rituals by the Shang ruling class to make contact with their ancestors. As both the source and the proof of the elite's authority, these vessels were often buried in Shang tombs. The complex shapes and elaborate decorations testify to the artisans' skill.

Covered ritual 'Fang-yi' wine vessel with 'Tao-tie' motif, Shang Dynasty (cast bronze with grey patina), Chinese School, (12th century B.C.)/Arthur M. Sackler Museum, Harvard University Art Museums, USA/Bequest of Grenville L. Winthrop/The Bridgeman Art Library

Excavated tombs of Shang royal and elite families, primarily from the vicinity of Anyang (ahn-yahng) (see Map 4.1), contain large quantities of valuable objects made of metal, jade, bone, ivory, shell, and stone, including musical instruments, jewelry, mirrors, weapons, and bronze vessels. These vessels, intricately decorated with stylized depictions of real and imaginary animals, were used to make offerings to ancestral spirits. Possession of bronze objects was a sign of status and authority. The tombs also contain the bodies of family members, servants, and prisoners of war who were killed at the time of the burial. It appears that the objects and people were intended to serve the main occupant of the tomb in the afterlife.

Shang cities are not well preserved in the archaeological record, partly because of the climate of northern China and partly because of the building materials used. With stone in short supply, cities were protected by massive walls of pounded earth, and buildings were constructed with wooden posts and dried mud. A number of sites appear to have served at different times as centers of political control and religion, with palaces, administrative buildings and storehouses, royal tombs, shrines of gods and ancestors, and houses of the nobility. The common people lived in agricultural villages outside these centers.

MAP 4.1 **China in the Shang and Zhou Periods, 1750–221 B.C.E.** The Shang dynasty arose in the second millennium B.C.E. in the floodplain of the Yellow River. While southern China benefits from the monsoon rains, northern China depends on irrigation. As population increased, the Han Chinese migrated from their eastern homeland to other parts of China, carrying with them their technologies and cultural practices. Other ethnic groups predominated in more outlying regions, and the nomadic peoples of the northwest constantly challenged Chinese authority. © Cengage Learning

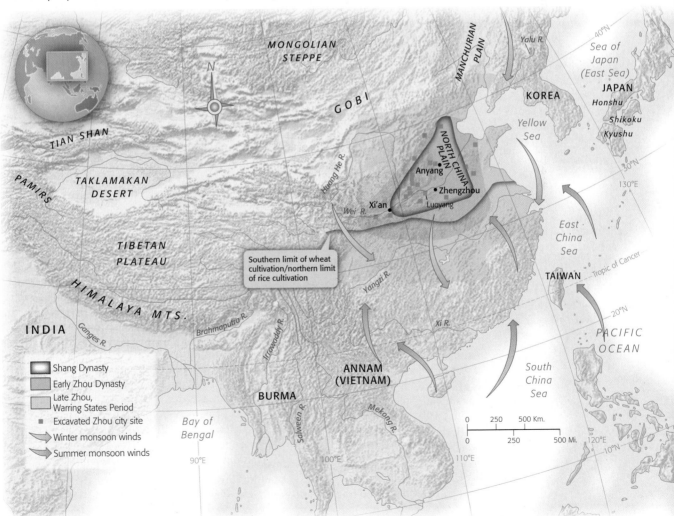

Divination in Ancient Societies

Many ancient peoples believed that the gods controlled the forces of nature and shaped destinies. Starting from this premise, they practiced various techniques of divination—the interpretation of phenomena in the natural world as signs of the gods' will and intentions. Through divination the ancients sought to communicate with the gods and thereby anticipate—even influence—the future.

The Shang ruling class in China frequently sought information from ancestors and other higher powers. The Shang monarch himself, with the help of religious experts, often functioned as the intermediary, since he had access to his own ancestors, who had a high ranking in the hierarchy of the spirit world. Chief among the tools of divination were oracle bones. Holes were first drilled in the shoulder bone of an ox or the bottom shell of a turtle to weaken it, and a red-hot pointed stick was applied, causing the bone or shell to crack. The cracks were then "read" by skilled interpreters as answers, on the part of the ancestor who was being consulted, to whatever questions had been asked. The questions, answers, and, often, confirmation of the accuracy of the prediction were subsequently incised on the shell or bone, providing a permanent record of matters of importance to the ruler, such as imminent weather, the yield of the upcoming harvest, the health of the king and his family, the proper performance of rituals, the prospects of military campaigns and hunting expeditions, and the mood of powerful royal ancestors and other divine forces. Tens of thousands of oracle bones survive as a major source of information about Shang life.

In Mesopotamia in the third and second millennia B.C.E. the most important type of divination involved close inspection of the form, size, and markings of the organs of sacrificed animals. Archaeologists have found models of sheeps' livers labeled with explanations of the meaning of various features.

Two other techniques of divination were following the trail of smoke from burning incense and examining the patterns that resulted when oil was thrown on water.

From about 2000 B.C.E. Mesopotamian diviners also foretold the future from their observation of the movements of the sun, moon, planets, stars, and constellations. In the centuries after 1000 B.C.E. celestial omens were the most important source of predictions about the future, and specialists maintained precise records of astronomical events. Mesopotamian mathematics, essential for calculations of the movements of celestial bodies, was the most sophisticated in the ancient Middle East. Astrology, with its division of the sky into the twelve segments of the zodiac and its use of the position of the stars and planets to predict an individual's destiny, developed out of long-standing Mesopotamian attention to the movements of celestial objects. Horoscopes—charts with calculations and predictions based on an individual's date of birth—have been found from shortly before 400 B.C.E.

Greeks and Romans frequently used oracles or divination before making decisions. Most famous among the many oracle sites in Greece was Delphi, in a stunning location overlooking the Gulf of Corinth, where advice was sought from the god Apollo. A private individual or the official envoy from a Greek community, after leaving the customary gift for the god and entering the temple, had his question conveyed to the priestess, who fell into a trance (recent geological studies have discovered that the temple lay directly above a fissure, and scholars speculate that a gas rising up into the chamber may have put the priestess into an intoxicated state) and delivered a wild utterance that was then "translated" and written down by the priests who administered the shrine. Information and advice from the god at Delphi helped Greek communities choose where to place new settlements during the centuries of colo-

The Zhou Period, 1045–221 B.C.E.

Zhou The people and dynasty that took over the dominant position in north China from the Shang and created the concept of the Mandate of Heaven to justify their rule. The Zhou era, particularly the vigorous early period (1045–771 B.C.E.), was remembered in Chinese tradition as a time of prosperity and benevolent rule.

In the mid-eleventh century B.C.E. the Shang were overthrown by the **Zhou** (joe), whose homeland lay several hundred miles to the west, in the valley of the Wei (way) River. While the ethnic origin of the Zhou is unclear (their traditions acknowledged that their ancestors had lived for generations among the western "barbarians"), they took over many elements of Shang culture. The Zhou line of kings was the longest lasting and most revered of all dynasties in Chinese history. The two founders were Wen, a vassal ruler who, after being held prisoner for a time by his Shang overlord, initiated a rebellion of disaffected Shang subjects; and his son, Wu, who mounted a successful attack on the Shang capital and was enthroned as the first ruler of the new dynasty.

Wu justified his achievement in a manner that became the norm throughout subsequent Chinese history. Claiming that the last Shang ruler was depraved and tyrannical, neglecting to honor gods and ancestors and killing and abusing his subjects, he invoked the highest Zhou deity, Tian (tyehn) ("Heaven"), who was more compassionate than the aloof Di of the Shang. Wu declared that Heaven granted authority and legitimacy to a ruler as long as he looked out for the welfare of his subjects; the monarch, accordingly, was called the "Son of Heaven." The proof of divine favor was the prosperity and stability of the kingdom. But if the ruler persistently failed in these duties and neglected the warning signs of flood, famine, invasion, or other disasters, Heaven could withdraw this "Mandate" and transfer it to another, more worthy ruler and family. This theory of the

Chinese Divination Shell After inscribing questions on a bone or shell, the diviner applied a red-hot point and interpreted the resulting cracks as a divine response. Courtesy of the Institute of History and Philology, Academia Sinica

nization throughout the Mediterranean and Black Seas, and Delphic priests may have collected information from the many travelers who came their way and then dispensed it by means of oracles.

Greek and Roman sources report on practices of divination among the Celts. Predicting the future is one of the many religious functions attributed to the Druids, as well as to a specialized group of "seers." Among their methods was careful observation of the flight patterns of birds and of the appearance of sacrificial offerings. In Ireland a ritual specialist ate the meat of a freshly killed bull, lay down to sleep on the bull's hide, and then had prophetic dreams. The most startling form of Celtic divination is described by the geographer Strabo:

The Romans put a stop to [the] customs . . . connected with sacrifice and divination, as they were in conflict with our own ways: for example, they would strike a man who had been consecrated for sacrifice in the back with a sword, and make prophecies based on his death-spasms.

Such horrifying reports were used by the Romans to justify the conquest of Celtic peoples in order to "civilize" them.

Little is known about the divinatory practices of early American peoples. The Olmec produced polished stone mirrors whose concave surfaces gave off reflected images that were thought to emanate from a supernatural realm. In later Mesoamerican societies women threw maize kernels onto the surface of water-filled basins and noted the patterns by which they floated or sank. By this means they ascertained information useful to the family, such as the cause and cure of illness, the right time for agricultural tasks or marriage, and favorable names for newborn children.

It may seem surprising that divination is being treated here as a form of technology. Most modern people would regard such interpretations of patterns in everyday phenomena as mere superstition. However, for ancient peoples who believed that the gods directly controlled events in the natural world, divination amounted to the application of these principles of causation to the socially beneficial task of acquiring information about the future. These techniques were usually known only to a class of experts whose special training and knowledge gave them high status in their society.

Mandate of Heaven Chinese religious and political ideology developed by the Zhou, according to which it was the prerogative of Heaven, the chief deity, to grant power to the ruler of China and to take away that power if the ruler failed to conduct himself justly and in the best interests of his subjects.

Mandate of Heaven, which validated the institution of monarchy by connecting the religious and political spheres, served as the foundation of Chinese political thought for three thousand years.

Much more is known about the early centuries of Zhou rule (the Western Zhou Period, 1045–771 B.C.E.) than the preceding Shang era because of the survival of written texts, above all the *Book of Documents*, a collection of decrees, letters, and other historical and pseudo-historical (some allegedly written by the early emperors of legend) records, and the *Book of Songs*, an anthology of 305 poems, ballads, and folksongs that illuminate the lives of rulers, nobles, and peasants. Additionally, members of the Zhou elite recorded their careers and cited honors received from the rulers in bronze inscriptions.

To consolidate his power, King Wu distributed territories to his relatives and allies, which they were to administer and profit from so long as they remained loyal to him. These regional rulers then apportioned pieces of their holdings to their supporters, creating a pyramidal structure of political, social, and economic relations often referred to as "feudal," borrowing terminology from the European Middle Ages.

When Wu died, his son and heir, Cheng (chung), was too young to assume full powers, and for a time the kingdom was run by his uncles, especially the Duke of Zhou. The Duke of Zhou is one of the most famous figures in early Chinese history, in large part because the philosopher Confucius later celebrated him as the ideal administrator who selflessly served as regent for his young nephew at a delicate time for the new dynasty, then dutifully returned power as soon as the lawful ruler came of age.

The early Zhou rulers constructed a new capital city in their homeland (near modern Xi'an), and other urban centers developed in succeeding centuries. Cities were laid out on a grid plan aligned with the north polar star, with gates in the fortification walls opening to the cardinal directions and major buildings facing south. This was in keeping with an already ancient concern, known as *feng shui* (fung shway) ("wind and water"), to orient structures so that they would be in a harmonious relationship with the terrain, the forces of wind, water, and sunlight, and the invisible energy perceived to be flowing through the natural world.

Alongside the new primacy of the Zhou deity Tian and continuation of religious practices inherited from the Shang era, new forms of divination developed. One increasingly popular method involved throwing down a handful of long and short stalks of the milfoil or yarrow plant and interpreting the patterns they formed. Over time a multilayered text was compiled, called the *Book of Changes,* that explained in detail the meanings of each of the sixty-four standard patterns formed by the stalks. In later ages this practice and the accompanying text also came to be used as a vehicle for self-examination and contemplation of the workings of the world.

The *Book of Songs* provides extraordinary glimpses into the lives, activities, and feelings of a diverse cross-section of early Chinese people—elite and common, male and female, urban and rural. We can glean much from these poems about the situation of women in early China. Some describe men and women choosing each other and engaging in sex outside of marriage. Other poems tell of arranged marriages in which the young woman anxiously leaves home and birth family behind and journeys to the household of an unknown husband and new family. One poem describes the different ways that infant boys and girls were welcomed into an aristocratic family. The male was received like a little prince: placed on a bed, swaddled in expensive robes, and given a jade scepter to play with as a symbol of his future authority; the female was placed on the floor and given the weight from a weaving loom to indicate her future obligations of subservience and household labor.

Over the period from the eleventh to eighth centuries B.C.E. the power of the Zhou monarch gradually eroded, largely because of the feudal division of territory and power. In 771 B.C.E. the Zhou capital was attacked by a coalition of enemies, and the dynasty withdrew to a base farther east, at Luoyang (LWOE-yahng). This change ushers in the Eastern Zhou Period (770–221 B.C.E.), a long era in which the Zhou monarchs remained as figureheads, given only nominal allegiance by the rulers of many virtually independent states scattered across northern and central China.

The first part of the Eastern Zhou era is called the Spring and Autumn Period (770–481 B.C.E.) because of the survival of a text, the *Spring and Autumn Annals,* that provides a spare historical record of events in the small eastern state of Lu. Later writers added commentaries that fleshed out this skeletal record. The states of this era were frequently at odds with one another and employed various tactics to protect themselves and advance their interests, including diplomatic initiatives, shifting alliances, and coups and assassinations as well as conventional warfare. The overall trend was gradual consolidation into a smaller number of larger and more powerful kingdoms.

Warfare was a persistent feature of the period, and there were important transformations in the character and technology of war. In the Shang and early Zhou periods, warfare largely had been conducted by members of the elite, who rode in chariots, treated battle as an opportunity for displays of skill and courage, and adhered to a code of heroic conduct. But in the high-stakes conflicts of the Eastern Zhou era, there was a shift to much larger armies made up of conscripted farmers who fought bloody battles, unconstrained by noble etiquette, in which large numbers were slaughtered. Some men undertook the study of war and composed handbooks, such as Sunzi's *Art of War.* Sunzi (soon-zuh) approaches war as a chess game in which the successful general employs deception, intuits the energy potential inherent in the landscape, and psychologically manipulates both friend and foe. The best victories are achieved without fighting so that one can incorporate the unimpaired resources of the other side.

Technological advances also impacted warfare. In the last centuries of the Zhou, the Chinese learned from the nomadic peoples of the northern steppes to put fighters on horseback. By 600 B.C.E. iron began to replace bronze as the primary metal for tools and weapons. There is mounting evidence that ironworking also came to China from the nomadic peoples of the northwest. Metalworkers in China were the first in the world to forge steel by removing carbon during the iron-smelting process.

Another significant development was the increasing size and complexity of the governments that administered Chinese states. Rulers ordered the careful recording of the population, the land, and its agricultural products so that the government could compel peasants to donate labor for public works projects (digging and maintaining irrigation channels and building roads, defensive walls, and palaces), conscript them into the army, and collect taxes. Skilled officials supervised the expanding bureaucracies of scribes, accountants, and surveyors and advised the rulers on various matters. Thus there arose a class of educated and ambitious men who traveled from state to state offering their services to the rulers—and their theories of ideal government.

Confucianism, Daoism, and Chinese Society

The Eastern Zhou era, despite being plagued by political fragmentation, frequent warfare, and anxious uncertainty, was also a time of great cultural development. The two most influential "philosophical" systems of Chinese civilization—Confucianism and Daoism—had their roots in this period, though they would be further developed and adapted to changing circumstances in later times.

Kongzi (kohng-zuh) (551–479 B.C.E.), known in the West by the Latin form of his name, **Confucius**, withdrew from public life after unsuccessful efforts to find employment as an official and adviser to several rulers of the day. He attracted a circle of students to whom he presented his wide-ranging ideas on morality, conduct, and government. His sayings were handed down orally by several generations of disciples before being compiled in written form as the *Analects* (see Diversity and Dominance: Human Nature and Good Government in the *Analects* of Confucius and the Legalist Writings of Han Fei). This work, along with a set of earlier texts that were believed (probably wrongly) to have been edited by Confucius—the *Book of Documents*, the *Book of Songs*, the *Book of Changes*, and the *Spring and Autumn Annals*—became the core texts of Confucianism.

Confucius drew upon traditional institutions and values but gave them new shape and meaning. He looked back to the early Zhou period as a Golden Age of wise rulers and benevolent government, models to which the people of his own "broken" society should return. He also placed great importance on the "rituals," or forms of behavior, that guide people in their daily interactions with one another, since these promote harmony in human relations.

For Confucius the family was the fundamental component of society, and the ways in which family members regulated their conduct in the home prepared them to serve as subjects of the state. Each person had his or her place and duties in a hierarchical order that was determined by age and gender. The "filiality" of children to parents, which included obedience, reverence, and love, had its analogue in the devotion of subjects to the ruler. Another fundamental virtue for Confucius was *ren* (ruhn), sometimes translated as "humaneness," which traditionally meant the feelings between family members and was now expanded into a universal ideal of benevolence and compassion that would, ideally, pervade every activity. Confucianism placed immense value on the practical task of making society function smoothly at every level. It provided a philosophical and ethical framework for conducting one's life and understanding one's place in the world. But it was not a religion. While Confucius urged respect for gods, ancestors, and religious traditions, he felt that such supernatural matters were unknowable.

Confucius's ideas were little known in his own time, but his teachings were preserved and gradually spread to a wider audience. Some disciples took Confucianism in new directions. Mengzi (muhng-zuh) (known in the West as Mencius, 371–289 B.C.E.), who did much to popularize Confucian ideas in his age, believed in the essential goodness of all human beings and argued that, if people were shown the right way by virtuous leaders, they would voluntarily do the right thing. Xunzi (shoon-zuh) (ca. 310–210 B.C.E.), on the other hand, concluded that people had to be compelled to make appropriate choices. (This approach led to the development of a school of thought called Legalism, discussed later in this chapter.) As we shall see in Chapter 6, in the era of the emperors a revised Confucianism became the dominant political philosophy and the core of the educational system for government officials.

If Confucianism emphasized social engagement, its great rival, **Daoism (DOW-ism)**, urged withdrawal from the empty formalities, rigid hierarchy, and distractions of Chinese society. Laozi (low-zuh) is regarded as the originator of Daoism, although virtually nothing is known about him, and some scholars doubt his existence. Laozi is credited with the foundational text of Daoism, the *Classic of the Way of Virtue*, a difficult book full of ambiguity and paradox, beautiful poetic images, and tantalizing hints of "truths" that cannot be adequately explained with words. It raises questions about whether the material world in which we operate is real or a kind of dream that blocks us from perceiving a higher reality. It argues that education, knowledge, and rational analysis are obstacles to understanding and that we would be better off cultivating

Confucius Western name for the Chinese philosopher Kongzi (551–479 B.C.E.). His doctrine of duty and public service had a great influence on subsequent Chinese thought and served as a code of conduct for government officials.

Daoism Chinese school of thought, originating in the Warring States Period with Laozi. Daoism offered an alternative to the Confucian emphasis on hierarchy and duty.

Human Nature and Good Government in the *Analects* of Confucius and the Legalist Writings of Han Fei

While monarchy (the rule of one man) was the standard form of government in ancient China and was rarely challenged, political theorists and philosophers thought a great deal about the qualities of the ideal ruler, his relationship to his subjects, and the means by which he controlled them. These considerations about how to govern people were inevitably molded by fundamental assumptions about the nature of human beings. In the Warring States Period, as the major states struggled desperately with one another for survival and expansion, such discussions took on a special urgency, and the Confucians and Legalists came to represent two powerful, and largely contradictory, points of view.

The Analects *are a collection of sayings of Confucius, probably compiled and written down several generations after he lived, though some elements may have been added even later. They cover a wide range of matters, including ethics, government, education, music, and rituals. Taken as a whole, they are a guide to living an honorable, virtuous, useful, and satisfying life. While subject to reinterpretation according to the circumstances of the times, Confucian principles have had a great influence on Chinese values and behavior ever since.*

Han Fei (280–233 B.C.E.), who was, ironically, at one time the student of a Confucian teacher, became a Legalist writer and political adviser to the ruler of the ambitious state of Qin. Eventually he lost out in a power struggle at court and was forced to kill himself.

The following selections illuminate the profound disagreements between Confucians and Legalists over the essential nature of human beings and how the ruler should conduct himself in order to most effectively govern his subjects and protect his kingdom.

Confucius

4:5 Confucius said: "Riches and honors are what all men desire. But if they cannot be attained in accordance with the *dao* [the way] they should not be kept. Poverty and low status are what all men hate. But if they cannot be avoided while staying in accordance with the *dao,* you should not avoid them. If a Superior Man departs from *ren* [humaneness], how can he be worthy of that name? A Superior Man never leaves *ren* for even the time of a single meal. In moments of haste he acts according to it. In times of difficulty or confusion he acts according to it."

16:8 Confucius said: "The Superior Man stands in awe of three things: (1) He is in awe of the decree of Heaven. (2) He is in awe of great men. (3) He is in awe of the words of the sages. The inferior man does not know the decree of Heaven; takes great men lightly and laughs at the words of the sages."

4:14 Confucius said: "I don't worry about not having a good position; I worry about the means I use to gain position. I don't worry about being unknown; I seek to be known in the right way."

7:15 Confucius said: "I can live with coarse rice to eat, water for drink and my arm as a pillow and still be happy. Wealth and honors that one possesses in the midst of injustice are like floating clouds."

13:6 Confucius said: "When you have gotten your own life straightened out, things will go well without your giving orders. But if your own life isn't straightened out, even if you give orders, no one will follow them."

12:2 Zhonggong asked about the meaning of *ren.* The Master said: "Go out of your home as if you were receiving an important guest. Employ the people as if you were assisting at a great ceremony. What you don't want done to yourself, don't do to others. Live in your town without stirring up resentments, and live in your household without stirring up resentments."

1:5 Confucius said: "If you would govern a state of a thousand chariots (a small-to-middle-size state), you must pay strict attention to business, be true to your word, be economical in expenditure and love the people. You should use them according to the seasons."

2:3 Confucius said: "If you govern the people legalistically and control them by punishment, they will avoid crime, but have no personal sense of shame. If you govern them by means of virtue and control them with propriety, they will gain their own sense of shame, and thus correct themselves."

12:7 Zigong asked about government. The Master said, "Enough food, enough weapons and the confidence of the people." Zigong said, "Suppose you had no alternative but to give up one of these three, which one would be let go of first?" The Master said, "Weapons." Zigong said, "What if you had to give up one of the remaining two, which one would it be?" The Master said, "Food. From ancient times, death has come to all men, but a people without confidence in its rulers will not stand."

12:19 Ji Kang Zi asked Confucius about government saying: "Suppose I were to kill the unjust, in order to advance the just. Would that be all right?"

Confucius replied: "In doing government, what is the need of killing? If you desire good, the people will be good. The nature of the Superior Man is like the wind, the nature of the inferior man is like the grass. When the wind blows over the grass, it always bends."

2:19 The Duke of Ai asked: "How can I make the people follow me?" Confucius replied: "Advance the upright and set aside the crooked, and the people will follow you. Advance the crooked and set aside the upright, and the people will not follow you."

2:20 Ji Kang Zi asked: "How can I make the people reverent and loyal, so they will work positively for me?" Confucius said, "Approach them with dignity, and they will be reverent. Be filial and compassionate and they will be loyal. Promote the able and teach the incompetent, and they will work positively for you."

Han Fei

Past and present have different customs; new and old adopt different measures. To try to use the ways of a generous and lenient government to rule the people of a critical age is like trying to drive a runaway horse without using reins or whips. This is the misfortune that ignorance invites. . . .

Humaneness [*ren*] may make one shed tears and be reluctant to apply penalties, but law makes it clear that such penalties must be applied. The ancient kings allowed law to be supreme and did not give in to their tearful longings. Hence it is obvious that humaneness cannot be used to achieve order in the state. . . .

The best rewards are those that are generous and predictable, so that the people may profit by them. The best penalties are those that are severe and inescapable, so that the people will fear them. The best laws are those that are uniform and inflexible, so that the people can understand them. . . .

Hardly ten men of true integrity and good faith can be found today, and yet the offices of the state number in the hundreds. . . . Therefore the way of the enlightened ruler is to unify the laws instead of seeking for wise men, to lay down firm policies instead of longing for men of good faith. . . .

When a sage rules the state, he does not depend on people's doing good of themselves; he sees to it that they are not allowed to do what is bad. If he depends on people's doing good of themselves, then within his borders he can count fewer than ten instances of success. But if he sees to it that they are not allowed to do what is bad, then the whole state can be brought to a uniform level of order. Those who rule must employ measures that will be effective with the majority and discard those that will be effective with only a few. Therefore they devote themselves not to virtue but to law. . . .

When the Confucians of the present time counsel rulers, they do not praise those measures that will bring order today, but talk only of the achievements of the men who brought order in the past. . . . No ruler with proper standards will tolerate them. Therefore the enlightened ruler works with facts and discards useless theories. He does not talk about deeds of humaneness and rightness, and he does not listen to the words of scholars. . . .

Nowadays, those who do not understand how to govern invariably say, "You must win the hearts of the people!". . .

The reason you cannot rely on the wisdom of the people is that they have the minds of little children. If the child's head is not shaved, its sores will spread; and if its boil is not lanced, it will become sicker than ever . . . for it does not understand that the little pain it suffers now will bring great benefit later. . . .

Now, the ruler presses the people to till the land and open up new pastures so as to increase their means of livelihood, and yet they consider him harsh; he draws up a penal code and makes the punishments more severe in order to put a stop to evil, and yet the people consider him stern. . . . He makes certain that everyone within his borders understands warfare and sees to it that there are no private exemptions from military service; he unites the strength of the state and fights fiercely in order to take its enemies captive, and yet the people consider him violent. . . . [These] types of undertaking all ensure order and safety to the state, and yet the people do not have sense enough to rejoice in them.

QUESTIONS FOR ANALYSIS

1. What do Confucius and Han Fei believe about the nature of human beings? Are they intrinsically good and well-behaved, or bad and prone to misbehave?

2. What are the qualities of an ideal ruler for Confucius and Han Fei?

3. By what means can the ruler influence his subjects in Confucian thought? How should the ruler compel obedience in the people in Legalist thought?

4. What do Confucians and Legalists think about the value of the past as a model for the present?

5. Why might Confucius's passionate concern for ethical behavior on the part of officials and rulers arise at a time when the size and power of governments were growing?

Sources: Confucius selections from "The Analects of Confucius," translated by A. Charles Muller, from *http://www.acmuller.net/con-dao/analects.html*. Reprinted by permission of Charles Muller. Passages from "The Five Vermin," from Han Fei Tzu, translated by Burton Watson. Copyright (c) 1964 Columbia University Press. Reprinted with permission of the publisher.

our senses and trusting our intuitions. The primal world of the distant past was happy and blessed before civilization and "knowledge" corrupted it. The Daoist sage strives to lead a tranquil existence by retreating from the stresses and obligations of a chaotic society. He avoids useless struggles, making himself soft and malleable so that the forces that buffet people can flow harmlessly around him. He chooses not to "act" because such action almost always leads to a different outcome from the one desired, whereas inaction may bring the desired outcome. And he has no fear of death because, for all we know, death may be merely a transformation to another plane of existence. In the end, in a world that is always changing and lacks any absolute morality or meaning, all that matters is the individual's fundamental understanding of, and accommodation to, the *Dao*, the "path" of nature.

Daoism, like Confucianism, would continue to evolve for many centuries, adapting to changes in Chinese society and incorporating many elements of traditional religion, mysticism, and magic. Although Daoism and Confucianism may appear to be thoroughly at odds regarding the relationship of the individual and the larger society, many Chinese through the ages have drawn on both traditions, and it has been said that the typical Chinese scholar-official was a Confucian in his work and public life but a Daoist in the privacy of his study.

The classical Chinese patterns of family and property took shape in the later Zhou period. The kinship structures of the Shang and early Zhou periods, based on the clan (a relatively large group of related families), gave way to the three-generation family of grandparents, parents, and children as the fundamental social unit. Fathers had absolute authority over women and children, arranged marriages for their offspring, and could sell the labor of family members. Only men could conduct rituals and make offerings to the ancestors, though women helped maintain the household's ancestral shrines. A man was limited to one wife but was permitted additional sexual partners, who had the lower status of concubines. A man whose wife died had a duty to remarry in order to produce male heirs to keep alive the cult of the ancestors, whereas women were discouraged from remarrying.

yin/yang In Chinese belief, complementary factors that help to maintain the equilibrium of the world. Yang is associated with masculine, light, and active qualities; yin with feminine, dark, and passive qualities.

In Chinese tradition the concept of **yin/yang** represented the complementary nature of male and female roles in the natural order. The male principle (yang) was equated with the sun: active, bright, and shining; the female principle (yin) corresponded to the moon: passive, shaded, and reflective. Male toughness was balanced by female gentleness, male action and initiative by female endurance and need for completion, and male leadership by female supportiveness. In its earliest form, the theory considered yin and yang as equal and alternately dominant, like night and day, creating balance in the world. However, as a result of the changing role of women in the Zhou period and the pervasive influence of Confucian ideology, the male principle came to be seen as superior to the female.

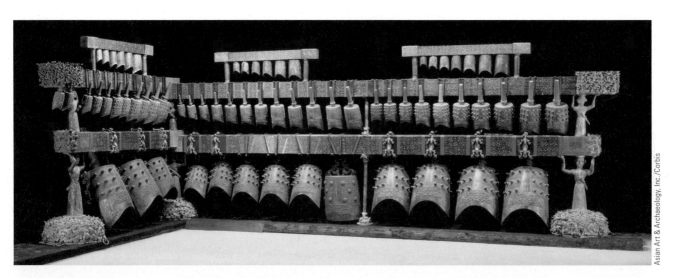

Asian Art & Archaeology, Inc./Corbis

Chinese Bronze Bells   This set of 65 bells was discovered in the tomb of Marquis Yi, the ruler of one of the warring states in the 5th century B.C.E. Bells in different sizes were central components of ancient Chinese "orchestras." In the Eastern Zhou era, each state had its own distinctive set of instruments, an assertion of independence and local pride.

The Warring States Period, 481–221 B.C.E.

The second half of the Eastern Zhou era is conventionally called the Warring States Period (480–221 B.C.E.) because the scale and intensity of rivalry and warfare between the states accelerated. More successful states conquered and absorbed less capable rivals, and by the beginning of the third century B.C.E. only seven major states remained. Each state sought security by any and all means: building walls to protect its borders; putting into the field the largest possible armies; experimenting with military organization, tactics, and technology; and devising new techniques of administration to produce the greatest revenues. Some wars were fought against non-Chinese peoples living on the margins of the states' territories or even in enclaves within the states. In addition to self-defense, the aim of these campaigns was often to increase the territory available for agriculture, since cultivated land was, ultimately, the source of wealth and manpower. The conquered peoples assimilated over time, becoming Chinese in language and culture.

The most innovative of all the states of this era was Qin (chin), on the western edge of the "Central States" (the term used for the Chinese lands of north and central China). Coming from the same Wei River Valley frontier region as the Zhou long before, and exposed to barbarian influences and attacks, the Qin rulers commanded a nation of hardy farmers and employed them in large, well-trained armies. The very vulnerability of their circumstances may have inspired the Qin rulers of the fourth and third centuries B.C.E. to take great risks, for they were the first to put into practice the philosophy and methods of the Legalist school of political theorists.

In the mid-fourth century B.C.E. Lord Shang was put in charge of the Qin government. He maintained that the Confucians were mistaken in looking to an idealized past for solutions and naïve in thinking that the ruler should worry about his subjects' opinions. In Lord Shang's view, the ruler should trust his own judgment and employ whatever means are necessary to compel obedience and good behavior in his subjects. In the end, Legalists were willing to sacrifice individual freedom to guarantee the security and prosperity of the state. To strengthen the ruler, Lord Shang moved to weaken the Qin nobility, sending out centrally appointed district governors, abolishing many of the privileges of the nobility, and breaking up large estates by requiring property to be divided equally among the surviving sons. Although he eventually became entangled in bitter intrigue at court and was killed in 338 B.C.E., the Qin rulers of the third century B.C.E. continued to employ Legalist advisers and pursue Legalist policies, and, as we shall see in Chapter 6, they converted the advantages gained from this approach into a position of unprecedented power.

SECTION REVIEW

- The challenges of engaging in agriculture in the varied environments of East Asia led to the formation of complex, hierarchical societies.

- The Shang and Zhou rulers of early China developed religious ideologies (oracle bone divination, Mandate of Heaven theories) that justified monarchic systems of government.

- The feudal organization of the Zhou state led, over time, to the weakening of the monarch's authority and the rise of many essentially independent states.

- The rivalry and conflict of Chinese states in the later Zhou era led to the rise of bureaucracies, administrative experts, and more deadly forms of warfare.

- This era also saw the rise and rivalry of major philosophical systems: Confucianism, Daoism, and Legalism.

- Although yin/yang theory regarded the female and male principles as interdependent, men were dominant in the family, and the influence of Confucianism led to a reduction in women's status and rights.

NUBIA, 2300 B.C.E.–350 C.E.

Since the first century B.C.E. the name *Nubia* has been applied to a 1,000-mile (1,600-kilometer) stretch of the Nile Valley lying between Aswan and Khartoum (kahr-TOOM) and straddling the southern part of the modern nation of Egypt and the northern part of Sudan (see Map 4.2). Nubia is the only continuously inhabited territory connecting sub-Saharan Africa (the lands south of the Sahara Desert) with North Africa. For thousands of years it has served as a corridor for trade between tropical Africa and the Mediterranean. Nubia was richly endowed with natural resources such as gold, copper, and semiprecious stones.

Nubia's location and natural wealth, along with Egypt's hunger for Nubian gold, explain the early rise of a civilization with a complex political organization, social stratification, metallurgy, monumental building, and writing. Scholars have moved away from the traditional view that Nubian civilization simply imitated Egypt, and they now emphasize the mutually beneficial interactions between Egypt and Nubia and the growing evidence that Nubian culture also drew on influences from sub-Saharan Africa.

Early Cultures and Egyptian Domination 2300–1100 B.C.E.

The central geographical feature of Nubia, as of Egypt, is the Nile River. This part of the Nile flows through a landscape of rocky desert, grassland, and fertile plain. River irrigation was essential for agriculture in a climate that was severely hot and, in the north, nearly without rainfall. Six cataracts, barriers formed by large boulders and rapids, obstructed boat traffic. Boats operating between the cataracts and caravans skirting the river made travel and trade possible.

In the fifth millennium B.C.E. bands of people in northern Nubia made the transition from seminomadic hunting and gathering to a settled life based on grain agriculture and cattle herding. From this time on, the majority of the population lived in agricultural villages alongside the river. Even before 3000 B.C.E. Egyptian craftsmen worked in ivory and in ebony wood—products of tropical Africa that came through Nubia.

Kush An Egyptian name for Nubia, the region alongside the Nile River south of Egypt, where an indigenous kingdom with its own distinctive institutions and cultural traditions arose beginning in the early second millennium B.C.E.

Nubia enters the historical record around 2300 B.C.E. in Old Kingdom Egyptian accounts of trade missions to southern lands. At that time Aswan, just north of the First Cataract, was the southern limit of Egyptian control. As we saw with the journey of Harkhuf at the beginning of this chapter, Egyptian officials stationed there led donkey caravans south in search of gold, incense, ebony, ivory, slaves, and exotic animals from tropical Africa. This was dangerous work, requiring delicate negotiations with local Nubian chiefs to secure protection, but it brought substantial rewards to those who succeeded.

During the Middle Kingdom (ca. 2040–1640 B.C.E.), Egypt adopted a more aggressive stance toward Nubia. Seeking to control the gold mines in the desert east of the Nile and to cut out the Nubian middlemen who drove up the cost of luxury goods from the tropics, the Egyptians erected a string of mud-brick forts on islands and riverbanks south of the Second Cataract. The forts regulated the flow of trade goods and protected the southern frontier of Egypt against Nubians and nomadic raiders from the desert. There seem to have been peaceable relations but little interaction between the Egyptian garrisons and the indigenous population of northern Nubia, which continued to practice its age-old farming and herding ways.

Farther south, where the Nile makes a great U-shaped turn in the fertile plain of the Dongola Reach (see Map 4.2), a more complex political entity was evolving from the chiefdoms of the third millennium B.C.E. The Egyptians gave the name **Kush** to the kingdom whose capital was located at Kerma, one of the earliest urbanized centers in tropical Africa. Beginning around 1750 B.C.E. the kings of Kush built fortification walls and monumental structures of mud brick. The dozens or even hundreds of servants and wives sacrificed for burial with the kings, as well as the rich objects found in their tombs, testify to the wealth and power of the rulers of Kush and imply a belief in an afterlife in which attendants and possessions would be useful. Kushite craftsmen were skilled in metalworking, whether for weapons or jewelry, and produced high-quality pottery.

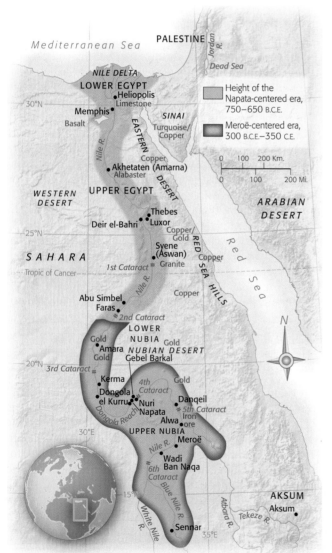

MAP 4.2 **Ancient Nubia** The land route alongside the Nile River as it flows through Nubia has long served as a corridor connecting sub-Saharan Africa with North Africa. Centuries of Egyptian occupation, as well as time spent in Egypt by Nubian hostages, mercenaries, and merchants, led to a marked Egyptian cultural influence in Nubia. Adapted from Map 15 from The Historical Atlas of Africa, ed. by J.F. Ajyi and Michael Crowder.   © Cengage Learning

KENNETH GARRETT/National Geographic Stock

Gebel Barkal The "Holy Mountain" of Nubia, located in northern Sudan at a great bend in the Nile near the Fourth Cataract. At its base sat the ancient city of Napata, first the capital of the New Kingdom Egyptian occupying forces, then of the independent state of Kush from the eighth to fourth centuries B.C.E. Several pillars survive from the temple of Amon, as well as a number of small burial pyramids.

During the expansionist New Kingdom (ca. 1532–1070 B.C.E.), the Egyptians penetrated more deeply into Nubia (see Chapter 3). They destroyed Kush and its capital (recent archaeological excavations have shown that the Egyptians constructed a new town and palace complex a half-mile north of the abandoned native city) and extended their frontier to the Fourth Cataract. A high-ranking Egyptian official called "Overseer of Southern Lands" or "King's Son of Kush" ruled Nubia from a new administrative center at Napata (nah-PAH-tuh), near Gebel Barkal (JEB-uhl BAHR-kahl), the "Holy Mountain," believed to be the home of a local god. Exploiting the mines of Nubia, Egypt supplied gold to the states of the Middle East. Fatalities were high among native workers in the brutal desert climate, and the army had to ward off attacks from desert nomads.

Five hundred years of Egyptian domination in Nubia left many marks. The Egyptian government imposed Egyptian culture on the native population. Children from elite families were brought to the Egyptian royal court to guarantee the good behavior of their relatives in Nubia; they absorbed Egyptian language, culture, and religion, which they later carried home with them. Other Nubians served as archers in the Egyptian armed forces. The manufactured goods that they brought back to Nubia have been found in their graves. The Nubians built towns on the Egyptian model and erected stone temples to Egyptian gods, particularly Amon. The frequent depiction of Amon with the head of a ram may reflect a blending of the chief Egyptian god with a Nubian ram deity.

The Kingdom of Meroë, 800 B.C.E.–350 C.E.

Egypt's weakness after 1200 B.C.E. led to the collapse of its authority in Nubia. In the eighth century B.C.E. a powerful new native kingdom emerged in southern Nubia. Its history can be divided into two parts. During the early period, between the eighth and fourth centuries B.C.E., Napata, the former Egyptian headquarters, was the primary center. During the later period, from the fourth century B.C.E. to the fourth century C.E., the center was farther south, at **Meroë** (MER-oh-ee), near the Sixth Cataract.

For half a century, from around 712 to 660 B.C.E., the kings of Nubia ruled all of Egypt as the Twenty-fifth Dynasty, conducting themselves in the age-old manner of Egyptian rulers. They were addressed by royal titles, depicted in traditional costume, and buried according to Egyptian custom. However, they kept their Nubian names and were depicted with the physical features of sub-Saharan Africans. They also inaugurated an artistic and cultural renaissance, building on a monumental scale for the first time in centuries and reinvigorating Egyptian art, architecture, and religion. The Nubian kings resided at Memphis, the Old Kingdom capital, while Thebes, the New Kingdom capital, was the residence of a celibate female member of the king's family who was titled "God's Wife of Amon."

The Nubian dynasty made a disastrous mistake in 701 B.C.E. when it offered help to local rulers in Palestine who were struggling against the Assyrian Empire. The Assyrians retaliated by invading Egypt and driving the Nubian monarchs back to their southern domain by 660 B.C.E.

Meroë Capital of a flourishing kingdom in southern Nubia from the fourth century B.C.E. to the fourth century C.E. In this period Nubian culture shows more independence from Egypt and the influence of sub-Saharan Africa.

Napata again became the chief royal residence and religious center of the kingdom. However, Egyptian cultural influences remained strong. Court documents continued to be written in Egyptian hieroglyphs, and the mummified remains of the rulers were buried in modestly sized sandstone pyramids along with hundreds of shawabti (shuh-WAB-tee) figurines.

By the fourth century B.C.E. the center of gravity had shifted south to Meroë, perhaps because Meroë was better situated for agriculture and trade, the economic mainstays of the Nubian kingdom. As a result, sub-Saharan cultural patterns gradually replaced Egyptian ones. Egyptian hieroglyphs gave way to a new set of symbols, still essentially undeciphered, for writing the Meroitic language. People continued to worship Amon as well as Isis, an Egyptian goddess connected to fertility and sexuality, but those deities had to share the stage with Nubian deities like the lion-god Apedemak. Meroitic art combined Egyptian, Greco-Roman, and indigenous traditions.

Women of the royal family played an important role in Meroitic politics, another reflection of the influence of sub-Saharan Africa. In their matrilineal system the king was succeeded by the son of his sister. Nubian queens sometimes ruled by themselves and sometimes in partnership with their husbands, playing a part in warfare, diplomacy, and the building of temples and pyramid tombs. They are depicted in scenes reserved for male rulers in Egyptian imagery, smiting enemies in battle and being suckled by the mother-goddess Isis.

Meroë was a huge city for its time, more than a square mile in area, dominating fertile grasslands and converging trade routes. Great reservoirs were dug to catch precious rainfall, and the city was a major center for iron smelting. Although much of the city is still buried under the sand, in 2002 archaeologists using a magnetometer to detect buried structures discovered a large palace. The Temple of Amon was approached by an avenue lined with stone rams, and the walled precinct of the "Royal City" was filled with palaces, temples, and administrative buildings. The ruler, who may have been regarded as divine, was assisted by a professional class of officials, priests, and army officers.

Meroë collapsed in the early fourth century C.E., overrun by nomads from the western desert who had become more mobile because of the arrival of the camel in North Africa. It had already been weakened when profitable commerce with the Roman Empire was diverted to the Red Sea and to the rising kingdom of Aksum (AHK-soom) (in present-day Ethiopia). Thus the end of the Meroitic kingdom was as closely linked to Nubia's role in long-distance commerce as its beginning.

SECTION REVIEW

- Nubia's natural wealth and location on the trade route between Egypt and sub-Saharan Africa, along with Egypt's hunger for Nubian gold, explain the early rise of a complex civilization there.

- During long periods of Egyptian domination, as well as a period in which Nubian rulers controlled Egypt, Nubian culture and technology were strongly influenced by Egyptian practices.

- During the Meroitic period, Nubia came under stronger cultural influences stemming from sub-Saharan Africa, as seen in the prominent role of queens.

- The city of Meroë was large and impressive, with monumental palaces, temples, and boulevards. It controlled agriculture and trade and was a center of metallurgy.

- Nubia's collapse in the early fourth century C.E. was due to shifting trade routes and attacks by desert nomads.

PASTORAL NOMADS OF THE EURASIAN STEPPES, 1000–100 B.C.E.

Early Nomadism

nomads People without permanent, fixed places of residence, whose way of life and means of subsistence require them to periodically migrate, often with their herds of domesticated animals, to a familiar series of temporary seasonal encampments.

Nomads (from a Greek word meaning "wanderers") are people who do not have a single, settled place of residence, but rather move from one temporary encampment to another, usually as a strategy for feeding themselves. For most of human history people were nomadic hunter-gatherers, moving about in search of wild plants they could harvest and animals they could kill. It was only with the Agricultural Revolutions—the domestication of plants and animals—beginning around 10,000 years ago that human groups were able to settle in one place, build permanent homes, acquire more possessions, and create more complex societies (see Chapter 1).

The domestication of herd animals, such as sheep, goats, and cattle, made possible a new kind of nomadism in which people lived off the products of their animals, consuming the meat, milk and other dairy products, clothing themselves with hair and hides, and utilizing animal manure to fuel fires. We have already seen several examples of nomadic peoples, initially living on the fringes of the settled, agricultural areas in early western Asia and, in some cases, eventually settling down and assimilating to the cultures of the more advanced agricultural peoples—the Amorites who migrated into southern Mesopotamia and founded Babylon in the early second millennium B.C.E. (see Chapter 2); the Aramaeans who settled in Syria-Palestine and whose language, Aramaic, became widespread in that region; and the early Israelites, whose migratory lifestyle was remembered in the traditions about the patriarchs Abraham, Isaac and Jacob (see Chapter 3). Many scholars believe that the proto-Indo-Europeans, speakers of the language or languages ancestral to the large family of Indo-European languages found across much of Europe and Asia, were nomadic herders who migrated from an original homeland north of the Black and Caspian Seas beginning in the third millennium B.C.E. They are believed to have first domesticated horses, which enhanced their ability to herd other animals (see Chapter 1).

Steppe Nomads

steppe An ecological region of grass- and shrub-covered plains that is treeless and too arid for agriculture.

Our concern here is with a new kind of pastoral nomadism that arose across the vast Eurasian Steppes in the first millennium B.C.E. **Steppe**—a word of Russian origin—is used to describe an ecological zone characterized by treeless, grass- and shrub-covered plains and marked by a relatively arid climate with too little precipitation for agriculture and radical extremes of temperature from summer to winter and day to night. The Eurasian Steppes extend from Hungary in eastern Europe across Ukraine and southern Russia, Central Asia, Mongolia, and southern Siberia (see Map 4.3). The peoples who occupied these lands became horse-riding warriors, driving their herds to seasonal camping grounds and being careful not to overexploit pastures

MAP 4.3 **Pastoral Nomads of the Eurasian Steppes** This map shows the vast steppes of Eurasia, arid grasslands extending from Hungary to Manchuria, and the nomadic pastoralist peoples who grazed their herds there. Steppe nomads sometimes traded with settled peoples, sometimes raided, forcing neighboring states like China to either buy them off or develop cavalry forces to fight them. Several of these groups, including Parthians, Scythians, and Yuezhi, migrated south to agricultural lands and created powerful states. © Cengage Learning

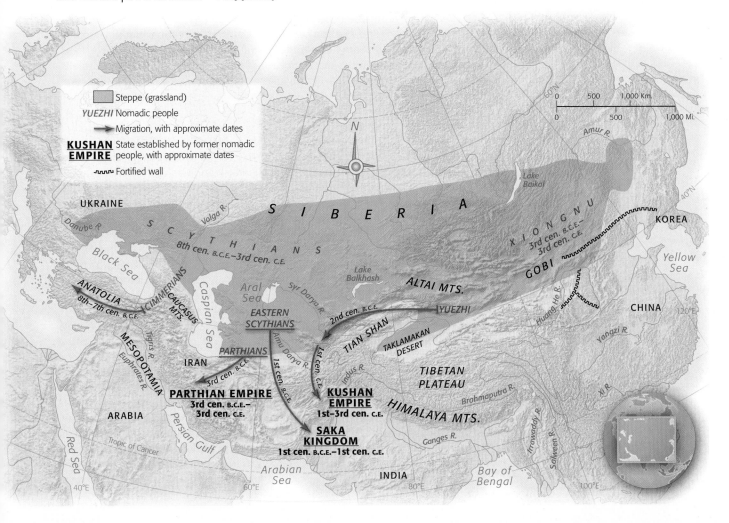

Scythian Gold Pectoral   This gold pectoral (decorative item worn over the breast), found in Ukraine and dating to the fourth century B.C.E., displays the beauty and quality of craftsmanship of Scythian art. The lower register shows griffins attacking a horse, while two men with quivers examine a fleece shirt in the upper register.

and water sources to the point that they could not recover and be used again. They didn't wander randomly, but rather operated within certain territorial bounds worked out with other groups. Normally they relocated to familiar encampments appropriate to their needs in different seasons. The success of this way of life also depended on a symbiotic interaction of the nomads with settled agricultural peoples, often by trading animal products (live animals, meat, hides, wool, cheese) for agricultural products and manufactured goods (metalwork and textiles), sometimes by raiding and stealing.

Because they lacked the technology of writing, we know relatively little about these peoples and must depend on the information provided by archaeology and the accounts of nomads in the records of literate ancient peoples. Greek and Roman texts tell us something about the peoples on the western range of the steppes, while Chinese sources inform us about the peoples of the eastern side. While there were, no doubt, significant ethnic and linguistic differences among these peoples, they shared many features of technology, culture, and political and social organization, due, in large part, to their mobility and the speed with which objects and ideas could move across this open landscape. Indeed, the steppe was the conduit by which products, such as wheat, and technologies, including bronze and iron metalworking, chariots, and cavalry warfare, traveled from western and Central Asia to East Asia.

While the origins of pastoral nomadism on the steppe are shrouded in the mists of prehistory, a picture begins to emerge in the centuries just after 1000 B.C.E. The first Greek historian, **Herodotus** (fifth century B.C.E.), claims that the nomadic Cimmerians, driven out of their northern homelands by another nomadic people, the **Scythians**, invaded Anatolia (modern Turkey) in the seventh century B.C.E., and the Cimmerians are also mentioned in Assyrian records from the late eighth and seventh centuries B.C.E.

Herodotus   Heir to the technique of historia ("investigation/research") developed by Greeks in the late archaic period. He came from a Greek community in Anatolia and traveled extensively, collecting information in western Asia and the Mediterranean lands. He traced the antecedents and chronicled the wars between the Greek city-states and the Persian Empire, thus originating the Western tradition of historical writing.

Scythians   Term used by the ancient Greeks for the nomadic peoples living on the steppe north of the Black and Caspian Seas.

The Scythians

Herodotus devoted many pages to an account of the Scythian lands and peoples. The Greeks used the term *Scythian* in a very broad and general way to describe peoples living to the north and east of their Aegean homeland: the lands north of the Black and Caspian Seas, or present-day Ukraine and southern Russia. While the Greeks lumped together various peoples who probably would not have regarded themselves as belonging to the same ethnic group, the Scythians were, according to most experts, speakers of languages belonging to the Iranian subgroup of the Indo-European language family. Because Greeks had established colonies around the coasts of the Black Sea, Herodotus was able to travel in this region, and his report, based primarily on information derived from Greek traders who traveled far inland and Scythian natives who interacted with the Greeks, is generally reliable. Some scholars have suggested that Herodotus is also employing the Scythians as a "mirror," emphasizing how different they were in lifestyle, culture, and values from the Greeks as an indirect way of highlighting aspects of Greek civilization.

For Herodotus, the fundamental quality of the Scythians was that they were nomads, people without cities or permanent homes who migrated with their herds of sheep, goats, and cattle and their prized horses, transporting their few possessions and living in carts. They belonged to tribal kinship groups ruled by kings. They are depicted as exceedingly warlike and savage; their chief god is equated with the Greek god of war, Ares, and they are said to drink the blood of their enemies, to cut off their enemies' heads as trophies, and to make goblets out of the skulls and napkins and coats from the skins. They had no images of the gods, no shrines and no altars, and employed a sacrificial ritual quite different from that of the Greeks that sometimes included human sacrifice. When their kings died, they were accompanied in the grave by murdered servants, guards, and horses. In an amusing passage, Herodotus betrays his puzzlement at how they threw brush (presumably cannabis, the plant source for marijuana) on a fire and appeared to be drunk, and how they cleaned their bodies by cavorting in cannabis steam baths. Herodotus also makes clear that not all Scythians were strictly nomadic; some engaged in a mixed pastoral and agricultural economy, and some (perhaps influenced by the nearby Greek settlers) were settled agriculturalists. These observations reinforce the idea that nomadic pastoralists required some form of access to agricultural peoples and the food and goods that they produced.

Herodotus then describes what he sees as the disastrous attempt of the Persian king Darius to invade the lands of the Scythians at the end of the sixth century B.C.E. Because the Scythians lacked permanent settlements and cultivated fields, there were no obvious targets for the Persians to attack and hold hostage. And because the nomads were exceedingly mobile, they were able to move away from the invaders, drawing them ever further into unknown territory and practicing a "scorched earth" policy of burning the grass and destroying the wells. They clearly felt that there was no shame in retreating, and when, at one point, the Persians were finally drawn up for battle with a contingent of Scythian troops, a hare darted across an open space and all the Scythians took off in pursuit of it. At this point, the Persian king realized that the Scythians were toying with him, and it was all he could do to make a successful escape home with part of his army. Herodotus is obviously taking pleasure at the discomfiture of the powerful Persians, and he may misunderstand Darius's purpose in the invasion—to drive the Scythians far from Persian-controlled lands. Nevertheless, he has brilliantly illustrated the unique difficulties that nomads presented to even powerful ancient states and empires, many of whom found it cheaper to just buy off the nomads by giving them "gifts" in return for not attacking.

China and the Nomads

Chinese sources provide glimpses of the nomadic peoples living at the other end of the Eurasian Steppes, and these accounts usually match up very closely with those of Herodotus and other Greek and Roman sources, proving the relative cultural and technological uniformity of the Eurasian steppe nomads. Again, it appears that an economy based on pastoral nomadism was taking shape on the steppes in central and eastern Asia in the early first millennium B.C.E. As the Chinese states of the Spring and Autumn and Warring States periods came under increasing pressure from raiding by swift-moving, horse-borne warriors, they began to build walls along their northern frontiers to keep the raiders out, and in the late fourth century B.C.E. the forward-thinking ruler of the state of Zhao took the unprecedented step of outfitting some of his troops with trousers and mounting them on horseback.

Sima Qian Chief astrologer for the Han dynasty emperor Wu. He composed a monumental history of China from its legendary origins to his own time and is regarded as the Chinese "father of history."

Our fullest Chinese account of the northern nomads comes from **Sima Qian (Sih-muh Chyen)** (ca. 100 B.C.E.), who in many ways corresponds to Herodotus as "the father of history" in East Asia. Like Herodotus, he may have been using his description of the Xiongnu **(Shawng-noo)** nomads to highlight characteristic aspects of Chinese civilization. Sima Qian served at the court of the Han emperor Wu and therefore had access to records in the imperial archives and earlier historical texts, as well as some experience traveling on official business among the barbarians.

Sima Qian reports that the Xiongnu had no cities, no fixed dwellings, no agriculture, and no writing. They migrated with their herds to pastures and sources of water. They were trained as warriors from an early age, and for this reason the young and fit were given preference over the old and useless. Though tough and warlike by nature, they felt no shame in retreating when necessary. Their armies lacked discipline and order, and they largely fought for their own personal gain. They swooped in like birds and vanished just as quickly, and they cut off the heads of their vanquished enemies. As with the Scythians, human sacrifice was a component of royal funerals. In Sima Qian's account, a former Chinese official who has defected to the nomads points out that, unlike the Chinese, their lives are simple and unencumbered by excessive rules, rituals, or bureaucracy. Again, the Xiongnu either controlled or were allied to groups that practiced agriculture, which gave them access to items they could not produce themselves. Many scholars believe that the Xiongnu and several other nomadic peoples on the East Asian steppe spoke Turkic languages, while the Yuezhi **(Yweh-juhr)**, located further west, spoke an Indo-European language.

In addition to information from ancient texts like those of Herodotus and Sima Qian, archaeological excavation has illuminated our understanding of the culture of pastoral nomads. Because of the lack of permanent settlements, the primary targets of archaeology have been the large burial mounds of the elite. In a number of cases the permafrost of Siberia has preserved materials, such as textiles, that normally do not survive in the archaeological record. The art of the nomads—mainly golden jewelry, horse fittings, and colorful carpets and other textiles—is beautiful to the modern eye, with its emphasis on animals, real and fantastic, often shown in combat and in twisting, interlocked poses that conform gracefully to the surface on which they are displayed.

- Humans were all nomadic until the Agricultural Revolutions, but the domestication of animals made possible the rise of a new form of pastoral nomadism.

- After 1000 B.C.E. pastoral nomads dominated the vast Eurasian Steppes but still needed goods produced by farming peoples, which they obtained by trading or raiding.

- Our information about the ancient steppe nomads comes primarily from archaeology and the accounts of Greek, Roman, and Chinese texts.

- The toughness and mobility of nomadic peoples posed a major challenge to states and empires.

As we will see in subsequent chapters, the nomadic pastoralists of the steppe were, at the least, a constant nuisance to the sedentary agricultural peoples living on their borders. Under normal circumstances the relatively small, fractious tribal groups were as prone to fight each other as to raid the lands and possessions of the farmers in neighboring areas. However, from time to time they united in great confederacies under charismatic leaders, and then they presented a serious military threat even to great states and empires. The Han Chinese emperors would be at war for centuries with the Xiongnu; the Parthians would take over Iran and much of Mesopotamia and become Rome's only great-power rival (see Chapter 6); the late Roman Empire would be hard-pressed by Avars and Huns; and in the medieval period the Mongols and several Turkic peoples would overrun most of Asia (see Chapter 13). While nomadism has become increasingly rare in the industrialized and urbanized modern world, it has been estimated that 30 to 40 million people still practice this ancient way of life, primarily in Central Asia and the West African Sahel region.

CELTIC EUROPE, 1000–50 B.C.E.

The southern peninsulas of Europe—present-day Spain, Italy, and Greece—share in the mild climate of all the Mediterranean lands and are separated from "continental" Europe to the north by high mountains (the Pyrenees and Alps). Consequently, the history of southern Europe in antiquity is primarily connected to that of the Mediterranean and Middle East, at least until the Roman conquests north of the Alps (see Chapters 3, 5, and 6).

Continental Europe (including the modern nations of France, Germany, Switzerland, Austria, the Czech Republic, Slovakia, Hungary, Poland, and Romania—see Map 4.4)—was well suited to agriculture and herding. It contained broad plains with good soil and had a temperate climate with cold winters, warm summers, and ample rainfall. It was well endowed with natural resources such as timber and metals, and large, navigable rivers facilitated travel and trade.

Humans had lived in this part of Europe for many thousands of years (see Chapter 1), but their lack of any system of writing severely limits our knowledge of the earliest inhabitants. Around 500 B.C.E., as Celtic peoples spread from their original homeland across a substantial portion of Europe, they came into contact with the literate societies of the Mediterranean and thereby entered the historical record. Information about the early **Celts** (kelts) comes from the archaeological record, the accounts of Greek and Roman travelers and conquerors, and the oral traditions of Celtic Wales and Ireland that were written down during the European Middle Ages.

Celts Peoples sharing common linguistic and cultural features that originated in central Europe in the first half of the first millennium B.C.E.

The Spread of the Celts

The term *Celtic* refers to a branch of the large Indo-European family of languages found throughout Europe and in western and southern Asia. Scholars link the Celtic language group to archaeological remains first appearing in parts of present-day Germany, Austria, and the Czech Republic after 1000 B.C.E. (see Map 4.4). Many early Celts lived in or near hill-forts—lofty natural locations made more defensible by earthwork fortifications. By 500 B.C.E. Celtic elites were trading with Mediterranean societies for crafted goods and wine. This contact may have stimulated the new styles of Celtic manufacture and art that appeared at this time.

These new cultural features coincided with a period in which Celtic groups migrated to many parts of Europe. The motives behind these population movements, the precise timing, and the manner in which they were carried out are not well understood. Celts occupied nearly all of France and much of Britain and Ireland, and they merged with indigenous peoples to create the Celtiberian culture of northern Spain. Other Celtic groups overran northern Italy (they sacked Rome in 490 B.C.E.), raided into central Greece, and settled in central Anatolia (modern

MAP 4.4 **The Celtic Peoples** Celtic civilization originated in central Europe in the early part of the first millennium B.C.E. Around 500 B.C.E. Celtic peoples began to migrate, making Celtic civilization the dominant cultural style in Europe north of the Alps. The Celts' interactions with the peoples of the Mediterranean, including Greeks and Romans, involved both warfare and trade. Adapted from Atlas of Classical History, Fifth Edition, by Michael Grant. © Cengage Learning

Turkey). By 300 B.C.E. Celtic peoples were spread across Europe north of the Alps, from present-day Hungary to Spain and Ireland. Their traces remain in many place names in Europe today.

These widely diffused Celtic groups shared elements of language and culture, but there was no Celtic "nation," for they were divided into hundreds of small, loosely organized kinship groups. In the past scholars built up a generic picture of Celtic society derived largely from the observations of Greek and Roman writers. Current scholarship is focusing attention on the differences as much as the similarities among Celtic peoples. It is unlikely that the ancient Celts identified themselves as belonging to anything akin to our modern conception of "Celtic civilization."

Greek and Roman writers were struck by the appearance of male Celts—their burly size, long red hair, shaggy mustaches, and loud, deep voices—and by their strange apparel, trousers (usually an indication of horse-riding peoples) and twisted gold neck collars. Particularly terrifying were the warriors who fought naked and made trophies of the heads of defeated enemies. Surviving accounts describe the Celts as wildly fond of war, courageous, childishly impulsive and emotional, and fond of boasting and exaggeration, yet quick-witted and eager to learn.

Celtic Society

One of the best sources of information about Celtic society is the account of the Roman general Gaius Julius Caesar, who conquered Gaul (present-day France) between 58 and 51 B.C.E. Many Celtic groups in Gaul had once been ruled by kings, but by the time of the Roman invasion they periodically chose public officials, perhaps under Greek and Roman influence.

Celtic society was divided into an elite class of warriors, professional groups of priests and bards (singers of poems about glorious deeds of the past), and commoners. The warriors owned land and flocks of cattle and sheep and monopolized both wealth and power. The common people labored on their land. The Celts built houses (usually round in Britain, rectangular in France) out of wattle and daub—a wooden framework filled in with clay and straw—with thatched straw

103

© Crown copyright. EH

Celtic Hill-Fort in England Hundreds of these fortresses have been found across Europe. They served as centers of administration, gathering points for Celtic armies, manufacturing centers, storage depots for food and trade goods, and places of refuge. The natural defense offered by a hill could be improved, as here, by the construction of ditches and earthwork walls. Particularly effective was the so-called Gallic Wall, made of a combination of earth, stone, and timber to create both strength and enough flexibility to absorb the pounding from siege engines.

Druids The class of religious experts who conducted rituals and preserved sacred lore among some ancient Celtic peoples.

roofs. Several such houses belonging to related families might be surrounded by a wooden fence for protection.

The warriors of Welsh and Irish legend reflect a stage of political and social development less complex than that of the Celts in Gaul. They raided one another's flocks, reveled in drunken feasts, and engaged in contests of strength and wit. At banquets warriors would fight to the death just to claim the choicest cut of the meat, the "hero's portion."

Druids, the Celtic priests in Gaul and Britain, formed a well-organized fraternity that performed religious, judicial, and educational functions. Trainees spent years memorizing prayers, secret rituals, legal precedents, and other traditions. The priesthood was the one Celtic institution that crossed tribal lines. The Druids sometimes headed off warfare between feuding groups and served as judges in cases involving Celts from different groups. In the first century C.E. the Roman government attempted to stamp out the Druids, probably because of concern that they might serve as a rallying point for Celtic opposition to Roman rule and also because of their involvement in human sacrifices.

The Celts supported large populations by tilling the heavy but fertile soils of continental Europe. Their metallurgical skills probably surpassed those of the Mediterranean peoples. Celts on the Atlantic shore of France built sturdy ships that braved ocean conditions, and they developed extensive trade networks along Europe's large, navigable rivers. One lucrative commodity was tin, which Celtic traders from southwest England brought to Greek buyers in southern France. By the first century B.C.E. some hill-forts were evolving into urban centers.

Women's lives were focused on child rearing, food production, and some crafts. Their situation was superior to that of women in the Middle East and in the Greek and Roman Mediterranean. Greek and Roman sources depict Celtic women as strong and proud. Welsh and Irish tales portray clever, self-assured women who sit at banquets with their husbands and engage in witty conversation. Marriage was a partnership to which both parties contributed property. Each had the right to inherit the estate if the other died. Celtic women also had greater freedom in their sexual relations than did their southern counterparts.

Tombs of elite women have yielded rich collections of clothing, jewelry, and furniture for use in the next world. Daughters of the elite were married to leading members of other tribes to create alliances. When the Romans invaded Celtic Britain in the first century C.E., they sometimes were opposed by Celtic tribes headed by queens, although some experts see this as an abnormal circumstance created by the Roman invasion itself.

Belief and Knowledge

Historians know the names of more than four hundred Celtic gods and goddesses, mostly associated with particular localities or kinship groups. More widely revered deities included Lug (loog), the god of light, crafts, and inventions; the horse-goddess Epona (eh-POH-nuh); and the horned god Cernunnos (KURN-you-nuhs). "The Mothers," three goddesses depicted together holding symbols of abundance, probably played a part in a fertility cult. Halloween and May Day preserve the ancient Celtic holidays of Samhain (SAH-win) and Beltaine (BEHL-tayn), respectively, which took place at key moments in the agricultural cycle.

The early Celts did not build temples but instead worshiped wherever they felt the presence of divinity—at springs, groves, and hilltops. At the sources of the Seine and Marne Rivers in

The Gundestrup Cauldron This silver vessel was found in a peat bog in Denmark, but it must have come from elsewhere. It is usually dated to the second or first century B.C.E. On the inside right are Celtic warriors on horse and on foot, with lozenge-shaped shields and long battle-horns. On the inside left is a horned deity, possibly Cernunnos. Universal History Archive/ Getty Images

SECTION REVIEW

- Around 500 B.C.E. Celtic-speaking peoples from central Europe began to spread across much of "continental" Europe.

- Most of what we know about the ancient Celts comes from archaeological discoveries and the written reports of Greek and Roman observers, who depict them as impulsive and fond of war.

- Celts lived in relatively small kinship (tribal) groups that were dominated by warrior elites. Hill-forts served as places of assembly and refuges.

- The Celts worshiped many gods in natural settings. The Druids, a priestly class in Gaul (France) and Britain, played a major role in religion, education, and intertribal legal matters.

- The Roman Empire's conquest of Celtic lands, followed later by Germanic invasions, pushed Celtic language and culture to the western edge of the European continent.

France, archaeologists have found huge caches of wooden statues thrown into the water by worshipers.

The burial of elite members of early Celtic society in wagons filled with extensive grave goods suggests belief in some sort of afterlife. In Irish and Welsh legends, heroes and gods pass back and forth between the natural and supernatural worlds much more readily than in the mythology of many other cultures, and magical occurrences are commonplace. Celtic priests set forth a doctrine of reincarnation—the rebirth of the soul in a new body.

The Roman conquest from the second century B.C.E. to the first century C.E. of Spain, southern Britain, France, and parts of central Europe curtailed the evolution of Celtic society, as the peoples in these lands were largely assimilated to Roman ways (see Chapter 6). As a result, the inhabitants of modern Spain and France speak languages that are descended from Latin. From the third century C.E. on, Germanic invaders weakened the Celts still further, and the English language has a Germanic base. Only on the western fringes of the European continent—in Brittany (northwest France), Wales, Scotland, and Ireland—did Celtic peoples maintain their language, art, and culture into modern times.

CONCLUSION

Environment and Organization

The civilizations of early China, Nubia, the Eurasian Steppes, and the Celts emerged in very different ecological contexts in widely separated parts of the Eastern Hemisphere, and the patterns of organization, technology, behavior, and belief that they developed were, in large part, responses to the challenges and opportunities of those environments.

In the North China Plain, as in the river-valley civilizations of Mesopotamia and Egypt, the presence of great, flood-prone rivers and the lack of dependable rainfall led to the formation of powerful institutions capable of organizing large numbers of people to dig and maintain irrigation channels and build dikes. An authoritarian central government has been a recurring feature of Chinese history from at least as early as the Shang monarchy.

In Nubia, the initial impetus for the formation of a strong state was the need for protection from desert nomads and from the Egyptian rulers who coveted Nubian gold and other resources. Control of these resources and of the trade route between sub-Saharan Africa and the north, as well as the agricultural surplus to feed administrators and specialists in the urban centers, made the rulers and elites of Kerma, Napata, and Meroë wealthy and powerful.

Pastoral nomads found ways to exploit the challenging environment of the Eurasian Steppes. The very nature of their lifestyle, based on migrating with their herds of domesticated animals to seasonal camping grounds, meant that they had no permanent settlements and maintained small, kinship-based groups. Thus, under normal circumstances, their political organization was relatively simple. However, in moments of crisis or when a charismatic military leader came to the fore, they could unite in formidable confederacies.

The Celtic peoples of continental Europe never developed a strong state. They occupied fertile lands with adequate rainfall for agriculture, grazing territory for flocks, and timber for fuel and construction. Kinship groups dominated by warrior elites and controlling compact territories were the usual form of organization. The Celtic elites of central Europe initially traded for luxury goods with the Mediterranean; when they began to expand into lands to the west and south after 500 B.C.E., they came into even closer contact with Mediterranean peoples. Eventually many Celtic groups were incorporated into the Roman Empire.

Religion and Power

In these, as in most human societies, the elites used religion to bolster their position. The Shang rulers of China were indispensable intermediaries between their kingdom and powerful and protective ancestors and gods. Bronze vessels were used to make offerings to ancestral spirits, and divination by means of oracle bones delivered information of value to the ruler and kingdom. Their Zhou successors developed the concept of the ruler as divine Son of Heaven who ruled in accord with the Mandate of Heaven.

In its religious practices, as in other spheres, the civilization that developed in Nubia was powerfully influenced by its interactions with the more complex and technologically advanced neighboring society in Egypt. Nubian rulers built temples and pyramid tombs on the Egyptian model, but they also synthesized Egyptian and indigenous gods, beliefs, and rituals.

While not much is known about the religious beliefs and practices of the steppe nomads, their mobility and lack of permanent settlements may account for the fact that they didn't build monumental religious shrines. Greco-Roman and Chinese accounts report, and archaeology confirms, that they sacrificed animals, and sometimes human victims, to their gods. The elaborate goods found in elite burials imply belief in an afterlife, and shamans were able to make contact with the gods and the dead.

Among the Celtic peoples of Gaul and Britain, the Druids constituted an elite class of priests who performed vital religious, legal, and educational functions. However, the Celts did not construct temples and ceremonial centers, and instead worshiped hundreds of gods and goddesses in natural surroundings, where they felt the presence of divinity.

A Tale of Two Hemispheres

This chapter has moved beyond the core area of the two oldest complex human societies (Mesopotamia and Egypt), and the neighboring peoples who came under their cultural influence, to focus on East Asia, sub-Saharan Africa, continental Europe, and the vast steppe region linking Europe, Central, and East Asia. It thus continues the discussion of the rise of complex societies in the Eastern Hemisphere.

The societies in the other half of the world, the Western Hemisphere, are discussed in Chapter 8. These civilizations—the Olmec in Mesoamerica and Chavín in South America—while contemporary with the societies featured in this chapter, emerged several millennia later than the earliest complex societies in the Eastern Hemisphere. Scholars have debated why powerful civilizations appeared many centuries later in the Western Hemisphere than in the Eastern Hemisphere, and recent theories have focused on environmental differences. The Eastern Hemisphere was home to a far larger number of wild plant and animal species that were particularly well suited to domestication. In addition, the natural east-west axis of the huge landmass of Europe and Asia allowed for the relatively rapid spread of domesticated plants and animals to climatically similar zones along the same latitudes. Settled agriculture led to population growth, more complex political and social organization, and increased technological sophistication. In the Americas, by contrast, there were fewer wild plant and animal species that could be domesticated, and the north-south axis of the continents made it more difficult for domesticated species to spread because of variations in climate at different latitudes. As a result, the processes that foster the development of complex societies evolved somewhat more slowly.

KEY TERMS

loess p. 84
Shang p. 85
Zhou p. 88
Mandate of Heaven p. 89

Confucius p. 91
Daoism p. 91
yin/yang p. 94
Kush p. 96

Meroë p. 97
nomads p. 98
steppe p. 99
Herodotus p. 100

Scythians p. 100
Sima Qian p. 101
Celts p. 102
Druids p. 104

SUGGESTED READING

Blunden, Caroline, and Mark Elvin. *Cultural Atlas of China.* 1983. Contains general geographic, ethnographic, and historical information about China through the ages, as well as many maps and illustrations.

Cunliffe, Barry. *The Ancient Celts.* 2000. An archaeologically based survey covering the extensive range of Celtic civilization in antiquity.

Davis-Kimball, Jeannine, ed. *Nomads of the Eurasian Steppes in the Early Iron Age.* 1995. This volume, which covers the vast extent and many peoples of the steppes, makes available in English the fundamental work of Russian archaeologists.

de Bary, Wm Theodore, and Irene Bloom. *Sources of Chinese Tradition,* vol. 1, 2d ed. 1999. A superb collection of translated excerpts from a wide range of sources, accompanied by perceptive introductions.

Diamond, Jared. *Guns, Germs, and Steel: The Fates of Human Societies.* 1997. Tackles the difficult question of why technological development occurred at different times and took different paths in the Eastern and Western Hemispheres.

Di Cosmo, Nicola. *Ancient China and Its Enemies: The Rise of Nomadic Power in East Asian History.* 2002. Sets the development of Chinese civilization in the broader context of interactions with nomadic neighbors.

Fisher, Marjorie, et al., eds. *Ancient Nubia: African Kingdoms on the Nile.* 2012. The most up-to-date survey of Nubian civilization.

Green, Miranda J. *The Celtic World.* 1995. A large and comprehensive collection of articles on many aspects of Celtic civilization.

Hansen, Valerie. *The Open Empire: A History of China to 1600.* 2000. Devotes substantial attention to ancient China and emphasizes China's connections with other cultures.

James, Simon. *The World of the Celts.* 2005. A concise, well-illustrated introduction to ancient Celtic civilization.

Loewe, Michael, and Edward L. Shaughnessy. *The Cambridge History of Ancient China: From the Origins of Civilization to 221 BC.* 1999. A detailed account of the archaeology, history, and literature of pre-Imperial China, with chapters written by leading experts.

O'Connor, David. *Ancient Nubia: Egypt's Rival in Africa.* 1993. Informative, well-illustrated text based on a major exhibition of Nubian antiquities.

Reeder, Ellen. *Scythian Gold.* 1999. The catalogue for a museum exhibition of gold artifacts from Ukraine, it contains essays by various experts on Scythian culture and art, as well as beautiful photographs of the artifacts.

Taylor, John H. *Egypt and Nubia.* 1991. Emphasizes the fruitful interaction of the Egyptian and Nubian cultures.

Van Norden, Bryan W. *Introduction to Classical Chinese Philosophy.* 2011. A clear and wide-ranging introduction to early Chinese political, ethical, and spiritual thought.

Animal Domestication

Because the earliest domestication of plants and animals took place long before the existence of written records, we cannot be sure how and when humans first learned to plant crops and make use of tamed animals. Historians usually link the two processes as part of an Agricultural Revolution, but they were not necessarily connected.

The domestication of plants is much better understood than the domestication of animals. Foraging bands of humans primarily lived on wild seeds, fruits, and tubers. Eventually some humans tried planting seeds and tubers, favoring varieties that they particularly liked, and a variety that may have been rare in the wild became more common. When such a variety suited human needs, usually by having more food value or being easier to grow or process, people stopped collecting the wild types and relied on farming and further developing their new domestic type.

In the case of animals, the basis of selection to suit human needs is less apparent. Experts looking at ancient bones and images interpret changes in hair color, horn shape, and other visible features as indicators of domestication. But these visible changes did not generally serve human purposes. It is usually assumed that animals were domesticated for their meat, but even this is questionable. Dogs, which may have become domestic tens of thousands of years before any other species, were not eaten in most cultures, and cats, which became domestic much later, were eaten even less often. As for the uses most commonly associated with domestic animals, some of the most important, such as milking cows, shearing sheep, and harnessing oxen and horses to pull plows and vehicles, first appeared hundreds and even thousands of years after domestication.

Cattle, sheep, and goats became domestic around ten thousand years ago in the Middle East and North Africa. Coincidentally, wheat and barley were being domesticated at roughly the same time in the same general area. This is the main reason

Nomadic Pastoralists on the Eurasian Steppe The domestication of animals engendered a new form of nomadism, enabling certain populations to live in the treeless grasslands of the steppe and move with their animals and portable dwellings to a sequence of water sources and grazing grounds.

historians generally conclude that plant and animal domestication are closely related. Yet other major meat animals, such as chickens, which originated as jungle fowl in Southeast Asia, and pigs, which probably became domestic separately in several parts of North Africa, Europe, and Asia, have no agreed-upon association with early plant domestication. Nor is plant domestication connected with the horses and camels that became domestic in western Asia and the donkeys that became domestic in the Sahara region around six thousand years ago. Moreover, though the wild forebears of these species were probably eaten, the domestic forms were usually not used for meat.

In the Middle East humans may have originally kept wild sheep, goats, and cattle for food, though wild cattle were large and dangerous and must have been hard to control. It is questionable whether, in the earliest stages, keeping these animals captive for food would have been more productive than hunting. It is even more questionable whether the humans who kept animals for this purpose had any reason to anticipate that life in captivity would cause them to become domestic.

Human motivations for domesticating animals can be better assessed after a consideration of the physical changes involved in going from wild to domestic. Genetically transmitted tameness, defined as the ability to live with and accept handling by humans, lies at the core of the domestication process. In separate experiments with wild rats and foxes in the twentieth century, scientists found that wild individuals with strong fight-or-flight tendencies reproduce poorly in captivity, whereas individuals with the lowest adrenaline levels have the most offspring in captivity. In the wild, the same low level of excitability would have made these individuals vulnerable to predators and kept their reproduction rate down. However, early humans probably preferred the animals that seemed the tamest and destroyed those that were most wild. In the rat and fox experiments, after twenty generations or so, the surviving animals were born with much smaller adrenal glands and greatly reduced fight-or-flight reactions. Since adrenaline production normally increases in the transition to adulthood, many of the low-adrenaline animals also retained juvenile characteristics, such as floppy ears and pushed-in snouts, both indicators of domestication.

Historians disagree about whether animal domestication was a deliberate process or the unanticipated outcome of keeping animals for other purposes. Some assume that domestication was an understood and reproducible process. Others argue that, since a twenty-generation time span for wild cattle and other large quadrupeds would have amounted to several human lifetimes, it is unlikely that the people who ended up with domestic cows had any recollection of how the process started. This would also rule out the possibility that people who had unwittingly domesticated one species would have attempted to repeat the process with other species, since they did not know what they and their ancestors had done to produce genetically transmitted tameness.

Historians who assume that domestication was an understood and reproducible process tend to conclude that humans domesticated every species that could be domesticated. This is unlikely. Twentieth-century efforts to domesticate bison, eland, and elk have not fully succeeded, but they have generally not been maintained for as long as twenty generations. Rats and foxes have more rapid reproduction rates, and the experiments with them succeeded.

Animal domestication is probably best studied on a case-by-case basis as an unintended result of other processes. In some instances, sacrifice probably played a key role. Religious traditions of animal sacrifice rarely utilize, and sometimes prohibit, the ritual killing of wild animals. It is reasonable to suppose that the practice of capturing wild animals and holding them for sacrifice eventually led to the appearance of genetically transmitted tameness as an unplanned result.

Horses and camels were domesticated relatively late, and most likely not for meat consumption. The societies within which these animals first appeared as domestic species already had domestic sheep, goats, and cattle for meat, and they used oxen to carry loads and pull plows and carts. Horses, camels, and later reindeer may represent successful experiments with substituting one draft animal for another, with genetically transmitted tameness an unexpected consequence of separating animals trained for riding or pulling carts from their wilder kin.

Once human societies had developed the full range of uses of domestic animals—meat, eggs, milk, fiber, labor, transport—the likelihood of domesticating more species diminished. In the absence of concrete knowledge of how domestication had occurred, it was usually easier for people to move domestic livestock to new locations than to attempt to develop new domestic species. Domestic animals accompanied human groups wherever they ventured, and this practice triggered enormous environmental changes as domestic animals, and their human keepers, competed with wild species for food and living space.

CHAPTER 5   Greece and Iran, 1000–30 B.C.E.

CHAPTER 6   An Age of Empires: Rome and Han China, 753 B.C.E.–330 C.E.

CHAPTER 7   India and Southeast Asia, 1500 B.C.E.–1025 C.E.

CHAPTER 8   Peoples and Civilizations of the Americas, from 1200 B.C.E.

DeA Picture Library/Art Resource, NY

Map of the Roman World, ca. 250 C.E.   The Peutinger Table, drawn on a 22-foot-long manuscript of the twelfth century C.E., is ultimately derived from a map of the world as known to inhabitants of the Roman Empire ca. 100 C.E.. This portion depicts (from top to bottom) southern Russia, Greece on the left, Anatolia on the right, the island of Crete, and the north coast of Africa. The main purpose appears to have been to show roads and distances, and sizes and geographical relationships of places are often distorted.

The Formation of New Cultural Communities, 1000 B.C.E.–400 C.E.

From 1000 B.C.E. to 400 C.E. important changes occurred in the ways of life established in the river-valley civilizations in the two previous millennia, and the scale of human institutions and activities increased. On the shores of the Mediterranean and in Iran, India, and Southeast Asia, new centers arose in lands watered by rainfall and worked by a free peasantry. Similarly, in the Americas new political and religious centers developed in southern Mesoamerica and in the Andes. These societies developed new patterns of political and social organization and economic activity, at the same time moving in new intellectual, artistic, and spiritual directions.

The rulers of the empires of this era constructed extensive networks of roads and promoted urbanization, measures that brought more rapid communication, trade over greater distances, and the broad diffusion of religious ideas, artistic styles, and technologies. Large cultural zones unified by common traditions emerged—Iranian, Hellenistic, Roman, Hindu, Mesoamerican, Andean, and Chinese—and exercised substantial influence on subsequent ages.

The expansion of agriculture and trade and improvements in technology led to population increases, the spread of cities, and the growth of new social classes. In many places iron replaced bronze as the preferred metal for weapons, tools, and utensils, and metals were available to more people than in the preceding age. People using iron tools cleared extensive forests around the Mediterranean, in India, and in eastern China, while iron weapons gave an advantage to the armies of Greece, Rome, and imperial China. Progress in metallurgy developed much more slowly in the Americas. Copper and copper-alloy production developed first in the Andes and only reached Mesoamerica after 500 C.E. Iron was only introduced with the arrival of Europeans.

New systems of writing, more easily and rapidly learned, moved the preservation and transmission of knowledge out of the control of specialists and gave birth to new ways of thinking, new genres of literature, and new types of scientific endeavor.

Chapter Outline

Ancient Iran, 1000–500 B.C.E.
➤ *How did the Persian Empire rise from its Iranian homeland and succeed in controlling vast territories and diverse cultures?*

The Rise of the Greeks, 1000–500 B.C.E.
➤ *What were the most distinctive elements of Greek civilization, and how and why did they evolve in the Archaic and Classical periods?*

The Struggle of Persia and Greece, 546–323 B.C.E.
➤ *How did the Persian Wars and their aftermath affect the politics and culture of ancient Greece and Iran?*

The Hellenistic Synthesis, 323–30 B.C.E.
➤ *How did Greeks and non-Greeks interact and develop new cultural syntheses during the Hellenistic Age?*

Conclusion

- **DIVERSITY + DOMINANCE** Persian and Greek Perceptions of Kingship
- **MATERIAL CULTURE** Wine and Beer in the Ancient World
- **ENVIRONMENT + TECHNOLOGY** Ancient Astronomy

Painted Cup of Arcesilas of Cyrene The ruler of this Greek community in North Africa supervises the weighing and export of silphium, a valuable medicinal plant.

Greek cup depicting Arcesilas II, King of Cyrene (c.560-550 BC) watching the weighing and loading of silphium, copy of a 6th century BC original (colour litho), French School, (19th century) / Bibliotheque Nationale, Paris, France/Archives Charmet/The Bridgeman Art Library

Greece and Iran, 1000–30 B.C.E.

The Greek historian Herodotus (heh-ROD-uh-tuhs) (ca. 485–425 B.C.E.) describes a famine on the island of Thera in the Aegean Sea in the seventh century B.C.E. that caused the desperate inhabitants to send out a portion of young men to found a new settlement called Cyrene on the coast of North Africa (modern Libya). This is one of our best descriptions of the process by which Greeks spread from their homeland to many parts of the Mediterranean and Black Seas between the eighth and sixth centuries B.C.E., carrying their language, technology, and culture with them. Cyrene became a populous and prosperous city-state, largely thanks to its exports of silphium—a plant valued for its medicinal properties—as seen on this painted cup with an image of Arcesilas, the ruler of Cyrene, supervising the weighing and transport of the product.

Greek Cyrene quietly submitted to the Persian king Cambyses (kam-BIE-sees) in the 520s B.C.E., in one of the more peaceful encounters of the city-states of Greece with the Persian Empire. This event reminds us that the Persian Empire (and the Hellenistic Greek kingdoms that succeeded it) brought together, in eastern Europe, western Asia, and northwest Africa, peoples and cultural systems that had little direct contact previously, thereby stimulating new cultural syntheses. The claim has often been made that the rivalry and wars of Greeks and Persians from the sixth to fourth centuries B.C.E. were the first act of a drama that has continued intermittently ever since: the clash of the civilizations of East and West, of two peoples and two ways of life that were fundamentally different and almost certain to come into conflict. Some see current tensions between the United States and Middle Eastern states such as Iran, Iraq, and Afghanistan as the latest manifestation of this age-old conflict.

Ironically, Greeks and Persians had more in common than they realized. Both spoke languages belonging to the same Indo-European language family found throughout Europe and western and southern Asia. Many scholars believe that all the ancient peoples who spoke languages belonging to this family inherited fundamental cultural traits, forms of social organization, and religious outlooks from their shared past.

ANCIENT IRAN, 1000–500 B.C.E.

Iran, the "land of the Aryans," links western Asia with southern and Central Asia, and its history has been marked by this mediating position (see Map 5.1). In the sixth century B.C.E. the vigorous Persians of southwest Iran created the largest empire the world had yet seen. Heirs to the long legacy of Mesopotamian culture, they introduced distinctly Iranian elements and developed new forms of political and economic organization in western Asia.

Relatively little written material from within the Persian Empire has survived, so we are forced to view it mostly through the eyes of the ancient Greeks—outsiders who were ignorant at best, often hostile, and interested primarily in events that affected themselves. (Iranian groups and individuals are known in the Western world by Greek approximations of their names; thus these familiar forms are used here, with the original Iranian names given in parentheses.) This Greek perspective leaves us less informed about developments in the central and eastern portions of the Persian Empire. Nevertheless, recent archaeological discoveries and close analysis of the limited written material from within the empire can supplement and correct the perspective of the Greek sources.

Geography and Resources

Iran is bounded by the Zagros (ZUHG-roes) Mountains to the west, the Caucasus (KAW-kuh-suhs) Mountains and Caspian Sea to the northwest and north, the mountains of Afghanistan and the desert of Baluchistan (buh-loo-chi-STAN) to the east and southeast, and the Persian Gulf to the southwest. The northeast is less protected by natural boundaries, and from that direction Iran was open to attacks by the nomads of Central Asia.

The fundamental topographical features of Iran are high mountains at the edges, salt deserts in the interior depressions, and mountain streams draining into interior salt lakes and marshes. Ancient Iran never had a dense population. The best-watered and most populous parts of the country lie to the north and west; aridity increases and population decreases as one moves south and east. On the interior plateau, oasis settlements sprang up beside streams or springs. The Great Salt Desert, which covers most of eastern Iran, and Baluchistan in the southeast corner were extremely inhospitable. Scattered settlements in the narrow plains beside the Persian Gulf were cut off from the interior plateau by mountain barriers.

In the first millennium B.C.E. irrigation enabled people to move down from the mountain valleys and open the plains to agriculture. To prevent evaporation of precious water in the hot, dry climate, they devised underground irrigation channels. Constructing and maintaining these channels and the vertical shafts that provided access to them was labor-intensive. Normally, local leaders oversaw the expansion of the network in each district. Activity accelerated when a strong central authority organized large numbers of laborers. Even so, human survival

MAP 5.1 **The Persian Empire Between 550 and 522** B.C.E. The Persians of southwest Iran, under their first two kings, Cyrus and Cambyses, conquered each of the major states of western Asia—Media, Babylonia, Lydia, and Egypt. The third king, Darius I, extended the boundaries as far as the Indus Valley to the east and the European shore of the Black Sea to the west. The first major setback came when the fourth king, Xerxes, failed in his invasion of Greece in 480 B.C.E. The Persian Empire was considerably larger than its predecessor, the Assyrian Empire. For their empire, the Persian rulers developed a system of provinces, governors, regular tribute, and communication by means of royal roads and couriers that allowed for efficient operations for two centuries. © Cengage Learning

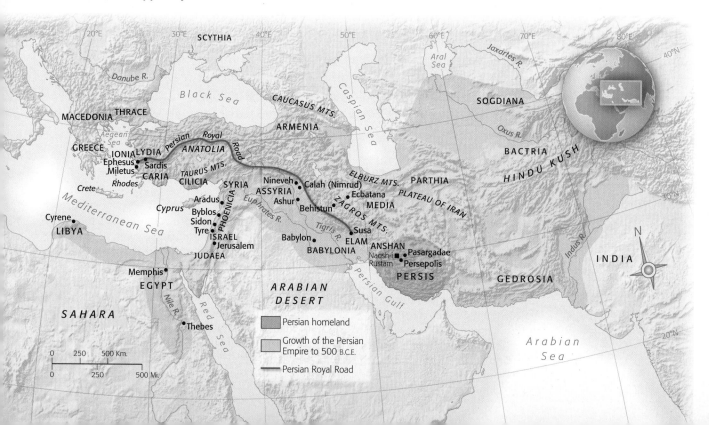

CHRONOLOGY

	Greece and the Hellenistic World	Persian Empire
1000 B.C.E.	1150–800 B.C.E. Greece's "Dark Age"	ca. 1000 B.C.E. Persians settle in southwest Iran
800 B.C.E.	ca. 800 B.C.E. Resumption of Greek contact with eastern Mediterranean 800–480 B.C.E. Greece's Archaic period ca. 750–550 B.C.E. Era of colonization ca. 700 B.C.E. Beginning of hoplite warfare ca. 650–500 B.C.E. Era of tyrants	
600 B.C.E.	594 B.C.E. Solon reforms laws at Athens 546–510 B.C.E. Pisistratus and sons hold tyranny at Athens	550 B.C.E. Cyrus overthrows Medes 550–530 B.C.E. Reign of Cyrus 546 B.C.E. Cyrus conquers Lydia 539 B.C.E. Cyrus takes control of Babylonia 530–522 B.C.E. Reign of Cambyses; Conquest of Egypt 522–486 B.C.E. Reign of Darius
500 B.C.E.	499–494 B.C.E. Ionian Greeks rebel against Persia 490 B.C.E. Athenians check Persian punitive expedition at Marathon 480–323 B.C.E. Greece's Classical period 477 B.C.E. Athens becomes leader of Delian League 461–429 B.C.E. Pericles dominant at Athens; Athens completes evolution to democracy 431–404 B.C.E. Peloponnesian War	480–479 B.C.E. Xerxes' invasion of Greece
400 B.C.E.	399 B.C.E. Trial and execution of Socrates 359 B.C.E. Philip II becomes king of Macedonia 338 B.C.E. Philip takes control of Greece	387 B.C.E. King's Peace makes Persia arbiter of Greek affairs 334–323 B.C.E. Alexander the Great defeats Persia and creates huge empire 323–30 B.C.E. Hellenistic period
300 B.C.E.	ca. 300 B.C.E. Foundation of the Museum in Alexandria 200 B.C.E. First Roman intervention in the Hellenistic East	
100 B.C.E.	30 B.C.E. Roman annexation of Egypt, the last Hellenistic kingdom	

depended on a delicate ecological balance, and a buildup of salt in the soil or a falling water table sometimes forced the abandonment of settlements.

Iran's mineral resources—copper, tin, iron, gold, and silver—were exploited on a limited scale in antiquity. Mountain slopes, more heavily wooded than they are now, provided fuel and materials for building and crafts. Because this austere land could not generate much of an agricultural surplus, objects of trade tended to be minerals and crafted goods such as textiles and carpets.

The Rise of the Persian Empire

In antiquity many groups of people, whom historians refer to collectively as "Iranians" because they spoke related languages and shared certain cultural features, spread across western and Central Asia—an area comprising not only the modern state of Iran but also Turkmenistan, Afghanistan, and Pakistan. Several of these groups arrived in western Iran near the end of the second millennium B.C.E. The first to achieve a complex level of political organization were the Medes (*Mada* in Iranian). They settled in the northwest and came under the influence of the ancient centers in Mesopotamia and Urartu (modern Armenia and northeast Turkey). The Medes played a major role in the destruction of the Assyrian Empire in the late seventh century B.C.E. According to Greek sources, Median kings extended their control westward across Assyria into Anatolia (modern Turkey) and also southeast toward the Persian Gulf, a region occupied by another Iranian people, the Persians (*Parsa*). However, some scholars doubt the Greek testimony about a well-organized Median kingdom controlling such extensive territories.

The Persian rulers—called Achaemenids (a-KEY-muh-nid) because they traced their lineage back to an ancestor named Achaemenes—cemented their relationship with the Median court through marriage. **Cyrus** (*Kurush*), the son of a Persian chieftain and a Median princess, united the various Persian tribes and overthrew the Median monarch around 550 B.C.E. His victory should perhaps be seen less as a conquest than as an alteration of the relations between groups, for Cyrus placed both Medes and Persians in positions of responsibility and retained the framework of Median rule. The differences between these two Iranian peoples were not great, and the Greeks could not readily tell them apart.

The early inhabitants of western Iran had a patriarchal family organization: the male head of the household had nearly absolute authority over family members. Society was divided into three social and occupational classes—warriors, priests, and peasants—with warriors being the dominant element. A landowning aristocracy, they took pleasure in hunting, fighting, and gardening. The king was the most illustrious member of this group. The priests, or Magi (*magush*), were ritual specialists who supervised the proper performance of sacrifices. The common people—peasants— were primarily village-based farmers and shepherds.

Over the course of two decades the energetic Cyrus (r. 550–530 B.C.E.) redrew the map of western Asia. In 546 B.C.E. he defeated the kingdom of Lydia, and all Anatolia, including the Greek city-states on the western coast, came under Persian control. In 539 B.C.E. he swept into Mesopotamia and overthrew the Neo-Babylonian dynasty that had ruled since the decline of Assyrian power (see Chapter 3). A skillful propagandist, Cyrus showed respect to the Babylonian priesthood and native traditions.

After Cyrus lost his life in 530 B.C.E. while campaigning against nomadic Iranians in the northeast, his son Cambyses (*Kambujiya*, r. 530–522 B.C.E.) set his sights on Egypt, the last of the great ancient kingdoms of the Middle East. After the Persians prevailed in a series of bloody battles, they sent exploratory expeditions south to Nubia and west to Libya. Greek sources depict Cambyses as a cruel and impious madman, but contemporary documents from Egypt show him operating in the same practical vein as his father, cultivating local priests and notables and respecting native traditions.

When Cambyses died in 522 B.C.E., a Persian nobleman distantly related to the royal family, **Darius I** (duh-RIE-uhs) (*Darayavaush*), seized the throne. His success in crushing many early challenges to his rule testifies to his skill, energy, and ruthlessness. From this reign forward, Medes played a lesser role, and the most important posts went to members of leading Persian families. Darius (r. 522–486 B.C.E.) extended Persian control eastward as far as the Indus Valley and westward into Europe, where he bridged the Danube River and chased the nomadic Scythian (SITH-ee-uhn) peoples north of the Black Sea. The Persians erected a string of forts in Thrace (modern-day

Cyrus Founder of the Achaemenid Persian Empire. Between 550 and 530 B.C.E. he conquered Media, Lydia, and Babylon. Revered in the traditions of both Iran and the subject peoples, he employed Persians and Medes in his administration and respected the institutions and beliefs of subject peoples.

Darius I Third ruler of the Persian Empire (r. 522–486 B.C.E.). He crushed the widespread initial resistance to his rule and gave major government posts to Persians rather than to Medes. He established a system of provinces and tribute, began construction of Persepolis, and expanded Persian control in the east (Pakistan) and west (northern Greece).

Gold Model of Four-Horse Chariot from the Eastern Achaemenid Empire This model is part of the Oxus Treasure, a cache of gold and silver objects discovered in Tajikistan. Seated on a bench next to the chariot driver, the main figure wears a long robe, a hood, and a torque around his neck, the garb of a Persian noble. It is uncertain whether this model was a child's toy or a votive offering to a deity.

Erich Lessing/Art Resource, NY

northeast Greece and Bulgaria) and by 500 B.C.E. were on the doorstep of Greece. Darius also promoted the development of maritime routes. He dispatched a fleet to explore the waters from the Indus Delta to the Red Sea, and he completed a canal linking the Red Sea with the Nile.

Imperial Organization

The empire of Darius I was the largest the world had yet seen (see Map 5.1). Stretching from eastern Europe and Libya to Pakistan, from southern Russia to Sudan, it encompassed multiple ethnic groups and many forms of social and political organization. Darius can rightly be considered a second founder of the Persian Empire, after Cyrus, because he created a new organizational structure that was maintained throughout the remaining two centuries of the empire's existence.

Darius divided the empire into about twenty provinces, each under the supervision of a Persian **satrap** (SAY-trap), or governor, who was often related or connected by marriage to the royal family. The satrap's court was a miniature version of the royal court. The tendency for the position of satrap to become hereditary meant that satraps' families lived in the province governed by their head, acquired knowledge about local conditions, and formed connections with the local elite. The farther a province was from the center of the empire, the more autonomy the satrap had, because slow communications made it impractical to refer most matters to the central administration.

One of the satrap's most important duties was to collect and send tribute to the king. Darius prescribed how much precious metal each province was to contribute annually. Some of it was disbursed for necessary expenditures, but most was hoarded. As precious metal was taken out of circulation, the price of gold and silver rose, and provinces found it increasingly difficult to meet their quotas. Evidence from Babylonia indicates a gradual economic decline setting in by the fourth century B.C.E. The increasing burden of taxation and official corruption may have inadvertently caused the economic downturn.

Well-maintained and patrolled royal roads connected the outlying provinces to the heart of the empire. Way stations were built at intervals to receive important travelers and couriers carrying official correspondence. Military garrisons controlled strategic points, such as mountain passes, river crossings, and important urban centers.

The king had numerous wives and children. Women of the royal family could become pawns in the struggle for power, as when Darius strengthened his claim to the throne by marrying two daughters and a granddaughter of Cyrus. Greek sources portray Persian queens as vicious intriguers, poisoning rival wives and plotting to win the throne for their sons. However, a recent study suggests that the Greek stereotype misrepresents the important role played by Persian women in protecting family members and mediating conflicts.[1] Both Greek sources and documents within the empire reveal that Persian elite women were politically influential, possessed substantial property, traveled, and were prominent on public occasions.

The king and his court moved with the seasons, living in luxurious tents on the road and in palaces in the ancient capitals of Mesopotamia and Iran. Besides the royal family, the king's large entourage included several other groups: (1) the sons of Persian aristocrats, who were educated at court and also served as hostages for their parents' good behavior; (2) many noblemen, who were expected to attend the king when they were not otherwise engaged; (3) the central administration, including officials and employees of the treasury, secretariat, and archives; (4) the royal bodyguard; and (5) countless courtiers and slaves. Long gone were the simple days when the king hunted and caroused with his warrior companions. Inspired by Mesopotamian conceptions of monarchy, the king of Persia had become an aloof figure of majesty and splendor: "The Great King, King of Kings, King in Persia, King of countries." He referred to everyone, even the Persian nobility, as "my slaves," and anyone who approached him had to bow down before him.

The king owned vast tracts of land throughout the empire. Some of it he gave to his supporters. Donations called "bow land," "horse land," and "chariot land" in Babylonian documents obliged the recipient to provide the corresponding form of military service. Scattered around the empire were gardens, orchards, and hunting preserves belonging to the king and high nobility. The *paradayadam* (meaning "walled enclosure"—the term has come into English as *paradise*), a green oasis in an arid landscape, advertised the prosperity that the king could bring to those who loyally served him.

Surviving administrative records from the Persian homeland reveal how the complex tasks of administration were managed. Government officials distributed food and other essential

satrap The governor of a province in the Achaemenid Persian Empire, often a relative of the king. He was responsible for protection of the province and for forwarding tribute to the central administration. Satraps in outlying provinces enjoyed considerable autonomy.

[1]Maria Brosius, *Women in Ancient Persia, 559–331 B.C.* (Oxford and New York: Oxford University Press, 1996).

commodities to large numbers of workers of many different nationalities. Some of these workers may have been prisoners of war brought to the center of the empire to work on construction projects, maintain and expand the irrigation network, and farm the royal estates. Workers were divided into groups of men, women, and children. Women received less than men of equivalent status, but pregnant women and women with babies received additional support. Men and women performing skilled jobs received more than their unskilled counterparts. Administrators were provided with authorizations to requisition food and other necessities while traveling on official business.

The central administration was not based in the Persian homeland but closer to the geographical center of the empire, in Elam and Mesopotamia, where it could employ the trained administrators and scribes of those ancient civilizations. The administrative center of the empire was Susa, the ancient capital of Elam, in southwest Iran near the present-day border with Iraq. It was to Susa that Greeks and others went with requests and messages for the king. A party of Greek ambassadors would need at least three months to make the journey. Additional time spent waiting for an audience with the Persian king, delays due to weather, and the duration of the return trip probably kept the ambassadors away from home a year or more.

However, on certain occasions the kings returned to one special place back in the homeland. Darius began construction of a ceremonial capital at **Persepolis** (per-SEH-poe-lis) (*Parsa*). An artificial platform was erected, and on it were built a series of palaces, audience halls, treasury buildings, and barracks. Here, too, Darius and his son Xerxes (ZERK-sees), who completed the project, were inspired by Mesopotamian traditions, for the great Assyrian kings had created new fortress-cities as advertisements of their wealth and power.

Ideology and Religion

Darius's approach to governing can be seen in the luxuriant relief sculpture that covers the foundations, walls, and stairwells of the buildings at Persepolis. Representatives of all the peoples of the empire—recognizable by their distinctive hair, beards, dress, hats, and footwear—are depicted bringing gifts to the king. In this exercise in what today we would call public relations or propaganda, Darius crafted a vision of an empire of vast extent and abundant resources in which all the subject peoples willingly cooperate. On his tomb Darius subtly contrasted the character of his rule with that of the Assyrian Empire, the Persians' predecessors in these lands (see Chapter 3). Where Assyrian kings had gloried in their power and depicted subjects staggering under the weight of a giant platform that supported the throne, Darius's artists showed erect subjects shouldering the burden willingly and without strain.

What actually took place at Persepolis? This opulent retreat in the homeland was the scene of events of special significance for the king and his people: the New Year's Festival, coronation, marriage, death, and burial. The kings from Darius on were buried in elaborate tombs cut into the cliffs at nearby Naqsh-i Rustam (NUHK-shee ROOS-tuhm).

Another perspective on what the Persian monarchy claimed to stand for is provided by several dozen royal inscriptions that have survived (see Diversity and Dominance: Persian and Greek Perceptions of Kingship). At Naqsh-i Rustam, Darius makes the following claim:

> Ahuramazda (ah-HOOR-uh-MAZZ-duh) [the chief deity], when he saw this earth in commotion, thereafter bestowed it upon me, made me king. . . . By the favor of Ahuramazda I put it down in its place. . . . I am of such a sort that I am a friend to right, I am not a friend to wrong. It is not my desire that the weak man should have wrong done to him by the mighty; nor is that my desire, that the mighty man should have wrong done to him by the weak.[2]

As this inscription makes clear, behind Darius and the empire stands the will of god. Ahuramazda made Darius king, giving him a mandate to bring order to a world in turmoil and ensure that all people be treated justly. Ahuramazda is the great god of a religion called **Zoroastrianism** (zo-roe-ASS-tree-uh-niz-uhm), and it is probable that Darius and his successors were Zoroastrians.

The origins of this religion are shrouded in uncertainty. The *Gathas,* hymns in an archaic Iranian dialect, are said to be the work of Zoroaster (zo-roe-ASS-ter) (*Zarathushtra*), who probably lived in eastern Iran sometime between 1700 and 500 B.C.E. He revealed that the world had been created by Ahuramazda, "the wise lord," but its original state of perfection and unity had been badly damaged by the attacks of Angra Mainyu (ANG-ruh MINE-yoo), "the hostile spirit,"

Persepolis A complex of palaces, reception halls, and treasury buildings erected by the Persian kings Darius I and Xerxes in the Persian homeland. It is believed that the New Year's festival was celebrated here, as well as the coronations, weddings, and funerals of the Persian kings, who were buried in cliff-tombs nearby.

Zoroastrianism A religion originating in ancient Iran that became the official religion of the Achaemenids. It centered on a single benevolent deity, Ahuramazda, who engaged in a struggle with demonic forces before prevailing and restoring a pristine world. It emphasized truth-telling, purity, and reverence for nature.

---

[2]Quoted in Roland G. Kent, *Old Persian: Grammar, Texts, Lexicon,* 2d ed. (New Haven, CT: American Oriental Society, 1953), 138, 140.

Sculpted Images on a Stairwell at Persepolis, ca. 500 B.C.E. Persepolis, in the Persian homeland, was built by Darius I and his son Xerxes, and it was used for ceremonies of special importance to the Persian king and people—coronations, royal weddings, funerals, and the New Year's Festival. Relief images like these on the stone foundations, walls, and stairways, representing members of the court and embassies bringing gifts, broadcast a vision of the grandeur and harmony of the Persian Empire. arazu/Shutterstock.com

backed by a host of demons. The struggle between good and evil plays out over thousands of years, with good ultimately destined to prevail. Humanity is a participant in this cosmic struggle, and individuals are rewarded or punished in the afterlife for their actions in life.

Darius has brilliantly joined the moral theology of Zoroastrianism to political ideology. In essence, he is claiming that the divinely ordained mission of the empire is to bring all the scattered peoples of the world back together again under a regime of justice and thereby to restore the perfection of creation.

SECTION REVIEW

- The Medes and the Persians of western Iran created complex societies in the seventh and sixth centuries B.C.E. under Mesopotamian influence.

- Cyrus, the founder of the Achaemenid Persian Empire, conquered most of western Asia, while his son Cambyses captured Egypt.

- Darius was a second founder of the empire, creating new systems for administration and collection of tribute.

- The king and his large entourage moved among several imperial centers: Susa was the administrative capital, and Persepolis in the homeland was the site of royal ceremonials.

- Darius was a brilliant propagandist, adapting Zoroastrian religious teachings to create an ideology justifying the empire.

- Zoroastrianism was one of the great religions of the ancient world, holding people to a high ethical standard, and may have influenced Judaism and Christianity.

In keeping with this Zoroastrian worldview, the Persians were sensitive to the beauties of nature and venerated beneficent elements, such as water, which was not to be polluted by human excretion, and fire, which was worshiped at fire altars. Corpses were exposed to wild beasts and the elements to prevent them from putrefying in the earth or tainting the sanctity of fire. Persians were also expected to keep promises and tell the truth. In his inscriptions Darius castigated evildoers as followers of "the Lie."

Zoroastrianism was one of the great religions of the ancient world. It preached belief in one supreme deity, held humans to a high ethical standard, and promised salvation. It traveled across western Asia with the advance of the Persian Empire, and it may have exerted a major influence on Judaism and thus, indirectly, on Christianity. God and the Devil, Heaven and Hell, reward and punishment, and the Messiah and the End of Time all appear to be legacies of this profound belief system. Because of the accidents of history—the fall of the Achaemenid Persian Empire in the later fourth century B.C.E. and the Islamic conquest of Iran in the seventh century C.E. (see Chapter 9)—Zoroastrianism has all but disappeared, except among a relatively small number of Parsees, as Zoroastrians are now called, in Iran and India.

Persian and Greek Perceptions of Kingship

An important internal source of information about the Persian Empire are the inscriptions commissioned by several kings. They provide valuable insights into how the kings conceived of the empire and their position as monarch, as well as the values they claimed to uphold. Darius carved the longest text into a cliff face at Behistun (beh-HISS-toon), high above the road leading from Mesopotamia to northwest Iran.

I am Darius, the great king, king of kings, the king of Persia, the king of countries, the son of Hystaspes, the grandson of Arsames, the Achaemenid . . . from antiquity we have been noble; from antiquity has our dynasty been royal. . . .

King Darius says: By the grace of Ahuramazda am I king; Ahuramazda has granted me the kingdom.

King Darius says: These are the countries which are subject unto me, and by the grace of Ahuramazda I became king of them: Persia, Elam, Babylonia, Assyria, Arabia, Egypt, the countries by the Sea, Lydia, the Greeks, Media, Armenia, Cappadocia, Parthia, Drangiana, Aria, Chorasmia, Bactria, Sogdiana, Gandara, Scythia, Sattagydia, Arachosia and Maka; twenty-three lands in all.

King Darius says: These are the countries which are subject to me; by the grace of Ahuramazda they became subject to me; they brought tribute unto me. Whatsoever commands have been laid on them by me, by night or by day, have been performed by them.

King Darius says: Within these lands, whosoever was a friend, him have I surely protected; whosoever was hostile, him have I utterly destroyed. . . .

King Darius says: As to these provinces which revolted, lies made them revolt, so that they deceived the people. Then Ahuramazda delivered them into my hand; and I did unto them according to my will.

King Darius says: You who shall be king hereafter, protect yourself vigorously from lies; punish the liars well, if thus you shall think, "May my country be secure!" . . .

King Darius says: On this account Ahuramazda brought me help, and all the other gods, all that there are, because I was not wicked, nor was I a liar, nor was I a tyrant, neither I nor any of my family. I have ruled according to righteousness . . . .

Another document, found at Persepolis, expands on the qualities of an exemplary ruler. Although it purports to be the words of Xerxes, it is almost an exact copy of an inscription of Darius, illustrating the continuity of concepts through several reigns.

A great god is Ahuramazda, who created this excellent thing which is seen, who created happiness for man, who set wisdom and capability down upon King Xerxes. . . .

The right, that is my desire. To the man who is a follower of the lie I am no friend. I am not hot-tempered. Whatever befalls me in battle, I hold firmly. I am ruling firmly my own will.

The man who is cooperative, according to his cooperation thus I reward him. Who does harm, him according to the harm I punish. It is not my wish that a man should do harm; nor indeed is it my wish that if he does harm he should not be punished . . . .

What a man does or performs, according to his ability, by that I become satisfied with him, and it is much to my desire, and I am well pleased, and I give much to loyal men. . . .

The royal inscriptions are certainly propaganda, but that does not mean they lack validity. To be effective, propaganda must be predicated on the moral values, political principles, and religious beliefs that are familiar and acceptable in a society, and thus it can provide us with a window on those views. The inscriptions also allow us to glimpse the personalities of Darius and Xerxes and how they wished to be perceived.

The Greek historian Herodotus creates a vivid portrait of Xerxes in his account of Xerxes' invasion of Greece in 480 B.C.E. He is drawing on information derived from Greeks who served in the Persian army, as well as the proud popular traditions of the Greek states that successfully resisted the invasion.

In this city Pythius son of Atys, a Lydian, sat awaiting them; he entertained Xerxes himself and all the king's army with the greatest hospitality, and declared himself willing to provide money for the war. . . . Xerxes was pleased with what he said and replied: "My Lydian friend, since I came out of Persia I have so far met with no man who was willing to give hospitality to my army, nor who came into my presence unsummoned

THE RISE OF THE GREEKS, 1000–500 B.C.E.

Because Greece was a relatively resource-poor region, the cultural developments of the first millennium B.C.E. were only possible because the Greeks had access to raw materials and markets abroad. Greek merchants, mercenaries, and travelers were in contact with other peoples and brought home foreign goods and ideas. Under the pressure of population, poverty, war, or political crisis, Greeks settled in other parts of the Mediterranean and Black Sea, bringing their language and culture and influencing other societies. Encounters with the different practices and beliefs of other peoples stimulated the formation of a Greek identity and sparked interest

and offered to furnish money for the war, besides you. But you have entertained my army nobly and offer me great sums. In return for this I give you these privileges: I make you my friend. . . . Remain in possession of what you now possess, and be mindful to be always such as you are; neither for the present nor in time will you regret what you now do." . . .

[some time later] As Xerxes led his army away, Pythius the Lydian, . . . encouraged by the gifts that he had received, came to Xerxes and said, "Master, I have a favor to ask that I desire of you, easy for you to grant and precious for me to receive." Xerxes supposed that Pythius would demand anything rather than what he did ask and answered that he would grant the request, bidding him declare what he desired. When Pythius heard this, he took courage and said: "Master, I have five sons, and all of them are constrained to march with you against Hellas. I pray you, O king, take pity on me in my advanced age, and release one of my sons, the eldest, from service, so that he may take care of me and of my possessions; take the four others with you, and may you return back with all your plans accomplished." Xerxes became very angry and thus replied: "Villain, you see me marching against Hellas myself, and taking with me my sons and brothers and relations and friends; do you, my slave, who should have followed me with all your household and your very wife, speak to me of your son? Be well assured of this, that a man's spirit dwells in his ears; when it hears good words it fills the whole body with delight, but when it hears the opposite it swells with anger. When you did me good service and promised more, you will never boast that you outdid your king in the matter of benefits; and now that you have turned aside to the way of shamelessness, you will receive a lesser requital than you merit. You and four of your sons are saved by your hospitality; but you shall be punished by the life of that one you most desire to keep." With that reply, he immediately ordered those who were assigned to do these things to find the eldest of Pythius's sons and cut him in half, then to set one half of his body on the right side of the road and the other on the left, so that the army would pass between them.

Xerxes has ordered a bridge to be built to transport his troops over the Hellespont strait.

The men who had been given this assignment made bridges starting from Abydos across to that headland; the Phoenicians one of flaxen cables, and the Egyptians a papyrus one.

From Abydos to the opposite shore it is a distance of seven stadia. But no sooner had the strait been bridged than a great storm swept down, breaking and scattering everything. When Xerxes heard of this, he was very angry and commanded that the Hellespont be whipped with three hundred lashes, and a pair of fetters be thrown into the sea. I have even heard that he sent branders with them to brand the Hellespont. He commanded them while they whipped to utter words outlandish and presumptuous, "Bitter water, our master thus punishes you, because you did him wrong though he had done you none. Xerxes the king will pass over you, whether you want it or not; in accordance with justice no one offers you sacrifice, for you are a turbid and briny river." He commanded that the sea receive these punishments and that the overseers of the bridge over the Hellespont be beheaded.

QUESTIONS FOR ANALYSIS

1. How does Darius justify his assumption of power in the Behistun inscription? What is his relationship to Ahuramazda, the Zoroastrian god, and what role does divinity play in human affairs?

2. How does Darius conceptualize his empire (look at a map and follow the order in which he lists the provinces), and what are the expectations and obligations that he places on his subjects? What does his characterization of his opponents as liars tell us about his view of human nature?

3. Looking at the document of Xerxes from Persepolis, what qualities (physical, mental, and moral) are desirable in a ruler? What is the Persian concept of justice?

4. How do the stories in Herodotus accord with the Persian conceptions of empire, kingship, and justice seen in the royal inscriptions? Where do we see gleeful Greek subversions of those ideals?

Sources: First selection from Behistun inscription translated by L. W. King and R. C. Thompson, *The Sculptures and Inscription of Darius the Great on the Rock of Behistun in Persia* (London, 1907) (http://www.livius.org/be-bm/behistun03 .html); second selection from Persepolis (http://www.livius.org); third selection from *Herodotus*, Volume III, Loeb Classical Library Volume 119, translated by A. D. Godley, pp. 27–29, 34–35, 38–39, 44–46, Cambridge, Mass.: Harvard University Press, Copyright 1922 by the President and Fellows of Harvard College, The Loeb Classical Library is a registered trademark of the President and Fellows of Harvard College.

in geography, ethnography, and history. A two-century-long rivalry with the Persian Empire helped shape the destinies of the Greek city-states.

Geography and Resources

Greece is part of an ecological zone encompassing the Mediterranean Sea and the lands surrounding it (see Map 3.5). This zone is bounded by the Atlantic Ocean to the west, the several ranges of the Alps to the north, the Syrian Desert to the east, and the Sahara to the south. The lands lying within this zone have a similar climate, a similar sequence of seasons, and similar plants and animals. In summer a weather front near the entrance of the Mediterranean impedes the passage of storms from the Atlantic, allowing hot, dry air from the Sahara to creep up over the region. In winter the front dissolves and ocean storms roll in, bringing waves, wind, and cold. It was relatively easy for people to migrate to new homes within this ecological zone without altering familiar cultural practices and means of livelihood.

Greek civilization arose in the lands bordering the Aegean Sea: the Greek mainland, the Aegean islands, and the western coast of Anatolia (see Map 5.2). Southern Greece is a dry and rocky land with small plains separated by low mountain ranges. No navigable rivers ease travel or the transport of commodities. The small islands dotting the Aegean were inhabited from early times. People could sail from Greece to Anatolia almost without losing sight of land. The sea was always a connector, not a barrier. From about 1000 B.C.E. Greeks began settling on the western edge of Anatolia. Broad and fertile river valleys near the coast made Ionia, as the ancient Greeks called this region, a comfortable place.

Greek farmers depended on rainfall to water their crops. The limited arable land, thin topsoil, and sparse rainfall in the south could not sustain large populations. Farmers planted grain (mostly barley, which was hardier than wheat) in the flat plain, olive trees at the edge of the plain, and grapevines on the terraced lower slopes of the foothills. Sheep and goats grazed in the hills during the growing season. In northern Greece, where the rainfall is greater and the land opens out into broad plains, cattle and horses were more abundant. These lands had few metal deposits and little timber, but both building stone, including fine marble, and clay for the potter were abundant.

The Greek mainland has a deeply pitted coastline with many natural harbors. A combination of circumstances—the difficulty of overland transport, the availability of good anchorages, and the need to import metals, timber, and grain—drew the Greeks to the sea. They obtained timber from the northern Aegean, gold and iron from Anatolia, copper from Cyprus, tin from the western Mediterranean, and grain from the Black Sea, Egypt, and Sicily. Sea transport was much cheaper and faster than overland transport. Thus, some Greeks reluctantly embarked upon the sea in their small, frail ships, hugging the coastline or island-hopping where possible.

The Emergence of the Polis

The first flowering of Greek culture in the Mycenaean civilization of the second millennium B.C.E., described in Chapter 3, was largely an adaptation to the Greek terrain of the imported institutions of Middle Eastern palace-dominated states. For several centuries after the destruction of the Mycenaean palace-states, Greece lapsed into a "Dark Age" (ca. 1150–800 B.C.E.), a time of depopulation, poverty, and backwardness that left few traces in the archaeological record.

During the Dark Age, the Greeks were largely isolated from the rest of the world. The importation of raw materials, especially metals, had been the chief source of Mycenaean prosperity. Lack of access to resources lay behind the poverty of the Dark Age. With fewer people to feed, the land was largely given over to grazing animals. Although there was continuity of language, religion, and other aspects of culture, there was a sharp break with the authoritarian Mycenaean political structure and centralized control of the economy. This opened the way for the development of new political, social, and economic forms rooted in the Greek environment.

The isolation of Greece ended by 800 B.C.E. when Phoenician ships began to visit the Aegean (see Chapter 3), inaugurating what scholars term the "Archaic" period of Greek history (ca. 800–480 B.C.E.). Soon Greek ships were also plying the waters of the Mediterranean in search of raw materials, trade opportunities, and fertile farmland.

New ideas arrived from the east, such as the depiction of naturalistic human and animal figures and imaginative mythical beasts on painted pottery. The most auspicious gift of the Phoenicians was a writing system. The Phoenicians used twenty-two symbols to represent the consonants in their language, leaving the vowel sounds to be inferred by the reader. To represent Greek vowel sounds, the Greeks utilized some of the Phoenician symbols for which there were no equivalent sounds in the Greek language. This was the first true alphabet, a system of writing that fully represents the sounds of spoken language. An alphabet offers tremendous advantages over systems of writing such as cuneiform and hieroglyphics, whose signs represent entire words or syllables. Because cuneiform and hieroglyphics required years of training and the memorization of hundreds of signs, they were known only by a scribal class whose elevated social position stemmed from their mastery of the technology. With an alphabet only a few dozen signs are required, and people can learn to read and write in a relatively short period of time.

Some scholars maintain that the Greeks first used alphabetic writing for economic purposes, such as to keep inventories of a merchant's wares. Others propose that it was created to preserve the

MAP 5.2 **Ancient Greece** By the early first millennium B.C.E. Greek-speaking peoples were dispersed throughout the Aegean region, occupying the Greek mainland, most of the islands, and the western coast of Anatolia. The rough landscape of central and southern Greece, with small plains separated by ranges of mountains, and the many islands in the Aegean favored the rise of hundreds of small, independent communities. The presence of adequate rainfall meant that agriculture was organized on the basis of self-sufficient family farms. As a result of the limited natural resources of this region, the Greeks had to resort to sea travel and trade with other lands in the Mediterranean to acquire metals and other vital raw materials. © Cengage Learning

oral epics so important to the Greeks. Whatever its first use, the Greeks soon applied the new technology to new forms of literature, law codes, religious dedications, and epitaphs on gravestones. This does not mean, however, that Greek society immediately became literate in the modern sense. For many centuries, Greece remained a primarily oral culture: people used storytelling, rituals, and performances to preserve and transmit information. Many of the distinctive intellectual and artistic creations of Greek civilization, such as theatrical drama, philosophical dialogues, and political and courtroom oratory, resulted from the dynamic interaction of speaking and writing.

The early Archaic period saw a veritable explosion of population. Studies of cemeteries in the vicinity of Athens show a dramatic population increase (perhaps fivefold or more) during the eighth century B.C.E. This was probably due, in part, to more intensive use of the land, as farming replaced herding and families began to work previously unused land on the margins of the plains. The accompanying shift to a diet based on bread and vegetables rather than meat may have increased fertility and life span. Another factor was increasing prosperity based on the importation of food and raw materials. Rising population density caused villages to merge and become urban centers. Freed from agricultural tasks, some members of the society were able to develop specialized skills in other areas, such as crafts and commerce.

Greece at this time consisted of hundreds of independent political entities, reflecting the facts of Greek geography—small plains separated by mountain barriers. The Greek **polis** (POE-lis) (usually translated "city-state") consisted of an urban center and the rural territory it controlled. City-states came in various sizes, with populations as small as several thousand or as large as several hundred thousand in the case of Athens.

Most urban centers had certain characteristic features. A hilltop *acropolis* (uh-KRAW-poe-lis) ("top of the city") offered refuge in an emergency. The town spread out around the base of this fortified high point. An *agora* (ah-go-RAH) ("gathering place") was an open area where citizens came together to ratify decisions of their leaders or to assemble with their weapons before military ventures. Government buildings were located there, but the agora developed into a marketplace as well, since vendors everywhere set out their wares wherever crowds gather. Fortified walls surrounded the urban center; but as the population expanded, new buildings went up beyond the perimeter.

City and country were not as sharply distinguished as they are today. The urban center depended on its agricultural hinterland to provide food, and many people living within the walls of the city worked on nearby farms during the day. Unlike the dependent workers on the estates of Mesopotamia, the rural populations of the Greek city-states were free members of the community.

Each polis was fiercely jealous of its independence and suspicious of its neighbors, leading to frequent conflict. By the early seventh century B.C.E. the Greeks had developed a new kind of warfare, waged by **hoplites** (HAWP-lite)—heavily armored infantrymen who fought in close formation. Protected by a helmet, a breastplate, and leg guards, each hoplite held a round shield over his own left side and the right side of the man next to him and brandished a thrusting spear, keeping a sword in reserve. The key to victory was maintaining the cohesion of one's own formation while breaking open the enemy's line. Most of the casualties were suffered by the defeated army in flight.

There was a close relationship between hoplite warfare and agriculture. Greek states were defended by armies of private citizens—mostly farmers—called up for brief periods of crisis, rather than by a professional class of soldiers. Although this kind of fighting called for strength to bear the weapons and armor, as well as courage to stand one's ground in battle, no special training was needed. Campaigns took place when farmers were available, in the windows of time between major tasks in the agricultural cycle. When a hoplite army marched into the fields of another community, the enraged farmers of that community, who had toiled to develop their land and buildings, rarely refused the challenge. Though brutal and terrifying, the clash of two hoplite lines provided a quick decision. Battles rarely lasted more than a few hours, and the survivors could promptly return home to tend their farms.

The expanding population soon surpassed the capacity of the small plains, and many communities sent excess population abroad to establish independent "colonies" in distant lands (see the story at the beginning of this chapter). Not every colonist left willingly. Sources tell of people being chosen by lot and forbidden to return on pain of death. Others, seeing an opportunity to escape from poverty, avoid the constraints of family, or find adventure, voluntarily sought their fortunes on the frontier. After obtaining the approval of the god Apollo from his sanctuary at Delphi, the colonists departed, carrying fire from the communal hearth of the "mother-city," a symbol of the kinship and religious ties that would connect the two communities. They settled by the sea in the vicinity of a hill or other natural refuge. The "founder," a prominent member of the mother-city, allotted parcels of land and drafted laws for the new community. In some cases the indigenous population was driven away or reduced to semiservile status; in other cases there was intermarriage between colonists and natives.

A wave of colonization from the mid-eighth through mid-sixth centuries B.C.E. spread Greek culture far beyond the land of its origins. New settlements sprang up in the northern Aegean area, around the Black Sea, and on the Libyan coast of North Africa. In southern Italy and on the island of Sicily (see Map 3.5) another Greek core area was established. Greek colonists were able to transplant their entire way of life because of the general similarity in climate and ecology in the Mediterranean lands.

polis The Greek term for a city-state, an urban center and the agricultural territory under its control. It was the characteristic form of political organization in southern and central Greece in the Archaic and Classical periods. Of the hundreds of city-states in the Mediterranean and Black Sea regions settled by Greeks, some were oligarchic, others democratic, depending on the powers delegated to the Council and the Assembly.

hoplite A heavily armored Greek infantryman of the Archaic and Classical periods who fought in the close-packed phalanx formation. Hoplite armies—militias composed of middle- and upper-class citizens supplying their own equipment—were for centuries superior to all other military forces.

Robert Harding Picture Library Ltd / Alamy

The Acropolis at Athens   This steep, defensible plateau jutting up from the Attic Plain served as a Mycenaean fortress in the second millennium B.C.E., and the site of Athens has been continuously occupied since that time. In the mid-sixth century B.C.E. the tyrant Pisistratus built a temple to Athena, the patron goddess of the community. It was destroyed by the Persians when they invaded Greece in 480 B.C.E. The Acropolis was left in ruins for three decades as a reminder of what the Athenians sacrificed in defense of Greek freedom, but in the 440s B.C.E. Pericles initiated a building program, using funds from the naval empire that Athens headed. These construction projects, including a new temple to Athena—the Parthenon—brought glory to the city and popularity to Pericles and to the new democracy that he championed.

Greeks began to use the term *Hellenes* (**HELL-leans**) (*Graeci* is what the Romans later called them) to distinguish themselves from *barbaroi* (the root of the English word *barbarian*). Interaction with new peoples and exposure to their different practices made the Greeks aware of the factors that bound them together: their language, religion, and lifestyle. It also introduced them to new ideas and technologies. Developments first appearing in the colonial world traveled back to the Greek homeland—urban planning, new forms of political organization, and new intellectual currents.

Coinage was invented in the early sixth century B.C.E., probably in Lydia (western Anatolia), and soon spread throughout the Greek world and beyond. A coin was a piece of metal whose weight and purity, and thus value, were guaranteed by the state. Silver, gold, bronze, and other metals were attractive choices for a medium of exchange: sufficiently rare to be valuable, relatively lightweight and portable, virtually indestructible, and therefore permanent. Prior to the invention of coinage, people weighed out quantities of metal in exchange for items they wanted to buy. Coinage allowed for more rapid exchanges of goods as well as for more efficient record keeping and storage of wealth. It stimulated trade and increased the total wealth of the society. Even so, international commerce could still be confusing because different states used different weight standards that had to be reconciled, just as people have to exchange currencies when traveling today.

By reducing surplus population, colonization helped relieve pressures within Archaic Greek communities. Nevertheless, this was an era of political instability. Kings ruled the Dark Age societies depicted in Homer's *Iliad* and *Odyssey*, but at some point councils composed of the heads of noble families superseded the kings. This aristocracy derived its wealth and power from ownership of large tracts of land. Peasant families worked this land, occupying small plots and handing over a portion of the crop to the owner. Debt-slaves, who had borrowed money or seed from the lord and lost their freedom when unable to repay the loan, also worked the land. Also living in a typical community were free peasants, who owned small farms, and urban-based craftsmen and merchants, who began to constitute a "middle class."

In the mid-seventh and sixth centuries B.C.E. in one city-state after another, a **tyrant**—a person who seized and held power in violation of the normal political traditions of the community—gained control. Greek tyrants were often disgruntled or ambitious members of the aristocracy who were backed by the emerging middle class. New opportunities for economic advancement and the declining cost of metals meant that more and more men could acquire arms and serve as hoplite soldiers in the local militias. These individuals must have demanded increased political rights as the price of their support for the tyrant.

Ultimately, the tyrants were unwitting catalysts in an evolving political process. Some were able to pass their positions on to their sons, but eventually the tyrant-family was ejected. Authority in the community developed along one of two lines: toward oligarchy (OLL-ih-gahr-key), the exercise of political privilege by the wealthier members of society, or toward **democracy**, the exercise of political power by all free adult males.

Greek religion encompassed a wide range of cults and beliefs. The ancestors of the Greeks brought a collection of sky-gods with them when they entered the Greek peninsula at the end of the third millennium B.C.E. Male gods predominated, but several female deities had important roles. Some gods represented forces in nature: for example, Zeus sent storms and lightning, and Poseidon was master of the sea and earthquakes. The two great epic poems of Homer, the *Iliad* and *Odyssey*, which Greek schoolboys memorized and professional performers recited, put a distinctive stamp on the personalities of these deities. The Homeric gods were anthropomorphic (an-thruh-puh-MORE-fik)—that is, conceived as humanlike in appearance (though taller, more beautiful, and far more powerful than mere mortals) and humanlike in their displays of emotion. Indeed, the chief difference between them and human beings was humans' mortality.

Worship of the gods at state-sponsored festivals was as much an expression of civic identity as of personal piety. **Sacrifice**, the central ritual of Greek religion, was performed at altars in front of the temples that the Greeks built to be the gods' places of residence. Greeks gave their gods gifts, often as humble as a small cake or a cup of wine poured on the ground, in the hope that the gods would favor and protect them. In more spectacular forms of sacrifice, a group of people would kill one or more animals, spray the altar with the victim's blood, burn parts of its body so that the aroma would ascend to the gods on high, and enjoy a rare feast of meat.

Greek individuals and communities sought advice or predictions about the future from oracles—sacred sites where they believed the gods communicated with humans. Especially prestigious was the oracle of Apollo at Delphi in central Greece. Petitioners left gifts in the treasuries, and the god responded to their questions through his priestess, who gave forth obscure utterances. Because most Greeks were farmers, a popular form of worship was the fertility cult, in which members worshiped and sought to enhance the productive forces in nature (usually conceived as female). This kind of popular religion is often hidden from modern view because of our dependence on literary texts privileging the values of an educated, urban elite.

New Intellectual Currents

The changes taking place in Greece in the Archaic period—new technologies, increasing prosperity, and social and political development—led to innovations in intellectual outlook and artistic expression. One distinctive feature of the period was a growing emphasis on the uniqueness and rights of the individual.

We see clear signs of individualism in the new lyric poetry—short verses in which the subject matter is intensely personal, drawn from the experience of the poet and expressing his or her feelings. Archilochus (ahr-KIL-uh-kuhs), a soldier and poet living in the first half of the seventh century B.C.E., made a surprising admission:

> *Some barbarian is waving my shield, since I was obliged to leave that perfectly good piece of equipment behind under a bush. But I got away, so what does it matter? Let the shield go; I can buy another one equally good.*[3]

---

[3]Richmond Lattimore, *Greek Lyrics*, 2d ed. (Chicago: University of Chicago Press, 1960), 2.

tyrant The term the Greeks used to describe someone who seized and held power in violation of the normal procedures and traditions of the community. Tyrants appeared in many Greek city-states in the seventh and sixth centuries B.C.E., often taking advantage of the disaffection of the emerging middle class and, by weakening the old elite, unwittingly contributing to the evolution of democracy.

democracy System of government in which all "citizens" (however defined) have equal political and legal rights, privileges, and protections, as in the Greek city-state of Athens in the fifth and fourth centuries B.C.E.

sacrifice A gift given to a deity, often with the aim of creating a relationship, gaining favor, and obligating the god to provide some benefit to the sacrificer, sometimes in order to sustain the deity and thereby guarantee the continuing vitality of the natural world.

Vase Painting Depicting a Sacrifice to the God Apollo, ca. 440 B.C.E.   For the Greeks, who believed in a multitude of gods who looked and behaved like humans, the central act of worship was the sacrifice, the ritualized offering of a gift. Sacrifice created a relationship between the human worshiper and the deity and raised expectations that the god would bestow favors in return. Here we see a number of male devotees, wearing their finest clothing and garlands in their hair, near a sacred outdoor altar and statue of Apollo. The god is shown at the far right, standing on a pedestal and holding his characteristic bow and laurel branch. The first worshiper offers the god bones wrapped in fat. All of the worshipers will feast on the meat carried by the boy.   Bildarchiv Preussischer Kulturbesitz/Art Resource, NY

Here Archilochus is poking fun at the heroic ideal that regarded dishonor as worse than death. In challenging traditional values and expressing personal views, lyric poets paved the way for the modern Western conception of poetry.

Some daring thinkers rejected traditional religious conceptions and sought rational explanations for events in nature. For example, in the sixth century B.C.E. Xenophanes (zeh-NOFF-uh-nees) called into question the kind of gods that Homer had popularized.

> *But if cattle and horses or lions had hands, or were able to draw with their hands and do the works that men can do, horses would draw the forms of the gods like horses, and cattle like cattle, and they would make their bodies such as they each had themselves.*[4]

These early philosophers were primarily concerned with how the world was created, what it is made of, and why changes occur. Some postulated various combinations of earth, air, fire, and water as the primal elements that combine or dissolve to form the numerous substances found in nature. One advanced the theory that the world is composed of microscopic atoms (from a Greek word meaning "indivisible") moving through the void of space, colliding randomly and combining in various ways to form many substances. This model, in some respects startlingly similar to modern atomic theory, was essentially a lucky intuition, but it attests to the sophistication of these thinkers. Most of these thinkers came from Ionia and southern Italy, where Greeks were in close contact with non-Greek peoples. The shock of encountering different ideas may have stimulated new lines of inquiry.

In Ionia in the sixth century B.C.E., a group of men referred to as logographers (loe-GOG-ruff-er) ("writers of prose accounts"), taking advantage of the nearly infinite capacity of writing to store information, gathered data on a wide range of topics, including ethnography (description of foreign people's physical characteristics and cultural practices), the geography of unfamiliar lands, foundation stories of important cities, and the origins of famous Greek families. They were the first to write in prose—the language of everyday speech—rather than poetry, which had long facilitated the memorization essential in an oral society. *Historia*, "investigation/research," was the Greek term for the method they used to collect, sort, and select information.

---

[4]G. S. Kirk and J. E. Raven, *The Presocratic Philosophers: A Critical History with a Selection of Texts* (Cambridge, England: Cambridge University Press, 1957), 169.

Herodotus Heir to the technique of *historia* ("investigation/research") developed by Greeks in the late Archaic period. He came from a Greek community in Anatolia and traveled extensively, collecting information in western Asia and the Mediterranean lands. He traced the antecedents and chronicled the wars between the Greek city-states and the Persian Empire, thus originating the Western tradition of historical writing.

An important successor to these early researchers was **Herodotus** (ca. 485–425 B.C.E.), who published his *Histories* in the later fifth century B.C.E. Early parts of the work are filled with the geographic and ethnographic reports, legends, and marvels dear to the logographers, but in later sections Herodotus focuses on the great event of the previous generation: the wars between the Greeks and the Persian Empire.

Herodotus declared his new conception of his mission in the first lines of the book:

> *I, Herodotus of Halicarnassus, am here setting forth my history, that time may not draw the color from what man has brought into being, nor those great and wonderful deeds, manifested by both Greeks and barbarians, fail of their report, and, together with all this, the reason why they fought one another.*[5]

In seeking to discover *why* Greeks and Persians came to blows, Herodotus became a historian, directing the all-purpose techniques of *historia* to the narrower service of *history* in the modern sense. For this achievement he is known as the "father of history."

Athens and Sparta

The two preeminent Greek city-states of the late Archaic and Classical periods were Athens and Sparta. The different character of these communities underscores the potential for diversity in human societies, even those arising in similar environmental and cultural contexts.

The ancestors of the Spartans migrated into the Peloponnese (PELL-uh-puh-neze), the southernmost part of the Greek mainland, around 1000 B.C.E. For a time Sparta followed a typical path of development, participating in trade and fostering the arts. Then in the seventh century B.C.E. something altered the character of the Spartan state. Like many other parts of Greece, the Spartan community was feeling the effects of increasing population and a shortage of arable land. However, instead of sending out colonists, the Spartans invaded the fertile plain of neighboring Messenia (see Map 5.2). They took over Messenia and reduced the native population to the status of helots (HELL-ut), or state-owned serfs, who became the most abused and exploited population on the Greek mainland.

Fear of a helot uprising led to the evolution of the unique Spartan way of life. The Spartan state became a military camp in a permanent state of preparedness. Territory in Messenia and Laconia (the Spartan homeland) was divided into several thousand lots and assigned to Spartan citizens. Helots worked the land and turned over a portion of what they grew to their Spartan masters, who were freed from food production and able to spend their lives in military training and service.

The Spartan soldier was the best in Greece, and the professional Spartan army was superior to the citizen militias of other Greek states. The Spartans, however, paid a huge personal price for their military readiness. At age seven, boys were taken from their families and put into barracks, where they were toughened by severe discipline, beatings, and deprivation. A Spartan male's whole life was subordinated to the needs of the state. Sparta essentially stopped the clock, declining to participate in the economic, political, and cultural renaissance taking place in the Archaic Greek world. There were no longer any poets or artists at Sparta. To maintain equality among citizens, precious metals and coinage were banned, and Spartans were forbidden to engage in commerce. The fifth-century B.C.E. Athenian historian Thucydides (thoo-SID-ih-dees) remarked that in his day Sparta appeared to be little more than a large village and that no future observer of the ruins of the site would be able to guess its power.

The Spartans, practicing a foreign policy that was cautious and isolationist, cultivated a mystique by rarely putting their reputation to the test. Reluctant to march far from home for fear of a helot uprising, the Spartans maintained regional peace through the Peloponnesian League, a system of alliances between Sparta and its neighbors.

In comparison with other Greek city-states, Athens possessed an unusually large and populous territory: the entire region of Attica, containing a number of moderately fertile plains and well suited for cultivation of olive trees. In addition to the urban center of Athens, located 5 miles (8 kilometers) from the sea where the sheer-sided Acropolis towered above the plain, the peninsula was dotted with villages and a few larger towns.

In 594 B.C.E., however, Athens was on the verge of civil war, and a respected member of the elite class, Solon, was appointed lawgiver and granted extraordinary powers. Solon divided

---

[5]Herodotus, *The History*, trans. David Grene (Chicago: University of Chicago Press, 1988), 33. (Herodotus 1.1)

- In the resource-poor Greek Aegean, prosperity and advancement depended on seaborne trade for metals and other vital materials.

- Hundreds of independent city-states existed in the fragmented Greek landscape. Rainfall-based agriculture allowed the land to be worked by independent farmers who were free citizens of their communities.

- Rapidly expanding population led to urbanization and to colonization, the migration of Greeks to new settlements around the Mediterranean and Black Seas.

- The rise of a middle class and the dependence of communities on a hoplite militia led to political unrest and an extension of political rights to more people.

- The Greeks created the first true alphabetic writing system, but Greece long remained a primarily oral society. New ideas challenged traditional notions, leading to individualism, science, and history.

- Sparta and Athens, though part of the same Greek civilization, evolved politically in different directions: Sparta toward a military oligarchy, Athens to democracy.

Pericles Aristocratic leader who guided the Athenian state through the transformation to full participatory democracy for all male citizens, supervised construction of the Acropolis, and pursued a policy of imperial expansion that led to the Peloponnesian War. He formulated a strategy of attrition but died from the plague early in the war.

Athenian citizens into four classes based on the annual yield of their farms. Those in the top three classes could hold state offices. Members of the lowest class, with little or no property, could participate in meetings of the Assembly. This arrangement, which made political rights a function of wealth, was far from democratic, but it broke the monopoly on power of a small circle of aristocratic families. Solon also abolished the practice of enslaving individuals for failure to repay their debts, thereby guaranteeing the freedom of Athenian citizens.

Nevertheless, political turmoil continued until 546 B.C.E., when an aristocrat named Pisistratus (pie-SIS-truh-tuhs) seized power. To strengthen his position and weaken the aristocracy, the tyrant enticed the largely rural population to identify with the urban center of Athens, where he was the dominant figure. He undertook a number of monumental building projects, including a Temple of Athena on the Acropolis. He also instituted or expanded several major festivals that drew people to Athens for religious processions, performances of plays, and athletic and poetic competitions.

Pisistratus passed the tyranny on to his sons, but with Spartan assistance the Athenians turned the tyrant-family out in the last decade of the sixth century B.C.E. In the 460s and 450s B.C.E. **Pericles** (PER-eh-kleez) and his political allies took the last steps in the evolution of Athenian democracy, transferring all power to popular organs of government: the Assembly, Council of 500, and People's Courts. Men of moderate or little means now could participate fully in the political process, being selected by lot to fill even the highest offices and being paid for public service so they could take time off from their work. The focal point of Athenian political life became the Assembly of all citizens. Several times a month proposals were debated; decisions were made openly, and any citizen could speak to the issues of the day.

During this century and a half of internal political evolution, Athens's economic clout and international reputation rose steadily. From the time of Pisistratus, Athenian exports, especially olive oil, became increasingly prominent all around the Mediterranean, crowding out the products of other Greek commercial powerhouses such as Corinth (see Map 5.2). Extensive trade increased the numbers and wealth of the middle class and helps explain why Athens took the path of increasing democratization.

THE STRUGGLE OF PERSIA AND GREECE, 546–323 B.C.E.

For many Greeks of the fifth and fourth centuries B.C.E., Persia was the great enemy and the wars with Persia were crucial events. The Persians probably were more concerned about threats farther east. Nevertheless, the encounters of Greeks and Persians over a period of two centuries were of profound importance for the history of the eastern Mediterranean and western Asia.

Early Encounters

Cyrus's conquest of Lydia in 546 B.C.E. led to the subjugation of the Greek cities on the Anatolian seacoast. In the years that followed, local groups or individuals who collaborated with the Persian government ruled their home cities with minimal Persian interference. All this changed when the Ionian Revolt, a great uprising of Greeks and other subject peoples on the western frontier, broke out in 499 B.C.E. The Persians needed five years and a massive infusion of troops and resources to stamp out the insurrection.

Persian Wars Conflicts between Greek city-states and the Persian Empire, ranging from the Ionian Revolt (499–494 B.C.E.) through Darius's punitive expedition that failed at Marathon (490 B.C.E.) and the defeat of Xerxes' massive invasion of Greece by the Spartan-led Hellenic League (480–479 B.C.E.). This first major setback for Persian arms launched the Greeks into their period of greatest cultural productivity. Herodotus chronicled these events in the first "history" in the Western tradition.

The failed revolt led to the **Persian Wars**—two Persian attacks on Greece in the early fifth century B.C.E. In 490 B.C.E. Darius dispatched a force to punish Eretria (er-EH-tree-uh) and Athens, two mainland states that had aided the Ionian rebels. Eretria was betrayed to the Persians, and the survivors were marched off to permanent exile in southwest Iran. The Athenians probably would have suffered a similar fate if their hoplites had not defeated the more numerous but lighter-armed Persian troops in a sharp engagement at Marathon, 26 miles (42 kilometers) from Athens.

In 480 B.C.E. Darius's son and successor, Xerxes (*Khshayarsha*, r. 486–465 B.C.E.), set out with a huge invasionary force consisting of the Persian army, contingents from all the peoples of the empire, and a large fleet of ships drawn from maritime subjects. Crossing the narrow Hellespont strait, Persian forces descended into central and southern Greece (see Map 5.2). Xerxes sent messengers ahead to most Greek states, demanding "earth and water"—tokens of submission.

Many Greek communities acknowledged Persian overlordship. But an alliance of southern Greek states bent on resistance was formed under the leadership of the Spartans. This Hellenic League initially failed to halt the Persian advance. At the pass of Thermopylae (thuhr-MOP-uh-lee) in central Greece, three hundred Spartans and their king gave their lives to buy time for their allies to escape. However, after the city of Athens had been sacked, the Persian navy was lured into the narrow straits of nearby Salamis (SAH-lah-miss), sacrificing their advantage in numbers and maneuverability, and suffered a devastating defeat. The following spring (479 B.C.E.), the Persian land army was routed at Plataea (pluh-TEE-uh), and the immediate threat to Greece receded. A number of factors account for the outcome: the Persians' difficulty in supplying their very large army in a distant land; their tactical error at Salamis; the superiority of heavily armed Greek hoplite soldiers over lighter-armed Asiatic infantry; and the tenacity of people defending their homeland and liberty.

The Greeks then went on the offensive. Athens's stubborn refusal to submit and the vital role played by the Athenian navy, which made up half the allied fleet, had earned the city a large measure of respect. The next phase of the war—driving the Persians away from the Aegean and liberating Greek states still under Persian control—was naval. Thus Athens replaced land-based, isolationist Sparta as leader of the campaign against Persia. In 477 B.C.E. the Delian (DEE-lih-yuhn) League was formed. Initially a voluntary alliance of Greek states to prosecute the war against Persia, in less than twenty years Athenian-led League forces swept the Persians from the waters of the eastern Mediterranean and freed all Greek communities except those in distant Cyprus (see Map 3.5).

The Height of Athenian Power

The Classical period of Greek history (480–323 B.C.E.) begins with the successful defense of the Greek homeland. Ironically, the Athenians, who had played such a crucial role, exploited these events to become an imperial power. A string of successful campaigns and the passage of time led many of their complacent Greek allies to contribute money instead of military forces. The Athenians used the money to build up and staff their navy. Eventually they saw the other members of the Delian League as their subjects and demanded annual contributions and other signs of submission. States that deserted the League were brought back by force, stripped of their defenses, and subordinated to Athens.

Athens's mastery of naval technology transformed Greek warfare and politics and brought great power and wealth to Athens itself. Unlike commercial ships, whose stable, round-bodied hulls were propelled by a single square sail, military vessels could not risk depending on the wind. By the late sixth century B.C.E. the **trireme** (TRY-reem), a sleek, fast vessel powered by 170 rowers, had become the premier warship. Athenian crews, by constant practice, became the best in the eastern Mediterranean, able to reach speeds of 7 knots and perform complex maneuvers.

trireme Greek and Phoenician warship of the fifth and fourth centuries B.C.E. It was sleek and light, powered by 170 oars arranged in three vertical tiers. Manned by skilled sailors, it was capable of short bursts of speed and complex maneuvers.

The effectiveness of the Athenian navy had significant consequences at home and abroad. The emergence at Athens of a democratic system in which each male citizen had an equal share is connected to the new primacy of the fleet. Hoplites, who had to provide their own armor and weapons, were members of the middle and upper classes. Rowers, in contrast, came from the lower classes, but because they were the source of Athens's power, they could insist on full rights.

The navy allowed Athens to project its power farther than would be possible with a hoplite militia, which could be kept in arms for only short periods of time. In previous Greek wars, the victorious state could not occupy a defeated neighbor permanently and was satisfied with booty and, perhaps, minor adjustments to boundary lines. Athens was able to continually dominate and exploit other, weaker communities in an unprecedented way.

Athens used its power to promote its economic interests. Its port, Piraeus (pih-RAY-uhs), became the most important commercial center in the eastern Mediterranean. The money collected from the subject states helped subsidize the increasingly expensive Athenian democracy as well as construction of beautiful buildings on the Acropolis, including the majestic new temple of Athena, the Parthenon. The Athenian leader Pericles redistributed the profits of empire to the many Athenians working on the construction and decoration of these monuments and gained extraordinary popularity.

Other cultural achievements were supported indirectly by the profits of empire. Wealthy Athenians paid the production costs of the tragedies and comedies performed at state festivals, and the most creative artists and thinkers in the Greek world were drawn to Athens. Traveling teachers called Sophists ("wise men") provided instruction in logic and public speaking to pupils who could afford their fees. The new discipline of rhetoric—the construction of attractive and persuasive arguments—gave those with training and quick wits a great advantage in politics and the courts.

These new intellectual currents came together in 399 B.C.E. when the philosopher **Socrates** (ca. 470–399 B.C.E.) was brought to trial. A sculptor by trade, Socrates spent most of his time in the company of young men who enjoyed conversing with him and observing him deflate the pretensions of those who thought themselves wise. He wryly commented that he knew one more thing than everyone else: that he knew nothing. At his trial, Socrates easily disposed of the charges of corrupting the youth and not believing in the gods of the city. He argued that the real basis of the hostility he faced was twofold: (1) He was being held responsible for the actions of several of his aristocratic students who had tried to overthrow the Athenian democracy. (2) He was being blamed for the controversial teachings of the Sophists, which were widely believed to contradict traditional religious beliefs and undermine morality.

In Athenian trials, juries of hundreds of citizens decided guilt and punishment, often motivated more by emotion than by legal principles. The vote that found Socrates guilty was close. But his lack of contrition in the penalty phase—he proposed that he be rewarded for his services to the state—led the jury to condemn him to death by drinking hemlock. Socrates's disciples regarded his execution as a martyrdom, and smart young men such as Plato withdrew from public life and dedicated themselves to the philosophical pursuit of knowledge and truth.

This period witnesses an important stage in the transition from orality to literacy. Socrates himself wrote nothing, preferring to converse with people. His student Plato (ca. 428–347 B.C.E.) may represent the first truly literate generation that gained much knowledge from books and

Socrates Athenian philosopher (ca. 470–399 B.C.E.) who shifted the emphasis of philosophical investigation from questions of natural science to ethics and human behavior. He attracted young disciples from elite families but made enemies by revealing the ignorance and pretensions of others, actions that culminated in his trial and execution by the Athenian state.

Replica of Ancient Greek Trireme Greek warships had a metal-tipped ram in front to pierce the hulls of enemy vessels and a pair of steering rudders in the rear. Though equipped with masts and sails, in battle these warships were propelled by 170 rowers. This modern, full-size replica, manned by international volunteer crews, is helping scholars to determine attainable speeds and maneuvering techniques.

Replica of the trireme 'Olympia' at sea (photo)/Private Collection/Ancient Art and Architecture Collection Ltd./Mike Andrews/The Bridgeman Art Library

habitually wrote down their thoughts. On the outskirts of Athens Plato founded the Academy, where young men could pursue a course of higher education. Yet even Plato retained traces of the orality of the world in which he had grown up. He wrote dialogues—an oral form—in which his protagonist, Socrates, uses the "Socratic method" of question and answer to reach a deeper understanding of values such as justice, excellence, and wisdom. Plato refused to write down the most advanced stages of the philosophical and spiritual training that took place at his Academy. He believed that full apprehension of a higher reality, of which our own sensible world is but a pale reflection, could be entrusted only to "initiates" who had completed the earlier stages.

The third of the great classical philosophers, Aristotle (384–322 B.C.E.), came from Stagira in the northern Aegean. After several decades of study at Plato's Academy, he was chosen by the king of Macedonia, Philip II, who had a high regard for Greek culture, to tutor his son Alexander. Later, Aristotle returned to Athens to found his own school, the Lyceum. Of a very different temperament than the mystical Plato, Aristotle collected and categorized a vast array of knowledge. He lectured and wrote about politics, philosophy, ethics, logic, poetry, rhetoric, physics, astronomy, meteorology, zoology, and psychology, laying the foundations for many modern disciplines.

Inequality in Classical Greece

Athens, the inspiration for the concept of democracy in the Western tradition, was a democracy only for the relatively small percentage of inhabitants who were citizens—free adult males of pure Athenian ancestry. Excluding women, children, slaves, and foreigners, this group amounted to 30,000 or 40,000 people out of a total population of approximately 300,000—only 10 or 15 percent.

Slaves, mostly of foreign origin, constituted perhaps one-third of the population of Attica in the fifth and fourth centuries B.C.E., and the average Athenian family owned one or more. Slaves were needed to run the shop or work on the farm while the master attended meetings of the Assembly or served on one of the boards that oversaw the day-to-day activities of the state. The slave was a "living piece of property," required to do any work, submit to any sexual acts, and receive any punishments the owner ordained. Most Greek slaves were domestic servants, often working on the same tasks as the master or mistress. Close daily contact between owners and slaves meant that a relationship often developed, making it hard for slave owners to deny the essential humanity of their slaves. Still, Aristotle rationalized the institution of slavery by arguing that *barbaroi* (non-Greeks) lacked the capacity to reason and thus were better off under the direction of rational Greek owners.

The position of women varied across Greek communities. The women of Sparta, who were expected to bear and raise strong children, were encouraged to exercise, and they enjoyed a level of public visibility and outspokenness that shocked other Greeks. Athens may have been at the opposite extreme as regards the confinement and suppression of women. Ironically, the exploitation of women in Athens, as of slaves, made possible the high degree of freedom enjoyed by men in the democratic state. Greek men justified the confinement of women by claiming that they were naturally promiscuous and likely to introduce other men's children into the household.

Athenian marriages were unequal affairs. A new husband might be thirty, reasonably well educated, a veteran of war, and experienced in business and politics. Under law he had nearly absolute authority over the members of his household. He arranged his marriage with the parents of his prospective wife, who was likely to be a teenager brought up with no formal education and only minimal training in weaving, cooking, and household management. Coming into the home of a husband she hardly knew, she had no political rights and limited legal protection. The primary function of marriage was to produce children, preferably male. It is likely that many more girls than boys were victims of infanticide—the killing through exposure of unwanted children.

Husbands and wives had limited contact. The man spent the day outdoors attending to work or political responsibilities; he dined with male friends at night; and usually he slept alone in the men's quarters (see Material Culture: Wine and Beer in the Ancient World). The woman stayed home to cook, clean, raise the children, and supervise the servants, going out only to attend funerals and religious rituals and to make discreet visits to female relatives. During the three-day Thesmophoria (thes-moe-FOE-ree-uh) festival, the women of Athens lived together and managed their own affairs in a great encampment, carrying out mysterious rituals to enhance the fertility of the land. The appearance of assertive women on the Athenian stage is also suggestive. Although the plays were written by men and probably reflect a male fear of strong women, the playwrights must have had models in their mothers, sisters, and wives.

Vase Painting Depicting Women at an Athenian Fountain House, ca. 520 B.C.E. Paintings on Greek vases provide the most vivid pictorial record of ancient Greek life. The subject matter usually reflects the interests of the aristocratic males who purchased the vases—warfare, athletics, mythology, drinking parties—but sometimes we are given glimpses into the lives of women and the working classes. These women are presumably domestic servants sent to fetch water for the household from the public fountain. The large water jars they are filling are like the one on which this scene is depicted. Scala/Art Resource, NY

The inequality of men and women posed obstacles to creating a "meaningful relationship" between the sexes. To find his intellectual and emotional equal, a man often looked to other men. Bisexuality was common in ancient Greece, as much a product of the social structure as of biological inclinations. A common pattern was that of an older man wooing a youth, in the process mentoring him and initiating him into the community of adult males.

Failure of the City-State and Triumph of the Macedonians

The emergence of Athens as an imperial power in the half century after the Persian invasion aroused the suspicions of other Greek states and led to open hostilities between former allies. In 431 B.C.E. the **Peloponnesian War** broke out, a nightmarish struggle between the Athenian and Spartan alliance systems that involved most of the Greek world.

Peloponnesian War A protracted (431–404 B.C.E.) and costly conflict between the Athenian and Spartan alliance systems that convulsed most of the Greek world. The war was largely a consequence of Athenian imperialism. Possession of a naval empire allowed Athens to fight a war of attrition, but ultimately Sparta prevailed because of Athenian errors and Persian financial support.

In this war unlike any previous Greek war, the Athenians used their naval power to insulate themselves from the dangers of a siege by land. In midcentury they had built three long walls connecting the city with the port of Piraeus and the adjacent shoreline. When the war began, Pericles, devising an unprecedented strategy, refused to engage the Spartan-led armies that invaded Attica each year, knowing that, as long as Athens controlled the sea lanes and was able to provision itself, the enemy hoplites must soon return to their farms and the city could not be starved into submission.

The Peloponnesian War dragged on for nearly three decades with great loss of life and squandering of resources. It sapped the morale of all Greece and ended only with the surrender of Athens after defeat in a naval battle in 404 B.C.E. Because the Persian Empire had bankrolled the construction of ships by the Spartan alliance, Sparta finally was able to take the conflict into Athens's own element, the sea.

The victorious Spartans, who had entered the war championing "the freedom of the Greeks," took over Athens's overseas empire until their own increasingly highhanded behavior aroused the opposition of other city-states. Indeed, the fourth century B.C.E. was a time of nearly continuous skirmishing among Greek states. The independent polis, from one point of view the glory of Greek culture, was also fundamentally flawed because it fostered rivalry, fear, and warfare among neighboring communities.

Internal conflict in the Greek world allowed the Persians to recoup old losses. By the terms of the King's Peace of 387 B.C.E., to which most of the states of war-weary Greece subscribed, all of western Asia, including the Greek communities of the Anatolian seacoast, were conceded to Persia. The Persian king became the guarantor of a status quo that kept the Greeks divided and weak. Luckily for the Greeks, rebellions in Egypt, Cyprus, and Phoenicia as well as intrigues among some of the satraps in the western provinces diverted Persian attention from thoughts of another Greek invasion.

Meanwhile, in northern Greece developments were taking place that would irrevocably alter the balance of power. Philip II (r. 359–336 B.C.E.) transformed his previously backward kingdom of Macedonia into the premier military power in the Greek world. (Although southern Greeks had long doubted the "Greekness" of the rough and rowdy Macedonians, many modern

Wine and Beer in the Ancient World

The most prized beverages of ancient peoples were wine and beer. Sediments found in jars excavated at a site in northwest Iran prove that techniques for the manufacture of wine were known as early as the sixth millennium B.C.E. Beer dates back at least as far as the fourth millennium B.C.E. Archaeological excavations have brought to light the equipment used in preparing, transporting, serving, and imbibing these beverages.

In Egypt and Mesopotamia, beer, made from wheat or barley by an elaborate process, was the staple drink of both the elite and the common people. Women prepared beer for the family in their homes, and breweries produced large

quantities for sale. Because the production process left chaff floating on the surface of the liquid, various means were employed to filter this out. Sculptures on Mesopotamian stone reliefs and seals show several drinkers drawing on straws immersed in a large bowl. Archaeologists have found examples of the perforated metal cones that fit over the submerged ends of the straws and filtered the liquid beer drawn through them.

The sharing of beer from a common vessel by several people probably was seen as creating a bond of friendship among the participants. Archaeologists have also found individual beer "mugs" resembling a modern watering can: closed bowls with a perforated spout to filter the chaff and a semicircular channel carrying the liquid into the drinker's mouth.

In Greece, Rome, and other Mediterranean lands, where the climate was suitable for cultivating grape vines, wine was the preferred beverage. Vines were prepared in February and periodically pinched and pruned. The full-grown grapes were picked in September and then crushed—with a winepress or by people trampling on them—to produce a liquid that was sealed in casks for fermentation. The new vintage

Photo By DEA/G. DAGLI ORTI/De Agostini/Getty Images

Dionysus in the Vineyard This Greek vase of the late sixth century B.C.E. depicts Dionysus, the god of wine. Carrying a large kantharos or drinking vessel, he is enveloped by vines carrying bunches of ripe grapes, and accompanied by several Satyrs (mythical creatures combining human features with those of goats or horses) and his human bride Ariadne. Greek drinking paraphernalia often depicted Dionysus and elements of his mythology and cult.

scholars regard their language and culture as Greek at base, though much influenced by contact with non-Greek neighbors.) Philip made a number of improvements to the traditional hoplite formation. He increased the striking power and mobility of his force by equipping soldiers with longer thrusting spears and less armor. Because horses thrived in the broad plains of the north, he experimented with the coordinated use of infantry and cavalry. His engineers also developed new kinds of siege equipment, including the first catapults—machines using the power of twisted cords to hurl arrows or stones great distances. For the first time it became possible to storm a fortified city rather than wait for starvation to take effect.

In 338 B.C.E. Philip defeated a coalition of southern states and established the Confederacy of Corinth as an instrument for controlling the Greek city-states. Philip had himself appointed military commander for a planned all-Greek campaign against Persia, and his generals established a bridgehead on the Asiatic side of the Hellespont. Philip apparently was following the advice of Greek thinkers who had pondered the lessons of the Persian Wars of the fifth century B.C.E. and urged a crusade against the national enemy as a means of unifying their quarrelsome countrymen.

We will never know how far Philip's ambitions extended, for an assassin killed him in 336 B.C.E. When **Alexander** (356–323 B.C.E.), his son and heir, crossed into Asia in 334 B.C.E., his avowed purpose was to exact revenge for Xerxes' invasion a century and half before. He defeated the Persian forces of King Darius III (r. 336–330 B.C.E.) in three pitched battles in Anatolia and Mesopotamia, and he ultimately campaigned as far as the Punjab region of modern Pakistan. After more than two centuries of domination in the Middle East, the Achaemenid Persian Empire had fallen.

Alexander King of Macedonia in northern Greece. Between 334 and 323 B.C.E. he conquered the Persian Empire, reached the Indus Valley, founded many Greek-style cities, and spread Greek culture across the Middle East. Later known as Alexander the Great.

was sampled the following February. Exuberant religious festivals marked key moments in the cycle. Initially expensive and therefore confined to the wealthy and for religious ceremonies, in later antiquity wine became available to a wider spectrum of people. Unlike beer, which requires refrigeration, wine can be stored for a long time in sealed containers and thus could be transported and traded across ancient lands. The usual containers for wine were long, conical pottery jars, which the Greeks called *amphoras.*

The Greeks, who normally mixed wine with water (and thought it scandalous that Persians drank undiluted wine), developed an elaborate array of vessels, made of pottery, metal, and glass, to facilitate mixing, serving, and drinking the precious liquid (see the photo on the facing page). *Kraters* were large mixing bowls into which the wine and water were poured. The *hydria* was used to carry water, and a heater could be used to warm the water when that was desired. Another special vessel could be used to chill the wine by immersion in cold water. Ladles and elegantly narrow vessels with spouts were used to pour the concoction into the drinkers' cups. The most popular shapes for individual drinking vessels were a shallow bowl with two handles, called a *kylix,* and the *kantharos,* a large, deep, two-handled cup. Another popular implement in Greece and western Asia was the *rhyton,* a horn-shaped vessel that tapered into the head and forepaws of an animal with a small hole at the base. The drinker would fill the horn, holding his thumb over the hole until he was ready to drink or pour, then move his thumb and release a thin stream of wine that appeared to be coming out of the animal's mouth.

The drinking equipment belonging to wealthy Greeks was often decorated with representations of the god of wine, Dionysus, holding a kantharos and surrounded by a dense tangle of vines and grape clusters. His entourage included the half-human, half-horse Centaurs; and the Maenads, literally "crazy women," female worshipers who drank wine and engaged in frenzied dancing until they achieved an ecstatic state and sensed the presence of the god.

Greeks, Romans, and other Mediterranean peoples used wine for more conventional religious ceremonies, pouring libations on the ground or on the altar as an offering to the gods. It was also used as a disinfectant and painkiller or as an ingredient in various medicines. Above all, wine was featured at the banquets and drinking parties that forged and deepened social bonds. In the Greek world, the *symposion* (meaning "drinking together") was held after the meal. The host presided over the affair, making the crucial decision about the proportion of water to wine, suggesting topics of conversation, and trying to keep some semblance of order. There might also be entertainment in the form of musicians, dancers, and acrobats.

In Shang China, magnificent bronze vessels whose surfaces were covered with abstract designs and representations of otherworldly animals were used in elaborate ceremonies at ancestral shrines (see photo on page 86). The vessels contained offerings of wine and food for the spirits of the family's ancestors, who were imagined to still need sustenance in the afterlife. The treasured bronze vessels were often buried with their owners so that they could continue to employ them after death. In later periods, as the ancestral sacrifices became less important, beautiful bronze vessels, as well as their ceramic counterparts, became part of the equipment at the banquets of the well-to-do.

QUESTIONS FOR ANALYSIS

1. What social benefits arise from drinking together?
2. How does wine serve religious purposes?
3. What evidence is there that collective drinking was practiced by the privileged social classes?

SECTION REVIEW

- The unsuccessful revolt of Greek city-states in western Anatolia led to two Persian attacks on Greece in the early fifth century B.C.E.

- An ambitious Athens took control of a naval empire in the Aegean. The wealth brought in by the empire subsidized Athenian democracy and culture.

- Ironically, Athenian male citizens were freed up to participate in government and politics by restricting the rights and exploiting the labor of slaves and women.

- The Spartans and their allies, frightened by the growing power of Athens, initiated the lengthy Peloponnesian War but were only able to win with Persian help.

- In the mid-fourth century B.C.E., Philip II made Macedonia into a military power and forcibly united the Greek city-states.

- His son Alexander the Great conquered and took over the Persian Empire.

Alexander the Great, as he came to be called, maintained the framework of Persian administration in the lands he conquered, recognizing that it was well adapted to local circumstances and familiar to the subject peoples. At first, he replaced Persian officials with his own Macedonian and Greek comrades. To control strategic points in his expanding empire, he established a series of Greek-style cities, beginning with Alexandria in Egypt, and settled wounded and aged former soldiers in them. After his decisive victory in northern Mesopotamia (331 B.C.E.), he began to experiment with leaving cooperative Persian officials in place. He also admitted some Persians and other Iranians into his army and the circle of his courtiers, and he adopted elements of Persian dress and court ceremonial. Finally, he married several Iranian women who had useful royal or aristocratic connections, and he pressed his leading subordinates to do the same.

Scholars have reached widely varying conclusions about why Alexander adopted these policies, which were fiercely resented by the Macedonian nobility. Alexander may have operated from a combination of pragmatic and idealistic motives. He set off on his Asian campaign with visions of glory, booty, and revenge. But the farther east he traveled, the more he began to see himself as the legitimate successor of the Persian king (a claim facilitated by the death of Darius III at the hands of subordinates). Besides recognizing that he had responsibilities to all the diverse peoples who fell under his control, he also may have realized the difficulty of holding down so vast an empire by brute force and without the cooperation of important elements among the conquered peoples. In this, he was following the example of the Achaemenids.

THE HELLENISTIC SYNTHESIS, 323–30 B.C.E.

Alexander died suddenly in 323 B.C.E. at the age of thirty-two, with no clear plan for the succession. This event ushered in a half century of chaos as the most ambitious and ruthless of his officers struggled for control of the vast empire. When the dust cleared, the empire had been broken up into three major kingdoms, each ruled by a Macedonian dynasty—the Seleucid (sih-LOO-sid), Ptolemaic (tawl-uh-MAY-ik), and Antigonid (an-TIG-uh-nid) kingdoms (see Map 5.3). Each kingdom faced a unique set of circumstances, and although they frequently were at odds with one another, a rough balance of power prevented any one from gaining the upper hand and enabled smaller states to survive by playing off the great powers.

Historians call the epoch ushered in by Alexander the "**Hellenistic Age**" (323–30 B.C.E.) because the lands in northeastern Africa and western Asia that came under Greek rule became "Hellenized"—that is, powerfully influenced by Greek culture. This was a period of large kingdoms with heterogeneous populations, great cities, powerful rulers, pervasive bureaucracies, and vast disparities in wealth—a far cry from the small, homogeneous, independent city-states of Archaic and Classical Greece. It was a cosmopolitan age of long-distance trade and communications, which saw the rise of new institutions like libraries and universities, new kinds of scholarship and science, and the cultivation of sophisticated tastes in art and literature.

The Seleucids, who took over the bulk of Alexander's conquests, faced the greatest challenges. The Indus Valley and Afghanistan soon split off, and over the course of the third and second centuries B.C.E. Iran was lost to the Parthians. From their capital at Syrian Antioch (AN-tee-awk), the Seleucid monarchs controlled Mesopotamia, Syria, and parts of Anatolia. Their sprawling territories were open to attack from many directions, and, like the Persians before them, they had to deal with many ethnic groups organized under various political and social forms. In the countryside, where most of the native peoples resided, the Seleucids largely maintained the Persian administrative system. They also continued Alexander's policy of founding Greek-style cities throughout their domains. These cities served as administrative centers and were also used to attract colonists from Greece, since the Seleucids needed Greek soldiers, engineers, and administrators.

The dynasty of the **Ptolemies** (TAWL-uh-meze) ruled Egypt and sometimes laid claim to adjacent Syria-Palestine. The people of Egypt belonged to only one ethnic group and were easily controlled because the vast majority were farmers in villages alongside the Nile. The Ptolemies essentially perfected

Hellenistic Age Historians' term for the era, usually dated 323–30 B.C.E., in which Greek culture spread across western Asia and northeastern Africa after the conquests of Alexander the Great. The period ended with the fall of the last major Hellenistic kingdom to Rome, but Greek cultural influence persisted until the spread of Islam in the seventh century C.E.

Ptolemies The Macedonian dynasty, descended from one of Alexander the Great's officers, that ruled Egypt for three centuries (323–30 B.C.E.). From their magnificent capital at Alexandria on the Mediterranean coast, the Ptolemies largely took over the system created by Egyptian pharaohs to extract the wealth of the land, rewarding Greeks and Hellenized non-Greeks serving in the military and administration.

Marshall Ikonography/Alamy

Marble Statue of a Naked Aphrodite Bathing This second century C.E. Roman copy of a Hellenistic original shows the goddess of love and sex crouching and trying to cover herself. While nude male figures were sculpted in previous eras, the female nude is a Hellenistic innovation, perhaps reflecting changing societal attitudes.

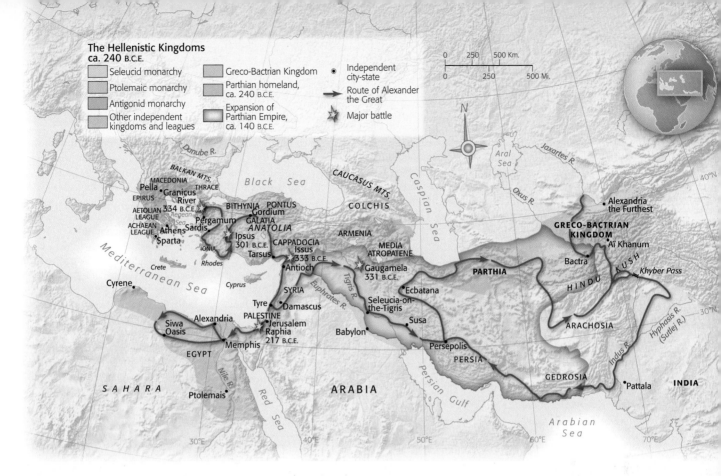

MAP 5.3 **Hellenistic Civilization** After the death of Alexander the Great in 323 B.C.E., his vast empire soon split apart into a number of large and small political entities. A Macedonian dynasty was established on each continent: the Antigonids ruled the Macedonian homeland and tried with varying success to extend their control over southern Greece; the Ptolemies ruled Egypt; and the Seleucids inherited the majority of Alexander's conquests in Asia, though they lost control of the eastern portions because of the rise of the Parthians of Iran in the second century B.C.E. This period saw Greeks migrating in large numbers from their overcrowded homeland to serve as a privileged class of soldiers and administrators on the new frontiers, where they replicated the lifestyle of the city-state. © Cengage Learning

Alexandria City on the Mediterranean coast of Egypt founded by Alexander. It became the capital of the Hellenistic kingdom of the Ptolemies. It contained the famous Library and the Museum, a center for leading scientific and literary figures. Its merchants engaged in trade with areas bordering the Mediterranean Sea and the Indian Ocean.

an administrative structure devised by the pharaohs to extract the surplus wealth of this populous and productive land. The Egyptian economy was centrally planned and highly controlled. Vast revenues poured into the royal treasury from rents (the king owned most of the land), taxes of all sorts, and royal monopolies on olive oil, salt, papyrus, and other key commodities.

The Ptolemies ruled from **Alexandria**, the first of the new cities laid out by Alexander himself. Whereas Memphis and Thebes, the capitals of ancient Egypt, had been located upriver, Alexandria was situated where the westernmost branch of the Nile runs into the Mediterranean Sea, linking Egypt and the Mediterranean world. In the language of the bureaucracy, Alexandria was technically "beside Egypt" rather than in it, as if to emphasize the gulf between rulers and subjects.

The Ptolemies also encouraged the immigration of Greeks from the homeland and, in return for their skills and collaboration in the military or civil administration, gave them land and a privileged position in the new society. But the Ptolemies did not plant Greek-style cities throughout the Egyptian countryside. Only the last Ptolemy, Queen Cleopatra (r. 51–30 B.C.E.), even bothered to learn the language of her Egyptian subjects. Periodic insurrections in the countryside were signs of the Egyptians' growing resentment of the Greeks' exploitation and arrogance.

The Antigonid dynasty ruled a compact and ethnically homogeneous kingdom in the Macedonian homeland and northern Greece. Garrisons at strong-points gave the Antigonids a toehold in central and southern Greece, and the shadow of Macedonian intervention always hung over the south. The southern states met the threat by banding together into confederations, such as the Achaean (uh-KEY-uhn) League in the Peloponnese, in which member-states maintained local autonomy but pooled resources and military power.

Athens and Sparta, the two leading cities of the Classical period, stood out from these confederations. The Spartans clung to the myth of their own invincibility and made a number of heroic but futile stands against Macedonian armies. Athens, which held a special place in the hearts of all Greeks because of the artistic and literary accomplishments of the fifth century

Ancient Astronomy

Long before the advent of writing, people studied the appearance and movement of objects in the sky and used this information for a variety of purposes. Ancient hunters, herders, and farmers all coordinated their activities with the cycle of seasons during the year so that they could follow the migrations of prey, find appropriate pastures for domestic animals, and perform vital agricultural tasks.

Ancient farmers drew on an intimate knowledge of the night sky. Hesiod (HEE-see-uhd), who lived around 700 B.C.E., composed a poem called *Works and Days* describing the annual cycle of tasks on a Greek farm. How did the ancient Greeks, with no clocks, calendars, or newspapers, know where they were in the cycle of the year? They oriented themselves by close observation of natural phenomena such as the movements of planets, stars, and constellations in the night sky. Hesiod gives the following advice for determining the proper times for planting and harvesting grain:

> *Pleiades rising in the dawning sky, Harvest is nigh.*
> *Pleiades setting in the waning night, Plowing is right.*

The Pleiades (PLEE-uh-dees) are a cluster of seven stars visible to the naked eye. The ancient Greeks observed that individual stars, clusters, and constellations moved from east to west during the night and appeared in different parts of the sky at different times of the year. (In fact, the apparent movement of the stars is due to the earth's rotation on its axis and orbit around the sun against a background of unmoving stars.) Hesiod is telling his audience that, when the Pleiades appear above the eastern horizon just before the light of the rising sun makes all the other stars invisible (in May on the modern calendar), a sensible farmer will cut down his grain crop. Some months later (in our September), when the Pleiades dip below the western horizon just before sunrise, it is time to plow the fields and plant seeds for the next year's harvest.

Farmers such as Hesiod were primarily concerned with the seasons of the year. However, there was also a need to divide the year up into smaller units. The moon, so easily visible in the night sky and with clear phases, offered the unit of the month. Unfortunately, the lunar and solar cycles do not fit comfortably together, since twelve lunar months falls eleven days short of the solar cycle of a 365-day year. Ancient peoples wrestled with ways of reconciling the two cycles, and the months of varying lengths and leap years in our present-day calendar are the legacy of this dilemma.

The complex societies that arose from the fourth millennium B.C.E. onward had additional needs for information derived from astronomical observation, and these needs reflected the distinctive characteristics of those societies. In ancient Egypt an administrative calendar was essential for record keeping and the regular collection of taxes by the government. The Egyptians discovered that a calendar based on lunar months could be kept in harmony with the solar year by inserting an extra month five times over a nineteen-year cycle. They also learned from experience that the flooding of the Nile River—so vital for Egyptian agriculture—happened at the time when Sirius, the brightest star in the sky, rose above the eastern horizon just before the sun came up.

In the second millennium B.C.E., the Babylonians began to make and record very precise naked-eye observations of the movements of the sun, the moon, and the visible planets,

B.C.E., pursued a policy of neutrality. The city became a large museum, filled with the relics and memories of a glorious past, as well as a university town that attracted the children of the well-to-do from all over the Mediterranean and western Asia.

In an age of cities, the greatest city of all was Alexandria, with a population of nearly half a million. At its heart was the royal compound, containing the palace and administrative buildings, as well as the magnificent Mausoleum of Alexander. (The first Ptolemy had stolen the body of Alexander on its way back to Macedonia for burial, seeking legitimacy for his dynasty by claiming the blessing of the great conqueror, who was declared to be a god.) Two harbors linked the commerce of the Mediterranean with the Red Sea and Indian Ocean. A great lighthouse—the first of its kind, a multistory tower with a fiery beacon visible at a distance of 30 miles (48 kilometers)—was one of the wonders of the ancient world.

Alexandria gained further luster from its famous Library, with several hundred thousand volumes, and from its Museum, or "House of the Muses" (divinities who presided over the arts and sciences), a research institution supporting the work of the greatest poets, philosophers, doctors, and scientists of the day. These well-funded institutions made possible significant advances in sciences such as mathematics, medicine, and astronomy (see Environment and Technology: Ancient Astronomy).

Greek residents of Alexandria enjoyed citizenship in a Greek-style polis with an Assembly, a Council, and officials who dealt with local affairs. Public baths and shaded arcades offered places to relax and socialize with friends. Ancient plays were revived in the theaters, and musical performances and demonstrations of oratory took place in the concert halls. Gymnasia, besides providing facilities for exercise, were where young men of the privileged classes were schooled in athletics, music, and literature. Jews had their own civic government, officials, and law courts

of occasional eclipses, and of other unusual celestial occurrences. Believing that the phenomena they saw in the sky sometimes contained messages and warnings of disaster, the rulers supported specialists who observed, recorded, and interpreted these "signs" from the gods. Using a sophisticated system of mathematical notation, they figured out the regularities of certain cycles and were able to predict future occurrences of eclipses and the movements of the planets.

Whereas Babylonian science observed and recorded data, Greek philosophers tried to figure out why the heavenly bodies moved as they did and what the actual structure of the *kosmos* (Greek for an "orderly arrangement") was. Aristotle pointed out that because the earth's shadow, as seen on the face of the moon during a lunar eclipse, was curved, the earth must be a sphere. Eratosthenes (eh-ruh-TOSS-thih-nees) made a surprisingly accurate calculation of the circumference of the earth. Aristarchus (ah-ris-TAWR-kiss) calculated the distances and relative sizes of the moon and sun. He also argued against the prevailing notion that the earth was the center of the universe, asserting that the earth and other planets revolved around the sun. Other Greek theorists pictured the earth as a sphere at the center of a set of concentric spheres that rotated, carrying along the seven visible "planets"—the moon, Mercury, Venus, the sun, Mars, Jupiter, Saturn—with the outermost ring containing the stars that maintain a fixed position relative to one another.

As a result of the conquests of Alexander the Great, Mesopotamia came under Greek control and Greek astronomers gained access to the many centuries of accumulated records of Babylonian observers. This more precise information allowed Greek thinkers to further refine their models for the structure and movement of celestial objects. The Greek conception of the universe, in the form set down by the second-century C.E. astronomer Claudius Ptolemy, became the basis of scientific

De Agostini/Getty Images

Tower of the Winds, Athens, Second Century B.C.E.
Designed in the Hellenistic period by the astronomer Andronicus of Cyrrhus, the eight sides are decorated with images of the eight directional winds. Sundials on the exterior showed the time of day, and a water-driven mechanism inside the tower revealed the hours, days, and phases of the moon.

thinking about these matters for the next 1,400 years in the Islamic Middle East and Christian Europe.

Source: From *Hesiod: Works and Days and Theogony*, translated by Stanley Lombardo. Copyright © 1993. Reprinted by permission of Hackett Publishing Company.

SECTION REVIEW

- In the Hellenistic Age, Greeks controlled western Asia and northwest Africa. Greek culture would have a strong influence in this region for a thousand years.

- Alexander's empire was broken up into three major successor kingdoms in Europe, Asia, and Africa, each with its own unique challenges.

- Alexandria in Egypt, capital of the Ptolemies, was the greatest city in the world. It had a large and diverse population and was a center of commerce for the Mediterranean Sea and Indian Ocean.

- The Ptolemies created the greatest library of antiquity and the Museum, a center of research fostering advances in scholarship, science, technology, and medicine.

- Ambitious and elite members of indigenous peoples learned Greek and adopted a Greek lifestyle in order to be part of the privileged ruling class, while Greeks borrowed from the ancient heritages of Egypt and Mesopotamia.

and predominated in two of the five main residential districts. Other quarters were filled with the sights, sounds, and smells of ethnic groups from Syria, Anatolia, and the Egyptian countryside.

In all the Hellenistic states, ambitious members of the indigenous populations learned the Greek language and adopted elements of Greek lifestyle, since this put them in a position to become part of the privileged and wealthy ruling class. For the ancient Greeks, to be Greek was primarily a matter of language and lifestyle rather than physical traits. In the Hellenistic Age there was a spontaneous synthesis of Greek and indigenous ways. Egyptians migrated to Alexandria, and Greeks and Egyptians intermarried in the villages of the countryside. Greeks living amid the monuments and descendants of the ancient civilizations of Egypt and western Asia were exposed to the mathematical and astronomical wisdom of Mesopotamia, the elaborate mortuary rituals of Egypt, and the many attractions of foreign religious cults. With little official planning or blessing, stemming for the most part from the day-to-day experiences and actions of ordinary people, a great multicultural experiment unfolded as Greek and Middle Eastern cultural traits clashed and merged.

139

CONCLUSION

Profound changes took place in the lands of the eastern Mediterranean and western Asia in the first millennium B.C.E., with Persians and Greeks playing pivotal roles. Let us compare the impacts of these two peoples and assess the broad significance of these centuries.

The empire of the Achaemenid Persians was the largest empire yet to appear in the world, encompassing a wide variety of landscapes, peoples, and social, political, and economic systems. How did the Persians manage this diverse collection of lands for more than two centuries? The answer did not lie entirely in brute force. The Persian government demonstrated flexibility and tolerance in its handling of the laws, customs, and beliefs of subject peoples. Persian administration, superimposed on top of local structures, left a considerable role for native institutions.

The Persians also displayed a flair for public relations. Their brand of Zoroastrian religion underlined the authority of the king as the appointee of god, champion of justice, and defender of world order against evil and destructive forces. In their art and inscriptions, the Persian kings broadcast an image of a benevolent empire in which the dependent peoples gladly contributed to the welfare of the realm.

Western Asia underwent significant changes in the period of Persian supremacy. By imposing a uniform system of law and administration and by providing security and stability, the Persian government fostered prosperity, at least for some. It also organized labor on a large scale to construct an expanded water distribution network and work the extensive estates of the Persian royal family and nobility.

Most difficult to assess is the cultural impact of Persian rule. A new synthesis of the long-dominant culture of Mesopotamia with Iranian elements is most visible in the art, architecture, and inscriptions of the Persian monarchs. The Zoroastrian religion may have spread across the empire and influenced other religious traditions, such as Judaism, but Zoroastrianism does not appear to have had broad, popular appeal. The Persian administration relied heavily on the scribes and written languages of its Mesopotamian, Syrian, and Egyptian subjects, and literacy remained the preserve of a small, professional class. Thus the Persian language does not seem to have been widely adopted by inhabitants of the empire.

Nearly two centuries of trouble with the Greeks on their western frontier vexed the Persians, but they were primarily concerned with the security of their eastern and northeastern frontiers, where they were vulnerable to attack by the nomads of Central Asia. The technological differences between Greece and Persia were not great. The only significant difference was the hoplite arms and military formation used by the Greeks, which often allowed them to prevail over the Persians. The Persian king's response in the later fifth and fourth centuries B.C.E. was to hire Greek mercenaries to employ hoplite tactics for his benefit.

Alexander's conquests brought changes to the Greek world almost as radical as those experienced by the Persians. Greeks spilled out into the sprawling new frontiers in northeastern Africa and western Asia, and the independent city-state became inconsequential in a world of large kingdoms. The centuries of Greek domination had a far more pervasive cultural impact on the Middle East than did the Persian period. Whereas Alexander had been inclined to preserve the Persian administrative apparatus, leaving native institutions and personnel in place, his successors relied almost exclusively on a privileged class of Greek soldiers, officers, and administrators.

Equally significant were the foundation of Greek-style cities, which exerted a powerful cultural influence on important elements of the native populations, and a system of easily learned alphabetic Greek writing, which led to more widespread literacy and more effective dissemination of information. The result was that the Greeks had a profound impact on the peoples and lands of the Middle East, and Hellenism persisted as a cultural force for a thousand years. And even after Islam spread over this region in the seventh century C.E., it absorbed and maintained elements of the Hellenistic legacy (see Chapter 10).

A final point should be made about the Greeks, one that is particularly apt for students of world history who are learning about the diversity of ways in which humans have addressed the challenges of living in the natural world and among other humans. Readers of this book are encouraged to compare Greek civilization to another great contemporary civilization where the sheer distance and lack of communication precluded any possibility of borrowing—ancient China in the Zhou era (see Chapter 4). Beyond discovering that the similarities are great, one is struck by the fact that the most innovative developments in both civilizations took place during periods of political fragmentation and persistent rivalry and warfare—the Archaic and Classical periods of Greek history and the Spring and Autumn and Warring States periods in China—rather than in the more stable centuries of imperial rule under the Roman and Han emperors (in Chapter 6 we will be making comparisons between Rome and early imperial China). The differences between Greek and early Chinese civilization are equally revealing and underlie the ways in which Western and East Asian civilizations have diverged, with implications for our own times.

KEY TERMS

Cyrus p. 116
Darius I p. 116
satrap p. 117
Persepolis p. 118
Zoroastrianism p. 118

polis p. 124
hoplite p. 124
tyrant p. 126
democracy p. 126
sacrifice p. 126

Herodotus p. 128
Pericles p. 129
Persian Wars p. 130
trireme p. 130
Socrates p. 131

Peloponnesian War p. 133
Alexander p. 134
Hellenistic Age p. 136
Ptolemies p. 136
Alexandria p. 137

SUGGESTED READING

Briant, Pierre. *From Cyrus to Alexander: A History of the Persian Empire.* 2002. The most up-to-date history of ancient Persia, by the leading scholar in this field.

Brosius, Maria. *Women in Ancient Persia, 559–331 B.C.* 1996. Gathers and evaluates the scattered evidence.

Bugh, Glenn R., ed. *The Cambridge Companion to the Hellenistic World.* 2006. Essays by leading authorities on many aspects of Hellenistic history and culture.

Cawkwell, George. *The Greek Wars: The Failure of Persia.* 2006. Examines the two-centuries-long encounter from a Persian perspective.

Curtis, John, and St. John Simpson, eds. *The World of Achaemenid Persia: The Diversity of Ancient Iran.* 2010. Contains up-to-date essays by leading scholars on Achaemenid history and culture.

Dillon, Matthew, and Lynda Garland, eds. *Ancient Greece: Social and Historical Documents from Archaic Times to the Death of Alexander.* 2010. A wide-ranging collection of documents in translation with explanatory notes.

Fantham, Elaine, Helene Peet Foley, Natalie Boymel Kampen, Sarah B. Pomeroy, and H. Alan Shapiro. *Women in the Classical World: Image and Text.* 1995. A strong exposition of the roles, experiences, and treatment of women in Greek and Roman society, combining texts and visual images with interpretation.

Grant, Michael, and Rachel Kitzinger, eds. *Civilization of the Ancient Mediterranean,* 3 vols. 1987. Essays by contemporary experts on nearly every aspect of ancient Greco-Roman civilization, with select bibliographies.

Hanson, Victor Davis. *The Other Greeks: The Family Farm and the Agrarian Roots of Western Civilization.* 1995. Emphasizes the centrality of farming to the development of Greek institutions and values.

Hanson, Victor Davis. *The Western Way of War: Infantry Battle in Classical Greece.* 1989. A clear and gripping description of every aspect of the most terrifying and effective form of combat in antiquity.

Havelock, Eric A. *The Muse Learns to Write: Reflections on Orality and Literacy from Antiquity to the Present.* 1986. Explores the profound effects of alphabetic literacy on the Greek mind.

Heckel, Waldemar, and Lawrence A. Trittle, eds. *Alexander the Great: A New History.* 2009. Essays by leading experts on Alexander's life, times, and legacy.

Kuhrt, Amelie. *The Persian Empire: A Corpus of Sources from the Achaemenid Period,* 2 vols. 2007. Makes available a wide range of documents in translation with explanatory notes.

Pomeroy, Sarah B., Stanley M. Burstein, Walter Donlan, and Jennifer Tolbert Roberts. *Ancient Greece: A Political, Social, and Cultural History,* 3d ed. 2011. An up-to-date, well-written account of Greek history and culture.

The Perseus Project (*www.perseus.tufts.edu*). A remarkable Internet site containing hundreds of ancient texts, thousands of photographs of artifacts and sites, maps, encyclopedias, dictionaries, and other resources for the study of Greek (and Roman) civilization.

CourseMate Go to the History CourseMate website for primary source links, study tools, and review materials for this chapter. www.cengagebrain.com

Chapter Outline

Rome's Creation of a Mediterranean Empire, 753 B.C.E.–330 C.E.
➤ *How did Rome create and maintain its vast Mediterranean empire?*

The Origins of Imperial China, 221 B.C.E.–220 C.E.
➤ *How did imperial China evolve under the Qin and Han dynasties?*

Conclusion
➤ *What were the most important similarities and differences between these two empires, and what do the similarities and differences tell us about the circumstances and the character of each?*

- **DIVERSITY + DOMINANCE**   Socioeconomic Mobility, Winners and Losers in Imperial Rome and Han China
- **ENVIRONMENT + TECHNOLOGY**   Ancient Glass

Scala/Art Resource, NY

Dancing Girl Wearing Silk Garment, Second–Third Century C.E.   This Roman mosaic depicts a musician accompanying a dancer who is wearing a sheer garment of silk imported from China.

An Age of Empires: Rome and Han China, 753 B.C.E.–330 C.E.

According to Chinese sources, in the year 166 C.E. a group of travelers identifying themselves as envoys from Andun, the king of distant Da Qin, arrived at the court of the Chinese emperor Huan, one of the Han dynasty rulers. Andun was Marcus Aurelius Antoninus, the emperor of Rome. As far as we know, these travelers were the first "Romans" to reach China, although they probably were residents of one of the eastern provinces of the Roman Empire, and they probably stretched the truth in claiming to be official representatives of the Roman emperor. More likely they were merchants hoping to set up a profitable trading arrangement at the source of the silk so highly prized in the West (see Environment and Technology: Ancient Glass). Chinese officials, however, were in no position to disprove their claim, since there was no direct contact between the Roman and Chinese Empires.

We do not know what became of these travelers, and their mission apparently did not lead to more regular contact between the empires. Even so, the episode raises some interesting points. First, the last centuries B.C.E. and the first centuries C.E. saw the emergence of two manifestations of a new kind of empire. Second, Rome and China were linked by far-flung international trading networks encompassing the entire Eastern Hemisphere, and they were dimly aware of each other's existence.

The Roman Empire encompassed all the lands surrounding the Mediterranean Sea as well as sizable portions of continental Europe and the Middle East. The Han Empire stretched from the Pacific Ocean to the oases of Central Asia. The largest empires the world had yet seen, they succeeded in centralizing control to a greater degree than earlier empires; their cultural impact on the lands and peoples they dominated was more pervasive; and they were remarkably stable and lasted for many centuries.

Thousands of miles separated Rome and Han China; neither influenced the other. Why did two such unprecedented political entities flourish at the same time? And why did they develop roughly similar solutions to certain problems? Historians have put forth theories stressing supposedly common factors—such as climate change and the pressure of nomadic peoples from Central Asia on the Roman and Chinese frontiers—but no theory has won general support.

ROME'S CREATION OF A MEDITERRANEAN EMPIRE, 753 B.C.E.–330 C.E.

Rome's central location contributed to its success in unifying Italy and then all the lands ringing the Mediterranean Sea (see Map 6.1). The middle of three peninsulas that jut from the European landmass into the Mediterranean, the boot-shaped Italian peninsula and the large island of Sicily constitute a natural bridge almost linking Europe and North Africa. Italy was a crossroads in the Mediterranean, and Rome was a crossroads within Italy. Rome lay at the midpoint of the peninsula, about 15 miles (24 kilometers) from the western coast, where a north-south road intersected an east-west river route. The Tiber River on one side and a double ring of seven hills on the other afforded natural protection to the site.

Italy is a land of hills and mountains. The Apennine range runs along its length like a spine, separating the eastern and western coastal plains, while the arc of the Alps shields it on the north. Many of Italy's rivers are navigable, and passes through the Apennines and through the snowcapped Alps allowed merchants and armies to travel overland. The mild Mediterranean climate affords a long growing season and conditions suitable for a wide variety of crops. The hillsides, largely denuded of cover today, were well forested in ancient times, providing timber for construction and fuel. The region of Etruria in the northwest was rich in iron and other metals.

Even though as much as 75 percent of the total area of the Italian peninsula is hilly, there is still ample arable land in the coastal plains and river valleys. Much of this land has extremely fertile volcanic soil and sustained a much larger population than was possible in Greece. While expanding within Italy, the Roman state created effective mechanisms for tapping the human resources of the countryside.

A Republic of Farmers, 753–31 B.C.E.

Popular legend maintained that Romulus was cast adrift on the Tiber River as a baby, was nursed by a she-wolf, and founded the city of Rome in 753 B.C.E. Archaeological research, however, shows that the Palatine Hill was occupied as early as 1000 B.C.E. The merging of several hilltop communities to form an urban nucleus, made possible by the draining of a swamp on the site of the future Roman Forum (civic center), took place shortly before 600 B.C.E. The Latin speech and cultural patterns of the inhabitants of the site were typical of the indigenous population of most of the peninsula. However, tradition remembered Etruscan immigrants arriving in the seventh century B.C.E. (the Etruscans, from the region north of Rome, were linguistically and culturally different and more technologically advanced than other peoples in Italy), and Rome came to pride itself on offering refuge to exiles and outcasts.

Agriculture was the essential economic activity in the early Roman state, and land was the basis of wealth. As a consequence, social status, political privilege, and fundamental values were related to land ownership. Most early Romans were self-sufficient farmers who owned small plots of land. A small number of families managed to acquire large tracts of land. The heads of these wealthy families were members of the Senate—a "Council of Elders" that played a dominant role in the politics of the Roman state. According to tradition, there were seven kings of Rome between 753 and 507 B.C.E. The first was Romulus; the last was the tyrannical Tarquinius Superbus. In 507 B.C.E. members of the senatorial class, led by Brutus "the Liberator," deposed Tarquinius Superbus and instituted a *res publica*, a "public possession," or republic.

The **Republic**, which lasted from 507 to 31 B.C.E., was not a democracy in the modern sense. Sovereign power resided in an Assembly of the male citizens where the votes of the wealthy classes counted for more than the votes of poor citizens. Each year a slate of officials was chosen, with members of the elite competing vigorously to hold offices in a prescribed order. The culmination of a political career was to be selected as one of the two consuls who presided over meetings of the Senate and Assembly and commanded the army on military campaigns.

The real center of power was the **Senate**. Technically an advisory council, first to the kings and later to the annually changing Republican officials, the Senate increasingly made policy and governed. Senators nominated their sons for public offices and filled Senate vacancies from the ranks of former officials. This self-perpetuating body, whose members served for life, brought together the state's wealth, influence, and political and military experience.

Republic The period from 507 to 31 B.C.E., during which Rome was largely governed by the aristocratic Roman Senate.

Senate A council whose members were the heads of wealthy, landowning families. Originally an advisory body to the early kings, in the era of the Roman Republic the Senate effectively governed the Roman state and the growing empire. Under Senate leadership, Rome conquered an empire of unprecedented extent in the lands surrounding the Mediterranean Sea.

CHRONOLOGY

	Rome	China
1000 B.C.E.	1000 B.C.E. First settlement on site of Rome	
500 B.C.E.	507 B.C.E. Establishment of the Republic	
		480–221 B.C.E. Warring States Period
300 B.C.E.	290 B.C.E. Defeat of tribes of Samnium gives Romans control of Italy 264–202 B.C.E. Wars against Carthage guarantee Roman control of western Mediterranean	221 B.C.E. Qin emperor unites eastern China
200 B.C.E.	200–146 B.C.E. Wars against Hellenistic kingdoms lead to control of eastern Mediterranean	202 B.C.E. Han dynasty succeeds Qin 140–87 B.C.E. Emperor Wu expands the Han Empire 109–91 B.C.E. Sima Qian writes history of China
100 B.C.E.	88–31 B.C.E. Civil wars and failure of the Republic 31 B.C.E.–14 C.E. Augustus establishes the Principate	9–23 C.E. Wang Mang usurps throne 25 C.E. Han capital transferred from Chang'an to Luoyang
50 C.E.	45–58 C.E. Paul spreads Christianity in the eastern Mediterranean	99 C.E. Ban Zhao composes "Lessons for Women"
200 C.E.	235–284 C.E. Third-Century Crisis	220 C.E. Fall of Han dynasty
300 C.E.	324 C.E. Constantine moves capital to Constantinople	

The inequalities in Roman society led to periodic conflict between the elite (called "patricians" [puh-TRISH-uhn]) and the majority of the population (called "plebeians" [pluh-BEE-uhn]), a struggle known as the Conflict of the Orders. On several occasions the plebeians refused to work or fight, and even physically withdrew from the city, in order to pressure the elite to make political concessions. One result was publication of the laws on twelve stone tablets ca. 450 B.C.E., which served as a check on arbitrary decisions by judicial officials. Another important reform was the creation of new officials, the tribunes (TRIH-byoon), who were drawn from the non-elite classes and who could veto, or block, actions of the Assembly or officials that threatened the interests of the lower orders. The elite, though forced to give in on key points, found ways to blunt the reforms, in large part by bringing the plebeian leadership into an expanded elite.

The basic unit of Roman society was the family, made up of the several living generations of family members plus domestic slaves. The oldest living male, the *paterfamilias*, exercised absolute authority over other family members. More generally, important male members of the society possessed *auctoritas*, a quality that elicited obedience from their inferiors.

patron/client relationship In ancient Rome, a fundamental social relationship in which the patron—a wealthy and powerful individual—provided legal and economic protection and assistance to clients, men of lesser status and means, and in return the clients supported the political careers and economic interests of their patron.

Complex ties of obligation, such as the **patron/client relationship**, bound together individuals of different classes. Clients sought the help and protection of patrons, men of wealth and influence. A patron provided legal advice and representation, physical protection, and loans of money in tough times. In turn, the client was expected to follow his patron into battle, work on his land, and support him in the political arena. Throngs of clients awaited their patrons in the morning and accompanied them to the Forum for the day's business. Especially large retinues brought great prestige. Middle-class clients of aristocrats might be patrons of poorer men. In Rome inequality was accepted, institutionalized, and turned into a system of mutual benefits and obligations.

Historical sources rarely report the activities of Roman women, largely because they played no public role, and nearly all our information pertains to the upper classes. In early Rome, a woman was like a child in the eyes of the law. She started out under the absolute authority of her paterfamilias, and when she married, she came under the jurisdiction of the paterfamilias of her husband's family. Unable to own property or represent herself in legal proceedings, she depended on a male guardian to protect her interests.

Despite these limitations, Roman women were less constrained than their Greek counterparts (see Chapter 5). Over time they gained greater personal protection and economic freedom:

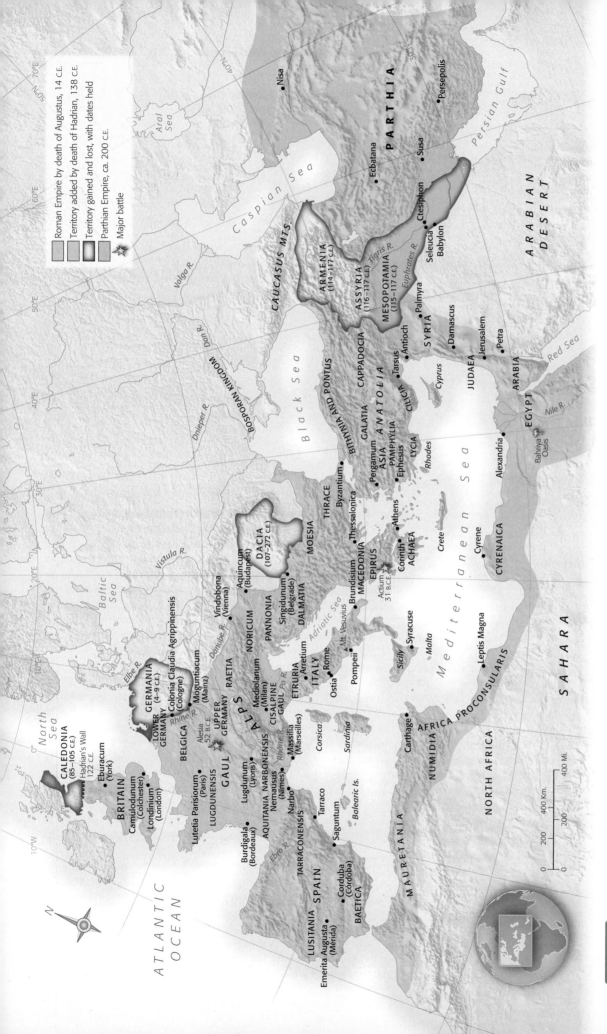

MAP 6.1 **The Roman Empire** The Roman Empire came to encompass all the lands surrounding the Mediterranean Sea, as well as parts of continental Europe. When Augustus died in 14 C.E., he left instructions to his successors not to expand beyond the limits he had set, but Claudius invaded southern Britain in the mid-first century and the soldier-emperor Trajan added Romania early in the second century. Deserts and seas provided solid natural boundaries, but the long and vulnerable river border in central and eastern Europe would eventually prove expensive to defend and vulnerable to invasion by Germanic and Central Asian peoples. © Cengage Learning

Legend:
- Roman Empire by death of Augustus, 14 C.E.
- Territory added by death of Hadrian, 138 C.E.
- Territory gained and lost, with dates held
- Parthian Empire, ca. 200 C.E.
- ★ Major battle

CALEDONIA (85–105 C.E.)
Hadrian's Wall 122 C.E.
Eburacum (York)
BRITAIN
Camulodunum (Colchester)
Londinium (London)

GERMANIA (4–9 C.E.)
LOWER GERMANY
Colonia Claudia Agrippinensis (Cologne)
BELGICA
UPPER GERMANY
Moguntiacum (Mainz)
Alesia 52 B.C.E.
GAUL
Lutetia Parisiorum (Paris)
LUGDUNENSIS
Lugdunum (Lyons)
AQUITANIA
NARBONENSIS
Nemausus (Nîmes)
Narbo
Massilia (Marseilles)
Burdigala (Bordeaux)
Tarraco
Saguntum
TARRACONENSIS
SPAIN
LUSITANIA
Emerita Augusta (Mérida)
Corduba (Córdoba)
BAETICA

ALPS
RAETIA
NORICUM
Vindobona (Vienna)
Aquincum (Budapest)
PANNONIA
Singidunum (Belgrade)
DALMATIA
DACIA (107–272 C.E.)
MOESIA
THRACE
Byzantium
Mediolanum (Milan)
CISALPINE GAUL
ETRURIA
Arretium
ITALY
Rome
Ostia
Pompeii
Mt. Vesuvius
Brundisium
EPIRUS
Actium 31 B.C.E.
MACEDONIA
Thessalonica
Corinth
ACHAEA
Athens
Crete
Corsica
Sardinia
Sicily
Syracuse
Malta
Leptis Magna
Carthage
AFRICA PROCONSULARIS
NUMIDIA
NORTH AFRICA
MAURETANIA
Balearic Is.

THRACE
BITHYNIA AND PONTUS
GALATIA
CAPPADOCIA
ASIA
ANATOLIA
Pergamum
Ephesus
PAMPHYLIA
LYCIA
CILICIA
Tarsus
Antioch
Rhodes
Cyprus
SYRIA
Palmyra
Damascus
JUDAEA
Jerusalem
Petra
ARABIA
CYRENAICA
Cyrene
EGYPT
Alexandria
Bahriya Oasis

ARMENIA (114–117 C.E.)
ASSYRIA (116–117 C.E.)
MESOPOTAMIA (115–117 C.E.)
Euphrates R.
Tigris R.
Ctesiphon
Seleucia
Babylon
PARTHIA
Ecbatana
Susa
Nisa
Persepolis
Persian Gulf
ARABIAN DESERT
SAHARA
Red Sea
Nile R.

CAUCASUS MTS.
Caspian Sea
Aral Sea
Black Sea
Adriatic Sea
Mediterranean Sea
North Sea
Baltic Sea
ATLANTIC OCEAN

BOSPORAN KINGDOM
Volga R.
Don R.
Dnieper R.
Vistula R.
Danube R.
Rhine R.
Elbe R.
Ebro R.
Rhône R.
Po R.

0   200   400 Mi.
0   200   400 Km.

Statue of a Roman Carrying Busts of His Ancestors, First Century B.C.E.   Roman society was extremely conscious of status, and the status of an elite Roman family was determined in large part by the public achievements of ancestors and living members. A visitor to a Roman home found portraits of distinguished ancestors in the entry hall, along with labels listing the offices they held. Portrait heads were carried in funeral processions. Alinari/Art Resource, NY

for instance, some employed a form of marriage that left a woman under the jurisdiction of her father and independent after his death. There are many stories of strong women with great influence on their husbands or sons who helped shape Roman history. From the first century B.C.E. on, Roman poets confess their love for educated and outspoken women.

Early Romans believed in invisible forces known as *numina*. Vesta, the living, pulsating energy of fire, dwelled in the hearth. Janus guarded the door. The Penates watched over food stored in the cupboard. Other deities resided in nearby hills, caves, grottoes, and springs. Romans made small offerings of cakes and liquids to win the favor of these spirits. Certain gods had larger spheres of operation—for example, Jupiter was the god of the sky, and Mars initially was a god of agriculture as well as war.

The Romans labored to maintain the *pax deorum* ("peace of the gods"), a covenant between the gods and the Roman state. Boards of priests drawn from the aristocracy performed sacrifices and other rituals to win the gods' favor. In return, the gods were expected to support the undertakings of the Roman state.

When the Romans came into contact with the Greeks of southern Italy (see Chapter 5), they equated their major deities with Greek gods—for example, Jupiter with Greek Zeus, Mars with Greek Ares—and they took over the myths attached to those gods.

Expansion in Italy and the Mediterranean

Around 500 B.C.E. Rome was a relatively unimportant city-state in central Italy. Three and a half centuries later, Rome was the center of a huge empire encompassing virtually all the lands surrounding the Mediterranean Sea. Expansion began slowly and then picked up momentum, reaching a peak in the third and second centuries B.C.E. Some scholars attribute this expansion to the greed and aggressiveness of a people fond of war. Others observe that the structure of the Roman state encouraged war, because the two consuls had only one year in office in which to gain military glory. The Romans invariably claimed that they were only defending themselves. The pattern was that the Romans, feeling insecure, expanded the territory under their control in order to provide a buffer against attack. However, each new conquest became vulnerable and led to further expansion.

The chief instrument of Roman expansion was the army. All male citizens owning a specified amount of land were subject to service. The Roman soldiers' equipment—body armor, shield, spear, and sword—was not far different from that of Greek hoplites, but the Roman battle line was more flexible than the phalanx, being subdivided into units that could maneuver independently. Roman armies were famous for their training and discipline. One observer noted that a Greek army would lazily seek a naturally defended hilltop to camp for the night, but a Roman army would always laboriously fortify an identical camp in the plain.

Rome's conquest of Italy was sparked by friction between the hill tribes of the Apennines, who drove their herds to seasonal grazing grounds, and the farmers of the coastal plains. In the fifth century B.C.E. Rome led a league of central Italian cities organized for defense against the hill tribes. On several occasions in the fourth century B.C.E. the Romans protected the wealthy and sophisticated cities of Campania, the region on the Bay of Naples possessing the

Cast of Trajan's Column, Detail of soldiers building fortifications in Dacia/De Agostini Picture Library/G. Dagli Orti/The Bridgeman Art Library

Scene from Trajan's Column, Rome, ca. 113 C.E. The Roman emperor Trajan erected a marble column 125 feet (38 meters) in height to commemorate his triumphant campaign in Dacia (modern Romania). The relief carving, which snakes around the column for 656 feet (200 meters), illustrates numerous episodes of the conquest and provides a detailed pictorial record of the equipment and practices of the Roman army in the field. This panel depicts soldiers building a fort.

richest farmland in Italy. By 290 B.C.E., in the course of three wars with the Samnite tribes of central Italy, the Romans had extended their "protection" over nearly the entire peninsula.

Unlike the Greeks, who were reluctant to share the privileges of citizenship with outsiders, the Romans often granted some or all of the political, legal, and economic privileges of Roman citizenship to conquered populations. They co-opted the most influential people in the conquered communities and made Rome's interests their interests. Rome demanded soldiers from its Italian subjects, and a seemingly inexhaustible reservoir of manpower was a key element of its military success. In a number of crucial wars, Rome was able to endure higher casualties than the enemy and to prevail by sheer numbers.

Between 264 and 202 B.C.E. Rome fought two protracted and bloody wars against the Carthaginians, those energetic descendants of Phoenicians from Lebanon who had settled in present-day Tunisia and dominated the commerce of the western Mediterranean (see Chapter 3). The Roman state emerged as the unchallenged master of the western Mediterranean and acquired its first overseas provinces in Sicily, Sardinia, and Spain (see Map 6.1). Between 200 and 146 B.C.E. a series of wars pitted the Roman state against the major Hellenistic kingdoms in the eastern Mediterranean. The Romans were at first reluctant to occupy such distant territories and withdrew their troops at the conclusion of several wars. But when the settlements that they imposed failed to take root—often because Rome's "friends" in the Greek world did not understand that they were expected to be deferential and obedient clients to their Roman patron—the frustrated Roman government took over direct administration of these lands. The conquest of the Celtic peoples of Gaul (modern France; see Chapter 4) by Rome's most brilliant general, Gaius Julius Caesar, between 59 and 51 B.C.E. led to Rome's first territorial acquisitions in Europe's heartland.

At first the Romans resisted extending their system of governance and citizenship rights to the distant provinces. Indigenous elite groups willing to collaborate with the Romans were given considerable autonomy, including responsibility for local administration and tax collection. Every year a senator who recently had held a high office was dispatched to each province to serve as governor. Accompanied by a small retinue of friends and relations who served as advisers and deputies, he was responsible for defending the province against outside attack and internal disruption, overseeing the collection of taxes and other revenues due Rome, and deciding legal cases.

Over time, this system of provincial administration proved inadequate. Officials were chosen because of their political connections and often lacked competence. Yearly changes of governor meant that incumbents had little time to gain experience or make local contacts. Although many governors were honest, some unscrupulously extorted huge sums of money from the provincial populace. While governing an ever-larger Mediterranean empire, the Romans were still relying on the institutions and attitudes that developed when Rome was merely a city-state.

The Failure of the Republic

Rome's success in creating a vast empire unleashed forces that eventually destroyed the Republican system of government. The frequent wars and territorial expansion of the third and second centuries B.C.E. produced profound changes in the Italian landscape. Most of the wealth generated by the conquest and control of new provinces ended up in the hands of the upper classes.

Italian farmers were away from home on military service for long periods of time, and while they were away, investors took over their farms by purchase, deception, or intimidation. The small, self-sufficient farms of the Italian countryside, whose peasant owners had been the backbone of the Roman legions, were replaced by *latifundia*, literally "broad estates," or ranches.

The owners of these large estates grazed herds of cattle or grew crops—such as grapes for wine—that brought in big profits, rather than growing wheat, the staple food of ancient Italy. As a result, the population in the burgeoning cities of Italy became dependent on expensive imported grain. Meanwhile, the cheap slave labor provided by prisoners of war made it hard for peasants who had lost their farms to find work in the countryside (see Diversity and Dominance: Socioeconomic Mobility, Winners and Losers in Imperial Rome and Han China). When they moved to Rome and other cities, they found no work there either, and they lived in dire poverty. The growing urban masses, idle and prone to riot, would play a major role in the political struggles of the late Republic.

One consequence of the decline of peasant farmers in Italy was a shortage of men who owned the property required for military service. At the end of the second century B.C.E. Gaius Marius—a "new man," as the Romans called politically active individuals who did not belong to the traditional ruling class—accepted into his legions poor, propertyless men and promised them farms upon retirement from military service. These troops became devoted to Marius and helped him get elected to an unprecedented (and illegal) six consulships.

Between 88 and 31 B.C.E., a series of ambitious individuals—Sulla, Pompey, Julius Caesar, Mark Antony, and Octavian—commanded armies more loyal to them than to the state. Their use of Roman troops to increase their personal power led to bloody civil wars. The city of Rome was taken by force on several occasions, and victorious commanders executed opponents and controlled the state.

The Roman Principate, 31 B.C.E.–330 C.E.

Principate A term used to characterize Roman government in the first three centuries C.E., based on the ambiguous title *princeps* ("first citizen") adopted by Augustus to conceal his military dictatorship.

Julius Caesar's grandnephew and heir, Octavian (63 B.C.E.–14 C.E.), eliminated all rivals by 31 B.C.E. and carefully set about refashioning the Roman system of government. He maintained the forms of the Republic—the offices, honors, and privileges of the senatorial class—but fundamentally altered the realities of power. A military dictator in fact, he never called himself king or emperor, claiming merely to be *princeps*, "first among equals," in a restored Republic. Thus, the period following the Republic is called the **Principate**.

Augustus, one of the many honorific titles that the Senate gave Octavian, connotes prosperity and piety, and it became the name by which he is best known to posterity. Augustus's patience and intuitive grasp of human nature enabled him to manipulate all the groups in Roman society. When he died in 14 C.E., after forty-five years of carefully veiled rule, few could remember the Republic. During his reign Egypt and parts of the Middle East and central Europe were added to the empire, leaving only the southern half of Britain and modern Romania to be added later.

Augustus Honorific name of Octavian, founder of the Roman Principate, the military dictatorship that replaced the failing rule of the Roman Senate. After defeating all rivals, between 31 B.C.E. and 14 C.E. he laid the groundwork for several centuries of stability and prosperity in the Roman Empire.

Augustus allied himself with the **equites** (EH-kwee-tays), the class of well-to-do Italian merchants and landowners second in wealth and social status to the senatorial class. This body of competent and self-assured individuals became the core of a new, paid civil service that helped run the Roman Empire. At last Rome had a governmental bureaucracy up to the task of managing a large empire with considerable honesty, consistency, and efficiency.

So popular was Augustus when he died that four members of his family succeeded to the position of "emperor" (as we call it) despite serious personal and political shortcomings. However, because of Augustus's calculated ambiguity about his role, the position of emperor was never automatically regarded as hereditary, and after the mid-first century C.E. other families obtained the post. In theory the early emperors were affirmed by the Senate; in reality they were chosen by the armies. By the second century C.E. a series of very capable emperors instituted a new mechanism of succession: each adopted a mature man of proven ability as his son and trained him as his successor.

equites In ancient Italy, prosperous landowners second in wealth and status to the senatorial aristocracy. The Roman emperors allied with this group to counterbalance the influence of the old aristocracy and used the *equites* to staff the imperial civil service.

While Augustus had felt it important to appeal to Republican traditions and conceal the source and extent of his power, this became less necessary over time, and later emperors exercised their authority more overtly. In imitation of Alexander the Great and the Hellenistic kings, many Roman emperors were officially deified (regarded as gods) after death. A cult of the living emperor developed as a way to increase the loyalty of subjects.

During the Republic a body of laws had developed, including decrees of the Senate, bills passed in the Assembly, and the practices of public officials who heard cases. In the later

Socioeconomic Mobility, Winners and Losers in Imperial Rome and Han China

Throughout human history, most people have been born into societies in which there was little opportunity or likelihood that they could significantly improve their social or economic circumstances. However, in complex and urbanized civilizations like imperial Rome or Han China, economic advancement (which is, then, generally linked to a higher social status) is more achievable for various reasons, including conditions of peace and stability favorable to commerce brought by the imperial power, the construction of roads over which goods can be conveyed, increased wealth and higher standards of living for many, the presence of large numbers of potential customers in urban centers, and innovative technologies for producing high-quality products. However, two further points need to be made. First, in situations of open economic competition, there are losers as well as winners. And, second, the existence of new forms of wealth and its acquisition by new groups of people tends to destabilize and threaten traditional institutions and values. We are fortunate in having texts from early imperial Rome and Han China that illustrate these processes from the vantage point of "the losers."

Juvenal wrote poetic satires at Rome in the late first and early second centuries C.E. Of course satire, by its very nature, exaggerates, but to be effective and funny it has to be based on something real. The main speaker in Juvenal's *Third Satire* is a friend of the poet named Umbricius, who has decided to abandon the ever more dangerous and frustrating city of Rome for a quieter town on the Bay of Naples.

...'There is no room in the city
for respectable skills,' he said, 'and no reward for one's efforts.
Today my means are less than yesterday; come tomorrow,
the little left will be further reduced...
What can I do in Rome? I can't tell lies; if a book

is bad I cannot praise it and beg for a copy; the stars
in their courses mean nothing to me; I'm neither willing nor able
to promise a father's death; I've never studied the innards
of frogs; I leave it to others to carry instructions and presents
to a young bride from her lover; none will get help from me
in a theft; that's why I never appear on a governor's staff;...
Who, these days, inspires affection except an accomplice – one
whose conscience boils and seethes with unspeakable secrets?...
I shan't mince words. My fellow Romans, I cannot put up with
a city of Greeks...
They make for the Esquiline, or the willow's Hill, intent on
    becoming
the vital organs and eventual masters of our leading houses.
Nimble wits, a reckless nerve, and a ready tongue...
What of the fact that the nation excels in flattery, praising
the talk of an ignorant patron, the looks of one who is ugly...
the whole country's a play. You chuckle, he shakes with a
    louder
guffaw; he weeps if he spots a tear in the eye of his patron,
yet he feels no grief; on a winter's day if you ask for a brazier,
he dons a wrap; if you say 'I'm warm,' he starts to perspire.
So we aren't on equal terms; he always has the advantage
who night and day alike is able to take his expression
from another's face, to throw up his hands and cheer if his
    patron
produces an echoing belch or pees in a good straight line...
There's no room here for any Roman...
That same man, moreover, provides a cause and occasion
for universal amusement if his cloak is ripped and muddy,
if his toga is a little stained, and one of his shoes gapes
    open...
Of all that luckless poverty involves, nothing is harsher
than the fact that it makes people funny.'

Republic legal experts began to analyze laws and legal procedures to determine the underlying principles; then they applied these principles to the creation of new laws required by a changing society. These experts were less lawyers in the modern sense than teachers, though they were sometimes consulted by officials or the parties to legal actions.

During the Principate the emperor became a major source of new laws. Roman law was studied and codified with a new intensity by the class of legal experts, and their interpretations often had the force of law. The basic divisions of Roman law—persons, things, and actions— reveal the importance of property and the rights of individuals in Roman eyes. The culmination of this long process of development and interpretation of the law was the sixth-century C.E. Digest of Justinian. Roman law has remained the foundation of European law to this day.

An Urban Empire

The Roman Empire of the first three centuries C.E. was an "urban" empire. This does not mean that most people lived in cities. Perhaps 80 percent of the 50 to 60 million people in the empire engaged in agriculture and lived in villages or isolated farms. The empire, however, was administered through a network of towns and cities, and the urban populace benefited most.

Numerous towns had several thousand inhabitants, while a few major cities had several hundred thousand. Rome itself had approximately a million residents. The largest cities strained

Umbricius complains about the difficulty that educated, middle-class Romans like Juvenal and himself have in finding gainful employment and making a decent living. They cannot compete with the swarms of "Greeks" (by which he means people from the Greek-speaking Eastern Mediterranean, which would include Greeks proper, Syrians, and Egyptians), who are such accomplished actors, flatterers, and liars that they ingratiate themselves with the rich and powerful and get all the good jobs and contracts. The real Romans, who have too much dignity to stoop to this level, are left on the outside looking in. As they descend into poverty in a city in which the cost of lodging, food, and everything else is exorbitantly high, they are scorned and humiliated.

We see in this poem a resurgence of long-standing Roman prejudice toward the Greeks. Ironically, the presence of so many Easterners in Rome is a product of the empire, both because large numbers of prisoners of war initially serving as slaves in Italy gained their freedom and Roman citizenship, and because the capital city was a magnet attracting the most able and ambitious people in the empire to come to Rome to make their fortune.

A striking Han Chinese parallel to Juvenal's *Third Satire* can be found in an essay on friendship written by Wang Fu. He lived in the first half of the second century CE and never obtained an official post, leading him to complain that the system was not operating with fairness.

People compete to flatter and to get close to those who are wealthy and prominent... People are also quick to snub those who are poor and humble... If a person makes friends with the rich and prominent, he will gain the benefits of influential recommendations for advancement in office and the advantages of generous presents and other emoluments. But if he makes friends with the poor and humble, he will lose money either from giving them handouts or from unrepaid loans... This is the reason that crafty, calculating individuals can worm their way up the official ladder while ordinary scholars slip ever more into obscurity. Unless the realm has a brilliant ruler, there may be no one to discern this... Alas! The gentlemen of today speak nobly

but act basely. Their words are upright, but their hearts are false. Their actions do not reflect their words, and their words are out of harmony with their thoughts... In their lofty speeches they refer to virtuous and righteous persons as being worthy. But when they actually recommend people for office, they consider only such requirements as influence and prominence. If a man is just an obscure scholar, even if he possesses the virtue of Yan Hui and Min Ziqian, even if he is modest and diligent, even if he has the ability of Yi Yin and Lu Shang, even if he is filled with the most devoted compassion for the people, he is clearly not going to be employed in this world.

As Wang Fu sees it, men of ambition focused all their attention on cultivating the rich and powerful in order to get the recommendations that led to official appointments, and in the process they ignored their real friends, whereas men of talent who could not or would not play this game were overlooked and scorned for their poverty. While appointment to public office was supposed to be meritocratic, based, first, on knowledge of the classic Confucian texts as determined by an exam and then by performance in office, Wang Fu's essay makes clear that what mattered most was connections to powerful people and the recommendations those people made to their peers in the government.

QUESTIONS FOR ANALYSIS

1. What kinds of abilities lead to success in imperial Rome and China?

2. Are the authors of these two texts just whining because they have had little success, or are they justified in claiming that the situation is unfair?

3. How are the new circumstances of increased socioeconomic mobility damaging traditional institutions and values?

Sources: First selection [translated by Niall Rudd, *Juvenal, The Satires* (Oxford 1992)]. Second selection [translated by Lily Hwa, in Patricia Buckley Ebrey (ed.), *Chinese Civilization*, A Sourcebook, 2d ed. (The Free Press, 1993)].

the technological capabilities of the ancients; providing adequate food and water and removing sewage were always problems.

In Rome the upper classes lived in elegant townhouses on one of the hills. The house was centered around an *atrium*, a rectangular courtyard with an open skylight that let in light and rainwater for drinking and washing. Surrounding the atrium were a large dining room for dinner and drinking parties, an interior garden, a kitchen, and possibly a private bath. Bedrooms were on the upper level. The floors were decorated with pebble mosaics, and the walls and ceilings were covered with frescoes (paintings done directly on wet plaster) of mythological scenes or outdoor vistas, giving a sense of openness in the absence of windows. The typical aristocrat also owned a number of villas in the Italian countryside to which the family could retreat to escape the pressures of city life.

The poor lived in crowded slums in the low-lying parts of the city. Damp, dark, and smelly, with few furnishings, these wooden tenements were susceptible to frequent fires. Fortunately, Romans could spend much of the day outdoors, working, shopping, eating, and socializing.

The cities, towns, and even the ramshackle settlements that sprang up on the edge of frontier forts were miniature replicas of the capital city in political organization and physical layout. A town council and two annually elected officials drawn from the local elite ran regional affairs with considerable autonomy. This "municipal aristocracy" imitated the manners and conduct of Roman senators, enhancing their status by endowing their communities with attractive elements of Roman urban life—civic buildings, temples, gardens, baths, theaters, amphitheaters—and putting on games and public entertainments.

In the countryside hard work and drudgery were relieved by occasional holidays and village festivals and by the everyday pleasures of sex, family, and conversation. Rural people had to fend for themselves in dealing with bandits, wild animals, and other hazards of country life. They had little direct contact with the Roman government other than occasional run-ins with bullying soldiers and the dreaded arrival of the tax collector.

The concentration of land ownership in ever fewer hands was temporarily reversed by the distribution of farms to veteran soldiers during the civil wars of the late Republic, but it resumed in the era of the emperors. However, after the era of conquest ended in the early second century C.E., slaves were no longer plentiful or inexpensive, and landowners needed a new source of labor. "Tenant farmers" cultivated plots of land in return for a portion of their crops. The landowners lived in the cities and hired foremen to manage their estates. Thus wealth was concentrated in the cities but was based on the productivity of rural laborers.

Some urban dwellers got rich from manufacture and trade. Commerce was greatly enhanced by the thousands of miles of well-built roads and by the **pax romana** ("Roman peace"), the safety and stability guaranteed by Roman might. Grain, meat, vegetables, and other bulk foodstuffs usually were exchanged locally because transportation was expensive and many products spoiled quickly. However, the city of Rome imported massive quantities of grain from Sicily and Egypt to feed its huge population, and special naval squadrons performed this vital task.

Glass, metalwork, delicate pottery, and other fine manufactured products were exported throughout the empire. The centers of production, originally located in Italy, moved into the provinces as knowledge of the necessary skills spread. Other merchants traded in luxury items from far beyond the boundaries of the empire, especially silk from China and spices from India and Arabia (see Environment and Technology: Ancient Glass).

pax romana Literally, "Roman peace," it connoted the stability and prosperity that Roman rule brought to the lands of the Roman Empire in the first two centuries C.E. The movement of people and trade goods along Roman roads and safe seas allowed for the spread of cultural practices, technologies, and religious ideas.

The Art Archive/Gianni Dagli Orti

Roman Shop Selling Food and Drink   The bustling town of Pompeii on the Bay of Naples was buried in ash by the eruption of Mt. Vesuvius in 79 C.E. Archaeologists have unearthed the streets, stores, and houses of this typical Roman town. Shops such as this sold hot food and drink served from clay vessels set into the counter. Shelves and niches behind the counter contained other items. In the background can be seen a well-paved street and a public fountain where the inhabitants could fetch water.

Roman armies stationed on the frontiers were a large market that promoted the prosperity of border provinces. The revenues collected by the central government transferred wealth from the rich interior provinces like Gaul (France) and Egypt, first to Rome to support the emperor and the central government, then to the frontier provinces to subsidize the armies.

Romanization—the spread of the Latin language and Roman way of life—was strongest in the western provinces, whereas Greek language and culture, a legacy of the Hellenistic kingdoms, predominated in the eastern Mediterranean (see Chapter 5). Modern Portuguese, Spanish, French, Italian, and Romanian evolved from the Latin language. The Roman government did not force Romanization; many provincials chose to adopt Latin and the cultural habits that went with it. There were advantages to speaking Latin and wearing a *toga* (the traditional cloak worn by Roman male citizens), just as people in today's developing nations see advantages in moving to the city, learning English, and wearing Western clothing. Latin facilitated dealings with the Roman administration and helped merchants get contracts to supply the military. Many also were drawn to the aura of success surrounding the language and culture of the dominant people.

The empire gradually granted Roman citizenship, with its privileges, legal protections, and exemptions from some types of taxation, to people living outside Italy. Men who completed a twenty-six-year term of service in the native military units that backed up the Roman legions were granted citizenship and could pass this coveted status on to their descendants. Emperors made grants of citizenship to individuals or entire communities as rewards for good service. Finally, in 212 C.E. the emperor Caracalla granted citizenship to all free, adult, male inhabitants of the empire.

The gradual extension of citizenship mirrored the empire's transformation from an Italian dominion into a commonwealth of peoples. As early as the first century C.E. some of the leading literary and intellectual figures came from the provinces. By the second century even the emperors hailed from Spain, Gaul, and North Africa.

The Rise of Christianity

During this period of general peace and prosperity, events were taking place in the East that, though little noted at the moment, would be of great historical significance. The Jewish homeland of Judaea (see Chapter 3), roughly equivalent to present-day Israel, came under direct Roman rule in 6 C.E. Over the next half century Roman governors insensitive to the Jewish belief in one god provoked opposition to Roman rule. Many waited for the arrival of the Messiah, the "Anointed One," a military leader who would drive out the Romans and liberate the Jewish people.

This is the context for the career of **Jesus**, a young Jewish carpenter from the Galilee region in northern Israel. Since the portrait of Jesus found in the New Testament largely reflects the viewpoint of followers a half century after his death, it is difficult to determine the motives and teachings of the historical Jesus. Some experts believe that he was essentially a rabbi, or teacher. Offended by Jewish religious and political leaders' excessive concern with money and power and by the perfunctory nature of mainstream Jewish religious practice in his time, he prescribed a return to the personal faith and spirituality of an earlier age. Others stress his connections to the apocalyptic fervor found in certain circles of Judaism, such as John the Baptist and the community that authored the Dead Sea Scrolls. They view Jesus as a fiery prophet who urged people to prepare themselves for the imminent end of the world and God's ushering in of a blessed new age. Still others see him as a political revolutionary, upset by the downtrodden condition of the peasants in the countryside and the poor in the cities, who determined to drive out the Roman occupiers and their collaborators among the Jewish elite.

Whatever the real nature of his mission, the charismatic Jesus eventually attracted the attention of the Jewish authorities in Jerusalem, who regarded popular reformers as potential troublemakers. They turned him over to the Roman governor, Pontius Pilate. Jesus was imprisoned, condemned, and executed by crucifixion, a punishment usually reserved for common criminals. After his death his followers, the Apostles, sought to spread his teachings among their fellow Jews and persuade them that he was the Messiah and had been resurrected (returned from death to life).

Paul, a Jew from the Greek city of Tarsus in southeast Anatolia, converted to the new creed. Between 45 and 58 C.E. he threw his enormous talent and energy into spreading the word. Traveling throughout Syria-Palestine, Anatolia, and Greece, he became increasingly frustrated with the refusal of most Jews to accept that Jesus was the Messiah and had ushered in a new age. Many Jews, on the other hand, were appalled by the failure of the followers of Jesus to maintain traditional Jewish practices. Discovering a spiritual hunger among many non-Jews, Paul redirected

Romanization The process by which the Latin language and Roman culture became dominant in the western provinces. Indigenous peoples in the provinces often chose to Romanize because of the political and economic advantages that it brought, as well as the allure of Roman success.

Jesus A Jew from Galilee in northern Israel who sought to reform Jewish beliefs and practices. He was executed as a revolutionary by the Romans. Hailed as the Messiah and son of God by his followers, he became the central figure in Christianity, a belief system that developed in the centuries after his death.

Paul A Jew from the Greek city of Tarsus in Anatolia, he initially persecuted the followers of Jesus but, after receiving a revelation on the road to Syrian Damascus, became a Christian. Taking advantage of his Hellenized background and Roman citizenship, he traveled throughout Syria-Palestine, Anatolia, and Greece, preaching the new religion and establishing churches. Finding his greatest success among pagans ("gentiles"), he began the process by which Christianity separated from Judaism.

his efforts toward them and set up a string of Christian (from the Greek name *christos*, meaning "anointed one," given to Jesus by his followers) communities in the eastern Mediterranean.

Paul's career exemplifies the cosmopolitan nature of the Roman Empire. Speaking both Greek and Aramaic, he moved comfortably between the Greco-Roman and Jewish worlds. He used Roman roads, depended on the peace guaranteed by Roman arms, called on his Roman citizenship to protect him from the arbitrary action of local authorities, and moved from city to city in his quest for converts. In 66 C.E. long-building tensions in Roman Judaea erupted into a full-scale revolt that lasted until 73. One of the casualties of the Roman reconquest of Judaea was the Jerusalem-based Christian community, which focused on converting the Jews. This left the field clear for Paul's non-Jewish converts, and Christianity began to diverge more and more from its Jewish roots.

For more than two centuries, the sect grew slowly but steadily. Many of the first converts were from disenfranchised groups—women, slaves, the urban poor. They received respect not accorded them in the larger society and obtained positions of responsibility when the members of early Christian communities democratically elected their leaders. However, as the religious movement grew and prospered, it developed a hierarchy of priests and bishops and became subject to bitter disputes over theological doctrine (see Chapter 11).

As monotheists forbidden to worship other gods, early Christians were persecuted by Roman officials, who regarded their refusal to worship the emperor as a sign of disloyalty. Despite occasional government-sponsored persecution and spontaneous mob attacks, or perhaps because of them, the young Christian movement continued to gain strength and attract converts. By the late third century C.E. its adherents were a sizable minority within the Roman Empire and included many educated and prosperous people with posts in the local and imperial governments.

The expansion of Christianity should be seen as part of a broader religious tendency. In the Hellenistic and Roman periods, a number of cults gained popularity by claiming to provide secret information about the nature of life and death and promising a blessed afterlife to their adherents. Arising in the eastern Mediterranean, they spread throughout the Greco-Roman lands in response to a growing spiritual and intellectual hunger not satisfied by traditional pagan practices. These included the worship of the mother-goddess Cybele in Anatolia, the Egyptian goddess Isis, and the Iranian sun-god Mithra. As we shall see, the ultimate victory of Christianity over these rivals had as much to do with historical circumstances as with its spiritual appeal.

Technology and Transformation

The relative safety and ease of travel brought by Roman arms and roads enabled merchants to sell their wares and early Christians to spread their faith. Surviving remnants of roads, fortification walls, aqueducts, and buildings testify to the engineering expertise of the ancient Romans. Using the labor of military personnel was one of the ways in which the Roman government kept large numbers of soldiers busy in peacetime. Some of the best engineers also served with the army, building bridges, siege works, and ballistic weapons that hurled stones and shafts.

Among the technological achievements of the Romans was the use of arches, which allow even distribution of great weights without thick supporting walls. With the invention of concrete—a mixture of lime powder, sand, and water that could be poured into molds—the Romans could create vast vaulted and domed interior spaces, unlike the rectilinear pillar-and-post construction of the Greeks. A third achievement was the **aqueduct**—a long elevated or underground conduit that carried water from a source to an urban center using only the force of gravity. Made of large cut stones closely fitted and held together by mortar, aqueducts were elevated atop walls or bridges, making it difficult for unauthorized parties to tap the water line for their own use. Sections of aqueduct that crossed rivers presented the same construction challenges as bridges. Roman engineers lowered prefabricated wooden cofferdams—large, hollow cylinders—into the riverbed and pumped out the water so workers could descend and construct cement piers to support the arched segments of the bridge. When an aqueduct reached the outskirts of a city, the water flowed into a reservoir, where it was stored. Pipes connected the reservoir to public fountains and the houses of the rich in different parts of the city.

Defending borders that stretched for thousands of miles was a major challenge. Augustus advised against further expanding the empire because the costs of administering and defending subsequent acquisitions would be greater than the revenues. The Roman army was then reorganized and redeployed to reflect the shift from an offensive to a defensive strategy. At most points the empire was protected by mountains, deserts, and seas. But the lengthy Rhine

aqueduct A conduit, either elevated or underground, that used gravity to carry water from a source to a location—usually a city—that needed it. The Romans built many aqueducts in a period of substantial urbanization.

and Danube river frontiers in Germany and central Europe were vulnerable, guarded only by a string of forts with small garrisons adequate for dealing with raiders. On particularly desolate frontiers, such as in Britain and North Africa, the Romans built long walls to keep out intruders.

Most of Rome's neighbors were less technologically advanced and more loosely organized and so did not pose a serious threat to the security of the empire. The one exception was the Parthian kingdom, heir to the Mesopotamian and Persian Empires, which controlled the lands on the eastern frontier (today's Iran and Iraq). For centuries Rome and Parthia engaged in a rivalry that sapped both sides without any significant territorial gain by either party.

The Roman state prospered for two and a half centuries after Augustus's reforms, but in the third century C.E. cracks in the edifice became visible. Historians use the expression "**Third-Century Crisis**" to refer to the period from 235 to 284 C.E., when political, military, and economic problems beset and nearly destroyed the Roman Empire. The most visible symptom of the crisis was the frequent change of rulers: twenty or more men claimed the office of emperor during this period. Most reigned for only a few months or years before being overthrown by rivals or killed by their own troops. Germanic tribesmen on the Rhine/Danube frontier took advantage of the frequent civil wars and periods of anarchy to raid deep into the empire. For the first time in centuries, Roman cities began to erect walls for protection. Several regions, feeling that the central government was not adequately protecting them, broke away and turned power over to a leader who promised to put their interests first.

These crises had a devastating impact on the empire's economy. Buying the loyalty of the armies and defending the increasingly permeable frontiers drained the treasury. The unending demands of the central government for more tax revenues, as well as the interruption of

Third-Century Crisis Historians' term for the political, military, and economic turmoil that beset the Roman Empire during much of the third century C.E.: frequent changes of ruler, civil wars, barbarian invasions, decline of urban centers, and near-destruction of long-distance commerce and the monetary economy. After 284 C.E. Diocletian restored order by making fundamental changes.

Roman Aqueduct near Tarragona, Spain   The growth of towns and cities challenged Roman officials to provide an adequate supply of water. Aqueducts channeled water from a source, sometimes many miles away, to an urban complex using only the force of gravity. To bring an aqueduct from high ground into the city, Roman engineers designed long, continuous rows of arches that maintained a steady downhill slope. Scholars sometimes can roughly estimate the population of an ancient city by calculating the amount of water that was available to it.

Lenar Musin/Shutterstock.com

Ancient Glass

Glass was a highly prized commodity in antiquity. While glass was manufactured in various places in the Eastern Hemisphere, glass production reached unparalleled heights of technological and aesthetic sophistication in the Roman Empire of the early centuries C.E. It was also widely available and had many uses. The Chinese, who did not acquire this level of glass technology for another fifteen centuries, eagerly imported Roman glass. The story of this commodity illuminates the far-reaching commercial conduits that linked the empires at either end of the hemisphere.

Glassmaking originated in the Middle East in the third millennium B.C.E., with the earliest products being beads. By the mid-second millennium B.C.E. the first hollow vessels were being produced in Egypt and Mesopotamia. The primary ingredient in glass is silica, usually in the form of sand, which is compounded with soda (sodium carbonate) to reduce the temperature at which the sand melts and then stabilized by calcium, which may already exist naturally in the sand as limestone particles. Early glass production was an expensive procedure, requiring access to soda and the ability to achieve high temperatures. Raw strips of glass were wrapped around a metal and clay core and heated until the strips fused. When the core was removed, the glass object was small and thick-walled. These expensive containers, used to hold perfume or other precious liquids, were only available to the rich and powerful.

A major breakthrough occurred in the late first century B.C.E. or early first century C.E. with the discovery of techniques for glassblowing, that is, inflating the glass while it is in liquid form. Blown glass vessels use far less glass, have thinner walls, and can be formed into a wide variety of shapes. A variation of the technique involved blowing into preformed molds. This technological breakthrough probably occurred along the eastern coast of the Mediterranean, at that time part of the Roman Empire. The glass industry of that era had two components. First, raw glass was produced in bulk in the eastern Mediterranean, since the major source of soda was in Egypt, and larger furnaces were developed that could produce huge glass slabs weighing many tons. Second, the raw glass was then exported to workshops throughout the empire and melted down again to produce finished objects. Glass became affordable for many more people.

A peculiarity of glass is that it can be recycled. Both archaeological evidence (e.g., shipwrecks) and texts reveal that broken glass was collected, melted back into raw glass, and turned into new objects.

Early glass was usually brightly colored (color comes from minerals introduced into the glass compound), probably in imitation of gemstones. But Romans of the first century C.E. developed a taste for clear, uncolored glass that imitated highly prized rock crystal. Glass was used not only for beads and dishware but also for mosaic tiles, and there was early experimentation with flat window glass. Many techniques were developed for decorating glass objects, including enameling (melting a thin layer of glass powder onto an object), creating a cameo effect by superimposing opaque glass forms on the body of a glass vessel, incising, and embedding gold foil between layers of glass.

The author Petronius tells a story (which we should not necessarily believe) that reveals the admiration, even awe, in which this material was held. A man secured an audience with the Emperor Tiberius and proceeded to show off his remarkable invention—glass that was unbreakable—by dashing a vessel to the ground without consequence. The astute emperor immediately ordered the inventor to be executed, arguing that such a substance would reduce the value of the gold and silver in his treasury.

Glass manufacturing came considerably later to East Asia than to western Asia and the Mediterranean. The earliest Chinese glass dates to the fifth century B.C.E. and was initially used to make "eye beads," imitations of beads imported from western Asia that were composed of several layers of glass that had the appearance of an eye. The first vessels were produced during the Han period. The Chinese did not pursue the possibilities of glass to the same extent as their Roman counterparts. They seem to have used it as a less expensive alternative to jade, producing imitations of such jade objects as a special kind of disk placed in the grave of the dead and suits of scale armor, and they preferred jadelike shades of green.

Not possessing the technology of glassblowing, the ancient Chinese valued the elegant and diverse shapes of Roman glassware. One text claims that Emperor Wu (second century B.C.E.) sent agents to the "Southern Sea" (probably India or Southeast Asia) to acquire glass, and Roman texts specify glass as an important component in the Indian Ocean trade (see Chapter 9). Roman glass, which can be distinguished from locally made glass by analysis of its chemical composition, is found in Chinese tombs of the Han era.

James L. Amos/Corbis

Roman Glass The discovery of the technique of glassblowing by the first century C.E. allowed Roman craftsmen to create elegant, thin-walled vessels in varied shapes and sizes. The color comes from trace elements in the sand from which the glass was made.

commerce by fighting, eroded the towns' prosperity. Shortsighted emperors, desperate for cash, secretly reduced the amount of precious metal in coins and pocketed the excess. The public quickly caught on, and the devalued coinage became less and less acceptable in the market-place. The empire reverted to a barter economy, a far less efficient system that further curtailed large-scale and long-distance commerce.

The municipal aristocracy, once the most vital and public-spirited class in the empire, was slowly crushed out of existence. As town councilors, its members were personally liable for shortfalls in taxes owed to the state. The decline in trade eroded their wealth, and many began to evade their civic duties and even went into hiding.

Population shifted out of the cities and into the countryside. Many sought employment and protection from both raiders and government officials on the estates of wealthy and powerful country landowners. The shrinking of cities and movement of the population to the country estates were the first steps in a demographic shift toward the social and economic structures of the European Middle Ages—roughly seven hundred years during which wealthy rural lords dominated a peasant population tied to the land (see Chapter 11).

Just when things looked bleakest, one man pulled the empire back from the brink of disaster. Like many rulers of that age, Diocletian came from one of the eastern European provinces most vulnerable to invasion. A commoner by birth, he had risen through the ranks of the army and gained power in 284. The proof of his success is that he ruled for more than twenty years and died in bed.

Diocletian implemented radical reforms that saved the Roman state by transforming it. To halt inflation (the process by which prices rise as money becomes worth less), Diocletian issued an edict specifying the maximum prices for various commodities and services. He froze many people into professions regarded as essential and required them to train their sons to succeed them. This unprecedented government regulation of prices and vocations had unforeseen consequences. A "black market" arose among buyers and sellers who ignored the government's price controls (and threats to impose the death penalty on violators). Many inhabitants of the empire began to see the government as an oppressive entity that no longer deserved their loyalty.

When Diocletian resigned in 305, the old divisiveness reemerged as various claimants battled for the throne. The eventual winner was **Constantine** (r. 306–337), who reunited the entire empire under his sole rule by 324.

In 312 Constantine won a key battle at the Milvian Bridge near Rome. He later claimed that he had seen a cross—the sign of the Christian God—superimposed on the sun before the battle. Believing that the Christian God had helped him achieve the victory, in the following year Constantine issued the Edict of Milan, ending the persecution of Christianity and guaranteeing freedom of worship to Christians and all others. Throughout his reign he supported the Christian church, although he tolerated other beliefs as well. Historians disagree about whether Constantine was spiritually motivated or pragmatically seeking to unify the peoples of the empire under a single religion. In either case, his embrace of Christianity was of tremendous significance. Large numbers of people began to convert when they saw that Christians seeking political office or government favors had clear advantages over non-Christians.

In 324 Constantine transferred the imperial capital from Rome to Byzantium, an ancient Greek city on the Bosporus (BAHS-puhr-uhs) strait leading from the Mediterranean into the Black Sea. The city was renamed Constantinople (cahn-stan-tih-NO-pul), "City of Constantine." This move both reflected and accelerated changes already taking place. Constantinople was closer than Rome to the most-threatened borders in eastern

Constantine Roman emperor (r. 312–337). After reuniting the Roman Empire, he moved the capital to Constantinople and made Christianity a favored religion.

SECTION REVIEW

- Rome's central location in Italy and the Mediterranean, and its ability to draw on the manpower resources of Italy, were important factors in its rise to empire.

- Early Rome was ruled by kings, but the Republic, inaugurated shortly before 500 B.C.E., was guided by the Senate, a council of the heads of wealthy families.

- Roman expansion, first in Italy, then throughout the Mediterranean, was due to several factors: the ambition and desire for glory of its leaders, weaker states appealing to Rome for protection, and Roman fear of others' aggression.

- Within Italy, and later in the overseas provinces, Rome co-opted the elites of subject peoples and extended its citizenship. Many subjects in the western provinces adopted the Latin language and Roman lifestyle.

- The civil wars that brought down the Republic were fought by armies more loyal to their leaders than to the state.

- Augustus developed a new system of government, the Principate, and while claiming to restore the Republic, he really created a military dictatorship.

- The Third-Century Crisis almost destroyed Rome, but Diocletian and Constantine saved the empire by transforming it.

- Christianity originated in the turbulent province of Judaea in the first century C.E., and despite official and spontaneous persecution, it grew steadily. Constantine's embrace of Christianity in the early fourth century C.E. made it virtually the official religion of the empire.

Europe (see Map 6.1). The urban centers and middle class in the eastern half of the empire had better withstood the Third-Century Crisis than those in the western half. In addition, more educated people and more Christians were living in the eastern provinces.

The conversion of Constantine and the transfer of the imperial capital are sometimes seen as the end of Roman history. But many of the important changes that culminated during Constantine's reign had their roots in events of the previous two centuries, and the Roman Empire as a whole survived for at least another century. The eastern, or Byzantine, portion of the empire (discussed in Chapter 11) survived Constantine by more than a thousand years. Nevertheless, the Roman Empire of the fourth and fifth centuries C.E. was fundamentally different from the earlier empire, and it is convenient to see Constantine's reign as the beginning of a new epoch.

THE ORIGINS OF IMPERIAL CHINA, 221 B.C.E.–220 C.E.

Qin A people and state in the Wei River Valley of eastern China that conquered rival states and created the first Chinese empire (221–206 B.C.E.). The Qin ruler, Shi Huangdi, standardized many features of Chinese society and ruthlessly marshaled subjects for military and construction projects, engendering hostility that led to the fall of his dynasty shortly after his death. The Qin framework was largely taken over by the succeeding Han dynasty.

Shi Huangdi Founder of the short-lived Qin dynasty and creator of the Chinese Empire (r. 221–210 B.C.E.). He is remembered for his ruthless conquests of rival states, standardization of practices, and forcible organization of labor for military and engineering tasks. His tomb, with its army of life-size terracotta soldiers, has been partially excavated.

Han A term used to designate (1) the ethnic Chinese people who originated in the Yellow River Valley and spread throughout regions of China suitable for agriculture and (2) the dynasty of emperors who ruled from 202 B.C.E. to 220 C.E.

The early history of China (described in Chapter 4) was characterized by the fragmentation that geography dictated. The Shang (ca. 1750–1045 B.C.E.) and Western Zhou (1045–771 B.C.E.) dynasties ruled over a compact zone in northeastern China. The last few centuries of nominal Zhou rule—the Warring States Period—saw frequent hostilities among a group of small states with somewhat different languages and cultures.

In the second half of the third century B.C.E. one of the warring states—the **Qin (chin)** state of the **Wei (way)** River Valley—rapidly conquered its rivals and created China's first empire (221–206 B.C.E.). Built at great cost in human lives and labor, the Qin Empire barely survived the death of its founder, **Shi Huangdi (shih wahng-dee)**. Power soon passed to a new dynasty, the **Han**, which ruled China from 202 B.C.E. to 220 C.E. (see Map 6.2). Thus began the long history of imperial China—a tradition of political and cultural unity and continuity that lasted into the early twentieth century and still has meaning for the very different China of our time.

The Qin Unification of China, 221–206 B.C.E.

From the mid-third century B.C.E., Qin began to methodically conquer and incorporate the other Chinese states, and by 221 B.C.E. it had unified northern and central China in the first Chinese "empire." The name *China*, by which this land is known in the Western world, is probably derived from *Qin*. Qin emerged as the ultimate winner because of a combination of factors: the toughness and military preparedness of a frontier state long accustomed to defending itself against "barbarian" neighbors, the wholehearted adoption of severe Legalist methods for exploiting the natural and human resources of the kingdom (see Chapter 4), and the surpassing ambition of a ruthless and energetic young king.

The Qin monarch, Zheng **(jahng)**, came to the throne at the age of thirteen in 246 B.C.E. Guided by a circle of Legalist advisers, he launched a series of wars of conquest. After defeating the last of his rivals in 221 B.C.E., he gave himself a title that symbolized the new state of affairs—Shi Huangdi, or "First Emperor"—and claimed that his dynasty would last ten thousand generations.

The new regime eliminated rival centers of authority. Its first target was the landowning aristocracy of the conquered states and the system on which aristocratic wealth and power had been based. The Qin government abolished primogeniture, the right of the eldest son to inherit all the landed property, requiring estates to be broken up and passed on to several heirs. A new, centrally controlled administrative structure was put in place, with district officials appointed by the king and watched over by his agents.

The Qin government's commitment to standardization helped create a unified Chinese civilization. A code of law, in force throughout the empire, applied punishments evenhandedly to all members of society. The Qin also imposed standardized weights and measures, a single coinage, a common system of writing, and even a specified axle-length for carts so that they would create a single set of ruts in the road.

Li Si **(luh suh)**, the Legalist prime minister, persuaded Shi Huangdi that the scholars (primarily Confucian rivals of the Legalists; see Chapter 4) were subverting the goals of the regime. The Legalists viewed Confucian expectations of benevolent and nonviolent conduct from rulers as an intolerable check on the government's absolute power. Furthermore, the Confucians' appeal to the past impeded the new order being created by the Qin. A crackdown on the scholars ensued in which many Confucian books were publicly burned and many scholars brutally executed.

Shi Huangdi was determined to secure the northern border against nomadic raids on Chinese territory. Pastoralists and farmers had always exchanged goods on the frontier. Herders sought food and crafted goods produced by farmers and townsfolk, and farmers depended on the herders for animals and animal products. Sometimes, however, nomads raided the settled lands and took what they needed. For centuries the Chinese kingdoms had struggled with these tough, horse-riding warriors, building long walls along the frontier to keep them away from vulnerable farmlands (see Chapter 4). Shortly before the Qin unification of China, several states had begun to train soldiers on horseback to contend with the mobile nomads.

Shi Huangdi sent a large force to drive the nomads far north. His generals succeeded momentarily, extending Chinese territory beyond the great northern loop of the Yellow River. They also connected and extended earlier walls to create a continuous fortification, the ancestor of the Great Wall of China. A recent study concludes that, contrary to the common belief that the purpose of the wall was defensive—to keep the "barbarians" out of China—its primary function was offensive, to take in newly captured territory, to which large numbers of Chinese peasants were now dispatched and ordered to begin cultivation.[1]

Shi Huangdi's attack on the nomads had an unanticipated consequence. The threat to their way of life created by the Chinese invasion drove the normally fragmented and quarreling nomad groups to unite in a great confederacy under the dynamic leadership of Maodun (mow-doon). This **Xiongnu** (SHE-OONG-noo) Confederacy would pose a huge military threat to China for centuries, with frequent wars and high costs in lives and resources.

Needing many people to serve in the armies, construct roads and walls on the frontiers, and build new cities, palaces, and a monumental tomb for the ruler, the Qin government instituted an oppressive program of compulsory military and labor services and relocated large numbers of people. The recent discovery of a manual of Qin laws used by an administrator, with prescriptions less extreme than expected, suggests that the sins of the Qin may have been exaggerated by later sources. Nevertheless, the widespread uprisings that broke out after the death of Shi Huangdi attest to the harsh nature of the Qin regime.

When Shi Huangdi died in 210 B.C.E., several officials schemed with one of his sons to place him on the throne. The First Emperor was buried in a monumental tomb whose layout mirrored the geography of China, and the tomb was covered with a great mound of earth. Nearby were buried life-size sculptures of seven thousand soldiers to guard him in the afterlife, a more humane alternative to the human sacrifices of earlier eras. This terracotta (baked clay) army was discovered in the 1970s C.E., but the burial mound remains unexcavated.

The new emperor proved to be weak. Uprisings broke out on many fronts, reflecting both the resentment of the old aristocracies that had been deprived of wealth and privilege, and the anger of the commoners against excessive compulsory labor, forced relocations, and heavy taxation. By 206 B.C.E. Qin rule had been broken—the "ten-thousand-generation dynasty" had lasted only fifteen years. Nevertheless, the most important achievements of the Qin, the unification of China and the creation of a single, widely dispersed Chinese style of civilization, would endure.

The Long Reign of the Han, 202 B.C.E.–220 C.E.

Despite the overthrow of the Qin, fighting continued among various rebel groups. In 202 B.C.E. Liu Bang (le-oo bahng) prevailed and inaugurated a new dynasty, the Han, that would govern China for more than four centuries (202 B.C.E.–220 C.E.). The Han created the machinery and ideology of imperial government that would prevail for two millennia, and Chinese people today refer to themselves ethnically as "Han."

The new emperor, generally known by the throne name **Gaozu** (gow-zoo), came from a modest background. Stories stress his peasant qualities: fondness for drink, blunt speech, and easy manner. Gaozu and his successors courted popularity and consolidated their rule by denouncing the harshness of the Qin and renouncing many Qin laws. In reality, however, they maintained—with sensible modifications—many Legalist-inspired institutions of the Qin to control far-flung territories and diverse populations.

The early Han rulers faced tough challenges. China had been badly damaged by the harsh exactions of the Qin and the widespread fighting in the period of rebellions. Because the economy needed time to recover, Gaozu and his immediate successors had to be frugal, keeping

Xiongnu A confederation of nomadic peoples living beyond the northwest frontier of ancient China. Chinese rulers tried a variety of defenses and stratagems to ward off these "barbarians," as they called them, and finally succeeded in dispersing the Xiongnu in the first century C.E.

Gaozu The throne name of Liu Bang, one of the rebel leaders who brought down the Qin and founded the Han dynasty in 202 B.C.E.

[1] Nicola Di Cosmo, *Ancient China and Its Enemies: The Rise of Nomadic Power in East Asian History* (Cambridge: Cambridge University Press, 2002), 155–158.

costs down to reduce taxes and undertaking measures to improve the state of agriculture. For instance, during prosperous times the government collected and stored surplus grain that could be sold at reasonable prices in times of shortage.

Gaozu reverted to the traditional feudal grants the Qin had abolished. The eastern parts of China were parceled out to relatives and major supporters, while the rest was divided into "commanderies" directly controlled by the central government. Over the next few reigns, these fiefs were reabsorbed as rebellions or deaths of the rulers provided the opportunity.

When Gaozu marched north to confront a Xiongnu incursion, he and his troops were trapped, and he had to negotiate a safe passage home for his army. Realizing the inferiority of Han troops and the limited funds for a military buildup, he adopted a policy of appeasing the Xiongnu. This essentially meant buying them off by dispatching annual "gifts" of rice, silk, and wine, as well as marrying a Han princess to the Xiongnu ruler.

While the throne passed to a young child when Gaozu died in 195 B.C.E., real power lay with Gaozu's formidable wife, Empress Lü (lyew). Throughout the Han era, empresses played a key role in determining which of the many sons (the emperors had multiple wives and concubines) would succeed to the throne, and they often chose minors or weak figures whom they and their male relatives could control. Under such circumstances Wu came to the throne as a teenager in 141 B.C.E.

MAP 6.2 **Han China** The Qin and Han rulers of northeast China extended their control over all of eastern China and extensive territories to the west. A series of walls in the north and northwest, built to check the incursions of nomadic peoples from the steppes, were joined together to form the ancestor of the present-day Great Wall of China. An extensive network of roads connecting towns, cities, and frontier forts promoted rapid communication and facilitated trade. The Silk Road carried China's most treasured products to Central, South, and West Asia and the Mediterranean lands. © Cengage Learning

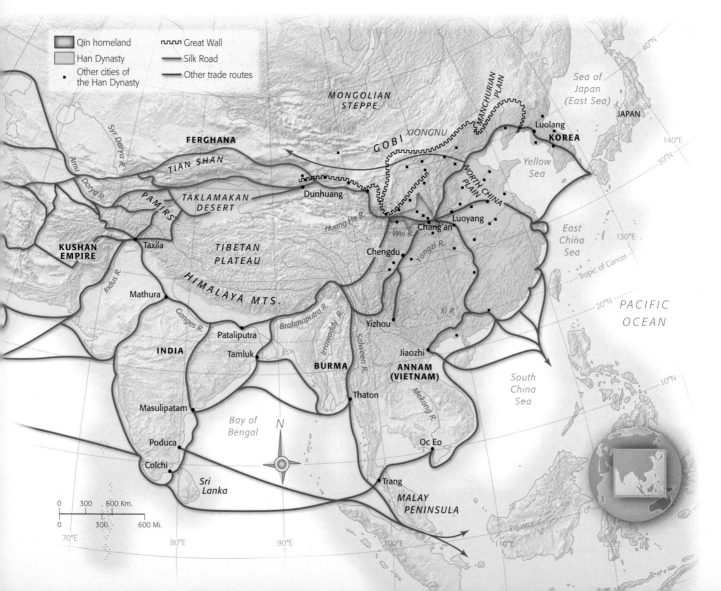

Terracotta Soldiers from the Tomb of Shi Huangdi, "First Emperor" of China, Late Third Century B.C.E. Near the monumental tomb that he built for himself, the First Emperor filled a huge underground chamber with more than seven thousand life-size baked-clay statues of soldiers. The terra-cotta army was unearthed in the 1970s.

Digital Vision/Getty Images

Sima Qian Chief astrologer for the Han dynasty emperor Wu. He composed a monumental history of China from its legendary origins to his own time and is regarded as the Chinese "father of history."

The deaths of his grandmother and uncle soon opened the way for him to rule in his own right, and thus began one of the longest and most eventful reigns in the history of the dynasty (141–87 B.C.E.).

We know much about the personality and policies of this emperor because of **Sima Qian (sih-muh chyehn)** (ca. 145–85 B.C.E.), who created the definitive form of historical writing in China. Serving as "chief astrologer" at the Han court, Sima Qian was castrated by Wu for defending a disgraced general. He therefore presents a generally negative view, portraying Wu as being manipulated by religious charlatans promising him magical powers, immortality, and séances with the dead. Reading his account critically, however, one could also conclude that Wu used religious pageantry to boost his own power.

Indeed, Wu did much to increase the power of the emperor. He launched military operations south as far as northern Vietnam, and north into Manchuria and North Korea. He abandoned the policy of appeasing the Xiongnu, concluding that this approach had failed since the nomads still made periodic attacks on the northern frontier. Wu built up his military, especially the cavalry, and went on the offensive. Thus began decades of bitter, costly fighting between China and the Xiongnu. In the long run Wu and his successors prevailed, and by the mid-first century C.E. the Xiongnu Confederacy had disintegrated, though nomad groups still threatened Chinese lands.

Wu dispatched forces to explore and conquer territories northwest of the Chinese heartland, essentially modern Gansu and Xinjiang **(SHIN-jyahng)**. His goals were to improve access to large numbers of horses for his expanding cavalry and to pressure the Xiongnu on their western flank. Thus began the incorporation of this region into greater China. This expansion also brought new economic opportunities, laying the foundations for the Silk Road over which silk and other lucrative trade goods would be carried to Central, southern, and western Asia (see Chapter 9).

The military buildup and frequent wars with the Xiongnu were expensive, forcing Wu to find new revenues. One solution was government monopolies on several high-profit commodities: salt, iron, and alcoholic beverages. These measures were highly controversial.

Another momentous development was the adoption of Confucianism—modified to meet the circumstances of the era—as the official ideology of the imperial system. A university was opened on the outskirts of the capital city, Chang'an **(chahng-ahn)**, and local officials were ordered to send a certain number of promising students from their districts each year. For two thousand years Chinese government would depend on scholar-officials promoted for their performance on exams probing their knowledge of Confucian texts. This alliance of Confucians and the imperial government, fraught with tensions, required compromises on both sides. The Confucians gained access to employment and power but had to accommodate ethical principles to the reality of far-from-perfect rulers. The emperors won the backing and services of a class of competent, educated

Gold Belt Buckle, Xiongnu, Second Century B.C.E. The Xiongnu, herders in the lands north of China, shared the artistic conventions of nomadic peoples across the steppes of Asia and eastern Europe, such as this fluid, twisting representation of the animals on which they depended for their livelihood. Shi Huangdi's military incursion into their pasturelands in the late third century B.C.E. catalyzed the formation of the Xiongnu Confederacy, whose horse-riding warriors challenged the Chinese for centuries. The Metropolitan Museum of Art. Image source/Art Resource, NY

people but had to deal with the Confucians' expectation that rulers should model ethical behavior and their insistence on giving often unwelcome advice.

Chinese Society

The Chinese government periodically conducted a census of inhabitants, and the results for 2 C.E. revealed 12 million households and 60 million people. Then, as now, the vast majority lived in the eastern river-valley regions where intensive agriculture could support a dense population.

The fundamental unit was the family, including not only the living but all previous generations. The Chinese believed their ancestors maintained an interest in the fortunes of living family members, so they consulted, appeased, and venerated them. Each generation must produce sons to perpetuate the family and maintain the ancestor cult that provided a kind of immortality to the deceased. In earlier times multiple generations and groups of families lived together, but by the imperial era independent nuclear families were the norm.

Within the family was a clear-cut hierarchy headed by the oldest male. Each person had a place and responsibilities, based on gender, age, and relationship to other family members, and people saw themselves as part of an interdependent unit rather than as individual agents. Parents' authority over children did not end with the passing of childhood, and parents occasionally took mature children to court for disobedience. The family inculcated the basic values of Chinese society: loyalty, obedience to authority, respect for elders and ancestors, and concern for honor and appropriate conduct. Because the hierarchy in the state mirrored the hierarchy in the family—peasants, soldiers, administrators, and rulers all made distinctive contributions to the welfare of society—these same attitudes carried over into the relationship between individuals and the state.

Traditional beliefs about conduct appropriate for women are preserved in a biography of the mother of the Confucian philosopher Mencius (Mengzi):

> A woman's duties are to cook the five grains, heat the wine, look after her parents-in-law, make clothes, and that is all!... [She] has no ambition to manage affairs outside the house.... She must follow the "three submissions." When she is young, she must submit to her parents. After her marriage, she must submit to her husband. When she is widowed, she must submit to her son.[2]

In reality, a woman's status depended on her "location" within various social institutions. Women of the royal family, such as wives of the emperor or queen-mothers, could be influential political figures. A young bride, whose marriage had been arranged by her parents, would go to live with her husband's family, where she was, initially, a stranger who had to prove herself. Mothers-in-law had authority over their sons' wives, and mothers, sisters, and wives competed for influence with the men of the household and a larger share of the family's resources.

"Lessons for Women," written at the end of the first century C.E. by Ban Zhao (bahn jow), illuminates the unresolved tensions in Han society's attitudes toward women. Instructing her own daughters on how to conduct themselves as proper women, Zhao urges them to conform to traditional expectations by obeying males, maintaining their husbands' households, performing domestic chores, and raising the children. Yet she also makes an impassioned plea for the education of girls and urges husbands to respect and not beat their wives.

People lived in various milieus—cities, rural villages and farms, or military camps on the frontiers—and their activities and the quality of their lives were shaped by these contexts. From 202 B.C.E. to 25 C.E.—the period of the Early, or Western, Han—the capital was at **Chang'an** (modern Xi'an [shee-ahn]), in the Wei River Valley, an ancient seat of power from

Chang'an City in the Wei River Valley in eastern China. It became the capital of the early Han Empire. Its main features were imitated in the cities and towns that sprang up throughout the Han Empire.

---

[2]Patricia Buckley Ebrey, ed., *Chinese Civilization and Society: A Sourcebook* (New York: Free Press, 1981), 33–34.

which the Zhou and Qin dynasties had emerged. Protected by a ring of hills but with ready access to the fertile plain, Chang'an was surrounded by a wall of pounded earth and brick 15 miles (24 kilometers) in circumference. In 2 C.E. its population was 246,000. Part of the city was carefully planned. Broad thoroughfares running north and south intersected with others running east and west. High walls protected the palaces, administrative offices, barracks, and storehouses of the imperial compound, to which access was restricted. Temples and marketplaces were scattered about the civic center. Chang'an became a model of urban planning, its main features imitated in cities and towns throughout China (it is estimated that between 10 and 30 percent of the population lived in urban centers). From 25 to 220 C.E. the Later, or Eastern, Han established its base farther east, in the more centrally located Luoyang (LWOE-yahng).

Han literature describes the appearance of the capitals and the activities taking place in the palace complexes, public areas, and residential streets. Moralizing writers criticized the excesses of the elite. Living in multistory houses, wearing fine silks, traveling in ornate horse-drawn carriages, well-to-do officials and merchants devoted their leisure time to art and literature, occult religious practices, elegant banquets, and various entertainments—music and dance, juggling and acrobatics, dog and horse races, and cock and tiger fights. In stark contrast, the common people inhabited a sprawling warren of alleys, living in dwellings packed "as closely as the teeth of a comb."

While the upper echelons of scholar-officials resided in the capital, lower-level bureaucrats were scattered throughout smaller cities and towns serving as headquarters for regional governments. These scholar-officials shared a common Confucian culture and ideology. Exempt from taxes and compulsory military or labor services, they led comfortable lives by the standards of the time. While the granting of government jobs on the basis of performance on the exams theoretically should have given everyone an equal chance, in reality the sons of officials had distinct advantages in obtaining the requisite education in classical texts. Thus the scholar-officials became a self-perpetuating, privileged class. The Han depended on local officials for day-to-day administration of their far-flung territories. They collected taxes, regulated conscription for the army and labor projects, provided protection, and settled disputes.

Merchant families also were based in the cities, and some became very wealthy. However, ancient Chinese society viewed merchants with suspicion, accusing them of greedily driving prices up through speculation and being parasites who lived off the work of others. Advisers to the emperors periodically blamed merchants for the economic ills of China and proposed harsh measures, such as banning them and their children from holding government posts.

The Western Han state required two years of military service from able-bodied males, but by the Eastern Han period the military was staffed by professional soldiers. Large numbers of Chinese men spent long periods away from home in distant frontier posts, building walls and forts, keeping an eye on barbarian neighbors, fighting when necessary, and growing crops to support themselves. Poems written by soldiers complain of rough conditions in the camps, tyrannical officers, and the dangers of confrontations with enemy forces, but above all they are homesick, missing and worrying about aged parents and vulnerable wives and children.

Silk Burial Banner from Mawangdui   This banner was placed on the coffin containing the mummified body of Lady Dai, wife of the ruler of a dependent kingdom in southern China, in the mid-second century B.C.E. The lower and upper portions depict the Underworld and Heaven, while the middle register shows the deceased and her family offering sacrifices to help her soul ascend to Heaven.

New Forms of Thought and Belief

The Han period was rich in intellectual developments, thanks to the relative prosperity of the era, the growth of urban centers, and state support of scholars. In their leisure time scholar-officials read and wrote in a range of genres, including poetry, philosophy, history, and technical subjects.

The Chinese had been preserving historical records since the early Zhou period. However, Sima Qian, the aforementioned "chief astrologer" of Emperor Wu, is regarded as "the father of history" in China, both because he created an organizational framework that became the standard for subsequent historical writing and because he sought the causes of events. Sima's monumental history, covering 2,500 years from legendary early emperors to his own time, was organized in a very different way from Western historical writing. It was divided into five parts: dynastic histories, accounts of noble families, biographies of important individuals and groups (such as Confucian scholars, assassins, barbarian peoples), a chart of historical events, and essays on special topics such as the calendar, astrology, and religious ceremonies. The same event may be narrated in more than one section, sometimes in a different way, inviting the reader to compare and interpret the differences. Sima may have utilized this approach to offer carefully veiled interpretations of past and present. Historians and other scholars in Han China had the advantage, as compared to their Western counterparts, of being employed by the government, but the disadvantage of having to limit their criticism of that government.

There were advances in science and technology. Widespread belief in astrology engendered astronomical observation of planets, stars, and other celestial objects. The watermill, which harnessed the power of running water to turn a grindstone, was used in China long before it appeared in Europe. The development of a horse collar that did not constrict breathing allowed Chinese horses to pull heavier loads than European horses. The Chinese first made paper, perhaps as early as the second century B.C.E., replacing the awkward bamboo strips of earlier eras. Improvements in military technology included horse breeding techniques to supply the cavalry and a reliable crossbow trigger. One clever inventor even created an early seismometer to register earthquakes and indicate the direction where the event took place.

The Qin and Han built thousands of miles of roads—comparable in scale to the roads of the Roman Empire—to connect parts of the empire and move armies quickly. They also built a network of canals connecting the river systems of northern and southern China, at first for military purposes but eventually for transporting commercial goods as well. Ultimately, a network of waterways permitted continuous transport of goods between the latitudes of Beijing and Guangzhou (Canton), a distance of 1,250 miles (2,012 kilometers). Some of these canals are still in use.

Chinese religion encompassed a wide spectrum of beliefs. Like the early Romans, the Chinese believed that divinity resided within nature. Most people believed in ghosts and spirits. The state maintained shrines to the lords of rain, winds, and soil, as well as to certain great rivers and high mountains. Sima Qian devoted an essay to the connection between religion and power, showing how emperors used ancient ceremonies and new-fangled cults to secure their authority. Daoism (see Chapter 4) became popular with the common people, incorporating an array of mystical and magical practices, including alchemy (the art of turning common materials into precious metals such as gold) and the search for potions that would impart immortality. Because Daoism questioned tradition and rejected the hierarchy and rules of the Confucian elite classes, charismatic Daoist teachers led several popular uprisings in the unsettled last decades of the Han dynasty.

Perhaps as early as the first century C.E. Buddhism (BOOD-izm) began to trickle into China. Originating in northern India in the fifth century B.C.E. (see Chapter 7), it slowly spread through South Asia and into Central Asia, carried by merchants on the Silk Road. Certain aspects of Buddhism fit comfortably with Chinese values: reverence for classic texts was also a feature of Confucianism, and the emphasis on severing attachments to material goods and pleasures found echoes in Daoism. But in other ways the Chinese were initially put off by Buddhist practices. The fact that Buddhist monks withdrew from their families to live in monasteries, shaved off their hair, and abstained from sex and procreation of children was repugnant to traditional Chinese values, which emphasized the importance of family ties, the body as an inviolable gift from parents, and the need to produce children to maintain the ancestor cult. Gradually Buddhism gained acceptance and was reshaped to fit the Chinese context, a process accelerated by the non-Chinese dynasties that dominated the north after the fall of the Han.

Decline of the Han

A break in the long sequence of Han rulers occurred early in the first century C.E. when an ambitious official named Wang Mang (wahng mahng) seized power (9–23 C.E.). The new ruler implemented major reforms to address serious economic problems and to cement his popularity with the common people, including limiting the size of the estates of the rich and giving the surplus land to landless peasants. However, a cataclysmic flood that changed the course of the Yellow River caused large numbers of deaths and economic losses. Members of the Han family and other elements of the elite resisted their loss of status and property, and widespread poverty engendered a popular uprising of the "Red Eyebrows," as the insurgents were called. Wang Mang was besieged in his palace and killed, and a member of the Han royal family was soon installed as emperor. In 25 C.E. Guangwu, founder of the Eastern Han dynasty, moved the capital east to Luoyang.

The dynasty continued for another two centuries, but the imperial court was frequently plagued by weak leadership and court intrigue, with royal spouses and their families jockeying for power behind immature or ineffectual monarchs. Poems from this period complain of corrupt officials, unchecked attacks by barbarians, uprisings of desperate and hungry peasants, the spread of banditry, widespread poverty, and despair.

Several factors contributed to the fall of the Han. Continuous military vigilance along the frontier burdened Han finances and exacerbated the economic troubles of later Han times. Despite the earnest efforts of Qin and early Han emperors to reduce the power and wealth of the aristocracy and turn land over to a free peasantry, by the end of the first century B.C.E. nobles and successful merchants again controlled huge tracts of land. Many peasants sought their protection against the demands of the imperial government, which was thereby deprived of tax revenues and manpower. The Eastern Han rulers abandoned the system of military conscription and were forced to hire more and more foreign soldiers and officers, men willing to serve for pay but not necessarily loyal to the Han state. By the end of the second century the empire was convulsed by civil wars, and in 220 C.E., with the former empire broken up into three kingdoms ruled by warlords, the last Han emperor was forced to abdicate.

With the fall of the Han, China entered a period of political fragmentation that lasted until the rise of the Sui (sway) and Tang (tahng) dynasties in the late sixth and early seventh centuries C.E., a story we take up in Chapter 12. In this period the north was dominated by a series of barbarian peoples who combined elements of their own practices with the foundation of Chinese culture. Many ethnic Chinese migrated south into the Yangzi Valley, where Chinese rulers prevailed, and in this era the center of gravity of both the population and Chinese culture shifted to the south.

SECTION REVIEW

- The tough, disciplined frontier kingdom of Qin conquered all rival kingdoms and unified China by 221 B.C.E. The First Emperor and his Legalist advisers imposed standardization in many spheres and compelled the labor of many people.

- The Qin attack on the northern nomads led to the formation of the formidable Xiongnu Confederacy, which long posed a military threat to China.

- The Han dynasty added to the Qin foundation, creating fundamental patterns of imperial government that lasted for two millennia.

- Emperor Wu went on the offensive against the nomads, extended Chinese control in the northwest, and began to use Confucian scholars as government officials.

- The family, with its strict hierarchy, roles for each member, and values of deference and obedience, prepared citizens for their obligations to the state.

- The layout, buildings, and activities in the capital city, Chang'an, were replicated in cities and towns across China. Regional administration was based on this network of urban centers.

- The Han era saw major intellectual and technological developments, as well as the arrival of Buddhism in China.

- The fall of the Han dynasty early in the third century C.E. was followed by the takeover of the northern plain by barbarian peoples. Many Chinese fled south to the Yangzi River Valley, which became the new center of gravity for Chinese civilization.

CONCLUSION

Both the Roman Empire and the first Chinese empire arose from relatively small states that, because of their discipline and military toughness, were initially able to subdue their neighbors. Ultimately they unified widespread territories under strong central governments.

Agriculture was the fundamental economic activity and source of wealth. Government revenues primarily derived from a percentage of the annual harvest. Both empires depended initially on sturdy independent farmers pressed into military service or other forms of compulsory labor, though later they came to rely on professional troops. Conflicts over who owned the land and how it was used were at the heart of political and social turmoil. The autocratic rulers of the Roman and Chinese states secured their positions by breaking the power of the old aristocratic families, seizing their excess land, and giving land to small farmers. The later reversal of this process, when wealthy noblemen again gained control of vast tracts of land and reduced the peasants to dependent tenant farmers, signaled the erosion of state authority.

Both empires spread out from an ethnically homogeneous core to encompass widespread territories containing diverse ecosystems, populations, and ways of life. Both brought those regions a cultural unity that has persisted, at least in part, to the present day. This development involved far more than military conquest and political domination. As the population of the core areas outstripped available resources, Italian and Han settlers moved into new regions, bringing their languages, beliefs, customs, and technologies. Many people in the conquered lands were attracted to the culture of the ruler nation and chose to adopt these practices and attach themselves to a "winning cause." Both empires found similar solutions to the problems of administering far-flung territories and large populations in an age when communication depended on men on horseback or on foot. The central government had to delegate considerable autonomy to local officials based in the cities and towns—in the Roman case local elites, in China officials dispatched by the central administration. In both empires a kind of civil service developed, staffed by educated and capable members of a prosperous middle class.

Technologies that facilitated imperial control also fostered cultural unification and improvements in the general standard of living. Roads built to expedite the movement of troops became the highways of commerce and the spread of imperial culture. A network of cities and towns linked the parts of the empire, providing local administrative bases, promoting commerce, and radiating imperial culture into the surrounding countryside. The majority of the population still resided in the countryside, but those living in urban centers enjoyed most of the advantages of empire. Cities and towns modeled themselves on the capital cities of Rome and Chang'an. Travelers found the same types of buildings and public spaces, and similar features of urban life, in outlying regions that they had seen in the capital.

The empires of Rome and Han China faced similar problems of defense: long borders located far from the administrative center and aggressive neighbors who coveted their prosperity. Both had to build walls and maintain chains of forts and garrisons to protect against incursions. The cost of frontier defense was staggering and eventually eroded the economic prosperity of the two empires. As imperial governments demanded more taxes and services from the hard-pressed civilian population, they lost the loyalty of their own people, many of whom sought protection on the estates of powerful rural landowners. As rough neighbors gradually learned the skills that had given the empires an initial advantage and were able to close the "technology gap," the Roman and Han governments eventually came to rely on soldiers hired from the same "barbarian" peoples who were pressing on the frontiers. Eventually, both empires were so weakened that their borders were overrun and their central governments collapsed. Ironically, the newly dominant immigrant groups were so deeply influenced by imperial culture that they maintained it to the best of their abilities.

In referring to the eventual failure of these two empires, we are brought up against important differences that led to different long-term outcomes. In China the imperial model was revived in subsequent eras, but the lands of the Roman Empire never again achieved the same level of unification. Several interrelated factors account for the different outcomes.

First, these cultures had different attitudes about the relationship of individuals to the state. In China the individual was more deeply embedded in the larger social group. The Chinese family, with its emphasis on a precisely defined hierarchy, unquestioning obedience, and solemn rituals of deference to elders and ancestors, served as the model for society and the state. Moreover, Confucianism, which sanctified hierarchy and provided a code of conduct for public officials, arose long before the imperial system and could be revived and tailored to fit changing political circumstances. Although the Roman family had its own hierarchy and traditions of obedience, the cult of ancestors was not as strong as among the Chinese, and the family was not the organizational model for Roman society and the Roman state. Also, there was no Roman equivalent of Confucianism—no ideology of political organization and social conduct that could survive the dissolution of the Roman state.

Another difference was that opportunities for economic and social mobility were greater in the Roman Empire than in ancient China. Whereas the merchant class in China was frequently disparaged and constrained by the government, the absence of government interference in the Roman Empire resulted in greater economic mobility and a thriving and influential middle class in the towns and cities. The Roman army, because it was composed of professional soldiers in service for decades and constituting a distinct and increasingly privileged group, frequently played a decisive role in political conflict. In China, on the other hand, the army was long drawn from draftees who served for two years and was much less likely to take the initiative in struggles for power.

Although Roman emperors tried to create an ideology to bolster their position, they were hampered by the persistence of Republican traditions and the ambiguities about the position of emperor deliberately cultivated by Augustus. As a result, Roman rulers were likely to be chosen by the army or by the Senate; the dynastic principle never took deep root; and the cult of the emperor had little spiritual content. This stands in sharp contrast to the unambiguous Chinese belief that the emperor was the divine Son of Heaven with privileged access to the beneficent power of the royal ancestors. Thus, in the lands that had once constituted the western part of the Roman Empire, there was no compelling basis for reviving the position of emperor and the territorial claims of empire in later ages.

Finally, Christianity, with its insistence on monotheism and one doctrine of truth, negated the Roman emperor's pretensions to divinity and was unwilling to compromise with pagan beliefs. The spread of Christianity through the provinces during the Late Roman Empire, and the decline of the western half of the empire in the fifth century C.E. (see Chapter 11), constituted an irreversible break with the past. On the other hand, Buddhism, which came to China in the early centuries C.E. and flourished in the post-Han era (see Chapter 12), was more easily reconciled with traditional Chinese values and beliefs.

KEY TERMS

Republic p. 144

Senate p. 144

patron/client relationship p. 145

Principate p. 149

Augustus p. 149

equites p. 149

pax romana p. 152

Romanization p. 153

Jesus p. 153

Paul p. 153

aqueduct p. 154

Third-Century Crisis p. 155

Constantine p. 157

Qin p. 158

Shi Huangdi p. 158

Han p. 158

Xiongnu p. 159

Gaozu p. 159

Sima Qian p. 161

Chang'an p. 162

SUGGESTED READING

Aldrete, Gregory S. *Daily Life in the Roman City: Rome, Pompeii, and Ostia.* 2009. Combines discussion of the institutions and practices that typified daily life with a description of the physical features of three exemplary cities.

Cherry, David, ed. *The Roman World: A Sourcebook.* 2001. A selection of thematically organized ancient sources in translation.

Clark, Gillian. *Christianity and Roman Society.* 2004. Investigates the rise of Christianity.

de Bary, Wm. Theodore, and Irene Bloom, eds. *Sources of Chinese Tradition*, vol. 1, 2d ed. 2000. A broad selection of ancient sources in translation with explanatory notes.

Di Cosmo, Nicola. *Ancient China and Its Enemies: The Rise of Nomadic Power in East Asian History.* 2002. Explores the interactions of Chinese and nomads on the northern frontier.

Dyson, Stephen L. *The Creation of the Roman Frontier.* 1985. Examines Roman military expansion and defense of the frontiers.

Hinsch, Bret. *Women in Early Imperial China.* 2002. A stimulating analysis of women's many roles in the early imperial period.

Lewis, Mark Edward. *The Early Chinese Empires: Qin and Han.* 2007. A thorough, up-to-date account of the first imperial dynasties.

Liu, Xinru. *The Silk Road in World History.* 2010. A concise overview that explores the political, economic, and cultural dimensions of the Silk Road in the ancient and medieval periods.

Loewe, Michael. *Everyday Life in Early Imperial China During the Han Period, 202 B.C.–A.D. 220.* 1988. Examines many typical facets of Chinese society in the Han era.

Millar, Fergus. *The Emperor in the Roman World (31 B.C.–A.D. 337).* 1977. A comprehensive study of the position of the princeps.

Nagle, D. Brendan. *Ancient Rome: A History.* 2009. A well-written and insightful new survey of Roman history.

Scheidel, Walter, ed. *Rome and China: Comparative Perspectives on Ancient World Empires.* 2009. Leading scholars make illuminating comparisons of political, legal, military, social, and economic factors.

Turcan, Robert. *The Gods of Ancient Rome: Religion in Everyday Life from Archaic to Imperial Times.* 2000. An accessible introduction to Roman religion in its public and private manifestations.

Ward-Perkins, Bryan. *The Fall of Rome and the End of Civilization.* 2005. Examines the momentous changes occurring in Rome's last centuries.

Chapter Outline

Foundations of Indian Civilization, 1500 B.C.E.–300 C.E.
➤ *What historical forces led to the development of complex social groupings in ancient India?*

Imperial Expansion and Collapse, 324 B.C.E.–650 C.E.
➤ *How, in the face of powerful forces that tended to keep India fragmented, did two great empires—the Mauryan Empire of the fourth to second centuries B.C.E. and the Gupta Empire of the fourth to sixth centuries C.E.—succeed in unifying much of India?*

Southeast Asia, 50–1025 C.E.
➤ *How did a number of states in Southeast Asia become wealthy and powerful by exploiting their position on the trade routes between China and India?*

Conclusion

- **ENVIRONMENT + TECHNOLOGY**   Indian Mathematics
- **DIVERSITY + DOMINANCE**   Relations Between Women and Men in the *Kama Sutra* and the *Arthashastra*

The Thousand Pillared Hall in the Temple of Minakshi at Madurai   At the annual Chittarai Festival, the citizens of this city in south India celebrate the wedding of their local patron goddess, Minakshi, to the high god Shiva.

Simon Reddy/Alamy

India and Southeast Asia, 1500 B.C.E.–1025 C.E.

In the *Bhagavad-Gita* (BUH-guh-vahd GEE-tuh), the most renowned Indian sacred text, the legendary warrior Arjuna (AHR-joo-nuh) rides out in his chariot to the open space between two armies preparing for battle. Torn between his social duty to fight for his family's claim to the throne and his conscience, which balks at the prospect of killing relatives, friends, and former teachers in the enemy camp, Arjuna slumps down in his chariot and refuses to fight. But his driver, the god Krishna (KRISH-nuh) in disguise, persuades him, in a carefully structured dialogue, both of the necessity to fulfill his duty as a warrior and of the proper frame of mind for performing these acts. In the climactic moment of the dialogue Krishna endows Arjuna with a "divine eye" and permits him to see the true appearance of God:

> It was a multiform, wondrous vision,
> with countless mouths and eyes
> and celestial ornaments,
>
> Everywhere was boundless divinity
> containing all astonishing things,
> wearing divine garlands and garments,
> anointed with divine perfume.
>
> If the light of a thousand suns
> were to rise in the sky at once,
> it would be like the light
> of that great spirit.
>
> Arjuna saw all the universe
> in its many ways and parts,
> standing as one in the body
> of the god of gods.[1]

In all of world literature, this is one of the most compelling attempts to depict the nature of deity. Graphic images emphasize the vastness, diversity, and multiplicity of the god, but in the end we learn that Krishna is the organizing principle behind all creation, that behind diversity and multiplicity lies a higher unity.

This is an apt metaphor for Indian civilization. The enormous variety of the Indian landscape is mirrored in the patchwork of ethnic and linguistic groups that occupy it, the political fragmentation that has marked most of Indian history, the elaborate hierarchy of social groups into which the Indian population is divided, and the thousands of deities who are worshiped at innumerable holy places that dot the subcontinent. Yet, in the end, one can speak of an Indian civilization united by shared views and

---

[1]Barbara Stoler Miller, *The Bhagavad-Gita: Krishna's Counsel in Time of War* (New York: Bantam, 1986), 98–99.

values. The photograph shows the interior of a temple in the city of Madurai in southern India. Here the ten-day Chittarai Festival, the most important religious event of the year in that district, celebrates the wedding of a local goddess, Minakshi, and the great Hindu god Shiva, symbolizing the reconciliation of local and national deities, southern and northern cultural practices, and male and female potentialities.

This chapter surveys the history of South and Southeast Asia from approximately 1500 B.C.E. to 1025 C.E., highlighting the evolution of defining features of Indian civilization. Considerable attention is given to Indian religious conceptions, due both to religion's profound role in shaping Indian society and the sources of information available to historians. For reasons that will be explained below, writing came late to India, and ancient Indians did not develop the same kind of historical consciousness as other peoples of antiquity and took little interest in recording specific historical events.

FOUNDATIONS OF INDIAN CIVILIZATION, 1500 B.C.E.–300 C.E.

India is called a *subcontinent* because it is a large—roughly 2,000 miles (3,200 kilometers) in both length and breadth—and physically isolated landmass. It is set off from the rest of Asia to the north by the Himalayas (him-uh-LAY-uhs), the highest mountains on the planet, and by the Indian Ocean on its eastern, southern, and western sides (see Map 7.1). The most permeable frontier, used by invaders and migrating peoples, lies to the northwest, but people using this corridor must cross the mountain barrier of the Hindu Kush (HIHN-doo KOOSH) (via the Khyber [KIE-ber] Pass) and the Thar (tahr) Desert east of the Indus River.

The Indian Subcontinent

The subcontinent—which encompasses the modern nations of Pakistan, Nepal, Bhutan, Bangladesh, India, and the adjacent island of Sri Lanka—divides into three distinct topographical zones. The mountainous northern zone contains the heavily forested foothills and high meadows on the edge of the Hindu Kush and Himalaya ranges. Next come the great basins of the Indus and Ganges (GAHN-jeez) Rivers. Originating in the snow-clad Tibetan mountains to the north, these rivers have repeatedly overflowed their banks and deposited layer on layer of silt, creating large alluvial plains. Northern India is divided from the third zone, the peninsula proper, by the Vindhya range and the Deccan (de-KAN), an arid, rocky plateau. The tropical coastal strip of Kerala (Malabar) in the west, the Coromandel Coast in the east with its web of rivers descending from the central plateau, the flatlands of Tamil Nadu on the southern tip of the peninsula, and the island of Sri Lanka often have followed paths of political and cultural development separate from those of northern India.

The northern rim of mountains shelters the subcontinent from cold Arctic winds and gives it a subtropical climate. The most dramatic source of moisture is the **monsoon** (seasonal wind). The Indian Ocean is slow to warm or cool, while the vast landmass of Asia swings between seasonal extremes of heat and cold. The temperature difference between water and land acts like a bellows, producing a great wind. The southwest monsoon begins in June, absorbing huge amounts of moisture from the Indian Ocean and dropping it over a swath of India that encompasses the rain forest belt on the western coast and the Ganges Basin. Three harvests a year are possible in some places. Rice is grown in the moist, flat Ganges Delta (modern Bengal). Elsewhere the staples are wheat, barley, and millet. The Indus Valley, in contrast, gets little precipitation (see Chapter 2), and agriculture requires extensive irrigation.

Although invasions and migrations usually came by land through the northwest corridor, the ocean has not been a barrier to travel and trade. Mariners learned to ride the monsoon winds across open waters from northeast to southwest in January and to make the return voyage in July. Ships sailed west across the Arabian Sea to the Persian Gulf, the southern coast of Arabia, and East Africa, and east across the Bay of Bengal to Indochina and Indonesia (see Chapter 9).

monsoon Seasonal winds in the Indian Ocean caused by the differences in temperature between the rapidly heating and cooling landmasses of Africa and Asia and the slowly changing ocean waters. These strong and predictable winds have long been ridden across the open sea by sailors, and the large amounts of rainfall that they deposit on parts of India, Southeast Asia, and China allow for the cultivation of several crops a year.

CHRONOLOGY

	India	Southeast Asia
2000 B.C.E.		ca. 2000 B.C.E. Swidden agriculture ca. 1600 B.C.E. Beginning of migrations from mainland Southeast Asia to islands in Pacific and Indian Oceans
1500 B.C.E.	ca. 1500 B.C.E. Migration of Indo-European peoples into northwest India	
1000 B.C.E.	ca. 1000 B.C.E. Indo-European groups move into the Ganges Plain	
500 B.C.E.	ca. 500 B.C.E. Siddhartha Gautama founds Buddhism; Mahavira founds Jainism 324 B.C.E. Chandragupta Maurya becomes king of Magadha and lays foundation for Mauryan Empire 273–232 B.C.E. Reign of Ashoka 184 B.C.E. Fall of Mauryan Empire	
1 C.E.	320 C.E. Chandra Gupta establishes Gupta Empire	ca. 50–560 C.E. Funan dominates southern Indochina and the Isthmus of Kra
500 C.E.	550 C.E. Collapse of Gupta Empire 606–647 C.E. Reign of Harsha Vardhana	ca. 500 C.E. Trade route develops through Strait of Malacca 683 C.E. Rise of Srivijaya in Sumatra 770–825 C.E. Construction of Borobodur in Java
1000 C.E.		1025 C.E. Chola attack on Palembang and decline of Srivijaya

Many characteristic features of later Indian civilization may derive from the Indus Valley civilization of the third and early second millennia B.C.E., but proof is hard to come by because writing from that period has not yet been deciphered. That society, with its advanced social organization and technology, succumbed around 1900 B.C.E. to some kind of environmental crisis (see Chapter 2).

The Vedic Age

Vedas Early Indian sacred "knowledge"—the literal meaning of the term—long preserved and communicated orally by Brahmin priests and eventually written down. These religious texts, including the thousand poetic hymns to various deities contained in the *Rig Veda*, are our main source of information about the Vedic period (ca. 1500–500 B.C.E.).

Historians call the period from 1500 to 500 B.C.E. the Vedic Age, after the **Vedas** (VAY-duhs), religious texts that are our main source of information about the period. The foundations for Indian civilization were laid in the Vedic Age. Most historians believe that new groups of people—animal-herding warriors speaking Indo-European languages—migrated into northwest India around 1500 B.C.E. Some argue for a much earlier Indo-European presence in this region in conjunction with the spread of agriculture. In any case, in the mid-second millennium B.C.E. northern India entered a new historical period associated with the dominance of Indo-European groups.

After the collapse of the Indus Valley civilization there was no central authority to direct irrigation efforts, and the region became home to kinship groups that depended mostly on their herds of cattle for sustenance. These societies were patriarchal, with the father dominating the family as the king ruled the tribe. Members of the warrior class boasted of their martial skill and courage, relished combat, celebrated with lavish feasts of beef and rounds of heavy drinking, and filled their leisure time with chariot racing and gambling.

After 1000 B.C.E. some groups migrated east into the Ganges Plain. New technologies made this advance possible. Iron tools—harder than bronze and able to hold a sharper edge—allowed settlers to fell trees and work the newly cleared land with plows pulled by oxen. The soil of the Ganges Plain was fertile, well watered by the annual monsoon, and able to sustain two or three crops a year. As in Greece at roughly the same time (see Chapter 5), the use of iron tools to open new land for agriculture must have led to a significant increase in population.

Stories about this era, not written down until much later but long preserved by memorization and oral recitation, speak of bitter warfare between two groups of people: the Aryas, relatively light-skinned speakers of Indo-European languages, and the Dasas, dark-skinned speakers of

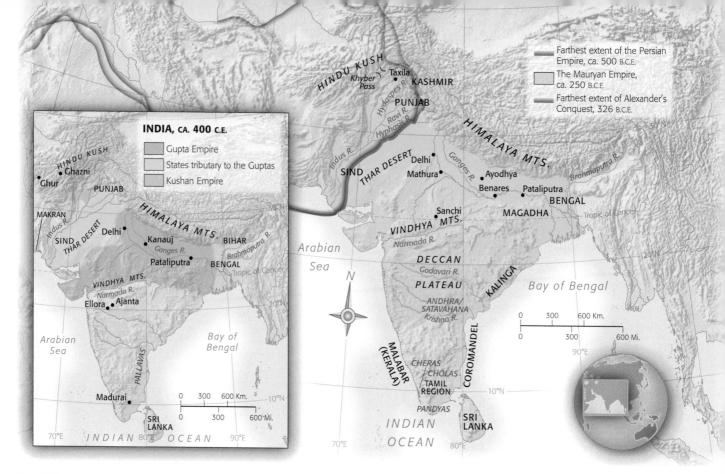

MAP 7.1 **Ancient India** Mountains and ocean largely separate the Indian subcontinent from the rest of Asia. Migrations and invasions usually came through the Khyber Pass in the northwest. Seaborne commerce with western Asia, Southeast Asia, and East Asia often flourished. Peoples speaking Indo-European languages migrated into the broad valleys of the Indus and Ganges Rivers in the north. Dravidian-speaking peoples remained the dominant population in the south. The diversity of the Indian landscape, the multiplicity of ethnic groups, and the primary identification of people with their class and caste lie behind the division into many small states that has characterized much of Indian political history. © Cengage Learning

varna/jati Two categories of social identity of great importance in Indian history. *Varna* are the four major social divisions: the Brahmin priest class, the Kshatriya warrior/administrator class, the Vaishya merchant/farmer class, and the Shudra laborer class. Within the system of varna are many *jati*, regional groups of people who have a common occupational sphere and who marry, eat, and generally interact with other members of their group.

Dravidian languages. It is possible that some Dasas were absorbed into Arya populations and that elites from both groups merged. For the most part, however, Aryas pushed the Dasas south into central and southern India, where their descendants still live. Today Indo-European languages are primarily spoken in northern India, while Dravidian speech prevails in the south.

Skin color has been a persistent concern of Indian society and is one of the bases for its historically sharp internal divisions. Over time there evolved a system of **varna**—literally "color," though the word came to indicate something akin to "class." Individuals were born into one of four classes: *Brahmin*, comprising priests and scholars; *Kshatriya* (kshuh-TREE-yuh), warriors and officials; *Vaishya* (VIESH-yuh), merchants, artisans, and landowners; or *Shudra* (SHOOD-ra), peasants and laborers. The designation *Shudra* originally may have been reserved for Dasas, who were given the menial jobs in society. Indeed, the very term *dasa* came to mean "slave." Eventually a fifth group was marked off: the Untouchables. They were excluded from the class system, and members of the other groups literally avoided them because of the demeaning or polluting work to which they were relegated—such as leather tanning, which involved touching dead animals, and sweeping away ashes of the dead after cremations.

People at the top of the social pyramid could explain why this hierarchy existed. According to one creation myth, a primordial creature named Purusha allowed itself to be sacrificed. From its mouth sprang the class of Brahmin priests, the embodiment of intellect and knowledge. From its arms came the Kshatriya warrior class, from its thighs the Vaishya landowners and merchants, and from its feet the Shudra workers.

The varna system was just one of the mechanisms developed to regulate relations between different groups. Within the broad class divisions, the population was further subdivided into numerous **jati**, or birth groups (sometimes called *castes*, from a Portuguese term meaning "breed"). Each jati had its proper occupation, duties, and rituals. Individuals who belonged to a given jati lived with members of their group, married within the group, and ate only with members of the group. Elaborate rules governed their interactions with members of other groups. Members of higher-status groups feared pollution from contact with lower-caste individuals and had to undergo elaborate rituals of purification to remove any taint.

The class and caste systems came to be connected to a widespread belief in reincarnation. The Brahmin priests taught that every living creature had an immortal essence: the *atman*, or "breath." Separated from the body at death, the atman was later reborn in another body. Whether the new body was that of an insect, an animal, or a human depended on the **karma**, or deeds, of the atman in its previous incarnations. People who lived exemplary lives would be reborn into the higher classes. Those who misbehaved would be punished in the next life by being relegated to a lower class or even a lower life form. The underlying message was: You are where you deserve to be, and the only way to improve your lot in the next cycle of existence is to accept your current station and its attendant duties.

The dominant deities in Vedic religion were male and associated with the heavens. To release the dawn, Indra, god of war and master of the thunderbolt, daily slew the demon encasing the universe. Varuna, lord of the sky, maintained universal order and dispensed justice. Agni, the force of fire, consumed the sacrifice and bridged the spheres of gods and humans.

Sacrifice—the dedication to a god of a valued possession, often a living creature—was the essential ritual. The purpose of these offerings was to invigorate the gods and thereby sustain their creative powers and promote stability in the world.

Brahmin priests controlled the sacrifices, for only they knew the rituals and prayers. The *Rig Veda*, a collection of more than a thousand poetic hymns to various deities, and the *Brahmanas*, detailed prose descriptions of procedures for ritual and sacrifice, were collections of priestly lore couched in the Sanskrit language of the Arya upper classes. This information was handed down orally from one generation of priests to the next. The priests' "knowledge" (the term *veda* means just that) was the basis of their economic well-being. They were amply rewarded for officiating at sacrifices, and their knowledge gave them social and political power because they were the indispensable intermediaries between gods and humans. Some scholars hypothesize that the Brahmins resisted the introduction of writing in order to preserve their control of sacred knowledge. This might explain why writing came into widespread use in India later than in other societies of equivalent complexity. However, we may be unaware of earlier uses of writing because it involved perishable materials that have not survived in the archaeological record.

It is difficult to uncover the experiences of women in early India. Limited evidence indicates that women in the Vedic period studied sacred lore, composed religious hymns, and participated in the sacrificial ritual. They could own property and usually did not marry until reaching their middle or late teens. Strong and resourceful women appear in the Indian epic poems originating in this era.

The sharp internal divisions and complex hierarchy of Indian society served important social functions. They provided each individual with a clear identity and role and offered the benefits of group solidarity and support. Moreover, there is evidence that groups sometimes were able to upgrade their status. Thus the elaborate system of divisions was not static and provided a mechanism for working out social tensions. Many of these features have persisted into modern times.

Challenges to the Old Order: Jainism and Buddhism

After 700 B.C.E. various forms of reaction against Brahmin power and privilege emerged. People who objected to the rigid hierarchy of classes and castes or the community's demands on the individual could retreat to the nearby forest that still covered much of ancient India. These wild places symbolized freedom from societal constraints.

Certain charismatic individuals who abandoned their town or village and moved to the forest attracted bands of followers. Calling into question the priests' exclusive claims to wisdom and the necessity of Vedic chants and sacrifices, they offered an alternate path to salvation: the individual pursuit of insight into the nature of the self and the universe through physical and mental discipline (*yoga*), special dietary practices, and meditation. They taught that by distancing oneself from desire for the things of this world, one could achieve **moksha**, or "liberation." This release from the cycle of reincarnations and union with the divine force that animates

karma In Indian tradition, the residue of deeds performed in past and present lives that adheres to a "spirit" and determines what form it will assume in its next life cycle. The doctrines of *karma* and reincarnation were used by the elite in ancient India to encourage people to accept their social position and do their duty.

moksha The Hindu concept of the spirit's "liberation" from the endless cycle of rebirths. There are various avenues—such as physical discipline, meditation, and acts of devotion to the gods—by which the spirit can distance itself from desire for the things of this world and be merged with the divine force that animates the universe.

the universe sometimes was likened to "a deep, dreamless sleep." The *Upanishads* (ooh-PAH-nee-shad)—a collection of more than one hundred mystical dialogues between teachers and disciples—reflect this questioning of the foundations of Vedic religion.

The most serious threat to Vedic religion and Brahmin prerogatives came from two new religions that emerged around this time: Jainism and Buddhism. Mahavira (540–468 B.C.E.) was known to his followers as Jina, "the Conqueror," from which is derived *Jainism* (JINE-iz-uhm), the belief system that he established. Emphasizing the holiness of the life force animating all living creatures, Mahavira and his followers practiced strict nonviolence. They wore masks to prevent accidentally inhaling small insects, and they carefully brushed off a seat before sitting down. Those who gave themselves over completely to Jainism practiced extreme asceticism and nudity, ate only what they were given by others, and eventually starved themselves to death. Less zealous Jainists, restricted from agricultural work by the injunction against killing, were city dwellers engaged in commerce and banking.

Far more significant for Indian and world history was the rise of Buddhism. So many stories were told about Siddhartha Gautama (563–483 B.C.E.), known as the **Buddha**, "the Enlightened One," that it is difficult to separate fact from legend. He came from a Kshatriya family of the Sakyas, a people in the foothills of the Himalayas. As a young man he enjoyed the princely lifestyle to which he had been born, but at some point he abandoned family and privilege to become a wandering ascetic. After six years of self-deprivation, he came to regard asceticism as no more likely to produce spiritual insight than the luxury of his previous life, and he decided to adhere to a "Middle Path" of moderation. Sitting under a tree in a deer park near Benares on the Ganges River, he gained a sudden and profound insight into the true nature of reality, which he set forth as "Four Noble Truths": (1) life is suffering; (2) suffering arises from desire; (3) the solution to suffering lies in curbing desire; and (4) desire can be curbed if a person follows the "Eightfold Path" of right views, aspirations, speech, conduct, livelihood, effort, mindfulness, and meditation. Rising up, the Buddha preached his First Sermon, a central text of Buddhism, and set into motion the "Wheel of the Law." He soon attracted followers, some of whom took vows of celibacy, nonviolence, and poverty.

Buddha An Indian prince named Siddhartha Gautama who renounced his wealth and social position to search for truth. After becoming "enlightened" (the meaning of *Buddha*), he enunciated the principles of Buddhism, which evolved and spread throughout India and to Southeast, East, and Central Asia.

Carved Stone Gateway Leading to the Great Stupa at Sanchi Pilgrims traveled long distances to visit stupas, mounds containing relics of the Buddha. The complex at Sanchi, in central India, was begun by Ashoka in the third century B.C.E., though the gates probably date to the first century C.E. This relief shows a royal procession bringing the remains of the Buddha to the city of Kushinagara.

Sculpture of the Buddha, Second or Third Century C.E. This depiction of the Buddha, showing the effects of a protracted fast before he abandoned asceticism for the path of moderation, is from Gandhara in the northwest. It displays the influence of Greek artistic styles emanating from Greek settlements established in that region by Alexander the Great in the late fourth century B.C.E. Seated Buddha in meditation, Greco-Buddhist style, 1st-4th century (bronze), Pakistani School/Lahore Museum, Lahore, Pakistan/Giraudon/The Bridgeman Art Library

In its original form, Buddhism centered on the individual. Although not quite rejecting the existence of gods, it denied their usefulness to a person seeking enlightenment. What mattered was living one's life with moderation, in order to minimize desire and suffering, and searching for spiritual truth through self-discipline and meditation. The ultimate reward was *nirvana*, literally "snuffing out the flame." With nirvana came release from the cycle of reincarnations and achievement of a state of perpetual tranquility. The Vedic tradition emphasized the eternal survival of the atman, the "breath" or nonmaterial essence of the individual. In contrast, Buddhism regarded the individual as a composite without any soul-like component that survived upon entering nirvana.

When the Buddha died, he left no final instructions, instead urging his disciples to "be their own lamp." As the Buddha's message—contained in philosophical discourses memorized by his followers—spread throughout India and into Central, Southeast, and East Asia, its very success began to subvert the individualistic and essentially atheistic tenets of the founder. Buddhist monasteries were established, and a hierarchy of Buddhist monks and nuns came into being. Worshipers erected *stupas* (STOO-puh) (large earthen mounds symbolizing the universe) over relics of the cremated founder. Believers began to worship the Buddha himself as a god. Many Buddhists also revered *bodhisattvas* (boe-dih-SUT-vuh), saintly men and women who had achieved enlightenment and were on the threshold of nirvana but chose to be reborn into mortal bodies to help others along the path to salvation.

The makers of early pictorial images refused to show the Buddha as a living person and represented him only indirectly, through symbols such as his footprints, his begging bowl, or the tree under which he achieved enlightenment, as if to emphasize his achievement of a state of nonexistence. From the second century C.E., however, statues of the Buddha and bodhisattvas began to proliferate, done in native sculptural styles and in a style that showed the influence of the Greek settlements established in Bactria (modern Afghanistan) by Alexander the Great (see Chapter 5). A schism emerged within Buddhism. Devotees of **Mahayana (mah-huh-YAH-nuh)** ("Great Vehicle") **Buddhism** embraced the popular new features, while practitioners of **Theravada (there-uh-VAH-duh)** ("Teachings of the Elders") **Buddhism** followed most of the original teachings of the founder.

Mahayana Buddhism "Great Vehicle" branch of Buddhism followed in China, Japan, and Central Asia. The focus is on reverence for Buddha and for bodhisattvas, enlightened persons who have postponed nirvana to help others attain enlightenment.

Theravada Buddhism "Way of the Elders" branch of Buddhism followed in Sri Lanka and much of Southeast Asia. Theravada remains close to the original principles set forth by the Buddha; it downplays the importance of gods and emphasizes austerity and the individual's search for enlightenment.

Hinduism A general term for a wide variety of beliefs and ritual practices that have developed in the Indian subcontinent since antiquity. Hinduism has roots in ancient Vedic, Buddhist, and south Indian religious concepts and practices. It spread along the trade routes to Southeast Asia.

The Evolution of Hinduism

Challenged by new, spiritually satisfying, and egalitarian movements, Vedic religion made important adjustments, evolving into **Hinduism**, the religion of hundreds of millions of people in South Asia today. The foundation of Hinduism is the Vedic religion of the Arya peoples of northern India. But Hinduism also incorporated elements drawn from the Dravidian cultures of the south, such as an emphasis on intense devotion to the deity and the prominence of fertility rituals. Also present are elements of Buddhism.

The process by which Vedic religion was transformed into Hinduism by the fourth century C.E. is largely hidden from us. The Brahmin priests maintained their high social status and influence. But sacrifice, though still part of traditional worship, was less central, and there was more opportunity for direct contact between gods and individual worshipers.

The gods were altered, both in identity and in their relationships with humanity. Two formerly minor deities, Vishnu (VIHSH-noo) and Shiva (SHEE-vuh), became preeminent.

Hinduism emphasized the worshiper's personal devotion to a particular deity, usually Vishnu, Shiva, or Devi **(DEH-vee)** ("the Goddess"). Both Shiva and Devi appear to be derived from the Dravidian tradition, in which fertility cults and female deities played a prominent role. Vishnu, who has a clear Arya pedigree, remains more popular in northern India, while Shiva is dominant in the Dravidian south. These gods can appear in many guises. They are identified by various cult names and are represented by a complex symbolism of stories, companion animals, birds, and objects.

Vishnu, the preserver, is a benevolent deity who helps his devotees in time of need. Hindus believe that whenever demonic forces threaten the cosmic order, Vishnu appears on earth in one of a series of *avataras*, or incarnations. Among his incarnations are the legendary hero Rama, the popular cowherd-god Krishna, and the Buddha (a clear attempt to co-opt the rival religion's founder). Shiva, who lives in ascetic isolation on Mount Kailasa in the Himalayas, is a more ambivalent figure. He represents both creation and destruction, for both are part of a single, cyclical process. He often is represented performing dance steps that symbolize the acts of creation and destruction. Devi manifests herself in various ways—as a full-bodied mother-goddess who promotes fertility and procreation, as the docile and loving wife Parvati, and as the frightening deity who, under the name Kali or Durga, lets loose a torrent of violence and destruction.

The multiplicity of gods (330 million according to one tradition), sects, and local practices within Hinduism is dazzling, reflecting the ethnic, linguistic, and cultural diversity of India. Yet within this variety there is unity. Ultimately, all the gods and spirits are seen as manifestations of a single divine force that pervades the universe. This sense of underlying unity is expressed in texts, such as the passage from the *Bhagavad-Gita* quoted at the beginning of this chapter; in the different potentials of women represented in the various manifestations of Devi; and in composite statues that are split down the middle—half Shiva, half Vishnu—as if to say that they are complementary aspects of one cosmic principle.

Hindu Temple at Khajuraho This sandstone temple of the Hindu deity Shiva, representing the celestial mountain of the gods, was erected at Khajuraho, in central India, around 1000 C.E., but it reflects the architectural symbolism of Hindu temples developed in the Gupta period. Worshipers made their way through several rooms to the image of the deity, located in the innermost "womb-chamber" directly beneath the tallest tower.

Borromeo/Art Resource, NY

Vishnu Rescuing the Earth Goddess, Fifth Century C.E.   This sculpture, carved into the rock wall of a cave at Udayagiri in eastern India, depicts Vishnu in his incarnation as a boar rescuing the Earth Goddess from the vast ocean. As the god treads triumphantly on a subdued snake demon and the joyful goddess clings to his snout, a chorus of gods and sages applaud the miracle.

SECTION REVIEW

- The Aryas, pastoralist warriors, migrated into the Indus River Valley ca. 1500 B.C.E. and the Ganges Plain after 1000 B.C.E., driving the Dasas into the southern part of the peninsula.

- The system of classes and castes, a mechanism for regulating the interactions of different groups, was linked to the concept of reincarnation and used to justify the power of the higher classes.

- Brahmin domination was challenged by new religions—Jainism and Buddhism.

- Theravada Buddhism remained close to the ideas of the founder, but Mahayana Buddhism developed gods, saints, monasteries, and shrines.

- Hinduism, created from a Vedic base but including Dravidian and Buddhist elements, preserved Brahmin status and privilege but allowed worshipers to make direct contact with the supernatural.

- Behind the diversity and multiplicity of Indian religion lies an ultimate unity.

Hinduism offers the worshiper a variety of ways to approach god and obtain divine favor—through special knowledge of sacred truths, mental and physical discipline, or extraordinary devotion to the deity. Worship centers on the temples, which range from humble village shrines to magnificent, richly decorated stone edifices built under royal patronage. Beautifully proportioned statues in which the deity may take up temporary residence are adored and beseeched by eager worshipers. A common form of worship is *puja*, service to the deity, which can take the form of bathing, clothing, or feeding the statue. Potent blessings are conferred on the man or woman who glimpses the divine image.

Pilgrimage to famous shrines and attendance at festivals offer worshipers additional opportunities to show devotion. The entire Indian subcontinent is dotted with sacred places where worshipers can directly sense and benefit from the inherent power of divinity. Mountains, caves, and certain trees, plants, and rocks are enveloped in an aura of mystery and sanctity. Hindus consider the Ganges River especially sacred, and each year millions of devoted worshipers bathe in its waters and receive their restorative and purifying power. The habit of pilgrimage has promoted contact and the exchange of ideas among people from different parts of India and has helped create a broad Hindu identity and the concept of India as a single civilization, despite enduring political fragmentation.

Religious duties may vary, depending not only on the worshiper's social standing and gender but also his or her stage of life. A young man from one of the three highest classes undergoes a ritual rebirth through the ceremony of the sacred thread, marking the attainment of manhood and readiness to receive religious knowledge. From this point, the ideal life cycle passes through four stages: (1) the young man becomes a student and studies the sacred texts; (2) he then becomes a householder, marries, has children, and acquires material wealth; (3) when his grandchildren are born, he gives up home and family and becomes a forest dweller, meditating on the nature and meaning of existence; (4) he abandons his personal identity altogether and becomes a wandering ascetic awaiting death. In the course of a virtuous life he has fulfilled first his duties to society and then his duties to himself, so that by the end he is so disconnected from the world that he can achieve *moksha* (liberation).

The successful transformation of a religion based on Vedic antecedents and the ultimate victory of Hinduism over Buddhism—Buddhism was driven from the land of its birth, though it maintains deep roots in Central, East, and Southeast Asia (see Chapters 9 and 11)—are remarkable phenomena. Hinduism responded to the needs of people for personal deities with whom they could establish direct connections. The austerity of Buddhism in its most authentic form, its denial of the importance of gods, and its expectation that individuals find their own path to enlightenment may have demanded too much of ordinary people. The very features that made Mahayana Buddhism more accessible to the populace—gods, saints, and myths—also made it more easily absorbed into the vast social and cultural fabric of Hinduism.

IMPERIAL EXPANSION AND COLLAPSE, 324 B.C.E.–650 C.E.

Political unity in India, on those rare occasions when it has been achieved, has not lasted long. A number of factors have contributed to India's habitual political fragmentation. Different terrains called forth varied forms of organization and economic activity, and peoples occupying diverse zones differed in language and cultural practices. Perhaps the most significant barrier to political unity lay in the complex social hierarchy. Individuals identified themselves primarily in terms of their class and caste; allegiance to a higher political authority was secondary.

Despite these divisive factors, two empires arose in the Ganges Plain in antiquity: the Mauryan (MORE-yuhn) Empire of the fourth to second centuries B.C.E. and the Gupta (GOOP-tuh) Empire of the fourth to sixth centuries C.E. Each extended political control over much of the subcontinent and fostered the formation of a common Indian civilization.

The Mauryan Empire, 324–184 B.C.E.

Around 600 B.C.E. independent kinship groups and states dotted the landscape of north India. The kingdom of Magadha, in eastern India south of the Ganges (see Map 7.1), began to play an increasingly influential role, however, thanks to wealth based on agriculture, iron mines, and its strategic location astride the trade routes of the eastern Ganges Basin. In the late fourth century B.C.E. Chandragupta Maurya (MORE-yuh), a young man from the Vaishya or Shudra class, gained control of Magadha and expanded it into the **Mauryan Empire**—India's first centralized empire. He may have been inspired by the example of Alexander the Great, who had followed up his conquest of the Persian Empire with a foray into the Punjab (northern Pakistan) in 326 B.C.E. (see Chapter 5). Chandragupta (r. 324–301 B.C.E.) and his successors Bindusara (r. 301–273 B.C.E.) and Ashoka (r. 273–232 B.C.E.) extended Mauryan control over the entire subcontinent except the southern tip. Not until the height of the Mughal Empire of the seventeenth century C.E. was so much of India again under the control of a single government.

Tradition holds that Kautilya, a crafty elderly Brahmin, guided Chandragupta in his conquests and consolidation of power. Kautilya is said to have written a surviving treatise on government, the *Arthashastra* (ahr-thuh-SHAHS-truh). Although recent studies have shown that the *Arthashastra* in its present form is a product of the third century C.E., its core text may well go back to Kautilya. This coldly pragmatic guide to political success and survival advocates the

Mauryan Empire The first state to unify most of the Indian subcontinent. It was founded by Chandragupta Maurya in 324 B.C.E. and survived until 184 B.C.E. From its capital at Pataliputra in the Ganges Valley it grew wealthy from taxes on agriculture, iron mining, and control of trade routes.

so-called *mandala* (man-DAH-luh) (circle) theory of foreign policy: "My enemy's enemy is my friend." It also presents schemes for enforcing and increasing the collection of tax revenues, and it prescribes the use of spies to keep watch on everyone in the kingdom.

A tax equivalent to as much as one-fourth the value of the harvest supported the Mauryan kings and government. Other revenues came from tolls on trade; government monopolies on mining, liquor sales, and the manufacture of weapons; and fees charged to those using the irrigation network. Close relatives and associates of the king governed administrative districts based on traditional ethnic boundaries. A large imperial army—with infantry, cavalry, and chariot divisions and the fearsome new element of war elephants—further secured power. Standard coinage issued throughout the empire was used to pay government and military personnel and promoted trade.

The Mauryan capital was at Pataliputra (modern Patna), where five tributaries join the Ganges. Surrounded by rivers and further protected by a timber wall and moat, the city extended along the riverbank for 8 miles (13 kilometers). Busy and crowded (the population has been estimated at 270,000), it was governed by six committees with responsibility for manufacturing, trade, sales, taxes, the welfare of foreigners, and the registration of births and deaths.

Ashoka, Chandragupta's grandson, is an outstanding figure in early Indian history. At the beginning of his reign he engaged in military campaigns that extended the boundaries of the empire. During his conquest of Kalinga, a coastal region southeast of Magadha, hundreds of thousands of people were killed, wounded, or deported. Overwhelmed by the brutality of this victory, the young monarch became a convert to Buddhism and preached nonviolence, morality, moderation, and religious tolerance in both government and private life.

Ashoka publicized this program by inscribing edicts on great rocks and polished pillars of sandstone scattered throughout his enormous empire. Among the inscriptions that have survived—they constitute the earliest decipherable Indian writing—is the following:

> *For a long time in the past, for many hundreds of years have increased the sacrificial slaughter of animals, violence toward creatures, unfilial conduct toward kinsmen, improper conduct toward Brahmins and ascetics. Now with the practice of morality by King [Ashoka], the sound of war drums has become the call to morality. . . . You [government officials] are appointed to rule over thousands of human beings in the expectation that you will win the affection of all men. All men are my children. Just as I desire that my children will fare well and be happy in this world and the next, I desire the same for all men. . . . King [Ashoka] . . . desires that there should be the growth of the essential spirit of morality or holiness among all sects. . . . There should not be glorification of one's own sect and denunciation of the sect of others for little or no reason. For all the sects are worthy of reverence for one reason or another.[2]*

Ashoka, however, was not naive. Despite his commitment to peaceful means, he reminded potential transgressors that "the king, remorseful as he is, has the strength to punish the wrongdoers who do not repent."

Commerce and Culture in an Era of Political Fragmentation

The Mauryan Empire prospered for a time after Ashoka's death in 232 B.C.E. Then, weakened by dynastic disputes and the expense of maintaining a large army and administrative bureaucracy, it collapsed from the pressure of attacks in the northwest in 184 B.C.E. Five hundred years passed before another indigenous state exercised control over northern India.

In the meantime, a series of foreign powers dominated the northwest, present-day Afghanistan and Pakistan, and extended their influence east and south. The first was the Greco-Bactrian kingdom (180–50 B.C.E.), descended from troops and settlers left in Afghanistan by Alexander the Great. Greek influence is evident in the art of this period and in the designs of coins. Occupation by two nomadic groups from Central Asia followed, resulting from large-scale movements of peoples set off by the pressure of Han Chinese forces on the Xiongnu (see Chapter 6). The Shakas, an Iranian people driven southwest along the mountain barrier of the Pamirs and

Ashoka Third ruler of the Mauryan Empire in India (r. 273–232 B.C.E.). He converted to Buddhism and broadcast his precepts on inscribed stones and pillars, the earliest surviving Indian writing.

---

[2]B. G. Gokhale, *Asoka Maurya* (New York: Twayne, 1966), 152–153, 156–157, 160.

Himalayas, were dominant from 50 B.C.E. to 50 C.E. They were followed by the Kushans (KOO-shahn), originally from Xinjiang in northwest China, who were preeminent from 50 to 240 C.E. At its height the Kushan kingdom controlled much of present-day Uzbekistan, Afghanistan, Pakistan, and northwest India, fostering trade and prosperity by connecting to both the overland Silk Road and Arabian seaports (see Chapter 9). The eastern Ganges region reverted to a patchwork of small principalities, as it had been before the Mauryan era.

Despite political fragmentation in the five centuries after the Mauryan collapse, there were many signs of economic, cultural, and intellectual vitality. The network of roads and towns that had sprung up under the Mauryans fostered lively commerce within the subcontinent, and India was at the heart of international land and sea trade routes that linked China, Southeast Asia, Central Asia, the Middle East, East Africa, and the lands of the Mediterranean. The growth of crafts (metalwork, cloth making and dying, jewelry, perfume, glass, stone and terracotta sculpture), the increasing use of coins, and the development of local and long-distance commerce fostered the expansion and prosperity of urban centers. In the absence of a strong central authority, guilds of merchants and artisans became politically powerful in the towns. They were wealthy patrons of culture and endowed the religious sects to which they adhered—particularly Buddhism and Jainism—with richly decorated temples and monuments.

During the last centuries B.C.E. and first centuries C.E. the two greatest Indian epics, the *Ramayana* (ruh-muh-YAH-nuh) and the *Mahabharata* (muh-huh-BAH-ruh-tuh), based on oral predecessors dating back many centuries, achieved their final form. The events that both epics describe are said to have occurred several million years in the past, but the political forms, social organization, and other elements of cultural context—proud kings, beautiful queens, wars among kinship groups, heroic conduct, and chivalric values—seem to reflect the conditions of the early Vedic period, when Arya warrior societies were moving onto the Ganges Plain.

Mahabharata A vast epic chronicling the events leading up to a cataclysmic battle between related kinship groups in early India. It includes the *Bhagavad-Gita*.

Bhagavad-Gita The most important work of Indian sacred literature, a dialogue between the great warrior Arjuna and the god Krishna on duty and the fate of the spirit.

The vast pageant of the **Mahabharata** (it is eight times the length of the Greek *Iliad* and *Odyssey* combined) tells the story of two sets of cousins, the Pandavas and Kauravas, whose quarrel over succession to the throne leads them to a cataclysmic battle at the field of Kurukshetra. The battle is so destructive on all sides that the eventual winner, Yudhishthira, is reluctant to accept the fruits of so tragic a victory.

The **Bhagavad-Gita**, quoted at the beginning of this chapter, is a self-contained (and perhaps originally separate) episode set in the midst of those events. The great hero Arjuna, at first reluctant to fight his own kinsmen, is tutored by the god Krishna and learns the necessity of fulfilling his duty as a warrior. Death means nothing in a universe in which souls will be reborn again and again. The climactic moment comes when Krishna reveals his true appearance—awesome and overwhelmingly powerful—and his identity as time itself, the force behind all creation and destruction. The *Bhagavad-Gita* offers an attractive resolution to the tension in Indian civilization between duty to society and duty to one's own soul. Disciplined action—that is, action taken without regard for any personal benefits that might derive from it—is a form of service to the gods and will be rewarded by release from the cycle of rebirths.

This era also saw significant advances in science and linguistics. Indian doctors had a wide knowledge of herbal remedies. Panini (late fourth century B.C.E.) undertook a detailed analysis of Sanskrit word forms and grammar. His work led to the standardization of Sanskrit, arresting its natural development and turning it into a formal, literary, and administrative language. Prakrits—popular dialects—emerged to become the ancestors of the modern Indo-European languages of northern and central India.

This period of political fragmentation in the north also saw the rise of the Satavahana dynasty (also called Andhra) in the Deccan Plateau from the second century B.C.E. to the early third century C.E. (see Map 7.1). Elements of north Indian technology and culture—including iron metallurgy, rice-paddy agriculture, urbanization, writing, coinage, and Brahmin religious authority—spread throughout central India, and indigenous kinship groups were absorbed into the Hindu system of class and caste.

Tamil kingdoms The kingdoms of southern India, inhabited primarily by speakers of Dravidian languages, which developed in partial isolation, and somewhat differently, from the Arya north. They produced epics, poetry, and performance arts. Elements of Tamil religious beliefs were merged into the Hindu synthesis.

In the southernmost parts of the peninsula were the three **Tamil kingdoms** of Cholas, Pandyas, and Cheras. While in frequent conflict with one another and experiencing periods of ascendancy and decline, they persisted in one form or another for over two thousand years. The period from the third century B.C.E. to the third century C.E. was a "classical" period of great literary and artistic productivity. Under the patronage of the Pandya kings and the intellectual leadership of an academy of five hundred authors, works of literature on a wide range of topics—grammatical treatises, collections of ethical proverbs, epics, and short poems about love, war, wealth, and the beauty of nature—were produced, and music, dance, and drama were performed.

The Gupta Empire, 320–550 C.E.

Gupta Empire A powerful Indian state based, like its Mauryan predecessor, on a capital at Pataliputra in the Ganges Valley. It controlled most of the Indian subcontinent through a combination of military force and its prestige as a center of sophisticated culture.

In the early fourth century C.E., following the decline of the Kushan and Satavahana regimes in northern and central India, a new imperial entity took shape in the north. Like its Mauryan predecessor, the **Gupta Empire** emerged from the Ganges Plain and had its capital at Pataliputra. The founder, consciously modeling himself on the first Mauryan king, called himself Chandra Gupta (r. 320–335). The monarchs of this dynasty never controlled territories as extensive as those of the Mauryans. Nevertheless, over the fifteen-year reign of Chandra Gupta and the forty-year reigns of his three successors—the war-loving Samudra Gupta, Chandra Gupta II, a famed patron of artists and scholars, and Kumara Gupta—Gupta power and influence reached across northern and central India, west to Punjab and east to Bengal, north to Kashmir, and south into the Deccan Plateau (see Map 7.1).

This new empire enjoyed the same strategic advantages as its Mauryan predecessor, sitting astride important trade routes, exploiting the agricultural productivity of the Ganges Plain, and controlling nearby iron deposits. Although similar methods for raising revenue and administering broad territories were adopted, Gupta control was never as effectively centralized as Mauryan authority, and the Gupta administrative bureaucracy and intelligence network were smaller and less pervasive. A standing army, whose strength lay in the excellent horsemanship (learned from the nomadic Kushans) and skill with bow and arrow of its cavalry, maintained tight control and taxation in the core of the empire. Governors, whose position often passed from father to son, had a freer hand in the more outlying areas. Distant subordinate kingdoms and areas inhabited by kinship groups made annual donations of tribute, and garrisons were stationed at key frontier points. At the local level, villages were managed by a headman and council of elders, while the guilds of artisans and merchants had important administrative roles in the cities.

theater-state Historians' term for a state that acquires prestige and power by developing attractive cultural forms and staging elaborate public ceremonies (as well as redistributing valuable resources) to attract and bind subjects to the center. Examples include the Gupta Empire in India and Srivijaya in Southeast Asia.

Limited in its ability to enforce its will on outlying areas, the empire found ways to "persuade" others to follow its lead. One medium of persuasion was the splendor, beauty, and orderliness of life at the capital and royal court. The Gupta Empire is a good example of a **"theater-state."** A constant round of solemn rituals, dramatic ceremonies, and exciting cultural events was a potent advertisement for the benefits of association with the empire. The center collected luxury goods and profits from trade and redistributed them to dependents through the exchange of gifts and other means. Subordinate princes gained prestige by emulating the Gupta center on whatever scale they could manage, and they maintained close ties through visits, gifts, and marriages to the Gupta royal family.

Astronomers, mathematicians, and other scientists received royal support. Indian mathematicians invented the concept of zero and developed the "Arabic" numerals and system of place-value notation used in most parts of the world today (see Environment and Technology: Indian Mathematics). The Gupta monarchs also supported poets and dramatists and the compilation of law codes and grammatical texts.

Because of the moist climate of the Ganges Plain, few archaeological remains from the Gupta era have survived. An eyewitness account, however, provides valuable information about Pataliputra, the capital city. A Chinese Buddhist monk named Faxian (fah-shee-en) made a pilgrimage to the homeland of his faith around 400 C.E. and left a record of his journey:

> *The royal palace and halls in the midst of the city, which exist now as of old, were all made by spirits which [King Ashoka] employed, and which piled up the stones, reared the walls and gates, and executed the elegant carving and inlaid sculpture-work—in a way which no human hands of this world could accomplish. . . . By the side of the stupa of Ashoka, there has been made a Mahayana [Buddhist] monastery, very grand and beautiful; there is also a Hinayana [Theravada] one; the two together containing six hundred or seven hundred monks. The rules of demeanor and the scholastic arrangements in them are worthy of observation.*[3]

---

[3]James Legge, *The Travels of Fa-hien: Fa-hien's Record of Buddhistic Kingdoms* (Delhi: Oriental Publishers, 1971), 77–79.

Indian Mathematics

The so-called Arabic numerals used in most parts of the world today were developed in India. The Indian system of place-value notation was far more efficient than the unwieldy numerical systems of Egyptians, Greeks, and Romans, and the invention of zero was a profound intellectual achievement. This system is used even more widely than the alphabet derived from the Phoenicians (see Chapter 3) and is, in one sense, the only truly global language.

In its fully developed form the Indian method of arithmetic notation employed a base-ten system. It had separate columns for ones, tens, hundreds, and so forth, as well as a zero sign to indicate the absence of units in a given column. This system makes possible the economical expression of even very large numbers. It also allows for the performance of calculations not possible in a system like the numerals of the Romans, where any real calculation had to be done mentally or on a counting board.

A series of early Indian inscriptions using the numerals from 1 to 9 are deeds of property given to religious institutions by kings or other wealthy individuals. They were incised in the Sanskrit language on copper plates. The earliest known example has a date equivalent to 595 C.E. A sign for zero is attested by the eighth century, but textual evidence leads to the inference that a place-value system and the zero concept were already known in the fifth century.

This Indian system spread to the Middle East, Southeast Asia, and East Asia by the seventh century. Other peoples quickly recognized its capabilities and adopted it, sometimes using indigenous symbols. Europe received the new technology somewhat later. Gerbert of Aurillac, a French Christian monk, spent time in Spain between 967 and 970, where he was exposed to the mathematics of the Arabs. A great scholar and teacher who eventually became Pope Sylvester II (r. 999–1003), he spread word of the "Arabic" system in the Christian West.

Knowledge of the Indian system of mathematical notation eventually spread throughout Europe, partly through the use of a mechanical calculating device—an improved version of the Roman counting board, with counters inscribed with variants of the Indian numeral forms. Because the counters could be turned sideways or upside down, at first there was considerable variation in the forms. But by the twelfth century they had become standardized into forms close to those in use today.

Copper Plate with Indian Numerals   This property deed from western India shows an early form of the symbol system for numbers that spread to the Middle East and Europe and today is used all over the world.   Facsimile by Georges Ifrah. Reproduced by permission of Georges Ifrah.

As the capabilities of the place-value system for calculations became clear, the counting board fell into disuse. This led to the adoption of the zero sign—not necessary on the counting board, where a column could be left empty—by the twelfth century. Leonardo Fibonacci, a thirteenth-century C.E. Italian who learned algebra in Muslim North Africa and employed the Arabic numeral system in his mathematical treatise, gave additional impetus to the movement to discard the traditional system of Roman numerals.

Why was this marvelous system of mathematical notation invented in ancient India? The answer may lie in the way its range and versatility correspond to elements of Indian cosmology. The Indians conceived of immense spans of time—trillions of years (far exceeding current scientific estimates of the age of the universe as approximately 14 billion years)—during which innumerable universes like our own were created, existed for a finite time, then were destroyed. In one popular creation myth, Vishnu is slumbering on the coils of a giant serpent at the bottom of the ocean, and worlds are being created and destroyed as he exhales and inhales. In Indian thought our world, like others, has existed for a series of epochs lasting more than 4 million years, yet the period of its existence is but a brief and insignificant moment in the vast sweep of time. The Indians developed a number system that allowed them to express concepts of this magnitude.

There was a decline in the status of women in this period (see Diversity and Dominance: Relations Between Women and Men in the *Kama Sutra* and the *Arthashastra*). As in Mesopotamia, Greece, and China, several factors—urbanization, increasingly complex political and social structures, and the emergence of a nonagricultural middle class that placed high value on the acquisition and inheritance of property—led to a loss of women's rights and an increase in male control over women's behavior.

Women in India lost the right to own or inherit property. They were also barred from studying sacred texts and participating in sacrificial rituals. In many respects, they were treated as equivalent to the lowest class, the Shudra. A woman was expected to obey first her father, then her husband, and finally her sons. Girls were married at an increasingly early age, sometimes as young as six or seven. This practice meant that the prospective husband could be sure of his

Wall Painting from the Caves at Ajanta, Fifth Century C.E. During and after the Gupta period, natural caves in the Deccan were turned into shrines decorated with sculpture and painting. This painting, while depicting one of the earlier lives of the Buddha, also gives us a glimpse of contemporary life at the Gupta court. King Mahajanaka, about to give up his throne and leave his family to become a monk, receives a ritual bath. Norma Joseph/Alamy

wife's virginity and, by bringing her up in his own household, could train her to suit his purposes. The most extreme form of control took place in parts of India where a widow was expected to cremate herself on her husband's funeral pyre. This ritual, called *sati* (suh-TEE), was seen as a way of keeping a woman "pure." Women who declined to make this ultimate gesture of devotion were forbidden to remarry, shunned socially, and given little opportunity to earn a living.

Some women escaped male control by entering a Jainist or Buddhist religious community. Status also gave women more freedom. Women who belonged to powerful families and courtesans trained in poetry and music as well as ways of providing sexual pleasure had high social standing and sometimes gave money for the erection of religious shrines.

The Mauryans had been Buddhists, but the Gupta monarchs were Hindus. They revived ancient Vedic practices to bring an aura of sanctity to their position. This period also saw a reassertion of the importance of class and caste and the influence of Brahmin priests. In return for the religious validation of their rule given by the Brahmins, the Guptas gave the priests extensive grants of land. The Brahmins became wealthy from the revenues, which they collected directly from the peasants, and they even exercised administrative and judicial authority over the villages in their domains. Nevertheless, it was an era of religious tolerance. The Gupta kings were patrons for Hindu, Buddhist, and Jain endeavors. Buddhist monasteries with hundreds or even thousands of monks and nuns in residence flourished in the cities, and a Buddhist university was established at Nalanda. Northern India was the destination of Buddhist pilgrims from Southeast and East Asia, traveling to visit the birthplace of their faith.

The classic form of the Hindu temple evolved during the Gupta era. Sitting atop a raised platform surmounted by high towers, the temple was patterned on the sacred mountain or palace in which the gods of mythology resided and represented the inherent order of the universe. From an exterior courtyard worshipers approached the central shrine, where the statue of the deity stood. Paintings or sculptured depictions of gods and mythical events covered the walls of the best-endowed sanctuaries. Cave-temples carved out of rock were also richly adorned with frescoes or sculpture.

Relations Between Women and Men in the *Kama Sutra* and the *Arthashastra*

The ancient Indians articulated three broad areas of human concern: dharma—the realm of religious and moral behavior; artha—the acquisition of wealth and property; and kama—the pursuit of pleasure. The Kama Sutra, which means "Treatise on Pleasure," while best known in the West for its detailed descriptions of erotic activities, is actually far more than a sex manual. It addresses, in a very broad sense, the relations between women and men in ancient Indian society, providing valuable information about the activities of men and women, the psychology of relationships, the forms of courtship and marriage, the household responsibilities of married women, appropriate behavior, and much more. The author of this text, Vatsyayana, lived in the third century C.E.

When a girl of the same caste, and a virgin, is married in accordance with the precepts of Holy Writ, the results of such a union are the acquisition of Dharma and Artha, offspring, affinity, increase of friends, and untarnished love. For this reason a man should fix his affections upon a girl who is of good family, whose parents are alive, and who is three years or more younger than himself. She should be born of a highly respectable family, possessed of wealth, well connected, and with many relations and friends. She should also be beautiful, of a good disposition, with lucky marks on her body, and with good hair, nails, teeth, ears, eyes and breasts, neither more nor less than they ought to be, and no one of them entirely wanting, and not troubled with a sickly body. . . . But at all events, says Ghotakamukha [an earlier writer], a girl who has been already joined with others (i.e., no longer a maiden) should never be loved, for it would be reproachable to do such a thing.

Now in order to bring about a marriage with such a girl as described above, the parents and relations of the man should exert themselves, as also such friends on both sides as may be desired to assist in the matter. These friends should bring to the notice of the girl's parents the faults, both present and future, of all the other men that may wish to marry her, and should at the same time extol even to exaggeration all the excellencies, ancestral and paternal, of their friend, so as to endear him to them. . . . Others again should rouse the jealousy of the girl's mother by telling her that their friend has a chance of getting from some other quarter even a better girl than hers.

A girl should be taken as a wife, as also given in marriage, when fortune, signs, omens, and the words of others are favourable, for, says Ghotakamukha, a man should not marry at any time he likes. A girl who is asleep, crying, or gone out of the house when sought in marriage, or who is betrothed to another, should not be married. The following also should be avoided:

- One who is kept concealed
- One who has an ill-sounding name
- One who has her nose depressed
- One who has her nostril turned up
- One who is formed like a male
- One who is bent down
- One who has crooked thighs
- One who has a projecting forehead
- One who has a bald head
- One who does not like purity
- One who has been polluted by another
- One who is disfigured in any way
- One who has fully arrived at puberty
- One who is a friend
- One who is a younger sister
- One who is a Varshakari [prone to extreme perspiration]

But some authors say that prosperity is gained only by marrying that girl to whom one becomes attached, and that therefore no other girl but the one who is loved should be married by anyone. . . .

A virtuous woman, who has affection for her husband, should act in conformity with his wishes as if he were a divine being, and with his consent should take upon herself the whole care of his family. She should keep the whole house well cleaned, and arrange flowers of various kinds in different parts of it, and make the floor smooth and polished so as to give the whole a neat and becoming appearance. She should surround the house with a garden, and place ready in it all the materials required for the morning, noon and evening sacrifices. Moreover she should herself revere the sanctuary of the Household Gods. . . .

As regards meals, she should always consider what her husband likes and dislikes and what things are good for him, and what are injurious to him. When she hears the sounds of his

The vibrant commerce of the previous era continued into the Gupta period, with artisan guilds playing an influential role in the economic, political, and religious life of the towns. The Guptas sought control of the ports on the Arabian Sea but saw a decline in trade with the weakened Roman Empire. In compensation, trade with Southeast and East Asia was on the rise. Adventurous merchants from the ports of eastern and southern India made the sea voyage to the Malay (muh-LAY) Peninsula and islands of Indonesia to exchange Indian cotton cloth, ivory,

footsteps coming home she should at once get up and be ready to do whatever he may command her, and either order her female servant to wash his feet, or wash them herself. When going anywhere with her husband, she should put on her ornaments, and without his consent she should not either give or accept invitations, or attend marriages and sacrifices, or sit in the company of female friends, or visit the temples of the Gods. And if she wants to engage in any kind of games or sports, she should not do it against his will. In the same way she should always sit down after him, and get up before him, and should never awaken him when he is asleep.

The core of the Arthashastra, *which means "Science of Wealth," may have been composed in the later third century* B.C.E. *by Kautilya, an adviser to the first Mauryan ruler, Chandragupta, but the text as we have it includes later additions. While the* Arthashastra *is primarily concerned with how the ruler may gain and keep power, it includes prescriptions on other aspects of life, including the kinds of problems that may threaten or destroy marriages.*

If a woman either brings forth no live children, or has no male issue, or is barren, her husband shall wait for eight years before marrying another. If she bears only a dead child, he has to wait for ten years. If she brings forth only females, he has to wait for twelve years. Then, if he is desirous to have sons, he may marry another. . . . If a husband either is of bad character, or is long gone abroad, or has become a traitor to his king, or is likely to endanger the life of his wife, or has fallen from his caste, or has lost virility, he may be abandoned by his wife. . . .

Women of refractive natures shall not be taught manners by using such expressions as "You, half-naked!; you, fully-naked; you, cripple; you, fatherless; you, motherless." Nor shall she be given more than three beats, either with a bamboo bark or with a rope or with the palm of the hand, on her hips. . . .

A woman who hates her husband, who has passed the period of seven turns of her menses, and who loves another, shall immediately return to her husband both the endowment and jewelry she has received from him, and allow him to lie down with another woman. A man, hating his wife, shall allow her to take shelter in the house of a beggar woman, or of her lawful guardians or of her kinsmen. . . . A woman, hating her husband, cannot divorce her husband against his will. Nor can a man divorce his wife against her will. But from mutual enmity divorce may be obtained. . . .

If a woman engages herself in amorous sports, or drinking in the face of an order to the contrary, she shall be fined three panas. She shall pay a fine of six panas for going out at daytime to sports or to see a woman or spectacles. She shall pay a fine of twelve panas if she goes out to see another man or for sports. For the same offences committed at night the fines shall be doubled. If a woman goes out while the husband is asleep or intoxicated, or if she shuts the door of the house against her husband, she shall be fined twelve panas. If a woman keeps him out of the house at night, she shall pay double the above fine. If a man and a woman make signs to each other with a view to sensual enjoyment, or carry on secret conversation for the same purpose, the woman shall pay a fine of twenty-four panas and the man double that amount. . . . For holding conversation in suspicious places, whips may be substituted for fines. In the center of the village, an outcaste person may whip such women five times on each of the sides of their body. . . .

A Kshatriya who commits adultery with an unguarded Brahman woman shall be punished with the highest amercement; a Vaishya doing the same shall be deprived of the whole of his property; and a Shudra shall be burnt alive wound round in mats. . . . A man who commits adultery with a woman of low caste shall be banished, with prescribed marks branded on his forehead, or shall be degraded to the same caste. A Shudra or an outcaste who commits adultery with a woman of low caste shall be put to death, while the woman shall have her ears and nose cut off.

QUESTIONS FOR ANALYSIS

1. In what ways are women given essentially equal treatment to men in these excerpts? In what ways are they treated unequally?

2. On what bases do men and women choose spouses and lovers? How does the class status of the two individuals play a part in these choices?

3. What were the most important household responsibilities of ancient Indian women? What social, intellectual, and cultural activities did they engage in?

4. In light of the prescriptions for how a married woman should treat her husband, what do you think was the nature of the emotional relationship of husband and wife? How might this differ from marriages in our society? Why did some marriages fail in ancient India?

Sources: First selection from Sir Richard Burton and F. F. Arbuthnot, *The Kama Sutra of Vatsyayana* (1883), sections III.1, III.4, III.5, IV.1, found at http://www.sacredtexts.com/sex/kama/index.htm. Second selection from R. Shamasastry, *Kautilya's Arthashastra*, 2d ed. (1923), sections III.2, III.3, IV.13, from Internet Indian History Sourcebook at http://www.fordham.edu/halsall/india/kautilya2.html.

metalwork, and animals for Chinese silk or Indonesian spices. The overland Silk Road from China was also in operation but was vulnerable to disruption by Central Asian nomads (see Chapter 9).

By the later fifth century C.E. the Gupta Empire was coming under pressure from the Huns, nomadic invaders from the steppes of Central Asia who poured into the northwest corridor. Defense of this distant frontier region eventually exhausted the imperial treasury, and the empire collapsed by 550.

SECTION REVIEW

- The Mauryan Empire, founded in the late fourth century B.C.E. by Chandragupta Maurya, eventually controlled most of the subcontinent.

- King Ashoka, a convert to Buddhism, inscribed stones and pillars with a call to nonviolence, moderation, and religious toleration.

- After the Mauryan fall in 184 B.C.E., foreign occupiers—Indo-Greeks, Shakas, and Kushans—controlled the northwest.

- Despite political fragmentation, commerce and culture thrived.

- A renaissance of art and literature occurred in the Tamil kingdoms of south India between the third century B.C.E. and the third century C.E.

- The Gupta Empire, while not as extensive as the Mauryan Empire, fostered scholarship, science, and the arts from the fourth to sixth centuries C.E.

The early seventh century saw a brief revival of imperial unity. Harsha Vardhana (r. 606–647), ruler of the region around Delhi, extended his power over the northern plain and moved his capital to Kanauj on the Ganges River. By this time cities and commerce were in decline, much of the land had been given as grants to Brahmin priests and government officials, and the administration was decentralized, depending on the allegiance of largely autonomous vassal rulers. In many respects the situation was parallel to that of the later Roman Empire in Europe (see Chapter 6), as India moved toward a more feudal social and economic structure. After Harsha's death, northern India reverted to its customary state of political fragmentation and remained divided until the Islamic invasions of the eleventh and twelfth centuries (see Chapter 15).

During and after the centuries of Gupta ascendancy and decline in the north, the Deccan Plateau and the southern part of the peninsula followed an independent path. In this region, where the landscape is segmented by mountains, rocky plateaus, tropical forests, and sharply cut river courses, there were many small centers of power. From the sixth to twelfth centuries, the Pallavas, Chalukyas, and other warrior dynasties collected tribute and plundered as far as their strength permitted, storing their wealth in urban fortresses. These rulers sought legitimacy and fame as patrons of religion and culture, and much of the distinguished art and architecture of the period were produced in the kingdoms of the south. Many elements of northern Indian religion and culture spread in the south, including the class and caste system, Brahmin religious authority, and worship of Vishnu and Shiva. These kingdoms also served as the conduit through which Indian religion and culture reached Southeast Asia.

SOUTHEAST ASIA, 50–1025 C.E.

Southeast Asia consists of three geographical zones: the Indochina mainland, the Malay Peninsula, and thousands of islands extending on an east-west axis far out into the Pacific Ocean (see Map 7.2). Encompassing a vast area of land and water, this region is now occupied by the countries of Myanmar (myahn-MAH) (Burma), Thailand, Laos, Cambodia, Vietnam, Malaysia, Singapore, Indonesia, Brunei (broo-NIE), and the Philippines. Poised between the ancient centers of China and India, Southeast Asia has been influenced by the cultures of both civilizations. The region first rose to prominence and prosperity because of its intermediate role in the trade exchanges between southern and eastern Asia.

The strategic importance of Southeast Asia is enhanced by the region's natural resources. This is a geologically active zone; the islands are the tops of a chain of volcanoes. Lying along the equator, Southeast Asia has a tropical climate. The temperature hovers around 80 degrees Fahrenheit (30 degrees Celsius), and the monsoon winds provide dependable rainfall throughout the year. Thanks to several growing cycles each year, the region is capable of supporting a large human population. The most fertile agricultural lands lie along the floodplains of the largest silt-bearing rivers or contain rich volcanic soil deposited by ancient eruptions.

Early Civilization

Rain forest covers much of Southeast Asia. As early as 2000 B.C.E. people in this region practiced swidden agriculture, clearing land for farming by cutting and burning the vegetation. The cleared land was farmed for several growing seasons. When the soil was exhausted, the farmers abandoned the patch, allowing the forest to reclaim it, while they cleared and cultivated other nearby fields in similar fashion. Rice was the staple food—labor-intensive (see Chapter 4) but able to support a large population. A number of plant and animal species spread from Southeast

MAP 7.2 **Southeast Asia** Southeast Asia's position between the ancient centers of civilization in India and China had a major impact on its history. In the first millennium C.E. a series of powerful and wealthy states arose in the region by gaining control of major trade routes: first Funan, based in southern Vietnam, Cambodia, and the Malay Peninsula, then Srivijaya on the island of Sumatra, then smaller states on the island of Java. Shifting trade routes led to the rise and fall of the various centers. © Cengage Learning

Asia to other regions, including rice, soybeans, sugar cane, yams, bananas, coconuts, chickens, and pigs.

The Malay peoples who became the dominant population in this region were the product of several waves of migration from southern China beginning around 3000 B.C.E. Some indigenous peoples merged with the Malay newcomers; others retreated to remote mountain and forest zones. Subsequently (beginning, perhaps, around 1600 B.C.E.), rising population and disputes within communities prompted streams of people to leave the Southeast Asian mainland for the islands. By the first millennium B.C.E. Southeast Asians had developed impressive navigational skills. They knew how to ride the monsoon winds and interpret the patterns of swells, winds, clouds, and bird and sea life. Over a period of several thousand years groups of Malay peoples in large, double outrigger canoes spread out across the Pacific and Indian Oceans—half the circumference of the earth—to settle thousands of islands.

The inhabitants of Southeast Asia clustered along riverbanks or in fertile volcanic plains. Their fields and villages were never far from the rain forest, with its wild animals and numerous plant species. Forest trees provided fruit, wood, and spices, and the shallow waters surrounding the islands teemed with fish. This region was also an early center of metallurgy. Metalsmiths heated copper and tin ore to the right temperature for producing and shaping bronze implements by using hollow bamboo tubes to funnel oxygen to the furnace.

Northern Indochina, by its geographic proximity, was vulnerable to Chinese pressure and cultural influences, and it was under Chinese political control for a thousand years (111 B.C.E.–939 C.E.). Farther south, larger states emerged in the early centuries C.E. in response to two powerful forces: commerce and Hindu-Buddhist culture.

Southeast Asia was situated along the trade routes that merchants used to carry Chinese silk westward to India and the Mediterranean. The movements of nomadic peoples had disrupted the old land route across Central Asia, but Indian demand for silk was increasing—both for domestic use and for transshipment to satisfy the fast-growing luxury market in the Roman Empire. Gradually merchants extended this exchange network to include goods from Southeast Asia, such as aromatic woods, resins, and cinnamon, pepper, cloves, nutmeg, and other spices. Southeast Asian centers rose to prominence by serving this trade network and controlling key points. **187**

The other force leading to the rise of larger political entities was the influence of Hindu-Buddhist culture imported from India. Commerce brought Indian merchants and sailors into the ports of Southeast Asia. As Buddhism spread, Southeast Asia became a way station for Indian missionaries and East Asian pilgrims going to and coming from the birthplace of their faith. Shrewd Malay rulers looked to Indian traditions as a rich source of ideas and prestige. They borrowed Sanskrit terms such as *maharaja* (mah-huh-RAH-juh) (great king), utilized Indian models of bureaucracy, ceremonial practices, and forms of artistic representation, and employed priests, administrators, and scribes skilled in Sanskrit writing to expedite government business. Their special connection to powerful gods and higher knowledge raised them above their rivals.

However, the Southeast Asian kingdoms were not just passive recipients of Indian culture. They took what was useful to them and synthesized it with indigenous beliefs, values, and institutions—for example, local concepts of chiefship, ancestor worship, and forms of oaths. Moreover, they trained their own people in the new ways, so that the bureaucracy contained both foreign experts and native disciples. The whole process amounted to a cultural dialogue between India and Southeast Asia in which both were active participants.

The first major Southeast Asian center, called "**Funan**" (FOO-nahn) by Chinese visitors, flourished between the first and sixth centuries C.E. (see Map 7.2), with its capital at the modern site of Oc-Eo in southern Vietnam. Funan occupied the delta of the Mekong (MAY-kawng) River, a "rice bowl" capable of supporting a large population, and its rulers mobilized large numbers of laborers to dig irrigation channels and prevent destructive floods. By extending its control over most of southern Indochina and the Malay Peninsula, Funan was able to dominate the trade route from India to China. The route began in the ports of northeast India, crossed the Bay of Bengal, continued by land over the Isthmus of Kra on the Malay Peninsula, and then continued across the South China Sea (see Map 7.2). Indian merchants found that offloading their goods from ships and carrying them across the narrow strip of land was safer than making the 1,000-mile (1,600-kilometer) voyage around the Malay Peninsula—a dangerous trip marked by treacherous currents, rocky shoals, and pirates. Once the portage across the isthmus was finished, the merchants needed food and lodging while waiting for the monsoon winds to shift so they could make the last leg of the voyage to China by sea. Funan stockpiled food and provided security for those engaged in this trade—in return for customs duties and other fees.

Chinese observers have left reports of the prosperity and sophistication of Funan, emphasizing the presence of walled cities, palaces, archives, systems of taxation, and state-organized agriculture. Nevertheless, Funan declined in the sixth century. The most likely explanation is that international trade routes changed and Funan no longer held a strategic position.

The Srivijayan Kingdom

By the sixth century a new, all-sea route had developed. Merchants and travelers from south India and Sri Lanka now sailed through the Strait of Malacca (between the west side of the Malay Peninsula and the northeast coast of the island of Sumatra) and into the South China Sea. Although presenting both human and navigational hazards, the new route significantly shortened the journey.

A new center of power, **Srivijaya** (sree-vih-JUH-yuh)—Sanskrit for "Great Conquest"—dominated the new southerly route by 683 C.E. The capital of the Srivijayan kingdom was at modern-day Palembang in southeastern Sumatra, 50 miles (80 kilometers) up the broad and navigable Musi River, with a good natural harbor. The kingdom was well situated to control the southern part of the Malay Peninsula, Sumatra, parts of Java and Borneo, and the Malacca (muh-LAH-kuh) and Sunda straits—vital passageways for shipping (see Map 7.2).

Funan An early complex society in Southeast Asia between the first and sixth centuries C.E. Centered in the rich rice-growing region of southern Vietnam, it controlled the passage of trade across the Malaysian isthmus.

Srivijaya A state based on the Indonesian island of Sumatra between the seventh and eleventh centuries C.E. It amassed wealth and power by a combination of selective adaptation of Indian technologies and concepts, control of the lucrative trade routes between India and China, and skillful showmanship and diplomacy in holding together a disparate realm of inland and coastal territories.

Srivijaya-Style Stupa in Thailand, Eighth Century C.E. This brick and mortar shrine at Chaiya shows that the influence of Srivijaya reached far into the Southeast Asian mainland. Michael Freeman/ORBIS

Aerial View of the Buddhist Monument at Borobodur, Java This great monument of volcanic stone was more than 300 feet (90 meters) in length and over 100 feet (30 meters) high. Pilgrims made a 3-mile-long (nearly 5-kilometer-long) winding ascent through ten levels intended to represent the ideal Buddhist journey from ignorance to enlightenment. Numerous sculptured reliefs depicting Buddhist legends provide glimpses of daily life in early Java. Robert Harding Picture Library Ltd/Alamy

The Srivijayan kingdom gained ascendancy over its rivals and assumed control of the international trade route by fusing four distinct ecological zones into an interdependent network. The core area was the productive agricultural plain along the Musi River. The king and his clerks, judges, and tax collectors controlled this zone directly. Control was less direct over the second zone, the upland regions of Sumatra's interior, with its commercially valuable forest products. Local rulers there were bound to the center by oaths of loyalty, elaborate court ceremonies, and the sharing of profits from trade. The third zone consisted of river ports that had been Srivijaya's main rivals. They were conquered and controlled thanks to an alliance between Srivijaya and neighboring sea nomads, pirates who served as a Srivijayan navy in return for a steady income.

The fourth zone was a fertile "rice bowl" on the central plain of the nearby island of Java—a region so productive, because of its volcanic soil, that it houses and feeds the majority of the population of present-day Indonesia. Srivijayan monarchs maintained alliances, cemented by intermarriage, with several ruling dynasties in this region, and the Srivijayan kings claimed descent from the main Javanese dynasty. These arrangements gave Srivijaya access to large quantities of foodstuffs that people living in the capital and merchants and sailors visiting the various ports needed.

The kings of Srivijaya who constructed and maintained this complex network of social, political, and economic relationships were men of energy and skill. Although their authority depended in part on force, it owed more to diplomatic and even theatrical talents. Like the Gupta monarchy, Srivijaya was a theater-state, securing its preeminence and binding dependents by its sheer splendor and its ability to attract labor, talent, and luxury products. The court was the scene of ceremonies designed to dazzle observers and reinforce an image of wealth, power, and sanctity. Subordinate rulers took oaths of loyalty carrying dire threats of punishment for violations, and in their home locales they imitated the splendid ceremonials of the capital.

The Srivijayan king, drawing upon Buddhist conceptions, presented himself as a bodhisattva, one who had achieved enlightenment and utilized his precious insights for the betterment

Borobodur A massive stone monument on the Indonesian island of Java, erected by the Sailendra kings around 800 C.E. The winding ascent through ten levels, decorated with rich relief carving, is a Buddhist allegory for the progressive stages of enlightenment.

of his subjects. The king was believed to have magical powers, controlling powerful forces of fertility associated with the rivers in flood and mediating between the spiritually potent realms of the mountains and the sea. He was also said to be so wealthy that he deposited bricks of gold in the river estuary to appease the local gods, and a hillside near town was covered with silver and gold images of the Buddha. The gold originated in East or West Africa and came to Southeast Asia through trade with the Muslim world (see Chapter 9).

The kings built and patronized Buddhist monasteries and schools. In central Java local dynasties allied with Srivijaya built magnificent temple complexes to advertise their glory. The most famous of these, **Borobodur** (booh-roe-boe-DOOR), built between 770 and 825 C.E., was the largest human construction in the Southern Hemisphere.

The kings of Srivijaya carried out this marvelous balancing act for centuries. But the system was vulnerable to shifts in the pattern of international trade. Some such change must have contributed to the decline of Srivijaya in the eleventh century, even though the immediate cause was a destructive raid on the capital Palembang by forces of the Chola kingdom of southeast India in 1025 C.E.

After the decline of Srivijaya, leadership passed to new, vigorous kingdoms on the eastern end of Java, and the maritime realm of Southeast Asia remained prosperous and connected to international trade networks. Through the ages Europeans remained dimly aware of this region as a source of spices and other luxury items. Some four centuries after the decline of Srivijaya, an Italian navigator serving under the flag of Spain—Christopher Columbus—sailed westward across the Atlantic Ocean, seeking to establish a direct route to the fabled "Indies" from which the spices came.

SECTION REVIEW

- Climate and resources enabled Southeast Asia to support large human populations.

- Located on the trade and pilgrimage routes between China and India, Southeast Asia came under strong Hindu and Buddhist influence.

- Shrewd rulers used Indian knowledge and personnel to enhance their power and prestige.

- Funan rose to prominence between the first and sixth centuries C.E. by controlling the trade route across the Malay Peninsula.

- The Srivijayan kingdom flourished between the seventh and eleventh centuries C.E. and dominated the new international trade route through the Strait of Malacca.

CONCLUSION

This chapter traces the emergence of complex societies in India and Southeast Asia between the second millennium B.C.E. and the first millennium C.E. Because of migrations, trade, and the spread of belief systems, an Indian style of civilization spread throughout the subcontinent and adjoining regions and eventually made its way to the mainland and island chains of Southeast Asia. In this period were laid cultural foundations that in large measure still endure.

The development and spread of belief systems—Vedism, Buddhism, Jainism, and Hinduism—have a central place in this chapter because nearly all the sources of information are religious. A museum visitor examining artifacts from ancient Mesopotamia, Egypt, the Greco-Roman Mediterranean, and China will find many objects of a religious nature. Only the Indian artifacts, however, will be almost exclusively from the religious sphere.

Writing came later to India than to other parts of the Eastern Hemisphere, for reasons particular to the Indian situation. Like Indian artifacts, most ancient Indian texts are of a religious nature. Ancient Indians did not develop a historical consciousness and generate historiographic texts like their Israelite, Greek, and Chinese contemporaries, primarily because they held a strikingly different view of time. The distinctive Indian conception—of vast epochs in which universes are created and destroyed again and again and the essential spirit of living creatures is reincarnated repeatedly—made the particulars of any brief moment seem relatively insignificant.

The tension between divisive and unifying forces can be seen in many aspects of Indian life. Political and social division has been the norm throughout much of the history of India, a consequence of the topographical and environmental diversity of the subcontinent and the complex mix of ethnic and linguistic groups inhabiting it. The elaborate structure of classes and castes was a response to this diversity—an attempt to organize the population and position individuals within an accepted hierarchy, as well as to regulate group interactions. Strong central governments, such as those of the Mauryan and Gupta kings, gained ascendancy for a time and promoted prosperity and development. They rose to dominance by gaining control of metal resources and important trade routes, developing effective military and administrative institutions, and creating cultural forms that inspired admiration and emulation. However, as in archaic Greece and Warring States China, the periods of fragmentation and multiple small centers of power seemed as economically and intellectually dynamic as the periods of unity.

Many distinctive social and intellectual features of Indian civilization—the class and caste system, models of kingship and statecraft, and Vedic, Jainist, and Buddhist belief systems—originated in the great river valleys of the north, where descendants of Indo-European immigrants predominated. Hinduism then embraced elements drawn from the Dravidian cultures of the south as well as from Buddhism. The capacity of the Hindu tradition to assimilate a wide range of popular beliefs facilitated the spread of a common Indian civilization across the subcontinent, although there was, and is, considerable variation from one region to another.

KEY TERMS

monsoon p. 170
Vedas p. 171
varna p. 172
jati p. 172
karma p. 172

moksha p. 173
Buddha p. 174
Mahayana Buddhism p. 175
Theravada Buddhism p. 175
Hinduism p. 175

Mauryan Empire p. 178
Ashoka p. 179
Mahabharata p. 180
Bhagavad-Gita p. 180
Tamil kingdoms p. 180

Gupta Empire p. 181
theater-state p. 181
Funan p. 188
Srivijaya p. 188
Borobodur p. 190

SUGGESTED READING

Allen, Charles. *Ashoka: The Search for India's Lost Emperor.* 2012. A detailed study of the most interesting and important Mauryan king.

Avari, Burjor. *India: The Ancient Past: A History of the Indian Sub-Continent from c. 7000 BC to AD 1200.* 2007. A clear, concise introduction to ancient Indian history.

Embree, Ainslee T. *Sources of Indian Tradition*, vol. 1, 2d ed. 1988. Contains translations of primary texts, with the emphasis almost entirely on religion and few materials from southern India.

Huntington, Susan L., and John C. Huntington. *The Art of Ancient India.* 1985. Focuses on the art and architecture of antiquity.

Kinnard, Jacob. *The Emergence of Buddhism.* 2006. A clear presentation of the antecedents, origins, evolution, and spread of Buddhism, with primary documents.

Kinsley, David R. *Hinduism: A Cultural Perspective.* 1982. Presents fundamental Indian social and religious conceptions.

Lang, Karen. "Women in Ancient India," in *Women's Roles in Ancient Civilizations: A Reference Guide*, ed. Bella Vivante. 1999. An up-to-date overview of women in ancient India, with bibliography.

Miller, Barbara Stoler. *The Bhagavad-Gita: Krishna's Counsel in Time of War.* 1986. A readable translation of this ancient classic with a useful introduction and notes.

Ramaswamy, T. N. *Essentials of Indian Statecraft: Kautilya's Arthashastra for Contemporary Readers.* 1962. A fascinating treatise on state building supposedly composed by the adviser to the founder of the Mauryan Empire.

Schmidt, Karl J. *An Atlas and Survey of South Asian History.* 1995. Maps and facing text illustrating geographic, environmental, cultural, and historical features of South Asian civilization.

Sedlar, Jean W. *India and the Greek World: A Study in the Transmission of Culture.* 1980. Explores the interaction of Greek and Indian civilizations.

Shaffer, Lynda. *Maritime Southeast Asia to 1500.* 1996. Focuses on early Southeast Asian history in a world historical context.

Singh, Upinder. *A History of Ancient and Early Medieval India: From the Stone Age to the 12th Century.* 2009. A comprehensive history that surveys the many geographical regions of the subcontinent and takes full advantage of archaeological as well as literary evidence.

Tarling, Nicholas, ed. *The Cambridge History of Southeast Asia (Part 1).* 2000. Chapters written by experts on archaeology, politics, economy, and religion.

SUGGESTED VIEWING

Brook, Peter, director. *The Mahabharata* (3 videos). 1989. This filmed version of a stage production generated much controversy because of its British director and multicultural cast, but it is a painless introduction to the plot and main characters of the great Indian epic.

CourseMate   **Go to the History CourseMate website** for primary source links, study tools, and review materials for this chapter. www.cengagebrain.com

Chapter Outline

Formative Civilizations of the Olmec and Chavín, 1200–200 B.C.E.
➤ *How did Olmec and Chavín influence later Mesoamerican and Andean civilizations?*

Classic-Era Culture and Society in Mesoamerica, 200–900
➤ *What were the most important shared characteristics of Mesoamerican cultures in the classic period?*

The Postclassic Period in Mesoamerica, 900–1300
➤ *What role did warfare play in the postclassic period of Mesoamerica?*

Northern Peoples
➤ *In what ways did Mesoamerica influence the cultural centers in North America?*

Andean Civilizations, 200–1400
➤ *How did the Amerindian peoples of the Andean area adapt to their environment and produce socially complex and politically advanced societies?*

Conclusion

- **DIVERSITY + DOMINANCE** Burials as Historical Texts
- **ENVIRONMENT + TECHNOLOGY** The Maya Writing System

Maya Scribe Maya scribes used a complex writing system to record religious concepts and memorialize the actions of their kings. An artisan painted this picture of a scribe on a ceramic plate.

Peoples and Civilizations of the Americas, from 1200 B.C.E.

The ancient Mesoamerican civilization of the Maya (MY-ah) developed a complex written language that enabled scribes like the one in this illustration to record the important actions of rulers and military events. Recent translations give us a glimpse into the life of a Maya princess. In late August 682 C.E. the Maya princess Lady Wac-Chanil-Ahau (wac-cha-NEEL-ah-HOW) walked down the steps from her family's residence and mounted a litter decorated with rich textiles and animal skins. As the procession exited from the urban center of Dos Pilas (dohs PEE-las), her military escort spread out through the fields and woods to prevent ambush by enemies. Lady Wac-Chanil-Ahau's destination was the Maya city of Naranjo (na-RAHN-hoe), where she was to marry a powerful nobleman. Her father had arranged her marriage to reestablish the royal dynasty of Naranjo, a dynasty eliminated when Caracol, the region's major military power, had conquered that city. Lady Wac-Chanil-Ahau's passage to Naranjo symbolized her father's desire to forge a military alliance that could resist Caracol. For us, the story of Lady Wac-Chanil-Ahau illustrates the importance of marriage and lineage in the politics of the classic-period Maya.

K'ak Tiliw Chan Chaak (kahk tee-lew CHAN cha-ahk) , the son of Lady Wac-Chanil-Ahau, ascended the throne of Naranjo as a five-year-old in 693 C.E. During his long reign he proved to be a careful diplomat and formidable warrior. He was also a prodigious builder, leaving behind an expanded and beautified capital as part of his legacy. Mindful of the importance of his mother and her lineage from Dos Pilas, he erected numerous steles (carved stone monuments) that celebrated her life.[1]

The world of Wac-Chanil-Ahau was challenged by warfare and by dynastic crisis as population increased and competition for resources grew more violent. In this environment the rise of Caracol undermined long-standing commercial and political relations in much of southern Mesoamerica and led to more than a century of conflict. Eventually, the dynasty created at Dos Pilas by the heirs of Lady Wac-Chanil-Ahau challenged Caracol. Despite a shared culture and religion, the great Maya cities remained divided by the dynastic ambitions of their rulers.

As the story of Lady Wac-Chanil-Ahau's marriage and her role in the development of a Maya dynasty suggests, the peoples of the Americas were in constant competition for resources. Members of hereditary elites organized their societies to meet these challenges, even as their ambition for greater power predictably ignited new conflicts. No single set of political institutions or technologies worked in every environment, and enormous cultural diversity existed in the ancient Americas. In Mesoamerica (most of Mexico and Central America) and in the Andean region of South

---

[1]This summary closely follows the historical narrative and translation of names offered by Linda Schele and David Freidel in *A Forest of Kings: The Untold Story of the Ancient Maya* (New York: Morrow, 1990), 182–186.

America, Amerindian peoples developed an extraordinarily productive and diversified agriculture. They also built great cities that rivaled the capitals of the Chinese and Roman Empires in size and beauty. The Olmec of Mesoamerica and Chavín (cha-VEEN) of the Andes were among the earliest civilizations of the Americas. In other regions of the hemisphere, indigenous peoples adapted combinations of hunting and agriculture to maintain a wide variety of settlement patterns, political forms, and cultural traditions. Despite differences, all the cultures and civilizations of the Americas experienced cycles of expansion and contraction as they struggled with the challenges of environmental change, population growth, and war.

FORMATIVE CIVILIZATIONS OF THE OLMEC AND CHAVÍN, 1200–200 B.C.E.

The domestication of new plant varieties, especially potatoes, corn, squash, and sweet potatoes, and a limited development of trade helped promote social stratification and the beginnings of urbanization in both Mesoamerica and the Andes. By 2000 B.C.E. a number of urban centers had begun to project their political and cultural power over neighboring territories, but very few of these early urban places had populations in excess of 2,500. Two of the hemisphere's most impressive cultural traditions, the Olmec of Mesoamerica (Mexico and northern Central America), and Chavín of the mountainous Andean region of South America, developed from these humble origins around 1200 B.C.E. Before their eclipse before 200 B.C.E., each had established a cultural legacy that would persist for more than a thousand years.

The Mesoamerican Olmec, 1200–400 B.C.E.

Mesoamerica is a region of great geographic and climatic diversity. It is extremely active geologically, experiencing both earthquakes and volcanic eruptions. Mountain ranges break the region into microenvironments, including the temperate climates of the Valley of Mexico and the Guatemalan highlands, the tropical forests of the Petén and Gulf of Mexico coast, the rain forest of the southern Yucatán and Belize, and the drier scrub forest of the northern Yucatán (see Map 8.1).

Within each of these ecological niches, Amerindian peoples developed specialized technologies that exploited indigenous plants and animals, as well as minerals like obsidian, quartz, and jade. The ability of farmers to produce dependable surpluses of maize, beans, squash, and other locally domesticated plants permitted the first stages of craft specialization and urbanization. Eventually, contacts across environmental boundaries led to trade and cultural exchange with emerging centers across the region and ultimately with Central and South America. Enhanced trade, increasing agricultural productivity, and rising population created the conditions for social stratification.

Scholars refer to the period 1500 B.C.E. to 200 C.E. in Mesoamerica as the preclassic period. The most important civilization in this period was the **Olmec**, which flourished between 1200 and 400 B.C.E. near the tropical Atlantic coast of Mexico (see Map 8.1). It is unclear whether Olmec urban centers were rival city-states or were subject to a centralized political authority, but scholars agree that San Lorenzo (1200–900 B.C.E.), with a population of between 10,000 to 18,000, was the largest and most important Olmec center. San Lorenzo's cultural influence ultimately extended south and west to the Pacific coast of Central America and north to central Mexico, suggesting its ability to project political and military power. Also founded around 1200 B.C.E., La Venta (LA BEN-tah) became the preeminent Olmec center when San Lorenzo was abandoned or destroyed around 900 B.C.E. After La Venta's collapse around 600 B.C.E., Tres Zapotes (TRACE zah-POE-tace) survived as the largest Olmec center, although it was much smaller than either of its predecessors.

San Lorenzo and other Olmec cities served primarily as religious centers. The urban elite's power grew with the development of persuasive religious ideologies and compelling religious rituals that helped organize and subordinate neighboring rural populations. As a result, urban centers were dominated by religious architecture that included pyramids, monumental mounds, and raised platforms. Constructed by thousands of laborers recruited in surrounding

Olmec The first Mesoamerican civilization. Between ca. 1200 and 400 B.C.E., the Olmec people of central Mexico created a vibrant civilization that included intensive agriculture, wide-ranging trade, ceremonial centers, and monumental construction. The Olmec had great cultural influence on later Mesoamerican societies, passing on artistic styles, religious imagery, sophisticated astronomical observation for the construction of calendars, and a ritual ball game.

CHRONOLOGY

	Mesoamerica	Northern Peoples	Andean Region
	Before 5000 B.C.E. Domestication of maize, beans, and squash		Before 5000 B.C.E. Domestication of potato, quinoa, manioc, and llama
5000 B.C.E.	Before 2000 B.C.E. Early urbanization	Before 2000 B.C.E. Domestication of squash and seed crops like sunflower	Before 2000 B.C.E. Urbanization
2000 B.C.E.	1200 B.C.E. Beginning of Olmec civilization		2000 B.C.E. Metallurgy; domestication of sweet potato
1000 B.C.E.			900 B.C.E. Beginning of Chavín civilization
500 B.C.E.	400 B.C.E. End of Olmec civilization		200 B.C.E. End of Chavín civilization
100 C.E.	100 First stage of Teotihuacan temple complex 200 Maya early classic period begins	100–400 Hopewell culture in Ohio River Valley	200 Moche begin to dominate Peruvian coast
500 C.E.	450 Teotihuacan dominates central Mexico 750 Teotihuacan destroyed 800–900 Maya classic-era cities abandoned 968 Toltec capital of Tula founded	700 beginnings of Anasazi culture in Four Corners region 800 beginnings of Mississippian culture	500–1000 Tiwanaku and Wari control Andean highlands 700 End of Moche domination 900 Chimú begin to dominate Peruvian coast
1000 C.E.	1175 Tula destroyed	1050–1250 Cahokia reaches peak population	1150 Anasazi center of Pueblo Bonito abandoned; other Anasazi centers enter crisis after 1200
1500 C.E.	Until 1300 Culhuacán and Cholula continue Toltec tradition		1470s End of Chimú domination

agricultural zones, the massive urban architecture was embellished with religious symbols tied to the official cult. The elite dominated collective religious life and built their residences on raised platforms located near the most sacred ritual spaces.

The Olmec were polytheistic, and most of their deities had both male and female natures. The motifs found on ceramics, sculptures, and buildings also show that human and animal characteristics were blended. Rulers were especially associated with the jaguar. Priests and shamans who foretold the future, cured the sick, and led collective rituals claimed the ability to make direct contact with supernatural powers by transforming themselves into powerful animals, such as crocodiles, snakes, and sharks. These transformative powers were also associated with a ballgame played with a solid rubber ball in banked courts located near the center of temple precincts. Versions of this game survived until the arrival of Europeans in the sixteenth century.

Olmec religious practice included the close observation of the heavens, and all their major ceremonial centers were laid out in alignment with the paths of certain stars. This concern for astronomic observation led to the development of an accurate calendar that was used to predict seasonal rains and guide planting and harvesting. The Olmec also developed a form of writing (as yet undeciphered) that scholars believe influenced later innovations among the Maya.

Little is known about Olmec political structure, but it seems likely that the rise of major urban centers coincided with the appearance of a form of kingship that combined religious and secular roles. Rulers and their close kin came to be associated with the gods through

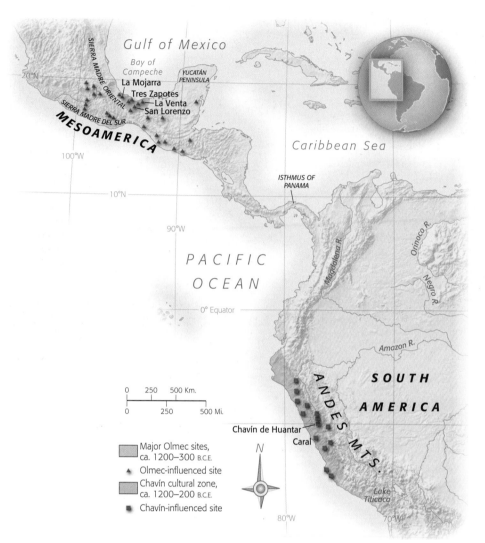

MAP 8.1 **Olmec and Chavín Civilizations** The regions of Mesoamerica (most of modern Mexico and Central America) and the Andean highlands of South America have hosted impressive civilizations since early times. The civilizations of the Olmec and Chavín were the originating civilizations of these two regions, providing the foundations of architecture, city planning, and religion. © Cengage Learning

bloodletting ceremonies and human sacrifice and through the staging of elaborate rituals that brought together urban and rural populations. The authority of the rulers is suggested by a series of colossal carved stone heads discovered buried near the major urban centers, especially San Lorenzo. These heads, some as large as 11 feet (3.4 meters) high, are the best-known monuments of Olmec culture. Archaeologists believe that they were carved to memorialize individual rulers. Some were depicted wearing the padded helmet used as protection in the sacred ballgame.

The first stage of urbanization was tied to the exploitation of products like salt, cacao (chocolate beans), and clay used for ceramics. Control of these resources led to the development of specialized crafts and to trade. In the largest urban centers, skilled artisans were full-time residents who decorated buildings with religious carvings and sculptures. They also produced high-quality crafts, such as exquisite carved jade figurines, necklaces, and ceremonial obsidian knives and axes. The diffusion of these Olmec products among distant locations suggests the existence of a specialized class of merchants.

The mounting wealth and power of the elite and the growing populations of Olmec cities depended on a bargain struck with the much larger populations of the surrounding countryside. The rural masses provided the labor that constructed the pyramids, platforms, and ball courts of the urban centers as well as the food that sustained urban populations, but they also received benefits. As a relief from their routines of heavy labor, they participated in awe-inspiring ceremonies at San Lorenzo and other centers. Here the official cult directed by the elite explained human origins and unforeseen natural events and helped to guide collective life. It provided practical benefits to the rural masses as well. The elite used its authority to organize labor to

Georg Gerster/Photo Researchers, Inc.

Olmec Head   Giant heads sculpted from basalt are a widely recognized legacy of Olmec culture. Sixteen heads have been found, the largest approximately 11 feet (3.4 meters) tall. Experts in Olmec archaeology believe the heads are portraits of individual rulers, warriors, or ballplayers.

dig drainage canals and construct the raised fields that allowed agriculture in wetlands, thus expanding food production.

Ultimately, every major Olmec center was abandoned, its monuments defaced and buried, and its buildings destroyed. Even the portrait heads were dragged from the centers, defaced, and buried. Archaeologists interpret these events differently; some see them as evidence of internal upheavals or military attacks by neighboring peoples, whereas others suggest that they were rituals associated with the death or overthrow of a ruler or evidence of social conflict. Regardless of the causes for Olmec decline, the influence of this civilization endured for centuries. Every subsequent Mesoamerican civilizations utilized the rich legacy of Olmec material culture, technology, religious belief and ritual, political organization, art, architecture, and sports.

Early South American Civilization: Chavín, 900–200 B.C.E.

Geography and environment played a critical role in the development of human society in the Andes. The region's diverse environments—a mountainous core, arid coastal plain, and dense interior tropical forests—challenged human populations, encouraging the development of specialized regional production as well as social institutions and cultural values that facilitated interregional exchanges and shared labor responsibilities.

Chavín The first major urban civilization in South America (900–250 B.C.E.). Its capital, Chavín de Huántar, was located high in the Andes Mountains of Peru. Chavín became politically and economically dominant in a densely populated region that included two distinct ecological zones, the Peruvian coastal plain and the Andean foothills.

Scholars use the term *Early Horizon* for the period 900 B.C.E. to 200 C.E. in Andean history. The earliest urban centers in this region were villages of a few hundred people built along the coastal plain or in the foothills near the coast, where an abundance of fish and mollusks provided a dependable food supply. The later introduction of corn (maize) cultivation from Mesoamerica increased the food supplies of the coast and interior foothills, allowing greater levels of urbanization. Trade between the peoples of the coastal region and Andean foothills also led to the exchange of ceremonial practices, religious motifs, and aesthetic ideas.

Between 900 and 250 B.C.E. **Chavín** dominated a densely populated region that included large areas of the Peruvian coastal plain and Andean foothills. The capital city of Chavín de Huantar **(cha-BEAN day WAHN-tar)** was located at 10,300 feet (3,139 meters) in the eastern range of the Andes north of the modern city of Lima (see Map 8.1). Its location facilitated exchanges among ecologically distinct zones, linking the coast to inland producers of quinoa (a local grain), maize, and potatoes, llama herders in high mountain valleys, and tropical producers of coca (the leaves were chewed, producing a mild narcotic effect) on the eastern flank of the Andes.

The development of these trade networks led to reciprocal labor obligations that permitted the construction and maintenance of roads, bridges, temples, palaces, and large irrigation and drainage projects, as well as textile production. These reciprocal labor obligations were organized initially by groups of related families who held land communally and claimed descent from a common ancestor. Group members thought of themselves as brothers and sisters and were obliged to aid one another. In the time of Chavín these groups were organized collectively by the state to provide labor to build temples, elite residences, and irrigation works.

Llamas, first bred in the mountainous interior of Peru, were the only domesticated beasts of burden in the Americas, and they played an important role in the integration of the Andean region. Llamas provided meat and wool and decreased the labor needed to transport goods. A single driver could control ten to thirty animals, each carrying up to 70 pounds (32 kilograms), while a human porter could carry only about 50 pounds (22.5 kilograms). By moving goods from one ecological zone to another, llamas promoted specialization of production and increased trade. Thus they were crucial to Chavín's development, not unlike the camel in the evolution of trans-Saharan trade (see Chapter 9).

Class distinctions appear to have increased in this period. Modern scholars see evidence that a powerful chief or king dominated Chavín's politics, while a class of priests directed religious life. The most common decorative motif in sculpture, pottery, and textiles was a jaguar-man similar in conception to the contemporary Olmec symbol. In both civilizations this powerful predator provided an enduring image of religious authority.

Chavín housed a large complex of multilevel platforms made of packed earth or rubble and faced with cut stone or adobe (sun-dried brick made of clay and straw). Small buildings used for ritual purposes or as elite residences were built on these platforms. Nearly all the structures were decorated with relief carvings of serpents, condors, jaguars, or human forms. The largest building at Chavín de Huantar measured 250 feet (76 meters) on each side and rose to a height of 50 feet (15 meters). Its hollow interior contained narrow galleries and small rooms that may have housed the remains of royal ancestors.

Metallurgy in the Western Hemisphere was first developed in the Andean region around 2000 B.C.E. The later introduction of metallurgy in Mesoamerica, like the appearance of maize agriculture in the Andes, suggests sustained trade and cultural contacts between the two regions. Archaeological investigations of Chavín de Huantar have uncovered remarkable silver, gold, and gold alloy ornaments that represent a clear advance over earlier technologies. Improvements in both the manufacture and decoration of textiles are also associated with the rise of Chavín.

Excavations of graves reveal that superior-quality textiles as well as gold crowns, breastplates, and jewelry distinguished rulers from commoners. These rich objects, the quality and abundance of pottery, and the monumental architecture of the major centers all indicate the presence of highly skilled artisans. The enormous scale of the capital and the dispersal of Chavín's pottery styles, religious motifs, and architectural forms over a wide area suggest that Chavín imposed political and economic control over its neighbors by military force. Most scholars believe, however, that, as in the case of the Olmec civilization, Chavín's influence depended more on the development of an attractive religious belief system and related rituals.

There is no convincing evidence, like defaced buildings or broken images, that the eclipse of Chavín (unlike the Olmec centers) was associated with conquest or rebellion. However, recent investigations have suggested that increased warfare throughout the region disrupted Chavín's trade and undermined the authority of the governing elite. Regardless of what caused the collapse of this powerful culture, the technologies, material culture, statecraft, architecture, and urban planning associated with Chavín influenced the Andean region for centuries.

llama A hoofed animal indigenous to the Andes Mountains in South America. It was the only domesticated beast of burden in the Americas before the arrival of Europeans. It provided meat and wool. The use of llamas to transport goods made possible specialized production and trade among people living in different ecological zones and fostered the integration of these zones by Chavín and later Andean states.

SECTION REVIEW

- Well before 3000 B.C.E. newly domesticated plants, new technologies, and trade led to greater social stratification and the beginnings of urbanization in Mesoamerica and the Andean region of South America.

- The Olmec of Mesoamerica (1200–400 B.C.E.) and the Chavín civilization (900–250 B.C.E.) in the Andes each coordinated exchanges of goods between different ecological zones. Their styles were widely emulated and persisted long afterward.

- Ruling elites residing in urban centers staged elaborate religious ceremonies designed to impress subjects and enhance their prestige.

- Olmec urban centers were probably ruled by kings, who were depicted by giant stone heads. Olmec shamans communicated with the spirit world, supervised the calendar, and created a system of writing.

- Chavín utilized llamas, the only domesticated beasts of burden in the hemisphere, to transport goods between regions.

CLASSIC-ERA CULTURE AND SOCIETY IN MESOAMERICA, 200–900

Between about 200 and 900 C.E. the peoples of Mesoamerica entered a period of remarkable cultural creativity. Despite enduring differences in language and the absence of regional political integration, Mesoamericans were unified by similarities in material culture, religious beliefs and practices, and social structures first forged in the Olmec era. Building on this legacy, the peoples of the area that is now Central America and south and central Mexico developed new forms of political organization, made great strides in astronomy and mathematics, and improved the productivity of their agriculture. Archaeologists call this mix of achievements the classic period. During this period, a growing population traded a greater variety of products over longer distances, and social hierarchies became more complex. Great cities were constructed that served as centers of political life and as arenas of religious ritual and spiritual experience. These political and cultural innovations did not result from the introduction of new technologies. Instead, the achievements of the classic era depended on the ability of increasingly powerful elites to organize and command growing numbers of laborers and soldiers.

Teotihuacan

Teotihuacan A powerful city-state in central Mexico (100–750 C.E.). Its population was more than 125,000 at its peak in 450 C.E.

Located about 30 miles (48 kilometers) northeast of modern Mexico City, **Teotihuacan** (teh-o-tee-WAH-kahn) (100–750 C.E.) was one of Mesoamerica's most important classic-period civilizations (see Map 8.3 on page 204). At the height of its power around 450 C.E., it was the largest city in the Americas. With between 125,000 and 150,000 inhabitants, it was larger than all but a small number of contemporary European and Asian cities.

The city center was dominated by religious architecture that was situated to align with nearby sacred mountains and with the movement of the stars. The people of Teotihuacan recognized and worshiped many gods and lesser spirits. Enormous pyramids and more than twenty smaller temples devoted to these gods were arranged along a central avenue. The largest pyramids were dedicated to the Sun and the Moon and to Quetzalcoatl (kate-zahl-CO-ah-tal), the feathered serpent, a culture-god believed to be the originator of agriculture and the arts. Murals suggest that another pair of powerful gods, the storm-god Tlaloc and a powerful female

The Temple of the Sun The temple of the sun in background is the largest pyramid in Tenochtitlan. The smaller temple of Quetzalcoatl in foreground displays the serpent images associated with this culture god common to most Mesoamerican civilizations.

G.Dagli Orti/The Art Archive

MAP 8.2 **Maya Civilization, 250–1400 C.E.** The Maya never created an integrated and unified state. Instead Maya civilization developed as a complex network of independent city-states. © Cengage Learning

chinampas Raised fields constructed along lakeshores in Mesoamerica to increase agricultural yields.

god associated with fertility, were also central figures in the city's religious life. Like the earlier Olmec, Teotihuacan's population practiced human sacrifice, illustrated by the discovery of more than a hundred sacrificial victims during the modern excavation of the temple of Quetzalcoatl. Scholars believe that residents viewed sacrifice as a sacred duty to the gods and as essential to the well-being of society.

The rapid growth in urban population initially resulted from a series of volcanic eruptions that disrupted agriculture. Later, as the city elite increased their power, they forced farm families from the smaller villages in the region to relocate to the urban core. The elite organized these new labor resources to bring marginal lands into production, drain swamps, construct irrigation canals, and build terraces into hillsides. They also expanded the use of **chinampas (chee-NAM-pahs)**, sometimes called "floating gardens." These were narrow artificial islands constructed along lakeshores or in marshes by heaping lake muck and waste material on beds of reeds and anchoring them to the shore. Chinampas permitted year-round agriculture—because of subsurface irrigation and resistance to frost—and thus played a crucial role in sustaining the region's growing population.

The city's role as a religious center and commercial power provided both divine approval of and a material basis for the elite's increased wealth and status. Members of the elite controlled the government, tax collection, and commerce. Their rich and ornate clothing, their abundant diet, and their large, well-made residences signaled the wealth and power of aristocratic families. Temple and palace murals make clear the authority and great prestige of the priestly class as well. Teotihuacan's wealth and religious influence drew pilgrims from distant regions, and many became permanent residents.

Unlike other classic-period civilizations, the people of Teotihuacan did not concentrate power in the hands of a single ruler. There is no clear evidence that individual rulers or a ruling dynasty gained overarching political power. In fact, some scholars suggest that allied elite families or weak kings who were the puppets of these powerful families ruled Teotihuacan.

Historians debate the role of the military in the development of Teotihuacan. The absence of walls and other defensive structures before 500 C.E. suggests that Teotihuacan enjoyed relative peace during its early development. Archaeological evidence, however, reveals that the city created a powerful military to protect long-distance trade and to compel peasant agriculturalists to transfer their surplus production to the city. Unlike later postclassic civilizations, however, Teotihuacan was not an imperial state controlled by a military elite.

It is unclear what forces brought about the collapse of Teotihuacan about 750 C.E. By 500 C.E. the urban population had declined to about 40,000 and the city's residents had begun to build defensive walls. Pictorial evidence from murals indicates that the city's final decades were violent. Scholars have uncovered evidence that the elite had mismanaged resources and then divided into competing factions, leading to class conflict and the breakdown of public order. In the final collapse the most important temples in the city center were destroyed and religious images defaced. Elite palaces were also systematically burned and many of their residents killed. Regardless of the causes, the eclipse of Teotihuacan was felt throughout Mexico and into Central America.

Maya Mesoamerican civilization concentrated in Mexico's Yucatán Peninsula and in Guatemala and Honduras but never unified into a single empire. Major contributions were in mathematics, astronomy, and development of the calendar.

The Maya

During Teotihuacan's ascendancy in the north, the **Maya** developed an impressive civilization in the region that today includes Guatemala, Honduras, Belize, and southern Mexico (see Map 8.2). Given the difficulties imposed by a tropical climate and fragile soils, the cultural and architectural achievements of the Maya were remarkable. Although they shared a single culture, the Maya never created a single, unified state. Instead, rival kingdoms led by hereditary rulers

The Great Plaza at Tikal   The impressive architectural and artistic achievements of the classic-era Maya are still visible in the ruins of Tikal, in modern Guatemala. Maya centers provided a dramatic setting for the rituals that dominated public life. Construction of Tikal began before 150 B.C.E.; the city was abandoned about 900 C.E. A ball court and residences for the elite were part of the Great Plaza.

struggled with each other for regional dominance, much like the Mycenaean-era Greeks (see Chapter 5).

Today Maya farmers prepare their fields by cutting down small trees and brush and then burning the dead vegetation to fertilize the land. Such swidden agriculture (also called shifting agriculture or slash and burn agriculture) can produce high yields for a few years. However, it uses up the soil's nutrients, eventually forcing farmers to move to more fertile land. The high population levels of the Maya classic period (200–900 C.E.) required more intensive forms of agriculture. Maya living near the major urban centers achieved high agricultural yields by draining swamps and building elevated fields. They used irrigation in areas with long dry seasons, and they terraced hillsides in the cooler highlands. Maya agriculturists also managed nearby forests, favoring the growth of the trees and shrubs that were most useful to them, as well as promoting the conservation of deer and other animals hunted for food.

During the classic period, Maya city-states proliferated. The most powerful cities controlled groups of smaller dependent cities and a broad agricultural zone by building impressive temples and by creating rituals that linked the power of kings to the gods. Open plazas were surrounded by high pyramids and by elaborately decorated palaces often built on high ground or on constructed mounds. The effect was to awe the masses drawn to the centers for religious and political rituals.

The Maya loved decoration. Carved decorations painted in bright colors covered nearly all public buildings. Religious allegories, the genealogies of rulers, and important historical events were the most common motifs. The Maya also erected beautifully carved altars and stone monoliths near major temples. As was true throughout the hemisphere, this rich legacy of monumental architecture was constructed without the aid of wheels—no pulleys, wheelbarrows, or

The Mesoamerican Ball Game From Guatemala to Arizona, archaeologists have found evidence of an ancient ball game played with a solid rubber ball on slope-sided courts shaped like a capital T. Among the Maya the game was associated with a creation myth and thus had deep religious meaning. Evidence suggests that some players were sacrificed. In this scene from a ceramic jar, players wearing elaborate ritual clothing—which includes heavy, protective pads around the chest and waist—play with a ball much larger than the ball actually used in such games. Some representations show balls drawn to suggest a human head. Chrysler Museum of Art/Justin Kerr

carts—or metal tools. Masses of men and women aided only by levers and stone tools cut and carried construction materials and lifted them into place.

The Maya divided the cosmos into three layers connected along a vertical axis that traced the course of the sun. The earthly arena of human existence held an intermediate position between the heavens, conceptualized as a sky-monster, and a dark underworld. The Maya believed that a sacred tree rose through the three layers; its roots were in the underworld, and its branches reached into the heavens. The temple precincts of Maya cities physically represented essential elements of this religious cosmology. The pyramids were sacred mountains reaching to the heavens. The doorways of the pyramids were portals to the underworld.

Rulers and other members of the elite served both priestly and political functions. They decorated their bodies with paint and tattoos and wore elaborate costumes of textiles, animal skins, and feathers to project both secular power and divine sanction. These lords communicated directly with the supernatural residents of the other worlds and with deified royal ancestors through bloodletting rituals and hallucinogenic trances.

The Maya infused warfare with religious meaning and celebrated it in elaborate rituals. Battle scenes and the depiction of the torture and sacrifice of captives were frequent decorative themes. Typically, Maya military forces fought to secure captives rather than territory. The king, his kinsmen, and other ranking nobles actively participated in war. Elite captives were nearly always sacrificed; captured commoners were more likely to be forced to labor for their captors.

Few women directly ruled Maya kingdoms, but Maya women of the ruling lineages did play important political and religious roles. The consorts of male rulers participated in bloodletting rituals and in other important public ceremonies, and their noble blood helped legitimate the power of their husbands. Although Maya society was patrilineal (tracing descent in the male line), there is clear evidence that some male rulers traced their lineages bilaterally (in both the male and female lines). Others, like Lady Wac-Chanil-Ahau's son discussed earlier, emphasized the female line if it held higher status. Little is known about the lives of poorer women, but scholars believe that women played a central role in the religious rituals of the home and some were healers and shamans. Women were essential to the household economy, maintaining essential garden plots and weaving, and in the management of family life.

Building on earlier Olmec achievements, the Maya made important contributions to the development of the Mesoamerican calendar and to mathematics and writing. Time was a central concern, and they developed an accurate calendar system that identified each day by three separate dating systems. The Maya calendar tracked a ritual cycle (260 days divided into thirteen months of 20 days). A second calendar tracked the solar year (365 days divided into eighteen months of 20 days, plus 5 unfavorable days at the end of the year). The Maya believed that the very survival of humanity was threatened every fifty-two years when the two calendars coincided. Alone among Mesoamerican peoples, the Maya also maintained a continuous "long count" calendar, which began with creation in 3114 B.C.E.

Maya mathematics and writing provided the foundations for both the calendars and the astronomical observations on which they were based. Their system of mathematics incorporated the concept of the zero and place value but had limited notational signs. Maya writing was a form of hieroglyphic inscription that signified whole words or concepts as well as phonetic cues or syllables (see Environment and Technology: The Maya Writing System). Scribes recorded aspects of public life, religious belief, and the biographies of rulers and their ancestors in books, on pottery, and on the stone columns and monumental buildings of the urban centers. In this sense every Maya city was a sacred text.

Between 800 and 900 C.E. the Maya abandoned many of their major urban centers. Many cities were destroyed by violence, although a small number of classic-period centers survived for centuries. Decades of urban decline, social conflict, and increased levels of warfare preceded this collapse in many areas. The earlier collapse of Teotihuacan around 750 had disrupted long-distance trade in ritual goods and may have begun to undermine the legitimacy of Maya rulers tied to that distant center. Certainly, rising regional population, climatic change, and environmental degradation undermined the fragile agricultural system that sustained Maya cities long before the collapse. But it was the growing scale and destructiveness of warfare that finally undermined the political legitimacy of ruling lineages and disrupted the web of economic relationships that tied rural agriculturalists to Maya cities.

SECTION REVIEW

- Teotihuacan, one of the largest Mesoamerican cities, was ruled by elites who used religious rituals and military power to legitimize their authority over the many laborers who worked the surrounding fields.

- Teotihuacan's impressive urban architecture, complex agriculture, and extensive trade made it a dominating cultural presence throughout Mesoamerica. Its collapse around 750 C.E. resulted from conflicts within the elite and resource mismanagement.

- The Maya shared a single culture but never created a single, unified state. Instead they developed numerous powerful city-states. Each city, filled with highly decorated monumental architecture, was a religious and political center for the surrounding region.

- Religious architecture dominated the centers of Teotihuacan and Maya cities. Many gods were worshiped, and religious ritual, including human sacrifice, organized collective life.

- The Maya devised an elaborate calendar system, the concept of zero, and writing.

- After centuries of expansion, the power of the Maya cities declined due to an intensified struggle for resources, leading to class conflict and warfare.

THE POSTCLASSIC PERIOD IN MESOAMERICA, 900–1300

The division between the classic and postclassic periods is somewhat arbitrary. Not only is there no single explanation for the collapse of Teotihuacan and the abandonment of many Maya centers, but these events occurred over more than a century and a half. While many smaller polities survived into the new period, the Mesoamerican world went through centuries of adjustment that ultimately led to the appearance of powerful new urban centers of culture and politics. Two of these, Tula and Cholula, had been deeply influenced by Teotihuacan before its eclipse.

Mesoamerican population expanded in the postclassic period. At the same time long-distance trade intensified, linking the producers of high-value goods like obsidian, cloth, and metal products to fast-growing cities. Resulting pressures on resources and competition for commercial advantage led to political instability and to increased warfare. The governing elites of major postclassic states, especially the Toltecs, responded to these harsh realities by increasing the size of their armies and by developing political institutions that facilitated their control of large and culturally diverse territories acquired through conquest.

Toltecs Powerful postclassic state in central Mexico (900–1175 C.E.) that influenced much of Mesoamerica. Aztecs later claimed ties to this civilization.

The Toltecs

While modern archaeology has revealed the civilizations of the Maya and Teotihuacan in previously unimaginable detail, the history of the **Toltecs** (TOLL-teks) remains in dispute. The Aztecs, the dominant late postclassic civilization (see Chapter 15), regarded the Toltecs as powerful and influential predecessors, much as the Romans regarded the Greeks. They erroneously

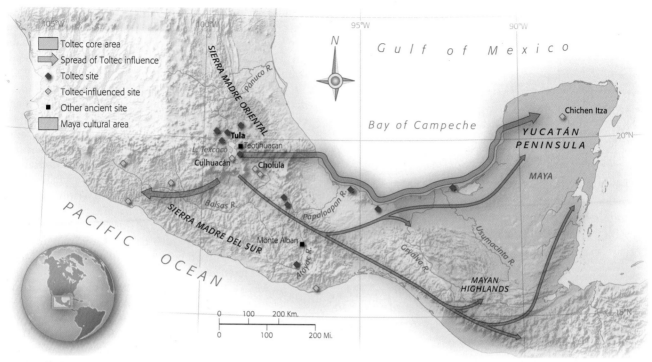

MAP 8.3 **Postclassic Mesoamerica** From their capital, Tula, the Toltecs exercised political and cultural influence across a vast region. © Cengage Learning

believed that the Toltecs were the source of nearly all important cultural achievements. As one Aztec source later recalled:

> *In truth [the Toltecs] invented all the precious and marvelous things. . . . All that now exists was their discovery. . . . And these Toltecs were very wise; they were thinkers, for they originated the year count, the day count. All their discoveries formed the book for interpreting dreams. . . . And so wise were they [that] they understood the stars which were in the heavens.*[2]

In fact, all these contributions to Mesoamerican culture were in place long before Toltec power spread across central Mexico. Some scholars speculate that the Toltecs were originally a satellite population that Teotihuacan had placed on the northern frontier to protect against the incursions of nomads. Regardless of their origins, it is clear that Toltec culture was deeply influenced by Teotihuacan, including its preservation of the religious architecture and rituals associated with the feathered serpent god, Quetzalcoatl. It also utilized agricultural technologies, like irrigation and terraced hillsides, so important to Teotihuacan.

In this more violent era, the Toltecs created a state that depended on military power. This dependence was illustrated by the use of violent images, like impaled skulls, in the decoration of public buildings. The Toltecs' influence ultimately extended to distant Central America from their political capital at Tula **(TOO-la)**, founded in 968 C.E. north of modern Mexico City. At its peak Tula covered 5.4 square miles (14 square kilometers) and had a population of approximately 60,000. The massive architecture of the city center featured impressive statues of warriors and serpents, colonnaded patios, raised stone platforms, and numerous temples.

Like the earlier Teotihuacan, Tula and its subject dependencies had a multiethnic character, hosting distinct cultural and language communities. The apex of Toltec power also coincided with the development of an alliance with another multiethnic state with historic ties to Teotihuacan located to the south, Culhuacán **(kool whah KHAN)**. The exact nature of this alliance is unclear, but the presence of Toltec groups in Culhuacán is undeniable. Together the two cities benefited from a military alliance and from networks of tribute and trade established throughout the central Mexican region.

To understand the end of Toltec power, historians rely primarily on written sources from the era of the Spanish conquest, including accounts told to Catholic priests by native informants. According to most of these sources, two chieftains or kings shared power at Tula, and

[2]From the Florentine Codex, quoted in Inga Clendinnen, *Aztecs* (New York: Cambridge University Press, 1991), 213.

DEA/G. DAGLI ORTI/Getty Images

Tula The capital of the Toltecs was dominated by massive public architecture like these carved stone figures.

this division of responsibility eventually weakened Toltec power. Sometime around 1150 C.E. a struggle between elite groups identified with rival religious cults led to violent clashes within Toltec society and encouraged attacks by rival states. Legends that survived among the Aztecs claimed that Topiltzin (tow-PEELT-zeen)—one of the two rulers and a priest of the cult of Quetzalcoatl—and his followers were forced into exile in the east, "the land of the rising sun." One of the ancient texts relates these events in the following manner:

> *Thereupon he [Topiltzin] looked toward Tula, and then wept. . . . And when he had done these things . . . he went to reach the seacoast. Then he fashioned a raft of serpents. When he had arranged the raft, he placed himself as if it were his boat. Then he set off across the sea.[3]*

Some scholars used this Aztec tale to suggest a Toltec conquest of the Maya region, an argument fortified by similarities in decorative motifs, architecture, and urban planning at Tula and at the Maya postclassic center of Chichen Itza (CHEECH-ehn EET-zah) in the Yucatán. Scholars now dispute this story, suggesting instead that these regions were linked by long-term cultural exchanges, not conquest.

Nevertheless, it is clear that Tula and the Toltec state entered a period of steep decline after 1150 C.E. that included internal power struggles and an external military threat from the north. The historical Topiltzin was closely linked to the fate of Tula, but his story was more complex than that indicated by Aztec legend. His father Mixcoatl (mish-coh-AHT-til) was a Toltec military leader active in Culhuacán and in Cholula, where another satellite Toltec population resided. Topiltzin was probably born in Culhuacán, not Tula. He attempted to save the beleaguered Toltec capital of Tula, but he ultimately failed and retired from power around 1175. While disaster then befell the once-dominant city of Tula, an independent Toltec legacy survived until at least 1300 C.E. in Culhuacán and in nearby Cholula.

SECTION REVIEW

- In the postclassic era, large, professional militaries allowed Mesoamerican elites to create empires through conquest, resulting in increasingly hierarchical societies.

- The Toltecs used military conquest and political alliances to create a powerful empire with its capital at Tula. Their influence spread across central Mexico.

- The architecture of Tula was decorated with militaristic themes and images of human sacrifice, indicating the increased violence of the postclassic period.

- Tula, Culhuacán, and Cholula were ethnically and religiously diverse cities as well as centers of long-distance trade.

- After the collapse of the Toltec capital Tula in the twelfth century, elements of Toltec culture and religious practice survived in Culhuacán and Cholula.

Cholula

Located near the modern Mexican city of Puebla, Cholula developed at about the same time as Teotihuacan. It was situated to serve as a trade center and religious pilgrimage destination linking the Valley of Mexico with Maya regions to the southeast and with the Mixtec peoples to the southwest. Among the largest cities of postclassic Mesoamerica, Cholula had a large culturally and linguistically diverse population, including a large Toltec community. Cholula's original ties to the Toltecs is unclear, but sometime after 1000 C.E. the resident Toltec population appealed to Culhuacán for military assistance. Just as Topiltzin would later try to save Tula, his father, Mixcoatl, went to the aid Cholula. While the fate of this vulnerable Toltec community is not known, Cholula survived as an important regional power until the Spanish conquest, thus connecting the legacies of both Teotihuacan and the Toltecs to the later rise of the powerful Aztec Empire (see Chapter 15).

[3]Quoted in Nigel Davies, *The Toltec Heritage: From the Fall of Tula to the Rise of Tenochtitlán* (Norman: University of Oklahoma Press, 1980), 3.

NORTHERN PEOPLES

By the end of the classic period in Mesoamerica, around 900 C.E., important cultural centers had appeared in the southwestern desert region and along the Ohio and Mississippi River Valleys of what is now the United States (see Map 8.4). The peoples of the Southwest benefited from the early introduction of maize and other Mesoamerican cultigens (before 1000 B.C.E.). The resulting improvement to agricultural productivity led before 500 C.E. to rising population, the beginnings of urbanization, and increased social stratification. Maize arrived among the Amerindian peoples of the Ohio Valley sometime after 200 C.E., but only became the region's chief staple after 800. Once widely adopted this useful crop accelerated the development of large population centers and new political institutions.

The two regions evolved different political traditions. The Anasazi (ah-nah-SAH-zee) and their neighbors in the Southwest maintained a relatively egalitarian social structure and retained collective forms of political organization based on kinship and age. The mound builders of the eastern river valleys evolved more hierarchical political institutions, which subordinated groups of small towns and villages to a political center ruled by a hereditary chief who wielded both secular and religious authority.

Southwestern Desert Cultures

Around 300 B.C.E. in what is today Arizona, contacts with Mesoamerica led to the introduction of agriculture based on irrigation. Because irrigation allowed the planting of two maize crops per year, the population grew and settled village life soon appeared. Of all the southwestern cultures, the Hohokam of the Salt and Gila River Valleys show the strongest Mesoamerican influence. Hohokam sites have platform mounds and ball courts similar to those of Mesoamerica. Hohokam pottery, clay figurines, cast copper bells, and turquoise mosaics also reflect this influence. By 1000 C.E. the Hohokam had constructed an elaborate irrigation system. Hohokam agricultural and ceramic technology then spread over to neighboring peoples, but it was the Anasazi to the north who left the most vivid legacy of these desert cultures.

Anasazi Important culture of what is now the southwest United States (700–1300 C.E.). Centered on Chaco Canyon in New Mexico and Mesa Verde in Colorado, the Anasazi culture built multistory residences and worshiped in subterranean buildings called kivas.

Archaeologists use **Anasazi**, a Navajo word meaning "ancient ones," to identify a number of dispersed, though similar, desert cultures located in what is now the Four Corners region of Arizona, New Mexico, Colorado, and Utah (see Map 8.4). In the centuries before 700 C.E. the Anasazi developed an economy based on maize, beans, and squash. As irrigation and other technologies increased their productivity, they formed larger villages and evolved a much more complex cultural life centered on underground buildings called kivas. They produced pottery decorated with geometric patterns, learned to weave cotton cloth, and, after 900 C.E., began to construct large multistory residential and ritual centers.

One of the largest Anasazi communities was located in Chaco Canyon in what is now northwestern New Mexico. There were twelve towns in the canyon and surrounding mesas, suggesting a regional population of 15,000. Pueblo Bonito (founded in 919 C.E.) had more than 650 rooms arranged in a four-story block of residences and storage rooms; it also had thirty-eight kivas, including a great kiva more than 65 feet (19 meters) in diameter. Hunting, trade, and the need to maintain irrigation works often drew men away from the village. Women shared in agricultural tasks, were specialists in many crafts, and were responsible for food preparation and childcare. At Chaco Canyon the high-quality construction, the size and number of kivas, and the system of roads linking the canyon to outlying towns all suggest that Pueblo Bonito and its nearest neighbors exerted political and cultural dominance over a large region.

As had been the case with the Olmec center of San Lorenzo and Chavín de Huantar in Peru nearly a thousand years earlier, Pueblo Bonito's ascendancy depended on its identity as a sacred site and on the elaboration of an intense cycle of religious rituals that attracted pilgrims from distant locations.

Early archaeologists suggested that the Chaco Canyon culture originated as a colonial appendage of Mesoamerica, but the archaeological record provides little evidence for this theory. Merchants from Chaco did provide Toltec-period peoples of northern Mexico with turquoise in exchange for shell jewelry, copper bells, macaws, and trumpets, but these exchanges occurred late in Chaco's development. More importantly, the signature elements of Mesoamerican influence, such as pyramid-shaped mounds and ball courts, are missing at Chaco.

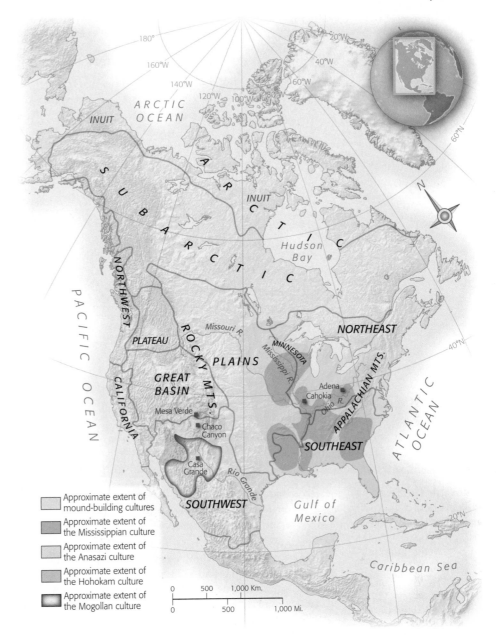

MAP 8.4 **Culture Areas of North America** In each of the large ecological regions of North America, native peoples evolved distinctive cultures and technologies. Here the Anasazi of the arid Southwest and the mound-building cultures of the Ohio and Mississippi River Valleys are highlighted. © Cengage Learning

The abandonment of the major sites in Chaco Canyon in the twelfth century most likely resulted from a long drought that undermined the culture's fragile agricultural economy. Nevertheless, the Anasazi continued in the Four Corners region for more than a century after the abandonment of Chaco Canyon, with major centers at Mesa Verde in present-day Colorado and at Canyon de Chelly and Kiet Siel in Arizona. The construction of these settlements in large natural caves high above valley floors suggests increased levels of warfare, probably provoked by population pressure on the region's limited arable land.

Mound Builders: The Hopewell and Mississippian Cultures

chiefdom Form of political organization with rule by a hereditary leader who held power over a collection of villages and towns. Less powerful than kingdoms and empires, chiefdoms were based on gift giving and commercial links.

From around 100 C.E. the Hopewell culture spread through the Ohio River Valley. Hopewell people constructed large villages and monumental earthworks. Once established, their influence spread west to Illinois, Michigan, and Wisconsin, east to New York and Ontario, and south to Alabama, Louisiana, Mississippi, and even Florida (see Map 8.4). For the necessities of daily life the Hopewell depended on hunting and gathering and on a limited agriculture. They are an early example of a North American **chiefdom**—populations as large as 10,000 and rule by a hereditary chief with both religious and secular responsibilities. Chiefs organized periodic rituals of feasting and gift giving to link diverse kinship groups and guarantee access to specialized crops and craft goods. They also managed long-distance trade for luxury goods and additional food supplies.

Mesa Verde Cliff Dwelling   Located in southern Colorado, the Anasazi cliff dwellings of the Mesa Verde region hosted a population of about 7,000 in 1250 c.e. The construction of housing complexes and religious buildings in the area's large caves was prompted by increased warfare in the region.   Kenneth Murray/Photo Researchers, Inc.

The largest Hopewell towns in the Ohio River Valley had several thousand inhabitants and served as ceremonial and political centers. Large mounds built to house burials and serve as platforms for religious rituals dominated major Hopewell centers. Some mounds were oriented to reflect sunrise and moonrise patterns. The abandonment of major sites around 400 c.e. marked the decline of Hopewell culture.

Hopewell influenced the development of the Mississippian culture (800–1500 c.e.). As in the case of the Anasazi, some experts have suggested that contacts with Mesoamerica influenced early Mississippian culture, but there is no convincing evidence to support this theory. It is true that maize, beans, and squash, all first domesticated in Mesoamerica, were crucial to the urbanized Mississippian culture. But these plants and related technologies were most likely acquired via intervening cultures.

The development of urbanized Mississippian chiefdoms resulted instead from the accumulated effects of small increases in agricultural productivity and the expansion of trade networks. An improved economy led to population growth, the building of cities, and social stratification. The largest towns shared a common urban plan based on a central plaza surrounded by large platform mounds.

The Mississippian culture reached its highest stage of evolution at the great urban center of Cahokia, located near the modern city of East St. Louis, Illinois (see Map 8.4). Cahokia, like Chavín de Huantar, the Olmec cities, and contemporary Pueblo Bonito served as a religious center and pilgrimage site. Subordinated rural populations were organized by the Cahokia elite through obligations of tribute, shared labor, and ritual. At the center of this site was the largest mound constructed in North America, a terraced structure 100 feet (30 meters) high and 1,037 by 790 feet (316 by 241 meters) at the base. Chunkey, a game infused with religious meaning and accompanied by gambling, helped establish Cahokia's cultural influence over a large region, as had the ballgame developed by the Olmec. Played with a stone disk and sticks, the game drew contestants and spectators from dependent towns and was used by the elite to organize tribute payments and labor for the construction of massive public works.

In this hierarchical society, commoners lived on the periphery of the ceremonial center where elite housing and temples were located. At its height in about 1200 C.E., Cahokia had a population of approximately 20,000—about the same as some of the postclassic Maya cities.

Cahokia controlled surrounding agricultural lands and a large number of secondary towns. Its political and economic influence depended on its location near the confluence of the Missouri, Mississippi, and Illinois Rivers, a location that facilitated commercial exchanges as far away as the coasts of the Atlantic and the Gulf of Mexico. Traders brought seashells, copper, mica, and flint to the city, where they were used in manufacture of ritual goods and tools. Burial evidence suggests that the rulers of Cahokia were rich and powerful. In one burial more than fifty young female and male retainers were sacrificed to accompany a ruler after death.

The construction of defensive walls around the ceremonial center and elite residences after 1250 C.E. provides some evidence that the decline and eventual abandonment of Cahokia were tied to the effects of military defeat or civil war, as had been true in Teotihuacan. There is also evidence that climate change and population pressures, exacerbated by environmental degradation caused by deforestation and more intensive farming practices, undermined Cahokia's viability. By 1300 Cahokia had lost control of its dependencies and its population was in precipitous decline. Despite its collapse, smaller Mississippian centers that preserved elements of Cahokian culture continued to flourish in the Southeast of the present-day United States until the arrival of Europeans.

SECTION REVIEW

- Transfer of irrigation and corn agriculture from Mesoamerica stimulated the development of Hohokam and Anasazi cultures.

- The Anasazi concentrated in the Four Corners region of the southwestern United States, especially in Chaco Canyon, where they built cities with underground kivas.

- Hopewell culture, organized around chiefdoms in the Ohio River Valley, was based on long-distance trade and religious ritual life centered on large mounds.

- The political organization, trade practices, and mound building of Hopewell were continued by the Mississippian culture, with its largest city, Cahokia, at the site of East St. Louis.

- Environmental changes probably undermined both Anasazi and Mississippian cultures.

ANDEAN CIVILIZATIONS, 200–1400

The Andean region of South America was an unlikely environment for the development of rich and powerful civilizations (see Map 8.5). Much of the region's mountainous zone is at altitudes that seem too high for agriculture and human habitation. Along the Pacific coast an arid climate posed a difficult challenge to the development of agriculture. To the east of the Andes Mountains, the hot and humid tropical environment of the Amazon headwaters also offered formidable obstacles to the organization of complex societies. Yet the Amerindian peoples of the Andean area produced some of the most socially complex and politically advanced societies of the Western Hemisphere. The very harshness of the environment compelled the development of productive and reliable agricultural technologies and attached them to a complex fabric of administrative structures and social relationships that became the central features of Andean civilization.

Cultural Response to Environmental Challenge

From the time of Chavín all of the great Andean civilizations succeeded in connecting the distinctive resources of the coastal region, with its abundant fisheries and irrigated maize fields, to the mountainous interior with its herds of llamas and rich mix of grains and tubers. Both regions faced significant environmental challenges. Droughts and shifting sands that clogged irrigation works periodically overwhelmed the coastal region's fields, and the mountainous interior presented enormous environmental challenges, since it averaged between 250 and 300 frosts per year.

The development of compensating technologies required an accurate calendar to time planting and harvests and the domestication of frost-resistant varieties of potatoes and grains. Native peoples learned to practice dispersed farming at different altitudes to reduce risks from frosts, and they terraced hillsides to create micro environments within a single area. They

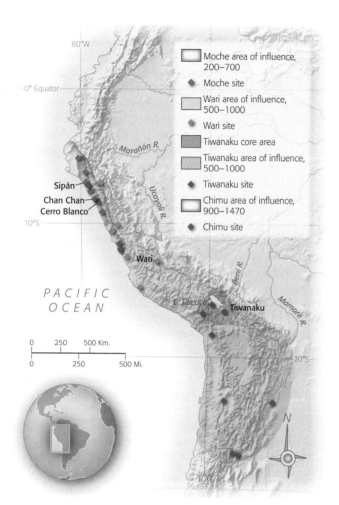

MAP 8.5 **Andean Civilizations, 200 B.C.E.–1532 C.E.** In response to these difficult environmental challenges, Andean peoples evolved complex social and technological adaptations. Irrigation systems, the domestication of the llama, metallurgy, and shared labor obligations helped provide a firm economic foundation for powerful, centralized states.

© Cengage Learning

ayllu Andean lineage group or kin-based community.

mita Andean labor system based on shared obligations to help kinsmen and work on behalf of rulers or religious organizations.

Moche Civilization of north coast of Peru (200–700 C.E.). An important Andean civilization that built extensive irrigation networks as well as impressive urban centers dominated by brick temples.

also discovered how to use the cold, dry climate to produce freeze-dried vegetable and meat products that prevented famine when crops failed. The domestication of the llama and alpaca also proved crucial, providing meat, wool, and long-distance transportation that linked coastal and mountain economies.

It was the clan, or **ayllu** (aye-YOU), that provided the foundation for Andean achievement. Members of an ayllu held land communally. Ayllu members thought of each other as brothers and sisters and were obligated to aid each other in tasks that required more labor than a single household could provide. These reciprocal obligations provided the model for the organization of labor and the distribution of goods at every level of Andean society. Just as individuals and families were expected to provide labor to kinsmen, ayllus were collectively expected to provide labor and goods to their rulers.

With the development of territorial states ruled by hereditary aristocracies and kings after 1000 B.C.E., these obligations were organized on a larger scale. The **mita** (MEET-ah) was a rotational labor draft that organized members of ayllus to work the fields and care for the llama and alpaca herds owned by religious establishments, the royal court, and the aristocracy. Mita laborers built and maintained roads, bridges, temples, palaces, and large irrigation and drainage projects. They also produced textiles and goods essential to ritual life, such as beer made from maize and coca (dried leaves chewed as a stimulant and now also the source of cocaine).

The ayllu was intimately tied to a uniquely Andean system of production and exchange. Because the region's mountain ranges created a multitude of small ecological areas with specialized resources, each community sought to control a variety of environments so as to guarantee access to essential goods. Coastal regions produced maize, fish, and cotton. Mountain valleys contributed quinoa (the local grain) as well as potatoes and other tubers. Higher elevations contributed the wool and meat of llamas and alpacas, and the Amazonian region provided coca and fruits. Ayllus sent out colonists to exploit the resources of these distinct ecological niches, retaining the loyalty of the colonists by arranging marriages and coming together for rituals. Historians commonly refer to this system of controlled exchange across ecological boundaries as vertical integration, or verticality.

The Early Intermediate Period Moche

Scholars of the Andes call the period 200 to 600 C.E. the Early Intermediate period. The **Moche** (MO-che) were among the most influential and powerful Andean civilizations of this period, dominating the north coastal region of Peru. While they did not establish a formal empire or create unified political structures, they did exercise authority over a broad geographic region. The most powerful of the Moche urban centers, such as Cerro Blanco located near the modern Peruvian city of Trujillo (see Map 8.5), first established hegemony over neighboring towns and villages and then extended political and economic control over more distant neighbors militarily. Key to this expansion was the elaboration of a potent ideology that tied hereditary rulers to the gods through elaborate religious rituals in the major Moche cities.

Archaeological evidence indicates that the Moche cultivated maize, quinoa, beans, manioc, and sweet potatoes with the aid of massive irrigation works, a complex network of canals and aqueducts that connected fields with water sources as far away as 75 miles (121 kilometers). Moche rulers forced commoners and subject peoples to build and maintain these hydraulic works. The Moche also relied on large herds of alpacas and llamas to transport goods across the region's difficult terrain. Their wool, along with cotton provided by farmers, provided the raw material for the thriving Moche textile production.

Evidence from surviving murals and decorated ceramics suggests that Moche society was highly stratified and theocratic. Wealth and power were concentrated, along with political control, in the hands of priests and military leaders. The military conquest of neighboring regions reinforced this hierarchy. Because the elite constructed their residences atop large platforms at Moche ceremonial centers, the powerful literally looked down on the commoners whose labor supported them. Evidence, such as ceramic portrait vessels, suggests that the power of the elite was highly individualized and associated with divine sanction. Moche rulers and other members of the elite wore tall headdresses and rich garments as well as elaborate gold jewelry that reinforced their connections to the gods. Moche burial practices reflected these deep social distinctions. A recent excavation in the Lambeyeque Valley discovered the tomb of a warrior-priest buried with a rich treasure of gold, silver, and copper jewelry, textiles, feather ornaments, and shells (see Diversity and Dominance: Burials as Historical Texts). A group of retainers and servants were executed and then buried with this powerful man in order to serve him in the afterlife.

Most commoners, on the other hand, devoted their time to subsistence farming and to the payment of labor dues owed to their ayllu and to the elite. Both men and women were involved in agriculture, care of llama herds, and the household economy. They lived with their families in one-room buildings clustered in the outlying areas of cities and in surrounding agricultural zones.

The high quality of Moche textiles, ceramics, and metallurgy indicates the presence of numerous skilled artisans. Women had a special role in the production of textiles, and even elite women devoted time to weaving. Moche culture developed a brilliant representational art. Craftsmen produced highly individualized portrait vases and decorated other ceramics with representations of myths and rituals. They were also accomplished metal-smiths, producing beautiful gold and silver religious objects and jewelry for elite adornment. Metallurgy served more practical ends as well: artisans produced a range of tools made of heavy copper and copper alloy for agricultural and military purposes.

The archaeological record makes clear that the rapid decline of major Moche centers coincided with a succession of natural disasters in the sixth century as well as with long-term climate changes. A thirty-year drought expanded the area of coastal sand dunes during the sixth century, and powerful winds pushed sand onto fragile agricultural lands, overwhelming the irrigation system. As the land dried, periodic heavy rains caused erosion that damaged fields and weakened the economy that had sustained ceremonial and residential centers. Despite massive efforts to keep the irrigation canals open and despite the construction of new urban centers in less vulnerable valleys to the north, Moche civilization never fully recovered. In the eighth century, the rise of a new military power, the Wari (see below), also contributed to the disappearance of the Moche by putting pressure on trade routes that linked the coastal region with the highlands.

Moche Warrior The Moche of ancient Peru were among the most accomplished ceramic artists of the Americas. Moche potters produced representations of gods and spirits, scenes of daily life, and portrait vases of important people. This warrior is armed with a mace, shield, and protective helmet. The Trustees of the British Museum/Art Resource, NY

Tiwanaku and Wari

Tiwanaku Name of capital city and empire centered on the region near Lake Titicaca in modern Bolivia (500–1000 C.E.).

Between 500 and 1000 C.E., what Andean scholars call the Middle Horizon period, two powerful civilizations dominated the highlands. The ruins of **Tiwanaku (tee-wah-NA-coo)** (see Map 8.5) stand at nearly 13,000 feet (3,962 meters) near Lake Titicaca in modern Bolivia. Tiwanaku's expansion depended on the adoption of technologies that increased agricultural productivity. Modern excavations provide the outline of vast drainage projects that reclaimed nearly 200,000 acres (80,000 hectares) of rich lakeside marshes for agriculture. This system of raised fields and ditches permitted intensive cultivation similar to that achieved by the use of chinampas in

Burials as Historical Texts

Efforts to reveal the history of the Americas before the arrival of Europeans depend on the work of archaeologists. The burials of rulers and other members of elites can be viewed as historical texts that describe how textiles, precious metals, beautifully decorated ceramics, and other commodities were used to reinforce the political and cultural power of ruling lineages. In public, members of the elite were always surrounded by the most desirable goods and rarest products as well as by elaborate rituals and ceremonies. The effect was to create an aura of godlike power. The material elements of political and cultural power were also integrated into the experience of death and burial as members of the elite were sent into the afterlife.

The first photograph is of an excavated Moche tomb in Sipán, Peru. The Moche (200–ca. 700 C.E.) were one of the most important of the pre-Inka civilizations of the Andean region, masters of metallurgy, ceramics, and textiles. The excavations at Sipán revealed a "warrior-priest" buried with an amazing array of gold ornaments, jewels, textiles, and ceramics. Also buried with him were five human sacrifices, two women, perhaps wives or concubines, two male servants, and a warrior. Three of these victims—the warrior, one woman, and a male servant—are each missing a foot, perhaps cut off to guarantee their continued faithfulness to the deceased ruler in the afterlife.

The second photograph shows the excavation of a classic-era (200–ca. 800 C.E.) Maya burial at Río Azul in Guatemala. After death this elite male was laid out on a carved wooden platform and cotton mattress and his body was painted with decorations. Mourners covered his body in rich textiles and surrounded him with valuable goods. These included a necklace of individual stones carved in the shape of heads, perhaps a symbol of his prowess in battle, and high-quality ceramics, some filled with foods consumed by the elite like cacao. The careful preparation of the burial chamber had required the work of numerous artisans and laborers, as was the case in the burial of the Moche warrior-priest. In death, as in life, these early American civilizations acknowledged the high status, political power, and religious authority of their elites.

QUESTIONS FOR ANALYSIS

1. If these burials are texts, what are stories?
2. Are there any visible differences in the two burials?
3. What questions might historians ask of these burials that cannot be answered?
4. Can modern burials be read as texts in similar ways to these ancient burials?

Burials Reveal Ancient Civilizations   (Left) Buried around 300 C.E., this Moche warrior-priest was buried amid rich tribute at Sipán in Peru. Also buried were the bodies of retainers or kinsmen probably sacrificed to accompany this powerful man. The body lies with the head on the right and the feet on the left. (Right) Similarly, the burial of a member of the Maya elite at Río Azul in northern Guatemala indicates the care taken to surround the powerful with fine ceramics, jewelry, and other valuable goods.

The Ritual Center of Tiwanaku   During the Middle Horizon period Tiwanaku was one of the most impressive cities in the Andean region. The ritual center was characterized by beautiful stone construction, sunken plazas, and by large carved stone representations of the gods.

Paulo Afonso/Shutterstock.com

Mesoamerica. Fish from the nearby lake and llamas added protein to a diet largely dependent on potatoes and grains. Llamas were also crucial for the maintenance of long-distance trade relationships that brought in corn, coca, tropical fruits, and medicinal plants. The resulting abundance permitted a dense cycle of feasting and religious observance that fueled the rise of a powerful elite.

Tiwanaku was distinguished by the scale of its urban construction and by the high quality of its stone masonry. Thousands of laborers were mobilized to cut and move the large stones used to construct large terraced pyramids, sunken plazas, walled enclosures, and a reservoir. Despite a limited metallurgy that produced only tools of copper alloy, Tiwanaku's artisans built large structures of finely cut stone that required little mortar to fit the blocks. They also produced gigantic human statuary. The largest example, a stern figure with a military bearing, was cut from a single block of stone that measures 24 feet (7 meters) high. These sacred constructions were oriented to reflect celestial cycles and distant Andean peaks infused with religious significance. Collectively, they provided an awe-inspiring setting for the religious rituals that legitimized the city's control of distant territories and peoples and for the elite's domination of society.

Archaeological evidence suggests that Tiwanaku at its height around 800 C.E. had a full-time population of around 60,000, including communities attracted from distant regions by the city's religious rituals and trade. It is clear that Tiwanaku was a highly stratified society ruled by a hereditary elite. This elite initially organized and controlled the ayllus of the surrounding region, but, as their military power grew, eventually utilized drafted labor from conquered and incorporated populations as well. As Tiwanaku's power and wealth grew, thousands of skilled craftsmen constantly expanded and embellished the ceremonial architecture and produced the metal goods, textiles, and pottery consumed by the elite. Military conquests and the establishment of distant colonial populations provided dependable supplies of more exotic products from ecologically distinct zones, such as colorful shells, gold and copper, and fine textiles.

Sometime after 1000 C.E. urban Tiwanaku was abandoned. While the exact cause is uncertain, we know the eclipse of this great civilization took a long time. There is evidence that years of severe drought led to precipitous population loss and to the breakdown of the long-distance trade in elite goods. This period was associated with the destruction of monumental effigies and other religious symbols, suggesting that worsening material conditions undermined the legitimacy of the elite.

The Maya Writing System

Of all the cultures of pre-Columbian America, only the Maya produced a written literature that has survived to the modern era. The literary legacy of the Maya is inscribed on stone monuments, ceramics, jade, shell, and bone. Books of bark paper were the original and most common medium of Maya scribes, but only four of these books exist today.

balam

ba-balam

balam-ma

ba-balam-ma

ba-la-m(a)

Maya Glyphs   The Maya developed a sophisticated written language expressed in stylized images (glyphs) conceptually similar to Egyptian hieroglyphics.   © Cengage Learning

The historical and literary importance of the written record of the Maya has been recognized only recently. In the early nineteenth century, visitors to southern Mexico and Guatemala began to record and decipher the symbols they found on stone monuments. By the end of the nineteenth century, the Maya system of numbers and the Maya calendar were decoded.

Not until the 1960s did scholars recognize that Maya writing reflects spoken language by having a set word order. We now know that Maya writing was capable of capturing the rich meaning of spoken language.

Maya scribes could use signs that represented sounds or signs that represented whole words. *Jaguar* (*balam* in Maya) could be written by using the head of this big cat in symbolic form. Because there were other large cats in the Maya region, scribes commonly added a pronunciation cue like a prefix or suffix to the front or back of the symbol to clarify meaning. In this case they might affix the syllable sign *ba* to the front of the jaguar head or the syllable sign *ma* to the end. Because no other Maya word for feline began with *ba* or ended with *ma*, the reader knew to pronounce the word as *balam* for "jaguar." Alternatively, because the last vowel was not sounded, *balam* could be written with three syllable signs: *ba la ma*.

These signs were expressed in a rich and varied array of stylized forms, much like illustrated European medieval texts, that make translation difficult. But these stylistic devices helped convey meaning. Readers detected meaning not only in what the text "said" but also in how and where the text was written.

The work of Maya scribes was not intended as mass communication, since few Maya could read these texts. Instead, as two of the most respected experts in this field explain, "Writing was a sacred proposition that had the capacity to capture the order of the cosmos, to inform history, to give form to ritual, and to transform the profane material of everyday life into the supernatural."

Source: Text and illustration based on Linda Schele and David Freidel, *A Forest of Kings: The Untold Story of the Ancient Maya*. New York: William Morrow & Co., Inc., 1990.

Wari   Andean civilization culturally linked to Tiwanaku, perhaps beginning as a colony of Tiwanaku.

The contemporary site of **Wari** (WAH-ree) was located about 450 miles (751 kilometers) to the northwest of Tiwanaku, near the modern Peruvian city of Ayacucho. Wari clearly shared elements of the culture and technology of Tiwanaku, but the exact nature of the relationship between these civilizations remains unclear. Some scholars argue that Wari began as a dependency of Tiwanaku, while others suggest that they were joint capitals of a single empire. Most now argue that Wari was a distinct culture that evolved a politically centralized state and powerful military. Recent research indicates an aggressive imperial expansion lubricated by captive-taking and human sacrifice.

Urban Wari was larger than Tiwanaku, measuring nearly 4 square miles (10 square kilometers). A massive wall surrounded the city center, which was dominated by a large temple and multifamily housing for elites and artisans. Housing for commoners was located in a sprawling suburban zone. The small scale of its monumental architecture relative to Tiwanaku and the near absence of cut stone masonry in public and private buildings suggest either the weakness of the elite or the absence of specialized construction crafts compared with other Andean centers. A distinctive Wari ceramic style allows experts to trace Wari's influence to the coastal area and to the northern highlands. This expansion occurred at a time of climate change and increasing warfare throughout the Andes that led ultimately to the eclipse of both Tiwanaku and Wari after 1000 C.E. In the centuries that followed the collapse of these two powerful centers, the Andean highlands experienced increased levels of violence, as evidenced by the construction of numerous fortifications by the smaller polities and villages that now contended for power.

Chimú

Chimú A powerful civilization, also called Kingdom of Chimor, that developed on the northern coast of Peru from about 1200 to its conquest by an expanding Inka empire in the 1470s. Its capital city was Chan Chan.

On the north coast of Peru in the region previously dominated by the Moche, a powerful new imperial state appeared after 900 C.E., the period called Late Intermediate (1000–1476 C.E.) in Andean history. The **Chimú** Empire, or Chimor, with its capital of Chan Chan, eventually controlled more than 600 miles (966 kilometers) of the Pacific coast from Ecuador in the north to central Peru. Building upon the legacy of the Moche who earlier controlled this area, the Chimú depended on the abundant production of an irrigated agricultural hinterland and on the labor provided by conquered dependencies.

While the grandeur of Wari and Tiwanaku can still be seen in surviving monumental stone architecture, the once-great city of Chan Chan, built from adobe, has been much diminished by a thousand years of erosion. Nevertheless, the imperial character of the city remains clear. Nine large residential compounds provide the urban nucleus. Each one is believed to have housed a ruler and his family during his life and become his mausoleum upon his death. With each succession the new ruler would be forced to organize the labor and materials necessary to construct a new palace compound. In addition to the family residence of the ruler, each compound contained a U-shaped room used for official functions and numerous smaller rooms used to store food and other tribute items sent from dependent jurisdictions. This system depended ultimately on a potent military and a series of conquests that only ended in the fifteenth century with the appearance of a more powerful rival, the Inka (see Chapter 15).

While Chan Chan was the center of imperial government and hosted a large aristocratic population in addition to the reigning family, there was little urban planning. Elite residential compounds were separated by high walls from the humble habitations of commoners dispersed across the city. Chan Chan served primarily as the residential precinct of the elite and those who provided the elite with luxury goods like gold jewelry and high-quality textiles and pottery, rather than as a religious or even commercial center. These patterns were repeated on a modest scale in the regional political capitals that organized the labor necessary to maintain irrigation works and collect the tribute that sustained Chan Chan.

Both the urban architecture and the organization of labor expressed the profound social and economic distance that separated royalty and populace. With a population of only 25,000 to 30,000 at its peak, we know the massive Chimú capital city was built and maintained by labor tributes imposed on dependent rural populations. As the city grew, the construction of large structures like palaces and religious monuments was subdivided into multiple small tasks assigned to parties of tribute workers from distinct regions who made their own adobe bricks.

The Chimú Empire (Chimor) survived for over four centuries in the difficult arid environment of the Peruvian coast, expanding the scale of Moche irrigation works by developing a larger, more efficient bureaucracy that could organize thousands of conscripted laborers for ever more ambitious irrigation tasks. As this empire expanded, the improved agricultural productivity that resulted from these projects compensated dependent peoples for their labor and for their loss of autonomy. Unlike earlier Andean

SECTION REVIEW

- Andean societies developed by devising solutions to problems posed by their complex environment of arid coastlands, cold highlands, and tropical forests.

- The ayllu and mita provided the social base for Andean economic and political organization.

- The Moche developed a powerful state based on irrigated agriculture, exchange between ecological regions, and a powerful religious elite.

- The construction of canals and the development of raised field agriculture made possible the rise of the religious and political center of Tiwanaku.

- Both Tiwanaku and Wari used their powerful militaries to extend their power over large regions and create long-distance networks of trade.

- The Chimú created a powerful new empire in the region previously dominated by the Moche.

civilizations, the Chimú did not collapse because of environmental catastrophe or social unrest. Instead, in the 1470s, they fell victim to the rapid imperial expansion of the Inka, who then freely borrowed Chimú's technologies and political institutions.

CONCLUSION

The Toltec Empire and Cholula of Mesoamerica and Chimor of the Andean region were all powerful states that depended upon religious practices, technologies, political institutions, and social forms that had developed over nearly two thousand years. In some cases crucial elements of political life, culture, and economy dated from the era of the Olmec and Chavín. Despite these continuities, rising populations and competition for resources led inevitably to new cycles of violence in both regions. The survival of these states ultimately depended on the power of their armies as much as on the productivity of their economies or the wisdom of their rulers.

Mesoamerica and the Andean region were environmentally challenging regions where a succession of native states found ways to produce and distribute products from distinct ecological regions as well as ways to organize ethnically diverse populations into coherent polities. From the beginning rulers in both regions legitimized their authority religiously, serving as priestly intermediaries with the gods or claiming direct descent from them. The major cities of every important civilization from the time of the Olmec and Chavín to 1400 C.E. operated as religious as well as political centers. Their urban centers were dominated by monumental religious architecture decorated with symbols connecting elites to the gods through creation myths. Dense cycles of religious ritual conducted by priests and rulers in elaborate costumes legitimized the power of cities over the countryside and habituated rural populations to the transfer of goods and labor that made the achievements of these civilizations possible.

With the important exception of metallurgy developed in the Andes and transferred to Mesoamerica after 500 C.E., technology developed slowly in the Americas after the era of the Olmec and Chavín. The dominant powers of each successive era—Teotihuacan and the Moche and, ultimately, the Toltecs and Cholula and Chimú—all depended on the mobilization of ever-larger workforces to meet environmental challenges and support growing urbanization, rather than on new technologies. The construction of irrigation canals, raised fields, terraced hillsides, and, in the case of Mesoamerica, chinampas multiplied agricultural productivity, subsidized craft specialization, and, through trade, overcame environmental constraints, but all these technologies were in place for nearly a thousand years before the Toltec, Cholula, and Chimú periods. The growing size of cities, the mounting power of government, and the expanding scale of empire all depended on the refinement of ancient technologies and the mobilization of ever-larger workforces.

There were important differences between Mesoamerica and the Andean region. Mesoamerican cultures developed elementary markets to distribute specialized regional production, although the forced payment of goods as tribute remained important to sustain cities like Toltec Tula. In the postclassic period standardized quantities of cacao beans, metal goods, and cloth were being used as money in these markets. In the Andes reciprocal labor obligations and managed exchange relationships were used to allocate goods. There were important regional political differences as well. In Mesoamerica the Toltecs imposed tribute obligations on defeated peoples but left local hereditary elites in place. The Chimú of the Andes, in contrast, created a more centralized imperial administrative structure managed by a trained bureaucracy and used compulsory labor obligations to produce and distribute goods.

We can find similar patterns in North America. The transfer of agricultural technology from Mesoamerica, with its dependence on corn, beans, and squash, influenced the mound-building cultures of the Ohio and Mississippi River Valleys and the desert cultures of the Southwest. In the desert region of what is now the Southwest of the United States, the Anasazi and other peoples also utilized irrigated agriculture, a technology crucial to both Mesoamerican and Andean cultures. Both the desert and mound-building cultures of North America experienced cycles when powerful new political centers expanded the territories they controlled and consolidated their power until overwhelmed by environmental challenges or displaced by military rivals.

Beginning in the eleventh century the Toltec Empire weakened. The ultimate collapse of Tula left Culhuacán and Cholula as heirs of a much-diminished Toltec presence in central Mexico. Chimor persisted until the fifteenth century, when it also lost momentum and was militarily overwhelmed by the rising Inka Empire around 1470. Great civilizations in both Mesoamerica and the Andean region had risen and then been overwhelmed in earlier epochs as well, as had the major powers of the Four Corners desert region and the Ohio and Mississippi River Valleys. In all these cases, a long period of cultural and political adjustment led eventually to the creation of new indigenous institutions, the adoption of new technologies, and the appearance of new centers of power in new locations. With the appearance of the Aztec and Inka Empires in the fourteenth century, America would experience its final cycle of autonomous indigenous crisis and adjustment. At the end of that century the future of Amerindian peoples would become linked to the cultures of the Old World (See Chapter 15).

KEY TERMS

Olmec p. 194
Chavín p. 197
llama p. 198
Teotihuacan p. 199

chinampas p. 200
Maya p. 200
Toltecs p. 204
Anasazi p. 206

chiefdom p. 207
ayllu p. 210
mita p. 210
Moche p. 210

Tiwanaku p. 211
Wari p. 214
Chimú p. 215

SUGGESTED READING

Bawden, Garth. *The Moche.* 1996. Among the best studies of this early culture in Peru.

Bruhns, Karen Olsen. *Ancient South America.* 1994. An introduction to current scholarship on early Andean societies.

Crown, Patricia L., and W. James Judge, eds. *Chaco and Hohokam.* 1991. A good summary of current research issues in the American Southwest.

Dickason, Olive Patricia. *Canada's First Nations.* 1992. A well-written survey that traces the history of Canada's Amerindian peoples to the modern era.

Fiedel, Stuart. *Prehistory of the Americas.* 1987. An excellent summary of the early history of the Western Hemisphere.

Janusek, John Wayne. *Ancient Tiwanaku.* 2012. The best introduction to this topic.

Kellogg, Susan. *Weaving the Past.* 2005. Early chapters provide an excellent synthesis of the place of women in early Mesoamerican and Andean societies.

Mastache, Alba Guadalupe, Robert H. Cobean, and Dan M. Healan. *Ancient Tollan, Tula and the Toltec Heartland.* 2002. Among the best studies of the Toltec era and controversies over the location of Tula.

Nicholson, H. B. *Topiltzin Quetzalcoatl: The Once and Future Lord of the Toltecs.* 2001. Examination of both the archaeological record and mythologies of Topiltzin and the Toltecs.

Pasztori, Esther. *Teotihuacan.* 1997. A good summary of recent research.

Pauketat, Timothy R. *Ancient Cahokia and the Mississippians.* 2004. The best summary of modern research on Cahokia and its legacy.

Schele, Linda, and David Freidel. *A Forest of Kings.* 1990. An excellent summary of recent research on the classic-period Maya.

Shutler, Richard, Jr. *Early Man in the New World.* 1983. A good brief introduction.

Silverberg, Robert. *Mound Builders of Ancient America.* 1968. A good introduction to this topic.

Tung, Tiffiny A. *Violence, Ritual, and the Wari Empire: A Social Bioarchaeology of Imperialism in the Ancient Andes.* 2012. A challenging synthesis of recent research.

Oral Societies and the Consequences of Literacy

The availability of written documents is a key factor used by historians to divide human prehistory from history. When we can read what people of the past thought and said about their lives, we begin to understand their cultures, institutions, values, and beliefs in ways that are not possible based only on the material remains unearthed by archaeologists.

Literacy and nonliteracy are not absolute alternatives. Personal literacy ranges from illiteracy through many shades of partial literacy (the ability to write one's name or to read simple texts with difficulty) to the fluent ability to read that is possessed by anyone reading this textbook. And there are degrees of societal literacy, ranging from nonliteracy through so-called craft literacy—in which a small specialized elite uses writing for limited purposes, such as administrative record keeping—up to the near-universal literacy and the use of writing for innumerable purposes that is the norm in the developed world in our times.

The vast majority of human beings of the last five to six thousand years, even those living in societies that possessed the technology of writing, were not themselves literate. If most people in a society rely on the spoken word and memory, that culture is essentially "oral" even if some members know how to write. The differences between oral and literate cultures are immense, affecting not only the kinds of knowledge that are valued and the forms in which information is preserved, but also the very use of language, the categories for conceptualizing the world, and ultimately the hard-wiring of the individual human brain (now recognized by neuroscientists to be strongly influenced by individual experience and mental activity).

Ancient Greece of the Archaic and Classical periods (ca. 800–323 B.C.E.) offers a particularly instructive case study because we can observe the process by which writing was introduced into an oral society as well as the far-reaching consequences. The Greeks of the Dark Age and early Archaic period lived in a purely oral society; all knowledge was preserved in human memory and passed on by telling it to others.

The *Iliad* and the *Odyssey* (ca. 700 B.C.E.), Homer's epic poems, reflect this state of affairs. Scholars recognize that the creator of these poems was an oral poet, almost certainly not literate, who had heard and memorized the poems of predecessors and retold them his own way. The poems are treasuries of information that this society regarded as useful—events of the past; the conduct expected of warriors, kings, noblewomen, and servants; how to perform a sacrifice, build a raft, put on armor, and entertain guests; and much more.

Embedding this information in a story and using the colorful language, fixed phrases, and predictable rhythm of poetry made it easier for poet and audience to remember vast amounts of material. The early Greek poets, drawing on their strong memories, skill with words, and talent for dramatic performance, developed highly specialized techniques to assist them in memorizing and presenting their tales. They played a vital role in the preservation and transmission of information and thus enjoyed a relatively high social standing and comfortable standard of living. Analogous groups can be found in many other oral cultures of the past, including the bards of medieval Celtic lands, Norse *skalds*, west African *griots*, and the tribal historians of Native American peoples.

Nevertheless, human memory, however cleverly trained and well practiced, can only do so much. Oral societies must be extremely selective about what information to preserve in the limited storage medium of human memory, and they are slow to give up old information to make way for new.

Sometime in the eighth century B.C.E. the Greeks borrowed the system of writing used by the Phoenicians of Lebanon and, in adapting it to their language, created the first purely alphabetic writing, employing several dozen symbols to express the sounds of speech. The Greek alphabet, although relatively simple to learn as compared to the large and cumbersome sets of symbols in such craft literacy systems as cuneiform, hieroglyphics, or Linear B, was probably known at first only to a small number of people and used for restricted purposes. Scholars believe that it may have taken three or four centuries for knowledge of reading and writing to spread to large numbers of Greeks and for the written word to become the primary storage medium for the accumulated knowledge of Greek civilization. Throughout that time Greece was still primarily an oral society, even though some Greeks, mostly highly educated members of the upper classes, were beginning to write down poems, scientific speculations, stories about the past, philosophic musings, and the laws of their communities.

It is no accident that some of the most important intellectual and artistic achievements of the Greeks, including early science, history, drama, and rhetoric, developed in the period when oral and literate ways existed side by side. Scholars have persuasively argued that writing, by opening up a virtually limitless capacity to store information, released the human mind from the hard discipline of memorization and ended the need to be so painfully selective about what was preserved. This made previously unimaginable innovation and experimentation possible. The Greeks began to organize and categorize information in linear ways, perhaps inspired by the linear sequence of the alphabet; and they began to engage in abstract thinking now that it was no longer necessary to put everything in a story format. We can observe changes in the Greek language as it developed a vocabulary full of abstract nouns, accompanied by increasingly complex sentence structure now that the reader had time to go back over the text.

Nevertheless, all the developments associated with literacy were shaped by the deeply rooted oral habits of Greek culture. It is often said that Plato (ca. 429–347 B.C.E.) and his contemporaries of the later Classical Period may have been the first generation of Greeks who learned much of what they knew from books. Even so, Plato was a disciple of the philosopher Socrates, who wrote nothing, and Plato employed the oral form of the dialogue, a dramatized sequence of questions and answers, to convey his ideas in written form.

The transition from orality to literacy met stiff resistance in some quarters. Groups whose position in the oral culture was based on the special knowledge only they possessed—members of the elite who judged disputes, priests who knew the time-honored formulas and rituals for appeasing the gods, oral poets who preserved and performed the stories of a heroic past—resented the consequences of literacy. They did what they could to inflame the common people's suspicions of the impiety of literate men who sought scientific explanations for phenomena, such as lightning and eclipses, that had traditionally been attributed to the will and action of the gods. The elite attacked the so-called Sophists, or "wise men," who charged fees to teach what they claimed were the skills necessary for success, accusing them of subverting traditional morals and corrupting the young.

Other societies, ancient and modern, offer parallel examples of these processes. Oral "specialists" in antiquity, including the Brahmin priests of India and the Celtic Druids, preserved in memory valuable religious information about how to win the favor of the gods. These groups jealously guarded their knowledge because it was the basis of their livelihood and social standing. In their determination to select and to maintain control over those who received this knowledge, they resisted committing it to writing, even after that technology was available. The ways in which oral authorities feel threatened by writing and resist it can be seen in the following quotation from a twentieth-century C.E. "griot," an oral rememberer and teller of the past in Mali in West Africa:

We griots are depositories of the knowledge of the past. . . . Other peoples use writing to record the past, but this invention has killed the faculty of memory among them. They do not feel the past anymore, for writing lacks the warmth of the human voice. With them everybody thinks he knows, whereas learning should be a secret. . . . What paltry learning is that which is congealed in dumb books! . . . For generations we have passed on the history of kings from father to son. The narrative was passed on to me without alteration, for I received it free from all untruth.[1]

This point of view is hard for us to grasp, living as we do in an intensely literate society in which the written word is often felt to be more authoritative and objective than the spoken word. It is important, in striving to understand societies of the past, not to superimpose our assumptions on them and to appreciate the complex interplay of oral and literate patterns in many of them.

NOTE

1. D. T. Niane, *Sundiata: An Epic of Old Mali* (Harlow, UK: Longman, 1986), 41.

PART

III

CHAPTER 9   Networks of Communication and Exchange, 300 B.C.E.–1100 C.E.

CHAPTER 10   The Sasanid Empire and the Rise of Islam, 200–1200

CHAPTER 11   Christian Societies Emerge in Europe, 600–1200

CHAPTER 12   Inner and East Asia, 400–1200

Werner Forman/Universal Images Group/Getty Images

Christian World Map from Muslim Spain   The east is shown at the top of the map with Adam and Eve in the Garden of Eden. Next to them is the holy city of Jerusalem represented by an arched gate suggestive of Andalusian architecture. Alexandria is below the bend of the Nile River at Adam's feet. The Mediterranean Sea is vertical with rectangular islands, and the red stripe to the right is the Red Sea and Indian Ocean.

Growth and Interaction of Cultural Communities, 300 B.C.E.–1200 C.E.

In 300 B.C.E., societies had only limited contacts beyond their frontiers. By 1200 C.E., this situation had changed, as traders, migrating peoples, and missionaries brought peoples together. Products and technologies also moved along long-distance trade networks: the Silk Road across Asia, Saharan caravan routes, and sea-lanes connecting the Indian Ocean coastlands.

During this period migrating Bantu peoples from West Africa spread iron and new farming techniques through much of sub-Saharan Africa and helped foster a distinctive African culture. Conquering Arabs from the Arabian peninsula, inspired by the Prophet Muhammad, established Muslim rule from Spain to India, laying the foundation of a new culture.

In Asia, missionaries and pilgrims helped Buddhism spread from India to Sri Lanka, Tibet, Southeast Asia, and East Asia. The new faith interacted with older philosophies and religions to produce distinctive cultural patterns. Simultaneously, the Tang Empire in China disseminated Chinese culture and technologies throughout Inner and East Asia.

In Europe, monks and missionaries spread Christian beliefs that became enmeshed with new political and social structures: a struggle between royal and church authority in western Europe; a union of religious and imperial authority in the Byzantine east; and a similar but distinctive society in Kievan Russia. The Crusades reconnected western Europe with the lands of the east.

CHAPTER 9

Chapter Outline

The Silk Road
➤ *What factors contributed to the growth of trade along the Silk Road?*

The Indian Ocean Maritime System
➤ *How did geography affect Indian Ocean trade routes?*

Routes Across the Sahara
➤ *Why did trade begin across the Sahara Desert?*

Sub-Saharan Africa
➤ *What accounts for the substantial degree of cultural unity in Africa south of the Sahara?*

The Spread of Ideas
➤ *Why do some goods and ideas travel more easily than others?*

Conclusion

● **DIVERSITY + DOMINANCE**   Travel Accounts of Africa and India
● **ENVIRONMENT + TECHNOLOGY**   Camel Saddles

Indian Ocean Sailing Vessel   Ships like this one, in a rock carving on the Buddhist temple of Borobodur in Java, probably carried colonists from Indonesia to Madagascar.

Networks of Communication and Exchange, 300 B.C.E.–1100 C.E.

Inspired by the tradition of the Silk Road, a Chinese poet named Po Zhuyi (boh joo-yee) nostalgically wrote:

Iranian whirling girl, Iranian whirling girl—
Her heart answers to the strings,
Her hands answer to the drums.
At the sound of the strings and drums, she raises her arms,
Like whirling snowflakes tossed about, she turns in her twirling dance.
Iranian whirling girl,
You came from Sogdiana (sog-dee-A-nuh).
In vain did you labor to come east more than ten thousand tricents.
For in the central plains there were already some who could do the Iranian whirl,
And in a contest of wonderful abilities, you would not be their equal.[1]

The western part of Central Asia, the region around Samarkand (SAM-mar-kand) and Bukhara (boh-CAR-ruh) known in the eighth century C.E. as Sogdiana, was 2,500 miles (4,000 kilometers) from the Chinese capital of Chang'an (chahng-ahn). Caravans took more than four months to trek across the mostly unsettled deserts, mountains, and grasslands.

The Silk Road connecting China and the Middle East across Central Asia fostered the exchange of agricultural goods, manufactured products, and ideas. Musicians and dancing girls traveled, too—as did camel pullers, merchants, monks, and pilgrims. The Silk Road was not just a means of bringing peoples and parts of the world into contact; it was also a social system.

With every expansion of territory, the growing wealth of temples, kings, and emperors enticed traders to venture ever farther afield for precious goods. For the most part, the customers were wealthy elites. But the new products, agricultural and industrial processes, and foreign ideas and customs these long-distance traders brought with them sometimes affected an entire society.

Travelers and traders seldom owned much land or wielded political power. Socially isolated (sometimes by law) and secretive because any talk about markets, products, routes, and travel conditions could help their competitors, they nevertheless contributed more to drawing the world together than did all but a few kings and emperors.

This chapter examines the social systems and historical impact of exchange networks that developed between 300 B.C.E. and 1100 C.E. in Europe, Asia, and Africa. The Silk Road and the Indian Ocean maritime system illustrate the nature of long-distance trade in this era.

---

[1] Victor H. Mair, ed., *The Columbia Anthology of Traditional Chinese Literature* (New York: Columbia University Press, 1994), 485; translated by Victor H. Mair.

Trading networks were not the only medium for the spread of new ideas, products, and customs. This chapter also compares developments along trade routes with folk migration by looking at the beginnings of contact across the Sahara and the simultaneous spread of Bantu-speaking peoples within sub-Saharan Africa. Chapter 6 discussed a third pattern of cultural contact and exchange, that taking place with the beginning of Christian missionary activity in the Roman Empire. This chapter further explores the process by examining the spread of Buddhism in Asia and Christianity in Africa and Asia.

THE SILK ROAD

Silk Road Caravan routes connecting China and the Middle East across Central Asia and Iran.

Archaeology and linguistic studies show that the peoples of Central Asia engaged in long-distance movement and exchange from at least 1500 B.C.E. In Roman times Europeans became captivated by the idea of a trade route linking the lands of the Mediterranean with China by way of Mesopotamia, Iran, and Central Asia. The **Silk Road**, as it came to be called in modern times, experienced several periods of heavy use (see Map 9.1). The first began around 100 B.C.E.

Origins and Operations

Parthians Iranian ruling dynasty between ca. 250 B.C.E. and 226 C.E.

The Seleucid kings who succeeded to the eastern parts of Alexander the Great's empire in the third century B.C.E. focused their energies on Mesopotamia and Syria. This allowed an Iranian nomadic leader to establish an independent kingdom in northeastern Iran. The **Parthians**, a people originally from east of the Caspian Sea, had become a major force by 247 B.C.E. They left few written sources, and recurring wars with Greeks and Romans to the west prevented travelers from the Mediterranean region from gaining firm knowledge of their kingdom. It seems likely, however, that they helped foster the Silk Road by being located on the threshold of Central Asia and sharing customs with steppe nomads farther to the east.

In 128 B.C.E. a Chinese general named Zhang Jian (jahng jee-en) made his first exploratory journey across the deserts and mountains of Inner Asia on behalf of Emperor Wu of the Han dynasty. After crossing the broad and desolate Tarim Basin north of Tibet, he reached the fertile valley of Ferghana (fer-GAH-nuh) and for the first time encountered westward-flowing rivers. There he found horse breeders whose animals far outclassed any horses he had seen. Later Chinese historians looked on General Zhang, who ultimately led eighteen expeditions, as the originator of overland trade with the western lands, and they credited him with personally introducing a whole garden of new plants and trees to China.

Long-distance travel suited the people of the steppes more than the Chinese. The populations of Ferghana and neighboring regions included many nomads who followed their herds. Their migrations had little to do with trade, but they provided pack animals and controlled transit across their lands. The trading demands that brought the Silk Road into being were Chinese eagerness for western products, especially horses, and on the western end, the organized Parthian state, which had captured the flourishing markets of Mesopotamia from the Seleucids and maintained relations with other markets in India.

By 100 B.C.E., Greeks could buy Chinese silk from Parthian traders in Mesopotamian border entrepôts. Yet caravans also bought and sold goods along the way in prosperous Central Asian cities like Samarkand and Bukhara. These cities grew and flourished, often under the rule of local princes.

General Zhang definitely seems to have brought two plants to China: alfalfa and wine grapes. The former provided the best fodder for horses. In addition, Chinese farmers adopted pistachios, walnuts, pomegranates, sesame, coriander, spinach, and other new crops. Chinese artisans and physicians made good use of other trade products, such as jasmine oil, oak galls (used in tanning animal hides, dyeing, and making ink), sal ammoniac (for medicines), copper oxides, zinc, and precious stones.

Traders going west from China carried new fruits such as peaches and apricots, which the Romans mistakenly attributed to other eastern lands, calling them Persian plums and Armenian plums, respectively. They also carried cinnamon, ginger, and other spices that could not be grown in the West.

CHRONOLOGY

	Silk Road	Indian Ocean Trade	Saharan Trade
500 B.C.E.	247 B.C.E. Parthian rule begins in Iran		500 B.C.E.–ca. 1000 C.E. Bantu migrations
			ca. 200 B.C.E. Camel nomads in southern Sahara
	128 B.C.E. General Zhang Jian reaches Ferghana		
	100 B.C.E.–300 C.E. Kushans rule northern Afghanistan and Sogdiana		46 B.C.E. First mention of camels in northern Sahara
1 C.E.	1st cent. C.E. First evidence of the stirrup	1st cent. C.E. *Periplus of the Erythraean Sea;* Indonesian migration to Madagascar	
300 C.E.			ca. 300 Beginning of camel nomadism in northern Sahara
	ca. 400 Buddhist pilgrim Faxian travels Silk Road		

Nomadism in Central and Inner Asia

The Silk Road could not have functioned without pastoral nomads to provide animals, animal handlers, and protection. As discussed in Chapter 4, descriptions of steppe nomads known as Scythians appear in the sixth century B.C.E. in the history of the Greek writer Herodotus, who portrays them as superb riders, herdsmen, and hunters living in Central Asia, the lands to the north of the Black and Caspian Seas. Moving regularly and efficiently with flocks and herds of enormous size prevented overgrazing. Though the Scythians were fearsome horse archers, their homes, which were made of felt spread over a lightweight framework, were transported on two- or four-wheeled wagons drawn by oxen. This custom continued in some parts of Inner Asia, the grasslands and deserts extending eastward from Central Asia to the borders of China, for another two thousand years.

Nomads were not unfamiliar with agriculture or unwilling to use products grown by farmers, but their ideal was self-sufficiency. Since their wanderings with their herds normally took them far from any farming region, self-sufficiency dictated foods they could provide for themselves—primarily meat and milk—and clothing made from felt, leather, and furs. Women oversaw the breeding and birthing of livestock and the preparation of skins. They were also responsible for relocating the portable dwellings.

Lee Boltin/The Bridgeman Art Library

Scythian Breastplate   This superbly crafted gold ornament from the fourth century B.C.E. features animal combat in the lower tier, flower motifs in the center, and scenes from Scythian pastoral life in the upper. Two men prepare a fleece garment in the middle of the upper tier while on either side young animals are suckling and a ewe is being milked. Note the contrast between the simplicity of nomadic life and the luxury represented by the gold ornament itself.

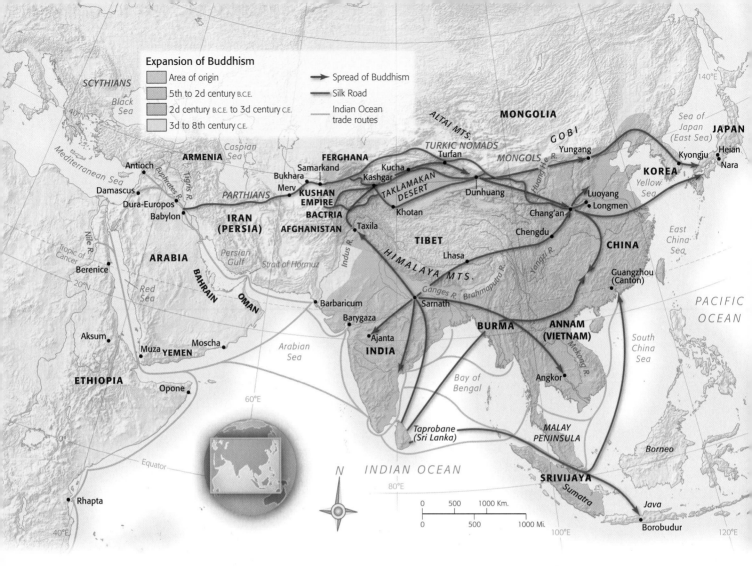

MAP 9.1 **Asian Trade and Communication Routes** The overland Silk Road was vulnerable to political disruption, but it was much shorter than the maritime route from the South China Sea to the Red Sea, and ships were more expensive than pack animals. Moreover, China's political centers were in the north. © Cengage Learning

Nomads were most dependent on settled regions for the bronze or iron used in bridles, stirrups, cart fittings, and weapons. They acquired metal implements in trade and reworked them to suit their purposes. Scythians in the Ukraine worked extensively with iron as early as the fourth century B.C.E., and Turkic-speaking peoples had large ironworking stations south of the Altai Mountains in western Mongolia in the 600s C.E. Steppe nomads situated near settled areas also traded wool, leather, and horses for wood, silk, vegetables, and grain.

The Impact of the Silk Road

As trade became a more important part of Central Asian life, the Iranian-speaking peoples increasingly settled in trading cities and surrounding farm villages. By the sixth century C.E., nomads originally from the Altai Mountains farther east had spread across the steppes and become the dominant pastoral group. These peoples spoke Turkic languages unrelated to the Iranian tongues. The nomads continued to live in the round, portable felt huts called yurts, or in Mongolia *gers*, that can still occasionally be seen in Central Asia, but prosperous individuals, both Turks and Iranians, built stately homes decorated with brightly

SECTION REVIEW

- The rise of the Parthian kingdom helped foster the Silk Road to meet European demand for Chinese silk and Chinese demand for horses.

- General Zhang first discovered Ferghana and then led expeditions that established the route from China through Central Asia.

- Central Asian nomads facilitated the movement of goods through their lands by providing animals and protection.

- Central Asian trading cities grew as a result of Silk Road trade.

- In addition to silk, agricultural products traveled both ways along the Silk Road.

Iranian Rider on Silk Road Camel   Glazed ceramic figurines of camels and horses are found in many Inner Asian burials of the Tang period. Most of the camel riders, like this one, have beards and big noses stereotyping people from Central Asia far to the west. Soft pointed caps first appear in images of Scythians living north of Iran. The absence of a saddle and the rider's diminutive size suggest a humorous caricature.

Werner Forman/Universal Images Group/Getty Images

colored wall paintings. The paintings show people wearing Chinese silks and Iranian brocades and riding on richly outfitted horses and camels. They also indicate an avid interest in Buddhism (discussed later in this chapter), which competed with Nestorian Christianity, Manichaeism, and Zoroastrianism in a lively and inquiring intellectual milieu.

Missionary influences exemplify the impact of foreign customs and beliefs on the peoples along the Silk Road. Military technology affords an example of the opposite phenomenon, steppe customs radiating into foreign lands. Chariot warfare and the use of mounted bowmen originated in Central Asia and spread eastward and westward through military campaigns and folk migrations that began in the second millennium B.C.E. and recurred throughout the period of the Silk Road.

Evidence of the **stirrup**, one of the most important inventions, comes first from the Kushan people who ruled northern Afghanistan in approximately the first century C.E. At first a solid bar, then a loop of leather to support the rider's big toe, and finally a device of leather and metal or wood supporting the ball of the foot, the stirrup gave riders far greater stability in the saddle—which itself was in all likelihood an earlier Central Asian invention.

stirrup Device for securing a horseman's feet, enabling him to wield weapons more effectively. First evidence of the use of stirrups was among the Kushan people of northern Afghanistan in approximately the first century C.E.

Using stirrups, a mounted warrior could supplement his bow and arrow with a long lance and charge his enemy at a gallop without fear that the impact of his attack would push him off his mount. Far to the west, the stirrup made possible the armored knights who dominated the battlefields of Europe (see Chapter 11), and it contributed to the superiority of the Tang cavalry in China (see Chapter 12).

THE INDIAN OCEAN MARITIME SYSTEM

Indian Ocean Maritime System In premodern times, a network of seaports, trade routes, and maritime culture linking countries on the rim of the Indian Ocean from Africa to Indonesia.

While a land route was established in Central Asia, a multilingual, multiethnic society of seafarers established the **Indian Ocean Maritime System**, a trade network across the Indian Ocean and the South China Sea. Although these people left few records and seldom played a visible part in the rise and fall of kingdoms and empires, they forged increasingly strong economic and social ties between the coastal lands of East Africa, southern Arabia, the Persian Gulf, India, Southeast Asia, and southern China.

This trade took place in three distinct regions: (1) In the South China Sea, Chinese and Malays (including Indonesians) dominated trade. (2) From the east coast of India to the islands of Southeast Asia, Indians and Malays were the main traders. (3) From the west coast of India to the Persian Gulf and the east coast of Africa, merchants and sailors were predominantly Persians and Arabs. However, Chinese and Malay sailors could and did voyage to East Africa, and Arab and Persian traders reached southern China.

From the time of Herodotus in the fifth century B.C.E., Greek writers regaled their readers with stories of marvelous voyages down the Red Sea into the Indian Ocean or around Africa from the west. Most often, they attributed such trips to the Phoenicians, the most fearless of Mediterranean seafarers. Occasionally a Greek appears. One such was Hippalus, a Greek ship's pilot who was said to have discovered the seasonal monsoon winds that facilitate sailing across the Indian Ocean (see Diversity and Dominance: Travel Accounts of Africa and India).

Of course, the regular, seasonal alternation of steady winds could not have remained unnoticed for thousands of years, waiting for an alert Greek to happen along. The great voyages and discoveries made before written records became common should surely be attributed to the

Travel Accounts of Africa and India

The most revealing description of ancient trade in the Indian Ocean and of the diversity and economic forces shaping the Indian Ocean trading system is found in The Periplus of the Erythraean Sea, *a sailing itinerary (*periplus *in Greek) that was composed in the first century* C.E. *by an unknown Greco-Egyptian merchant. It highlights the diversity of peoples and products from the Red Sea to the Bay of Bengal. Historians believe that the descriptions of market towns were based on firsthand experience. The following passages deal with East Africa and the coastal lands of the Indian subcontinent (see Maps 9.1 and 9.2).*

Of the designated ports on the Erythraean Sea [Indian Ocean], and the market-towns around it, the first is the Egyptian port of Mussel Harbor. To those sailing down from that place, on the right hand . . . there is Berenice. The harbors of both are at the boundary of Egypt. . . .

On the right-hand coast next below Berenice is the country of the Berbers. Along the shore are the Fish-Eaters, living in scattered caves in the narrow valleys. Further inland are the Berbers, and beyond them the Wild-flesh-Eaters and Calf-Eaters, each tribe governed by its chief; and behind them, further inland, in the country towards the west, there lies a city called Meroe.

Below the Calf-Eaters there is a little market-town on the shore . . . called Ptolemais of the Hunts, from which the hunters started for the interior under the dynasty of the Ptolemies. . . . But the place has no harbor and is reached only by small boats. . . .

Beyond this place, the coast trending toward the south, there is the Market and Cape of Spices, an abrupt promontory, at the very end of the Berber coast toward the east. . . . A sign of an approaching storm . . . is that the deep water becomes more turbid and changes its color. When this happens they all run to a large promontory called Tabae, which offers safe shelter. . . .

Beyond Tabae [lies] . . . another market-town called Opone. . . . [I]n it the greatest quantity of cinnamon is produced . . . and slaves of the better sort, which are brought to Egypt in increasing numbers . . . .

[Ships also come] from the places across this sea, from . . . Barygaza, bringing to these . . . market-towns the products of their own places; wheat, rice, clarified butter, sesame oil, cotton cloth . . . and honey from the reed called sacchari [sugar cane]. Some make the voyage especially to these market-towns, and others exchange their cargoes while sailing along the coast. This country is not subject to a King, but each market-town is ruled by its separate chief.

Beyond Opone, the shore trending more toward the south . . . this coast [the Somali region of Azania, or East Africa] is destitute of harbors . . . until the Pyralax islands [Zanzibar]. . . . [A] little to the south of south-west . . . is the island Menuthias [Madagascar], about three hundred stadia from the mainland, low and wooded, in which there are rivers and many kinds of birds and the mountain-tortoise. There are no wild beasts except the crocodiles; but there they do not attack men. In this place there are sewed boats, and canoes hollowed from single logs. . . .

Two days' sail beyond, there lies the very last market-town of the continent of Azania, which is called Rhapta [Dar es-Salaam]; which has its name from the sewed boats (*rhapton ploiarion*) . . . ; in which there is ivory in great quantity, and tortoise-shell. Along this coast live men of piratical habits, very great in stature, and under separate chiefs for each place. . . .

And these markets of Azania are the very last of the continent that stretches down on the right hand from Berenice; for beyond these places the unexplored ocean curves around toward the west, and running along by the regions to the south of Aethiopia and Libya and Africa, it mingles with the western sea. . . .

Now the whole country of India has very many rivers, and very great ebb and flow of the tides. . . . But about Barygaza [Broach] it is much greater, so that the bottom is suddenly seen, and now parts of the dry land are sea, and now it is dry where ships were sailing just before; and the rivers, under the inrush of the flood tide, when the whole force of the sea is directed against them, are driven upwards more strongly against their natural current. . . .

The country inland from Barygaza is inhabited by numerous tribes. . . . Above these is the very warlike nation of the Bactrians, who are under their own king. And Alexander, setting out from these parts, penetrated to the Ganges. . . . [T]o the present day ancient drachmae are current in Barygaza, coming from this country, bearing inscriptions in Greek letters, and the devices of those who reigned after Alexander. . . .

Inland from this place and to the east, is the city called Ozene [Ujjain]. . . . [F]rom this place are brought down all things needed for the welfare of the country about Barygaza, and many things for our trade: agate and carnelian, Indian muslins. . . .

There are imported into this market-town wine, Italian preferred, also Laodicean and Arabian; copper, tin, and lead; coral and topaz; thin clothing and inferior sorts of all kinds . . . gold and silver coin, on which there is a profit when

peoples who lived around the Indian Ocean rather than to interlopers from the Mediterranean Sea. The story of Hippalus resembles the Chinese story of General Zhang Jian, whose role in opening trade with Central Asia overshadows the anonymous contributions made by the indigenous peoples. The Chinese may indeed have learned from General Zhang and the Greeks from Hippalus, but other people played important roles anonymously.

exchanged for the money of the country. . . . And for the King there are brought into those places very costly vessels of silver, singing boys, beautiful maidens for the harem, fine wines, thin clothing of the finest weaves, and the choicest ointments. There are exported from these places [spices], ivory, agate and carnelian . . . cotton cloth of all kinds, silk cloth. . . .

Beyond Barygaza the adjoining coast extends in a straight line from north to south. . . . The inland country back from the coast toward the east comprises many desert regions and great mountains; and all kinds of wild beasts—leopards, tigers, elephants, enormous serpents, hyenas, and baboons of many sorts; and many populous nations, as far as the Ganges. . . .

This whole voyage as above described . . . they used to make in small vessels, sailing close around the shores of the gulfs; and Hippalus was the pilot who by observing the location of the ports and the conditions of the sea, first discovered how to lay his course straight across the ocean. . . .

About the following region, the course trending toward the east, lying out at sea toward the west is the island Palae-simundu, called by the ancients Taprobane [Sri Lanka]. . . . It produces pearls, transparent stones, muslins, and tortoiseshell. . . .

Beyond this, the course trending toward the north, there are many barbarous tribes, among whom are the Cirrhadae, a race of men with flattened noses, very savage; another tribe, the Bargysi; and the Horse-faces and the Long-faces, who are said to be cannibals.

After these, the course turns toward the east again, and sailing with the ocean to the right and the shore remaining beyond to the left, Ganges comes into view. . . . And just opposite this river there is an island in the ocean, the last part of the inhabited world toward the east, under the rising sun itself; it is called Chryse; and it has the best tortoise-shell of all the places on the Erythraean Sea.

After this region under the very north, the sea outside ending in a land called This, there is a very great inland city called Thinae, from which raw silk and silk yarn and silk cloth are brought on foot. . . . But the land of This is not easy of access; few men come from there, and seldom.

The Chinese traveler Xuanzang (600–664) journeyed across Inner Asia to India, making pilgrimage to Buddhist holy places and searching for Sanskrit scriptures to take back to China with him. His descriptions of the places he visited reflect his interests. The following passages come from his description of India.

Towns and Buildings

The towns and villages have inner gates; the walls are wide and high; the streets and lanes are tortuous, and the roads winding. The thoroughfares are dirty and the stalls arranged on both sides of the road with appropriate signs. Butchers, fishers, dancers, executioners, and scavengers, and so on, have their abodes without the city. In coming and going these persons are bound to keep on the left side of the road till they arrive at their homes. Their houses are surrounded by low walls, and form the suburbs. The earth being soft and muddy, the walls of the town are mostly built of brick or tiles. The towers on the walls are constructed of wood or bamboo; the houses have balconies and belvederes, which are made of wood, with a coating of lime or mortar, and covered with tiles. The different buildings have the same form as those in China: rushes, or dry branches, or tiles, or boards are used for covering them. The walls are covered with lime and mud, mixed with cow's dung for purity. At different seasons they scatter flowers about. Such are some of their different customs.

Dress and Appearance

Their clothing is not cut or fashioned; they mostly affect fresh-white garments; they esteem little those of mixed color or ornamented. The men wind their garments round their middle, then gather them under the armpits, and let them fall down across the body, hanging to the right. The robes of the women fall down to the ground; they completely cover their shoulders. They wear a little knot of hair on their crowns, and let the rest of their hair fall loose. Some of the men cut off their moustaches, and have other odd customs. . . . In North India, where the air is cold, they wear short and close-fitting garments. . . . The dress and ornaments worn by the nonbelievers are varied and mixed. Some wear peacocks' feathers; some wear as ornaments necklaces made of skull bones; some have no clothing, but go naked; some wear leaf or bark garments; some pull out their hair and cut off their moustaches; others have bushy whiskers and their hair braided on the top of their heads. The costume is not uniform, and the color, whether red or white, not constant.

QUESTIONS FOR ANALYSIS

1. **How do the differing interests of a trader and a religious pilgrim show up in what they report?**

2. **How do these narratives show the influence of the countries the authors are coming from?**

3. **Given the different viewpoints of travelers, what is the value of travel accounts as sources for history?**

Source: Samuel Beal, *Buddhist Records of the Western World, Translated from the Chinese of Hiuen Tsiang (A.D. 629)* (London: Trubner and Company, 1884; reprint Delhi: Oriental Books Reprint Corporation, 1969), 73–76.

The ships used in the Indian Ocean differed from those used in the west. Whereas Mediterranean sailors of the time of Alexander used square sails and long banks of oars to maneuver among the sea's many islands and small harbors, Indian Ocean vessels relied on roughly triangular lateen sails and normally did without oars in running before the wind on long ocean stretches. Whereas Mediterranean shipbuilders nailed their vessels together, the planks of

Indian Ocean ships were pierced, tied together with palm fiber, and caulked with bitumen. Mediterranean sailors rarely ventured out of sight of land. Indian Ocean sailors, thanks to the monsoon winds, could cover long reaches entirely at sea.

These technological differences prove that the world of the Indian Ocean developed differently than the world of the Mediterranean Sea, where the Phoenicians and Greeks established colonies that maintained contact with their home cities (see Chapters 3 and 5). The traders of the Indian Ocean, where distances were greater and contacts less frequent, seldom retained political ties with their homelands. The colonies they established were sometimes socially distinctive but rarely independent of the local political powers.

Origins of Contact and Trade

By 2000 B.C.E. Sumerian records indicate regular trade between Mesopotamia, the islands of the Persian Gulf, Oman, and the Indus Valley. However, this early trading contact broke off, and later Mesopotamian trade references mention East Africa more often than India.

A similarly early chapter in Indian Ocean history concerns migrations from Southeast Asia to Madagascar, the world's fourth largest island, situated off the southeastern coast of Africa. About two thousand years ago, people from one of the many Indonesian islands of Southeast Asia established themselves in that forested, mountainous land 6,000 miles (9,500 kilometers) from home. They could not possibly have carried enough supplies for a direct voyage across the Indian Ocean, so their route must have touched the coasts of India and southern Arabia. No physical remains of their journeys have been discovered, however.

Apparently, the sailing canoes of these people plied the seas along the increasingly familiar route for several hundred years. Settlers farmed the new land and entered into relations with Africans who found their way across the 250-mile-wide (400-kilometer-wide) Mozambique (moe-zam-BEEK) Channel around the fifth century C.E. Descendants of the seafarers preserved the language of their homeland and some of its culture, such as the cultivation of bananas, yams, and other native Southeast Asian plants. These food crops spread to mainland Africa. But the memory of their distant origins gradually faded, not to be recovered until modern times, when scholars unraveled the linguistic link between the two lands.

The Impact of Indian Ocean Trade

The demand for products from the coastal lands inspired mariners to persist in their long ocean voyages. Africa produced exotic animals, wood, and ivory. Since ivory also came from India, Mesopotamia, and North Africa, the extent of African ivory exports cannot be determined. The highlands of northern Somalia and southern Arabia grew the scrubby trees whose aromatic resins were valued as frankincense and myrrh. Pearls abounded in the Persian Gulf, and evidence of ancient copper mines has been found in Oman in southeastern Arabia. India shipped spices and manufactured goods, and more spices came from Southeast Asia, along with manufactured items, particularly pottery, obtained in trade with China. In sum, the Indian Ocean trading region had a great variety of highly valued products. Given the long distances and the comparative lack of islands, however, the volume of trade there was undoubtedly much lower than in the Mediterranean Sea.

Hellenistic South Arabian Coins These coins minted in southern Arabia around the third century B.C.E. imitate the coinage of Athens, at that time the dominant currency in the Mediterranean region. The head of the goddess Athena appears on the obverse and an owl symbolizing her wisdom on the reverse. The use of these coin designs indicates the involvement of southern Arabia in the Red Sea-Indian Ocean trading network that stretched from the Mediterranean lands to India. Philippe Maillard/akg-images

The culture of the Indian Ocean ports was often isolated from the hinterlands, particularly in the west. The coasts of the Arabian peninsula, the African side of the Red Sea, southern Iran, and northern India (today's Pakistan) were mostly barren desert. Ports in all these areas tended to be small, and many suffered from meager supplies of fresh water. Farther south in India, the monsoon provided ample water, but steep mountains cut off the coastal plain from the interior of the country. Thus few ports between Zanzibar and Sri Lanka had substantial inland populations within easy reach. The head of the Persian Gulf was one exception: ship-borne trade was possible from the port of Apologus (later called Ubulla, the precursor of modern Basra) as far north as Babylon and, from the eighth century C.E., nearby Baghdad.

By contrast, eastern India, the Malay Peninsula, and Indonesia afforded more hospitable and densely populated shores with easier access to inland populations. Though the fishers, sailors, and traders of the western Indian Ocean system supplied a long series of kingdoms and empires, none of these consumer societies became primarily maritime in orientation, as the Greeks and Phoenicians did in the Mediterranean. In contrast, seaborne trade and influence seem to have been important even to the earliest states of Southeast Asia.

In coastal areas throughout the Indian Ocean system, small groups of seafarers sometimes had a significant social impact despite their usual lack of political power. Women seldom accompanied the men on long sea voyages, so sailors and merchants often married local women in port cities. The families thus established were bilingual and bicultural. As in many other situations in world history, women played a crucial though not well-documented role as mediators between cultures. Not only did they raise their children to be more cosmopolitan than children from inland regions, but they also introduced the men to customs and attitudes that they carried with them when they returned to sea. As a consequence, the designation of specific seafarers as Persian, Arab, Indian, or Malay often conceals mixed heritages and a rich cultural diversity.

SECTION REVIEW

- The Indian Ocean Maritime System grew from the voyages of a collection of diverse seafaring traders.

- The system originated in early Mesopotamian trade routes and the migrations of Southeast Asian peoples to Madagascar.

- Unlike the Mediterranean, the Indian Ocean developed no network of colonies with home ties, but traders intermarried with indigenous peoples to create distinct cultures.

- Trade in a broad range of goods flourished.

ROUTES ACROSS THE SAHARA

trans-Saharan caravan routes
Trading network linking North Africa with sub-Saharan Africa across the Sahara.

The windswept Sahara, a desert stretching from the Red Sea to the Atlantic Ocean and broken only by the Nile River, isolates sub-Saharan Africa from the Mediterranean world (see Map 9.2). The current dryness of the Sahara dates only to about 2500 B.C.E. The period of drying out that preceded that date lasted twenty-five centuries and encompassed several cultural changes. During that time, travel between a slowly shrinking number of grassy areas was comparatively easy. However, by 300 B.C.E., scarcity of water was restricting travel to a few difficult routes initially known only to desert nomads. Trade over **trans-Saharan caravan routes**, at first only a trickle, eventually expanded into a significant stream.

Early Saharan Cultures

Sprawling sand dunes, sandy plains, and vast expanses of exposed rock make up most of the great desert. Stark and rugged mountain and highland areas separate its northern and southern portions. The cliffs and caves of these highlands, the last spots where water and grassland could be found as the climate changed, preserve rock paintings and engravings that constitute the primary evidence for early Saharan history.

Though dating is difficult, what appear to be the earliest images, left by hunters in much wetter times, include elephants, giraffes, rhinoceroses, crocodiles, and other animals that have long been extinct in the region. Overlaps in the artwork indicate that the hunting societies were gradually joined by new cultures based on cattle breeding and well adapted to the sparse grazing that remained. Domestic cattle probably originated separately in northern Africa, western Asia, and southern Pakistan. They certainly reached the Sahara before it became completely dry. The beautiful paintings of cattle and scenes of daily life seen in the Saharan rock art depict

Cattle Herders in Saharan Rock Art   These paintings represent the most artistically accomplished type of Saharan art. Herding societies of modern times living in the Sahel region south of the Sahara strongly resemble the society depicted here.

pastoral societies that bear little similarity to any in western Asia. The people seem physically akin to today's West Africans, and the customs depicted, such as dancing and wearing masks, as well as the breeds of cattle, particularly those with piebald coloring (splotches of black and white), strongly suggest later societies to the south of the Sahara. These factors support the hypothesis that some southern cultural patterns originated in the Sahara.

Overlaps in artwork also show that horse herders succeeded the cattle herders. The rock art changes dramatically in style, from the superb realism of the cattle pictures to sketchier images that are often strongly geometric. Moreover, the horses are frequently shown drawing light chariots. According to the most common theory, intrepid charioteers from the Mediterranean shore drove their flimsy vehicles across the desert and established societies in the few remaining grassy areas of the central Saharan highlands. Some scholars suggest possible chariot routes that refugees from the collapse of the Mycenaean and Minoan civilizations of Greece and Crete (see Chapter 5) might have followed deep into the desert around the twelfth century B.C.E. However, no archaeological evidence of actual chariot use in the Sahara has been discovered, and it is difficult to imagine large numbers of refugees from the politically chaotic Mediterranean region driving chariots into a waterless, trackless desert in search of a new homeland somewhere to the south.

As with the cattle herders, therefore, the identity of the Saharan horse breeders and the source of their passion for drawing chariots remain a mystery. Only with the coming of the camel is it possible to make firm connections with the Saharan nomads of today through the depiction of objects and geometric patterns still used by the veiled, blue-robed Tuareg (TWAH-reg) people of the highlands in southern Algeria, Niger, and Mali.

Some historians maintain that the Romans inaugurated an important trans-Saharan trade, but they lack firm archaeological evidence. More plausibly, Saharan trade relates to the spread of camel domestication. Supporting evidence comes from rock art, where overlaps of images imply that camel riders in desert costume constitute the latest Saharan population. The camel-oriented images are decidedly the crudest to be found in the region.

The first mention of camels in North Africa comes in a Latin text of 46 B.C.E. Since the native camels of Africa probably died out before the era of domestication, the domestic animals most

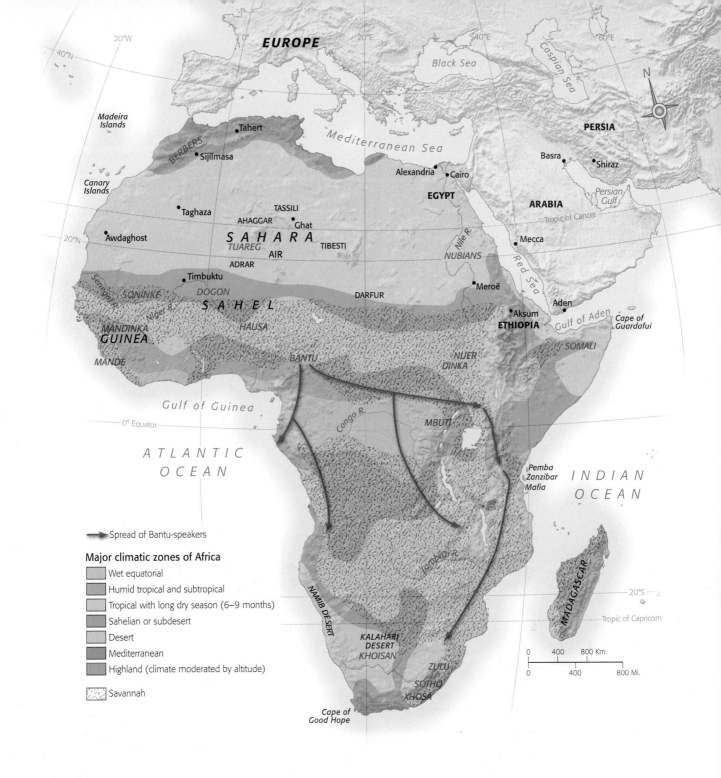

MAP 9.2 **Africa and the Trans-Saharan Trade Routes** The Sahara and the surrounding oceans isolated most of Africa from foreign contact before 1000 C.E. The Nile Valley, a few trading points on the east coast, and limited transdesert trade provided exceptions to this rule; but the dominant forms of sub-Saharan African culture originated far to the west, north of the Gulf of Guinea. © Cengage Learning

likely reached the Sahara from Arabia, probably by way of Egypt in the first millennium B.C.E. They could have been adopted by peoples farther and farther to the west, from one central Saharan highland to the next, only much later spreading northward and coming to the attention of the Romans. Camel herding made it easier for people to move away from the Saharan highlands and roam the deep desert (see Environment and Technology: Camel Saddles).

Camel Saddles

As seemingly simple a technology as saddle design can indicate a society's economic structure. The south Arabian saddle, a Tunisian example of which is shown to the right, was good for riding, and baggage could easily be tied to the wooden arches at its front. It was militarily inefficient, however, because the rider knelt on the cushion behind the camel's hump, which made it difficult to use weapons.

The north Arabian saddle was a significant improvement that came into use in the first centuries B.C.E. The two arches anchoring the front end of the south Arabian saddle were separated and greatly enlarged, one arch going in front of the hump and the other behind. This formed a solid wooden framework to which loads could easily be attached, but the placement of the prominent front and back arches seated the rider on top of the camel's hump instead of behind it and thereby gave warriors a solid seat and the advantage of height over enemy horsemen. Arabs in northern Arabia used these saddles to take control of the caravan trade through their lands.

The lightest and most efficient riding saddles, shown below, come from the southern Sahara, where personal travel and warfare took priority over trade. These excellent war saddles could not be used for baggage because they did not offer a convenient place to tie bundles.

Private collection

Fred Bavendam/Minden Pictures

Camel Saddles The militarily inefficient south Arabian saddle (above) seats the rider behind the animal's hump atop its hindquarters. The rider controls his mount by tapping its neck with a long camel stick. The Tuareg saddle (below) seats the rider over the animal's withers, leaving his hands free to wield a sword and letting him control his mount with his toes.

Trade Across the Sahara

Linkage between two different trading systems, one in the south, the other in the north, developed slowly. Southern traders concentrated on supplying salt from large deposits in the southern desert to the peoples of sub-Saharan Africa. Traders from the equatorial forest zone brought forest products, such as kola nuts (a condiment and source of caffeine) and edible palm oil, to trading centers near the desert's southern fringe. Each received the products they needed in their homelands from the other, or from the farming peoples of the **Sahel** (SAH-hel)—literally "the coast" in Arabic, the southern borderlands of the Sahara (see Map 9.2). Middlemen who were native to the Sahel played an important role in this trade, but precise historical details are lacking.

Sahel Belt south of the Sahara; literally "coastland" in Arabic.

In the north, Roman colonists supplied Italy with agricultural products, primarily wheat and olives. Surviving mosaic pavements depicting scenes from daily life show that people living on the farms and in the towns of the interior consumed Roman manufactured goods and shared Roman styles. This northern pattern began to change only in the third century C.E. with the decline of the Roman Empire, the abandonment of many Roman farms, the growth of nomadism, and a lessening of trade across the Mediterranean.

SECTION REVIEW

- Rock paintings show that early Saharan cultures included hunting societies and, in isolated areas, groups of cattle breeders.

- Later, horse and camel herders joined these groups.

- Camel-riding nomads most likely pioneered the trans-Saharan trade routes, linking North African and sub-Saharan trade networks.

SUB-SAHARAN AFRICA

sub-Saharan Africa Portion of the African continent lying south of the Sahara.

The Indian Ocean network and later trade across the Sahara provided **sub-Saharan Africa**, the portion of Africa south of the Sahara, with a few external contacts. The most important African network of cultural exchange from 300 B.C.E. to 1100 C.E., however, arose within the region and took the form of folk migration. These migrations and exchanges put in place enduring characteristics of African culture.

A Challenging Geography

Many geographic obstacles impede access to and movement within sub-Saharan Africa (see Map 9.2). The Sahara, the Atlantic and Indian Oceans, and the Red Sea form the boundaries of the region. With the exception of the Nile, a ribbon of green traversing the Sahara from south to north, the major river systems empty into oceans: the Senegal, Niger, and Zaire (zah-EER) Rivers empty into the Atlantic, and the Zambezi River empties into the Mozambique Channel of the Indian Ocean. Rapids limit the use of these rivers for navigation.

steppe An ecological region of grass- and shrub-covered plains that is treeless and too arid for agriculture.

savanna Tropical or subtropical grassland, either treeless or with occasional clumps of trees. Most extensive in sub-Saharan Africa but also present in South America.

tropical rain forest High-precipitation forest zones of the Americas, Africa, and Asia lying between the Tropic of Cancer and the Tropic of Capricorn.

Stretching over 50 degrees of latitude, sub-Saharan Africa encompasses dramatically different environments. A 4,000-mile (6,500-kilometer) trek from the southern edge of the Sahara to the Cape of Good Hope would take a traveler from the flat, semiarid **steppes** of the Sahel region to tropical **savanna** covered by long grasses and scattered forest, and then to **tropical rain forest** on the lower Niger and in the Zaire Basin. The rain forest gives way to another broad expanse of savanna, followed by more steppe and desert, and finally by a region of temperate highlands at the southern extremity, located as far south of the equator as Greece and Sicily are to its north. East-west travel is comparatively easy in the steppe and savanna regions—a caravan from Senegal to the Red Sea would have traversed a distance comparable to that of the Silk Road—but difficult in the equatorial rain-forest belt and across the mountains and deep rift valleys that abut the rain forest to the east and separate East from West Africa.

The Development of Cultural Unity

"great traditions" Historians' term for a literate, well-institutionalized complex of religious and social beliefs and practices adhered to by diverse societies over a broad geographical area.

"small traditions" Historians' term for a localized, usually nonliterate, set of customs and beliefs adhered to by a single society, often in conjunction with a "great tradition."

Cultural heritages shared by the educated elites within each region of the world—heritages that some anthropologists call "**great traditions**"—typically include a written language, common legal and belief systems, ethical codes, and other intellectual attitudes. They loom large in written records as traditions that rise above the diversity of local customs and beliefs commonly distinguished as "**small traditions**."

By the year 1 C.E. sub-Saharan Africa had become a distinct cultural region, though one not shaped by imperial conquest or characterized by a shared elite culture, a "great tradition." The cultural unity of sub-Saharan Africa rested on similar characteristics shared to varying degrees by many popular cultures, or "small traditions." These had developed during the region's long period of isolation from the rest of the world after the drying up of the Sahara and had been refined, renewed, and interwoven by repeated episodes of migration and social interaction. Historians know little about this complex prehistory beyond what archaeology indicates for the beginnings of ironworking and the spread of domesticated grains, such as pearl millet (from Mali) and teff (from Ethiopia), around the third millennium B.C.E. Thus, to a greater degree than in other regions, they call on anthropological descriptions, oral history, and comparatively late records of various "small traditions" to reconstruct the broad outlines of cultural formation.

Sub-Saharan Africa's cultural unity is less immediately apparent than its diversity. By one estimate, Africa is home to two thousand distinct languages, many corresponding to social and belief systems endowed with distinctive rituals and cosmologies. There are likewise numerous food production systems, ranging from hunting and gathering—very differently carried out by the Mbuti (m-BOO-tee) Pygmies of the equatorial rain forest and the Khoisan (KOI-sahn) peoples of the southwestern deserts—to the cultivation of bananas, yams, and other root crops in forest clearings and of sorghum, originally from Egypt, and millet in the savanna lands. Pastoral societies, particularly those depending on cattle, display somewhat less diversity across the Sahel and savanna belt from Senegal to Kenya. Equatorial regions have distinctive breeds of dwarf goats that are resistant to tsetse fly infection.

Sub-Saharan Africa covered a larger and more diverse area than any other cultural region in the first millennium C.E. and had a lower overall population density. Thus societies and polities had ample room to form and reform, and a substantial amount of space separated different groups. The contacts that did occur did not last long enough to produce rigid cultural uniformity.

In addition, for centuries external conquerors could not penetrate the region's natural barriers and impose a uniform culture. The Egyptians occupied Nubia, and some traces of Egyptian influence appear in Saharan rock art farther west, but the Nile cataracts and the vast swampland in the Nile's upper reaches blocked movement farther south. The Romans sent expeditions against pastoral peoples living in the Libyan Sahara but could not incorporate them into the Roman world. Not until the nineteenth century did outsiders gain control of the continent and begin the process of establishing an elite culture—that of European imperialism.

African Cultural Characteristics

European travelers who got to know the sub-Saharan region well in the nineteenth and twentieth centuries observed broad commonalities underlying African life and culture. In agriculture, the common technique was cultivation by hoe and digging stick. Plows were never used despite an abundance of cattle in the Sahel. Musically, different groups of Africans played many instruments, especially types of drums, but common features, particularly in rhythm, gave African music as a whole a distinctive character. Music played an important role in social rituals, as did dancing and wearing masks, which often showed great artistry in their design.

African kingdoms varied, but kingship displayed common features, most notably the ritual isolation of the king himself. Fixed social categories—age groupings, kinship divisions, distinct gender roles and relations, and occupational groupings—also show resemblances from one region to another, even in societies too small to organize themselves into kingdoms. Though not hierarchical, these categories played a role similar to the divisions between noble, commoner, and slave prevalent where kings ruled.

Some historians hypothesize that these common cultural features emanated from the peoples who once occupied the southern Sahara. In Paleolithic times, periods of dryness alternated with periods of wetness as the Ice Age that locked up much of the world's fresh water in glaciers and icecaps came and went. When European glaciers receded with the waning of the Ice Age, a storm belt brought increased wetness to the Saharan region. Rushing rivers scoured deep canyons. Now filled with fine sand, those canyons are easily visible on flights over the southern parts of the desert. As the glaciers receded farther, the storm belt moved northward to Europe, and dryness set in gradually after 5000 B.C.E. As a consequence, runs the hypothesis, the region's population migrated southward, becoming increasingly concentrated in the Sahel, which may have been the initial incubation center for Pan-African cultural patterns.

Increasing dryness and the resulting difficulty in supporting the population would have driven some people out of this core into more sparsely settled lands to the east, west, and south. In a parallel development farther to the east, migration away from the growing aridity of the desert seems to have contributed to the settling of the Nile Valley and the emergence of the Old Kingdom of Egypt (see Chapter 2). The archaeological site of Nabta Playa **(NEB-tuh PLY-uh)** in the totally barren desert west of the Nile in southern Egypt marks a stage in this process. Originally cattle herders around a lake in the tenth millennium B.C.E., the local population had developed large villages with deep wells, sorghum and millet cultivation, and sheep and goat herding by the seventh millennium. The fifth millennium witnessed their construction of an astronomically oriented ring of stones two thousand years older than Stonehenge, along with a cattle cult featuring animals buried in stone-built chambers. The excavators see a likely connection between that cult and later cattle worship in dynastic Egypt.

The Advent of Iron and the Bantu Migrations

Archaeology confirms that agriculture had become common between the equator and the Sahara by the early second millennium B.C.E. It then spread southward, displacing hunting and gathering as a way of life. Moreover, botanical evidence indicates that banana trees, probably introduced to southeastern Africa from Southeast Asia, made their way north and west, retracing in the opposite direction the presumed migration routes of early agriculturists.

Traces of copper mining appear in the Sahara from the early first millennium B.C.E. Copper appears in the Niger Valley somewhat later and in the Central African copper belt after 400 C.E. Most important of all, iron smelting began in northern sub-Saharan Africa in the early first millennium C.E. and spread southward from there.

Many historians believe that the secret of smelting iron, which requires very high temperatures, was discovered only once, by the Hittites of Anatolia (modern Turkey) around 1500 B.C.E. (see Chapter 3). If that is the case, it is hard to explain how iron smelting reached sub-Saharan Africa. The earliest evidence of ironworking from the kingdom of Meroë, situated on the upper Nile and in cultural contact with Egypt, is no earlier than the evidence from West Africa (northern Nigeria). Even less plausible than the Nile Valley as a route of technological diffusion is the idea of a spread southward from Phoenician settlements in North Africa, since archaeological evidence has failed to substantiate the vague Greek and Latin accounts of Phoenician excursions to the south.

A more plausible scenario focuses on Africans' discovering for themselves how to smelt iron. Some historians suggest that they might have done so while firing pottery in kilns. No firm evidence exists to prove or disprove this theory.

Linguistic analysis provides the strongest evidence of extensive contacts among sub-Saharan Africans in the first millennium C.E.—and offers suggestions about the spread of iron. More than three hundred languages spoken south of the equator belong to the branch of the Niger-Congo family known as **Bantu**, after the word meaning "people" in most of the languages.

Bantu Collective name of a large group of sub-Saharan African languages and of the peoples speaking these languages.

The distribution of the Bantu languages both north and south of the equator is consistent with a divergence beginning in the first millennium B.C.E. By comparing core words common to most of the languages, linguists have drawn some conclusions about the original Bantu-speakers, whom they call "proto-Bantu." These people engaged in fishing, using canoes, nets, lines, and hooks. They lived in permanent villages on the edge of the rain forest, where they grew yams and grains and harvested wild palm nuts from which they pressed oil. They possessed domesticated goats, dogs, and perhaps other animals. They made pottery and cloth. Linguists surmise that the proto-Bantu homeland was near the modern boundary of Nigeria and Cameroon.

Because the presumed home of the proto-Bantu lies near the known sites of early iron smelting, migration by Bantu-speakers seems a likely mechanism for the southward spread of iron. The migrants probably used iron axes and hoes to hack out forest clearings and plant crops. According to this scenario, their actions would have established an economic basis for new societies capable of sustaining much denser populations than could earlier societies dependent on hunting and gathering alone. Thus the period from 500 B.C.E. to 1000 C.E. saw a substantial transfer of Bantu traditions and practices southward, eastward, and westward and their transformation, through intermingling with preexisting societies, into Pan-African traditions and practices.

SECTION REVIEW

- An environmentally diverse region, sub-Saharan Africa includes many barriers to travel and communication.

- Sub-Saharan Africa achieved a cultural unity of similar "small traditions."

- Shared characteristics include agricultural methods, approaches to music, forms of kingship, and fixed social categories.

- The likely mechanism of this unity was the Bantu migrations, which were also responsible for the spread of iron smelting throughout sub-Saharan Africa.

THE SPREAD OF IDEAS

Ideas, like social customs, religious attitudes, and artistic styles, can spread along trade routes and through folk migrations. In both cases, documenting the dissemination of ideas, particularly in preliterate societies, poses a difficult historical problem.

Ideas and Material Evidence

Historians know about some ideas only through the survival of written sources. Other ideas do not depend on writing but are inherent in material objects studied by archaeologists and anthropologists. Customs surrounding the eating of pork are a case in point. Scholars disagree about whether pigs became domestic in only one place, from which the practice of pig keeping spread elsewhere, or whether several peoples hit on the same idea at different times and in different places.

Southeast Asia was an important early center of pig domestication. Anthropological studies tell us that the eating of pork became highly ritualized in this area and that it was sometimes allowed only on ceremonial occasions. On the other side of the Indian Ocean, wild swine were common in the Nile swamps of ancient Egypt. There, too, pigs took on a sacred role, being associated with the evil god Set, and eating them was prohibited. The biblical prohibition on the Israelites' eating pork, echoed later by the Muslims, probably came from Egypt in the second millennium B.C.E.

In a third locale in eastern Iran, an archaeological site dating from the third millennium B.C.E. provides evidence of another religious taboo relating to pork. Although the area around the site was swampy and home to many wild pigs, not a single pig bone has been found. Yet small pig figurines seem to have been used as symbolic religious offerings, and the later Iranian religion associates the boar with an important god.

What accounts for the apparent connection between domestic pigs and religion in these far-flung areas? There is no way of knowing. It has been hypothesized that pigs were first domesticated in Southeast Asia by people who had no herd animals—sheep, goats, cattle, or horses—and who relied on fish for most of their animal protein. The pig therefore became a special animal to them. The practice of pig herding, along with religious beliefs and rituals associated with the consumption of pork, could conceivably have spread from Southeast Asia along the maritime routes of the Indian Ocean, eventually reaching Iran and Egypt. But no evidence survives to support this hypothesis. In this case, therefore, material evidence can only hint at the spread of religious ideas, leaving the door open for other explanations.

A more certain example of objects' indicating the spread of an idea is the practice of hammering a carved die onto a piece of precious metal and using the resulting coin as a medium of exchange. From its origin in the Lydian kingdom in Anatolia in the first millennium B.C.E. (see Chapter 5), the idea of trading by means of struck coinage spread rapidly to Europe, North Africa, and India. Was the low-value copper coinage of China, made by pouring molten metal into a mold, also inspired by this practice from far away? It may have been, but it might also derive from indigenous Chinese metalworking. There is no way to be sure.

The Spread of Buddhism

While material objects associated with religious beliefs and rituals are important indicators of the spread of spiritual ideas, written sources deal with the spread of today's major religions. Buddhism grew to become, with Christianity and Islam (see Chapter 10), one of the most popular and widespread religions in the world. In all three cases, the religious ideas spread without dependency on a single ethnic or kinship group.

King Ashoka, the Mauryan ruler of India, and Kanishka, the greatest king of the Kushans of northern Afghanistan, promoted Buddhism between the third century B.C.E. and the second century C.E. However, monks, missionaries, and pilgrims who crisscrossed India, followed the Silk Road, or took ships on the Indian Ocean brought the Buddha's teachings to Southeast Asia, China, Korea, and ultimately Japan (see Map 9.1).

The Chinese pilgrim Faxian (fah-shee-en) (died between 418 and 423 C.E.) left a written account of his travels. Faxian began his trip in the company of a Chinese envoy to an unspecified ruler or people in Central Asia. After traveling from one Buddhist site to another across Afghanistan and India, he reached Sri Lanka, a Buddhist land, where he lived for two years. He

Gandharan Sculpture The art of Gandhara in northwest Pakistan featured Hellenistic styles and techniques borrowed from the cities founded by Alexander the Great in Afghanistan. Though much Gandharan art is Buddhist in spirit, this fourth-century C.E. image of a flower-bearer is strongly Greek in the naturalistic treatment of the head and left arm. Erich Lessing/Art Resource, NY

then embarked for China on a merchant ship with two hundred men aboard. A storm drove the ship to Java, which he chose not to describe since it was Hindu rather than Buddhist. After five months ashore, Faxian finally reached China on another ship.

Less reliable accounts make reference to missionaries traveling to Syria, Egypt, and Macedonia, as well as to Southeast Asia. One of Ashoka's sons allegedly led a band of missionaries to Sri Lanka. Later, his sister brought a company of nuns there, along with a branch of the sacred Bo tree under which the Buddha had received enlightenment. At the same time, there are reports of other monks traveling to Burma, Thailand, and Sumatra. Ashoka's missionaries may also have reached Tibet by way of trade routes across the Himalayas.

The different lands that received the story and teachings of the Buddha preserved or adapted them in different ways. Theravada Buddhism, "Teachings of the Elder," was centered in Sri Lanka. Holding closely to the Buddha's earliest teachings, it maintained that the goal of religion, available only to monks, is *nirvana*, the total absence of suffering and the end of the cycle of rebirth (see Chapter 7). This teaching contrasted with Mahayana, or "Great Vehicle" Buddhism, in later centuries the dominant form of the religion in East Asia, which stressed the goal of becoming a *bodhisattva*, a person who attains nirvana but chooses to remain in human company to help and guide others.

The Spread of Christianity

Armenia One of the earliest Christian kingdoms, situated in eastern Anatolia and the western Caucasus and occupied by speakers of the Armenian language.

Ethiopia East African highland nation lying east of the Nile River.

The post-Roman development of Christianity in Europe is discussed in Chapter 11. The Christian faith enjoyed an earlier spread in Asia and Africa before its confrontation with Islam (described in Chapter 10). Jerusalem in Palestine, Antioch in Syria, and Alexandria in Egypt became centers of Christian authority soon after the crucifixion, but the spread of Christianity to Armenia and Ethiopia illustrates the connections between religion, trade, and imperial politics.

Situated in eastern Anatolia (modern Turkey), **Armenia** served recurrently as a battleground between Iranian states to the south and east and Mediterranean states to the west. Each imperial power wanted to control this region so close to the frontier where Silk Road traders met their Mediterranean counterparts. In Parthian times, Armenia's kings favored Zoroastrianism. The invention of an Armenian alphabet in the early fifth century opened the way to a wider spread of Christianity. The Iranians did not give up domination easily, but within a century the Armenian Apostolic Church had become the center of Armenian cultural life.

Far to the south Christians similarly sought to outflank Iran. The Christian emperors in Constantinople (see Chapter 6) sent missionaries along the Red Sea trade route to seek converts in Yemen and **Ethiopia**. In the fourth century C.E. a Syrian philosopher traveling with two young relatives sailed to India. On the way back the ship docked at a Red Sea port occupied by Ethiopians from the prosperous kingdom of Aksum. Being then at odds with the Romans, the Ethiopians killed everyone on board except the two boys, Aedisius—who later narrated this story—and Frumentius. Impressed by their learning, the king made the former his cupbearer and the latter his treasurer and secretary.

When the king died, his wife urged Frumentius to govern Aksum on her behalf and that of her infant son, Ezana. As regent,

Werner Forman/Art Resource, NY

Stele of Aksum   This 70-foot (21-meter) stone is the tallest remnant of a field of steles, or standing stones, marking the tombs of Aksumite kings. The carvings of doors, windows, and beam ends imitate common features of Aksumite architecture, suggesting that each stele symbolized a multistory royal palace. The largest steles date from the fourth century C.E.

SECTION REVIEW

- Material evidence can only offer hints about the spread of some ideas; it cannot completely explain the connection between pigs and religion and the use of coins in different parts of the world.

- Material and documentary evidence show the spread of Buddhism from India along the land and sea trade routes to elsewhere in Asia, with some areas adopting Theravada Buddhism and others Mahayana Buddhism.

- Christianity spread through a combination of trade and imperial politics, with significant Christian societies emerging in Armenia and Ethiopia.

Frumentius sought out Roman Christians among the merchants who visited the country and helped them establish Christian communities. When he became king, Ezana, who may have become a Christian, permitted Aedisius and Frumentius to return to Syria. The patriarch of Alexandria, on learning about the progress of Christianity in Aksum, elevated Frumentius to the rank of bishop, though he had not previously been a clergyman, and sent him back to Ethiopia as the first leader of its church.

The spread of Christianity into Nubia, the land south of Egypt along the Nile River, proceeded from Ethiopia rather than Egypt. Politically and economically, Ethiopia became a power at the western end of the Indian Ocean trading system, occasionally even extending its influence across the Red Sea and asserting itself in Yemen (see Map 9.1).

CONCLUSION

Exchange facilitated by the early long-distance trading systems differed in many ways from the ebb and flow of culture, language, and custom that folk migrations brought about. Transportable goods and livestock and ideas about new technologies and agricultural products sometimes worked great changes on the landscape and in people's lives. But nothing resembling the commonality of African cultural features observed south of the Sahara can be attributed to the societies involved in the Silk Road, Indian Ocean, or trans-Saharan exchanges. Few people were directly involved in these complex social systems of travel and trade compared with the populations with whom they were brought into contact, and their lifestyles as pastoral nomads or seafarers isolated them still more. Communities of traders contributed to this isolation by their reluctance to share knowledge with people who might become commercial competitors.

The Bantu, however, if current theories are correct, spread far and wide in sub-Saharan Africa with the deliberate intent of settling and implanting a lifestyle based on iron implements and agriculture. The metallurgical skills and agricultural techniques they brought with them permitted much denser habitation and helped ensure that the languages of the immigrants would supplant those of their hunting and gathering predecessors. Where the trading systems encouraged diversity by introducing new products and ideas, the Bantu migrations brought a degree of cultural dominance that strongly affected later African history.

An apparent exception to the generalization that trading systems have less impact than folk migrations on patterns of dominance lies in the intangible area of ideas. Christianity and Buddhism both spread along trade routes, at least to some degree. Each instance of spread, however, gave rise to new forms of cultural diversity even as overall doctrinal unity made these religions dominant. As "great traditions," the new faiths based on conversion linked priests, monks, nuns, and religious scholars across vast distances. However, these same religions merged with myriad "small traditions" to provide for the social and spiritual needs of peoples living in many lands under widely varying circumstances.

KEY TERMS

Silk Road p. 224

Parthians p. 224

stirrup p. 227

Indian Ocean Maritime
System p. 227

trans-Saharan caravan
routes p. 231

Sahel p. 234

sub-Saharan Africa p. 235

steppe p. 235

savanna p. 235

tropical rain forest p. 235

"great traditions" p. 235

"small traditions" p. 235

Bantu p. 237

Armenia p. 239

Ethiopia p. 239

SUGGESTED READING

Ajayi, J. F. A., and Michael Crowder. *A History of West Africa*, vol. 1. 1976. A broad survey.

Bulliet, Richard W. *The Camel and the Wheel*. 1975. Deals with camel use in the Middle East, along the Silk Road, and in North Africa and the Sahara.

Chaudhuri, K. N. *Trade and Civilization in the Indian Ocean: An Economic History from the Rise of Islam to 1750*. 1985. First volume of a comprehensive history.

Curtin, Philip D. *Cross-Cultural Trade in World History*. 1985. A broad and suggestive overview on cross-cultural exchange.

Ehret, Christopher. *An African Classical Age: Eastern and Southern Africa in World History, 1000 B.C. to A.D. 400*. 2001. A historical survey.

Foltz, Richard. *Religions of the Silk Road*. 1999. An excellent brief introduction covering Buddhism, Zoroastrianism, and Islam.

Fowden, Garth. *Empire to Commonwealth: Consequences of Monotheism in Late Antiquity*. 1993. A history of early Christianity placing special stress on Africa and Asia.

Franck, Irene M., and David M. Brownstone. *The Silk Road: A History*. 1986. A readable overview.

Jettmar, Karl. *Art of the Steppes*, rev. ed. 1967. A well-illustrated introduction to early Central Asia.

Lattimore, Owen. *The Desert Road to Turkestan*. 1928. Gives a first-person account of traveling by camel caravan.

Lhote, Henri. *The Search for the Tassili Frescoes: The Story of the Prehistoric Rock-Paintings of the Sahara*. 1959. A well-illustrated account of discovering Saharan rock art.

Maquet, Jacques. *Africanity: The Cultural Unity of Black Africa*. 1972. An interpretation informed by anthropological insights.

Rolle, Renate. *The World of the Scythians*. 1989. Early evidence of the lifestyles of Central Asian nomads.

Toussaint, August. *History of the Indian Ocean*. 1966. A readable but sketchy historical overview.

Villiers, Alan. *Sons of Sinbad*. 1940. Recounts what it was like to sail between East Africa and the Persian Gulf.

CourseMate Go to the History CourseMate website for primary source links, study tools, and review materials for this chapter.
www.cengagebrain.com

CHAPTER

10

Chapter Outline

The Sasanid Empire, 224–651
➤ *How did the traditions and religious views of pre-Islamic peoples become integrated into the culture shaped by Islam?*

The Origins of Islam
➤ *How did the Muslim community of the time of Muhammad differ from the society that developed after the Arab conquests?*

The Rise and Fall of the Caliphate, 632–1258
➤ *Was the Baghdad caliphate really the high point of Muslim civilization?*

Islamic Civilization
➤ *How did regional diversity affect the development of Islamic civilization?*

Conclusion

- **DIVERSITY + DOMINANCE**   Secretaries, Turks, and Beggars
- **ENVIRONMENT + TECHNOLOGY**   Chemistry
- **MATERIAL CULTURE**   Head Coverings

Baghdad Bookstore   With the advent of papermaking, manufacturing books became increasingly common and inexpensive. As a result, bookstores also became more common. Notice how books are shelved on their sides in wall cubicles.

The Sasanid Empire and the Rise of Islam, 200–1200

Knowledge of papermaking, which spread from China to the Middle East after Arab conquests in the seventh century C.E. established an Islamic caliphate stretching from Spain to Central Asia, provided a medium that was superior to papyrus and parchment and well suited to a variety of purposes. Maps, miniature paintings, and, of course, books became increasingly common and inexpensive. With cheaper books came bookstores, and one of the most informative manuscripts of the period of the Islamic caliphate is a *Fihrist*, or descriptive catalogue, of the books sold at one bookstore in Baghdad.

Abu al-Faraj Muhammad al-Nadim, a man with good connections at the caliph's court, compiled the catalogue, though his father probably founded the bookstore. Its latest entry dates to ca. 990, al-Nadim's death date. Superbly educated, al-Nadim wrote such well-informed comments on books and authors that his catalogue presents a detailed survey of the intellectual world of Baghdad.

The first of the *Fihrist*'s ten books deals with Arabic language and sacred scriptures: the Quran, the Torah, and the Gospel. The second covers Arabic grammar, and the third writings from people connected with the caliph's court: historians, government officials, singers, jesters, and the ruler's boon companions. *Al-Nadim* means "book companion," so it is assumed that he knew this milieu well. After dealing with Arabic poetry, Muslim sects, and Islamic law in Books 3 through 6, he comes to Greek philosophy, science, and medicine in Book 7.

Most things we would find today in a bookstore are relegated to the final three chapters. Book 8 divides into three sections, the first being "Story Tellers and Stories." Here he lists a Persian book called *A Thousand Stories*, which in translation became *The Arabian Nights*. Al-Nadim's version no longer survives. The collection we have today comes from a manuscript written five hundred years later.

Then come books about "Exorcists, Jugglers, and Magicians," followed by "Miscellaneous Subjects and Fables." These include books on "Freckles, Twitching, Moles, and Shoulders," "Horsemanship, Bearing of Arms, the Implements of War," "Veterinary Surgery," "Birds of Prey, Sport with Them and Medical Care of Them," "Interpretation of Dreams," "Perfume," "Cooked Food," "Poisons," and "Amulets and Charms."

Non-Muslim sects and foreign lands—India, Indochina, and China—fill Book 9, leaving Book 10 for a few final notes on philosophers not mentioned previously.

All together, the thousands of titles and authors commented on by al-Nadim provide both a panorama of what interested book buyers in tenth-century Baghdad and a saddening picture of how profound the loss of knowledge has been since that glorious era.

THE SASANID EMPIRE, 224–651

Sasanid Empire Iranian empire, established around 224, with a capital in Ctesiphon, Mesopotamia. The Sasanid emperors established Zoroastrianism as the state religion. Islamic Arab armies overthrew the empire around 651.

The rise in the third century of a new Iranian state, the **Sasanid (SAH-suh-nid) Empire**, continued the old rivalry between Rome and the Parthians along the Euphrates frontier. However, behind this façade of continuity, a social and economic transformation took place that set the stage for a new and powerful religiopolitical movement: Islam.

Politics and Society

Ardashir, whose dynasty takes its name from an ancestor named Sasan, defeated the Parthians around 224 and established the Sasanid kingdom. To the west, the new rulers confronted the Romans, whom later historians frequently refer to as the Byzantines after about 330. Along their desert Euphrates frontier, the Sasanids subsidized nomadic Arab chieftains to protect their empire from invasion (the Byzantines did the same with Arabs on their Jordanian desert frontier). Arab pastoralists farther to the south remained isolated and independent. The rival empires launched numerous attacks on each other across that frontier between the 340s and 628. In times of peace, however, exchange between the empires flourished, allowing goods transported over the Silk Road to enter the zone of Mediterranean trade.

The mountains and plateaus of Iran proper formed the Sasanids' political hinterland, often ruled by the cousins of the shah (king) or by powerful families descending from the pre-Sasanid Parthian nobility. Cities there were small walled communities that served more as military strong-points than as centers of population and production. Society revolved around a local aristocracy that lived on rural estates and cultivated the arts of hunting, feasting, and war just like the warriors described in the sagas of ancient kings and heroes sung at their banquets. Despite the dominance of powerful aristocratic families, long-lasting political fragmentation of the medieval European variety did not develop (see Chapter 11). Also, although many nomads lived in the mountain and desert regions, no folk migration took place comparable to that of the Germanic peoples who defeated Roman armies and established kingdoms in formerly Roman territory from about the third century C.E. onward. The Sasanid and Byzantine Empires generally maintained central control of imperial finances and military power and found effective ways of integrating frontier peoples as mercenaries or caravaneers.

The Silk Road brought new products to Mesopotamia, some of which became part of the agricultural landscape. Sasanid farmers pioneered in planting sugar cane, rice, citrus trees, eggplants, and other crops adopted from India and China. Although the acreage devoted to new crops increased slowly, these products became important consumption and trade items during the succeeding Islamic period.

Sasanid Silver Plate with Gold Decoration The Sasanid aristocracy, based in the countryside, invested part of its wealth in silver plates and vessels. This image of a Sasanid king hunting on horseback also reflects a favorite aristocratic pastime. Erich Lessing /Art Resource, NY

CHRONOLOGY

	The Arab Lands	Iran and Central Asia
200		224–651 Sasanid Empire
	570–632 Life of the Prophet Muhammad	
600	634 Conquests of Iraq and Syria commence	
	639–642 Conquest of Egypt by Arabs	
	656–661 Ali caliph; first civil war	
	661–750 Umayyad Caliphate rules from Damascus	
700	711 Berbers and Arabs invade Spain from North Africa	711 Arabs capture Sind in India
		747 Abbasid revolt begins in Khurasan
	750 Beginning of Abbasid Caliphate	
	755 Umayyad state established in Spain	
	776–809 Caliphate of Harun al-Rashid	
800	835–892 Abbasid capital moved from Baghdad to Samarra	875 Independent Samanid state founded in Bukhara
900	909 Fatimids seize North Africa, found Shi'ite Caliphate	
	929 Abd al-Rahman III declares himself caliph in Córdoba	
	945 Shi'ite Buyids take control in Baghdad	945 Buyids from northern Iran take control of Abbasid Caliphate
	969 Fatimids conquer Egypt	
1000	1055 Seljuk Turks take control in Baghdad	1036 Beginning of Turkish Seljuk rule in Khurasan
	1099 First Crusade captures Jerusalem	
	1171 Fall of Fatimid Egypt	
	1187 Saladin recaptures Jerusalem	
	1250 Mamluks control Egypt	
	1258 Mongols sack Baghdad and end Abbasid Caliphate	
	1260 Mamluks defeat Mongols at Ain Jalut	

Religion and Empire

The Sasanids established their Zoroastrian faith (see Chapter 5), which the Parthians had not particularly stressed, as a state religion similar to Christianity in the Byzantine Empire (see Chapter 11), though other faiths may have competed effectively in eastern Iran. The proclamation of Christianity and Zoroastrianism as official faiths marked the fresh emergence of religion as an instrument of politics both within and between the empires, setting a precedent for the subsequent rise of Islam as the focus of a political empire.

Both Zoroastrianism and Christianity practiced intolerance. A late-third-century inscription in Iran boasts of the persecutions of Christians, Jews, and Buddhists carried out by the Zoroastrian high priest. Yet sizable Christian and Jewish communities remained, especially in Mesopotamia. Similarly, from the fourth century onward, councils of Christian bishops declared many theological beliefs heretical—so unacceptable that they were un-Christian.

Christians then became pawns in the political rivalry with the Byzantines and were sometimes persecuted, sometimes patronized, by the Sasanid kings. In 431 a council of bishops called by the Byzantine emperor declared the Nestorian Christians heretics for overemphasizing the humanness of Christ. The Nestorians believed that human characteristics and divinity coexisted in Jesus and that Mary was not the mother of God, as many other Christians maintained, but the mother of the human Jesus. After the bishops' ruling, the Nestorians sought refuge under the Sasanid shah and eventually extended their missionary activities along the Central Asian trade routes.

In the third century a preacher named Mani founded a new religion in Mesopotamia: Manichaeism. Mani preached a dualist faith—a struggle between Good and Evil—theologically derived from Zoroastrianism. Although at first he enjoyed the favor of the shah, he and many of his followers were martyred in 276. However, his religion survived and spread widely. Nestorian missionaries in Central Asia competed with Manichaean missionaries for converts. In later centuries, the term *Manichaean* was applied to all sorts of beliefs about a cosmic struggle between Good and Evil.

The Arabs became enmeshed in this web of religious conflict. The border protectors subsidized by the Byzantines adopted a Monophysite theology, which emphasized Christ's divine nature; the allies of the Sasanids, the Nestorian faith. Through them, knowledge of Christianity penetrated deeper into the Arabian peninsula during the fifth and sixth centuries.

Religion permeated all aspects of community life. Most subjects of the Byzantine emperors and Sasanid shahs identified themselves first and foremost as members of a religious community. Their schools and law courts were religious. They looked on priests, monks, rabbis, and the Zoroastrian mobads (priests officiating in fire temples) as moral guides in daily life. Most books discussed religious subjects. In some areas, religious leaders represented their flocks even in such secular matters as tax collection.

SECTION REVIEW

- Originating in southern Iran, the Sasanids overthrew the Parthians and continued their predecessors' rivalry with Rome.

- Sasanid farmers pioneered the cultivation of Silk Road crops.

- Sasanid kings made Zoroastrianism the state religion, and other religions, particularly Christianity, experienced both toleration and persecution.

- Silk Road trade encouraged movements of peoples in Iran and Central Asia, as well as the exchange of religious ideas and military technology.

THE ORIGINS OF ISLAM

The Arabs of 600 C.E. lived exclusively in the Arabian peninsula and on the desert fringes of Syria, Jordan, and Iraq. Along their Euphrates frontier, the Sasanids subsidized nomadic Arab chieftains to protect their empire from invasion. The Byzantines did the same with Arabs on their Jordanian frontier. Arab pastoralists farther to the south remained isolated and independent, seldom engaging the attention of the shahs and emperors. It was in these interior Arabian lands that the religion of Islam took form.

The Arabian Peninsula Before Muhammad

Throughout history more people living on the Arabian peninsula have subsisted as farmers than as pastoral nomads. Farming villages supported the comparatively dense population of Yemen, where abundant rainfall waters the highlands during the spring monsoon. Small inlets along the southern coast favored fishing and trading communities. The enormous sea of sand known as the "Empty Quarter" isolated many southern regions from the Arabian interior. In the seventh century, most people in southern Arabia knew more about Africa, India, and the Persian Gulf than about the forbidding interior and the scattered camel- and sheep-herding nomads who lived there.

The Arab pastoralists inhabiting the desert between Syria and Mesopotamia supplied camels and guides and played a significant role as merchants and organizers of caravans. The militarily efficient North Arabian camel saddle (see Chapter 9, Environment and Technology: Camel Saddles), developed around the third century B.C.E., provided another key to Arab prosperity. The Arabs used it to take control of the caravan trade in their territories and thereby became so important as suppliers of animal power, even in agricultural districts, that wheeled vehicles— mostly ox carts and horse-drawn chariots—had all but disappeared by the sixth century C.E.

Caravan trading provided a rare link among peoples. Nomads derived income from providing camels, guides, and safe passage to merchants bringing the primary product of the south, the aromatic resins frankincense and myrrh, to northern customers. Return caravans brought manufactured products from Mesopotamia and Syria.

Arabs who accompanied the caravans became familiar with the cultures and lifestyles of the Sasanid and Byzantine Empires, and many of those who pastured their herds on the imperial frontiers adopted one form or another of Christianity. Even in the interior deserts, Semitic

MAP 10.1 **Early Expansion of Muslim Rule** Arab conquests of the first Islamic century brought vast territory under Muslim rule, but conversion to Islam proceeded slowly. In most areas outside the Arabian peninsula, the only region where Arabic was then spoken, conversion did not accelerate until the third century after the conquest. © Cengage Learning

polytheism, with its worship of natural forces and celestial bodies, began to encounter more sophisticated religions.

Mecca City in western Arabia; birthplace of the Prophet Muhammad and ritual center of the Islamic religion.

Mecca, a late-blooming caravan city, occupies a barren mountain valley halfway between Yemen and Syria and somewhat inland from the Red Sea coast (see Map 10.1). A nomadic kin group known as the Quraysh (koo-RAYSH) settled in Mecca in the fifth century and assumed control of trade. Mecca rapidly achieved a measure of prosperity, partly because it was too far from Byzantine Syria, Sasanid Iraq, and Ethiopian-controlled Yemen for them to attack it.

A cubical shrine with idols inside called the Ka'ba (KAH-buh), a holy well called Zamzam, and a sacred precinct surrounding the two wherein killing was prohibited contributed to the emergence of Mecca as a pilgrimage site. Some Meccans associated the shrine with stories known to Jews and Christians. They regarded Abraham (Ibrahim in Arabic) as the builder of the Ka'ba, and they identified a site outside Mecca as the location where God asked Abraham to sacrifice his son. The son was not Isaac (Ishaq in Arabic), the son of Sarah, but Ishmael (Isma'il in Arabic), the son of Hagar, cited in the Bible as the forefather of the Arabs.

Muhammad in Mecca and Medina

Muhammad Arab prophet (570–632 C.E.); founder of religion of Islam.

Born in Mecca in 570, **Muhammad** grew up an orphan in the house of his uncle. He engaged in trade and married a Quraysh widow named Khadija (kah-DEE-juh), whose caravan interests he superintended. Their son died in childhood, but several daughters survived. Around 610 Muhammad began meditating at night in the mountainous terrain around Mecca. During one night vigil, known to later tradition as the "Night of Power and Excellence," a being whom Muhammad later understood to be the angel Gabriel (Jibra'il in Arabic) spoke to him:

> *Proclaim! In the name of your Lord who created. Created man from a clot of congealed blood. Proclaim! And your Lord is the Most Bountiful. He who has taught by the pen. Taught man that which he knew not.*[1]

[1]Quran, Sura 96, verses 1–5.

For three years Muhammad shared this and subsequent revelations only with close friends and family members. This period culminated in his conviction that he was hearing the words of God (Allah [AH-luh] in Arabic). Khadija, his uncle's son Ali, his friend Abu Bakr (ah-boo BAK-uhr), and others close to him shared this conviction. The revelations continued until Muhammad's death in 632.

Like most people of the time, including Christians and Jews, the Arabs believed in unseen spirits: gods, demonic *shaitans*, and desert spirits called *jinns* who were thought to possess seers and poets. Therefore, when Muhammad recited his rhymed revelations in public, many people believed he was inspired by an unseen spirit, even if it was not, as Muhammad asserted, the one true god.

Muhammad's earliest revelations called on people to witness that one god had created the universe and everything in it, including themselves. At the end of time, their souls would be judged, their sins balanced against their good deeds. The blameless would go to paradise; the sinful would taste hellfire:

> By the night as it conceals the light;
> By the day as it appears in glory;
> By the mystery of the creation of male and female;
> Verily, the ends ye strive for are diverse.
> So he who gives in charity and fears God,
> And in all sincerity testifies to the best,
> We will indeed make smooth for him the path to Bliss.
> But he who is a greedy miser and thinks himself self-sufficient,
> And gives the lie to the best,
> We will indeed make smooth for him the path to misery.[2]

The revelation called all people to submit to God and accept Muhammad as the last of his messengers. Doing so made one a **Muslim**, meaning one who makes "submission," **Islam**, to the will of God.

Because earlier messengers mentioned in the revelations included Noah, Moses, and Jesus, Muhammad's hearers connected his message with Judaism and Christianity, religions they were already familiar with. Yet his revelations charged the Jews and Christians with being negligent in preserving God's revealed word. Thus, even though they identified Abraham/Ibrahim, whom Muslims consider the first Muslim, as the builder of the Ka'ba, which superseded Jerusalem as the focus of Muslim prayer in 624, Muhammad's followers considered his revelation more perfect than the Bible because it had not gone through an editing process.

Some scholars maintain that Muhammad appealed especially to people distressed over wealth replacing kinship as the most important aspect of social relations and over neglect of orphans and other powerless people. Most Muslims, however, put less emphasis on a social message than on the power and beauty of Muhammad's recitations.

Mecca's leaders feared that accepting Muhammad as the sole agent of the one true God would threaten their power and prosperity. They pressured his kin to disavow him and persecuted the weakest of his followers. Stymied by this hostility, Muhammad and his followers fled Mecca in 622 to take up residence in the agricultural community of **Medina** 215 miles (346 kilometers) to the north. This hijra (HIJ-ruh) marks the beginning of the Muslim calendar.

Formation of the Umma

Prior to the hijra, Medinan representatives had met with Muhammad and agreed to accept and protect him and his followers because they saw him as an inspired leader who could calm their perpetual feuding. Together, the Meccan migrants and major groups in Medina bound themselves into a single **umma** (UM-muh), a community defined by acceptance of Islam and of Muhammad as the "Messenger of God," his most common title. Partly because three Jewish kin groups chose to retain their own faith, the direction of prayer was changed from Jerusalem toward the Ka'ba in Mecca, now thought of as the "House of God."

Having left their Meccan kin groups, the immigrants in Medina felt vulnerable. During the last decade of his life, Muhammad took active responsibility for his umma. Fresh revelations

Muslim An adherent of the Islamic religion; a person who "submits" (in Arabic, *Islam* means "submission") to the will of God.

Islam Religion expounded by the Prophet Muhammad on the basis of his reception of divine revelations, which were collected after his death into the Quran. In the tradition of Judaism and Christianity, and sharing much of their lore, Islam calls on all people to recognize one creator god—Allah—who rewards or punishes believers after death according to how they led their lives.

Medina City in western Arabia to which the Prophet Muhammad and his followers emigrated in 622 to escape persecution in Mecca.

umma The community of all Muslims. A major innovation against the background of seventh-century Arabia, where traditionally kinship rather than faith had determined membership in a community.

[2]Quran, Sura 92, verses 1–10.

provided a framework for regulating social and legal affairs and stirred the Muslims to fight against the still-unbelieving city of Mecca. At various points during the war, Muhammad charged the Jewish kin groups, whom he had initially hoped would recognize him as God's messenger, with disloyalty, and he finally expelled or eliminated them. The sporadic war, largely conducted by raiding and negotiating with desert nomads, sapped Mecca's strength and convinced many Meccans that God favored Muhammad. In 630 Mecca surrendered, and Muhammad and his followers made the pilgrimage to the Ka'ba unhindered.

Muhammad stayed in Medina, which had grown into a bustling city-state. Delegations came to him from all over Arabia and returned home with believers who could teach about Islam and collect alms. Muhammad's mission to bring God's message to humanity had brought him unchallenged control of a state that was coming to dominate the Arabian peninsula.

Succession to Muhammad

In 632, after a brief illness, Muhammad died. Within twenty-four hours a group of Medinan leaders, along with three of Muhammad's close friends, determined that Abu Bakr, one of the earliest believers and the father of Muhammad's favorite wife A'isha (AH-ee-shah), should succeed him. They called him the *khalifa* (kah-LEE-fuh), or "successor," the English version of which is *caliph*. But calling Abu Bakr a successor did not clarify his powers. Everyone knew that neither Abu Bakr nor anyone else could receive revelations, and they likewise knew that Muhammad's revelations made no provision for succession or for any government purpose beyond maintaining the umma.

Abu Bakr continued and confirmed Muhammad's religious practices, notably the so-called Five Pillars of Islam: (1) avowal that there is only one god and Muhammad is his messenger, (2) prayer five times a day, (3) fasting during the lunar month of Ramadan, (4) paying alms, and (5) making the pilgrimage to Mecca at least once during one's lifetime. He also reestablished and expanded Muslim authority over Arabia's communities, some of which had abandoned their allegiance to Medina or followed various would-be prophets. Muslim armies fought hard to confirm the authority of the newborn **caliphate**. In the process, some fighting spilled over into non-Arab areas in Iraq.

Reportedly, Abu Bakr ordered the men who had written down Muhammad's revelations to collect them in a book. Hitherto written haphazardly on pieces of leather or bone, these now became a single document gathered into chapters. Muslims believe the **Quran** (kuh-RAHN), or the Recitation, acquired its final form around the year 650. They see it not as the words of Muhammad but as the unalterable word of God. Theologically, it compares not so much to the Bible, a book written by many hands over many centuries, as to the person of Jesus Christ, whom Christians consider an earthly manifestation of God.

Though united in accepting God's will, the umma soon disagreed over the succession to the caliphate. When rebels assassinated the third caliph, Uthman (ooth-MAHN), in 656, and the assassins nominated Ali, Muhammad's first cousin and the husband of his daughter Fatima, to succeed him, civil war broke out. Ali had been passed over three times previously, even though many people considered him to be the Prophet's natural heir. Those who believed Ali was the Prophet's heir came to be known as **Shi'ites**, after the Arabic term *Shi'at Ali* ("Party of Ali").

When Ali accepted the nomination to be caliph, two of Muhammad's close companions and his favorite wife A'isha challenged him. Ali defeated them in the Battle of the Camel (656), so called because the fighting raged around the camel on which A'isha was seated in an enclosed woman's saddle.

After the battle, the governor of Syria, Mu'awiya (moo-AH-we-yuh), a kinsman of the slain Uthman from the Umayya clan of the Quraysh, renewed the challenge. Inconclusive battle gave way to arbitration. The arbitrators decided that Uthman, whom his assassins considered corrupt, had not deserved death and that Ali had erred in accepting the caliphate. Ali rejected these findings, but before fighting could resume, one of his own supporters killed him for agreeing to the arbitration. Mu'awiya offered Ali's son Hasan a dignified retirement and thus emerged as caliph in 661.

Mu'awiya chose his own son, Yazid, to succeed him, thereby instituting the **Umayyad** (oo-MY-ad) **Caliphate**. When Hasan's brother Husayn revolted in 680 to reestablish the right of Ali's family to rule, Yazid ordered Husayn and his family killed. Sympathy for Husayn's martyrdom helped transform Shi'ism from a political movement into a religious sect.

caliphate Office established in succession to the Prophet Muhammad, to rule the Islamic empire; also the name of that empire.

Quran Book composed of divine revelations made to the Prophet Muhammad between around 610 and his death in 632; the sacred text of the religion of Islam.

Shi'ites Muslims belonging to the branch of Islam believing that God vests leadership of the community in a descendant of Muhammad's son-in-law Ali. Shi'ism is the state religion of Iran.

Umayyad Caliphate First hereditary dynasty of Muslim caliphs (661 to 750). From their capital at Damascus, the Umayyads ruled an empire that extended from Spain to India. Overthrown by the Abbasid Caliphate.

- Islam emerged among the nomadic pastoralists and caravan traders of the Arabian peninsula.

- Mecca grew as a caravan city and pilgrimage site identified with Jewish and Christian stories.

- Muhammad experienced revelations that called people to submit to God's will.

- Facing hostility in Mecca, Muhammad and his followers fled to Medina, where they formed the umma.

- As caliph succeeding Muhammad, Abu Bakr confirmed the Five Pillars of Islam and ordered the composition of the Quran.

- Civil war within the umma resulted in the Sunni/Shi'ite division and the foundation of the Umayyad Caliphate.

Several variations in Shi'ite belief developed, but Shi'ites all agree that Ali was the rightful successor to Muhammad and that God's choice as Imam, leader of the Muslim community, has always been one or another of Ali's descendants. They see the caliphal office as more secular than religious. Because the Shi'ites seldom held power, their religious feelings came to focus on outpourings of sympathy for Husayn and other martyrs and on messianic dreams that one of their Imams would someday triumph.

Those Muslims who supported the first three caliphs gradually came to be called "People of Tradition and Community"—in Arabic, *Ahl al-Sunna wa'l-Jama'a*, **Sunnis** for short. Sunnis consider the caliphs to be Imams. As for Ali's followers who had abhorred his acceptance of arbitration, they evolved into small and rebellious Kharijite sects (from *kharaja*, meaning "to secede or rebel") claiming righteousness for themselves alone. These three divisions of Islam, the last now quite minor, still survive.

THE RISE AND FALL OF THE CALIPHATE, 632–1258

The Islamic caliphate built on the conquests the Arabs carried out after Muhammad's death gave birth to a dynamic and creative religious society. By the late 800s, however, one piece after another of this huge realm broke away. Yet the idea of a caliphate, however unrealistic, remains today a touchstone of Sunni belief in the unity of the umma.

Sunnis Muslims belonging to branch of Islam believing that the community should select its own leadership. The majority religion in most Islamic countries.

Sunni Islam never gave a single person the power to define true belief, expel heretics, and discipline clergy. Thus, unlike Christian popes and patriarchs, the caliphs had little basis for reestablishing their universal authority once they lost political and military power.

The Islamic Conquests, 634–711

Arab conquests outside Arabia began under the second caliph, Umar (r. 634–644). Arab armies wrenched Syria (636) and Egypt (639–642) away from the Byzantine Empire and defeated the last Sasanid shah, Yazdigird III (r. 632–651). After a decade-long lull, expansion began again. Tunisia fell and became the governing center from which was organized, in 711, the conquest of Spain by an Arab-led army mostly composed of Berbers from North Africa. In the same year, Sind—the southern Indus Valley in today's Pakistan—succumbed to invaders from Iraq. The Muslim dominion remained roughly stable in size for three centuries until conquest began anew in the eleventh century. India and Anatolia experienced invasions; sub-Saharan Africa and other regions saw Islam expand peacefully by trade and conversion.

Muhammad's close companions, men of political and economic sophistication inspired by his charisma, guided the conquests. The social structure and hardy nature of Arab society lent itself to flexible military operations; and the authority of Medina, reconfirmed during the caliphate of Abu Bakr, ensured obedience.

The decision made during Umar's caliphate to prohibit Arabs from assuming ownership of conquered territory proved important. Umar tied army service, with its regular pay and windfalls of booty, to residence in military camps—two in Iraq (Kufa and Basra), one in Egypt (Fustat), and one in Tunisia (Qairawan). East of Iraq, Arabs settled around small garrison towns at strategic locations and in one large garrison at Marv in present-day Turkmenistan. This policy kept the armies together and ready for action and preserved normal life in the countryside, where some three-fourths of the population lived. Only a tiny proportion of the Syrian, Egyptian, Iranian, and Iraqi populations understood the Arabic language.

The million or so Arabs who participated in the conquests over several generations constituted a small, self-isolated ruling minority living on the taxes paid by a vastly larger non-Arab, non-Muslim subject population. The Arabs had little material incentive to encourage conversion, and there is no evidence of coherent missionary efforts to spread Islam during the conquest period.

The Umayyad and Early Abbasid Caliphates, 661–850

The Umayyad caliphs presided over an Arab realm rather than a religious empire. Ruling from Damascus, their armies consisted almost entirely of Muslim Arabs. Sasanid and Byzantine administrative practices continued in force. Only gradually did the caliphs replace non-Muslim secretaries and tax officials with Muslims and introduce Arabic as the language of government. Distinctively Muslim silver and gold coins introduced at the end of the seventh century symbolized the new order. Henceforward, silver dirhams and gold dinars bearing Arabic religious phrases circulated in monetary exchanges from Morocco to the frontiers of China.

The Umayyad dynasty fell in 750 after a decade of growing unrest. Converts to Islām numbered no more than 10 percent of the indigenous population, but they were still important because of the comparatively small number of Arab warriors. These converts resented Arab social domination. In addition, non-Syrian Arabs envied the Syrian domination of caliphal affairs, and pious Muslims looked askance at the secular and even irreligious behavior of the caliphs. Finally, Shi'ites and Kharijites attacked the Umayyad family's legitimacy as rulers, launching a number of rebellions.

In 750 one rebellion, begun in 747 in the region of Khurasan (kor-uh-SAHN) in what is today northeastern Iran, overthrew the last Umayyad caliph, though one family member escaped to Spain to found an Umayyad principality there in 755. Many Shi'ites supported the rebellion, thinking they were fighting for the family of Ali. As it turned out, the family of Abbas, one of Muhammad's uncles, controlled the secret organization that coordinated the revolt. Upon victory they established the **Abbasid (ah-BASS-id) Caliphate**. Some of the Abbasid caliphs who ruled after 750 befriended their relatives in Ali's family, and one even flirted with transferring the caliphate to them. The Abbasid family, however, held on to the caliphate until 1258, when Mongol invaders killed the last of them in Baghdad (see Chapter 13).

Initially, the Abbasid dynasty made a fine show of leadership and piety. Theology and religious law became preoccupations at court and among a growing community of scholars devoted to interpreting the Quran, collecting the sayings of the Prophet, and compiling Arabic grammar. (In recent years, some Western scholars have maintained that the Quran, the sayings of the Prophet, and the biography of the Prophet were all composed around this time to provide a foundation myth for the regime. This reinterpretation of Islamic origins has not been generally accepted either in the scholarly community or among Muslims.) Some caliphs sponsored ambitious projects to translate great works of Greek, Persian, and Indian thought into Arabic.

With its roots among the semi-Persianized Arabs of Khurasan, the new dynasty gradually adopted the ceremonies and customs of the Sasanid shahs. Government grew increasingly complex in Baghdad, the newly built capital city on the Tigris River. As more non-Arabs converted to Islam, the ruling elite became more cosmopolitan. Greek, Iranian, Central Asian, and African cultural currents met in the capital and gave rise to an abundance of literary works, a process facilitated by the introduction of papermaking from China. Arab poets neglected the traditional odes extolling life in the desert and wrote instead wine songs (despite Islam's prohibition of alcohol) or poems in praise of their patrons.

The translation of Aristotle into Arabic, the founding of the main currents of theology and law, and the splendor of the Abbasid court—reflected in stories of *The Arabian Nights* set in the time of the caliph Harun al-Rashid (hah-ROON al-rah-SHEED) (r. 776–809)—in some respects warrant calling the early Abbasid period a "golden age." Yet the refinement of Baghdad culture only slowly made its way into the provinces. Egypt remained predominantly Christian and Coptic-speaking in the early Abbasid period. Iran never adopted Arabic as a spoken tongue. Most of Berber-speaking North Africa rebelled and freed itself of direct caliphal rule after 740.

Gradual conversion to Islam among the conquered population accelerated in the second quarter of the ninth century. Social discrimination against non-Arab converts gradually faded, and the Arabs themselves—at least those living in cosmopolitan urban settings—lost their previously strong attachment to kinship and ethnic identity.

Political Fragmentation, 850–1050

Abbasid decline became evident in the second half of the ninth century as conversion to Islam accelerated (see Map 10.2). No government ruling so vast an empire could hold power easily. Caravans traveled only 20 miles (32 kilometers) a day, and the couriers of the caliphal post

Abbasid Caliphate Descendants of the Prophet Muhammad's uncle, al-Abbas, the Abbasids overthrew the Umayyad Caliphate and ruled an Islamic empire from their capital in Baghdad (founded 762) from 750 to 1258.

system usually did not exceed 100 miles (160 kilometers) a day. News of frontier revolts took weeks to reach Baghdad. Military responses might take months.

During the first two Islamic centuries, revolts against Muslim rule had been a concern. The Muslim umma had therefore clung together, despite the long distances. But with the growing conversion of the population to Islam, fears that Islamic dominion might be overthrown faded. Once they became the overwhelming majority, Muslims realized that a highly centralized empire did not necessarily serve the interests of all the people.

By the middle of the ninth century, revolts targeting Arab or Muslim domination gave way to movements within the Islamic community concentrating on seizure of territory and formation of principalities. None of the states carved out of the Abbasid Caliphate after that time repudiated or even threatened Islam. They did, however, cut the flow of tax revenues to Baghdad, thereby increasing local prosperity.

Increasingly starved for funds by breakaway provinces and by an unexplained fall in revenues from Iraq itself, the caliphate experienced a crisis in the late ninth century. Distrusting generals and troops from outlying areas, the caliphs purchased Turkic slaves, **mamluks** (MAM-luke), from Central Asia and established them as a standing army. Well trained and hardy, the Turks proved an effective but expensive military force. When the government could not pay them, the mamluks took it on themselves to seat and unseat caliphs, a process made easier by the construction of a new capital at Samarra, north of Baghdad on the Tigris River.

The Turks dominated Samarra without interference from an unruly Baghdad populace that regarded them as rude and highhanded. However, the money and effort that went into the huge city, which was occupied only from 835 to 892, further sapped the caliphs' financial strength and deflected labor from more productive pursuits.

In 945, after several attempts to find a strongman to save it, the Abbasid Caliphate fell under the control of rude mountain warriors from Daylam in northern Iran. Led by the Shi'ite Buyid (BOO-yid) family, they conquered western Iran as well as Iraq. Each Buyid commander ruled his own principality. After two centuries of glory, the sun began to set on Baghdad. The Abbasid caliph remained, but the Buyid princes controlled him. Being Shi'ites, the Buyids had no special reverence for the Sunni caliph. The Shi'ite teachings they followed held that the twelfth and last Imam had disappeared around 873 and would return as a messiah only at the end of time. Thus they had no Shi'ite Imam to defer to and retained the caliph only to help control their predominantly Sunni subjects.

Dynamic growth in outlying provinces paralleled the caliphate's gradual loss of temporal power. In the east in 875, the dynasty of the Samanids (sah-MAN-id), one of several Iranian families to achieve independence, established a glittering court in Bukhara, a major city on the Silk Road (see Map 10.2). Samanid princes patronized literature and learning, but the language they favored was Persian written in Arabic letters. For the first time, a non-Arabic literature rose to challenge the eminence of Arabic within the Islamic world.

In the west, the Berber revolts against Arab rule led to the appearance after 740 of the city-states of Sijilmasa (sih-jil-MAS-suh) and Tahert (TAH-hert) on the northern fringe of the Sahara. The Kharijite beliefs of these states' rulers interfered with their east-west overland trade and led them to develop the first regular trade across the Sahara desert (see Chapter 9). Once traders looked to the desert, they discovered that Berber speakers in the southern Sahara were already carrying salt from the desert into the Sahel region. The northern traders found that they could trade salt for gold by providing the southern nomads, who controlled the salt sources but had little use for gold, with more useful products, such as copper and manufactured goods. Sijilmasa and Tahert became wealthy cities, the former minting gold coins that circulated as far away as Egypt and Syria.

The earliest known sub-Saharan beneficiary of the new exchange system was the kingdom of **Ghana** (GAH-nuh). It first appears in an Arabic text of the late eighth century as the "land of gold." Few details survive about the early years of this realm, which was established by the Soninke (soh-NIN-kay) people and covered parts of Mali, Mauritania, and Senegal, but it prospered until 1076, when it was conquered by nomads from the desert. It was one of the first lands outside the orbit of the caliphate to experience a gradual and peaceful conversion to Islam.

The North African city-states lost their independence after the Fatimid (FAH-tuh-mid) dynasty, whose members claimed (perhaps falsely) to be Shi'ite Imams descended from Ali, established itself in Tunisia in 909. After consolidating their hold on northwest Africa, the Fatimids culminated their rise to power by conquering Egypt in 969. Claiming the title of caliph in a direct challenge to the Abbasids, the Fatimid rulers governed from a palace complex outside the

mamluks Under the Islamic system of military slavery, Turkic military slaves formed an important part of the armed forces of the Abbasid Caliphate of the ninth and tenth centuries. Mamluks eventually founded their own state, ruling Egypt and Syria (1250–1517).

Ghana First known kingdom in sub-Saharan West Africa between the sixth and thirteenth centuries C.E. Also the modern West African country once known as the Gold Coast.

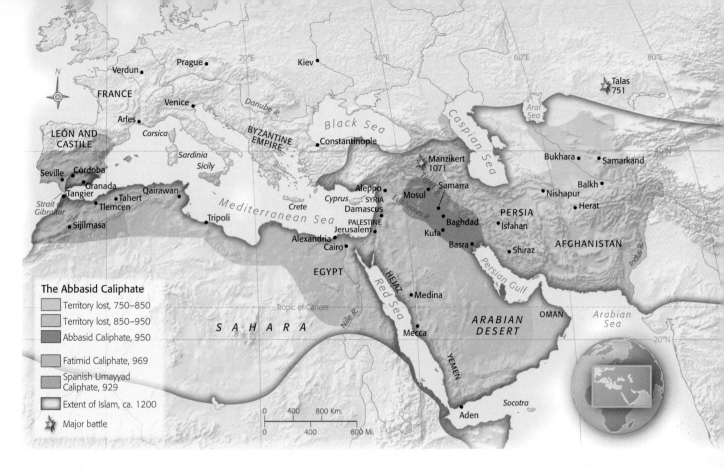

MAP 10.2 **Rise and Fall of the Abbasid Caliphate** Though Abbasid rulers occupied the caliphal seat in Iraq from 750 to 1258, when Mongol armies destroyed Baghdad, real political power waned sharply and steadily after 850. The rival caliphates of the Fatimids (909–1171) and Spanish Umayyads (929–976) were comparatively short-lived. © Cengage Learning

old conquest-era garrison city of Fustat **(fuss-TAHT)**. They named the complex Cairo. For the first time Egypt became a major cultural, intellectual, and political center of Islam. The abundance of Fatimid gold coinage, now channeled to Egypt from West Africa, made the Fatimids an economic power in the Mediterranean.

Cut off from the rest of the Islamic world by the Strait of Gibraltar and, from 740 onward, by independent city-states in Morocco and Algeria, Umayyad Spain developed a distinctive Islamic culture blending Roman, Germanic, and Jewish traditions with those of the Arabs and Berbers. Historians disagree on how rapidly and completely the Spanish population converted to Islam. If we assume a process similar to that in the eastern regions, it seems likely that the most rapid surge in Islamization occurred in the middle of the tenth century.

As in the east, governing cities symbolized the Islamic presence in al-Andalus, as the Muslims called their Iberian territories. Córdoba, Seville, Toledo, and other cities grew substantially, becoming much larger and richer than contemporary cities in neighboring France. Converts to Islam and their descendants, unconverted Arabic-speaking Christians, and Jews joined with the comparatively few descendants of Arab settlers to create new architectural and literary styles. In the countryside, where the Berbers preferred to settle, a fusion of preexisting agricultural technologies with new crops, notably citrus fruits, and irrigation techniques from the east gave Spain the most diverse and sophisticated agricultural economy in Europe.

The rulers of al-Andalus took the title *caliph* only in 929, when Abd al-Rahman **(AHB-d al–ruh-MAHN)** III (r. 912–961) did so in response to a similar declaration by the newly established (909) Fatimid ruler in Tunisia. By the century's end, however, this caliphate encountered challenges from breakaway movements that eventually splintered al-Andalus into a number of small states. Political decay did not impede cultural growth. Some of the greatest writers and thinkers in Jewish history worked in Muslim Spain in the eleventh and twelfth centuries, sometimes writing in Arabic, sometimes in Hebrew. Judah Halevi (1075–1141) composed exquisite poetry and explored questions of religious philosophy. Maimonides (1135–1204) made a major compilation of Judaic law and expounded on Aristotelian philosophy. At the same time, Islamic thought in Spain attained its loftiest peaks in Ibn Hazm's (994–1064) treatises on love and other subjects, the Aristotelian philosophical writings of Ibn Rushd **(IB-uhn RUSHED)** (1126–1198, known in

Mosque of Ibn Tulun in Fustat Completed in 877, this mosque symbolized Egypt becoming for the first time a quasi-independent province under its governor. The kiosk in the center of the courtyard contains fountains for washing before prayer. Before its restoration in the thirteenth century, the mosque had a spiral minaret and a door to an adjoining governor's palace.

Latin as Averroës [uh-VERR-oh-eez]) and Ibn Tufayl (IB-uhn too-FILE) (d. 1185), and the mystic speculations of Ibn al-Arabi (IB-uhn ahl–AH-rah-bee) (1165–1240). Christians, too, shared in the intellectual and cultural dynamism of al-Andalus. Translations from Arabic to Latin made during this period had a profound effect on the later intellectual development of western Europe (see Chapter 11).

The Samanids, Fatimids, and Spanish Umayyads, three of many regional principalities, represent the political diversity and awakening of local awareness that coincided with Abbasid decline. Yet drawing and redrawing political boundaries did not result in the rigid division of the Islamic world into kingdoms. Religious and cultural developments, particularly the rise in cities of a social group of religious scholars known as the **ulama** (oo-leh-MAH)—Arabic for "people with (religious) knowledge"—worked against any permanent division of the Islamic umma.

Assault from Within and Without, 1050–1258

The role played by Turkish mamluks in the decline of Abbasid power established an enduring stereotype of the Turk as a ferocious, unsophisticated warrior. This image gained strength in the 1036 when the Seljuk (sel-JOOK) family established a Turkish Muslim state based on nomadic power. Taking the Arabic title *Sultan*, meaning "power," and the revived Persian title *Shahan-shah*, or King of Kings, the Seljuk ruler Tughril (TUUG-ruhl) Beg created a kingdom that stretched from northern Afghanistan to Baghdad, which he occupied in 1055. After a century under the thumb of the Shi'ite Buyids, the Abbasid caliph breathed easier under the slightly lighter thumb of the Sunni Turks. The Seljuks pressed on into Syria and Anatolia, administering a lethal blow to Byzantine power at the Battle of Manzikert (MANZ-ih-kuhrt) in 1071. The Byzantine army fell back on Constantinople, leaving Anatolia open to Turkish occupation.

Under Turkish rule, which coincided with a severe climatic cooling that reduced harvests in Iran, Iraq, and eastern Anatolia, cities shrank as pastoralists overran their agricultural hinterlands. Irrigation works suffered from lack of maintenance in the unsettled countryside. Tax revenues fell. Quarreling twelfth-century princes fought over cities, but few Turks participated in urban cultural and religious life. The gulf between a religiously based urban society and the culture and personnel of the government deepened. When factional riots broke out between

ulama Muslim religious scholars. From the ninth century onward, the primary interpreters of Islamic law and the social core of Muslim urban societies.

Tomb of the Samanids in Bukhara This early-tenth-century structure has the basic layout of a Zoroastrian fire temple: a dome on top of a cube. However, geometric ornamentation in baked brick marks it as an early masterpiece of Islamic architecture. The Samanid family achieved independence as rulers of northeastern Iran and western Central Asia in the tenth century.

Bridgeman-Giraudon/Art Resource, NY

Sunnis and Shi'ites, or between rival schools of Sunni law, rulers generally remained aloof, even as destruction and loss of life mounted.

By the early twelfth century, unrepaired damage from floods, fires, and civil disorder had reduced old Baghdad on the west side of the Tigris to ruins. The withering of Baghdad reflected a broader environmental problem: the collapse of the canal system on which agriculture in the Tigris and Euphrates Valley depended. For millennia a center of world civilization, Mesopotamia underwent substantial population loss and never again regained its geographical importance.

The Turks alone cannot be blamed for the demographic and economic misfortunes of Iran and Iraq. Too-robust urbanization, spurred largely by a boom in Iranian cotton production, resulted in strained food resources when the climate deteriorated after 1000. Baghdad, a city with a torrid climate today, experienced heavy winter snowfalls that killed date trees. In addition, the growing practice of paying soldiers and courtiers with land grants led to absentee landlords using agents to collect taxes. These agents gouged villagers to meet their quotas and took little interest in improving production, thus intensifying the agricultural crisis.

Internecine feuding was preoccupying the Seljuk family when the first Christian Crusaders reached the Holy Land and captured Jerusalem in 1099 (see Chapter 11). Though charged with the stuff of romance, the Crusades had little lasting impact on the Islamic lands. The four Crusader principalities of Edessa, Antioch, Tripoli, and Jerusalem simply became pawns in the shifting pattern of politics already in place. Newly arrived knights eagerly attacked the Muslim enemy, whom they called "Saracens" **(SAR-uh-suhn)**; but veteran Crusaders recognized that practicing diplomacy and seeking partners of convenience among rival Muslim princes offered a sounder strategy.

The Muslims finally unified to face the European enemy in the mid-twelfth century. Nur al-Din ibn Zangi **(NOOR uhd–DEEN ib-uhn ZAN-gee)** established a strong state based in Damascus and sent an army to terminate the Fatimid Caliphate in Egypt. A nephew of the Kurdish commander of that expedition, Salah-al-Din, known in the West as Saladin, took advantage of Nur al-Din's timely death to seize power and unify Egypt and Syria. The Fatimid dynasty fell in 1171. In 1187 Saladin recaptured Jerusalem from the Europeans. He then took the title

Spanish Muslim Textile of the Twelfth Century This fragment of woven silk, featuring peacocks and Arabic writing, is one of the finest examples of Islamic weaving. The cotton industry flourished in the early Islamic centuries, but silk remained a highly valued product. Some fabrics were treasured in Christian Europe.

Khadim al-Haramain **(KAH-dim al–ha-ra-MAYN)**, literally "Servant of the Two Holy Places," meaning Mecca and Medina, in a challenge to the caliph's claim to be the paramount Sunni potentate. Revitalizing the pilgrimage became a core concern for later rulers in Egypt and Syria, particularly after the termination of the Baghdad caliphate in 1258.

Saladin's descendants fought off subsequent Crusades. After one such battle, however, in 1250, Turkish mamluk troops seized control of the government in Cairo, ending Saladin's dynasty. In 1260 these mamluks rode east to confront a new invading force. At the Battle of Ain Jalut **(ine jah-LOOT)** (Spring of Goliath) in Syria, they met and defeated an army of Mongols from Central Asia (see Chapter 13), thus stemming an invasion that had begun several decades before and legitimizing their claim to dominion over Egypt and Syria.

During the ensuing Mamluk period a succession of slave-soldier sultans ruled Egypt and Syria until 1517. Fear of new Mongol attacks receded after 1300, but by then the new ruling system had become fixed. Young Turkish or Circassian slaves, the latter from the eastern end of the Black Sea, were imported from non-Muslim lands, raised in training barracks, and converted to Islam. Owing loyalty to the Mamluk officers who purchased them, they formed a military class that was socially disconnected from the Arabic-speaking native population.

The Mongol invasions, especially their destruction of the Abbasid Caliphate in Baghdad in 1258, shocked the world of Islam. The Mamluk sultan enthroned a relative of the last Baghdad caliph in Cairo, but the Egyptian Abbasids were mere puppets serving Mamluk interests. From Iraq eastward, non-Muslim rule lasted for much of the thirteenth century. Although the Mongols left few ethnic or linguistic traces in these lands, their initial destruction of cities and slaughter of civilian populations, their diversion of Silk Road trade from Baghdad to more northerly routes ending at Black Sea ports, and their casual disregard, even after conversion to Islam, for Muslim religious life and urban culture hastened currents of change already under way.

SECTION REVIEW

- By 711, Arab armies had conquered an empire stretching from Sind in the east to Spain in the west.

- The Umayyad caliphs ruled an ethnic empire; they governed from Damascus using Sasanid and Byzantine administrative methods.

- The Umayyads fell to rebels who established the Abbasid Caliphate at Baghdad, while surviving Umayyads fled to Spain.

- Influenced by Persian culture, the Abbasids presided over significant spiritual, intellectual, and artistic activity.

- Abbasid decline led to fragmentation of the caliphate into independent states, but the Islamic umma remained intact.

- Political divisions continued as successor states to the former caliphate fell, replaced by Seljuk Turk, Crusader, Mamluk, and Mongol states.

ISLAMIC CIVILIZATION

Though increasingly unsettled in its political dimension and subject to economic disruptions caused by war, the ever-expanding Islamic world underwent a fruitful evolution in law, social structure, and religious expression. Religious conversion and urbanization reinforced each other to create a distinct Islamic civilization. The immense geographical and human diversity of the Muslim lands allowed many "small traditions" to coexist with the developing "great tradition" of Islam.

Law and Dogma

The Shari'a, the law of Islam, provides the foundation of Islamic civilization. Yet aside from certain Quranic verses conveying specific divine ordinances—most pertaining to personal and family matters—Islam had no legal system in the time of Muhammad. Arab custom and the Prophet's own authority offered the only guidance. After Muhammad died, the umma tried to follow his example. This became harder and harder to do, however, as those who knew Muhammad best passed away and many Arabs found themselves living in far-off lands. Non-Arab converts to Islam, who at first tried to follow Arab customs they had little familiarity with, had an even harder time.

Islam slowly developed laws to govern social and religious life. The full sense of Islamic civilization, however, goes well beyond the basic Five Pillars mentioned earlier. Some Muslim thinkers felt that the reasoned consideration of a mature man offered the best resolution of issues not covered by Quranic revelation. Others argued for the sunna, or tradition, of the Prophet as the best guide. To understand that sunna they collected and studied thousands of reports, called **hadith** (hah-DEETH), purporting to convey the precise words or deeds of Muhammad. It became customary to precede each hadith with a chain of oral authorities leading back to the person who had direct acquaintance with the Prophet.

hadith A tradition relating the words or deeds of the Prophet Muhammad; next to the Quran, the most important basis for Islamic law.

Many hadith dealt with ritual matters, such as how to wash before prayer. Others provided answers to legal questions not covered by Quranic revelation or suggested principles for deciding such matters. By the eleventh century most legal thinkers had accepted the idea that Muhammad's personal behavior provided the best role model and that the hadith constituted the most authoritative basis for law after the Quran itself.

Yet the hadith posed a problem because the tens of thousands of anecdotes included both genuine and invented reports, the latter sometimes politically motivated, as well as stories derived from non-Muslim religious traditions. Only a specialist could hope to separate a sound from a weak tradition. As the hadith grew in importance, so did the branch of learning devoted to their analysis. Scholars discarded thousands for having faulty chains of authority. The most reliable they collected into books that gradually achieved authoritative status. Sunnis placed six books in this category; Shi'ites, four.

As it gradually evolved, the Shari'a embodied a vision of an umma in which all subscribed to the same moral values and political and ethnic distinctions lost importance. Every Muslim ruler was expected to abide by and enforce the religious law. In practice, this expectation often lost out in the hurly-burly of political life. But the Shari'a proved an important basis for an urban lifestyle that varied surprisingly little from Morocco to India.

Converts and Cities

Conversion to Islam, more the outcome of people's learning about the new rulers' religion than an escape from the tax on non-Muslims, as some scholars have suggested, helped spur urbanization. Conversion did not require extensive knowledge of the faith. To become a Muslim, a person simply stated, in the presence of a Muslim: "There is no God but God, and Muhammad is the Messenger of God."

Few converts spoke Arabic, and fewer could read the Quran. Many converts knew no more of the Quran than the verses they memorized for daily prayers. Muhammad had established no priesthood to define and spread the faith. Thus new converts, whether Arab or non-Arab, faced the problem of finding out for themselves what Islam was about and how they should act as Muslims. This meant spending time with Muslims, learning their language, and imitating their practices.

In many areas, conversion involved migrating to an Arab governing center. The alternative, converting to Islam but remaining in one's home community, was difficult because religion had become the main component of social identity in Byzantine and Sasanid times. Converts to Islam thus encountered discrimination if they stayed in their Christian, Jewish, or Zoroastrian communities. Migration both averted discrimination and took advantage of the economic opportunities opened up by tax revenues flowing into the Arab governing centers.

The Arab military settlements of Kufa and Basra in Iraq blossomed into cities and became important centers for Muslim cultural activities. As conversion rapidly spread in the mid-ninth century, urbanization accelerated in other regions, most visibly in Iran, where most cities previously had been quite small. Nishapur in the northeast grew from fewer than 10,000 pre-Islamic

Model of a Water-Lifting Device The artist's effort to render a three-dimensional construction in two dimensions shows a talent for schematic drawing.

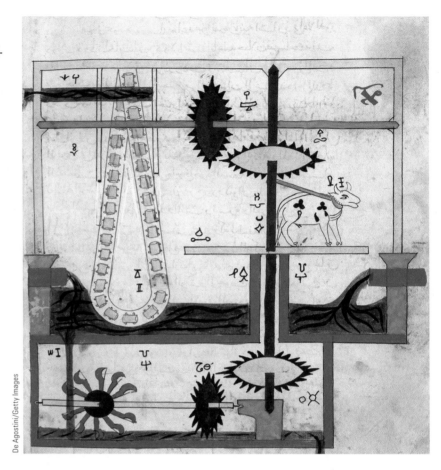

De Agostini/Getty Images

inhabitants to between 100,000 and 200,000 by the year 1000. Other Iranian cities experienced similar growth. In Iraq, Baghdad and Mosul joined Kufa and Basra as major cities. In Syria, Aleppo and Damascus flourished under Muslim rule. Fustat in Egypt developed into Cairo, one of the largest and greatest Islamic cities. The primarily Christian patriarchal cities of Jerusalem, Antioch, and Alexandria, not being Muslim governing centers, shrank and stagnated.

Conversion-related migration meant that cities became heavily Muslim before the countryside did. This reinforced the urban orientation deriving from the fact that Muhammad and his first followers came from the commercial city of Mecca. Mosques in large cities served both as ritual centers and as places for learning and social activities.

Islam colored all aspects of urban social life (see Diversity and Dominance: Secretaries, Turks, and Beggars). Initially the new Muslims imitated Arab dress and customs, particularly favoring plain linen or cotton over the silk brocade of the non-Muslim Iranian elite, and emulated people they regarded as particularly pious. In the absence of a central religious authority, local variations developed in the way people practiced Islam and in the hadith they attributed to the Prophet. This gave the rapidly growing religion the flexibility to accommodate many different social situations.

By the tenth century, urban growth was affecting the countryside by expanding the consumer market. Citrus fruits, rice, and sugar cane, introduced by the Sasanids, increased in acreage and spread to new areas. Cotton became a major crop in Iran and elsewhere and stimulated textile production. Irrigation works expanded. Abundant coinage facilitated a flourishing intercity and long-distance trade that provided regular links between isolated districts and integrated the pastoral nomads, who provided pack animals, into the region's economy. Trade encouraged the manufacture of cloth, metal goods, and pottery.

Science and technology also flourished (see Environment and Technology: Chemistry). Building on Hellenistic traditions and their own observations and experience, Muslim doctors and astronomers developed skills and theories far in advance of their European counterparts. Working in Egypt in the eleventh century, the mathematician and physicist Ibn al-Haytham **(IB-uhn al–HY-tham)** wrote more than a hundred works. Among other things, he determined that the Milky Way lies far beyond earth's atmosphere, proved that light travels from a seen object to the eye and not the reverse, and explained why the sun and moon appear larger on the horizon than overhead.

Women Playing Chess in Muslim Spain   As shown in this thirteenth-century miniature, women in their own quarters, without men present, wore whatever clothes and jewels they liked. Notice the henna decorating the hands of the woman in the middle. The woman on the left, probably a slave, plays an oud.   Album/Art Resource, NY

Women and Islam

Women seldom traveled. Those living in rural areas worked in the fields and tended animals. Urban women, particularly members of the elite, lived in seclusion and did not leave their homes without covering themselves (see Material Culture: Head Coverings). Seclusion of women and veiling in public already existed in Byzantine and Sasanid times. Through interpretation of specific verses from the Quran, these practices now became fixtures of Muslim social life. Although women sometimes became literate and studied with relatives, they did so away from the gaze of unrelated men, and while they played influential roles within the family, public roles were generally barred. Only slave women could perform before unrelated men as musicians and dancers. A man could have sexual relations with as many slave concubines as he pleased, in addition to marrying as many as four wives.

Muslim women fared better legally under Islamic law than did Christian and Jewish women under their respective religious codes. Because Islamic law guaranteed daughters a share in inheritance equal to half that of a son, the majority of women inherited some amount of money or real estate. This remained their private property to keep or sell. Muslim law put the financial burden of supporting a family exclusively on the husband, who could not legally compel his wife to help out.

Women could also remarry if their husbands divorced them, and they received a cash payment upon divorce. Although a man could divorce his wife without stating a cause, a woman could initiate divorce under specified conditions. Women could also practice birth control. They could testify in court, although their testimony counted as half that of a man. They could go on pilgrimage. Nevertheless, a misogynistic tone sometimes appears in Islamic writings. One saying attributed to the Prophet observed: "I was raised up to heaven and saw that most of its denizens were poor people; I was raised into the hellfire and saw that most of its denizens were women."[3]

---

[3]Richard W. Bulliet, *Islam: The View from the Edge* (New York: Columbia University Press, 1994), 87.

Secretaries, Turks, and Beggars

The passages below fall into the category of Arabic literature known as adab, or belles-lettres. The purpose of adab was to entertain and instruct through a succession of short anecdotes, verses, and expository discussions. It attracted the finest writers of the Abbasid era and affords one of the richest sources for looking at everyday life, always keeping in mind that the intended readers were a restricted class of educated men, including merchants, court and government officials, and even men of religion.

One of the greatest masters of Arabic prose, Jahiz (776–869), was a famously ugly man—his name means "Popeyed"—of Abyssinian family origin. Spending part of his life in his native Basra, in southern Iraq, and part in Baghdad, the Abbasid capital, he wrote voluminously on subjects ranging from theology to zoology to miserliness. These excerpts are from two of his short essays, "Censure of the Conduct of Secretaries" and "The Virtues of the Turks."

Censure of the Conduct of Secretaries

Furthermore, the foundation on which writing is based [is] that only a subordinate should take [it] up and only one who is in a sense a servant [can] master it. We have never seen an important person undertake it for its own sake or share in his secretary's work. Every secretary is required to be loyal and requested to bear hardship patiently. The most diverse conditions are imposed on him and he is sorely tried. The secretary has no right to set any of those conditions. On the contrary, he is thought slow at the first lapse even if exhausted and censured at the first error even if unintentional. A slave is entitled to many complaints against his master. He can request his sale to another if he wishes. The secretary has no way to lay

claim to his late back wages or to leave his patron if he acts unfairly. He is governed by the rules for slaves. His status is that of a dolt.

It should be enough for you to know of this group that the noblest of them is at the bottom of the pay scale. The most wealthy of them are the least regarded by the ruler. The head of the secretariat who acts as spokesman to the nation earns a tenth of the income of the head of land tax. The scribe whose handwriting lends beauty to the communications of the caliph earns a fraction of the income of the head copyist in the land tax bureau. The correspondence secretary is not fetched for a disaster nor is his aid sought in a crisis. When the ministers have settled on a course of action and agreed in their appraisal, a note is tossed him with the gist of the order. He prepares the text. When he has finished his editing and straightened out the words, he brings in his copyist. He sits as near as anyone to the caliph, in a restricted location away from visitors. Once that task is completed, however, there is no difference between those two scribes and the common people.

The Virtues of the Turks

The Turk has with him at the moment of attack everything he needs for himself, his weapons, his mount, and equipment for it. His endurance is quite amazing for long riding, continuous travel, lengthy night trips, and crossing a land. . . . The Turk is more skilled than the veterinarian and better at teaching his mount what he wants than trainers. He bred it and raised it as a foal. It followed him if he called and galloped behind him when he galloped. . . . If you sum up the life of the Turk and reckon his days you will find he sits longer on the back of his mount than on the face of the earth.

In the absence of writings by women about women from this period, the status of women must be deduced from the writings of men. Two episodes involving the Prophet's wife A'isha, the daughter of Abu Bakr, provide examples of how Muslim men appraised women in society. Only eighteen when Muhammad died, A'isha lived for another fifty years. Early reports stress her status as Muhammad's favorite, the only virgin he married and the only wife to see the angel Gabriel. These reports emanate from A'isha herself, who was an abundant source of hadith. As a fourteen-year-old she had become separated from a caravan and rejoined it only after traveling through the night with a man who found her alone in the desert. Gossips accused her of being untrue to the Prophet, but a revelation from God proved her innocence. The second event was her participation in the Battle of the Camel, fought to derail Ali's caliphate. These two episodes came to epitomize what Muslim men feared most about women: sexual infidelity and meddling in politics. Even though the earliest literature dealing with A'isha stresses her position as Muhammad's favorite, his first wife, Khadija, and his daughter, Ali's wife Fatima, eventually surpassed A'isha as ideal women. Both appear as model wives and mothers with no suspicion of sexual irregularity or political manipulation.

As the seclusion of women became commonplace in urban Muslim society, some writers extolled homosexual relationships, partly because a male lover could appear in public or go on a journey. Although Islam deplored homosexuality, one ruler wrote a book advising his son to

If he is unable to hunt people, he hunts wild animals. If he is unsuccessful in that or needs nourishment, he bleeds one of his riding animals. If thirsty he milks one of his mares. If he wants to rest the one under him he mounts another without touching the ground. There is no one on earth besides him whose body would not reel against eating only meat. His mount is likewise satisfied with stubble, grass, and shrubs. He does not shade it from the sun or cover it against the cold. . . .

The Turk is a herdsman, groom, trainer, trader, veterinarian, and rider. A single Turk is a nation in himself.

Though rulers, warriors, and religious scholars dominate the traditional narratives, the society that developed over the early centuries of Islam was remarkably diverse. Beggars, tricksters, and street performers belonged to a single loose fraternity: the Banu Sasan, or Tribe of Sasan. Tales of their tricks and exploits amused staid, pious Muslims, who often encountered them in cities and on their scholarly travels. The tenth-century poet Abu Dulaf al-Khazraji, who lived in Iran, studied the jargon of the Banu Sasan and their way of life and composed a long poem in which he cast himself as one of the group. However, he added a commentary to each verse to explain the jargon words that his sophisticated court audience would have found unfamiliar.

We are the beggars' brotherhood, and no one can deny
    us our lofty pride. . . .
And of our number is the feigned madman and mad
    woman, with metal charms strung from their necks.
And the ones with ornaments drooping from their ears,
    and with collars of leather or brass round their
    necks. . . .
And the one who simulates a festering internal wound,
    and the people with false bandages round their
    heads and sickly, jaundiced faces.
And the one who slashes himself, alleging that he
    has been mutilated by assailants, or the one who

darkens his skin artificially pretending that he has
    been beaten up and wounded. . . .
And the one who practices as a manipulator and quack
    dentist, or who escapes from chains wound round
    his body, or the one who uses almost invisible silk
    thread mysteriously to draw off rings. . . .
And of our number are those who claim to be refugees
    from the Byzantine frontier regions, those who go
    round begging on pretext of having left behind cap-
    tive families. . . .
And the one who feigns an internal discharge, or who
    showers the passers-by with his urine, or who farts
    in the mosque and makes a nuisance of himself,
    thus wheedling money out of people. . . .
And of our number are the ones who purvey objects of
    veneration made from clay, and those who have
    their beards smeared with red dye.
And the one who brings up secret writing by immersing
    it in what looks like water, and the one who simi-
    larly brings up the writing by exposing it to burning
    embers.

QUESTIONS FOR ANALYSIS

1. **Why might the ruling elite have found the descriptions of diverse social groups entertaining?**

2. **What role does religion appear to play in the culture that patronized this type of literature?**

3. **How does the personality of the author show up in these passages?**

Sources: First selection excerpts from *Nine Essays of al-Jahiz*, trans. William M. Hutchins, pp. 56, 64, 196. Copyright © 1989. Second selection excerpts from Clifford Edmund Bosworth, *The Mediaeval Islamic Underworld: The Banu Sasan in Arabic Society and Literature*, pp. 191–199. Copyright © 1976.

follow moderation in all things and thus share his affections equally between men and women. Another ruler and his slave-boy became models of perfect love in the verses of mystic poets.

Islam allowed slavery but forbade Muslims from enslaving other Muslims or so-called People of the Book—Jews, Christians, and Zoroastrians, who revered holy books respected by the Muslims. Being enslaved as a prisoner of war, a fate that befell many women captured in the camps of defeated armies, constituted an exception. Later centuries saw a constant flow of slaves into Islamic territory from Africa and Central Asia. A hereditary slave society, however, did not develop. Usually slaves converted to Islam, and many masters then freed them as an act of piety. The offspring of slave women and Muslim men were born free.

The Recentering of Islam

Early Islam centered on the caliphate, the political expression of the unity of the umma. No formal organization or hierarchy, however, directed the process of conversion. Thus there emerged a multitude of local Islamic communities so disconnected from each other that numerous competing interpretations of the developing religion arose. Inevitably, the centrality of the caliphate diminished (see Map 10.2). The appearance of rival caliphates in Tunisia and Córdoba accentuated the problem of decentralization.

Chemistry

Muslim scientists developed sophisticated chemical processes and used them to produce a broad range of goods, including glazes for pottery, rosewater (the distilled essence of roses), hard soap, gunpowder, and various types of glass. The words *chemistry* and *alchemy* are both related to the Arabic term for these activities, *al-kimiya*, and many chemical processes passed from the Muslim world to Europe.

Distillation was used at Baku in Azerbaijan to produce a light flammable liquid called "white *naft*," roughly equivalent to kerosene, from crude oil. Special military units wearing fire-resistant clothing were trained to use white *naft* as an incendiary weapon. Flaming liquids, whose exact composition is still uncertain, could be put into pots and thrown, placed in containers attached to arrows, or pumped from a tube.

Collection of The Corning Museum of Glass, 68.1.1

Islamic Glassware   This glass bottle from Syria shows the skill of Muslim chemists and artisans in producing clear, transparent glass. The scratched decoration reflects the Muslim taste for geometric design.

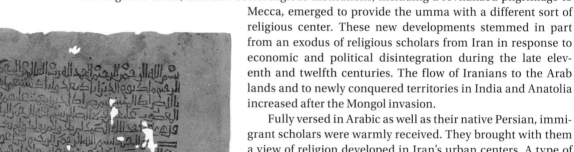

The rise of the ulama as community leaders did not prevent growing fragmentation because the ulama themselves divided into contentious factions. During the twelfth century factionalism began to abate, and new socioreligious institutions, including a revitalized pilgrimage to Mecca, emerged to provide the umma with a different sort of religious center. These new developments stemmed in part from an exodus of religious scholars from Iran in response to economic and political disintegration during the late eleventh and twelfth centuries. The flow of Iranians to the Arab lands and to newly conquered territories in India and Anatolia increased after the Mongol invasion.

Fully versed in Arabic as well as their native Persian, immigrant scholars were warmly received. They brought with them a view of religion developed in Iran's urban centers. A type of religious college, the *madrasa* (MAH-dras-uh), gained sudden popularity outside Iran, where madrasas had been known since the tenth century. Scores of madrasas, many founded by local rulers, appeared throughout the Islamic world. In the fourteenth century, Mecca became a major educational center for the first time since Muhammad's generation.

Iranians also contributed to the growth of mystic groups known as *Sufi* brotherhoods in the twelfth and thirteenth centuries. The doctrines and rituals of certain Sufis spread from

Quran Page Printed from a Woodblock   Printing from woodblocks or tin plates existed in Islamic lands between approximately 800 and 1400. Most prints were narrow amulets designed to be rolled and worn around the neck in cylindrical cases. Less valued than handwritten amulets, many prints came from Banu Sasan con men. Why block-printing had so little effect on society in general and eventually disappeared is unknown.   By permission of the Syndics of Cambridge University Library

Head Coverings

Covering the head is one of the most universal of human cultural characteristics. It is also one of the most common ways of signaling social status. Examples can be drawn from every part of the world, from earliest times down to the modern era. In premodern Chinese society, the color and design of a man's cap indicated his rank as clearly as the insignia on military head coverings does today. In most European societies in the seventeenth and eighteenth centuries, men and frequently women of the higher social orders wore wigs, a practice that still survives in the costume of British judges.

Head coverings were particularly important for royalty. From ancient Egypt, where the earliest Pharaonic crowns symbolized the union of the northern and southern parts of the Nile Valley, down to the twentieth century and the jewel-studded crown of the shah of Iran, each land developed its own distinctive royal headdress. This also held true for Native American societies in pre-Columbian times and for African and Polynesian societies. In some societies, such as Sasanid Iran and the Ottoman Empire in what is today Turkey, each ruler's crown or turban had a distinctive design that symbolized his rule.

Head coverings have also played significant roles in religion. In orthodox Judaism, for example, men wear hats or skullcaps, and married women wear wigs, as signs of acceptance of God's laws. In Islam, head coverings for women, borrowed from pre-Islamic practice in the Middle East, have become politically controversial in recent years; but prior to the twentieth century it was considered equally improper for a Muslim man to go bareheaded.

Wearing no hat at all was usually a characteristic of slaves or of the poorest elements in society. But it could also signify a deliberate desire to be regarded as humble. Sumerian priests, Buddhist monks and nuns, and certain Sufis in the Muslim world shaved their heads clean. In Europe, early Christian monks and priests shaved the crown of their heads in the Roman Catholic tradition. This form of tonsure competed with and eventually superseded an Irish Catholic practice of shaving the front of the head. Yet head shaving did not always signify humility. Japanese samurai, or warriors, also shaved the front of their heads.

Head coverings for women, as well as wigs and hairdressing styles, sometimes show greater diversity than those for men. This has been particularly true in societies where women of high status mix with men on public occasions. A magnificent wig, hat, or coiffure under these circumstances might speak as much for the social rank of the woman's husband as for her own.

Given this long history of distinctive head coverings, the abandonment of both men's and women's hats in the second half of the twentieth century marked a major turning point in

Muslim Head Coverings   The man standing before a governor in this thirteenth-century miniature painting wears a simple skullcap indicating his low social status. The two attendants wear turbans, but the governor's turban is built into a high, conical shape. The folds and tails of turbans signified not only rank, but also place of origin. To this day, men from western Afghanistan wear tightly wound white turbans with long tails while men from eastern Afghanistan wear loose colorful turbans.   Abu Zayd standing before the governor of Ramba in Baghdad, Arabic miniature, 1237. /De Agostini Picture Library/J.E. Bulloz/The Bridgeman Art Library

the history of symbolism. Around the world, the hat-making industry has greatly contracted. Whether one visits China, Egypt, India, France, or Brazil, one finds it difficult to determine the rank or status of most people by looking at what they have on their heads. Heads of government typically pose for group photographs with no hats on at all. Aside from conservative religious groups, the head coverings that remain most often indicate occupations: military, police, construction, athletics, and so on.

The reasons for this change are unclear. The spread of democracy and decline of aristocracy may have contributed to it, but hats have become equally uncommon in dictatorships. A more likely cause is the worldwide role of news photographs, movies, and other pictorial media. The media developed in Europe and the United States tend to take Western customs as normal and exoticize non-Western styles as "native costumes." People everywhere have thus felt pressure to switch to Western styles, including bareheadedness, to fit into the image of the modern world.

QUESTIONS FOR ANALYSIS

1. What might covering the head, or removing a head cover, signify in America today?

2. How desirable is it to be able to distinguish a person's job or social position by looking at his or her head covering?

3. What does wearing a baseball cap convey?

city to city, giving rise to the first geographically extensive Islamic religious organizations. Sufi doctrines varied, but a quest for a sense of union with God through rituals and training was a common denominator. Sufism had begun in early Islamic times and had doubtless benefited from the ideas and beliefs of people from religions with mystic traditions who converted to Islam.

The early Sufis had been saintly individuals given to ecstatic and poetic utterances and wonder-working. They attracted disciples but did not try to organize them. The growth of brotherhoods, a less ecstatic form of Sufism, set a tone for society in general. It soon became common for most Muslim men, particularly in the cities, to belong to at least one brotherhood.

A sense of the social climate the Sufi brotherhoods fostered can be gained from a twelfth-century manual:

> *Every limb has its own special ethics. . . . The ethics of the tongue. The tongue should always be busy in reciting God's names (dhikr) and in saying good things of the brethren, praying for them, and giving them counsel. . . . The ethics of hearing. One should not listen to indecencies and slander. . . . The ethics of sight. One should lower one's eyes in order not to see forbidden things.*[4]

Special dispensations allowed people who merely wanted to emulate the Sufis and enjoy their company to follow less demanding rules:

> *It is allowed by way of dispensation to possess an estate or to rely on a regular income. The Sufis' rule in this matter is that one should not use all of it for himself, but should dedicate this to public charities and should take from it only enough for one year for himself and his family. . . .*
>
> *There is a dispensation allowing one to watch all kinds of amusement. This is, however, limited by the rule: What you are forbidden from doing, you are also forbidden from watching.*[5]

Some Sufi brotherhoods spread in the countryside, and local shrines and pilgrimages to the tombs of Muhammad's descendants and saintly Sufis became popular.

SECTION REVIEW

- The foundation of Islamic civilization is the Shari'a, which is derived from the Quran and hadith.

- Urbanization and religious conversion reinforced each other and prompted the expansion of agriculture, trade, science, and technology.

- Women in general enjoyed relatively high status under Islamic law, though urban women tended to live in seclusion.

- Islamic attitudes toward homosexuality were ambivalent, and slavery was an accepted and continuous practice.

- Migrations of Iranian scholars centered Islam on the madrasa and contributed to the rise of Sufism.

CONCLUSION

The Sasanid Empire that held sway in Iran and Iraq from the third to the seventh century resembled the contemporary realm of the eastern Roman emperors ruling from Constantinople. Both states forged strong relations between the ruler and the dominant religion, Zoroastrianism in the former empire, Christianity in the latter. Priestly hierarchies paralleled state administrative structures, and the citizenry came to think of themselves more as members of a faith community than as subjects of a ruler. This gave rise to conflict among religious sects and also raised the possibility of the founder of a new religion commanding both political and religious loyalty on an unprecedented scale. This possibility was realized in the career of the prophet Muhammad in the seventh century.

Islam culminated the trend toward identity based on religion. The concept of the umma united all Muslims in a universal community embracing enormous diversity of language, appearance, and social custom. Though Muslim communities adapted to local "small traditions," by the twelfth century a religious scholar could travel anywhere in the Islamic world and blend easily into the local Muslim community.

By the ninth century, the forces of conversion and urbanization fostered social and religious experimentation in urban settings. From the eleventh century onward, political disruption, the

---

[4]Abu Najib al-Suhrawardi, *A Sufi Rule for Novices*, trans. Menahem Milson (Cambridge, MA: Harvard University Press, 1975), 45–58.

[5]Ibid., 73–82.

spread of pastoral nomadism, and climatic deterioration slowed this early economic and technological dynamism. Muslim communities then turned to new religious institutions, such as the madrasas and Sufi brotherhoods, to create the flexible and durable community structures that carried Islam into new regions and protected ordinary believers from capricious political rule.

KEY TERMS

Sasanid Empire p. 244
Mecca p. 247
Muhammad p. 247
Muslim p. 248
Islam p. 248

Medina p. 248
umma p. 248
caliphate p. 249
Quran p. 249
Shi'ites p. 249

Umayyad Caliphate p. 249
Sunnis p. 251
Abbasid Caliphate p. 251
mamluks p. 252
Ghana p. 252

ulama p. 254
hadith p. 257

SUGGESTED READING

al-Hassan, Ahmad Y., and Donald R. Hill. *Islamic Technology: An Illustrated History.* 1986. Introduces a little-studied field.

Armstrong, Karen. *Muhammad: A Biography of the Prophet.* 1993. A sympathetic work with an ecumenical tone.

Berkey, Jonathan. *The Formation of Islam: Religion and Society in the Near East, 600–1800.* 2003. A short and lively survey.

Bloom, Jonathan. *Paper Before Print.* 2001. A superb study of paper and papermaking in medieval Islamic culture.

Bulliet, Richard W. *Cotton, Climate, and Camels in Early Islamic Iran.* 2009. Discusses the economic impact of a cotton boom followed by climatic cooling.

Bulliet, Richard W. *Islam: The View from the Edge.* 1993. An approach that concentrates on the lives of converts to Islam and local religious notables.

Choksy, Jamsheed K. *Conflict and Cooperation: Zoroastrian Subalterns and Muslim Elites in Medieval Iranian Society.* 1997. Exploits Arabic and Middle Persian sources to detail the interaction of religious communities.

Donner, Fred. *Narratives of Islamic Origins.* 1998. Discusses the new school of thought that rejects the traditional accounts of Muhammad's life and of the origins of the Quran.

Glick, Thomas F. *From Muslim Fortress to Christian Castle: Social and Cultural Change in Medieval Spain.* 1995. Questions standard ideas about Christians and Muslims from a geographical and technological standpoint.

Lapidus, Ira M. *A History of Islamic Societies,* 2d ed. 2002. A lengthy work that focuses on social developments and includes Islam outside the Middle East.

Laroui, Abdallah. *The History of the Maghrib: An Interpretive Essay.* 1977. Challenges traditional French scholarship on North Africa.

Lassner, Jacob. *A Mediterranean Society: An Abridgement in One Volume.* 1999. Summary of S. D. Goitein's multivolume study of the Jews of medieval Egypt.

Pourshariati, Parvaneh. *Decline and Fall of the Sasanian Empire: The Sasanian-Parthian Confederacy and the Arab Conquest of Iran.* 2008. Revisionist interpretation of the transition from Sasanid to Islamic rule in Iran.

Sells, Michael. *Approaching the Qur'an: The Early Revelations.* 1999. An insightful reading of parts of the Quran, which Muslims regard as untranslatable. Most "interpretations" in English adhere reasonably closely to the Arabic text.

Spellberg, Denise. *Politics, Gender, and the Islamic Past: The Legacy of A'isha bint Abi Bakr.* 1994. A pathbreaking work on the methodology of women's history.

Waines, David. *An Introduction to Islam.* 1995. A reliable starting point for studying the religion of Islam.

CourseMate Go to the History CourseMate website for primary source links, study tools, and review materials for this chapter. www.cengagebrain.com

Chapter Outline

The Byzantine Empire, 600–1200
➤ *How did the Byzantine Empire maintain Roman imperial traditions in the east?*

Early Medieval Europe, 600–1000
➤ *How did the culture of early medieval Europe develop in the absence of imperial rule?*

The Western Church
➤ *What role did the Western Church play in the politics and culture of Europe?*

Kievan Russia, 900–1200
➤ *What was the significance of the adoption of Orthodox Christianity by Kievan Russia?*

Western Europe Revives, 1000–1200
➤ *How did Mediterranean trade help revive western Europe?*

The Crusades, 1095–1204
➤ *What were the origins and impact of the Crusades?*

Conclusion

● **ENVIRONMENT + TECHNOLOGY** Iron Production
● **DIVERSITY + DOMINANCE** The Struggle for Christian Morality

Building ships under the orders of Duke William, detail from the Bayeux Tapestry, before 1082 (wool embroidery on linen), French School, (11th century)/Musee de la Tapisserie, Bayeux, France/With special authorisation of the city of Bayeux/The Bridgeman Art Library

Boatbuilding Scene from the Bayeaux Tapestry Eleventh-century shipwrights prepare vessels for William of Normandy's invasion of England.

Christian Societies Emerge in Europe, 600–1200

Christmas Day in 800 found Charles, king of the Franks, in Rome instead of at his palace at Aachen in northwestern Germany. At six-foot-three, Charles towered over the average man of his time, and his royal career had been equally gargantuan. Crowned king in his mid-twenties in 768, he had crisscrossed Europe for three decades, waging war on Muslim invaders from Spain, Avar (ah-vahr) invaders from Hungary, and a number of German princes.

Charles had subdued many enemies and had become protector of the papacy. So not all historians believe the eyewitness report of his secretary and biographer that Charles was surprised when, as the king rose from his prayers, Pope Leo III placed a new crown on his head. "Life and victory to Charles the August, crowned by God the great and pacific Emperor of the Romans," proclaimed the pope.[1] Then, amid the cheers of the crowd, he humbly knelt before the new emperor.

Charlemagne (SHAHR-leh-mane) (from Latin *Carolus magnus*, "Charles the Great") was the first in western Europe to bear the title *emperor* in over three hundred years. Rome's decline and Charlemagne's rise marked a shift of focus for Europe—away from the Mediterranean and toward the north and west. German custom and Christian piety transformed the Roman heritage to create a new civilization. While the memory of Greek and Roman philosophy faded, Irish monks preaching in Latin became important intellectual influences in some parts of Europe. Urban life continued the decline that had begun in the later days of the Roman Empire. Historians originally called this era "**medieval**," literally "middle age," because it comes between the era of Greco-Roman civilization and the intellectual, artistic, and economic changes of the Renaissance in the fourteenth century; but research has uncovered many aspects of medieval culture that are as rich and creative as those that came earlier and later.

Charlemagne was not the only ruler in Europe to claim the title emperor. Another emperor held sway in the Greek-speaking east, where Rome's political and legal heritage continued. The Eastern Roman Empire was often called the **Byzantine Empire** after the seventh century, and it was known to the Muslims as Rum (room). While western Europeans lived amid the ruins of empire, the Byzantines maintained and reinterpreted Roman traditions. The authority of the Byzantine emperors blended with the influence of the Christian church to form a cultural synthesis that helped shape the emerging kingdom of **Kievan Russia**. Byzantium's centuries-long conflict with Islam helped spur the crusading passion that overtook western Europe in the eleventh century.

The comparison between western and eastern Europe appears paradoxical. Byzantium inherited a robust and self-confident late Roman society and economy,

Charlemagne King of the Franks (r. 768–814); emperor (r. 800–814). Through a series of military conquests he established the Carolingian Empire, which encompassed all of Gaul and parts of Germany and Italy. Though illiterate himself, he sponsored a brief intellectual revival.

medieval Literally "middle age," a term that historians of Europe use for the period around 500 to 1500, signifying its intermediate point between Greco-Roman antiquity and the Renaissance.

Byzantine Empire Historians' name for the eastern portion of the Roman Empire from the fourth century onward, taken from "Byzantium," an early name for Constantinople, the Byzantine capital city. The empire fell to the Ottomans in 1453.

Kievan Russia State established at Kiev in Ukraine around 880 by Scandinavian adventurers asserting authority over a mostly Slavic farming population.

[1]Lewis G. M. Thorpe, *Two Lives of Charlemagne* (Harmondsworth, England: Penguin, 1969).

while western Europe could not achieve political unity and suffered severe economic decline. Yet by 1200 western Europe was showing renewed vitality and flexing its military muscles, while Byzantium was showing signs of decline and military weakness. As we explore the causes and consequences of these different historical paths, we must remember that the emergence of Christian Europe included both developments.

THE BYZANTINE EMPIRE, 600–1200

The Byzantine emperors established Christianity as their official religion (see Chapter 6). They also represented a continuation of Roman imperial rule and tradition that was largely absent in the kingdoms that succeeded Rome in the west. Whereas only provincial forms of Roman law survived in the west, Byzantium inherited imperial law intact. Combining the imperial role with political oversight over the Christian church, the emperors made a comfortable transition into the role of all-powerful Christian monarchs. The Byzantine drama, however, played on a steadily shrinking stage. Territorial losses and almost constant military pressure from north and south deprived the empire of long periods of peace.

An Empire Beleaguered

Having a single ruler endowed with supreme legal and religious authority prevented the breakup of the Eastern Empire into petty principalities, but a series of territorial losses sapped the empire's strength. Between 634 and 650, Arab armies destroyed the Sasanid Empire and captured Byzantine Egypt, Syria, and Tunisia (see Chapter 10). Islam posed a religious as well as a political challenge. By the end of the twelfth century, some two-thirds of the Christians in these former Byzantine territories had adopted the Muslim faith (see Map 11.1 on page 271).

The loss of such populous and prosperous provinces shook the empire and reduced its power. Although it had largely recovered and reorganized militarily by the tenth century, it never regained the lost lands. Though Crusaders from western Europe established short-lived Christian principalities at the eastern end of the Mediterranean Sea at the very end of the eleventh century, the Byzantines found them almost as hostile as the Muslims (see the section below on the Crusades). Eventually the empire succumbed to Muslim conquest in 1453.

The later Byzantine emperors faced new enemies in the north and south. Following the wave of Germanic migrations (see Chapter 6), Slavic and Turkic peoples appeared on the northern frontiers as part of centuries-long and poorly understood population migrations in Eurasian steppe lands. Other Turks led by the Seljuk family became the primary foe in the south (see Chapter 10).

At the same time, relations with the popes and princes of western Europe steadily worsened. In the mid-ninth century the patriarchs of Constantinople (cahn-stan-tih-NO-pul) had challenged the territorial jurisdiction of the popes of Rome and some of the practices of the Latin Church. These arguments worsened

Byzantine Church from a Twelfth-Century Manuscript The upper portion shows the church façade and domes. The lower portion shows the interior with a mosaic of Christ enthroned at the altar end. Image Asset Management Ltd./SuperStock

CHRONOLOGY

	Western Europe	Eastern Europe
600		634–650 Muslims conquer Byzantine provinces of Syria, Egypt, and Tunisia
	711 Muslim conquest of Spain 732 Battle of Tours	
800	800 Coronation of Charlemagne 843 Treaty of Verdun divides Carolingian Empire among Charlemagne's grandsons	
		ca. 880 Varangians take control of Kiev
	910 Monastery of Cluny founded 962 Beginning of Holy Roman Empire	
		980 Vladimir becomes grand prince of Kievan Russia
1000	1054 Formal schism between Latin and Orthodox Churches 1066 Normans under William the Conqueror invade England 1076–1078 Climax of investiture controversy	
		1081–1118 Alexius Comnenus rules Byzantine Empire, calls for western military aid against Muslims
	1095 Pope Urban II preaches First Crusade	
1200		1204 Western knights sack Constantinople in Fourth Crusade

schism A formal split within a religious community.

over time and in 1054 culminated in a formal **schism** (SKIZ-uhm) between the Latin Church and the Orthodox Church—a break that has been only partially mended.

Society and Urban Life

Imperial authority and urban prosperity in the eastern provinces of the Late Roman Empire initially sheltered Byzantium from many of the economic reverses and population losses suffered by western Europe. However, the two regions shared a common demographic crisis during a sixth-century epidemic of bubonic plague known as "the plague of Justinian," named after the emperor who ruled from 527 to 565. A similar though gradual and less pronounced social transformation set in around the seventh century, possibly sparked by further epidemics and the loss of Egypt and Syria to the Muslims. Formal histories tell us little, but popular narratives of saints' lives show a transition from stories about educated saints hailing from cities to stories about saints who originated as peasants. In many areas, barter replaced money transactions; some cities declined in population and wealth; and the traditional class of local urban notables nearly disappeared.

As the urban elite class shrank, the importance of high-ranking aristocrats at the imperial court and of rural landowners increased. Power organized by family began to rival power from class-based officeholding. By the end of the eleventh century, a family-based military aristocracy had emerged. Of Byzantine emperor Alexius Comnenus (uh-LEX-see-uhs kom-NAY-nuhs) (r. 1081–1118) it was said: "He considered himself not a ruler, but a lord, conceiving and calling the empire his own house."[2] The situation of women changed, too. Although earlier Roman family life was centered on a legally all-powerful father, women had enjoyed comparative freedom in public. After the seventh century women increasingly found themselves confined to the home. Some sources indicate that when they went out, they concealed their faces behind veils. The only men they socialized with were family members. Paradoxically, however, from 1028 to 1056 women ruled the Byzantine Empire alongside their husbands. These social changes and the apparent increase in the seclusion of women resemble simultaneous developments in neighboring Islamic countries, but historians have not uncovered any firm linkage between them.

[2]A. P. Kazhdan and Ann Wharton Epstein, *Change in Byzantine Culture in the Eleventh and Twelfth Centuries* (Berkeley: University of California Press, 1985), 71.

Economically, the Byzantine emperors continued the Late Roman inclination to set prices, organize grain shipments to the capital, and monopolize trade in luxury goods like Tyrian purple cloth. Such government intervention may have slowed technological development and economic innovation. So long as merchants and pilgrims hastened to Constantinople from all points of the compass, aristocrats could buy rare and costly goods. Just as the provisioning and physical improvement of Rome overshadowed the development of other cities at the height of the Roman Empire, so other Byzantine cities suffered from the intense focus on Constantinople. In the countryside, Byzantine farmers continued to use slow oxcarts and light scratch plows, which were efficient for many, but not all, soil types, long after farmers in western Europe had begun to adopt more efficient techniques (discussed later in this chapter).

Because Byzantium's Roman inheritance remained so much more intact than western Europe's, few people recognized the slow deterioration. Gradually, however, pilgrims and visitors from the west saw the reality beyond the awe-inspiring, incense-filled domes of cathedrals and beneath the glitter and silken garments of the royal court. An eleventh-century French visitor wrote:

> *The city itself [Constantinople] is squalid and fetid and in many places harmed by permanent darkness, for the wealthy overshadow the streets with buildings and leave these dirty, dark places to the poor and to travelers; there murders and robberies and other crimes which love the darkness are committed. Moreover, since people live lawlessly in this city, which has as many lords as rich men and almost as many thieves as poor men, a criminal knows neither fear nor shame, because crime is not punished by law and never entirely comes to light. In every respect she exceeds moderation; for, just as she surpasses other cities in wealth, so too, does she surpass them in vice.*[3]

A Byzantine contemporary, Anna Comnena, the brilliant daughter of Emperor Alexius Comnenus, expressed the view from the other side. She scornfully described a prominent churchman and philosopher who happened to be from Italy: "Italos . . . was unable with his barbaric, stupid temperament to grasp the profound truths of philosophy; even in the act of learning he utterly rejected the teacher's guiding hand, and full of temerity and barbaric folly, [believed] even before study that he excelled all others."[4]

Cultural Achievements

Though the greatest Byzantine architectural monument, Constantinople's Hagia Sophia (AH-yah SOH-fee-uh) ("Sacred Wisdom") cathedral, dates to the reign of Justinian, artistic creativity continually manifested itself in the design and ornamentation of other churches and monasteries. Justinian also ordered the collection of all Roman imperial edicts in a massive law code known as the *Corpus Juris Civilis*, or Body of Civil Law. Byzantine religious art, featuring stiff but arresting images of holy figures against gold backgrounds, strongly influenced painting in western Europe down to the thirteenth century, and Byzantine musical traditions strongly affected the chanting employed in medieval Latin churches.

Another important Byzantine achievement dates to the empire's long period of political decline. In the ninth century brothers named Cyril and Methodius embarked on a highly successful mission to the Slavs of Moravia (part of the modern Czech Republic). They preached in the local language, and their followers perfected a writing system, called Cyrillic (sih-RIL-ik), that came to be used by Slavic Christians adhering to the Orthodox—that is, Byzantine—rite. Their careers also mark the beginning of a competition between the Greek and Latin forms of Christianity for the allegiance of the Slavs. The use today of the Cyrillic alphabet among the Russians and other Slavic peoples of Orthodox Christian faith, and of the Roman alphabet among the Poles, Czechs, and Croatians, testifies to this competition (see the section on Kievan Russia).

SECTION REVIEW

- Unlike the Western Roman Empire, the Eastern Roman Empire retained its unity and became the Byzantine Empire, headed by an emperor who held both political and religious power.

- A schism split the Orthodox Church from the Catholic Church in the west.

- The Byzantine Empire suffered territorial losses, and its urban centers gradually declined.

- The culture of the Byzantine Empire made many important aesthetic contributions to the art of Europe.

- Byzantine missionaries spread their faith and the Cyrillic alphabet into eastern Europe.

[3]Ibid., 248.
[4]Ibid., 255.

EARLY MEDIEVAL EUROPE, 600–1000

The disappearance of the imperial legal framework that had persisted to the final days of the Western Roman Empire (see Chapter 6) and the rise of various kings, nobles, and chieftains changed the legal and political landscape of western Europe. In region after region, the family-based traditions of the Germanic peoples, which often fit local conditions better than previous practices, supplanted the edicts of the Roman emperors (see Map 11.2).

Fear and physical insecurity led communities to seek the protection of local strongmen. In places where looters and pillagers might appear at any moment, a local lord with a castle at which peasants could take refuge counted for more than a distant king. Dependency of weak people on strong people became a hallmark of the post-Roman period in western Europe.

The Time of Insecurity

In 711 a frontier raiding party of Arabs and Berbers, acting under the authority of the Umayyad caliph in Syria, crossed the Strait of Gibraltar and overturned the kingdom of the Visigoths in Spain (see Chapter 10). The disunited Europeans could not stop them from consolidating their hold on the Iberian Peninsula. After pushing the remaining Christian chieftains into the northern

MAP 11.1 **The Spread of Christianity** By the early eighth century, Christian areas around the southern Mediterranean from northern Syria to northern Spain, accounting for most of the Christian population, had fallen under Muslim rule; the slow process of conversion to Islam had begun. This change accentuated the importance of the patriarchs of Constantinople, the popes in Rome, and the later converting regions of northern and eastern Europe. © Cengage Learning

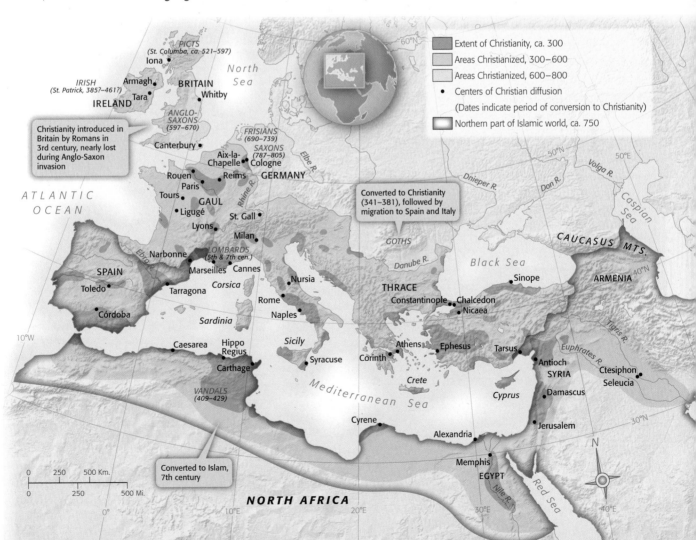

mountains, the Muslims moved on to France. They occupied much of the southern coast and penetrated as far north as Tours, less than 150 miles (240 kilometers) from the English Channel, before Charlemagne's grandfather, Charles Martel, stopped their most advanced raiding party in 732.

Military effectiveness was the key element in the rise of the Carolingian **(kah-roe-LIN-gee-uhn)** family (from Latin *Carolus*, "Charles"), first as protectors of the Frankish (French) kings, then as kings themselves under Charlemagne's father Pepin (r. 751–768), and finally, under Charlemagne, as emperors. At the peak of Charlemagne's power, the Carolingian Empire encompassed all of Gaul and parts of Germany and Italy, with the pope ruling part of the latter. When Charlemagne's son, Louis the Pious, died, the Germanic tradition of splitting property among sons led to the Treaty of Verdun (843), which split the empire into three parts. French-speaking in the west (France) and middle (Burgundy), and German-speaking in the east (Germany), the three regions never reunited. Nevertheless, the Carolingian economic system based on landed wealth and a brief intellectual revival sponsored personally by Charlemagne—though he himself was illiterate—provided a common heritage.

A new threat to western Europe appeared in 793, when the Vikings, sea raiders from Scandinavia, attacked and plundered a monastery on the English coast, the first of hundreds of such raids. Local sources from France, the British Isles, and Muslim Spain attest to widespread dread of Viking warriors descending from multi-oared, dragon-prowed boats to pillage monasteries, villages, and towns. Viking shipbuilders made versatile vessels that could brave the stormy North Atlantic and also maneuver up rivers to attack inland towns. As we shall see, in the ninth century raiders from Denmark and Norway harried the British and French coasts while Varangians **(va-RAN-gee-anz)** (Swedes) pursued raiding and trading interests, and eventually the building of kingdoms, along the rivers of eastern Europe and Russia. Although many Viking raiders sought booty and slaves, in the 800s and 900s Viking captains organized the settlement of Iceland, Greenland, and, around the year 1000, Vinland on the northern tip of Newfoundland.

Vikings long settled on lands they had seized in Normandy (in northwestern France) organized the most important and ambitious expeditions in terms of numbers of men and horses and long-lasting impact. William the Conqueror, the duke of Normandy, invaded England in 1066 and brought Anglo-Saxon domination of the island to an end. Other Normans (from "north men") attacked Muslim Sicily in the 1060s and, after thirty years of fighting, permanently severed it from the Muslim world.

MAP 11.2 **Germanic Kingdoms** Though German kings asserted authority over most of western Europe, German-speaking peoples were most numerous east of the Rhine River. In most other areas, Celtic languages, for example, Breton on this map, or languages derived from Latin predominated. Though the Germanic Anglo-Saxon tongue increasingly supplanted Welsh and Scottish in Britain, the absolute number of Germanic settlers seems to have been fairly limited. © Cengage Learning

Viking Runestone Pre-Christian symbols and myths from northern Europe appear on stones like this one from Sweden. An inscription containing names written in the runic alphabet had elaborately intertwined ornaments at the ends, a feature that reappears in the Christian Book of Kells (see page 280). The scene at the top is thought to depict Odin, the chief god of the Vikings. Werner Forman/Art Resource, NY

A Self-Sufficient Economy

Archaeology and records kept by Christian monasteries and convents reveal a profound economic transformation that accompanied the new Germanic political order. The new rulers cared little for the urban-based civilization of the Romans, which accordingly shrank in importance. Though the pace of change differed from region to region, most cities lost population, in some cases becoming villages. Roman roads fell into disuse and disrepair. Small thatched houses sprang up beside abandoned villas, and public buildings made of marble became dilapidated in the absence of the laborers, money, and civic leadership needed to maintain them. Paying for purchases in coin largely gave way to bartering goods and services.

Trade across the Mediterranean did not entirely stop after the Muslim conquests. Archaeological investigations of sunken ships show a continuation of contact, but more with North African ports than with Egypt and Syria. Nevertheless, most of western Europe came to rely on meager local resources. These resources, moreover, underwent redistribution.

Roman centralization had channeled the wealth and production of the empire to the capital, which in turn radiated Roman cultural styles and tastes to the provinces. As Roman governors were replaced by Germanic territorial lords, who found the riches of their own culture more appealing than those of Rome, local self-sufficiency became more important. The decline of literacy and other aspects of Roman life made room for the growth of Germanic cultural traditions.

The diet in the northern countries featured beer, lard or butter, and bread made of barley, rye, or wheat, all supplemented by pork from herds of swine fed on forest acorns and beechnuts, and by game from the same forests. Nobles ate better than peasants, but even the peasant diet was reasonably balanced. The Roman diet based on wheat, wine, and olive oil persisted in the south. The average western European of the ninth century was probably better nourished than his or her descendants three hundred years later, when population was increasing and the nobility monopolized the resources of the forests.

manor In medieval Europe, a large, self-sufficient landholding consisting of the lord's residence (manor house), outbuildings, peasant village, and surrounding land.

In both north and south, self-sufficient farming estates known as **manors** became the primary centers of agricultural production. Fear of attack led many common farmers in the most vulnerable regions to give their lands to large landowners in return for political and physical protection. The warfare and instability of the post-Roman centuries made unprotected country houses especially vulnerable to pillaging. Isolated by poor communications and lack of organized government, landowners depended on their own resources for survival. Many became warriors or maintained a force of armed men. Others swore allegiance to landowners who had armed forces to protect them.

A well-appointed manor possessed fields, gardens, grazing lands, fishponds, a mill, a church, workshops for making farm and household implements, and a village where the farmers dependent on the lord of the manor lived. Depending on local conditions, protection ranged from a ditch and wooden stockade to a stone wall surrounding a fortified keep (a stone building). Fortification tended to increase until the twelfth century, when stronger monarchies made it less necessary.

serf In medieval Europe, an agricultural laborer legally bound to a lord's property and obligated to perform set services for the lord.

Manor life reflected personal status. Nobles and their families exercised almost unlimited power over the **serfs**—agricultural workers who belonged to the manor, tilled its fields, and owed other dues and obligations. Serfs could not leave the manor where they were born and attach themselves to another lord. Most peasants in England, France, and western Germany were unfree serfs in the tenth and eleventh centuries. However, in Bordeaux (bore-DOE), Saxony, and a few other regions, free peasantry survived based on the egalitarian social structure of the Germanic peoples during their period of migration. Outright slavery, the mainstay of the Roman economy (see Chapter 6), diminished as more and more peasants became serfs in return for a lord's protection. At the same time, the enslavement of prisoners to serve as laborers became less important as an object of warfare.

Early Medieval Society in the West

Europe's reversion to a self-sufficient economy limited the freedom and potential for personal achievement of most people, but an emerging class of nobles reaped great benefits. During the Germanic migrations and later among the Vikings of Scandinavia, men regularly answered the call to arms issued by war chiefs, to whom they swore allegiance. All warriors shared in the booty gained from raiding. As settlement enhanced the importance of agricultural tasks, laying down the plow and picking up the sword at the chieftain's call became harder.

Those who, out of loyalty or desire for adventure, continued to join the war parties included a growing number of horsemen. Mounted warriors became the central force of the Carolingian army. At first, fighting from horseback did not make a person either a nobleman or a landowner. By the tenth century, however, nearly constant warfare to protect land rights or support the claims of a lord brought about a gradual transformation in the status of the mounted warrior, which led, at different rates in different areas, to landholding becoming almost inseparable from military service.

In trying to understand long-standing traditions of landholding and obligation, lawyers in the sixteenth century and later simplified thousands of individual agreements into a neat system they called "feudalism," from Latin *feodum*, meaning a land awarded for military service. It became common to refer to medieval Europe as a "feudal society" in which kings and lords gave land to "vassals" in return for sworn military support. By analyzing original records, more recent historians have discovered this to be an oversimplification. Relations between landholders and serfs and between lords and vassals differed too much from one place to another, and from one time to another, to fit together in anything resembling a regular system.

The German foes of the Roman legions had equipped themselves with helmets, shields, and swords, spears, or throwing axes. Some rode horses, but most fought on foot. Before the invention of the stirrup by Central Asian pastoralists in approximately the first century C.E., horsemen had gripped their mounts with their legs and fought with bows and arrows, throwing javelins, stabbing spears, and swords. Stirrups allowed a rider to stand in the saddle, lean forward, and absorb the impact when his lance struck an enemy at full gallop. This type of warfare required grain-fed horses that were larger and heavier than the small, grass-fed animals of the Central Asian nomads, though smaller and lighter than the draft horses bred in later times for hauling heavy loads. Thus agricultural Europe rather than the grassy steppes produced the charges of armored knights that came to dominate the battlefield.

By the eleventh century, the knight, called by different terms in different places, had emerged as the central figure in medieval warfare. He wore an open-faced helmet and a long linen shirt, or hauberk (HAW-berk), studded with small metal disks (see Environment and Technology: Iron Production). A century later, knightly equipment commonly included a visored helmet that covered the head and neck and a hauberk of chain mail.

Each increase in armor for knight and horse entailed a greater financial outlay. Since land was the basis of wealth, a knight needed financial support from land revenues. Accordingly, kings began to reward armed service with grants of land from their own property. Lesser nobles with extensive properties built their own military retinues the same way.

fief In medieval Europe, land granted in return for a sworn oath to provide specified military service.

A grant of land in return for a pledge to provide military service was often called a **fief**. At first, kings granted fiefs to their noble followers, known as **vassals**, on a temporary basis. By the tenth century, most fiefs could be inherited as long as the specified military service continued to be provided. Though patterns varied greatly, the association of landholding with military service made the medieval society of western Europe quite different from the contemporary city-based societies of the Islamic world.

vassal In medieval Europe, a sworn supporter of a king or lord committed to rendering specified military service to that king or lord.

Kings and lords might be able to command the service of their vassals for only part of the year. Vassals could hold land from several different lords and owe loyalty to each one. Moreover, the allegiance that a vassal owed to one lord could entail military service to that lord's master in time of need.

A "typical" medieval realm—actual practices varied between and within realms—consisted of lands directly owned by a king or a count and administered by his royal officers. The king's or count's major vassals held and administered other lands, often the greater portion, in return for military service. These vassals, in turn, granted land to their own vassals.

Noblewoman Directing Construction of a Church   This picture of Berthe, wife of Girat de Rousillon, acting as mistress of the works comes from a tenth-century manuscript that shows a scene from the ninth century. Wheelbarrows rarely appear in medieval building scenes.

Copyright Brussels, Royal Library of Belgium

The lord of a manor provided local governance and justice, direct royal government being quite limited. The king had few financial resources and seldom exercised legal jurisdiction at a local level. Members of the clergy, as well as the extensive agricultural lands owned by monasteries and nunneries, fell under the jurisdiction of the church, which further limited the reach and authority of the monarch.

Noblewomen became enmeshed in this tangle of obligations as heiresses and as candidates for marriage. A man who married the widow or daughter of a lord with no sons could gain control of that lord's property. Marriage alliances affected entire kingdoms. Noble daughters and sons had little say in marriage matters; issues of land, power, and military service took precedence. Noblemen guarded the women in their families as closely as their other valuables.

Nevertheless, women could own land. A noblewoman sometimes administered her husband's estates when he was away at war. Nonnoble women usually worked alongside their menfolk, performing agricultural tasks such as raking and stacking hay, shearing sheep, and picking vegetables. As artisans, women spun, wove, and sewed clothing. The Bayeux (bay-YUH) Tapestry, a piece of embroidery 230 feet (70 meters) long and 20 inches (51 centimeters) wide depicting William the Conqueror's invasion of England in 1066, was designed and executed entirely by women, though historians do not agree on who those women were.

SECTION REVIEW

- In the west, German kingdoms divided territory seized from Rome, and German lifestyles gradually replaced Roman ones.

- Raids by warrior peoples, including Muslims and Vikings, forced an emphasis on warfare.

- The Carolingians created an empire that was later split into three realms.

- Society focused on rural villages and estates—manors—rather than cities.

- Rulers and nobles granted land to vassals in return for military service, thus creating the armed knight.

THE WESTERN CHURCH

Just as the Christian populations in eastern Europe followed the religious guidance of the patriarch of Constantinople appointed by the Byzantine emperor, so the pope commanded similar authority over church affairs in western Europe. And just as missionaries in the east spread Christianity among the Slavs, so missionaries in the west added territory to Christendom with forays into the British Isles and the lands of the Germans. Throughout the period covered by this chapter, Christian society was emerging and changing in both areas.

papacy The central administration of the Roman Catholic Church, of which the pope is the head.

In the west, Roman nobles lost control of the **papacy**—the office of the pope—and it became a more powerful international office after the tenth century. Councils of bishops—which normally set rules, called canons, to regulate the priests and laypeople (men and women who were not members of the clergy) under their jurisdiction—became increasingly responsive to papal direction.

Iron Production

Despite the collapse of the Roman economy, ironworking expanded throughout Europe. The iron swords of the Germans outperformed traditional Roman weapons, which became obsolete. The spreading use of armor also increased the demand for iron. Archaeologists have found extensive evidence of iron smelting well beyond the frontiers of the Roman Empire. Helg Island in a lake near Stockholm, Sweden, had a large walled settlement that relied entirely on iron trading. Discoveries of a Buddha from India and a christening spoon from Egypt, both datable to the sixth century C.E., indicate the range of these trade contacts. At Zelechovice in the Czech Republic, remains of fifty "slag-pit" furnaces have been dated to the ninth century.

Most iron smelting was done on a small scale. Ore containing iron oxide was shoveled onto a charcoal fire in an open-air hearth pit. The carbon in the charcoal combined with the oxygen in the ore to form carbon dioxide gas, leaving behind a soft glowing lump of iron called a "bloom." This bloom was then pounded on a stone to remove the remaining impurities, like sand and clay, before being turned over to the blacksmith for fabricating into swords or armor.

During the post-Roman centuries, smelters learned to build walls around the hearth pits and then to put domes and chimneys on them. The resulting "slag-pit" furnaces produced greater amounts of iron. They also consumed great amounts of wood. Twelve pounds of charcoal, made from about 25 pounds of wood, were needed to produce 1 pound of bloom iron, and about 3 pounds of useless slag. Though bellows were developed to force oxygen into the fire, temperatures in slag-pit furnaces never became high enough to produce molten metal.

Iron Smelting Two bellows blowing alternately provide a constant stream of air to the furnace. The man on the right pounds the bloom into bars or plates that a blacksmith will reheat and shape. Sloane 3983 fol.5

Blacksmiths at work, from 'Liber Astrologiae' (vellum), Netherlandish School, (14th century)/British Library, London, UK/© British Library Board. All Rights Reserved/The Bridgeman Art Library

Nevertheless, regional disagreements over church regulations, shortages of educated and trained clergy, difficult communications, political disorder, and the general insecurity of the period posed formidable obstacles to unifying church standards and practices (see Diversity and Dominance: The Struggle for Christian Morality). Clerics in some parts of western Europe were still issuing prohibitions against the worship of rivers, trees, and mountains as late as the eleventh century. Church problems included lingering polytheism, lax enforcement of prohibitions against marriage of clergy, nepotism (giving preferment to one's close kin), and simony (selling ecclesiastical appointments, often to people who were not members of the clergy). The persistence of the papacy in asserting its legal jurisdiction over clergy, combating polytheism and heretical beliefs, and calling on secular rulers to recognize the pope's authority, including unpopular rulings like a ban on first-cousin marriage, constituted a rare force for unity and order in a time of disunity and chaos.

Politics and the Church

Holy Roman Empire Loose federation of mostly German states and principalities, headed by an emperor elected by the princes. It lasted from 962 to 1806.

In politically fragmented western Europe, the pope needed allies. Like his son, Charlemagne's father Pepin was a strong supporter of the papacy. The relationship between kings and popes was tense, however, since both thought of themselves as ultimate authorities. In 962 the pope crowned the first "Holy Roman Emperor" (Charlemagne never held this full title). This designation of a secular political authority as the guardian of general Christian interests proved more apparent then real. Essentially a loose confederation of German princes who named one of their own to the highest office, the **Holy Roman Empire** had little influence west of the Rhine River.

Although the pope crowned the early Holy Roman Emperors, this did not signify political superiority because the law of the church (known as canon law because each law was called a canon) gave the pope exclusive legal jurisdiction over all clergy and church property wherever located. However, since bishops who held land as vassals owed military support or other services and dues to kings and princes, the secular rulers argued that they should have the power to appoint those bishops because that was the only way to guarantee fulfillment of their duties as vassals. The popes disagreed.

In the eleventh century, this conflict over the control of ecclesiastical appointments came to a head. Hildebrand (HILL-de-brand), an Italian monk, capped a career of reorganizing church finances when the cardinals (a group of senior bishops) meeting in Rome selected him to be Pope Gregory VII in 1073. His personal notion of the papacy (preserved among his letters) represented an extreme position, stating among other claims, that

§ *The pope can be judged by no one;*
§ *The Roman church has never erred and never will err till the end of time;*
§ *The pope alone can depose and restore bishops;*
§ *He alone can call general councils and authorize canon law;*
§ *He can depose emperors;*
§ *He can absolve subjects from their allegiance;*
§ *All princes should kiss his feet.*[5]

investiture controversy Dispute between the popes and the Holy Roman Emperors over who held ultimate authority over bishops in imperial lands.

Such claims antagonized lords and monarchs, who had become accustomed to *investing*—that is, conferring a ring and a staff as symbols of authority on bishops and abbots in their domains. Historians apply the term **investiture controversy** to the medieval struggle between the church and the lay lords to control ecclesiastical appointments; the term also refers to the broader conflict of popes versus emperors and kings. When Holy Roman Emperor Henry IV defied Gregory's reforms, Gregory excommunicated him in 1076, thereby cutting him off from church rituals. Stung by the resulting decline in his influence, Henry stood barefoot in the snow for three days outside a castle in northern Italy waiting for Gregory, a guest there, to receive him. Henry's formal act of penance induced Gregory to forgive him and restore him to the church; but the reconciliation, an apparent victory for the pope, did not last. In 1078 Gregory declared Henry deposed. The emperor then forced Gregory to flee from Rome to Salerno, where he died two years later.

The struggle between the popes and the emperors continued until 1122, when a compromise was reached at Worms, a town in Germany. In the Concordat of Worms, Emperor Henry V renounced his right to choose bishops and abbots or bestow spiritual symbols upon them. In return, Pope Calixtus II permitted the emperor to invest papally appointed bishops and abbots with any lay rights or obligations before their spiritual consecration. Such compromises did not fully solve the problem, but they reduced tensions between the two sides.

Assertions of royal authority triggered other conflicts as well. Though barely twenty when he became king of England in 1154, Henry II, a great-grandson of William the Conqueror, instituted reforms designed to strengthen the power of the Crown and weaken the nobility. He appointed traveling justices to enforce his laws and made juries, a holdover from traditional Germanic law, into powerful legal instruments. He also established the principle that criminal acts violated the "king's peace" and should be tried and punished in accordance with charges brought by the Crown instead of in response to charges brought by victims.

Henry had a harder time controlling the church. His closest friend and chancellor, or chief administrator, Thomas à Becket (ca. 1118–1170), lived the grand and luxurious life of a courtier. In 1162 Henry persuaded Becket to become a priest and assume the position of archbishop of Canterbury, the highest church office in England. Becket agreed but cautioned that from then on he would act solely in the interest of the church if it came into conflict with the Crown. When Henry sought to try clerics accused of crimes in royal instead of ecclesiastical courts, Archbishop Thomas, now leading an austere and pious life, resisted.

In 1170 four of Henry's knights, knowing that the king desired Becket's death, murdered the archbishop in Canterbury Cathedral. Their crime backfired, and an outpouring of sympathy caused Canterbury to become a major pilgrimage center. In 1173 the pope declared the

---

[5]R. W. Southern, *Western Society and the Church in the Middle Ages* (Harmondsworth, England: Penguin, 1970), 102.

The Struggle for Christian Morality

Ireland

The medieval church believed that Christians could be absolved of their sins by performing public or private penalties, or acts of humiliation. Priests listened to the believers confess their sins and then set the nature and duration of the penance. Books called penitentials guided the priests by stipulating the appropriate penance for specific sins. These books varied over time and tended to reflect local conditions. One of the earliest is attributed to Saint Patrick, who began his missionary work in Ireland in 432. The selections below deal not just with penalties for sin but also with efforts to impose church discipline on priests.

§ There shall be no wandering cleric in a parish.

§ If any cleric, from sexton [church caretaker] to priest, is seen without a tunic, and does not cover the shame and nakedness of his body; and if his hair is not shaven according to the Roman custom, and if his wife goes about with her head unveiled, he shall be alike despised by laymen and separated from the Church.

§ A monk and a virgin, the one from one place, the other from another, shall not dwell together in the same inn, nor travel in the same carriage from village to village, nor continually hold conversation with each other.

§ It is not permitted to the Church to accept alms from pagans.

§ A Christian who believes that there is a vampire in the world, that is to say, a witch, is to be anathematized [condemned by the Church]; whoever lays that reputation upon a living being, shall not be received into the Church until he revokes with his own voice the crime that he has committed and accordingly does penance with all diligence.

§ A Christian who defrauds anyone with respect to a debt in the manner of the pagans, shall be excommunicated [barred from Christian society] until he pays the debt.

England and Southern Germany

Boniface (ca. 675–754), a widely esteemed bishop of the southern German city of Mainz, began life with the name Winfrid in Anglo-Saxon Britain. After working as a missionary in Frisia in the Netherlands, he devoted the bulk of his life to establishing Christianity and respect for Christian law and morality in southern Germany. His letters reflect his passion for reforming personal behavior along Christian lines.

Boniface to Pope Zacharias, 742

We must confess, our father and lord, that after we learned from messengers that your predecessor in the apostolate [i.e., papacy], Gregory of reverend memory . . . had been set free from the prison of the body and had passed on to God, nothing gave us greater joy or happiness than the knowledge that the Supreme Arbiter had appointed your fatherly clemency to administer the canon law and to govern the Apostolic See. . . .

Some of the ignorant common people, Alemanians, Bavarians, and Franks, hearing that many of the offenses prohibited by us are practiced in the city of Rome imagine that they are allowed by the priests there and reproach us for causing them to incur blame in their own lives. They say that on the first day of January year after year, in the city of Rome and in the neighborhood of St. Peter's church by day or night, they have seen bands of singers parading the streets in pagan fashion, shouting and chanting sacrilegious songs and loading tables with food day and night, while no one in his own house is willing to lend his neighbor fire or tools or any other convenience. They say also that they have seen there women with amulets and bracelets of heathen fashion on their arms and legs, offering them for sale to willing buyers. . . .

Boniface and Other Bishops to King Ethelbald of Mercia (a Saxon Kingdom in England), 746–747

We have heard that you are very liberal in almsgiving, and congratulate you thereon. . . . We have heard also that you repress robbery and wrongdoing, perjury, and rapine with a strong hand, and that you have established peace within your kingdom. . . .

But amidst all this, one evil report as to the manner of life of Your Grace has come to our hearing, which has greatly grieved

---

monasticism Living in a religious community apart from secular society and adhering to a rule stipulating chastity, obedience, and poverty. It was a prominent element of medieval Christianity and Buddhism. Monasteries were the primary centers of learning and literacy in medieval Europe.

martyred Becket a saint. Henry allowed himself to be publicly whipped twice in penance for the crime, but his authority had been badly damaged.

Henry II's conflict with Thomas à Becket, like the Concordat of Worms, yielded no clear victor. The problem of competing legal traditions made political life in western Europe more complicated than in Byzantium or the lands of Islam (see Chapter 10). Feudal law, rooted in Germanic custom, gave supreme power to the king. Canon law, based on Roman precedent, visualized a single hierarchical legal institution with jurisdiction over all of Western Christendom. In the eleventh century Roman imperial law, contained in the *Corpus Juris Civilis* (see above), added a third tradition.

Monasticism

Monasticism featured prominently in the religious life of almost all medieval Christian lands. The origins of group monasticism lay in the eastern lands of the Roman Empire. Pre-Christian

us and which we would wish were not true. We have learned from many sources that you have never taken to yourself a lawful wife. . . . If you had willed to do this for the sake of chastity and abstinence . . . we should rejoice, for that is not worthy of blame but rather of praise. But if, as many say—but which God forbid!—you have neither taken a lawful spouse nor observed chastity for God's sake but, moved by desire, have defiled your good name before God and man by the crime of adulterous lust, then we are greatly grieved because this is a sin in the sight of God and is the ruin of your fair fame among men.

And now, what is worse, our informants say that these atrocious crimes are committed in convents with holy nuns and virgins consecrated to God, and this, beyond all doubt, doubles the offense. . . .

Northern Germany and Scandinavia

Adam of Bremen's History of the Archbishops of Hamburg-Bremen *consists of four sections. The third is devoted to the Archbishop Adalbert, whose death in 1072 stirred Adam to write. References to classical poets, the lives of saints, and royal documents show that Adam, a churchman, had a solid education and access to many sources, including conversations with kings and nobles.*

This remarkable man [i.e., Archbishop Adalbert] may . . . be extolled with praise of every kind in that he was noble, handsome, wise, eloquent, chaste, temperate. All these qualities he comprised in himself and others besides, such as one is wont to attach to the outer man: that he was rich, that he was successful, that he was glorious, that he was influential. All these things were his in abundance. Moreover, in respect of the mission to the heathen, which is the first duty of the Church at Hamburg, no one so vigorous could ever be found. . . .

As soon as the metropolitan [i.e., Archbishop Adalbert] had entered upon his episcopate, he sent legates to the kings of the north in the interest of friendship. There were also dispersed throughout all Denmark and Norway and Sweden and to the ends of the earth admonitory letters in which he exhorted the bishops and priests living in those parts . . . fearlessly to forward the conversion of the pagans. . . . [One Danish king] forgot the heavenly King as things prospered with him and married a blood relative from Sweden. This mightily displeased the lord archbishop, who sent legates to the rash king, rebuking him severely for his sin, and

who stated finally that if he did not come to his senses, he would have to be cut off with the sword of excommunication. Beside himself with rage, the king then threatened to ravage and destroy the whole diocese of Hamburg. Unperturbed by these threats, our archbishop, reproving and entreating, remained firm, until at length the Danish tyrant was prevailed upon by letters from the pope to give his cousin a bill of divorce. . . .

In Norway . . . King Harold surpassed all the madness of tyrants in his savage wildness. Many churches were destroyed by that man; many Christians were tortured to death by him. But he was a mighty man and renowned for the victories he had previously won in many wars with barbarians in Greece and in the Scythian regions [i.e., while assisting the Byzantine empress Zoë fight the Seljuk Turks]. After he came into his fatherland, however, he never ceased from warfare; he was the thunderbolt of the north. . . . And so, as he ruled over many nations, he was odious to all on account of his greed and cruelty. He also gave himself up to the magic arts and, wretched man that he was, did not heed the fact that his most saintly brother [i.e., Saint Olaf, one of Harold's predecessors] had eradicated such illusions from the realm and striven even unto death for the adoption of the precepts of Christianity. . . .

Across the Elbe [i.e., east of the river Hamburg is on] and in Slavia our affairs were still meeting with great success. For Gottschalk . . . married a daughter of the Danish king and so thoroughly subdued the Slavs that they feared him like a king, offered to pay tribute, and asked for peace with subjection. Under these circumstances our Church at Hamburg enjoyed peace, and Slavia abounded in priests and churches. . . .

QUESTIONS FOR ANALYSIS

1. How are the practices of non-Christians used as good and bad examples for Christians?

2. What limits, if any, do church officials recognize in their role as moral judges?

3. How does the church confront royal authority?

Sources: Excerpts from John T. McNeill and Helena M. Gamer, *Medieval Handbooks of Penance* (New York: Columbia University Press, 1938), 77–78; *The Letters of Saint Boniface,* tr. Ephraim Emerton (New York: Columbia University Press, 2000), 56, 59–60, 103–105; and *History of the Archbishops of Hamburg-Bremen,* tr. Francis J. Tschan (New York: Columbia University Press, 1959 [new ed. 2002]), 114–133.

practices such as celibacy, continual devotion to prayer, and living apart from society (alone or in small groups) came together in Christian form in Egypt.

The most important form of monasticism in western Europe, however, involved groups of monks or nuns living together in organized communities. The person most responsible for introducing this originally Egyptian practice in the Latin west was Benedict of Nursia (ca. 480–547) in Italy. Benedict began his pious career as a hermit in a cave but eventually organized several monasteries, each headed by an abbot. In the seventh century monasteries based on his model spread far beyond Italy. The Rule Benedict wrote to govern the monks' behavior envisions a balanced life of devotion and work, along with obligations of celibacy, poverty, and obedience to the abbot. Those who lived by this or other monastic rules became *regular clergy,* in contrast to *secular clergy,* priests who lived in society instead of in seclusion and did not follow a formal code of regulations. The Rule of Benedict was the starting point for most forms of western European monastic life and remains in force today in Benedictine monasteries.

Trinity College Library Dublin/The Bridgeman Art Library

Illustrated Manuscript from Monastic Library This page from the Book of Kells, written around 800 in Ireland, combines an icon-like image of a gospel writer with complex interwoven patterns in the margin that derive from the pre-Christian art of northern Europe. Note the evangelist's blonde hair.

Though monks and nuns, women who lived by monastic rules in convents, made up a small percentage of the total population, their secluded way of life reinforced the separation of religious affairs from ordinary politics and economics. Monasteries followed Jesus' axiom to "render unto Caesar what is Caesar's and unto God what is God's" better than the many town-based bishops who behaved like lords.

Although some rulers, like Charlemagne, encouraged scholarship at court, many illiterate lay nobles interested themselves only in warfare and hunting. Thus it was monasteries that preserved literacy and learning in the early medieval period. Monks (but seldom nuns) saw copying manuscripts and even writing books as a religious calling, and monastic scribes preserved many ancient Latin works that would otherwise have disappeared. The survival of Greek works depended more on Byzantine and Muslim scribes in the east.

Monasteries and convents served other functions as well. A few planted Christianity in new lands, as Irish monks did in parts of Germany. Most serviced the needs of travelers, organized agricultural production on their lands, and took in infants abandoned by their parents. Convents provided refuge for widows and other women who lacked male protection in the harsh medieval world or who desired a spiritual life. These religious houses presented problems of oversight to the church, however. A bishop might have authority over an abbot or abbess (head of a convent), but he could not exercise constant vigilance over what went on behind monastery walls.

The failure of some abbots to maintain monastic discipline led to the growth of a reform movement centered on the Benedictine abbey of Cluny (KLOO-nee) in eastern France. Founded in 910 by William the Pious, the first duke of Aquitaine, who completely freed it of lay authority, Cluny gained similar freedom from the local bishop a century later. Its abbots pursued a vigorous campaign, eventually in alliance with reforming popes like Gregory VII, to improve monastic discipline and administration. A magnificent new abbey church symbolized Cluny's claims to eminence. With later additions, it became the largest church in the world.

At the peak of Cluny's influence, nearly a thousand Benedictine abbeys and priories (lower-level monastic houses) in various countries accepted the authority of its abbot. Whereas the Benedictine Rule had presumed that each monastery would be independent, the Cluniac reformers stipulated that every abbot and every prior (head of a priory) be appointed by the abbot of Cluny and have personal experience of the religious life of Cluny. Monastic reform also gained new impetus in the second half of the twelfth century with the rapid rise of the Cistercian order, which emphasized a life of asceticism and poverty. These movements set the pattern for the monasteries, cathedral clergy, and preaching friars that would dominate ecclesiastical life in the thirteenth century.

SECTION REVIEW

- Christianity in western Europe focused on the pope in Rome, but conflict with Holy Roman Emperors led to the investiture controversy.

- Likewise, conflict grew between Henry of England and the archbishop Thomas à Becket, leading to Becket's martyrdom.

- One religious constant was life in monasteries; Benedict of Nursia founded the Benedictine Rule, and later the need for greater discipline over monks and nuns led to the founding of Cluny, a center of monastic reform.

- Monasteries provided many charitable services and preserved learning.

KIEVAN RUSSIA, 900–1200

Though Latin and Orthodox Christendom followed different paths in later centuries, which of them had a more promising future was not apparent in 900. The Poles and other Slavic peoples living in the north eventually accepted the Christianity of Rome as taught by German priests and missionaries. The Serbs and other southern Slavs took their faith from Constantinople.

The conversion of Kievan Russia, farther to the east, shows how economics, politics, and religious life were closely intertwined. The choice of orthodoxy over Catholicism had important consequences for later European history.

The Rise of the Kievan Empire

The territory between the Black and Caspian Seas in the south and the Baltic and White Seas in the north divides into a series of east-west zones. Frozen tundra in the far north gives way to a cold forest zone, then to a more temperate forest, then to a mix of forest and steppe grass-lands, and finally to grassland only. Several navigable rivers, including the Volga, the Dnieper (d-NYEP-er), and the Don, run from north to south across these zones.

Early historical sources reflect repeated linguistic and territorial changes, seemingly under pressure from poorly understood population migrations. Most of the Germanic peoples, along with some Iranian and west Slavic peoples, migrated into eastern Europe from Ukraine and Russia in Roman times. The peoples who remained behind spoke eastern Slavic languages, except in the far north and south: Finns and related peoples lived in the former region, Turkic-speakers in the latter.

Forest dwellers, farmers, and steppe nomads complemented each other economically. Nomads traded animals for the farmers' grain; and honey, wax, and furs from the forests became important exchange items. Traders could travel east and west by steppe caravan (see Chapters 9 and 13), or they could use boats on the rivers to move north and south.

Hoards containing thousands of Byzantine and Islamic coins buried in Poland and on islands in the Baltic Sea where fairs were held attest to the trading activity of Varangians (Swedish Vikings) who sailed across the Baltic and down Russia's rivers. The Varangians exchanged forest products and slaves for manufactured goods and coins, which they may have used as jewelry rather than as money, at markets controlled by the Khazar Turks, a powerful kingdom centered around the mouth of the Volga River.

Historians debate the early meaning of the word *Rus* (from which *Russia* is derived), but at some point it came to refer to Slavic-speaking peoples ruled by Varangians. Unlike western European lords, the Varangian princes and their *druzhina* (military retainers) lived in cities, while the Slavs farmed. The princes occupied themselves with trade and fending off enemies. The Rus of the city of Kiev (KEE-yev), which was taken over by Varangians around 880, controlled trade on the Dnieper River and dealt more with Byzantium than with the Muslim world because the Dnieper flows into the Black Sea. The Rus of Novgorod (NOHV-goh-rod) played the same role on the Volga. The semilegendary account of the Kievan Rus conversion to Christianity must be seen against this background.

In 980 Vladimir (VLAD-ih-mir) I, a ruler of Novgorod who had fallen from power, returned from exile to Kiev with a band of Varangians and made himself the grand prince of Kievan Russia (see Map 11.3). Though his grandmother Olga had been a Christian, Vladimir built a temple on Kiev's heights and placed there the statues of the six gods his Slavic subjects worshiped. The earliest Russian chronicle reports that Vladimir and his advisers decided against Islam as the official religion because of its ban on alcohol, rejected Judaism (the religion to which the Khazars had converted) because they thought that a truly powerful god would not have let the ancient Jewish kingdom be destroyed, and even spoke with German emissaries advocating Latin Christianity. Why Vladimir chose Orthodox Christianity over the Latin version is not precisely known. The magnificence of Constantinople seems to have been a consideration. After visiting Byzantine churches, his agents reported: "We knew not whether we were in heaven or on earth, for on earth there is no such splendor of [sic] such beauty, and we are at a loss how to describe it. We know only that God dwells there among men, and their service is finer than the ceremonies of other nations."[6]

After choosing a reluctant bride from the Byzantine imperial family, Vladimir converted to Orthodox Christianity, probably in 988, and opened his lands to Orthodox clerics and

---

[6]S. A. Zenkovsky, ed., *Medieval Russia's Epics, Chronicles, and Tales* (New York: New American Library, 1974), 67.

MAP 11.3 **Kievan Russia and the Byzantine Empire in the Eleventh Century** By the mid-eleventh century, the princes of Kievan Russia had brought all the eastern Slavs under their rule. The loss of Egypt, Syria, and Tunisia to Arab invaders in the seventh to eighth century had turned Byzantium from a far-flung empire into a fairly compact state. From then on the Byzantine rulers looked to the Balkans and Kievan Russia as the primary arena for extending their political and religious influence. © Cengage Learning

missionaries. The patriarch of Constantinople appointed a metropolitan (chief bishop) at Kiev to govern ecclesiastical affairs; churches arose in Kiev, one of them on the ruins of Vladimir's earlier hilltop temple; and writing was introduced, using the Cyrillic alphabet devised earlier for the western Slavs. This extension of Orthodox Christendom northward provided a barrier against the eastward expansion of Latin Christianity. Kiev became firmly oriented toward trade with Byzantium and turned its back on the Muslim world, though the Volga trade continued through Novgorod.

Struggles within the ruling family and with other enemies, most notably the steppe peoples of the south, marked the later political history of Kievan Russia. But down to the time of the Mongols in the thirteenth century (see Chapter 13), the state remained and served as an instrument for the Christianization of the eastern Slavs.

Cathedral of Saint Dmitry in Vladimir Built between 1193 and 1197, this Russian Orthodox cathedral shows Byzantine influence. The three-arch façade, small dome, and symmetrical Greek Cross floor plan strongly resemble features of the Byzantine church shown on page 268.

Society and Culture

The manorial agricultural system of western Europe never developed in Kievan Russia because its political power derived from trade rather than from landholding. Farmers practiced shifting cultivation of their own lands. They would burn a section of forest, then lightly scratch the ash-strewn surface with a plow. When fertility waned, they would move to another section of forest. Poor land and a short growing season in the most northerly latitudes made food scarce. Living on their own estates, the druzhina evolved from infantry into cavalry and focused their efforts more on horse breeding than on agriculture.

Large cities like Kiev and Novgorod may have reached thirty thousand or fifty thousand people—roughly the size of contemporary London or Paris, but far smaller than Constantinople or major Muslim metropolises like Baghdad and Nishapur. Many cities amounted to little more than fortified trading posts. Yet they served as centers for the development of crafts, some, such as glassmaking, based on skills imported from Byzantium. Artisans enjoyed higher status in society than peasant farmers. Construction relied on wood from the forests, although Christianity brought the building of stone cathedrals and churches on the Byzantine model.

Christianity penetrated the general population slowly. Several polytheist uprisings occurred in the eleventh century, particularly in times of famine, and passive resistance led some groups to reject Christian burial and persist in cremating the dead and keeping the bones of the deceased in urns. Women continued to use polytheist designs on their clothing and bracelets, and as late as the twelfth century they were still turning to polytheist priests for charms to cure sick children. Traditional Slavic marriage practices involving casual and polygamous relations particularly scandalized the clergy.

Christianity eventually triumphed, and its success led to increasing church engagement in political and economic affairs. In the twelfth century, Christian clergy became involved in government administration, some of them collecting fees and taxes related to trade. Direct and indirect revenue from trade provided the rulers with the money they needed to pay their soldiers. The rule of law also spread as Kievan Russia experienced its peak of culture and prosperity in the century before the Mongol invasion of 1237.

SECTION REVIEW

- Power in Kievan Russia depended on trade rather than agriculture; thus there was no manorial system, and lords ruled from cities.

- Varangian traders established political dominion over Slavic peoples.

- The cities of Kiev and Novgorod provided the nucleus of Russian principalities.

- The Kievan ruler Vladimir I made Orthodox Christianity the official religion in Kievan Russia, though it penetrated the population slowly.

- Kievan cities reflected some aspects of Byzantine culture, especially in crafts such as glassmaking.

WESTERN EUROPE REVIVES, 1000–1200

Between 1000 and 1200 western Europe slowly emerged from nearly seven centuries of subsistence economy—in which most people who worked on the land could meet only their basic needs for food, clothing, and shelter. With the climate somewhat warmer than in previous centuries, population and agricultural production climbed, and a growing food surplus found its way to town markets, speeding the return of a money-based economy and providing support for larger numbers of craftspeople, construction workers, and traders.

Historians have attributed western Europe's revival to population growth spurred by new technologies and to the appearance in Italy and Flanders, on the coast of the North Sea, of self-governing cities devoted primarily to seaborne trade. For monarchs, the changes facilitated improvements in central administration, greater control over vassals, and consolidation of realms on the way to becoming stronger kingdoms.

The Role of Technology

A lack of concrete evidence confirming the spread of technological innovations frustrates efforts to relate the exact course of Europe's revival to technological change. Nevertheless, most historians agree that technology played a significant role in the near doubling of the population of western Europe between 1000 and 1200. The population of England seems to have risen from 1.1 million in 1086 to 1.9 million in 1200, and the population of the territory of modern France seems to have risen from 5.2 million to 9.2 million over the same period.

Examples that illustrate the difficulty of drawing historical conclusions from scattered evidence of technological change were a new type of plow and the use of efficient draft harnesses for pulling wagons. The Roman plow, which farmers in southern Europe and Byzantium continued to use, scratched shallow grooves, as was appropriate for loose, dry Mediterranean soils. The new plow cut deep into the soil with a knifelike blade, while a curved board mounted behind the blade lifted the cut layer and turned it over. This made it possible to farm the heavy, wet clays of the northern river valleys. Pulling the new plow took more energy, which could mean harnessing several teams of oxen or horses.

Horses plowed faster than oxen but were more delicate. Iron horseshoes, which were widely adopted in this period, helped protect their feet, but like the plow itself, they added to the farmer's expenses. Roman horse harnesses, inefficiently modeled on the yoke used for oxen, put such pressure on the animal's neck that a horse pulling a heavy load risked strangulation. A mystery surrounds the adoption of more efficient designs. The **horse collar**, which moves the point of traction from the animal's throat to its shoulders, first appeared around 800 in a miniature painting, and it is shown clearly as a harness for plow horses in the Bayeux Tapestry, embroidered after 1066. The breast-strap harness, which is not as well adapted for the heaviest work but was preferred in southern Europe, seems to have appeared around 500. In both cases, linguists have tried to trace key technical terms to Chinese or Turko-Mongol words and have argued for technological diffusion across Eurasia. Yet third-century Roman farmers in Tunisia and Libya used both types of harness to hitch horses and camels to plows and carts. This technology, which is still employed in Tunisia, appears clearly on Roman bas-reliefs and lamps; but there is no more concrete evidence of its movement northward into Europe than there is of similar harnessing moving across Asia. Thus the question of where efficient harnessing came from and whether it began in 500 or in 800, or was known even earlier but not extensively used, cannot be easily resolved.

Hinging on this problem is the question of when and why landowners in northern Europe began to use teams of horses to pull plows through moist, fertile river-valley soils that were too heavy for teams of oxen. Horses moved faster but cost more, particularly after the population increase raised the prices of the grain needed to feed them. Thus, it is difficult to say that one technology was always better: although agricultural surpluses did grow and better plowing did play a role in this growth, areas that continued to use oxen and even old-style plows seem to have shared in the general population growth of the period.

horse collar Harnessing method that increased the efficiency of horses by shifting the point of traction from the animal's neck to the shoulders; its adoption favors the spread of horse-drawn plows and vehicles.

Cities and the Rebirth of the Trade

Independent cities governed and defended by communes appeared first in Italy and Flanders and then elsewhere. Communes were groups of leading citizens who banded together to defend their cities and demand the privilege of self-government from their lay or ecclesiastical lord. Lords who granted such privileges benefited from the commune's economic dynamism. Lacking extensive farmlands, these cities turned to manufacturing and trade, which they encouraged through the laws they enacted. Laws making serfs free once they came into the city, for example, attracted many workers from the countryside. Cities in Italy that had shrunk within walls built by the Romans now pressed against those walls, forcing the construction of new ones. Pisa built a new wall in 1000 and expanded it in 1156. Other twelfth-century cities that built new walls include Florence, Brescia (BREH-shee-uh), Pavia, and Siena (see-EN-uh).

The city of Venice was organized by settlers on a group of islands at the northern end of the Adriatic Sea that had been largely uninhabited in Roman times. In the eleventh century it became the dominant sea power in the Adriatic and competed with Pisa and Genoa, its rivals on the western side of Italy, for leadership in the trade with Muslim ports in North Africa and the eastern Mediterranean. A somewhat later merchant's list mentions trade in some three thousand "spices" (including dyestuffs, textile fibers, and raw materials), some of them products of Muslim lands and some coming via the Silk Road or the Indian Ocean Maritime System (see Chapter 9). Among them were eleven types of alum (for dyeing), eleven types of wax, eight types of cotton, four types of indigo, five types of ginger, four types of paper, and fifteen types of sugar, along with cloves, caraway, tamarind, and fresh oranges. By the time of the Crusades (see below), maritime commerce throughout the Mediterranean had come to depend heavily on ships from Genoa, Venice, and Pisa. At the same time, the climate-driven decline of agriculture in Iran and Iraq, which became colder while Europe enjoyed unusual warmth, caused more and more trade from the Indian Ocean and Asia to flow through Egypt and Syria.

SECTION REVIEW
• Western Europe became more dynamic after 1000.
• Population grew, and cities expanded both in area and commercial activity, with some cities gaining independence from religious and lay authorities.
• New technologies, such as better plows and horse collars, probably contributed to the economic revival, though how they arrived is unclear.
• Northern Italy and Flanders took the lead as maritime trading centers.
• Gold coinage reappeared after centuries of disuse.

Ghent, Bruges **(broozh)**, and Ypres **(EEP-r)** in Flanders rivaled the Italian cities in prosperity, trade, and industry. Enjoying comparable independence based on privileges granted by the counts of Flanders, these cities centralized the fishing and wool trades of the North Sea region. Around 1200 raw wool from England began to be woven into woolen cloth for a very large market.

More abundant coinage also signaled the upturn in economic activity. In the ninth and tenth centuries most gold coins had come from Muslim lands and the Byzantine Empire. Being worth too much for most trading purposes, they seldom reached Germany, France, and England, where the widely imitated Carolingian silver penny sufficed. With the economic revival of the twelfth century, however, minting of silver coins began in Scandinavia, Poland, and other outlying regions, and in the following century the reinvigoration of Mediterranean trade made possible a new and abundant gold coinage.

THE CRUSADES, 1095–1204

Crusades (1095–1204) Armed pilgrimages to the Holy Land by Christians determined to recover Jerusalem from Muslim rule. The Crusades brought an end to western Europe's centuries of intellectual and cultural isolation.

Western European revival coincided with and contributed to the **Crusades**, a series of religiously inspired Christian military campaigns against Muslims in the eastern Mediterranean that dominated the politics of Europe from 1095 to 1204 (see Chapter 10 and Map 11.4). Four great expeditions, the last redirected against the Byzantines and resulting in the Latin capture of Constantinople, constituted the region's largest military undertakings since the fall of Rome. As a result of the Crusades, noble courts and burgeoning cities in western Europe consumed more goods from the east. This set the stage for the later adoption of ideas, artistic styles, and industrial processes from Byzantium and the lands of Islam.

The Roots of the Crusades

Several social and economic currents of the eleventh century contributed to the Crusades. First, reforming leaders of the Latin Church, seeking to soften the warlike tone of society, popularized the Truce of God. This movement limited fighting between Christian lords by specifying times of truce, such as during Lent (the forty days before Easter) and on Sundays. Many knights welcomed a religiously approved alternative to fighting other Christians. Second, ambitious rulers, like the Norman chieftains who invaded England and Sicily, were looking for new lands to conquer. Nobles, particularly younger sons in areas where the oldest son inherited everything, were hungry for land and titles to maintain their status. Third, Italian merchants wanted to increase trade in the eastern Mediterranean and acquire trading posts in Muslim territory. However, without the rivalry between popes and kings already discussed, and without the desire of the church to demonstrate political authority over western Christendom, the Crusades might never have occurred.

pilgrimage Journey to a sacred shrine by Christians seeking to show their piety, fulfill vows, or gain absolution for sins. Other religions also have pilgrimage traditions, such as the Muslim pilgrimage to Mecca and the pilgrimages made by early Chinese Buddhists to India in search of sacred Buddhist writings.

Several factors focused attention on the Holy Land, which had been under Muslim rule for four centuries. **Pilgrimages** played an important role in European religious life. In western Europe, pilgrims traveled under royal protection, with a few in their number actually being tramps, thieves, beggars, peddlers, and merchants for whom pilgrimage was a safe way of traveling. Genuinely pious pilgrims often journeyed to visit the old churches and sacred relics preserved in Rome or Constantinople. The most intrepid went to Jerusalem, Antioch, and other cities under Muslim control to fulfill a vow or to atone for a sin.

Knights who followed a popular pilgrimage route across northern Spain to pray at the shrine of Santiago de Compostela learned of the expanding efforts of Christian kings to dislodge the Muslims. The Umayyad Caliphate in al-Andalus had broken up in the eleventh century, leaving its smaller successor states prey to Christian attacks from the north (see Chapter 10). This was the beginning of a movement of reconquest that culminated in 1492 with the surrender of the last Muslim kingdom. The word *crusade*, taken from Latin *crux* for "cross," was first used in Spain. Stories also circulated of the war conducted by seafaring Normans against the Muslims in Sicily, whom they finally defeated in the 1090s after thirty years of fighting.

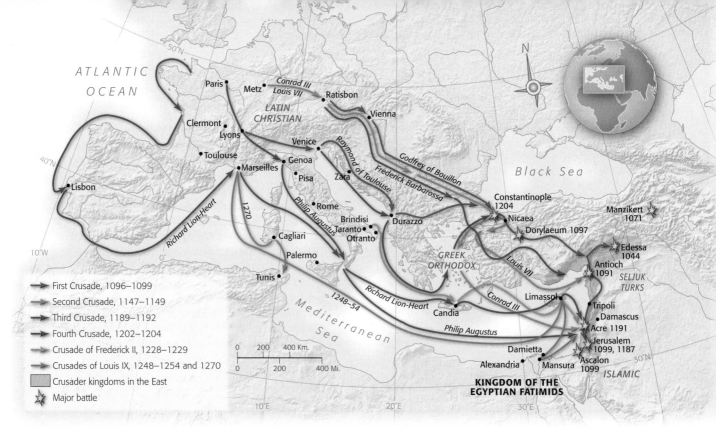

MAP 11.4 **The Crusades** The first two Crusades proceeded overland through Byzantine territory. The Third Crusade included contingents under the French and English kings, Philip Augustus and Richard Lion-Heart, that traveled by sea, and a contingent under the Holy Roman Emperor Frederick Barbarossa that took the overland route. Frederick died in southern Anatolia. Later Crusades were mostly seaborne, with Sicily, Crete, and Cyprus playing important roles. © Cengage Learning

The tales of pilgrims returning from Palestine further induced both churchmen and nobles to consider the Muslims a proper target for Christian militancy. Muslim rulers, who had controlled Jerusalem, Antioch, and Alexandria since the seventh century, generally tolerated and protected Christian pilgrims. But after 1071, when a Seljuk army defeated the Byzantine emperor at the Battle of Manzikert (see Chapter 10), Turkish nomads spread throughout the region, and security along the pilgrimage route through Anatolia, already none too good, deteriorated further. The decline of Byzantine power threatened ancient centers of Christianity, such as Ephesus in Anatolia, previously under imperial control.

Despite the theological differences between the Orthodox and Roman churches, the Byzantine emperor Alexius Comnenus asked the pope and western European rulers to help him confront the Muslim threat and reconquer what the Christians termed the Holy Land, the early centers of Christianity in Palestine and Syria. Pope Urban II responded; at the Council of Clermont in 1095, he addressed a huge crowd of people gathered in a field and called on them, as Christians, to stop fighting one another and go to the Holy Land to fight Muslims.

"God wills it!" exclaimed voices in the crowd. People cut cloth into crosses and sewed them on their shirts to symbolize their willingness to march on Jerusalem. Thus began the holy war now known as the "First Crusade." People at the time more often used the word *peregrinatio*, "pilgrimage." Urban promised to free Crusaders who had committed sins from their normal penance, or acts of atonement, the usual reward for peaceful pilgrims to Jerusalem.

The First Crusade captured Jerusalem in 1099 and established four Crusader principalities, the most important being the Latin Kingdom of Jerusalem. The next two expeditions strove with diminishing success to protect these gains. Muslim forces retook Jerusalem in 1187. By the time of the Fourth Crusade in 1204, the original religious ardor had so diminished that the commanders agreed, at the urging of the Venetians, to sack Constantinople first to help pay the cost of transporting the army by ship.

The Impact of the Crusades

Exposure to Muslim culture in Spain, Sicily, Mediterranean seaports, and the Crusader principalities established in the Holy Land made many Europeans aware of things lacking in their own lives. Borrowings from Muslim society occurred gradually and are not always easy

Armored Knights in Battle   This painting from around 1135 shows the armament of knights at the time of the Crusades. Chain mail, a helmet, and a shield carried on the left side protect the rider. The lance carried underarm and the sword are the primary weapons. Notice that riders about to make contact with lances have their legs straight and braced in the stirrups, while riders with swords and in flight have bent legs.   Pierpont Morgan Library/ Art Resource, NY

to date, but Europeans eventually learned how to manufacture pasta, paper, sugar, cotton cloth, colored glass, and many other items that had formerly been imported. Arabic translations of and commentaries on Greek philosophical, scientific, and medical works, and equally important original works by Arabs and Iranians, provided a vital stimulus to European thought.

Some works were brought directly into the Latin world through the conquests of Sicily, parts of Spain and the Holy Land, and Constantinople (for Greek texts). Others were rendered into Latin by translators who worked in parts of Spain that continued under Muslim rule. Generations passed before all these works were studied and understood, but they eventually transformed the intellectual world of the western Europeans, who previously had had little familiarity with Greek writings. The works of Aristotle and the Muslim commentaries on them were of particular importance to theologians, but Muslim writers like Avicenna (Ibn Sina) (980–1037) were of parallel importance in medicine.

Changes affecting the lifestyle of the nobles took place more quickly. Eleanor of Aquitaine (1122?–1204), one of the most influential women of the crusading era, accompanied her husband, King Louis VII of France, on the Second Crusade (1147–1149). The court life of her uncle Raymond, ruler of the Crusader principality of Antioch, particularly appealed to her. After her return to France, a lack of male offspring led to an annulment of her marriage with Louis, and in 1151 she married Henry of Anjou, who inherited the throne of England as Henry II three years later. Eleanor's sons—Richard Lion-Heart, famed in romance as the chivalrous foe of Saladin during the Third Crusade (1189–1192), and John—rebelled against their father but eventually succeeded him as kings of England.

In Aquitaine, a powerful duchy in southern France, Eleanor maintained her own court for a time. The poet-singers called troubadours who enjoyed her favor made her court a center for new music based on the idea of "courtly love," an idealization of feminine beauty and grace that influenced later European ideas of romance. Thousands of troubadour melodies survive in manuscripts, and some show the influence of the poetry styles then current in Muslim Spain. The favorite troubadour instrument, moreover, was the lute, a guitarlike instrument with a bulging belly whose design and name (Arabic *al-ud*) come from Muslim Spain. In centuries to come the lute would become the mainstay of Renaissance music in Italy.

SECTION REVIEW

- The Crusades began because of the Truce of God, which asked Christians to stop fighting one another, and hunger for land and trade.
- Pilgrimages to the Holy Land brought attention to that area, and Pope Urban's sermon initiated the Crusader effort.
- The Crusaders captured Jerusalem and established four principalities.
- Muslim counterattacks provoked additional Crusades, and as energy flagged the Crusaders sacked Constantinople.
- The cultural contact with Muslim lands brought to Europe Muslim interpretations of ancient Greek learning and stimulated other changes in European thought and society.
- Eleanor of Aquitaine, the spouse and later the mother of crusading monarchs, promoted the culture of courtly love.

CONCLUSION

The legacy of Roman rule affected eastern and western Europe in different ways. Byzantium inherited the grandeur, pomp, and legal supremacy of the imperial office and merged it with leadership of the Christian church. Although it guarded its shrinking frontiers against foreign invasion, it gradually contracted around Constantinople, its imperial capital, as more and more territory was lost. By contrast, no Roman core survived in the west. The Germanic peoples overwhelmed the legions guarding the frontiers and established kingdoms based on their own traditions. The law of the king and the law of the church did not echo each other. Yet memories of Roman grandeur and territorial unity resurfaced with the idea of a Holy Roman Empire, however unworkable that empire proved to be.

The competition between the Orthodox and Catholic forms of Christianity complicated the role of religion in the emergence of medieval European society and culture. The Byzantine Empire, constructed on a Roman political and legal heritage that had largely passed away in the west, was generally more prosperous than the Germanic kingdoms of western Europe, and its arts and culture were initially more sophisticated. Furthermore, Byzantine society became deeply Christian well before a comparable degree of Christianization had been reached in western Europe. Yet despite their success in transmitting their version of Christianity and imperial rule to Kievan Russia, and in the process erecting a barrier between the Orthodox Russians and the Catholic Slavs to their west, the Byzantines failed to demonstrate the dynamism and ferment that characterized both the Europeans to their west and the Muslims to their south. Byzantine armies played only a supporting role in the Crusades, and the emperors lost their capital and their power, at least temporarily, to western Crusaders in 1204.

Technology and commerce deepened the political and religious gulf between the two Christian zones. Changes in military techniques in western Europe increased battlefield effectiveness, while new agricultural technologies accompanied population increases that revitalized urban life and contributed to the crusading movement by making the nobility hunger for new lands. At the same time, the need to import food for growing urban populations contributed to the growth of maritime commerce in the Mediterranean and North Seas. Culture and manufacturing benefited greatly from the increased pace of communication and exchange. Lacking parallel developments of a similar scale, the Byzantine Empire steadily lost the dynamism of its early centuries and by the end of the period had clearly fallen behind western Europe in prosperity and cultural innovation.

KEY TERMS

Charlemagne p. 267
medieval p. 267
Byzantine Empire p. 267
Kievan Russia p. 267
schism p. 269

manor p. 273
serf p. 273
fief p. 274
vassal p. 274
papacy p. 275

Holy Roman Empire p. 276
investiture controversy p. 277
monasticism p. 278
horse collar p. 284

Crusades p. 285
pilgrimage p. 285

SUGGESTED READING

Collins, Roger. *Early Medieval Europe, 300–1000*. 1991. A lively survey that concentrates on religious and political developments.

Duby, Georges. *Rural Economy and Country Life in the Medieval West*. 1990. A detailed introduction to agricultural history.

Keller, Amy. *Eleanor of Aquitaine and the Four Kings*. 1950. Lively biography of a major female figure.

Labarge, Margaret Wade. *A Small Sound of the Trumpet: Women in Medieval Life*. 1986. A look at the lives of women at all social levels.

Martin, Janet. *Medieval Russia, 980–1584*. 1995. An up-to-date survey work.

Riley-Smith, Jonathan. *The Crusades: A Short History*. 1987. The current standard work in this field.

Southern, Richard W. *Western Society and the Church in the Middle Ages*. 1970. One of many good books on medieval Christendom.

Treadgold, Warren. *A History of Byzantine State and Society*. 1997. A recent general survey.

White, Lynn, Jr. *Medieval Technology and Social Change*. 1962. Classic starting point for history of technology.

Chapter Outline

The Sui and Tang Empires, 581–755
➤ *What is the importance of Inner and Central Asia as a region of interchange during the Tang period?*

China and Its Rivals
➤ *What were the effects of the fracturing of power in Central Asia and China?*

New Kingdoms in East Asia
➤ *How did East Asia develop between the fall of the Tang and 1200?*

Conclusion

- **DIVERSITY + DOMINANCE** Law and Society in China and Japan
- **ENVIRONMENT + TECHNOLOGY** Writing in East Asia, 400–1200

A detail of a scroll called "Going Up the River at the Qingming (Spring) Festival" by Zhang Zeduan/Werner Forman Archive/The Bridgeman Art Library

Going Up the River   Song cities hummed with commercial and industrial activity, much of it concentrated on the rivers and canals linking the capital Kaifeng to the provinces. This detail from *Going Upriver at the Qingming [Spring] Festival* shows a tiny portion of the scroll painting's panorama. Painted by Zhang Zeduan sometime before 1125, its depiction of daily life makes it an important source of information on working people. Before open shop fronts and tea houses a camel caravan departs, donkey carts are unloaded, a scholar rides loftily (if gingerly) on horseback, and women of wealth go by enclosed sedan-chairs.

Inner and East Asia, 400–1200

After the Han Empire fell in 220 C.E. (see Chapter 6), China suffered four centuries of rule by short-lived and competing states. The powerful and expansive Tang Empire (618–907), discussed in this chapter, finally brought that period of turmoil to an end. Tang rule also encouraged the spread of Buddhism, brought by missionaries from India and by Chinese pilgrims returning with sacred Sanskrit texts. The Tang left an indelible mark on the Chinese imagination long after it too fell.

The origins of East Asia, characterized by a shared writing system, political ideology, and culture, can also be traced to the Sui and Tang Empires. The Tang Empire in particular became a model for emerging regimes on the Korean Peninsula, in northeast Asia, on the Japanese islands, and, to a certain extent, in continental Southeast Asia. But the formation of East Asia did not occur in isolation. Travelers from as far as India and Persia traveled to Tang China, bringing with them their native religions, artistic aesthetic, popular entertainments, technology, and even cuisine. Foreigners worked in the Tang bureaucracy, served in the military, and maintained close ties to the royal family.

The Song Empire that eventually succeeded the Tang Empire never approached the Tang's dominance over East Asia, nor was it as globally connected. However, it was extraordinarily productive and advanced in terms of technology, economy, and government. The sustainable boom in population during the Song Dynasty that fostered urbanization, and the expansion of domestic markets and international trade, played a major role in these seemingly modern developments. However, these were not simply Chinese achievements, newly introduced grain from Southeast Asia pushed the Song agriculture revolution.

THE SUI AND TANG EMPIRES, 581–755

After the fall of the Han dynasty, China was fragmented for several centuries. It was reunified under the Sui (sway) dynasty, father and son rulers who held power from 581 until Turks from Inner Asia (the part of the Eurasian steppe east of the Pamir Mountains) defeated the son in 615. He was assassinated three years later, and the Tang filled the political vacuum.

The small kingdoms of northern China and Inner Asia that had come and gone during the centuries following the fall of the Han Empire had structured themselves around a variety of political ideas and institutions. Some favored the Chinese tradition, with an emperor, a bureaucracy using the Chinese language exclusively, and a Confucian state philosophy (see Chapter 6). Others reflected Tibetan, Turkic, or other regional cultures and depended on Buddhism to legitimate their rule. Throughout the period the relationship between northern China and the deserts and steppe of Inner Asia remained a central focus of political life, a key commercial linkage, and a source of new ideas and practices.

Though northern China constituted the Sui heartland, population centers along the Yangzi (yahng-zeh) River in the south grew steadily and pointed to what would be the future direction of Chinese expansion. To facilitate communication and trade with the south, the Sui built

Grand Canal The 1,100-mile (1,771-kilometer) waterway linking the Yellow and the Yangzi Rivers. It was begun in the Han period and completed during the Sui Empire.

the 1,100-mile (1,771-kilometer) **Grand Canal** linking the Yellow River with the Yangzi, and they also constructed irrigation systems in the Yangzi Valley. On their northern frontier, the Sui also improved the Great Wall, the barrier against nomadic incursions that had been gradually constructed by several earlier states.

Sui military ambition, which extended to Korea and Vietnam as well as Inner Asia, required high levels of organization and mustering of resources—manpower, livestock, wood, iron, and food supplies. The same was true of their massive public works projects. These burdens proved more than the Sui could sustain. Overextension compounded the political dilemma stemming from the military defeat and subsequent assassination of the second Sui emperor. These circumstances opened the way for another strong leader to establish a new state.

In 618 the powerful Li family took advantage of Sui disorder to carve out an empire of similar scale and ambition. They adopted the dynastic name Tang (see Map 12.1 on page 294). The brilliant emperor **Li Shimin** (lee shir-meen) (r. 626–649) extended his power primarily westward into Inner Asia. Though he and succeeding rulers of the **Tang Empire** retained many Sui governing practices, they avoided overcentralization by allowing local nobles, gentry, officials, and religious establishments to exercise significant power (see Diversity and Dominance: Law and Society in China and Japan).

Li Shimin One of the founders of the Tang Empire and its second emperor (r. 626–649). He led the expansion of the empire into Central Asia.

Tang Empire Empire unifying China and part of Central Asia, founded 618 and ended 907. The Tang emperors presided over a magnificent court at their capital, Chang'an.

The Tang emperors and nobility descended from the Turkic elites that built small states in northern China after the Han, as well as from Chinese officials and settlers who had moved there. They appreciated the pastoral nomadic culture of Inner Asia (see Chapter 9) as well as Chinese traditions. Some of the most impressive works of Tang art, for example, are large pottery figurines of the horses and two-humped camels used along the Silk Road, brilliantly colored with glazes devised by Chinese potters. In warfare, the Tang combined Chinese weapons—the crossbow and armored infantrymen—with Inner Asian expertise in horsemanship and the use of iron stirrups. At their peak, from about 650 to 751, when they were defeated in Central Asia (present-day Kyrgyzstan) by an Arab Muslim army at the Battle of Talas River, the Tang armies were a formidable force.

Chang'an: Metropolis at the Center of East Asia

Much of the global interaction in China during the Sui and Tang dynasties occurred in the capital Chang'an (chahng-ahn), named in honor of the old Han capital. With a population of nearly 2 million, Chang'an and its surrounding suburbs constituted the largest metropolitan area in the world at the time. Its sophisticated gridlike layout, with its palace located in the north Pole Star position to reflect the celestial order, was imitated by Korean and Japanese capitals.

tributary system A system in which, from the time of the Han Empire, countries in East and Southeast Asia not under the direct control of empires based in China nevertheless enrolled as tributary states, acknowledging the superiority of the emperors in China in exchange for trading rights or strategic alliances.

Chang'an became the center of what is often called the **tributary system**, a type of political relationship dating from Han times by which independent countries acknowledged the Chinese emperor's supremacy. Each tributary state sent regular embassies to the capital to pay tribute. As symbols of China's political supremacy, these embassies sometimes meant more to the Chinese than to the tribute-payers, who might have seen them more as a means of accessing the vast Chinese market.

More than simply a political center, Chang'an was also the premier study-abroad destination in Asia. Rulers sent intellectuals to learn statecraft, the techniques of running a government, to bring back to their home governments. Nestorian Christian churches and even Jewish communities existed in Chang'an, as did many Daoist and Buddhist temples and monasteries. Monks from Korea and Japan could study with Chinese Buddhists and with Indian masters who taught there in Sanskrit. The diverse population also included Central Asian, Arab, and Persian merchants who became long-time residents of the city. So many Iranians lived in Chang'an, for example, that the government established a special office just to address Iranian-Tang affairs.

Buddhism and the Tang Empire

State cults based on Buddhism had flourished in Inner Asia and north China since the fall of the Han, and the Tang rulers followed these Inner Asian precedents in their political use of Buddhism. Some interpretations of Buddhist doctrine accorded kings and emperors the spiritual function of welding humankind into a harmonious Buddhist society. Protecting spirits were to help the ruler govern and prevent harm from coming to his people.

Mahayana (mah-HAH-YAH-nah), or "Great Vehicle," Buddhism predominated. Mahayana fostered faith in enlightened beings—bodhisattvas—who postpone nirvana (see Chapter 7) to

CHRONOLOGY

	Inner Asia	China	Northeast and Southeast Asia	Japan
200		220–589 China disunited 581–618 Sui unification	313–668 Three Korean kingdoms: Koguryō, Paekche, Silla	
600	751 Battle of Talas River	618 Tang Empire founded 626–649 Li Shimin reign 690–705 Wu Zhao reign 755–763 An Lushan rebellion	668 Silla victory in Korea	645–655 Taika era 710–784 Nara as capital 752 "Eye-opening" ceremony 794 Heian era
800		840 Suppression of Buddhism 879–881 Huang Chao rebellion 907 End of Tang Empire 960 Song Empire founded	916 Liao Empire founded 918 Koryo founded: Korean Peninsula unified 936 Annam becomes Dai Viet (northern Vietnam)	866–1180 Fujiwara influence
1000	1038–1227 Tanggut state on China's northwest frontier	1127–1279 Southern Song period	1115 Jin Empire founded	ca. 1000 *The Tale of Genji*
1200				1185 Kamakura Shogunate founded

help others achieve enlightenment. This permitted the absorption of local gods and goddesses into Mahayana sainthood and thereby made conversion more attractive to the common people. Mahayana also encouraged translating Buddhist scripture into local languages, and it accepted religious practices not based on written texts. The tremendous reach of Mahayana views, which proved adaptable to different societies and classes of people, invigorated travel, language learning, and cultural exchange.

Early Tang princes competing for political influence enlisted monastic leaders to pray for them, preach on their behalf, counsel aristocrats to support them, and—perhaps most important—contribute monastic wealth to their war chests. In return, the monasteries received tax exemptions, land privileges, and gifts.

As the Tang Empire expanded westward, contacts with Central Asia and India increased, and so did the complexity of Buddhist influence throughout China. The Mahayana network connecting Inner Asia and China intersected a vigorous commercial world in which material goods and cultural influences mixed. Though Buddhism and Confucianism proved attractive to many different peoples, regional cultures and identities remained strong, just as regional commitments to Tibetan, Uighur (WEE-ger), and other languages and writing systems coexisted with the widespread use of written Chinese. Textiles reflected Persian, Korean, and Vietnamese styles, while influences from every part of Asia appeared in sports, music, and painting. Many historians characterize the Tang Empire as "cosmopolitan" because of its breadth and diversity.

Upheavals and Repression, 750–879

The later years of the Tang Empire saw increasing turmoil as a result of conflict with Tibetans and Turkic Uighurs. One result was a backlash against "foreigners," which to Confucians included Buddhists. The Tang elites came to see Buddhism as undermining the Confucian idea of the family as the model for the state. The Confucian scholar Han Yu (768–824) spoke powerfully for a return to traditional Confucian practices. In "Memorial on the Bone of Buddha" written to the emperor in 819 on the occasion of ceremonies to receive a bone of the Buddha in the imperial palace, he scornfully disparages the Buddha and his followers:

> Now Buddha was a man of the barbarians who did not speak the language of China and wore clothes of a different fashion. His sayings did not concern the ways of our ancient kings, nor did his manner of dress conform to their laws. He understood neither the duties that bind sovereign and subject nor the affections of father and son. If he were still alive today and came to our court by order of his ruler, Your Majesty might condescend to receive him, but . . . he would then be escorted to the borders of the state, dismissed, and not allowed to delude the masses. How then, when he has long been dead, could his rotten bones, the foul and unlucky remains of his body, be rightly admitted to the palace? Confucius said, "Respect spiritual beings, while keeping at a distance from them."[1]

Buddhism was also attacked for encouraging women in politics. Wu Zhao (woo jow), a woman who had married into the imperial family, seized control of the government in 690 and declared herself emperor. She based her legitimacy on claiming to be a bodhisattva, an enlightened soul who had chosen to remain on earth to lead others to salvation. She also favored Buddhists and Daoists over Confucians in her court and government.

---

[1]Theodore de Bary, ed., *Sources of Chinese Tradition*, vol. 1, 2d ed. (New York: Columbia University Press, 1999), 584.

MAP 12.1   **The Tang Empire in Inner and Eastern Asia, 750**   For over a century the Tang Empire controlled China and a very large part of Inner Asia. The defeat of Tang armies in 751 by a force of Arabs, Turks, and Tibetans at the Talas River in present-day Kyrgyzstan ended Tang westward expansion. To the south the Tang dominated Annam, and Japan and the Silla kingdom in Korea were leading tributary states of the Tang.   © Cengage Learning

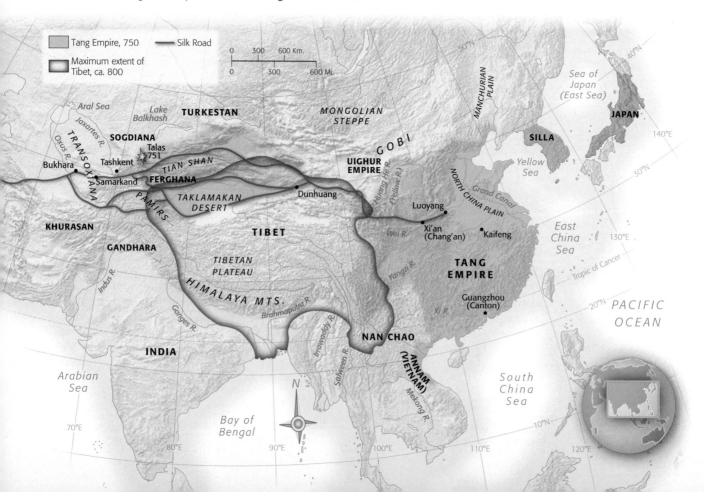

Iron Stirrups This bas-relief from the tomb of Li Shimin depicts the type of horse on which the Tang armies conquered China and Inner Asia. Saddles with high supports in front and back, breastplates, and cruppers (straps beneath the tail that help keep the saddle in place) point to the importance of high speeds and quick maneuvering. Central and Inner Asian horsemen had iron stirrups available from the time of the Huns (fifth century). Earlier stirrups were of leather or wood. Stirrups could support the weight of shielded and well-armed soldiers rising in the saddle to shoot arrows or use lances.

Horse figures, relief from Emperor T'ai Tsung's tomb in Hsi-An (Shensi), Chinese civilization, 7th century/De Agostini Picture Library/The Bridgeman Art Library

Later Confucian writers expressed contempt for Wu Zhao and other powerful women, such as the concubine Yang Guifei **(yahng gway-fay)**. Bo Zhuyi **(baw joo-ee)**, in his poem "Everlasting Remorse," lamented the influence of women at the Tang court, which had caused "the hearts of fathers and mothers everywhere not to value the birth of boys, but the birth of girls."[2] Confucian elites heaped every possible charge on prominent women who offended them, accusing Emperor Wu of grotesque tortures and murders, including tossing the dismembered but still living bodies of enemies into wine vats and cauldrons. They blamed Yang Guifei for the outbreak of the An Lushan rebellion in 755 (see later in this chapter).

Serious historians dismiss the stories about Wu Zhao as stereotypical characterizations of "evil" rulers. Eunuchs (castrated palace servants) charged by historians with controlling Chang'an and the Tang court and publicly executing rival bureaucrats represent a similar stereotype. In fact Wu seems to have ruled effectively and was not deposed until 705, when extreme old age (eighty-plus) incapacitated her. Nevertheless, traditional Chinese historians commonly describe unorthodox rulers and all-powerful women as evil, and the truth about Wu will never be known.

Even Chinese gentry living in safe and prosperous localities associated Buddhism with social ills. People who worried about "barbarians" ruining their society pointed to Buddhism as evidence of the foreign evil, since it had such strong roots in Inner Asia and Tibet. Moreover, because Buddhism shunned earthly ties, monks and nuns severed relations with the secular world in search of enlightenment. They paid no taxes, served in no army. They deprived their families of advantageous marriage alliances and denied descendants to their ancestors. The Confucian elites saw all this as threatening to the family and to the family estates that underlay the Tang economic and political structure.

By the ninth century, hundreds of thousands of people had entered tax-exempt Buddhist institutions. In 840 the government moved to crush the monasteries whose tax exemption had allowed them to accumulate land, serfs, and precious objects, often as gifts. Within five years 4,600 temples had been destroyed. Now an enormous amount of land and 150,000 workers were returned to the tax rolls.

---

[2]Quoted in David Lattimore, "Allusion in T'ang Poetry," in *Perspectives on the T'ang*, ed. Arthur F. Wright and David Twitchett (New Haven, CT: Yale University Press, 1973), 436.

Law and Society in China and Japan

The Tang law code, compiled in the early seventh century, served as the basis for the Tang legal system and as a model for later dynastic law codes. It combined the centralized authority of the imperial government, as visualized in the legalist tradition dating back to Han times, with Confucian concern for status distinctions and personal relationships. Like contemporary approaches to law in Christian Europe and the Islamic world, it did not fully distinguish between government as a structure of domination and law as an echo of religious and moral values.

Following a Preface, 502 articles, each with several parts, are divided into twelve books. Each article contains a basic ordinance with commentary, subcommentary, and sometimes additional questions. Excerpts from a single article from Book 1, General Principles, follow.

The Ten Abominations

Text: The first is called plotting rebellion.

Subcommentary: The *Gongyang* (GON-gwang) *Commentary* states: "The ruler or parent has no harborers [of plots]. If he does have such harborers, he must put them to death." This means that if there are those who harbor rebellious hearts that would harm the ruler or father, he must then put them to death.

The king occupies the most honorable position and receives Heaven's precious decrees. Like Heaven and Earth, he acts to shelter and support, thus serving as the father and mother of the masses. As his children, as his subjects, they must be loyal and filial. Should they dare to cherish wickedness and have rebellious hearts, however, they will run counter to Heaven's constancy and violate human principle. Therefore this is called plotting rebellion.

Text: The second is called plotting great sedition.

Subcommentary: This type of person breaks laws and destroys order, is against traditional norms, and goes contrary to virtue. . . .

Commentary: Plotting great sedition means to plot to destroy the ancestral temples, tombs, or palaces of the reigning house.

Text: The third is called plotting treason.

Subcommentary: The kindness of father and mother is like "great heaven, illimitable." . . . Let one's heart be like the *xiao* bird or the *jing* beast, and then love and respect both cease. Those whose relationship is within the five degrees of mourning are the closest of kin. For them to kill each other is the extreme abomination and the utmost in rebellion, destroying and casting aside human principles. Therefore this is called contumacy.

Commentary: Contumacy means to beat or plot to kill [without actually killing] one's paternal grandparents or parents; or to kill one's paternal uncles or their wives, or one's elder brothers or sisters, or one's maternal grandparents, or

one's husband, or one's husband's paternal grandparents, or his parents. . . .

Text: The fifth is called depravity.

Subcommentary: This article describes those who are cruel and malicious and who turn their backs on morality. Therefore it is called depravity.

Commentary: Depravity means to kill three members of a single household who have not committed a capital crime, or to dismember someone. . . .

Commentary: The offense also includes the making or keeping of poison or sorcery.

Subcommentary: This means to prepare the poison oneself, or to keep it, or to give it to others in order to harm people. But if the preparation of the poison is not yet completed, this offense does not come under the ten abominations. As to sorcery, there are a great many methods, not all of which can be described.

Text: The tenth is called incest.

Subcommentary: The *Zuo Commentary* states: "The woman has her husband's house; the man has his wife's chamber; and there must be no defilement on either side." If this is changed, then there is incest. If one behaves like birds and beasts and introduces licentious associates into one's family, the rules of morality are confused. Therefore this is called incest.

Commentary: This section includes having illicit sexual intercourse with relatives who are of the fourth degree of mourning or closer. . . .

In Japan during the same period, there appeared a set of governing principles attributed to Prince Shotoku (573–621) called the "Seventeen-Article Constitution." These principles, which continued to influence Japanese government for many centuries, reflect Confucian ideals even though the prince was himself a devout Buddhist. The complete text of five of these principles follows:

I

Harmony is to be valued, and contentiousness avoided. All men are inclined to partisanship and few are truly discerning. Hence there are some who disobey their lords and fathers and who maintain feuds with the neighboring villages. But when those above are harmonious and those below are conciliatory and there is concord in the discussion of all matters, the disposition of affairs comes about naturally. Then what is there that cannot be accomplished?

VIII

Let ministers and functionaries attend the courts early in the morning, and retire late. The business of the state does not admit of remissness, and the whole day is hardly enough for its accomplishment. If, therefore, the attendance at court is late, emergencies cannot be met; if officials retire soon, the work cannot be completed.

IX

Trustworthiness is the foundation of right. In everything let there be trustworthiness, for in this there surely consists the good and the bad, success and failure. If the lord and the vassal trust one another, what is there which cannot be accomplished? If the lord and the vassal do not trust one another, everything without exception ends in failure.

XIII

Let all persons entrusted with office attend equally to their functions. Owing to their illness or to their being sent on missions, their work may sometimes be neglected. But whenever they become able to attend to business, let them be as accommodating as if they had cognizance of it from before and not hinder public affairs on the score of their not having had to do with them.

XVII

Matters should not be decided by one person alone. They should be discussed with many others. In small matters, of less consequence, many others need not be consulted. It is only in considering weighty matters, where there is a suspicion that they might miscarry, that many others should be involved in debate and discussion so as to arrive at a reasonable conclusion.

QUESTIONS FOR ANALYSIS

1. Why is one of these documents called a law code and the other a constitution?

2. How is the Confucian concern for family relations, duty, and social status differently manifested in the Chinese and Japanese documents?

3. Do these documents seem intended for government officials or for common people?

Sources: First selection from JOHNSON WALLACE; THE TANG CODE, VOL. I. © 1979 Princeton University Press. Reprinted by permission of Princeton University Press. Second selection from *Sources of Japanese Tradition*, Vol. 1, 2e, by Wm. Theodore de Bary, Donald Keene, George Tanabe, and Paul Varely. Copyright © 2001 Columbia University Press. Reprinted with permission of the publisher.

Buddhist centers like the cave monasteries at Dunhuang were protected by local warlords loyal to Buddhist rulers in Inner Asia. Nevertheless, China's cultural heritage suffered a great loss in the dissolution of the monasteries. Some sculptures and grottoes survived only in defaced form. Wooden temples and façades sheltering great stone carvings burned to the ground. Monasteries became legal again in later times, but Buddhism never recovered the influence of early Tang times.

The End of the Tang Empire, 879–907

The campaigns of expansion in the seventh century had left the empire dependent on local military commanders and a complex tax collection system. Reverses like the Battle of the Talas River in 751, where Arabs halted Chinese expansion into Central Asia, led to military demoralization and underfunding. In 755 An Lushan, a Tang general on the northeast frontier, led about 200,000 soldiers in rebellion. The emperor fled Chang'an and executed his favorite concubine, Yang Guifei, who was rumored to be An Lushan's lover. The rebellion lasted for eight years and resulted in new powers for the provincial military governors who helped suppress it. Even so, Chang'an never recovered, and during the eighth century, its decline symbolized Tang's waning

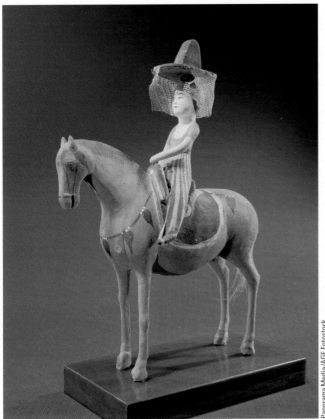

Panorama Media/AGE Fotostock

Tang Horsewoman This ceramic tomb figurine from the far northwest, a region populated largely by Turkic speaking peoples, is unusual in being painted rather than glazed. The woman's costume suggests that she is of high rank, but not Chinese. Note the difference between the rider's light, toe-only stirrup and the full iron military stirrup shown on page 295.

- After the period of disunity following the fall of the Han, China was united under the Sui, followed by the Tang with its founder Li Shimin.

- Tang culture was based on both Inner Asia nomadic culture and war expertise and Chinese tradition.

- The Tang Empire, along with the rival Uighur and Tibetan states, experienced political problems that steadily weakened it.

- In China, this turmoil resulted in a backlash against foreign and female cultural influences and especially Buddhism, as Tang elites led a neo-Confucian reaction.

- The Tang fell due to a combination of destabilizing forces.

influence over satellite states in Korea and Japan, which could no longer turn to China for support or inspiration.

A disgruntled member of the gentry, Huang Chao (wang show), led the most devastating uprising between 879 and 881. Despite his ruthless treatment of the villages he controlled, his rebellion attracted poor farmers and tenants who could not protect themselves from local bosses and oppressive landlords, or who simply did not know where else to turn in the deepening chaos. The new hatred of "barbarians" spurred the rebels to murder thousands of foreign residents in Canton and Beijing (bay-jeeng).

Local warlords finally wiped out the rebels, but Tang society did not find peace. Refugees, migrant workers, and homeless people became common sights. Residents of northern China fled to the southern frontiers as groups from Inner Asia moved into localities in the north. Though Tang emperors continued in Chang'an until a warlord terminated their line in 907, they never regained power after Huang Chao's rebellion.

CHINA AND ITS RIVALS

Song Empire Empire in central and southern China (960–1126) while the Liao people controlled the north. Empire in southern China (1127–1279; the "Southern Song") while the Jin people controlled the north. Distinguished for its advances in technology, medicine, astronomy, and mathematics.

In the aftermath of the Tang, three new states emerged and competed to inherit its legacy (see Map 12.2). The Liao (lee-OW) Empire of the Khitan (kee-THAN) people, pastoral nomads related to the Mongols living on the northeastern frontier, established their rule in the north. They centered their government on several cities, but the emperors preferred life in nomad encampments. On the Inner Asian frontier in northwestern China, the Minyak people (cousins of the Tibetans) established a state they called Tanggut (1038–1227) (TAHNG-gut) to show their connection with the fallen empire. The third state, the Chinese-speaking **Song Empire** came into being in 960 in central China.

These states embodied the political ambitions of peoples with different religious and philosophical systems—Mahayana Buddhism among the Liao, Tibetan Buddhism among the Tangguts, and Confucianism among the Song. Cut off from Inner Asia, the Song used advanced seafaring and sailing technologies to forge maritime connections with other states in East, West, and Southeast Asia. The Song elite shared the late Tang dislike of "barbaric" or "foreign" influences as they tried to cope with multiple enemies that heavily taxed their military capacities. Meanwhile, Korea, Japan, and some Southeast Asian states strengthened political and cultural ties with China.

The Liao and Jin Challenge

The Liao Empire of the Khitan people extended from Siberia to Inner Asia. Variations on the Khitan name became the name for China in these distant regions: "Kitai" for the Mongols, "Khitai" for the Russians, and "Cathay" for Italian merchants like Marco Polo who reported on China in Europe (see Chapter 13).

The Liao rulers prided themselves on their pastoral traditions as horse and cattle breeders, which were the continuing source of their military might, and they made no attempt to create a single elite culture. Instead they encouraged Chinese elites to use their own language, study their own classics, and see the emperor through Confucian eyes; and they encouraged other peoples to use their own languages and see the emperor as a champion of Buddhism or as a nomadic chieftain. On balance, Buddhism far outweighed Confucianism in this and other northern states, where rulers depended on their roles as bodhisattvas or as Buddhist kings to legitimate power. Liao rule lasted from 916 to 1125.

The Liao Empire was the most powerful East Asian empire at the time, with the largest army in East Asia. Superb horsemen and archers, the Khitans also challenged the Song with siege machines from China and Central Asia. A truce concluded in 1005 required the Song emperor

Buddhist Cave Painting at Dunhuang Hundreds of caves dating to the period when Buddhism enjoyed popularity and government favor in China survive in Gansu province, which was beyond the reach of the Tang rulers when they turned against Buddhism. This cave, dated to the period 565–576, depicts the historical Buddha flanked by bodhisattvas. Scenes of the Buddha preaching appear on the wall to the left.

Pierre Colombel/Corbis

to pay the Liao great quantities of cash and silk annually. A century later, the Song tired of paying tribute and secretly allied with the Jurchens of northeastern Asia, who also resented Liao rule. In 1115 the Jurchens first destroyed the Liao capital in Mongolia and proclaimed their own empire, the Jin (see Map 12.2), and then turned on the Song.

The Jurchens grew rice, millet, and wheat, but they also spent a good deal of time hunting, fishing, and tending livestock. Using Khitan military arts and political organization, they became formidable enemies in an all-out campaign against the Song in 1127, laying siege to the Song capital, Kaifeng (kie-fuhng), and capturing the Song emperor. Within a few years the Song withdrew south of the Yellow River and established a new capital at Hangzhou (hahng-jo), leaving central as well as northern China in Jurchen control (see Map 12.3). Annual payments to the Jin Empire staved off further warfare. Historians generally refer to this period as the "Southern Song" (1127–1279).

Song Industries

The Southern Song came closer to initiating an industrial revolution than any other premodern state. Many Song advances in technology, medicine, astronomy, and mathematics had come to China in Tang times, sometimes from very distant places. Song officials, scholars, and businessmen had the motivation and resources to adapt this Tang lore to meet their military, agricultural, and administrative needs.

Song mathematicians introduced the use of fractions, first employing them to describe the phases of the moon. From lunar observations, Song astronomers constructed a very precise calendar and, alone among the world's astronomers, noted the explosion of the Crab Nebula in 1054. Song inventors drew on their knowledge of celestial coordinates, particularly the Pole Star, to refine compass design. The magnetic compass, an earlier Chinese invention, shrank in size in Song times and gained a fixed pivot point for the needle. With a protective glass cover, the compass now became suitable for seafaring, a use first attested in 1090.

Development of the seaworthy compass coincided with new techniques in building China's main oceangoing ship, the **junk**. A stern-mounted rudder improved the steering of the large ship in uneasy seas, and watertight bulkheads helped keep it afloat in emergencies. The shipwrights of the Persian Gulf soon copied these features in their ship designs.

Because they needed iron and steel to make weapons for their army of 1.25 million men, the Song rulers fought their northern rivals for control of mines in north China. Production of coal and iron soared. By the end of the eleventh century, cast iron production reached about 125,000 tons (113,700 metric tons) annually, putting it on a par with the output of eighteenth-century

junk A very large flatbottom sailing ship produced in the Tang, Song, and Ming Empires, specially designed for long-distance commercial travel.

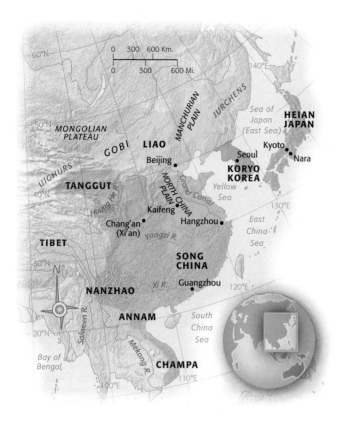

Britain. Engineers became skilled at high-temperature metallurgy using enormous bellows, often driven by water wheels, to superheat the molten ore. Military engineers used iron to buttress defensive works because it was impervious to fire or concussion. Armorers mass-produced body armor. Iron construction also appeared in bridges and small buildings. Mass-production techniques for bronze and ceramics in use in China for nearly two thousand years were adapted to iron casting and assembly.

To counter cavalry assaults, the Song experimented with **gunpowder**, which they initially used to propel clusters of flaming arrows. During the wars against the Jurchens in the 1100s, the Song introduced a new and terrifying weapon. Shells launched from Song fortifications exploded in the midst of the enemy, blowing out iron shrapnel and dismembering men and horses. The short range of these shells limited them to defensive uses.

Economy and Society in Song China

In a warlike era, Song elite culture idealized civil pursuits. Socially, the civil man outranked the military man. Private academies, designed to train young men for the official examinations, became influential in culture and politics. New interpretations of Confucian teachings became so important and influential that the term **neo-Confucianism** is used for Song and later versions of Confucian thought.

Zhu Xi (**jew she**) (1130–1200), the most important early neo-Confucian thinker, wrote in reaction to the many centuries during which Buddhism and Daoism had overshadowed the precepts of Confucius. He and others worked out a systematic approach to cosmology that focused on the central conception that human nature is moral, rational, and essentially good. To combat the Buddhist dismissal of worldly affairs as a transitory distraction, they reemphasized individual moral and social responsibility. Their human ideal was the sage, a person who could preserve mental stability and serenity while dealing conscientiously with troubling social problems. Whereas earlier Confucian thinkers had written about sage kings and political leaders, the neo-Confucians espoused the spiritual idea of universal sagehood, a state that could be achieved through proper study of the new Confucian principles and cosmology.

Popular Buddhist sects also persisted during the Song, demonstrating that anti-Buddhist feelings were not as ferocious as Confucian polemics against Buddhism might

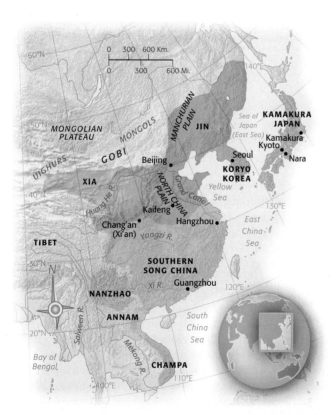

gunpowder A mixture of saltpeter, sulfur, and charcoal, in various proportions. The formula, brought to China in the 400s or 500s, was first used to make fumigators to keep away insect pests and evil spirits. In later centuries it was used to make explosives and grenades and to propel cannonballs, shot, and bullets.

neo-Confucianism Term used to describe new approaches to understanding classic Confucian texts that became the basic ruling philosophy of China from the Song period to the twentieth century.

Zen The Japanese word for a branch of Mahayana Buddhism based on highly disciplined meditation. It is known in Sanskrit as *dhyana*, in Chinese as *Chan*, and in Korean as *Son*.

movable type Type in which each individual character is cast on a separate piece of metal. It eventually replaced woodblock printing, allowing for the arrangement of individual letters and other characters on a page, rather than requiring the carving of entire pages at a time. Although China had an early form of moveable type in the eleventh century, Koreans invented durable, metal moveable type in the thirteenth century that may have influenced later print technology in China.

suggest. Some Buddhists elaborated on Tang-era folk practices derived from India and Tibet. The best known, Chan Buddhism (known as **Zen** in Japan and as Son in Korea), asserted that mental discipline alone could win salvation.

Meditation, a key Chan practice that was employed by Confucians as well as Buddhists, afforded prospective officials relief from studying for civil service examinations, which continued into the Song from the Tang period. Unlike the ancient Han policy of hiring and promoting on the basis of recommendations, Song-style examinations involved a large bureaucracy. Test questions, which changed each time the examinations were given, often related to economic management or foreign policy even though they were always based on Confucian classics.

Hereditary class distinctions meant less than they had in Tang times, when noble lineages played a greater role in the structure of power. The new system recruited the most talented men, whatever their origin. Yet men from wealthy families enjoyed an advantage. Preparation for the tests consumed so much time that peasant boys could rarely compete.

Success in the examinations brought good marriage prospects, the chance for a high salary, and enormous prestige. Failure could bankrupt a family and ruin a man both socially and psychologically. This put great pressure on candidates, who spent days writing essays in tiny, dim, airless examination cells.

During the Song era, a technical change from woodblock to an early form of **movable type** made printing cheaper. To promote its ideological goals, the Song government authorized the mass production of test preparation books in the years before 1000. Although a man had to be literate to read the preparation books and basic education was still rare, a growing number of candidates entered the Song bureaucracy without noble, gentry, or elite backgrounds.

The availability of printed books changed country life as well, since landlords gained access to expert advice on planting and irrigation techniques, harvesting, tree cultivation, threshing, and weaving. Landlords frequently gathered their tenants and workers to show them illustrated texts and explain their meaning. New agricultural land was developed south of the Yangtze River, and iron implements such as plows and rakes, first used in the Tang era, were adapted to southern wet-rice cultivation.

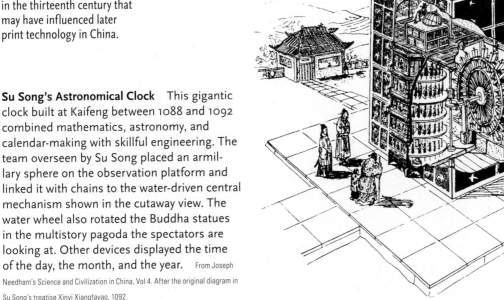

Su Song's Astronomical Clock This gigantic clock built at Kaifeng between 1088 and 1092 combined mathematics, astronomy, and calendar-making with skillful engineering. The team overseen by Su Song placed an armillary sphere on the observation platform and linked it with chains to the water-driven central mechanism shown in the cutaway view. The water wheel also rotated the Buddha statues in the multistory pagoda the spectators are looking at. Other devices displayed the time of the day, the month, and the year. From Joseph Needham's Science and Civilization in China, Vol 4. After the original diagram in Su Song's treatise Xinyi Xiangfayao, 1092.

The growing profitability of agriculture interested ambitious members of the gentry. Still a frontier for Chinese settlers under the Tang, the south saw increasing concentration of land in the hands of a few wealthy families. In the process, the indigenous inhabitants of the region, related to the modern-day populations of Malaysia, Thailand, and Laos, retreated into the mountains or southward toward Vietnam.

During the 1100s the total population of the Chinese territories, spurred by prosperity, rose above 100 million. The leading Song cities had fewer than a million inhabitants but were still among the largest cities in the world. Health and crowding posed problems in the Song capitals. Multistory wooden apartment houses fronted on narrow streets—sometimes only 4 or 5 feet (1.2 to 1.5 meters) wide—that were clogged by peddlers or families spending time outdoors. The crush of people called for new techniques in waste management, water supply, and firefighting.

In Hangzhou engineers diverted the nearby river to flow through the city, flushing away waste and disease. Arab and European travelers who had firsthand experience with the Song capital, and who were sensitive to urban conditions in their own societies, expressed amazement at Hangzhou's amenities: restaurants, parks, bookstores, wine shops, tea houses, theaters, and various entertainments.

The idea of credit, originating in the robust long-distance trade of the Tang period, spread widely under the Song. Intercity or interregional credit—what the Song called "flying money"—depended on the acceptance of guarantees that the paper could be redeemed for coinage at another location. The public accepted the practice because credit networks tended to be managed by families, so that brothers and cousins were usually honoring each other's certificates.

"Flying money" certificates differed from government-issued paper money, which the Song pioneered. In some years, military expenditures consumed 80 percent of the government budget. The state responded to this financial pressure by distributing paper money. But this made inflation so severe that by the beginning of the 1100s paper money was trading for only 1 percent of its face value. Eventually the government withdrew paper money and instead imposed new taxes, sold monopolies, and offered financial incentives to merchants.

Song River Transport This seventeenth-century painting shows the emperor Huizong (r. 1100–1126), in red, supervising the ceremonial transfer of pierced stones and a tree. The purpose of their transfer is unknown. Note the differences between the workshop at lower left and the residence at lower right where women, children, and even a pet dog are enjoying life outside the enclosed courtyard.

Chinese School/The Bridgeman Art Library/Getty Images

Female Musicians A group of entertainers from a Song period copy of a lost Tang painting titled "Night Revels of Han Xizai." The emperor ordered the painter to document the lifestyle of a man who preferred music, dance, and poetry to accepting appointment as Prime Minister. The mood of genteel indulgence appealed to Song era elites. Chinese women were not veiled, but foot-binding became common under the Song.

The Night Revelry of Han Xizai, by Gu Hongzhong the court painter sent by his suspicious monarch to spy on Han and to make a record of Han's licentious behaviour/Werner Forman Archive/The Bridgeman Art Library

Hard-pressed for the revenue needed to maintain the army, canals, roads, waterworks, and other state functions, the government finally resorted to tax farming: selling the rights to tax collection to private individuals. Tax farmers made their profit by collecting the maximum amount and sending an agreed-upon smaller sum to the government. This meant exorbitant rates for taxable services, such as tolls, and much heavier tax burdens on the common people.

Rapid economic growth undermined the remaining government monopolies and the traditional strict regulation of business. Now merchants and artisans as well as gentry and officials could make fortunes. With land no longer the only source of wealth, the traditional social hierarchy common to an agricultural economy weakened, while cities, commerce, consumption, and the use of money and credit boomed. Urban life reflected the elite's growing taste for fine fabrics, porcelain, exotic foods, large houses, and exquisite paintings and books.

In conjunction with the backlash against Buddhism and revival of Confucianism that began under the Tang and intensified under the Song, women experienced subordination, legal disenfranchisement, and social restriction. Merchants spent long periods away from home, and many maintained several wives in different locations. Frequently they depended on wives to manage their homes and even their businesses in their absence. But though women took on responsibility for the management of their husbands' property, their own property rights suffered legal erosion. Under Song law, a woman's property automatically passed to her husband, and women could not remarry if their husbands divorced them or died.

The subordination of women proved compatible with Confucianism, and it became fashionable to educate girls just enough to read simplified versions of Confucian philosophy that emphasized the lowly role of women. Modest education made these young women more desirable as companions for the sons of gentry or noble families and as literate mothers in lower-ranking families aspiring to improve their status. The poet Li Qingzhao (lee CHING-jow) (1083–1141) acknowledged and made fun of her unusual status as a highly celebrated female writer:

> *Although I've studied poetry for thirty years*
> *I try to keep my mouth shut and avoid reputation.*
> *Now who is this nosy gentleman talking about my poetry*
> *Like Yang Ching-chih* (yahng SHING-she)
> *Who spoke of Hsiang Ssu* (sang sue) *everywhere he went.*[3]

Her reference is to a hermit poet of the ninth century who was continually and extravagantly praised by a court official, Yang Ching-chih.

Female footbinding first appeared among slave dancers at the Tang court, but it did not become widespread until the Song period. The bindings forced the toes under and toward the

---

[3]Quoted at "Women's Early Music, Art, Poetry," http://music.acu.edu/www/iawm/pages/reference/tzusongs.html.

- Several rival states replaced the fallen Tang Empire, and the close relations between Central Asia and East Asia ended.

- The Liao and Jin Empires encouraged culturally diverse societies and confronted Song China with formidable military threats.

- The Song Empire of central and southern China built upon Tang achievements in technology and science and promoted civil ideals.

- Under the Song, print culture developed, urban populations rose, commercial activity grew through innovation, and women were subordinated to men.

heel, so that the bones eventually broke and the woman could not walk on her own. In noble and gentry families, footbinding began between ages five and seven. In less wealthy families, girls worked until they were older, so footbinding began only in a girl's teens.

Many literate men condemned the maiming of innocent girls and the general uselessness of footbinding. Nevertheless, bound feet became a status symbol. By 1200 a woman with unbound feet had become undesirable in elite circles, and mothers of elite status, or aspiring to such status, almost without exception bound their daughters' feet. They knew that girls with unbound feet faced rejection. Working women and the indigenous peoples of the south, where northern practices took a longer time to penetrate, did not practice footbinding. Consequently they enjoyed considerably more mobility and economic independence than did elite Chinese women.

NEW KINGDOMS IN EAST ASIA

The best possibilities for expanding the Confucian worldview of the Song lay with newly emerging kingdoms to the east and south. Korea, Japan, and Vietnam, like Song China, devoted great effort to the cultivation of rice. This practice fit well with Confucian social ideas, as tending the young rice plants, irrigating the rice paddies, and managing the harvest required coordination among many village and kin groups and rewarded hierarchy, obedience, and self-discipline.

Confucianism also justified using agricultural profits to support the education, safety, and comfort of the literate elite. In each of these new kingdoms Song civilization melded with indigenous cultural and historical traditions to create a distinctive synthesis.

Chinese Influences

Korea, Japan, and Vietnam had first centralized power under ruling houses in the early Tang period, and their state ideologies continued to resemble that of the early Tang, when Buddhism and Confucianism seemed compatible. Government offices went to noble families and did not depend on passing examinations on Confucian texts. Landowning and agriculture remained the major sources of income, and landowners faced no challenges from a merchant class or urban elite.

Nevertheless, learned men prized literacy in classical Chinese and a good knowledge of Confucian texts (see Environment and Technology: Writing in East Asia, 400–1200). Though formal education was available to only a small number of people, the ruling and landholding elites sought to instill Confucian ideals of hierarchy and harmony among the general population (see Diversity and Dominance: Law and Society in China and Japan).

Korea

shamanism The practice of identifying special individuals (shamans) who will interact with spirits for the benefit of the community. Characteristic of the Korean kingdoms of the early medieval period and of early societies of Central Asia.

Our first knowledge of Korea, Japan, and Vietnam comes from early Chinese officials and travelers. When the Qin Empire established its first colony in the Korean peninsula in the third century B.C.E., Chinese bureaucrats began documenting Korean history and customs. Han writers noted the horse breeding, strong hereditary elites, and **shamanism** (belief in the ability of certain individuals to contact ancestors and the invisible spirit world) of Korea's small kingdoms. But Korea quickly absorbed Confucianism and Buddhism.

Mountainous in the east and north, Korea was heavily forested until modern times. The land that can be cultivated (less than 20 percent) lies mostly in the south, where a warm climate and monsoon rains support two crops per year. Population movements from Manchuria, Mongolia, and Siberia to the north and to Japan in the south promoted the spread of languages that were very different from Chinese but distantly related to the Turkic tongues of Inner Asia.

In the early 500s the dominant landholding families made inherited status—the "bone ranks"—permanent in Silla (SILL-ah or SHILL-ah), a kingdom in the southeast of the peninsula. In the early 660s, Silla defeated the southwestern kingdom of Paekche, which had played a major role as a maritime power in transmitting Chinese culture to Japan. Then in 668 the northern Koguryō kingdom came to an end after prolonged conflict with the Sui and Tang. Koguryō was so influential in Northeast Asia that the Liao and Jin Empires, and subsequent Korean kingdoms, claimed to inherit its legacy.

Supported by the Tang, Silla now took control of much of the Korean peninsula. The Silla rulers imitated Tang government and examined officials on the Confucian classics. They also sent Buddhist monks to China. But the intellectual exchange was not one-directional: writings by the monk Wonhyo, known as the "Korean Commentary," greatly influenced Buddhism in China. The fall of the Tang in the early 900s coincided with Silla's collapse and enabled the ruling house of **Koryo** (KAW-ree-oh), from which the modern name "Korea" derives, to rule a united peninsula for the next three centuries. Threatened constantly by the Liao and then the Jin in northern China, Koryo maintained amicable relations with Song China in the south. The Koryo kings supported Buddhism and made superb printed editions of Buddhist texts.

Koryo Korean kingdom founded in 918 and destroyed by a Mongol invasion in 1259.

The oldest surviving woodblock print in Chinese characters comes from Korea in the middle 700s. Commonly used during the Tang period, woodblock printing required great technical skill. A calligrapher would write the text on thin paper, which would then be pasted upside down on a block of wood. Once wetted, the characters showed through from the back, and an artisan would carve away the wooden surface surrounding each character. A fresh block had to be carved for each printed page. Korean artisans developed their own advances in printing, including experiments with movable type. By Song times, Korean experiments reached China, where further improvements led to metal or porcelain type from which texts could be cheaply printed.

Japan

Japan consists of four main islands and many smaller ones stretching in an arc from as far south as Georgia to as far north as Maine. The nearest point of contact with the Asian mainland lies 100 miles away in southern Korea. In early times Japan was even more mountainous and heavily forested than Korea, with only 11 percent of its land area suitable for cultivation. Mild winters and monsoon rains supported the earliest population centers on the coastlands of the Inland Sea between Honshu and Shikoku Islands. The first rulers to extend their power broadly in the fourth and fifth centuries C.E. were based in the Yamato River Basin on the Kinai Plain at the eastern end of the sea.

The first Chinese description of Japan, dating from the fourth century, tells of an island at the eastern edge of the world that is divided into hundreds of small communities, with the largest one, called Yamatai, ruled over by a shamaness named Himiko or Pimiko. The location of the early Yamatai kingdom remains a source of debate and fascination in Japan, but archeological finds point to frequent interaction with China and Korea.

In the mid-600s the Yamatai rulers, acting on knowledge gained from Korean contacts and embassies to Chang'an sent by five different kings, implemented the Taika (TIE-kah) and other reforms, giving this regime the key features of Tang government. A legal code, an official variety of Confucianism, and an official reverence for Buddhism blended with the local recognition of indigenous and immigrant chieftains as territorial administrators. Within a century, a centralized government with a complex system of law had emerged, as attested by a massive history in the Confucian style.

Women from the aristocracy became royal consorts and thereby linked their kinsmen with the royal court. At the death of her husband in 592, Suiko, a woman from the immigrant aristocratic family of Soga, became empress. She occupied the throne until 628, enjoying a longer reign than

DeA Picture Library/Art Resource, NY

Silla Warrior This ewer—the projection in front is the pour spout—reflects Korea's early use of cavalry. Horses were probably introduced to Japan by way of Korea.

Writing in East Asia, 400–1200

An ideographic writing system that originated in China became a communications tool throughout East Asia. Variations on this system, based more on depictions of meanings than representations of sound, spread widely by the time of the Sui and Tang Empires. Many East Asian peoples adapted ideographic techniques to writing languages unrelated to Chinese in grammar or sound.

The Vietnamese, Koreans, and Japanese often simplified Chinese characters and associated them with the sounds of their own non-Chinese languages. For instance, the Chinese character *an*, meaning "peace" (Fig. 1), was pronounced "an" in Japanese and was familiar as a Chinese character to Confucian scholars in Japan's Heian (hay-ahn) period. However, nonscholars simplified the character and used it to write the Japanese sound "a" (Fig. 2). A set of more than thirty of these syllabic symbols adapted from Chinese characters could represent the inflected forms (forms with grammatical endings) of any Japanese word. Murasaki Shikibu used such a syllabic system when she wrote *The Tale of Genji*.

In Vietnam and later in northern Asia, phonetic and ideographic elements combined in new ways. The apparent circles in some *chu nom* writing from Vietnam (Fig. 3) derive from the Chinese character for "mouth" and indicate a primary sound association for the word. The Khitans, who spoke a language related to Mongolian, developed an ideographic system of their own, inspired by Chinese characters. The Chinese character *wang* (Fig. 4), meaning "king, prince, ruler," was changed to represent the Khitan word for "emperor" by adding an upward stroke representing a "superior" ruler (Fig. 5). Because the system was ideographic, we do not know the pronunciation of this Khitan word. The Khitan character for "God" or "Heaven" adds a top stroke representing the "supreme" ruler or power to the character meaning "ruler" (Fig. 6). Though inspired by Chinese characters, Khitan writings could not be read by anyone who was not specifically educated in them.

The Khitans developed another system to represent the sounds and grammar of their language. They used small, simplified elements arranged within an imaginary frame to indicate the sounds in any word. This idea might have come from the phonetic script used by the Uighurs. Here (Fig. 7) we see the word for horse in a Khitan inscription. Fitting sound elements within a frame also occurred later in *hangul*, the Korean phonetic system introduced in the 1400s. Here (Fig. 8) we see the two words making up the country name "Korea."

The Chinese writing system served the Chinese elite well. But peoples speaking unrelated languages continually experimented with the Chinese invention to produce new ways of expressing themselves. Some of the resulting sound-based writing systems remain in common use; others are still being deciphered.

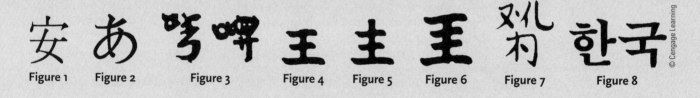

Figure 1   Figure 2   Figure 3   Figure 4   Figure 5   Figure 6   Figure 7   Figure 8

© Cengage Learning

any other ruler down to the nineteenth century. Asuka, her capital, saw a flowering of Buddhist art, and her nephew Shotoku opened relations with Sui China and is credited with promulgating a "Constitution" in 604 that had lasting influence on Japan's governing philosophy (see Diversity and Dominance: Law and Society in China and Japan).

The Japanese mastered Chinese building techniques so well that Nara (NAH-rah) (710-784) and Kyoto (794-1868), Japan's early capitals, provide invaluable evidence of the wooden architecture long since vanished from China. During the eighth century Japan in some ways surpassed China in Buddhist studies. In 752 dignitaries from all over Mahayana Buddhist Asia gathered at the enormous Todaiji temple, near Nara, to celebrate the "eye-opening" of the "Great Buddha" statue.

Though the Japanese adopted Chinese building styles and some street plans, Japanese cities were built without walls. One reason was that central Japan was not plagued by constant warfare. Also, the Confucian Mandate of Heaven, which justified dynastic changes, played no role in legitimating Japanese government. The *tenno*, or "heavenly sovereign"—often called "emperor" in English—belonged to a family believed to have ruled Japan since the beginning of history. The dynasty never changed. A prime minister and the leaders of the native religion, in later times called Shinto, the "way of the gods," exercised real control.

By 750 the government in Nara had reached its zenith. During the Nara and Early Heian periods, the rulers expanded their fledgling regime outward from central Japan. They did this by sending an army led by a "barbarian-subduing generalissimo," the shogun, into regions on the peripheries of the Japanese islands. The court extended Japanese rice-growing culture into the territory of the Hayato people of southern Kyushu and into northeastern Honshu, where the

Emishi, a mixed indigenous population, practiced slash-and-burn agriculture. A collection of poems dating from the eight century, called *Ten Thousand Leaves*, records the hopes and fears of those engaged in expanding the sovereign's contact with China, the Korean peninsula, and Japanese islands distant from the capital city:

> *A frontier-guard when I set out, Oh what turmoil there was! Of the work my wife should do, I said not a word and came away.*[4]

In 794 the central government moved to Kyoto, usually called by its ancient name, Heian (hay-ahn). Legally centralized government lasted there until 1185, though power became decentralized toward the end. In Kyoto members of the **Fujiwara** (foo-jee-WAH-rah) clan—a family of priests, bureaucrats, and warriors who had succeeded the Soga clan in influence—controlled power and protected the emperor. Fujiwara dominance favored men of Confucian learning over the generally illiterate warriors, and noblemen of the Fujiwara period read the Chinese classics and appreciated painting and poetry.

Gradually, however, the Fujiwara nobles began to entrust responsibility for local government, policing, and tax collection to their warriors, who were known as *samurai*, literally "one who serves." Though often of humble origins, a small number of these warriors had achieved wealth and power by the late 1000s. By the middle 1100s the nobility had lost control, and civil war between rival warrior clans engulfed the capital.

Like other East Asian states influenced by Confucianism, the elite families of Fujiwara Japan did not encourage education for women. The hero of the celebrated Japanese novel about Fujiwara court culture, *The Tale of Genji*, written around the year 1000 and often regarded as the world's first novel, remarks: "Women should have a general knowledge of several subjects, but it gives a bad impression if they show themselves to be attached to a particular branch of learning."[5] However, within the marriage politics of the day, having interesting and talented women helped the Fujiwara monopolize the monarch's attention on their own women rather than those of other families.

Fujiwara noblewomen lived in near-total isolation, generally spending their time on cultural pursuits and the study of Buddhism. To communicate with their families or among themselves, they depended on writing. The simplified syllabic script that they used represented the Japanese language in its fully inflected form (the Chinese classical script used by Fujiwara men could not do so).

Sei Shonagon (SAY SHOH-nah-gohn), a lady attending one of the royal consorts, composed her *Pillow Book* between 996 and 1021. Most likely named for being kept by the author's pillow so she could jot down occasional thoughts, this famous work begins:

> *Spring is best at dawn as gradually the hilltops lighten, while the light grows brighter until there are purple-tinged clouds trailing through the sky.*
> *Summer is best at night. That goes without saying when there is a full moon. But when fireflies flit here and there in a dark sky, that too is wonderful. It is even wonderful when it is raining.*[6]

Military clans acquired increasing importance during the period 1156–1185, when warfare between rival families culminated in the establishment of the **Kamakura** (kah-mah-KOO-rah) **Shogunate** in eastern Honshu, far from the old religious and political center at Kyoto. The standing of the Fujiwara family fell as nobles and the emperor hurried to accommodate the new warlords. *The Tale of the Heike*, an anonymously composed thirteenth-century epic account of the clan war, reflects a Buddhist appreciation of the impermanence of worldly things, a view that became common among the new warrior class. This class eventually absorbed some of the Fujiwara aristocratic values, but the monopoly of power by a nonmilitary civil elite had come to an end.

Fujiwara Aristocratic family that dominated the Japanese imperial court between the ninth and twelfth centuries.

Kamakura Shogunate The first of Japan's decentralized military governments (1185–1333).

Vietnam

Not until Tang times did the relationship between Vietnam and China become close enough for economic and cultural interchange to play an important role. Occupying the coastal regions east

---

[4]The Manyōshū: The Nippon Gakujutsu Shinkōkai translation of One Thousand poems, p. 254. Copyright © 1965 Columbia University Press. Reprinted with permission of the publisher.

[5]Quoted in Ivan Morris, *The World of the Shining Prince: Court Life in Ancient Japan* (New York: Penguin Books, 1979), 221–222.

[6]Quoted in Ivan Morris, trans., *The Pillow Book of Sei Shonagon* (New York: Columbia University Press, 1991), section 1.

Christian Kober/Alamy

Imperial Palace in Kyoto The first version of the palace was built in the eighth century 1.2 miles (2 kilometers) away from the current site. The Kyoto palace complex was the primary residence of the Japanese emperors until the middle of the nineteenth century, when the imperial capital moved to Tokyo. Being built of wood with cypress-bark roofing, the buildings have been repeatedly ravaged by fire, but each restoration has utilized traditional materials in an effort to preserve the historical forms. The latest rebuilding took place in 1855. The palace complex includes gardens and numerous buildings in a variety of styles particular to different periods in its history.

SECTION REVIEW

- Korea, Japan, and Vietnam adapted Chinese cultural and political models, including the Tang blend of Confucianism and Buddhism.

- In all three cultures, landowning and agriculture remained the principal source of wealth.

- The Korean peninsula, which was split into three rival kingdoms, became unified under the founder of the Koryo kingdom.

- In Japan, a warrior aristocracy in Kamakura gradually arose beginning in the twelfth century to rule alongside the court nobles and emperor who resided in Kyoto.

- Modern day Vietnam was originally split into several kingdoms that featured a unique blend of the culture and politics of China and Southeast Asian states.

of the mountainous spine of mainland Southeast Asia, Vietnam's economic and political life centered on two fertile river valleys, the Red River in the north and the Mekong **(may-KONG)** in the south. The rice-based agriculture of Vietnam made the region well suited for integration with southern China. In both regions the wet climate and hilly terrain demanded expertise in irrigation.

Early Vietnamese peoples may have preceded the Chinese in using draft animals in farming and working with metal. But in Tang and Song times the elites of Annam **(ahn-nahm)**—as the Chinese called early Vietnam—adopted Confucian bureaucratic training, Mahayana Buddhism, and other aspects of Chinese culture, and Annamese elites continued to rule in the Tang style after that dynasty's fall. In 936 Annam assumed the name Dai Viet **(die vee-yet)** and maintained good relations with Song China as an independent country.

Champa, located in what is now southern Vietnam, rivaled the Dai Viet state. The cultures of India and the Malay Peninsula strongly influenced Champa through maritime networks of trade and communication. During the Tang period, Champa fought with Dai Viet, but both kingdoms cooperated with the less threatening Song. Among the tribute gifts brought to the Song court by Champa emissaries was **Champa rice** (originally from India). Chinese farmers soon made use of this fast-maturing variety to improve their yields of the essential crop.

Vietnam shared the general Confucian interest in hierarchy, but attitudes toward women, like those in Korea and Japan, differed from the Chinese model. None of the societies adopted footbinding. In Korea strong family alliances that functioned like political and economic organizations allowed women a role in negotiating and disposing of property. Before the adoption of Confucianism, Annamese women had enjoyed higher status than women in China, perhaps because both women and men participated in wet-rice cultivation. The Trung sisters of Vietnam, who lived in the second century C.E. and led local farmers in resistance against the Han Empire, still serve as national symbols in Vietnam and as local heroes in southern China.

CONCLUSION

The Tang Empire put into place a solid system of travel, trade, and communications that allowed cultural and economic influences to move quickly from Inner Asia to Japan. In addition, diversity within the empire produced great wealth and new ideas. Eventually, however, tensions among rival groups weakened the political structure and led to great violence and misery.

The post-Tang fragmentation permitted regional cultures to emerge that experimented with and often improved on Tang military, architectural, and scientific technologies. In northern and

Champa rice Quick-maturing rice that can allow two harvests in one growing season. Originally introduced into Champa from India, it was later sent to China as a tribute gift by the Champa state.

Inner Asia, these refinements included state ideologies based on Buddhism, bureaucratic practices based on Chinese traditions, and military techniques combining nomadic horsemanship and strategies with Chinese armaments and weapons. In Song China, the spread of Tang technological knowledge resulted in the privatization of commerce, major advances in technology and industry, increased productivity in agriculture, and deeper exploration of ideas relating to time, cosmology, and mathematics.

The brilliant achievements of the Song period came from mutually reinforcing developments in economy and technology. Without the rampant warfare and exploitation of the economy in the mid to late Tang period, the Song economy, though much smaller than its predecessor, showed great productivity, circulating goods and money throughout East Asia and stimulating the economies of neighbors.

Korea, Japan, and Vietnam developed distinct social, economic, and political systems. Buddhism became the preferred religion in all three regions, but Chinese influences, largely deriving from a universal esteem for Confucian thought and writings, put down deep roots. All of these societies made advances in agricultural technology and productivity and raised their literacy rates as printing spread. In the absence of a land border with China, Japan retained greater political independence than Korea and Vietnam. The culture of its imperial center reached a high level of refinement, but the political system was ultimately based on a warrior aristocracy.

KEY TERMS

Grand Canal p. 292
Li Shimin p. 292
Tang Empire p. 292
tributary system p. 292
Song Empire p. 298
junk p. 299
gunpowder p. 301
neo-Confucianism p. 301
Zen p. 301
movable type p. 301
shamanism p. 304
Koryo p. 305
Fujiwara p. 307
Kamakura Shogunate p. 307
Champa rice p. 309

SUGGESTED READING

Barfield, Thomas. *The Perilous Frontier: Nomadic Empires and China.* 1992. An anthropologist's view of the relationship between pastoralists and agriculturists in the region.

Batten, B. L. *To the Ends of Japan: Premodern Frontiers, Boundaries, and Interactions.* 2003. Japan in the overall history of Northeast Asia.

Ch'oe, Yongho, et al., eds. *Sources of Korean Tradition.* 2000. Key texts and sound interpretations.

De Bary, W. T., W-T Chan, and B. Watson, compilers. *Sources of Chinese Tradition*, vol. 1, 2d ed. 1999. Key texts and sound interpretations of neo-Confucianism and Buddhism.

Ebrey, Patricia. *The Inner Quarters: Marriage and the Lives of Chinese Women in the Sung Period.* 1993. Uncommon study of Chinese women's history.

Elvin, Mark. *The Pattern of the Chinese Past.* 1973. A classic thesis on Song advancement (and Ming backwardness); see particularly Part II.

Hymes, Robert P. *Way and Byway: Taoism, Local Religion, and Models of Divinity in Sung China.* 2002. A study of post-Tang religious matters.

Lewis, Mark. *China's Cosmopolitan Empire: The Tang Empire.* 2009. Excellent introduction to Tang and its global interaction.

Nahm, Andrew C. *Introduction to Korean History and Culture.* 1993. A general survey.

Rossabi, Morris, ed. *China Among Equals: The Middle Kingdom and Its Neighbors, 10th–14th Centuries.* 1983. General account of post-Tang political relationships.

Taylor, Keith Weller. *The Birth of Vietnam.* 1983. A general survey.

Tsunoda, R., W. T. de Bary, and D. Keene, compilers. *Sources of Japanese Tradition*, vol. 1, 2d ed. 2002. Key texts and sound interpretations.

Varley, Paul H. *Japanese Culture.* 1984. A classic introduction.

Wright, Arthur F., and David Twitchett, eds. *Perspectives on the T'ang.* 1973. A variety of enduring essays.

Go to the History CourseMate website for primary source links, study tools, and review materials for this chapter. **CourseMate** www.cengagebrain.com

PART

IV

CHAPTER 13   Mongol Eurasia and Its Aftermath, 1200–1500

CHAPTER 14   Latin Europe, 1200–1500

CHAPTER 15   Southern Empires, Southern Seas, 1200–1500

CHAPTER 16   The Maritime Revolution, to 1550

Library of Congress

Martin Waldseemüller's Map of the World   This map, published in 1507 and included in a German geography book entitled *Cosmographiae Introductio*, marks the first usage of the name *America*, placed one-third of the way from the bottom of the New World's southern continent. After Amerigho (original spelling) Vespucci sailed twice to the New World as a navigator in 1499 and 1501, he wrote letters that misled the author of this map into thinking that Vespucci, and not Columbus, had been the first to land on the mainland. "I do not see what right any one would have to object to calling this part after Americus, who discovered it and who is a man of intelligence, [and so to name it] Amerige, that is, the Land of Americus, or America: since both Europa and Asia got their names from women."

Interregional Patterns of Culture and Contact, 1200–1550

Part IV begins with the Mongol conquests under Chinggis Khan, whose empire made Mongolia the center of an administrative and trading system linking Europe, the Middle East, Russia, and East Asia. Some lands flourished; others groaned under tax burdens and physical devastation.

Societies that escaped conquest also felt the Mongol impact. Around the eastern Mediterranean coast and in eastern Europe, Southeast Asia, and Japan, fear of Mongol attack stimulated defense planning and accelerated processes of urbanization, technological development, and political centralization.

By 1500, Mongol dominance had waned. A new Chinese empire, the Ming, was expanding its influence in Southeast Asia. The Ottomans had overthrown the Byzantine Empire, and Christian monarchs in Spain and Portugal, victorious over Muslim enemies, were laying the foundations of new overseas empires.

As Eurasia's overland trade faded, merchants, soldiers, and explorers took to the seas. From China, the admiral Zheng He made state-sponsored long-distance voyages that were spectacular but without long-term results. Meanwhile, Africans explored the Atlantic, and Polynesians colonized the central and eastern Pacific in the 1300s and 1400s. By 1500 Christopher Columbus had reached the Americas; within twenty-five years a Portuguese ship would sail around the world.

The overland routes of Eurasia had generated massive wealth in East Asia and a growing hunger for commerce in Europe. These factors similarly spurred the development of maritime trade. Exposure to the achievements, wealth, and resources of the Americas, sub-Saharan Africa, and Asia guaranteed the further expansion of European exploration and maritime power.

Chapter Outline

The Rise of the Mongols, 1200–1260
➤ *What accounts for the magnitude and speed of the Mongol conquests?*

The Mongols and Islam, 1260–1500
➤ *How did Mongol expansion and Islam affect each other?*

Regional Responses in Western Eurasia
➤ *What benefits resulted from the integration of Eurasia into the Mongol Empire?*

Mongol Domination in China, 1271–1368
➤ *How did Mongol rule in China foster cultural and scientific exchange?*

The Early Ming Empire, 1368–1500
➤ *In what ways did the Ming Empire continue or discontinue Mongol practices?*

Centralization and Militarism in East Asia, 1200–1500
➤ *What are some of the similarities and differences in how Korea and Japan responded to the Mongol threat?*

Conclusion

● **DIVERSITY + DOMINANCE**   Observations of Mongol Life
● **ENVIRONMENT + TECHNOLOGY**   From Gunpowder to Guns

The Granger Collection, New York

Defending Japan   Japanese warriors board Mongol warships with swords to prevent the landing of the invasion force in 1281.

Mongol Eurasia and Its Aftermath, 1200–1500

When Temüjin (TEM-uh-jin) was a boy, a rival group murdered his father. Temüjin's mother tried to shelter him, but she could not find a safe haven. At fifteen Temüjin sought refuge with the leader of the Keraits (keh-rates), a warring confederation whose people spoke Turkic and respected both Christianity and Buddhism. Temüjin learned the importance of religious tolerance, the necessity of dealing harshly with enemies, and the variety of Inner Asia's cultural and economic traditions.

In 1206 the **Mongols** and their allies acknowledged Temüjin as **Chinggis Khan** (CHING-iz KAHN) (sometimes known as Genghis), or supreme leader. His advisers spoke many languages and belonged to different religions. His deathbed speech, which cannot be literally true even though a contemporary recorded it, captures the strategy behind Mongol success: "If you want to retain your possessions and conquer your enemies, you must make your subjects submit willingly and unite your diverse energies to a single end."[1] By implementing this strategy, Chinggis Khan became the most famous conqueror in history, initiating an expansion of Mongol dominion that by 1250 stretched from Poland to northern China.

Scholars today stress the positive developments that transpired under Mongol rule. European and Asian sources of the time, however, vilify the Mongols as agents of death, suffering, and conflagration, a still-common viewpoint based on reliable accounts of horrible massacres.

The tremendous extent of the Mongol Empire promoted the movement of people and ideas from one end of Eurasia to the other. Trade routes improved, markets expanded, and the demand for products grew. Trade on the Silk Road, which had declined with the fall of the Tang Empire (see Chapter 12), revived.

Between 1218 and about 1350 in western Eurasia and down to 1368 in China, the Mongols focused on specific economic and strategic interests, usually permitting local cultures to survive and develop. In some regions, local reactions to Mongol domination sowed seeds of regional and ethnic identity that blossomed in the period of Mongol decline. Regions as widely separated as Russia, Iran, China, Korea, and Japan benefited from the Mongol stimulation of economic and cultural exchange and also found in their opposition to the Mongols new bases for political consolidation and affirmation of cultural difference.

Mongols A people of this name is mentioned as early as the records of the Tang Empire, living as nomads in northern Eurasia. After 1206 they established an enormous empire under Chinggis Khan, linking western and eastern Eurasia.

Chinggis Khan The title of Temüjin when he ruled the Mongols (1206–1227). It means the "oceanic" or "universal leader." Chinggis Khan was the founder of the Mongol Empire.

[1]Quotation adapted from Desmond Martin, *Chingis Khan and His Conquest of North China* (Baltimore: The John Hopkins Press, 1950), 303.

THE RISE OF THE MONGOLS, 1200–1260

nomadism A way of life, forced by a scarcity of resources, in which groups of people continually migrate to find pastures and water.

The Mongol Empire owed much of its success to the cultural institutions and political traditions of the Eurasian steppes (prairies) and deserts. The pastoral way of life known as **nomadism** gives rise to imperial expansion only occasionally, and historians disagree about what triggers these episodes. In the case of the Mongols, a precise assessment of the personal contributions of Chinggis Khan and his successors remains uncertain.

Nomadism in Central and Inner Asia

The pastoral nomads of the Eurasian steppes played an on-again, off-again role in European, Middle Eastern, and Chinese history for hundreds of years before the rise of the Mongols (see Chapter 9). The Mongol way of life probably did not differ materially from that of those earlier peoples (see Diversity and Dominance: Observations of Mongol Life). Traditional accounts maintain that the Mongols put their infants on goats to accustom them to riding. Moving regularly and efficiently with flocks and herds and homes carried on two-wheeled vehicles required firm decision making, and the independence of individual Mongols and their families made this decision making public, with many voices being heard. A council with representatives from powerful families ratified the decisions of the leader, the *khan*. Yet people who disagreed with a decision could strike out on their own. Even during military campaigns, warriors moved with their families and possessions.

Menial work in camps fell to slaves—either prisoners of war or people who sought refuge in slavery to escape starvation. Weak groups secured land rights and protection from strong groups by providing them with slaves, livestock, weapons, silk, or cash. More powerful groups, such as Chinggis Khan's extended family and descendants, lived almost entirely off tribute, so they spent less time and fewer resources on herding and more on warfare designed to secure greater tribute.

Leading families combined resources and solidified intergroup alliances through arranged marriages and acts of allegiance, a process that helped generate political federations. Marriages were arranged in childhood—in Temüjin's case, at the age of eight—and children thus became pawns of diplomacy. Women from prestigious families could wield power in negotiation and management, though they ran the risk of assassination or execution just like men.

The wives and mothers of Mongol rulers traditionally managed state affairs during the interregnum between a ruler's death and the selection of a successor. Princes and heads of ministries treated such regents with great deference and obeyed their commands without question. Since a female regent could not herself succeed to the position of khan, her political machinations usually focused on gaining the succession for a son or other male relative.

Families often included believers in two or more religions, most commonly Buddhism, Christianity, or Islam. Virtually all Mongols observed the practices of traditional shamanism, rituals in which special individuals visited and influenced the supernatural world. Whatever their faith, the Mongols believed in world rulership by a khan who, with the aid of his shamans, could speak to and for an ultimate god, represented as Sky or Heaven. This universal ruler transcended particular cultures and dominated them all.

The Mongol Conquests, 1215–1283

Shortly after his acclamation in 1206, Chinggis initiated two decades of Mongol aggression. By 1209 he had cowed the Tanggut (TAHNG-gut) rulers of northwest China, and in 1215 he captured the Jin capital of Yanjing, today known as Beijing (bay-jeeng). He turned westward in 1219 with an invasion of Khwarezm (kaw-REZM), a state east of the Caspian Sea that included much of Iran. After 1221, when most of Iran had fallen, Chinggis left the command of most campaigns to subordinate generals.

Ögödei (ERG-uh-day), Chinggis's son, became the Great Khan in 1227 after his father's death (see Figure 13.1). He completed the destruction of the Tanggut and the Jin and put their territories under Mongol governors. By 1234 he controlled most of northern China and was threatening the Southern Song (see Chapter 12). Two years later Chinggis's grandson Batu (BAH-too) (d. 1255) attacked Russian territories, took control of the towns along the Volga (VOHL-gah) River, and conquered Kievan Russia, Moscow, Poland, and Hungary in a five-year campaign. Only the

CHRONOLOGY

	Mongolia and China	Central Asia and Middle East	Russia	Korea, Japan, and Southeast Asia
1200	1206 Temüjin chosen Chinggis Khan of the Mongols	1219–1223 First Mongol attacks in Iran	1221–1223 First Mongol attacks on Russia	
	1227 Death of Chinggis Khan			
	1227–1241 Reign of Great Khan Ögödei			
	1234 Mongols conquer northern China		1240 Mongols sack Kiev	
			1242 Alexander Nevskii defeats Teutonic Knights	1258 Mongols conquer Koryo rulers in Korea
		1258 Mongols sack Baghdad and kill the caliph		
	1271 Founding of Yuan Empire	1260 Mamluks defeat Il-khans at Ain Jalut	1260 War between Il-khans and Golden Horde	
	1279 Mongol conquest of Southern Song			1274, 1281 Mongols attack Japan
				1283 Yuan invades Champa
1300		1295 Il-khan Ghazan converts to Islam		1293 Yuan attacks Java
		1349 End of Il-khan rule	1346 Plague outbreak at Kaffa	1333–1338 End of Kamakura Shogunate in Japan, beginning of Ashikaga
		ca. 1350 Egypt infected by plague		
	1368 Ming Empire founded			
		1370–1405 Reign of Timur		1392 Founding of Choson dynasty in Korea
1400	1403–1424 Reign of Yongle	1402 Timur defeats Ottoman sultan		
	1405–1433 Voyages of Zheng He	1453 Ottomans capture Constantinople	1462–1505 Ivan III establishes authority as tsar. Moscow emerges as major political center.	1471–1500 Dai Viet conquers Champa

death of Ögödei in 1241, which caused a suspension of campaigning, saved Europe from graver damage. With Chinggis's grandson Güyük (gi-yik) installed as the new Great Khan, the conquests resumed. In the Middle East a Mongol army sacked Baghdad in 1258 and executed the last Abbasid caliph (see Chapter 10).

Chinggis Khan's original objective had probably been collecting tribute, but the success of the Mongol conquests created a new situation. Ögödei unquestionably sought to rule a united empire based at his capital, Karakorum (kah-rah-KOR-um), and until his death he controlled the subordinate Mongol domains: the Golden Horde in Russia and the Chagatai (JAH-guh-die) domains in Central Asia (see Map 13.1). After Ögödei's death, however, family unity began to unravel; when Khubilai (KOO-bih-lie) declared himself Great Khan in 1260, the descendants of Chinggis's son Chagatai (d. 1242) and other branches of the family refused to accept him. As Karakorum was destroyed in the ensuing fighting, Khubilai transferred his court to the old Jin capital now renamed Beijing. In 1271 he declared himself founder of the **Yuan Empire**.

Yuan Empire Empire created in China and Siberia by Khubilai Khan.

Chagatai's descendants continued to dominate Central Asia and enjoyed close relations with the region's Turkic-speaking nomads. This, plus a continuing hatred of Khubilai, contributed to Central Asia becoming an independent Mongol center and to the spread of Islam there.

After the Yuan destroyed the Southern Song (see Chapter 12) in 1279, Mongol troops attacked Dai Viet—now northern Vietnam—and in 1283 invaded the kingdom of Champa in southern Vietnam. When the initially successful Mongols suffered a defeat, Khubilai was so infuriated that he postponed an invasion of Japan to focus on the Vietnamese kingdoms. In 1287, the Vietnamese troops, under the command of Tran Hung Dao, Vietnam's most famous military hero,

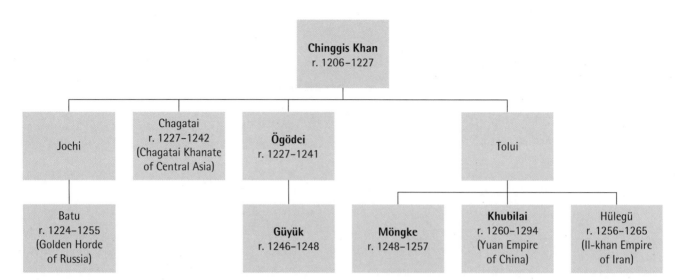

Jochi

Chagatai
r. 1227–1242
(Chagatai Khanate
of Central Asia)

Ögödei
r. 1227–1241

Tolui

Batu
r. 1224–1255
(Golden Horde
of Russia)

Güyük
r. 1246–1248

Möngke
r. 1248–1257

Khubilai
r. 1260–1294
(Yuan Empire
of China)

Hülegü
r. 1256–1265
(Il-khan Empire
of Iran)

FIGURE 13.1 **Mongol Rulers, 1206–1260** The names of the Great Khans are shown in bold type. Those who founded the regional khanates are listed with their dates of rule. © Cengage Learning

defeated the Mongol forces in a final battle. A plan to invade Java by sea also failed, as did two invasions of Japan in 1274 and 1281.

The Mongols seldom outnumbered their enemies, but they were extraordinary riders and utilized superior bows. The Central Asian bow, made by laminating layers of wood, leather, and bone, could shoot one-third farther (and was correspondingly more difficult to pull) than the bows used by sedentary enemies.

Rarely did an archer expend all of the five dozen arrows in his quiver. As the battle opened, arrows shot from a distance decimated enemy marksmen. Then the Mongols charged the enemy's infantry to fight with sword, lance, javelin, and mace. The Mongol cavalry met its match only at the Battle of Ain Jalut **(ine jah-LOOT)**, where an under-strength force confronted Turkic-speaking Mamluks whose war techniques matched their own (see Chapter 10).

The Mongols also fired flaming arrows and hurled enormous projectiles—sometimes flaming—from catapults. The first Mongol catapults, built on Chinese models, transported easily but had short range and poor accuracy. During western campaigns in Central Asia, however, the Mongols encountered a design that was half again as powerful. They used it to hammer the cities of Iran and Iraq.

Cities that resisted faced siege and annihilation. Surrender was the only option. The slaughter the Mongols inflicted on Balkh **(bahlk)** (in present-day northern Afghanistan) and other

Passport The Mongol Empire facilitated the movement of products, merchants, and diplomats over long distances. Travelers frequently encountered new languages, laws, and customs. The *paisa* (from a Chinese word for "card" or "sign"), with its inscription in Mongolian, proclaimed that the traveler had the ruler's permission to travel through the region. Europeans later adopted the practice, thus making the *paisa* the ancestor of modern passports. The Metropolitan Museum of Art/Image source/Art Resource, NY

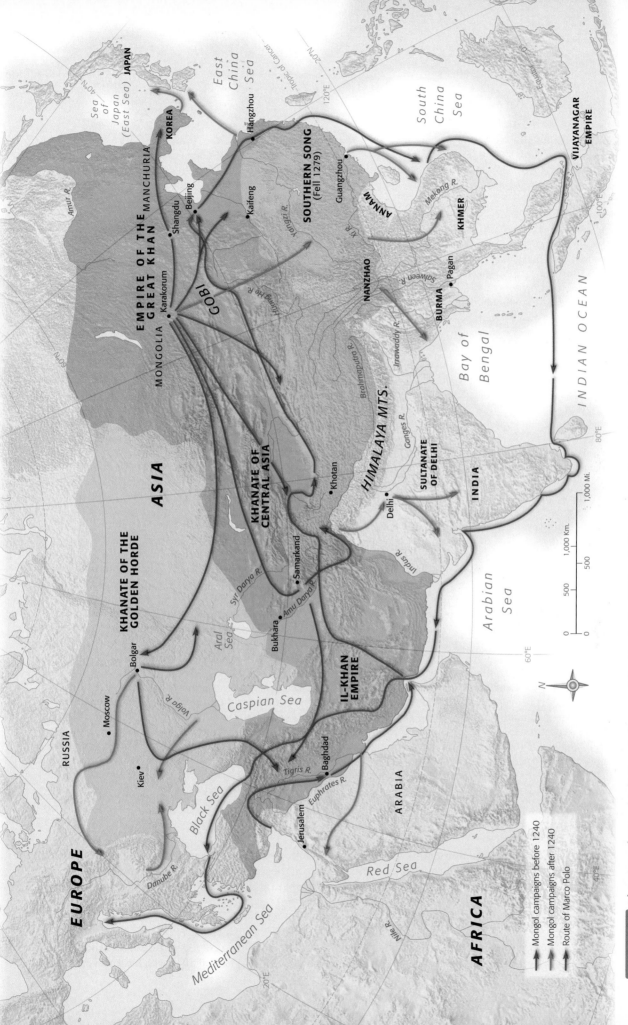

MAP 13.1 **The Mongol Domains in Eurasia in 1300** After the death of Chinggis Khan in 1227, his empire was divided among his sons and grandsons. Son Ögödei succeeded Chinggis as Great Khan. Grandson Khubilai expanded the domain of the Great Khan into southern China by 1279. Grandson Hülegü was the first Il-khan in the Middle East. Grandson Batu founded the Khanate of the Golden Horde in southern Russia. Son Chagatai ruled the Chagatai Khanate in Central Asia. © Cengage Learning

Mongol campaigns before 1240
Mongol campaigns after 1240
Route of Marco Polo

Observations of Mongol Life

The Mongols, despite the power, geographical extent, and durability of their empire, are known mainly from the observations made by non-Mongols who either traveled in their territory or worked for them. The following passages come from three such authors.

William of Rubruck, a Franciscan friar, journeyed to the court of the Great Khan Mönke in 1253–1255 after living for some period of time in crusader territory in the Middle East. He carried a letter from the French king, Louis IX (ruled 1226–1270), asking that the friar and a companion be allowed to stay with the Mongols, preach Christianity, and comfort German prisoners. William never made contact with the Germans, but his highly personal observations on Mongol life fascinated European readers.

The dwelling in which they sleep is based on a hoop of interlaced branches, and its supports are made of branches, converging at the top around a smaller hoop, from which projects a neck like a chimney. They cover it with white felt: quite often they also smear the felt with chalk or white clay and ground bones to make it gleam whiter, or sometimes they blacken it. . . . These dwellings are constructed to such a size as to be on occasion thirty feet across: I myself once measured a breadth of twenty feet between the wheeltracks of a wagon, and when the dwelling was on the wagon it protruded beyond the wheels by at least five feet on either side. I have counted twenty-two oxen to one wagon, hauling along a dwelling, eleven in a row, corresponding to the width of the wagon, and another eleven in front of them. The wagon's axle was as large as a ship's mast, and one man stood at the entrance of the dwelling on top of the wagon, driving the oxen. . . .

The married women make themselves very fine wagons. . . . One rich Mo'al [i.e., Mongol] or Tartar has easily a hundred or two hundred such wagons with chests. Baatu has twenty-six wives, each of whom has a large dwelling, not counting the other, smaller ones placed behind the large one, which are chambers, as it were, where the maids live: to each of these dwellings belong a good two hundred wagons. When they unload the dwellings, the chief wife pitches her residence at the westernmost end, and the others follow according to rank. . . . Hence the court of one wealthy Mo'al will have the appearance of a large town, though there will be very few males in it. . . . One woman will drive twenty or thirty wagons, since the terrain is level. The ox- or camel-wagons are lashed together in sequence, and the woman will sit at the front driving the ox, while all the rest follow at the same pace. If at some point the going happens to become difficult, they untie them and take them through one at a time. For they move slowly, at the pace at which a sheep or an ox can walk.

The History of the World-Conqueror by the Iranian historian 'Ata-Malik Juvaini, who worked for the Mongols in Iran, was written in elegant Persian during the 1250s. It combines a glorification of the Mongol rulers with an unflinching picture of the cruelties and devastation inflicted by their conquests.

He [i.e., Chingiz-Khan] paid great attention to the chase and used to say that the hunting of wild beasts was a proper occupation for the commanders of armies; and that instruction and training therein was incumbent on warriors and men-at-arms. . . . Whenever the Khan sets out on the great hunt (which takes place at the beginning of the winter season), he issues orders that the troops stationed around his headquarters and in the neighborhood. . .shall make preparation for the chase. . . .

The right wing, left wing and center of the army are drawn up and entrusted to the great emirs; and they set out together with the Royal Ladies and the concubines, as well as provisions of food and drink. For a month, or two, or three they form a hunting ring and drive the game slowly and gradually before them, taking care lest any escape from the ring. . . . Finally, when the ring has been contracted to a diameter of two or three parasangs [approximately 7 to 10 miles] they bind ropes together and cast felts over them; while the troops come to a halt all around the ring, standing shoulder to shoulder. The ring is now filled with the cries and commotion of every manner of game and the roaring and tumult of every kind of ferocious beast . . . lions becoming familiar with wild asses, hyaenas friendly with foxes, wolves intimate with hares.

When the ring has been so much contracted that the wild beasts are unable to stir, first the Khan rides in together with some of his retinue; then after he has wearied of the sport, they dismount upon high ground in the center . . . to watch the princes likewise entering the ring, and after them, in due order, the *noyans* [chiefs], the commanders and the troops. Several days pass in this manner; then, when nothing is left

cities spread terror and caused other cities to surrender. Each conquered area contributed men to the "Mongol" armies. In the Middle East, on the western fringe of their empire, a few Mongol officers commanded armies of recently recruited Turks and Iranians.

Overland Trade and Disease

Commercial integration under Mongol rule affected all parts of the empire. Like earlier nomad elites, Mongol nobles had the exclusive right to wear silk, almost all of which came from China.

of the game but a few wounded and emaciated stragglers, old men and greybeards humbly approach the Khan, offer up prayers for his well-being and intercede for the lives of the remaining animals asking that they be suffered to depart to someplace nearer to grass and water. . . .

Now war—with its killing, counting of the slain and sparing of the survivors—is after the same fashion, and indeed analogous in every detail, because all that is left in the neighborhood of the battlefield are a few broken-down wretches.

Hu Szu-hui, a physician of Chinese-Turkic family background, presented the Yuan emperor with a manual entitled Proper and Essential Things for the Emperor's Food and Drink *in 1330. His work reflects both the meat-heavy diet of the steppes and traditional Chinese concern with good nutrition.*

Foods That Cure Various Illnesses [60 entries]

Donkey's Head Gruel

It cures apoplexy-vertigo, debility of hand and foot, annoying pain of extremities, and trouble in speaking:

Black donkey's head (one; remove hair and wash clean), black pepper (two measures), tsaoko cardamom (two measures). Cook ingredients until overcooked. Add the five spices in fermented black bean juice. Flavor with the spices. Flavor evenly. Eat on an empty stomach.

Donkey's Meat Soup

It cures wind, mania and depression and pacifies the heart:

Meat of black donkey. (The quantity does not matter. Cut up.) Cook ingredient until overcooked in fermented black beans. When done add the five spices. Eat on an empty stomach.

Fox Meat Gruel

It cures infantile convulsion, epilepsy, spiritual confusion, indistinct speech, and inappropriate singing and laughing:

Fox meat. (The quantity does not matter. Include organ meat.) [To] ingredient add the five spices according to the regular method. Cook until overcooked. When done eat on an empty stomach.

Bear Meat Gruel

It cures the various winds, foot numbness-insensitivity, and five flaccidities, tendon and muscle spasms:

Bear meat (one measure). [To] ingredient add the five spices in fermented black beans. [Add] onions and sauce. Cook. When done eat on an empty stomach.

Foodstuffs That Mutually Conflict [55 entries]

Horse meat cannot be eaten together with granary rice.

Horse meat cannot be eaten with cocklebur. It can be eaten with ginger.

Pork cannot be eaten together with beef.

Sheep's liver cannot be eaten together with pepper. It wounds the heart.

Hare meat cannot be eaten together with ginger.

Beef cannot be eaten together with chestnuts.

Mare's milk cannot be eaten together with fish hash. It produces obstruction of the bowels.

Venison cannot be eaten together with catfish.

Beef stomach cannot be eaten together with dog meat. Quail meat cannot be eaten together with pork. The face will turn black.

Pheasant eggs cannot be eaten together with onions. It produces vermin.

Meat of sparrows cannot be eaten together with plums. Eggs cannot be eaten together with turtle meat.

QUESTIONS FOR ANALYSIS

1. Can you determine from the subject matter of these passages the different viewpoints of a European, an Iranian, and a Chinese?

2. Is there anything in these passages to indicate that the Mongols were Muslims, Christians, Buddhists, or Confucians?

3. Do you expect the observations of a traveler to be more or less valuable as historical sources than those of someone who served a Mongol ruler?

Sources: From *The Mission of Friar William of Rubruck. His Journey to the Court of the Great Khan Mönke 1253–1255*, translated by Peter Jackson, pp. 73–74. Copyright © 1990. From Ata-Malik Juvani's *The History of the World Conqueror*, translated by Andrew Boyle, pp. 27–29, Cambridge, Mass.: Harvard University Press, Copyright © 1958 by Manchester University Press. Paul D. Buell and Eugene N. Anderson, *A Soup for the Qan*, 2000, pp. 428–429, 438–440.

New styles and huge quantities of silk flowed westward to feed the luxury trade in the Middle East and Europe. Artistic motifs from Japan and Tibet reached as far as England and Morocco. Porcelain, another eastern luxury, became important in trade and strongly influenced later tastes in the Islamic world.

Merchants encountered ambassadors, scholars, and missionaries over the long routes to the Mongol courts. Some of the resulting travel literature, like the account of the Venetian Marco Polo (mar-koe POE-loe) (1254–1324), freely mixed the fantastic with the factual. Stories of immense wealth stimulated a European ambition to find easier routes to Asia.

SECTION REVIEW

- The society of the nomadic Mongols functioned through kinship and tribute ties, in which women often played important roles.

- Chinggis Khan began the period of Mongol conquest to win tribute from Eurasian kingdoms.

- His successors turned to territorial rule, yet internal politics split the empire into smaller ones in China and Central Asia.

- The Mongols won territory through superior battle tactics and integrated it into a vast overland commercial network.

- That network allowed the bubonic plague and other diseases to spread across Asia into Europe.

Exchange also spread disease. In the mid-thirteenth century, marmots and other rodents became infected and passed their disease to dogs and people. Though other diseases contributed to the mortality of the resulting pandemic, **bubonic plague**, which probably originated in Central Asia, was certainly involved. An alternative theory sees southern China as the point of origin, but the great distances involved and the unusually cold winters experienced in China from 1344 to 1353, which would have impeded the reproduction of fleas, indicate otherwise. Plague incapacitated the Mongol army during its assault on the city of Kaffa (KAH-fah) in Crimea (cry-MEE-ah) in 1346. They withdrew, but the plague remained. From Kaffa flea-infested rats reached Europe and Egypt by ship (see Chapter 14).

Typhus, influenza, and smallpox traveled the same route. The combination of these and other diseases created the "great pandemic" of 1347–1352 and caused deaths far in excess of what the Mongol armies inflicted. Epidemics like this one were exacerbated by the environmental devastation caused by the Mongol conquest. The Mongols destroyed dams, irrigation channels, farmland, and crops; they also cut down trees that helped keep the desert at bay, with the effect of turning large portions of China into steppe.

THE MONGOLS AND ISLAM, 1260–1500

bubonic plague A bacterial disease of fleas that can be transmitted by flea bites to rodents and humans; humans in late stages of the illness can spread the bacteria by coughing. Because of its very high mortality rate and the difficulty of preventing its spread, major outbreaks have created crises in many parts of the world.

Il-khan A "secondary" or "peripheral" khan based in Persia. The Il-khans' khanate was founded by Hülegü, a grandson of Chinggis Khan, and was based at Tabriz in the Iranian province of Azerbaijan. It controlled much of Iran and Iraq.

Golden Horde Mongol khanate founded by Chinggis Khan's grandson Batu. It was based in southern Russia and quickly adopted both the Turkic language and Islam. Also known as the Kipchak Horde.

From the perspective of Mongol imperial history, the issue of which branches of the family adopted Islam and which did not mostly concerns political rivalries. From the standpoint of Islamic history, however, recovery from the devastation that culminated in the destruction of the Abbasid Caliphate in Baghdad in 1258 attests to the vitality of the faith and the ability of Muslims to overcome adversity. Within fifty years of its darkest hour, Islam reemerged as a potent ideological and political force.

Mongol Rivalry

By 1260 the **Il-khan** (IL–con) state, established by Chinggis's grandson Hülegü, controlled Iran, Azerbaijan, Mesopotamia, and parts of Armenia. North of the Caspian Sea the Mongols who had conquered southern Russia established the capital of their Khanate of the **Golden Horde** (also called the Kipchak [KIP-chahk] Khanate) at Sarai (sah-RYE) on the Volga River. Like the Il-khans, they ruled an indigenous, mostly Turkic-speaking, Muslim population.

Some members of the Mongol imperial family professed Islam before the Mongol assault on the Middle East, and Turkic Muslims served the family in various capacities. Hülegü himself, though a Buddhist, had a trusted Shi'ite adviser and granted privileges to the Shi'ites. However, the Mongols under Hülegü's command came only slowly to Islam.

Islamic doctrines clashed with Mongol ways. Muslims abhorred the Mongols' worship of Buddhist and shamanist idols. Furthermore, Mongol law specified slaughtering animals without spilling blood, which involved opening the chest and stopping the heart. This horrified Muslims, who were forbidden to consume blood and slaughtered animals by slitting their throats and draining the blood.

Islam became a point of inter-Mongol tension when Batu's successor as leader of the Golden Horde declared himself a Muslim. He swore to avenge the murder of the Abbasid caliph and laid claim to the Caucasus—the mountains between the Black and Caspian Seas—which the Il-khans also claimed (see Map 13.2).

Some European leaders believed that if they helped the non-Muslim Il-khans repel the Golden Horde from the Caucasus, the Il-khans would help them relieve Muslim pressure on the Crusader principalities in Syria, Lebanon, and Palestine (see Chapter 10). This resulted in a brief correspondence between the Il-khan court and Pope Nicholas IV (r. 1288–1292) and a diplomatic mission that sent two Christian Turks to western Europe as Il-khan ambassadors in the late 1200s. The Golden Horde responded by seeking an alliance with the Muslim Mamluks in Egypt (see Chapter 10) against both the Crusaders and the Il-khans. These complicated efforts extended the life of the Crusader principalities, but the Mamluks finally ended their existence in the fifteenth century.

Before the Europeans' diplomatic efforts could bear fruit, a new Il-khan ruler, Ghazan (gaz-ZAHN) (1271–1304), declared himself a Muslim in 1295. Conflicting indications of Sunni and Shi'ite affiliation, such as divergent coin inscriptions, indicate that Ghazan had a casual attitude toward theological matters. It is similarly unclear whether the Muslim Turkic nomads who served in his army were Shi'ite or Sunni.

Islam and the State

The Il-khans gradually came to appreciate the traditional urban culture of the Muslim territories they ruled. Nevertheless, they used tax farming, a fiscal method developed earlier in the Middle East, to extract maximum wealth from their subjects. The government sold tax-collecting contracts to small partnerships, mostly consisting of merchants who might also finance caravans, small industries, or military expeditions. Whoever offered to collect the most revenue for the government won the contracts. They could collect by whatever methods they chose and keep anything in excess of the contracted amount.

Tax farming initially lowered administrative costs; but over the long term, the extortions of the tax farmers drove many landowners into debt and servitude. Agricultural productivity declined, making it hard to supply the army. So the government resorted to taking land to grow its own grain. Like property held by religious trusts, this land paid no taxes. Thus the tax base shrank even as the demands of the army and the Mongol nobility continued to grow.

Ghazan faced many economic problems. Citing Islam's humane values, he promised to reduce taxes. But the need for revenue kept the decrease from becoming permanent. The Chinese practice of printing paper money had been tried unsuccessfully by a predecessor. Now it was tried again. The experiment, to which the Il-khan's subjects responded negatively, pushed the economy into a depression that lasted beyond the end of the Il-khan state in 1349. Mongol nobles competed among themselves for the decreasing revenues, and fighting among Mongol factions destabilized the government.

While the Golden Horde and the Il-khan Empire quarreled, a new power was emerging in the Central Asian Khanate of Chagatai (see Map 13.1). The leader **Timur** (TEE-moor), known to Europeans as Tamerlane, maneuvered himself into command of the Chagatai forces and launched campaigns into western Eurasia, apparently seeing himself as a new Chinggis Khan. By ethnic background he was a Turk with only an in-law relationship to the family of the Mongol conqueror. This prevented him from assuming the title *khan*, but not from sacking the Muslim sultanate of Delhi in northern India in 1398 or defeating the sultan of the rising Ottoman Empire in Anatolia in 1402. He was reportedly preparing to march on China when he died in 1405. However, Timur's descendants could not hold the empire together.

Culture and Science in Islamic Eurasia

The Il-khans and Timurids (descendants of Timur) presided over a brilliant cultural flowering in Iran, Afghanistan, and Central Asia based on blending Iranian and Chinese artistic trends and cultural practices. The dominant cultural tendencies were Muslim, however. Timur died before he could reunite Iran and China, but by transplanting Middle Eastern scholars, artists, and craftsmen to his capital, Samarkand, he fostered the cultural achievements of his descendants.

The historian Juvaini (joo-VINE-nee) (d. 1283), who recorded Chinggis Khan's deathbed speech cited at the beginning of this chapter, came from the city of Balkh, which the Mongols had devastated in 1221. His family switched their allegiance to the Mongols, and both Juvaini and his older brother assumed high government posts. The Il-khan Hülegü, seeking to immortalize and justify his conquests, enthusiastically supported Juvaini's writing of the first comprehensive narrative of Chinggis Khan's empire.

Juvaini combined a florid style with historical objectivity, often criticizing the Mongols. This approach served as an inspiration to **Rashid al-Din** (ra-SHEED ad-DEEN), Ghazan's prime minister, when he attempted the first history of the world. Rashid al-Din's work included the earliest known general history of Europe, derived from conversations with European monks, and a detailed description of China based on information from an important

Timur Member of a prominent family of the Mongols' Chagatai Khanate, Timur through conquest gained control over much of Central Asia and Iran. He consolidated the status of Sunni Islam as orthodox, and his descendants, the Timurids, maintained his empire for nearly a century and founded the Mughal Empire in India.

Rashid al-Din Adviser to the Il-khan ruler Ghazan, who converted to Islam on Rashid's advice.

Chinese Muslim official stationed in Iran. The miniature paintings that accompanied some copies of Rashid al-Din's work included depictions of European and Chinese people and events and reflected the artistic traditions of both cultures. The Chinese compositional techniques helped inaugurate the greatest period of Islamic miniature painting under the Timurids.

Rashid al-Din traveled widely and collaborated with administrators from other parts of the far-flung Mongol dominions. His idea that government should be in accord with the moral principles of the majority of the population buttressed Ghazan's adherence to Islam. Administratively, however, Ghazan did not restrict himself to Muslim precedents but employed financial and monetary techniques that roughly resembled those used in Russia and China.

Under the Timurids, the tradition of the Il-khan historians continued. After conquering Damascus, Timur himself met there with the greatest historian of the age, Ibn Khaldun (ee-bin hal-DOON) (1332–1406), a Tunisian. In a scene reminiscent of Ghazan's answering Rashid al-Din's questions on the history of the Mongols, Timur and Ibn Khaldun exchanged historical, philosophical, and geographical viewpoints. Like Chinggis, Timur saw himself as a world conqueror. At their capitals of Samarkand and Herat (in western Afghanistan), later Timurid rulers sponsored historical writing in both Persian and Chagatai Turkish.

A Shi'ite scholar named **Nasir al-Din Tusi** (nah-SEER ad–DEEN TOO-si) represents the beginning of Mongol interest in the scientific traditions of the Muslim lands. Nasir al-Din may have joined the entourage of Hülegü during a campaign in 1256 against the Assassins, a Shi'ite religious sect derived from the Fatimid dynasty in Egypt and at odds with his more mainstream Shi'ite views (see Chapter 10). Although Nasir al-Din wrote on history, poetry, ethics, and religion, he made his most outstanding contributions in mathematics and cosmology. Following

Nasir al-Din Tusi Persian mathematician and cosmologist whose academy near Tabriz provided the model for the movement of the planets that helped to inspire the Copernican model of the solar system.

MAP 13.2 **Western Eurasia in the 1300s** Ghazan's conversion to Islam in 1295 upset the delicate balance of power in Mongol domains. European leaders abandoned their hope of finding an Il-khan ally against the Muslim defenders in Palestine, while an alliance between the Mamluks and the Golden Horde kept the Il-khans from advancing west. This helped the Europeans retain their lands in Palestine and Syria.   © Cengage Learning

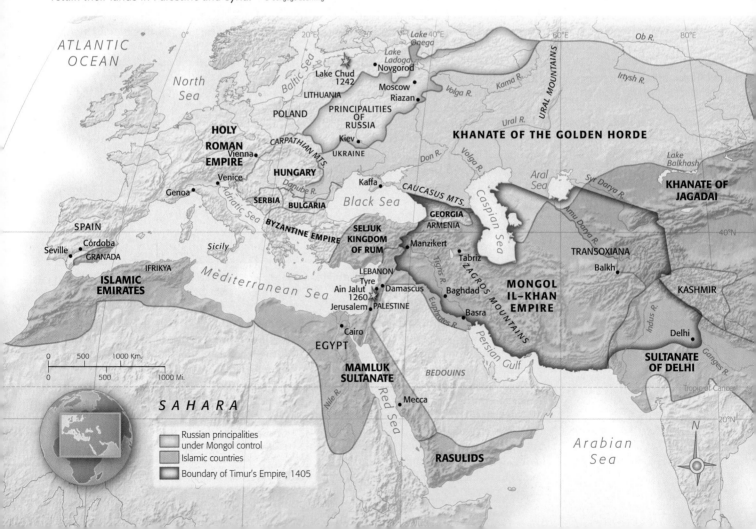

Tomb of Timur in Samarkand The turquoise tiles that cover the dome are typical of Timurid architectural decoration. Timur's family ornamented his capital with an enormous mosque, three large religious colleges facing one another on three sides of an open plaza, and a lane of brilliantly tiled Timurid family tombs in the midst of a cemetery. Timur brought craftsmen to Samarkand from the lands he conquered to build these magnificent structures.

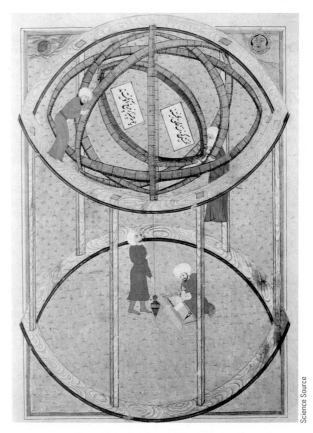

Astronomy and Engineering Observational astronomy went hand in hand not only with mathematics and calendrical science but also with engineering as the construction of platforms, instruments for celestial measurement, and armillary spheres became more sophisticated. This manual in Persian, completed in the 1500s but illustrating activities of the Il-khan period, illustrates the use of a plumb line with an enormous armillary sphere.

Omar Khayyam **(oh-mar kie-YAM)** (1038?–1131), a poet and mathematician of the Seljuk **(SEL-jook)** period, he laid new foundations for algebra and trigonometry. Some followers working at an observatory built for Nasir al-Din at Maragheh **(mah-RAH-gah)**, near the Il-khan capital of Tabriz, used the new mathematical techniques to reach a better understanding of celestial orbits.

Nasir al-Din's work led to major contributions in astronomy that had worldwide influence. Observational astronomy and calendar-making had engaged the interest of earlier Central Asian rulers, particularly the Uighurs **(WEE-ger)** and the Seljuks. Under the Il-khans, the astronomers of Maragheh excelled in predicting eclipses, and astrolabes, armillary spheres, three-dimensional quadrants, and other instruments acquired new precision. The remarkably accurate eclipse predictions and tables prepared by Il-khan and Timurid astronomers reached the hostile Mamluk lands in Arabic translation; Byzantine monks took them to Constantinople and translated them into Greek; Christian scholars working in Muslim Spain rendered them into Latin; and in India the sultan of Delhi ordered Sanskrit versions of them.

Following one of these routes, the mathematical tables and geometric models of lunar motion devised by one of Nasir al-Din's students somehow became known to Nicholas Copernicus (1473–1543), a Polish monk and astronomer (see Chapter 14). Copernicus adopted this lunar model as his own, virtually without revision, and then proposed it as the proper model for planetary movement as well—but with the planets circling the sun.

The Great Khan Khubilai (discussed later in this chapter) summoned a team of Iranians to Beijing to build an observatory for him. Timur's grandson Ulugh Beg **(oo-loog bek)** (1394–1449),

SECTION REVIEW

- For the Mongols of the Il-khan and Golden Horde states, Islam became a matter of political rivalry.

- In the Il-khan state Islamic values struggled with economic needs, and the resulting unrest left it open to invasions by Golden Horde Mongols.

- At the same time, Timur took control of the Chagatai territory and began his own imperial conquests.

- Under the Il-khans and Timurids, Iran and Central Asia experienced a flowering of Islamic culture.

- These rulers fostered great achievements in historical writing, literature, art, mathematics, and astronomy.

whose avocation was astronomy, constructed a great observatory in Samarkand and actively participated in compiling observational tables that were later translated into Latin and used by European astronomers.

A further advance made under Ulugh Beg came from the mathematician Ghiyas al-Din Jamshid al-Kashi (gee-YASS ad–DIN jam-SHEED al–KAH-shee), who noted that Chinese astronomers had long used one ten-thousandth of a day as a unit in calculating the occurrence of a new moon. This seems to have inspired him to employ decimal notation, by which quantities less than one could be represented by a marker to show place. Al-Kashi's proposed value for *pi* (π) was far more precise than any previously calculated. This innovation arrived in Europe by way of Constantinople, where a Greek translation of al-Kashi's work appeared in the fifteenth century.

REGIONAL RESPONSES IN WESTERN EURASIA

Safe, reliable overland trade benefited Mongol ruling centers and commercial cities along the Silk Road. But the countryside, ravaged by conquest, sporadic violence, and heavy taxes, suffered terribly. As Mongol control weakened, regional forces in Russia, eastern Europe, and Anatolia reasserted themselves. Sometimes this meant collaborating with the Mongols. At other times it meant using local ethnic or religious traditions to resist or roll back Mongol influence.

Russia and Rule from Afar

The Golden Horde, established after Chinggis's grandson Batu defeated a combined Russian and Kipchak (a Turkic people) army in 1223, started as a unified state but gradually lost unity as some districts crystallized into smaller khanates. The White Horde, for instance, ruled much of southeastern Russia in the fifteenth century, and the Crimean khanate on the northern shore of the Black Sea succumbed to Russian power only in 1783.

East-west routes across the steppe and north-south routes along the rivers of Russia and Ukraine (you-CRANE) conferred importance on certain trading entrepôts (places where goods are stored and from which they are distributed), as they had under Kievan Russia (see Chapter 11). The Golden Horde capital (Old) Sarai, just north of where the Volga flows into the Caspian Sea (see Map 13.1), ruled its Russian domains to the north and east from afar. To facilitate control, it granted privileges to the Orthodox Church, which then helped reconcile the Russian people to their distant masters.

The politics of language played a role in subsequent history. Old Church Slavonic, an ecclesiastical language, revived; but Russian steadily acquired greater importance and eventually became the dominant written language. Russian scholars shunned Byzantine Greek, previously the main written tongue, even after the Golden Horde permitted renewed contacts with Constantinople. The Golden Horde enlisted Russian princes to act as their agents, primarily as tax collectors and census takers.

The flow of silver and gold into Mongol hands starved the local economy of precious metal. Like the Il-khans, the Golden Horde attempted to introduce paper money as a response to the currency shortage. The unsuccessful experiment left such a vivid memory that the Russian word for money (*denga* [DENG-ah]) comes from the Mongolian word for the stamp (*tamga* [TAHM-gah]) used to create paper currency. In reality, commerce depended more on direct exchange of goods than on currency transactions.

Alexander Nevskii (nih-EFF-skee) (ca. 1220–1263), the prince of Novgorod, persuaded some fellow princes to submit to the Mongols. In return, the Mongols favored both Novgorod and the emerging town of Moscow, ruled by Alexander's son Daniel. As these towns eclipsed Kiev (earlier

Alexander Nevskii Prince of Novgorod (r. 1236–1263). He submitted to the invading Mongols in 1240 and received recognition as the leader of the Russian princes under the Golden Horde.

devastated by the Mongols) as political, cultural, and economic centers, they drew people northward to open new agricultural land far from the Mongol steppes. Decentralization continued in the 1300s, with Moscow only very gradually becoming Russia's dominant political center.

In appraising the Mongol era, some historians stress Mongol destructiveness and brutality in tax collecting. Ukraine, a fertile and well-populated region in the late Kievan period (1000–1230), suffered severe population loss from these sources. Isolated from developments to the west, Russia and parts of eastern Europe are portrayed as suffering under the "Mongol yoke."

Other historians point out that even before the Mongols struck Kiev had declined economically and ceased to mint coins. Yet the Russian territories regularly paid the heavy Mongol taxes in silver, indicating both economic surpluses and an ability to convert goods into cash. The burdensome taxes stemmed less from the Mongols than from their tax collectors, Russian princes who often exempted their own lands and shifted the load to the peasants.

tsar (czar) From Latin *caesar*, this Russian title for a monarch was first used in reference to a Russian ruler by Ivan III (r. 1462–1505).

As for Russia's cultural isolation, skeptics observe that before the Mongol invasion, the powerful and constructive role played by the Orthodox Church oriented Russia primarily toward Byzantium (see Chapter 11). This situation discouraged but did not eliminate contacts with western Europe. But repeated wars with the expanding Catholic principality of Lithuania on Russia's western border discouraged extensive relations.

The traditional structure of local government survived Mongol rule, as did the Russian princely families, who continued to battle among themselves for dominance. The Mongols merely added a new player to those struggles.

In the late 1400s Ivan (ee-VAHN) III, the prince of Moscow (r. 1462–1505), established himself as an autocratic ruler. Before Ivan, the title **tsar** (from *caesar*), of Byzantine origin, applied only to foreign rulers, whether the emperors of Byzantium or the Turkic khans of the steppe. Ivan's use of the title probably represents an effort to establish a basis for legitimate rule with the decline of the Golden Horde and the disappearance of the Byzantine Empire.

New States in Eastern Europe and Anatolia

Anatolia and parts of Europe responded dynamically to the Mongol challenges. Raised in Sicily, the Holy Roman Emperor Frederick II (r. 1212–1250) appreciated Muslim culture and did not recoil from negotiating with Muslims. When the pope threatened to excommunicate him unless he waged a crusade, Frederick nominally regained Jerusalem through a flimsy treaty with the Mamluk sultan in Egypt. Dissatisfied, the pope continued to quarrel with the emperor, leaving Hungary, Poland, and Lithuania to deal with the Mongol onslaught on their own. Many princes capitulated and went to (Old) Sarai to offer their submission to Batu.

However, the Teutonic (two-TOHN-ik) Knights resisted. This German-speaking order of Christian warriors, originally organized in the Holy Land, sought to Christianize the pagan populations of northern Europe and colonize their territories with German settlers. They also fought against other Christians. To protect Slav territory, Alexander Nevskii joined the Mongols in fighting the Teutonic Knights and their Finnish allies. The latter suffered

akg-images/RIA Nowosti

Transformation of the Kremlin Like other northern Europeans, the Russians preferred to build in wood, which was easy to handle and comfortable to live in. But they fortified important political centers with stone ramparts. In the 1300s, the city of Moscow emerged as a new capital, and its old wooden palace, the Kremlin, was gradually transformed into a stone structure.

a catastrophe in 1242, when many broke through an icy northern lake and drowned. This event destroyed the power of the Knights, and the northern Crusades virtually ceased.

The "Mongol" armies encountered by the Europeans consisted mostly of Turks, Chinese, Iranians, a few Europeans, and at least one Englishman, who went to crusade in the Middle East but joined the Mongols and served in Hungary. But most commanders were Mongol.

Initial wild theories describing the Mongols as coming from Hell or from caves where Alexander the Great confined the monsters of antiquity gradually yielded to a more sophisticated understanding as European embassies to Mongol courts returned with reliable intelligence. In some quarters terror gave way to appreciation. Europeans learned about diplomatic passports, coal mining, movable type, high-temperature metallurgy, higher mathematics, gunpowder, and, in the fourteenth century, the casting and use of bronze cannon. Yet with the outbreak of bubonic plague in the late 1340s (see Chapter 14), the memory of Mongol terror helped ignite religious speculation that God might again be punishing the Christians.

In the fourteenth century several regions, most notably Lithuania (lith-oo-WAY-nee-ah), escaped the Mongol grip. When Russia fell to the Mongols, Lithuania had experienced an unprecedented centralization and military strengthening. Like Alexander Nevskii, the Lithuanian leaders maintained their independence by cooperating with the Mongols. In the late 1300s Lithuania capitalized on its privileged position to dominate Poland and ended the Teutonic Knights' hope of regaining power.

Ottoman Empire Islamic state founded by Osman in northwestern Anatolia around 1300. After the fall of the Byzantine Empire, the Ottoman Empire was based at Istanbul (formerly Constantinople) from 1453 to 1922. It encompassed lands in the Middle East, North Africa, the Caucasus, and eastern Europe.

In the Balkans independent kingdoms separated themselves from the chaos of the Byzantine Empire and thrived amidst the political uncertainties of the Mongol period. The Serbian king Stephen Dushan (ca. 1308–1355) proved the most effective leader. Seizing power from his father in 1331, he took advantage of Byzantine weakness to turn the archbishop of Serbia into an independent patriarch. In 1346 the patriarch crowned him "tsar and autocrat of the Serbs, Greeks, Bulgarians, and Albanians," a title that fairly represents the wide extent of his rule. As in the case of Timur, however, his kingdom declined after his death in 1355 and disappeared entirely after a defeat by the Ottomans at the battle of Kosovo in 1389.

The Turkic nomads whose descendants established the **Ottoman Empire** came to Anatolia in the same wave of Turkic migrations as the Seljuks (see Chapter 10). Though Il-khan influence was strong in eastern Anatolia, a number of small Turkic principalities emerged in the west. The Ottoman principality was situated in the northwest, close to the Sea of Marmara. This not only put them in a position to cross into Europe and take part in the dynastic struggles of the declining Byzantine state, but it also attracted Muslim religious warriors who wished to do battle with Christians on the frontiers. The defeat of the Ottoman sultan by Timur in 1402 was only a temporary setback. In 1453 Sultan Mehmet II captured Constantinople and brought the Byzantine Empire to an end.

The Ottoman sultans, like the rulers of Russia, Lithuania, and Serbia, seized opportunities that arose with the decay of Mongol power. The powerful states they created put strong emphasis on religious and linguistic identity, factors that the Mongols themselves did not stress. As we shall see, Mongol rule stimulated similar reactions in the lands of East and Southeast Asia.

SECTION REVIEW

- Mongol conquest devastated Kievan Russia, but the Russian language achieved greater importance, and many Russian traditions survived.

- Mongol conquest prompted decentralization of Russian power away from Kiev, but the Golden Horde's decline set the stage for the rise of Russian autocracy.

- The decline of Mongol power and Byzantine weakness enabled the rise of Lithuania and Serbia in eastern Europe and of the Ottoman Empire in Anatolia.

MONGOL DOMINATION IN CHINA, 1271–1368

After conquering northern China in the 1230s, Great Khan Ögödei told a Confucian adviser that he planned to turn the heavily populated North China Plain into a pasture for livestock. The adviser reacted calmly but argued that taxing the cities and villages would bring greater wealth. The Great Khan agreed, but he imposed an oppressive tax-farming system instead of the fixed-rate method traditional to China.

The Chinese suffered under this system during the early years, but the Yuan Empire, established by Chinggis Khan's grandson Khubilai in 1271, also brought benefits: secure trade routes; exchange of experts between eastern and western Eurasia; and transmission of information, ideas, and skills.

The Yuan Empire, 1271–1368

Khubilai Khan Last of the Mongol Great Khans (r. 1260–1294) and founder of the Yuan Empire.

lama In Tibetan Buddhism, a teacher.

Beijing China's northern capital, first used as an imperial capital in 906 and now the capital of the People's Republic of China.

The Yuan sought a fruitful synthesis of the Mongol and Chinese traditions. **Khubilai Khan** gave his oldest son a Chinese name and had Confucianists participate in the boy's education. In public announcements and the crafting of laws, he took Confucian conventions into consideration. Buddhist and Daoist leaders who visited the Great Khan came away believing that they had all but convinced him of their beliefs.

Buddhist priests from Tibet called **lamas** (LAH-mah) became popular with some Mongol rulers. Their idea of a militant universal ruler bringing the whole world under control of the Buddha and thus pushing it nearer to salvation mirrored an ancient Inner Asian idea of universal rulership.

Beijing, the Yuan capital, became the center of cultural and economic life. Karakorum had been geographically remote, but Beijing served as the eastern terminus of caravan routes that began near Tabriz, the Il-khan capital, and (Old) Sarai, the Golden Horde capital. A horseback courier system utilizing hundreds of stations maintained communications along routes that were generally safe for travelers. Ambassadors and merchants arriving in Beijing found a city that was much more Chinese in character than Karakorum had been.

Called Great Capital (Dadu) or City of the Khan (*khan-balikh* [kahn-BAL-ik], Marco Polo's "Cambaluc"), Khubilai's capital included the Forbidden City, a closed imperial complex with wide streets and a network of linked lakes and artificial islands. In summer, Khubilai practiced riding and shooting at a palace and park in Inner Mongolia. This was Shangdu (shahng-DOO), the "Xanadu" (ZAH-nah-doo) with its "stately pleasure dome" celebrated by the English poet Samuel Taylor Coleridge.

Before the arrival of the Mongols, three separate states with different languages, writing systems, forms of government, and elite cultures competed in China (see Chapter 12), The Tanggut and Jin Empires controlled the north, and the Southern Song controlled most of the area south of the Yellow River. The Great Khans destroyed all three and encouraged the restoration or preservation of many features of Chinese government and society.

The Mongol-ruled Yuan state was cosmopolitan, attracting many non-Chinese who helped the Mongols govern China. By law, Mongols ranked highest. Below them came Central Asians and Middle Easterners, then northern Chinese, and finally southern Chinese. This ranking reflected a hierarchy of functions. The Mongols were the empire's warriors, the Central Asians and Middle Easterners its census takers and tax collectors. The northern Chinese outranked the southern Chinese because they came under Mongol control almost two generations earlier.

Though Khubilai included some "Confucians" (under the Yuan, a formal and hereditary status) in government, their position compared poorly with pre-Mongol times. The Confucians disparaged merchants, many of whom were from the Middle East or Central Asia, and physicians, whom they regarded as mere technicians or Daoist mystics. But the Yuan encouraged doctors and began the process of integrating Chinese medical approaches with those contained in Muslim and Hellenistic sources.

A Muslim governor from Central Asia, Sayyid Ajall Shams al-Din (SAY-id a-JELL Shams ad–DEEN), exemplifies a non-Chinese person who helped the Mongols rule and yet still promoted Confucian culture. The Mongols appointed him governor of Yunnan (YOON-nahn), their newly acquired territory in the southwest that became a key transit area for trade between Tibet, Burma, the Vietnamese kingdoms, and China. Some scholars have called this area the Southwest Silk Road. Shams al-Din walked a fine line between connecting Yunnan with the imperial center and relying upon native chieftains to stabilize the area. Moreover, he promoted Confucian education, dress, and rituals and built schools and Confucian temples. Yunnan, once considered only a periphery to earlier Chinese rulers, became an integral part of China under the Mongol rule and remains so to the present.

Like the Il-khans, the Yuan rulers stressed census taking and tax collecting. Persian, Arab, and Uighur administrators staffed the offices of taxation and finance, and Muslim scholars worked at calendar-making and astronomy. The Mongols organized all of China into provinces. Central appointment of provincial governors, tax collectors, and garrison commanders marked a radical change by systematizing control in all parts of the country.

Many cities seem to have prospered: in north China by being on the caravan routes; in the interior by being on the Grand Canal; and along the coast by participation in maritime grain shipments from south China. The reintegration of East Asia (though not Japan) with the overland Eurasian trade, which had lapsed with the fall of the Tang (see Chapter 12), stimulated the urban economies.

With merchants a privileged group, life in the cities changed. So few government posts were open to the old Chinese elite that families that had previously spent fortunes on educating sons for government service sought other opportunities. Many gentry families chose commerce. Corporations—investor groups that behaved as single commercial and legal units and shared the risk of doing business—handled most economic activities, starting with financing caravans and expanding into tax farming and lending money to the Mongol aristocracy. Central Asians and Middle Easterners headed most corporations in the early Yuan period; but as Chinese bought shares, many acquired mixed membership, or even complete Chinese ownership.

The agricultural base, damaged by war, overtaxation, and the passage of armies, could not satisfy the financial needs of the Mongol aristocracy. Following earlier precedent, the imperial government made up the shortfall with paper money. But people doubted the value of the notes, which were unsecured. Copper coinage partially offset the failure of the paper currency. During the Song, exports of copper to Japan, where the metal was scarce, had caused a severe shortage in China, leading to a rise in the value of copper in relation to silver. By cutting off trade with Japan, the Mongols intentionally or unintentionally stabilized the value of copper coins.

As city life increasingly catered to the tastes of merchants instead of scholars, many gentry families moved from their traditional homes in the countryside to engage in urban commerce. Specialized shops selling clothing, grape wine, furniture, and religiously butchered meats became common. Teahouses offered sing-song girls, drum singers, operas, and other entertainments previously considered coarse. Writers published works in the style of everyday speech. And the increasing influence of the northern, Mongolian-influenced Chinese language, often called Mandarin in the West, resulted in lasting linguistic change.

Cottage industries linked to the urban economies dotted the countryside, where 90 percent of the people lived. Some villages cultivated mulberry trees and cotton using dams, water wheels, and irrigation systems patterned in part on Middle Eastern models. Treatises on planting, harvesting, threshing, and butchering were published. One technological innovator, Huang Dao Po (hwahng DOW poh), brought knowledge of cotton growing, spinning, and weaving from her native Hainan Island to the fertile Yangzi Delta.

Yet on the whole, the countryside did poorly during the Yuan period. Initially, the Mongol princes evicted many farmers and subjected the rest to brutal tax collection. By the time the Yuan shifted to lighter taxes and encouragement of farming at the end of the 1200s, it was too late. Servitude or homelessness had overtaken many farmers. Neglect of dams and dikes caused disastrous flooding, particularly on the Yellow River.

According to Song records from before the Mongol conquest and the Ming census taken after their overthrow—each, of course, subject to inaccuracy or exaggeration—China's population may have shrunk by 40 percent during eighty years of Mongol rule, with many localities in northern China losing up to five-sixths of their inhabitants. Scholars have suggested several causes: prolonged warfare, rural distress causing people to resort to female infanticide, epidemics, a southward flight of refugees, and flooding on the Yellow River. The last helps explain why losses in the north exceeded those in the south and why the population along the Yangzi River markedly increased.

The Fall of the Yuan Empire

In the 1340s strife broke out among the Mongol princes, and within twenty years farmer rebellions and inter-Mongol feuds engulfed the land. Amidst the chaos, in 1368 a charismatic Chinese leader, Zhu Yuanzhang (JOO yuwen-JAHNG), mounted a campaign that destroyed the Yuan Empire and brought China under control of his new empire, the Ming. Many Mongols—as well as the Muslims, Jews, and Christians who had come with them—remained in China. Most of their descendants took Chinese names and became part of the diverse cultural world of China.

Many other Mongols, however, had never moved out of their home territories in Mongolia. Now they welcomed back refugees from the Yuan collapse. Though Turkic peoples were becoming predominant in the steppe regions in

SECTION REVIEW

- The Great Khans reunified China, expanded its borders, and fostered a synthesis of ideas and cultural traditions.

- Khubilai Khan made Beijing the capital of the Yuan Empire and presided over a social hierarchy with Mongols at the top and southern Chinese at the bottom.

- Mongol rule systematized government, but cities benefited more from Mongol policies than did the countryside.

- China's population shrank as a result of Mongol conquest and rule.

- Mongol-protected trade routes encouraged a steady exchange of scientific and cultural ideas.

- Internal strife weakened the Yuan Empire, which fell to the Ming in 1368, but many Mongols remained in China.

the west, including territories still ruled by descendants of Chinggis Khan, Mongols continued to predominate in Inner Asia, the steppe regions bordering on Mongolia. Some Mongol groups adopted Islam; others favored Tibetan Buddhism. But religious affiliation proved less important than Mongol identity in fostering a renewed sense of unity.

The Ming thus fell short of dominating all the Mongols. The Mongols of Inner Asia paid tribute to the extent that doing so facilitated their trade. Other Mongols, however, remained a continuing threat on the northern Ming frontier.

THE EARLY MING EMPIRE, 1368–1500

Ming Empire Empire based in China that Zhu Yuanzhang established after the overthrow of the Yuan Empire. The Ming emperor Yongle sponsored the building of the Forbidden City and the voyages of Zheng He. The later years of the Ming saw a slowdown in technological development and economic decline.

Historians of China, like historians of Russia and Iran, divide over the overall impact of the Mongol era. Since the **Ming Empire** reestablished many practices that are seen as purely Chinese, it receives praise from people who ascribe central importance to Chinese traditions. On the other hand, historians who look upon the Mongol era as a pivotal historical moment when communication across the vast interior of Eurasia served to bring east and west together sometimes see the inward-looking Ming as less productive than the Yuan.

Ming China on a Mongol Foundation

Zhu Yuanzhang, a former monk, soldier, and bandit, had watched his parents and other family members die of famine and disease, conditions he blamed on Mongol misrule. During the Yuan Empire's chaotic last decades, he vanquished rival rebels and assumed imperial power under the name Hongwu (r. 1368–1398).

Hongwu moved the capital to Nanjing (nahn-JING) ("southern capital") on the Yangzi River, turning away from the Mongol's Beijing ("northern capital"; see Map 13.3). Though Zhu Yuanzhang the rebel had espoused a radical Buddhist belief in a coming age of salvation, once in power he used Confucianism to depict the emperor as the champion of civilization and virtue.

Hongwu choked off relations with Central Asia and the Middle East and imposed strict limits on imports and foreign visitors. Silver replaced paper money for tax payments and commerce. These practices, illustrative of an anti-Mongol ideology, proved as economically unwise as some of the Yuan economic policies and did not last. Eventually, the Ming government came to resemble the Yuan. Ming rulers retained the provincial structure and continued to observe the hereditary professional categories of the Yuan period. Muslims made calendars and astronomical calculations at a new observatory at Nanjing, a replica of Khubilai's at Beijing. The Mongol calendar continued in use.

Yongle The third emperor of the Ming Empire (r. 1403–1424). He sponsored the building of the Forbidden City, a huge encyclopedia project, the expeditions of Zheng He, and the reopening of China's borders to trade and travel.

Zheng He An imperial eunuch and Muslim, entrusted by the Ming emperor Yongle with a series of state voyages that took his gigantic ships through the Indian Ocean, from Southeast Asia to Africa.

Continuities with the Yuan became more evident after an imperial prince seized power through a coup d'état to rule as the emperor **Yongle** (yoong-LAW) (r. 1403–1424). Yongle returned the capital to Beijing and enlarged and improved Khubilai's Forbidden City, which now acquired its present features: moats, orange-red outer walls, golden roofs, and marble bridges. He intended this combination fortress, religious site, bureaucratic center, and imperial residential park to overshadow Nanjing, and it survives today as China's most imposing traditional architectural complex.

Yongle also restored commercial links with the Middle East. Because hostile Mongols still controlled much of the caravan route, Yongle explored maritime connections. In Southeast Asia, Vietnam became a Ming province as the early emperors continued the Mongol program of aggression. This focus on the southern frontier helped inspire the naval expeditions of the trusted imperial eunuch **Zheng He** (jehng huh) from 1405 to 1433.

A Muslim eunuch whose father and grandfather had made the pilgrimage to Mecca, Zheng He had a good knowledge of the Middle East; and his religion eased relations with the states of the Indian subcontinent, where he directed his first three voyages. Subsequent expeditions reached Hormuz on the Persian Gulf, sailed the southern coast of Arabia and the Horn of Africa (modern Somalia), and possibly reached as far south as the Strait of Madagascar.

On early voyages Zheng He visited long-established Chinese merchant communities in Southeast Asia to cement their allegiance to the Ming Empire and collect taxes. When a community on the island of Sumatra resisted, he slaughtered the men to set an example. The expeditions added some fifty new tributary states to the Ming imperial universe, but trade did not increase as dramatically. Sporadic embassies reached Beijing from rulers in India, the Middle

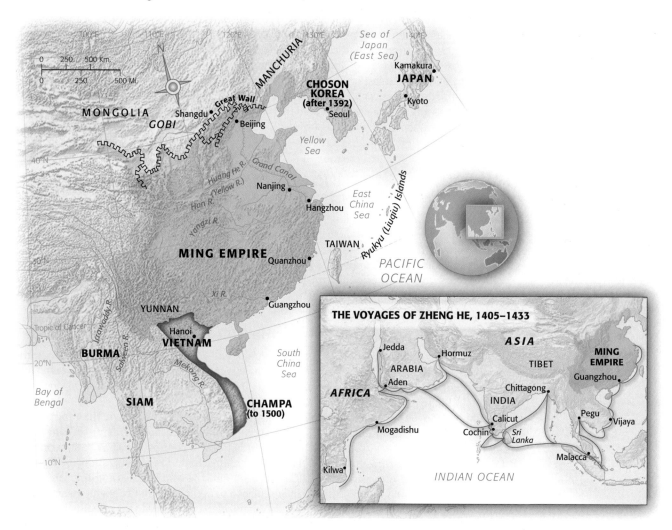

MAP 13.3 **The Ming Empire and Its Allies, 1368–1500** The Ming Empire controlled China but had a hostile relationship with peoples in Mongolia and Inner Asia who had been under the rule of the Mongol Yuan emperors. Mongol attempts at conquest by sea were continued by the Ming mariner Zheng He. Between 1405 and 1433 he sailed to Southeast Asia and then beyond, to India, the Persian Gulf, and East Africa. © Cengage Learning

East, Africa, and Southeast Asia. During one visit the ruler of Brunei (broo-NYE) died and received a grand burial at the Chinese capital. The expeditions stopped in the 1430s after the deaths of Yongle and Zheng He.

Why did the Chinese not develop seafaring for commercial and military gain? Contemporaries considered the voyages a personal project of Yongle, an upstart ruler who had always sought to prove his worthiness. Building the Forbidden City in Beijing and sponsoring gigantic encyclopedia projects might be taken to reflect a similar character. Yongle may also have been emulating Khubilai Khan's sea expeditions against Japan and Southeast Asia. This would fit with the rumor spread by Yongle's political enemies that he was actually a Mongol.

A less speculative approach starts with the fact that the new commercial opportunities fell short of expectations, despite bringing foreign nations into the Ming orbit. In the meantime, Japanese coastal piracy intensified, and Mongol threats in the north and west grew. The human and financial demands of fortifying the north, redesigning and strengthening Beijing, and outfitting campaigns against the Mongols ultimately took priority over the quest for maritime empire.

Technology and Population

The Ming government limited mining, partly to maintain the value of metal coins and partly to tax the industry. As a consequence, metal implements became more expensive for farmers. Techniques for making the high-quality bronze and steel used for weapons also declined. Japan quickly surpassed China in the production of extremely high-quality swords.

Vanni Archive/Art Resource, NY

Examination Cells   Students taking examinations on the Confucian classics to gain admission to the class of officials occupied these cells for 24 to 72 hours, depending on the level they were attempting. In the city of Guangdong there were 7,500 cells in long rows. Candidates were identified only by number, and their essays were rewritten to prevent their handwriting being recognized. Approximately 5 percent of the candidates passed the examination.

After the death of Emperor Yongle in 1424, shipbuilding skills deteriorated, and few advances occurred in printing, timekeeping, and agricultural technology. Agricultural production peaked around the mid-1400s and remained level for more than a century. New weaving techniques did appear, but technological development in this field had peaked by 1500.

Reactivation of the examination system for recruiting government officials (see Chapter 12) drew large numbers of ambitious men into a renewed study of the Confucian classics. This shift reduced the vitality of commerce, where they had previously been employed, just as population growth was creating a labor surplus. Records indicating a growth from 60 million at the end of the Yuan period in 1368 to nearly 100 million by 1400 may not be entirely reliable, but rapid population growth encouraged the production of staples—wheat, millet, and barley in the north and rice in the south—at the expense of commercial crops such as cotton that had stimulated many technological innovations under the Song. Staple crops yielded lower profits, which further discouraged capital improvements. New foods, such as sweet potatoes, became available but were little adopted. At the same time, population growth in southern and central China caused deforestation and raised the price of wood.

Against the Mongol horsemen in the north the Ming used scattershot mortars and explosive canisters. They even used a few cannon, which they knew about from contacts with the Middle East and later with Europeans (see Environment and Technology: From Gunpowder to Guns). Fearing a loss of technological secrets, the government censored the chapters on gunpowder and guns in early Ming encyclopedias. Shipyards and ports shut down to avoid contact with Japanese pirates and to prevent Chinese from migrating to Southeast Asia.

A technology gap with Korea and Japan opened up nevertheless. When superior steel was needed, supplies came from Japan. Korea moved ahead of China in the design and production of firearms and ships, in printing techniques, and in the sciences of weather prediction and calendar-making. The desire to tap the wealthy Ming market spurred some of these advances.

The Ming Achievement

In the late 1300s and the 1400s the wealth and consumerism of the early Ming stimulated high achievement in literature, the decorative arts, and painting. The plain writing of the Yuan period had produced some of the world's earliest novels. This genre flourished under the Ming. *Water Margin*, which originated in the raucous drum-song performances loosely related to Chinese opera, features dashing Chinese bandits who struggle against Mongol rule. Many authors had a hand in the final print version.

Luo Guanzhong (law gwahn-joong), one of the authors of *Water Margin*, is also credited with *Romance of the Three Kingdoms*, based on a much older series of stories that in some ways resemble the Arthurian legends. It describes the attempts of an upright but doomed war leader

From Gunpowder to Guns

Long before the invention of guns, gunpowder was used in China and Korea to excavate mines, build canals, and channel irrigation. Alchemists in China used related formulas to make noxious gas pellets to paralyze enemies and expel evil spirits. A more realistic benefit was eliminating disease-carrying insects, a critical aid to the colonization of malarial regions in China and Southeast Asia. The Mongol Empire staged fireworks displays on ceremonial occasions, delighting European visitors to Karakorum who saw them for the first time.

Anecdotal evidence in Chinese records gives credit for the introduction of gunpowder to a Sogdian Buddhist monk of the 500s. The monk described the wondrous alchemical transforma-

Wubeizhi ('On Warfare') (woodblock print), Chinese School/British Library, London, UK/The Bridgeman Art Library

tion of elements produced by a combination of charcoal and salt-peter. In this connection he also mentioned sulfur. The distillation of naphtha, a light, flammable derivative of oil or coal, seems also to have been first developed in Central Asia, the earliest evidence coming from the Gandhara region (in modern Pakistan).

By the eleventh century, the Chinese had developed flame-throwers powered by burning naphtha, sulfur, or gunpowder in a long tube. These weapons intimidated and injured foot soldiers and horses and also set fire to thatched roofs in hostile villages and, occasionally, the rigging of enemy ships.

In their long struggle against the Mongols, the Song learned to enrich saltpeter to increase the amount of nitrate in gunpowder. This produced forceful explosions rather than jets of fire. Launched from catapults, gunpowder-filled canisters could rupture fortifications and inflict mass casualties. Explosives hurled from a distance could sink or burn ships.

The Song also experimented with firing projectiles from metal gun barrels. The earliest gun barrels were broad and squat and were transported on special wagons to their emplacements. The mouths of the barrels projected saltpeter mixed with scattershot minerals. The Chinese and then the Koreans adapted gunpowder to shooting masses of arrows—sometimes flaming—at enemy fortifications.

In 1280 weapons makers of the Yuan Empire produced the first device featuring a projectile that completely filled the mouth of the cannon and thus concentrated the explosive force. The Yuan used cast bronze for the barrel and iron for the cannonball. The new weapon shot farther and more accurately, and was much more destructive, than the earlier Song devices.

Knowledge of the cannon and cannonball moved westward across Eurasia. By the end of the thirteenth century cannon were being produced in the Middle East. By 1327 small, squat cannon called "bombards" were being used in Europe.

Launching Flaming Arrows   Song soldiers used gunpowder to launch flaming arrows.

SECTION REVIEW

- The first Ming emperor, Hongwu, based his policies on an anti-Mongol ideology, but the Ming government came to adopt Yuan practices.

- Yongle reestablished international commerce and sent Zheng He to explore maritime connections to the Middle East.

- Technological innovation continued, but with less frequent advances and reduced output, and some techniques became guarded secrets.

- The Ming reestablished the Confucian examination system, reducing the vitality of commerce.

- The greatest Ming achievements were in literature, the arts, and porcelain production.

and his followers to restore the Han Empire of ancient times and resist the power of the cynical but brilliant villain. *Romance of the Three Kingdoms* and *Water Margin* express the militant but joyous pro-China sentiment of the early Ming era and remain among the most appreciated Chinese fictional works.

Probably the best-known product of Ming technological advance was porcelain. The imperial ceramic works at Jingdezhen (JING-deh-JUHN) experimented with new production techniques and new ways of organizing and rationalizing workers. "Ming ware," a blue-on-white style developed in the 1400s from Indian, Central Asian, and Middle Eastern motifs, became especially prized. Other Ming goods in high demand included furniture, lacquered screens, and silk, all of which found ready markets in Southeast Asia and the Pacific, India, the Middle East, and East Africa.

CENTRALIZATION AND MILITARISM IN EAST ASIA, 1200–1500

Korea, Japan, and the Vietnamese kingdoms, the other major states of East Asia, were all affected by confrontation with the Mongols, but with differing results. Japan and northern Vietnam escaped Mongol conquest but changed in response to the Mongol threat, becoming more effective and expansive regimes with enhanced commitments to independence.

As for Korea, just as the Ming stressed Chinese traditions and identity in the aftermath of Yuan rule, so Mongol domination contributed to revitalized interest in Korea's own language and history. The Mongols conquered Korea after a difficult war, and though Korea suffered socially and economically under Mongol rule, members of the elite associated closely with the Yuan Empire. After the fall of the Yuan, merchants continued the international connections established in the Mongol period, while Korean armies consolidated a new kingdom and fended off pirates.

Korea from the Mongols to the Choson Dynasty, 1231–1500

Choson The Choson dynasty ruled Korea from the fall of the Koryo kingdom to the colonization of Korea by Japan.

Korea was the answer to the Mongol search for coastal areas from which to launch naval expeditions and choke off the sea trade of their adversaries. By the time the Mongols attacked in 1231, the Choe family had assumed the role of military commander and protector of the Koryo (KAW-ree-oh) king (not unlike the shoguns of Japan). Four generations of Choe-led tyranny and years of defensive war left a ravaged countryside, exhausted armies, and burned treasure. The Choe's refusal to sue for peace, or emerge from their capital on Kanghwa Island to drive the Mongols from the Korean peninsula, led to widespread hardship among the populace and frustration among military men and nobles alike. The last of the Choe tyrants was killed by his underlings in 1258. Soon afterward the king surrendered to the Mongols and became a subject monarch by linking his family to the Great Khan by marriage.

By the mid-1300s the Koryo kings were of mostly Mongol descent and favored Mongol dress, customs, and language. The kings, their families, and their entourages often traveled between China and Korea, thus exposing Korea to the philosophical and artistic styles of Yuan China: neo-Confucianism, Chan Buddhism (called Son in Korea), and celadon (light green) pottery.

Mongol control broke down centuries of comparative isolation. Cotton was introduced in southern Korea; gunpowder came into use; and the art of calendar-making stimulated astronomical observation and mathematics. Avenues of advancement opened for Korean scholars willing to learn Mongolian, landowners willing to open their lands to falconry and grazing, and merchants servicing the new royal exchanges with Beijing. These developments contributed to the rise of a new landed and educated class.

When the Yuan Empire fell in 1368, the Koryo ruling family remained loyal to the Mongols until a rebellious general, Yi Songgye (YEE SONG-gye), forced it to recognize the new Ming Empire. In 1392, Yi Songgye established a new kingdom called **Choson** (cho-sun) with a capital in Seoul and sought to reestablish a distinctive Korean identity. Like Russia and Ming China, the Choson regime publicly rejected the period of Mongol domination. Yet the Choson government continued to employ Mongol-style land surveys, taxation in kind, and military garrison techniques.

Like the Ming emperors, the Choson kings revived the study of the Confucian classics, an activity that required knowledge of Chinese and showed the dedication of the state to learning. This revival may have led to a key technological breakthrough in printing technology.

Koreans had begun using Chinese woodblock printing in the 700s. This technology worked well in China, where a large number of buyers

Movable Type The improvement of cast bronze tiles, each showing a single character, eliminated the need to cast or carve whole pages. Individual tiles—the ones shown are Korean—could be moved from page frame to page frame and gave an even and pleasing appearance. All parts of East Asia eventually adopted this form of printing for cheap, popular books. In the mid-1400s Korea also experimented with a fully phonetic form of writing, which in combination with movable type allowed Koreans unprecedented levels of literacy and access to printed works.   SSPL/The Image Works

wanted copies of a comparatively small number of texts. But in Korea, the comparatively few literate men had interests in a wide range of texts. Movable wooden or ceramic type appeared in Korea in the early thirteenth century and may have been invented there, but the texts were frequently inaccurate and difficult to read. In the 1400s Choson printers, working directly with the king, developed a reliable device to anchor the pieces of type to the printing plate. By replacing the old beeswax adhesive with solid copper frames, they improved the legibility of the printed page, and high-volume, accurate production became possible. Combined with the phonetic *han'gul* (HAHN-goor) writing system, this printing technology laid the foundation for a high literacy rate in Korea.

Choson publications told readers how to produce and use fertilizer, transplant rice seedlings, and engineer reservoirs. Building on Eurasian knowledge imported by the Mongols and introduced under the Koryo, Choson scholars developed a meteorological science of their own. They invented or redesigned instruments to measure wind speed and rainfall and perfected a calendar based on minute comparisons of the Chinese and Islamic systems.

In agriculture, farmers expanded the cultivation of cash crops, the reverse of what was happening in Ming China. Cotton, the primary crop, enjoyed such high value that the state accepted it for tax payments. The Choson army used cotton uniforms, and cotton became the favored fabric of the Korean elite. With cotton gins and spinning wheels powered by water, Korea advanced more rapidly than China in mechanization and began to export considerable amounts of cotton to China and Japan.

Although both the Yuan and the Ming withheld the formula for gunpowder from the Korean government, Korean officials acquired the information by subterfuge. By the later 1300s they had mounted cannon on ships that patrolled against pirates and used gunpowder-driven arrow launchers against enemy personnel and the rigging of enemy ships. Combined with skills in armoring ships, these techniques made the small Choson navy a formidable defense force.

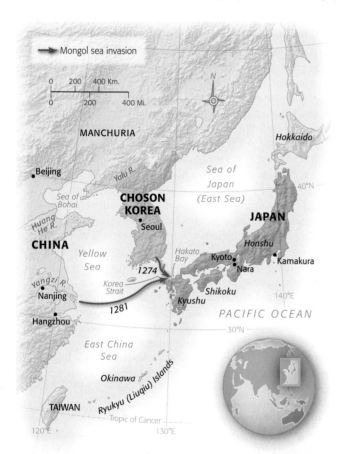

MAP 13.4 **Korea and Japan, 1200–1500** The proximity of Korea and northern China to Japan gave the Mongols the opportunity to launch enormous fleets against the Kamakura Shogunate, which controlled most of the three islands (Honshu, Shikoku, and Kyushu) of central Japan. © Cengage Learning

Political Transformation in Japan, 1274–1500

Having secured Korea, the Mongols looked toward Japan, a target they could easily reach from Korea. Their first 30,000-man invasion force in 1274 included Mongol cavalry and archers and sailors from Korea and northeastern Asia. Its weaponry included light catapults and incendiary and explosive projectiles of Chinese manufacture. The Mongol forces landed successfully and decimated the Japanese cavalry, but a great storm on Hakata (HAH-kah-tah) Bay on the north side of Kyushu (KYOO-shoo) Island (see Map 13.4) prevented the establishment of a beachhead and forced the Mongols to sail back to Korea.

The invasion hastened social and political changes that were already under way. Under the Kamakura (kah-mah-KOO-rah) Shogunate established in 1185—another powerful family actually exercised control—the shogun, or military leader, distributed land and privileges to his followers. In return they paid him tribute and supplied him with soldiers. This stable, but decentralized, system depended on balancing the power of regional warlords. Lords in the north and east of Japan's main island were remote from those in the south and west. Beyond devotion to the emperor and the shogun, little united them until the terrifying Mongol threat materialized.

After the return of his fleet, Khubilai sent envoys to Japan demanding submission. Japanese leaders executed them and prepared for war. The shogun then took steps to centralize his military government, effectively increasing the influence of warlords from the south and west of Honshu (Japan's main island) and from the island of Kyushu, where invasion seemed most likely. These local commanders acted under the shogun's orders.

Military planners studied Mongol tactics and retrained and outfitted Japanese warriors for defense against advanced weaponry, while farm laborers drafted from all over the country constructed defensive fortifications. This effort demanded, for the first time, a national system to move resources toward western points rather than toward the imperial or shogunal centers to the east.

The Mongols attacked again in 1281. They brought 140,000 warriors, including many non-Mongols, as well as thousands of horses, in hundreds of ships. However, the wall the Japanese had built to cut off Hakata Bay from the mainland deprived the Mongol forces of a reliable landing point. Japanese swordsmen rowed out and boarded the Mongol ships lingering offshore. Their superb steel swords shocked the invaders, while an epidemic decimated the Mongol troops. After a prolonged standoff, a typhoon struck and sank perhaps half of the Mongol ships. The remainder sailed away, never again to harass Japan. Religious institutions later claimed that their prayers for help brought a "divine wind"—***kamikaze*** (kah-me-kah-zay)—that drove away the Mongols.

Nevertheless, the Mongol threat continued to influence Japanese development. Prior to his death in 1294, Khubilai had in mind a third invasion. Although his successors did not carry through with it, the shoguns did not know that the Mongols had given up the idea and rebuilt coastal defenses well into the fourteenth century, helping to consolidate the social position of Japan's warrior elite and stimulating the development of a national infrastructure for trade and communication. But the Kamakura Shogunate, based on regionally collected and regionally dispersed revenues, suffered financial strain in trying to pay for centralized road and defense systems.

Between 1333 and 1338 the emperor Go-Daigo (go-DIE-go) broke the centuries-old tradition of imperial seclusion and aloofness from government and tried to reclaim power from the shoguns. This effort ignited a civil war that destroyed the Kamakura system. In 1338, with the Mongol threat waning, the **Ashikaga** (ah-shee-KAH-gah) **Shogunate** took control at the imperial center of Kyoto.

Under the new shogunate, provincial warlords enjoyed renewed independence. Around their imposing castles, they sponsored the development of market towns, religious institutions, and schools, while the application of technologies imported in earlier periods, including water wheels, improved plows, and Champa rice, increased agricultural productivity.

Growing wealth and relative peace stimulated artistic creativity, mostly reflecting Zen Buddhist beliefs held by the warrior elite. In the simple elegance of architecture and gardens, in the contemplative landscapes of artists, and in the eerie, stylized performances of the Noh theater, the aesthetic code of Zen became established in the Ashikaga era.

kamikaze The "divine wind," which the Japanese credited with blowing Mongol invaders away from their shores in 1281.

Ashikaga Shogunate The second of Japan's military governments headed by a shogun (a military ruler). Sometimes called the Muromachi Shogunate.

Noh Drama Performance This slow, rhythmic, chanted form of drama appealed to the military elite with its stories of warriors, women, gods, and demons. The minimal stage is normally bare except for a painting at the rear of a pine tree, symbolizing the means by which deities descend to earth. The actors wear masks and lavish costumes. Four instrumentalists playing flutes and three types of drums punctuate the chanting. Scenes of urban life under the 'Bakufu' government from a performance of Noh Drama, Tosa School, 1800, Japanese, (detail from six-fold screen, see 67712), (colour woodblock print). Private Collection/Photo © Bonhams, London, UK/The Bridgeman Art Library

Despite the technological advancement, artistic productivity, and rapid urbanization of this period, competition among warlords and their followers led to regional wars. By the later 1400s these conflicts resulted in the near destruction of the warlords. The great Onin War in 1477 left Kyoto devastated and the Ashikaga Shogunate a central government in name only. Ambitious but low-ranking warriors, some with links to trade with the continent, began to scramble for control of the provinces.

After the fall of the Yuan in 1368 Japan resumed overseas trade, exporting raw materials and swords, as well as folding fans, invented in Japan during the period of isolation. Japan's primary imports from China were books and porcelain. The volatile political environment in Japan gave rise to partnerships between warlords and local merchants. All worked to strengthen their own towns and treasuries through overseas commerce or, sometimes, through piracy.

The Emergence of Vietnam, 1200–1500

Before the first Mongol attack in 1257, the states of Dai Viet (northern Vietnam) and Champa (southern Vietnam) had clashed frequently. Dai Viet (once called Annam) looked toward China and had once been subject to the Tang. Chinese political ideas, social philosophies, dress, religion, and language heavily influenced its official culture. Champa related more closely to the trading networks of the Indian Ocean, and its official culture was strongly influenced by Indian religion, language, architecture, and dress. Champa's relationship with China depended in part on how close its enemy, Dai Viet, was to China at any particular time. During the Song period Dai Viet was neither formally subject to China nor particularly threatening to Champa militarily, so Champa inaugurated a trade and tribute relationship with China that spread fast-ripening Champa rice throughout East Asia.

The Mongols exacted tribute from both Dai Viet and Champa until the fall of the Yuan Empire in 1368. Mongol political and military ambitions were mostly focused elsewhere, however, which minimized their impact on politics and culture. The two Vietnamese kingdoms soon resumed their warfare. When Dai Viet moved its army to reinforce its southern border, Ming troops occupied the capital, Hanoi, and installed a puppet government. Almost thirty years elapsed before Dai Viet regained independence and resumed a tributary status. By then the Ming were turning to meet Mongol challenges to their north. In a series of ruthless campaigns, Dai Viet terminated Champa's independence, and by 1500 the ancestor of the modern state of Vietnam had been born.

The new state still relied on Confucian bureaucratic government and an examination system, but some practices differed from those in China. The Vietnamese legal code, for example, preserved group landowning and decision making within the villages, as well as women's property rights. Both developments probably had roots in an early rural culture based on the growing of rice in wet paddies; by this time the Dai Viet kingdom considered them distinctive features of its own culture.

SECTION REVIEW

- Mongol conquest devastated Korea, but Mongol rule opened it to new ideas and technologies.

- The Choson dynasty succeeded the Koryo and fostered local identity while encouraging economic expansion and technological innovation.

- In Japan, the Mongol threat forced military and organizational innovations, but the expense of these defenses weakened the Kamakura Shogunate.

- Go-Daigo's failed attempt to reassert imperial power resulted in the rise of the Ashikaga Shogunate.

- The warring states of Vietnam avoided Mongol conquest but paid tribute to the Yuan Empire.

- After the Ming withdrawal, Dai Viet conquered Champa, establishing a unified state on both Confucian and local practices.

CONCLUSION

Despite their brutality and devastation, the Mongol conquests brought a degree of unity to the lands between China and Europe that had never before been known. Nomadic mobility and expertise in military technology contributed to communication across vast spaces and initially, at least, an often-callous disregard for the welfare of farmers, as manifested in oppressive tax policies. By contrast, trade received active Mongol stimulation through the protection of routes and encouragement of industrial production.

The Mongols ruled with an unprecedented openness, employing talented people irrespective of their linguistic, ethnic, or religious affiliations. As a consequence, the period of comparative Mongol unity, which lasted less than a century, saw a remarkable exchange of ideas, techniques, and products across the breadth of Eurasia. Chinese gunpowder spurred the development of Ottoman and European cannon, while Muslim astronomers introduced new instruments and mathematical techniques to Chinese observatories.

However, rule over dozens of restive peoples could not endure. Where Mongol military enterprise reached its limit of expansion, it stimulated local aspirations for independence. Division and hostility among branches of Chinggis Khan's family—between the Yuan in China and the Chagatai in Central Asia or between the Golden Horde in Russia and the Il-khans in Iran—provided opportunities for achieving these aspirations. The Russians gained freedom from Mongol domination in western Eurasia, and the general political disruption and uncertainty of the Mongol era assisted the emergence of the Lithuanian, Serbian, and Ottoman states.

In the east, China, Korea, and Dai Viet similarly found renewed political identity in the aftermath of Mongol rule. The invasions expanded China's boundaries as never before, and they have changed little since. A resurgence of native Chinese culture blossomed in the following Ming dynasty. At the same time, Japan fought off two Mongol invasions and transformed its internal political and cultural identity in the process. In every case, the reality or threat of Mongol attack and domination encouraged centralization of government, improvement of military techniques, and renewed stress on local cultural identity. Thus, in retrospect, despite its traditional association with death and destruction, the Mongol period appears as a watershed, establishing new connections between widespread parts of Eurasia and leading to the development of strong, assertive, and culturally creative regional states.

KEY TERMS

Mongols p. 313
Chinggis Khan p. 313
nomadism p. 314
Yuan Empire p. 315
bubonic plague p. 320
Il-khan p. 320

Golden Horde p. 320
Timur p. 321
Rashid al-Din p. 321
Nasir al-Din Tusi p. 322
Alexander Nevskii p. 324
tsar p. 325

Ottoman Empire p. 326
Khubilai Khan p. 327
lama p. 327
Beijing p. 327
Ming Empire p. 329
Yongle p. 329

Zheng He p. 329
Choson p. 333
kamikaze p. 335
Ashikaga Shogunate p. 335

SUGGESTED READING

Adshead, S. A. M. *Central Asia in World History.* 1993. Central Asia after the conquests.

Allsen, Thomas T. *Commodity and Exchange in the Mongol Empire: A Cultural History of Islamic Textiles.* 2002. A look at exchange on the Silk Road.

Allsen, Thomas T. *Culture and Conquest in Mongol Eurasia.* 2001. A careful study of comparative practices in Mongol China and Iran.

Christian, David. *A History of Russia, Central Asia, and Mongolia.* 1998. A one-volume account of the Mongols in Russia.

Frank, André Gunder. *ReORIENT: Global Economy in the Asian Age.* 1998. An important interpretation of Ming economic achievement.

Hall, John W., and Toyoda Takeshi, eds. *Japan in the Muromachi Age.* 1977. History of a period of civil war.

Henthorn, William E. *Korea: The Mongol Invasions.* 1963. A less emphasized aspect of Mongol history.

Jackson, Peter. *The Mongols and the West: 1221–1410.* 2005. Europe's encounter with the Mongols.

Keene, Donald. *Yoshimasa and the Silver Pavilion: The Creation of the Soul of Japan.* 2003. A delightful introduction to the cultural changes of the fourteenth century.

Levathes, Louise. *When China Ruled the Seas.* 1993. Popular account of the voyages of Zheng He.

Manz, Beatrice Forbes. *The Rise and Rule of Tamerlane.* 1989. The most recent scholarly study of Timur.

Mokyr, Joel. *The Lever of Riches: Technological Creativity and Economic Progress.* 1990. Looks at comparative technological developments across Eurasia.

Morgan, David. *The Mongols.* 1986. An accessible introduction to the Mongol Empire.

Rossabi, Morris. *Khubilai Khan: His Life and Times.* 1988. China under Mongol rule.

Chapter Outline

Rural Growth and Crisis
➤ *How well did inhabitants of Latin Europe, rich and poor, urban and rural, deal with their natural environment?*

Urban Revival
➤ *What social and economic factors led to the growth of cities in late medieval Europe?*

Learning, Literature, and the Renaissance
➤ *What factors were responsible for the promotion of learning and the arts in Latin Europe?*

Political and Military Transformations
➤ *What social, political, and military developments contributed to the rise of European nations in this period?*

Conclusion

● **DIVERSITY + DOMINANCE**   Persecution and Protection of Jews, 1272–1349
● **ENVIRONMENT + TECHNOLOGY**   The Clock

Burying Victims of the Black Death   This scene from Tournai, Flanders, captures the magnitude of the plague.

Latin Europe, 1200–1500

I n the summer of 1454, a year after the Ottoman Turks captured the Greek Christian city of Constantinople, Aeneas Sylvius Piccolomini (uh-NEE-uhs SIL-vee-uhs pee-kuh-lo-MEE-nee), destined in four years to become pope, expressed doubts as to whether anyone could persuade the rulers of Christian Europe to take up a new crusade against the Muslims: "Christendom has no head whom all will obey—neither the pope nor the emperor receives his due."

At the time, the Christian states thought more of fighting each other. French and English armies had been battling for over a century; the German emperor presided over dozens of states but did not really control them; and the numerous kingdoms and principalities of Spain and Italy could not unite. The Catholic rulers of Hungary, Poland, and Lithuania, on the front line against the Muslim Ottomans, seemed very far away from the western monarchs. With only slight exaggeration, Aeneas Sylvius moaned, "Every city has its own king, and there are as many princes as there are households." He attributed this lack of unity to European preoccupation with personal welfare and material gain. Both pessimism about human nature and materialism had increased during the previous century, after a devastating plague had carried off a third of Europe's population.

Yet despite all these divisions, disasters, and wars, historians now see the period from 1200 to 1500 (Europe's later Middle Ages) as a time of unusual progress. Prosperous cities adorned with splendid architecture, institutions of higher learning, and cultural achievements counterbalanced the avarice and greed that Aeneas Sylvius lamented. While frequent wars caused havoc and destruction, they also promoted the development of military technology and more unified monarchies.

Although their Muslim and Byzantine neighbors commonly called Catholic Europeans "Franks," they ordinarily referred to themselves as "Latins," underscoring their allegiance to the Roman Catholic church and the Latin language used in its rituals.

RURAL GROWTH AND CRISIS

Between 1200 and 1500, the countries of western Europe brought more land under cultivation using new farming techniques and made greater use of machinery and mechanical forms of energy. Yet for the nine out of ten people who lived in the countryside, hard labor brought meager returns, and famine, epidemics, and war struck often. After the devastation of the Black Death between 1347 and 1351, social changes speeded up by peasant revolts released many persons from serfdom and brought some improvements to rural life.

By contrast, eastern Europe, a region of vast open spaces and sparse population, saw in increase in serfdom. Faced with a labor shortage, nobles agreed to force farm workers to till their lands.

Peasants, Population, and Plague

In 1200, most western Europeans lived as serfs tilling the soil on large estates owned by the nobility and the church (see Chapter 11). They owed their lord both a share of their harvests and numerous labor services. These obligations combined with inefficient farming practices meant that peasants received meager returns for their hard work. Even with numerous religious holidays, peasants labored some fifty-four hours a week, more than half the time in support of the local nobility. Each noble family, housed in its stone castle, required the labor of fifteen to thirty peasant families living in one-room thatched cottage containing little furniture and no luxuries.

Scenes of rural life show both men and women at work in the fields, but equality of labor did not mean equality at home. In the peasant's hut as elsewhere in medieval Europe, women were subordinate to men. The influential theologian Thomas Aquinas (uh-KWY-nuhs) (1225–1274) spoke for his age when he argued that although both men and women were created in God's image, there was a sense in which "the image of God is found in man, and not in woman: for man is the beginning and end of woman; as God is the beginning and end of every creature."[1]

Rural poverty resulted partly from rapid population growth. In 1200, China's population may have exceeded Europe's by two to one; by 1300, the population of each was about 80 million. China's population fell because of the Mongol conquest (see Chapter 13), while Europe's more than doubled between 1100 and 1445. Some historians believe the reviving economy stimulated the increase. Others argue that severe epidemics were few, and warmer-than-usual temperatures after 950, referred to as the Medieval Warm Period by climate historians, reduced mortality from starvation and exposure.

More people required more productive farming and new agricultural settlements. One widespread new technique, the **three-field system**, replaced the custom of leaving half the land fallow (uncultivated) every year to regain its fertility. Farmers grew crops on two-thirds of their land each year, alternating wheat and rye with oats, barley, or legumes. The third field was left fallow. The oats restored nitrogen to the depleted soil and produced feed for plow horses. In much of Europe, however, farmers continued to let half of their land lie fallow and use oxen (less efficient but cheaper than horses) to pull their plows.

Population growth also encouraged new agricultural settlements. In the twelfth and thirteenth centuries, large numbers of Germans migrated into the fertile lands east of the Elbe River from the Baltic Sea in the north to Transylvania (part of modern Romania) in the south. The Order of Teutonic Knights, founded in the Holy Land but given a (temporary) European base of operations by the king of Hungary, slaughtered or drove away native inhabitants who had not yet adopted Christianity. During the thirteenth century, they conquered, resettled, and administered a vast area along the Baltic that later became Prussia (see Map 14.3 on page 356).

Draining swamps and clearing forests also brought new land under cultivation. But as population continued to rise, some people had to farm lands with poor soils or vulnerability to flooding, frost, or drought. Average crop yields fell accordingly after 1250, and more people lived at the edge of starvation. According to one historian, "By 1300, almost every child born in western Europe faced the probability of extreme hunger at least once or twice during his expected 30 to 35 years of life."[2] One unusually cold spell at the end of the Medieval Warm Period produced the Great Famine of 1315–1317, which affected much of Europe north of the Alps.

three-field system A rotational system for agriculture in which two fields grow food crops and one lies fallow. It gradually replaced the two-field system in medieval Europe.

[1]Quoted in Marina Warner, *Alone of All Her Sex: The Myth and Cult of the Virgin Mary* (New York: Random House, 1983), 179.

[2]Harry Miskimin, *The Economy of the Early Renaissance, 1300–1460* (Englewood Cliffs, NJ: Prentice Hall, 1969), 26–27.

Kharbine-Tapabor/The Art Archive at Art Resource, NY

Rural French Peasants   Many scenes of peasant life in winter are visible in this small painting by the Flemish Limbourg brothers from the 1410s. Above the snow-covered beehives one man chops firewood, while another drives a donkey loaded with firewood to a little village. At the lower right a woman, blowing on her frozen fingers, heads past the huddled sheep and hungry birds to join other women warming themselves in the cottage (whose outer wall the artists have cut away).

CHRONOLOGY

	Technology and Environment	Culture	Politics and Society
1200	1200s Widespread use of crossbows and windmills		1200s Champagne fairs flourish 1204 Fourth Crusade
		1210s Teutonic Knights, Franciscans, Dominicans	1215 Magna Carta issued
		1225–1274 Philosopher-monk Thomas Aquinas	
1300		1300–1500 Rise of universities 1313–1375 Giovanni Boccaccio, human-ist writer	
	1315–1317 Great Famine		1337 Start of Hundred Years' War
	1347–1351 Black Death ca. 1350 Growing deforestation		1381 Wat Tyler's Rebellion
		ca. 1390–1441 Jan van Eyck, painter	
1400	1400s Cannon and hand-held firearms in use		1415 Portuguese take Ceuta 1431 Joan of Arc burned
		1452–1519 Leonardo da Vinci, artist	
	1454 Gutenberg Bible		1453 End of Hundred Years' War; Otto-mans take Constantinople
		1492 Expulsion of Jews from Spain	1492 Fall of Muslim state of Granada

Black Death An outbreak of bubonic plague that spread across Asia, North Africa, and Europe in the mid-fourteenth century, carrying off vast numbers of persons.

The **Black Death** reversed the population growth. This terrible plague originated in Inner Asia and spread westward with the Mongol armies (see Chapter 13). In 1346, the Mongols attacked the city of Kaffa (KAH-fah) on the Black Sea; a year later, Genoese (JEN-oh-eez) traders in Kaffa carried the disease to Italy and southern France. For two years, the Black Death spread across Europe, in some places carrying off two-thirds of the population. Average losses in western Europe amounted to one in three.

Victims developed boils the size of eggs in their groins and armpits, black blotches on their skin, foul body odors, and severe pain. In most cases, death came within a few days. Town officials closed their gates to people from infected areas and burned the victims' possessions. Such measures helped to spare some communities but could not halt the advance of the disease (see Map 14.1). Bubonic plague, the primary form of the Black Death, spreads from person to person and through the bites of fleas infesting the fur of certain rats. Even if the medieval doctors had understood the source of the disease, eliminating the rats that thrived on urban refuse would have been difficult.

The plague brought home to people how sudden and unexpected death could be. Some people became more religious, giving money to the church or lashing themselves with iron-tipped whips to atone for their sins. Others chose reckless enjoyment, spending their money on fancy clothes, feasts, and drinking.

Periodic returns of plague made recovery from population losses slow and uneven. Europe's population in 1400 equaled that in 1200. Not until after 1500 did it rise above its preplague level.

Social Rebellion

In addition to its demographic and psychological effects, the Black Death triggered social changes in western Europe. Workers who survived demanded higher pay for their services. When authorities tried to freeze wages at the old levels, peasants rose up against wealthy nobles and churchmen. During a widespread revolt in France in 1358, known as the Jacquerie, peasants looted castles and killed dozens of persons. In a large revolt in England in 1381 led by Wat Tyler, an estimated 50,000 peasants and craftsmen invaded London, calling for an end to serfdom and obligations to landowners and murdering the archbishop of Canterbury and other officials. Authorities put down these rebellions with great bloodshed and cruelty, but they could not stave off the higher wages and other social changes the rebels demanded.

Serfdom practically disappeared in western Europe as peasants bought their freedom or ran away. Some English landowners who could no longer hire enough fieldworkers began pasturing sheep for their wool. Others grew crops that required less care or made greater use of draft animals and laborsaving tools. Because the plague had not killed livestock and game, survivors had abundant meat and leather. Thus, the welfare of the rural masses generally improved after the Black Death, though the gap between rich and poor remained wide.

In urban areas, employers raised wages to attract workers. Guilds (discussed later in this chapter) shortened the period of apprenticeship. Competition within crafts also became more common. Although the overall economy shrank with the decline in population, per capita production actually rose.

Mills and Mines

Mining, primarily in Germany and east-central Europe, and metalworking and craft mechanization everywhere expanded so greatly in the centuries before 1500 that some historians speak of an "industrial revolution" in medieval Europe. This is too strong a term, but the landscape fairly bristled with mechanical devices. Mills powered by water or wind ground grain, sawed logs, crushed olives, operated bellows, and pounded linen rags for making paper.

Watermills multiplied at a faster rate than the population. In 1086, 5,600 watermills flanked England's many rivers. After 1200, mills spread rapidly across the European mainland. By the early fourteenth century, entrepreneurs had crammed 68 watermills into a 1-mile section of the Seine (sen) River in Paris. Undershot wheels that depended on the river flowing beneath them were less efficient than overshot wheels where water channeled to fall over the top of the wheel combined the force of gravity with the water's current. Windmills multiplied in comparatively dry lands like Spain and in northern Europe, where water wheels froze in winter.

MAP 14.1 **The Black Death in Fourteenth-Century Europe** Spreading out of Inner Asia along the routes opened by Mongol expansion, the plague reached the Black Sea port of Kaffa in 1346. This map documents its deadly progress year by year from there into the Mediterranean and north and east across the face of Europe. © Cengage Learning

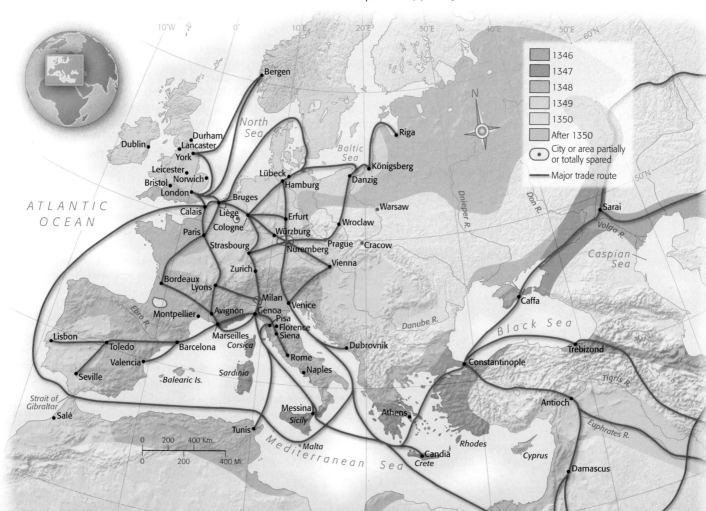

Designs for water mills dated back to Roman times, and the Islamic world, which inherited Hellenistic technologies, knew both water wheels and windmills. However, European-style heavy investment in water or wind power made no sense in Muslim lands because animal power from oxen and camels was so much cheaper where arid and semiarid wastes provided virtually free grazing. There comparatively cheap and simple single-animal mills and irrigation devices predominated. In Europe, by contrast, where grain farmers grew both human food and animal fodder, population growth increased the cost of animal energy, and of horsepower in particular. One result was that the family name *Miller* became very important in European languages but was rarely used in Arabic, Persian, or Turkish.

Owners invested heavily in building mills, but since nature furnished the energy to run them for free, they returned great profits. While individuals or monasteries constructed some mills, most were built by groups of investors. Rich millers often aroused the jealousy of their neighbors. In his *Canterbury Tales*, the English poet Geoffrey Chaucer (ca. 1340–1400) captured their unsavory reputation by portraying a miller as "a master-hand at stealing grain" by pushing down on the balance scale with his thumb.[3]

Waterpower aided the great expansion of iron making. Water powered the stamping mills that pulverized iron ore, the lifting devices that drained water from deep mines, and the bellows (first documented in the West in 1323) that raised temperatures to the point where liquid iron could be poured into molds. Blast furnaces producing high-quality iron are documented from 1380.

In addition to iron mines in many countries, new silver, lead, and copper mines in Austria and Hungary supplied metal for coins, church bells, cannon, and statues. Techniques of deep mining developed in central Europe spread west in the latter part of the fifteenth century. A building boom stimulated stone quarrying in France during the eleventh, twelfth, and thirteenth centuries.

Industrial growth changed the landscape. Towns grew outward and new ones were founded, dams and canals changed the flow of rivers, and quarries and mines scarred the hillsides. Urban tanneries (factories that cured and processed leather), the runoff from slaughterhouses, and human waste polluted streams. England's Parliament enacted the first recorded antipollution law in 1388, but enforcement proved difficult.

Deforestation accelerated. Trees provided timber for buildings and ships; tanneries stripped bark to make acid for tanning leather; and many forests gave way to farmland. The glass and iron industries used great quantities of charcoal, made by controlled burning of oak or other hardwood. A single iron furnace could consume all the trees within five-eighths of a mile (1 kilometer) in just forty days. Consequently, the later Middle Ages saw the end of many of western Europe's once-dense forests, except in places where powerful landowners established hunting preserves. Central and eastern Europe, being more lightly populated, experienced less environmental degradation.

SECTION REVIEW

- Population growth stimulated improved farming methods and agricultural expansion, but peasant life did not significantly improve.

- Famine and the Black Death reversed the population growth and resulted in social change throughout Europe.

- Improved mill designs and other technology stimulated further industrial growth, which, in turn, changed the landscape.

URBAN REVIVAL

In the tenth century, no town in the Latin Europe could compete in size, wealth, or comfort with the cities of Byzantium and Islam. Yet by the later Middle Ages, the Mediterranean, Baltic, and Atlantic coasts boasted wealthy port cities, as did some major rivers draining into these seas (see Map 14.2). Some Byzantine and Muslim cities still exceeded those of the West in size, but not in commercial, cultural, and administrative dynamism, as marked by impressive new churches, guild halls, and residences.

Trading Cities

Most urban growth after 1200 resulted from manufacturing and trade, both between cities and their hinterlands and over long distances. Northern Italy particularly benefited from maritime trade with the port cities of the eastern Mediterranean and, through them, the markets of the

---

[3]Quotations here and later in the chapter are from Geoffrey Chaucer, *The Canterbury Tales*, trans. Nevill Coghill (New York: Penguin Books, 1952), 25, 29, 32.

MAP 14.2 **Trade and Manufacturing in Later Medieval Europe** The economic revival of European cities was associated with great expansion of commerce. Notice the concentration of wool and linen textile manufacturing in northern Italy, the Netherlands, and England; the importance of trade in various kinds of foodstuffs; and the slave-exporting markets in Cairo, Kiev, and Rostov. © Cengage Learning

Hanseatic League An economic and defensive alliance of the free towns in northern Germany, founded about 1241 and most powerful in the fourteenth century.

Indian Ocean and East Asia. In northern Europe, commercial cities in the county of Flanders (roughly today's Belgium) and around the Baltic Sea profited from regional networks and from overland and sea routes to the Mediterranean.

A Venetian-inspired assault in 1204 against the city of Constantinople, misleadingly named the "Fourth Crusade," temporarily eliminated Byzantine control of the passage between the Mediterranean and the Black Sea and thereby allowed Venice to seize Crete and expand its trading colonies around the Black Sea. Another boon to Italian trade came from the westward expansion of the Mongol Empire, which opened trade routes from the Mediterranean to China that did not go through Iran and Iraq (see Chapter 13).

When Mongol decline interrupted the caravan trade in the fourteenth century, Venetian merchants purchased eastern silks and spices brought by other middlemen to Constantinople, Damascus, and Cairo. Three times a year, Venice dispatched convoys of two or three galleys, with sixty oarsmen each, capable of bringing back 2,000 tons of goods.

The sea trade of Genoa on northern Italy's west coast probably equaled that of Venice. Genoese merchants established colonies in the western and eastern Mediterranean and around the Black Sea. In northern Europe, an association of trading cities known as the **Hanseatic (han-see-AT-ik) League** traded extensively in the Baltic, including the coasts of Prussia, newly conquered by German knights. Their merchants ranged eastward to Novgorod in Russia and westward across the North Sea to London.

In the late thirteenth century, Genoese galleys from the Mediterranean and Hanseatic ships from the Baltic were converging on the trading and manufacturing cities in Flanders. Artisans in the Flemish towns of Bruges (broozh), Ghent (gent [hard g as in get]), and Ypres (EE-pruh) transformed raw wool from England into a fine cloth that was softer and smoother than the coarse "homespuns" from simple village looms. Dyed in vivid hues, these Flemish textiles appealed to wealthy Europeans, who also appreciated fine textiles from Asia.

Along the overland route connecting Flanders and northern Italy, important trading fairs developed in the Champagne (sham-PAIN) region of Burgundy. The Champagne fairs began as regional markets, exchanging manufactured goods, livestock, and farm produce once or twice a year. When the king of France gained control of Champagne at the end of the twelfth century, royal guarantees of safe conduct to merchants turned these markets into international fairs that were important for currency exchange and other financial transactions as well. A century later, fifteen Italian cities had permanent consulates in Champagne to represent the interests of their citizens. During the fourteenth century, the large volume of trade made it cheaper to ship Flemish woolens to Italy by sea than to pack them overland on animal backs. Champagne's fairs consequently lost some international trade, but they remained important as regional markets.

Flemish Weaver (engraving), English School, (19th century)/Private Collection/© Look and Learn/The Bridgeman Art Library

Flemish Weavers, Ypres The spread of textile weaving gave employment to many people in the Netherlands. The city of Ypres in Flanders (now northern Belgium) was an important textile center in the thirteenth century. This drawing from a fourteenth-century manuscript shows a man and a woman weaving cloth on a horizontal loom.

In the late thirteenth century, the English monarchy raised taxes on exports of raw wool, making cloth manufacture in England more profitable than in Flanders. Flemish specialists crossed the English Channel and introduced the spinning wheel, perhaps invented in India, and other devices to England. Annual raw wool exports fell from 35,000 sacks of wool at the beginning of the fourteenth century to 8,000 in the mid-fifteenth century, while English wool cloth production rose from 4,000 pieces just before 1350 to 54,000 a century later.

Florence also replaced Flemish imports with its own woolens industry financed by local banking families. In 1338, Florence manufactured 80,000 pieces of cloth, while importing only 10,000. Elsewhere in northern Italy a new industry appeared to manufacture cotton cloth, which had previously been imported across the Mediterranean. These changes in the textile industry show how competition promoted the spread of manufacturing and encouraged new specialties. Other Italian industries that grew on the basis of techniques borrowed from the Muslim world were papermaking, glassblowing, ceramics, and sugar refining.

In the fifteenth century, Venice surpassed its European rivals in the volume of its trade in the Mediterranean as well as across the Alps into central Europe. Its craftspeople manufactured luxury goods once obtainable only from eastern sources, including cotton and sugar grown with slave labor on the islands of Crete, Cyprus, and Sicily. This enterprise later became the model for the slave-based sugar economy of the New World (see Chapter 16). Exports of Italian and northern European woolens to the eastern Mediterranean also rose. In the space of a few centuries, western European cities had used the eastern trade to increase their prosperity and then reduce their dependence on eastern goods.

Civic Life

Most northern Italian and German cities were independent states, much like the port cities of the Indian Ocean Basin (see Chapter 15). Other European cities held royal charters exempting them from the authority of local nobles. Their autonomy enabled them to adapt to changing market conditions more quickly than cities controlled by imperial authorities, as in China and the Islamic world. Since anyone who lived in a chartered city for over a year could claim freedom, urban life promoted social mobility.

Europe's Jews mostly lived in cities. Spain had the largest communities because of the tolerance of earlier Muslim rulers, but there were also sizable populations as far east as Magdeburg in Prussia. Commercial cities generally welcomed Jews with manufacturing and business skills. Despite official protection by certain Christian princes and kings, however, Jews endured violent religious persecutions or expulsions in times of crisis, such as during the Black Death (see Diversity and Dominance: Persecution and Protection of Jews, 1272–1349). In 1492, the Spanish monarchs expelled all Jews in the name of religious and ethnic purity. Only the papal city of Rome left its Jews undisturbed throughout the centuries before 1500.

Within most towns and cities, powerful associations known as guilds dominated civic life. **Guilds** brought together craft specialists, such as silversmiths, or merchants working in a particular trade, to regulate business practices and set prices. Guilds also trained apprentices and promoted members' interests with the city government. By denying membership to outsiders and Jews, guilds protected the interests of families that already belonged to them. They also perpetuated male dominance of most skilled jobs.

guild In medieval Europe, an association of men (rarely women), such as merchants, artisans, or professors, who worked in a particular trade and banded together to promote their economic and political interests. Guilds were also important in other societies, such as the Ottoman and Safavid Empires.

Nevertheless, in a few places, women could join guilds either on their own or as the wives, widows, or daughters of male guild members. Large numbers of poor women also toiled in non-guild jobs in urban textile industries and in the food and beverage trades, generally receiving lower wages than men.

Some women advanced socially through marriage to wealthy men. One of Chaucer's *Canterbury Tales* concerns a woman from Bath, a city in southern England, who became wealthy by marrying a succession of old men for their money (and then two other husbands for love), "aside from other company in youth." She was also a skilled weaver, Chaucer says: "In making cloth she showed so great a bent, / She bettered those of Ypres and of Ghent."

By the fifteenth century, a new class of wealthy merchant-bankers was operating on a vast scale and specializing in money changing and loans and making investments on behalf of other parties. Merchants great and small used their services. They also handled the financial transactions of ecclesiastical and secular officials and arranged for the transmission to the pope of funds known as Peter's pence, a collection taken up annually in every church in Latin Europe. Princes and kings supported their wars and lavish courts with credit. Some merchant-bankers even developed their own news services, gathering information on any topic that could affect business.

Florentine financiers offered checking accounts, organized private shareholding companies (the forerunners of modern corporations), and improved bookkeeping techniques. In the fifteenth century, the Medici (MED-ih-chee) family of Florence operated banks in Italy, Flanders, and London. Medicis also controlled the government of Florence and commissioned art works. The Fuggers (FOOG-uhrz) of Augsburg, who had ten times the Medici bank's lending capital, topped Europe's banking fraternity by 1500. Beginning as cloth merchants under Jacob "the Rich" (1459–1525), the family's many activities included the trade in Hungarian copper, essential for casting cannon.

Since Latin Christians generally considered charging interest (usury) sinful, Jews predominated in moneylending. Christian bankers devised ways to get around the condemnation of usury. Some borrowers repaid loans in a different currency at a rate of exchange favorable to the lender. Others added to their repayment a "gift" for the lender. For example, in 1501, church officials agreed to repay a Fugger loan of 6,000 gold ducats in five months along with a "gift" of 400 ducats, amounting to an effective interest rate of 16 percent a year. In fact, the return was less since the church failed to repay the loan on time.

Yet most residents of European cities suffered poverty and ill health. European cities generally lacked civic amenities such as public baths and water supply systems that had existed in Roman times and still survived in Islamic lands.

Gothic Cathedrals

Gothic cathedrals Large churches originating in twelfth-century France; built in an architectural style featuring pointed arches, tall vaults and spires, flying buttresses, and large stained-glass windows.

Master builders and stone masons counted among the skilled people in greatest demand. Though cities competed with one another in the magnificence of their guild halls and town halls (see Environment and Technology: The Clock), **Gothic cathedrals**, first appearing about 1140 in France, cost the most and brought the greatest prestige. The pointed, or Gothic, arch, replacing the older round, or Romanesque, arch, signaled the new design. External (flying) buttresses stabilizing the high, thin, stone columns below the arches constituted another distinctive feature. This design enabled master builders to push the Gothic cathedrals to great heights and fill the outside walls between the arches with giant windows depicting religious scenes in brilliantly

Cathedral at Autun in Eastern France Begun around 1120 and sufficiently completed to receive the relics of St. Lazaire in 1146, this cathedral reflected Romanesque architectural design and artistic taste. In the fifteenth century a rebuilding program changed the cathedral's external appearance from Romanesque to Gothic, but the images above the west portal survive in their original form. Carved by a sculptor named Gislebertus between 1130 and 1135, they depict the Last Judgment, with Christ enthroned between the saved souls on his right and those condemned to Hell on his left. The sharply angular figures are typical of Romanesque style. Scenes like these taught important religious messages to illiterate worshipers. Scala/Art Resource, NY

Persecution and Protection of Jews, 1272–1349

Because they did not belong to the dominant Latin Christian faith, Jews suffered from periodic discrimination and persecution. For the most part, religious and secular authorities tried to curb such anti-Semitism. Jews, after all, were useful citizens who worshiped the same God as their Christian neighbors. Still, it was hard to know where to draw the line between justifiable and unjustifiable discrimination. The famous reviser of Catholic theology, St. Thomas Aquinas, made one such distinction in his Summa Theologica *with regard to attempts at forced conversion.*

Now, the practice of the Church never held that the children of Jews should be baptized against the will of their parents. . . . Therefore, it seems dangerous to bring forward this new view, that contrary to the previously established custom of the Church, the children of Jews should be baptized against the will of their parents.

There are two reasons for this position. One stems from danger to faith. For, if children without the use of reason were to receive baptism, then after reaching maturity they could easily be persuaded by their parents to relinquish what they had received in ignorance. This would tend to do harm to the faith.

The second reason is that it is opposed to natural justice . . . it [is] a matter of natural right that a son, before he has the use of reason, is under the care of his father. Hence, it would be against natural justice for the boy, before he has the use of reason, to be removed from the care of his parents, or for anything to be arranged for him against the will of his parents.

The "new view" Aquinas opposed was much in the air, for in 1272 Pope Gregory X issued a decree condemning forced baptism. The pope's decree reviews the history of papal protection given to the Jews, starting with a quotation from Pope Gregory I dating from 598, and decrees two new protections of Jews' legal rights.

Even as it is not allowed to the Jews in their assemblies presumptuously to undertake for themselves more than that which is permitted them by law, even so they ought not to suffer any disadvantage in those [privileges] which have been granted them.

Although they prefer to persist in their stubbornness rather than to recognize the words of their prophets and the mysteries of the Scriptures, and thus to arrive at a knowledge of Christian faith and salvation; nevertheless, inasmuch as they have made an appeal for our protection and help, we therefore admit their petition and offer them the shield of our protection through the clemency of Christian piety. In so doing we follow in the footsteps of our predecessors of happy memory, the popes of Rome—Calixtus, Eugene, Alexander, Clement, Celestine, Innocent, and Honorius.

We decree moreover that no Christian shall compel them or any one of their group to come to baptism unwillingly. But if any one of them shall take refuge of his own accord with Christians, because of conviction, then, after his intention will have been made manifest, he shall be made a Christian without any intrigue. For indeed that person who is known to come to Christian baptism not freely, but unwillingly, is not believed to possess the Christian faith.

Moreover, no Christian shall presume to seize, imprison, wound, torture, mutilate, kill, or inflict violence on them; furthermore no one shall presume, except by judicial action of the authorities of the country, to change the good customs in the land where they live for the purpose of taking their money or goods from them or from others.

In addition, no one shall disturb them in any way during the celebration of their festivals, whether by day or by night, with clubs or stones or anything else. Also no one shall exact any compulsory service of them unless it be that which they have been accustomed to render in previous times.

Inasmuch as the Jews are not able to bear witness against the Christians, we decree furthermore that the testimony of Christians against Jews shall not be valid unless there is among these Christians some Jew who is there for the purpose of offering testimony.

Since it occasionally happens that some Christians lose their Christian children, the Jews are accused by their enemies of secretly carrying off and killing these same Christian children, and of making sacrifices of the heart and blood of these very children. It happens, too, that the parents of these children, or some other Christian enemies of these Jews, secretly hide these very children in order that they may be able to injure these Jews, and in order that they may be able to extort from them a certain amount of money by redeeming them from their straits.

And most falsely do these Christians claim that the Jews have secretly and furtively carried away these children and killed them, and that the Jews offer sacrifice from the heart and the blood of these children, since their law in this matter precisely and expressly forbids Jews to sacrifice, eat, or drink the blood, or eat the flesh of animals having claws. This has been demonstrated many times at our court by Jews converted to the Christian faith: nevertheless very many Jews are often seized and detained unjustly because of this.

We decree, therefore, that Christians need not be obeyed against Jews in such a case or situation of this type, and we order that Jews seized under such a silly pretext be freed from imprisonment, and that they shall not be arrested henceforth on such a miserable pretext, unless—which we do not believe—they be caught in the commission of the crime. We decree that no Christian shall stir up anything against them, but that they should be maintained in that status and position in which they were from the time of our predecessors, from antiquity till now.

We decree, in order to stop the wickedness and avarice of bad men, that no one shall dare to devastate or to destroy a cemetery of the Jews or to dig up human bodies for the sake of getting money [by holding them for ransom]. Moreover, if anyone, after having known the content of this decree, should—which we hope will not happen—attempt audaciously to act contrary to it, then let him suffer punishment in his rank and position, or let him be punished by the penalty of excommunication, unless he makes amends for his boldness by proper recompense.

Moreover, we wish that only those Jews who have not attempted to contrive anything toward the destruction of the Christian faith be fortified by the support of such protection. . . .

Despite such decrees, violence against Jews might burst out when fears and emotions were running high. This selection is from the official chronicles of the upper-Rhineland towns.

In the year 1349 there occurred the greatest epidemic that ever happened. Death went from one end of the earth to the other, on that side and this side of the [Mediterranean] sea, and it was greater among the Saracens [Muslims] than among the Christians. In some lands everyone died so that no one was left. Ships were also found on the sea laden with wares; the crew had all died and no one guided the ship. The Bishop of Marseilles and priests and monks and more than half of all the people there died with them. In other kingdoms and cities so many people perished that it would be horrible to describe. The pope at Avignon stopped all sessions of court, locked himself in a room, allowed no one to approach him and had a fire burning before him all the time. And from what this epidemic came, all wise teachers and physicians could only say that it was God's will. And the plague was now here, so it was in other places, and lasted more than a whole year. This epidemic also came to Strasbourg in the summer of the above mentioned year, and it is estimated about sixteen thousand people died.

In the matter of this plague the Jews throughout the world were reviled and accused in all lands of having caused it through the poison which they are said to have put into the water and the wells—that is what they were accused of—and for this reason the Jews were burnt all the way from the Mediterranean into Germany, but not in Avignon, for the pope protected them there.

Nevertheless they tortured a number of Jews in Berne and Zofingen who admitted they had put poison into many wells, and they found the poison in the wells. Thereupon they burnt the Jews in many towns and wrote of this affair to Strasbourg, Freibourg, and Basel in order that they too should burn their Jews. . . . The deputies of the city of Strasbourg were asked what they were going to do with their Jews. They answered and said that they knew no evil of them. Then . . . there was a great indignation and clamor against the deputies from Strasbourg. So finally the Bishop and the lords and the Imperial Cities agreed to do away with the Jews. The result was that they were burnt in many cities, and wherever they were expelled they were caught by the peasants and stabbed to death or drowned. . . .

On Saturday—that was St. Valentine's Day—they burnt the Jews on a wooden platform in their cemetery. There were about two thousand people of them. Those who wanted to baptize themselves were spared. Many small children were taken out of the fire and baptized against the will of their fathers and mothers. And everything that was owed to the Jews was cancelled, and the Jews had to surrender all pledges and notes that they had taken for debts. The council, however, took the cash that the Jews possessed and divided it among the working-men proportionately. The money was indeed the thing that killed the Jews. If they had been poor and if the feudal lords had not been in debt to them, they would not have been burnt.

QUESTIONS FOR ANALYSIS

1. Why do Aquinas and Pope Gregory oppose prejudicial actions against Jews?

2. Why did prejudice increase at the time of the Black Death?

3. What factors account for the differences between the views of Christian leaders and the Christian masses?

Sources: First selection source is Pocket Books, a division of Simon & Schuster, Inc., and the Vernon & Janet Bourke Living Trust from *The Pocket Aquinas*, edited with translations by Vernon G. Bourke. Copyright © 1960 by Washington Square Press. Copyright renewed © 1988 by Simon & Schuster, Inc. Second and third selections from Jacob R. Marcus, ed., *The Jew in the Medieval World: A Source Book, 315–1791* (Cincinnati: Union of American Hebrew Congregations, 1938), 152–154, 45–47. Reprinted with permission of the Hebrew Union College Press, Cincinnati.

SECTION REVIEW

- After 1200, most cities grew through manufacture and trade, particularly those of northern Italy, Flanders, and the Baltic coast.

- Expanding trade and technological innovation ultimately reduced Europe's dependence on eastern goods.

- Cities fostered social mobility, but civic life was dominated by guilds, wealthy merchants, and bankers.

- Most urban residents lived in squalor without the amenities of Islamic Middle Eastern cities.

- Gothic cathedrals became signs of special civic pride and prestige in European cities.

colored stained glass. During the next four centuries, interior heights soared ever higher and walls became dazzling curtains of stained glass.

The men who designed and built the cathedrals had little or no formal education and limited understanding of the mathematical principles of civil engineering. Master masons sometimes miscalculated, causing parts of some overly ambitious cathedrals to collapse. The record-high choir vault of Beauvais Cathedral, for instance—154 feet (47 meters) in height—came tumbling down in 1284. But as builders gained experience and invented novel solutions to their problems, success rose from the rubble of their mistakes. The cathedral spire in Strasbourg reached 466 feet (142 meters) into the air—as high as a forty-story building. Such heights were unsurpassed until the nineteenth century.

The Clock

Clocks were a prominent feature of the western Europe in the late medieval period. The Song-era Chinese had built elaborate mechanical clocks centuries earlier (see Chapter 12), but the West was the first part of the world where clocks became a regular part of urban life. Whether mounted in a church steeple or placed on a bridge or tower, mechanical clocks proclaimed Western people's delight with mechanical objects and display of civic wealth. Precision timekeeping was a secondary concern given the crudeness of the first designs.

The word *clock* comes from a word for bell. The first mechanical clocks that appeared around 1300 in western Europe were simply bells with a device to strike the number of hours automatically. The most elaborate Chinese clock had been powered by falling water, but this was impractical in cold weather. The levers, pulleys, and gears of European clocks were powered by a weight hanging from a rope wound around a cylinder. An "escapement" lever regulated the slow, steady unwinding.

Prosperous merchants readily donated money to build a splendid clock that would display their city's wealth. The city of Strasbourg, for example, built a clock in the 1350s that included statues of the Virgin, the Christ Child, and the three Magi; a mechanical rooster; the signs of the zodiac; a perpetual calendar; and an astrolabe—and it could play hymns, too!

By the 1370s and 1380s clocks were common enough for their measured hours to displace the older system, which monks had long relied on, that varied the divisions of the day in proportion to the number of daylight hours. Previously, for example, the London hour had varied from thirty-eight minutes in winter to eighty-two minutes in summer. By 1500 clocks had numbered faces with hour and minute hands. Small clocks for indoor use were also in vogue. Some historians consider the clock the most important of the many technological advances of the later Middle Ages, but its value was not fully realized until the railroad era.

Medioimages/Photodisc/Getty Images

City Hall Clock of Prague This clock was installed in 1410; calendar dial added in 1490.

LEARNING, LITERATURE, AND THE RENAISSANCE

Throughout the Middle Ages, people in the western Europe lived amid reminders of the achievements of the Romans. They wrote and worshiped in a version of their language, traveled their roads, and obeyed some of their laws. The vestments and robes of popes, kings, and emperors followed the designs of Roman officials. Yet the learning of Greco-Roman antiquity virtually disappeared outside of Byzantium and the Muslim world.

The Renaissance

A small revival of learning at the court of Charlemagne in the ninth century was followed by a larger renaissance (rebirth) in the twelfth century, when cities became centers of intellectual and artistic life. The universities established across Latin Europe after 1200 contributed to this

Renaissance (European) A period of intense artistic and intellectual activity, said to be a "rebirth" of Greco-Roman culture. Usually divided into an Italian Renaissance, from roughly the mid-fourteenth to mid-fifteenth century, and a Northern (trans-Alpine) Renaissance, from roughly the early fifteenth to early seventeenth century.

cultural revival. In the mid-fourteenth century, the pace of intellectual and artistic life quickened in what is often called the **Renaissance**, which began in northern Italy and later spread to northern and eastern Europe. Some Italian authors saw the Italian Renaissance as a sharp break with an age of darkness.

Before 1100, Byzantine and Islamic scholarship generally surpassed scholarship in Latin Europe. But when Latin Christians wrested southern Italy from the Byzantines and Sicily and Toledo from the Muslims in the eleventh century, they acquired many manuscripts of Greek and Arabic works. These included works by Plato and Aristotle (AR-ih-stah-tahl) and Greek treatises on medicine, mathematics, and geography, as well as scientific and philosophical writings by Muslim writers. Latin translations of the Iranian philosopher Ibn Sina (IB-uhn SEE-nah) (980–1037), known in the West as Avicenna (av-uh-SEN-uh), had great influence because of their sophisticated blend of Aristotelian and Islamic philosophy. Jewish scholars contributed significantly to the translation and explication of Arabic and other manuscripts.

In a related development, the thirteenth century saw the foundation of two new religious orders, the Dominicans and the Franciscans. Living according to a rule but not confined to monasteries, these friars brought preaching to the common people and carried the Christian message abroad as missionaries. Some of their most talented members taught in the independent colleges that arose after 1200. Though some aspects of these institutions may derive from institutions of higher Islamic learning called *madrasas* that proliferated after 1100 (see Chapter 10), Latin Europe innovated the idea of **universities** as degree-granting corporations imparting both religious and nonreligious learning.

universities Degree-granting institutions of higher learning. Those that appeared in Latin Europe from about 1200 onward became the model of all modern universities.

Between 1300 and 1500, sixty universities, from St. Andrews in Scotland to Krakow and Prague in eastern Europe, joined the twenty established before that time. Students banded together to start some of them; guilds of professors founded others. Teaching guilds, like crafts guilds, set standards for the profession, trained apprentices and masters, and defended their professional interests.

Universities set curricula and instituted final examinations for degrees. Students who passed the exams that ended their apprenticeship received a "license" to teach, while those who completed longer training and defended a masterwork of scholarship became "masters" and "doctors." The University of Paris gradually absorbed the city's various colleges, but the colleges of Oxford and Cambridge remained independent, self-governing organizations.

Since all universities used Latin, students and masters moved freely across political and linguistic borders, seeking the courses and professors they wanted. Some universities offered specialized training. Legal training centered on Bologna in Italy (buh-LOHN-yuh); Montpellier in southern France and Salerno in Sicily focused on medicine; Paris and Oxford excelled in theology.

Some topics, such as astronomy, were studied outside the university. Both Greek and Arabic traditions presumed that the planets traced circular orbits around the earth, the circle being a perfect geometrical figure. Celestial observations did not always fit this presumption, however. Fifteenth-century astronomers in both Europe and the lands of Islam theorized explanations for the observational deviations. At the very end of the fifteenth century, the Polish-German astronomer Nicolaus Copernicus (co-PER-ni-cus), basing his ideas mainly on the Greek Ptolemy but also aware of more recent writings in Arabic, hit on the idea of planets orbiting the sun instead of the earth. His work, finally published as he lay dying of a stroke in 1543, would pose a challenge to the church's assumption that the earth was the center of God's universe.

Though the new learning sometimes raised inconvenient questions, students aspiring to ecclesiastical careers, and their professors, conferred special prominence on theology, seen as the "queen of the sciences" encompassing all true knowledge. Hence, thirteenth-century theologians sought to synthesize the rediscovered philosophical works of Aristotle and the commentaries of Avicenna with the Bible's revealed truth. These efforts to synthesize reason and faith were known as **scholasticism** (skoh-LAS-tih-sizm).

scholasticism A philosophical and theological system, associated with Thomas Aquinas, devised to reconcile Aristotelian philosophy and Roman Catholic theology in the thirteenth century.

Thomas Aquinas, a brilliant Dominican theology professor at the University of Paris, wrote the most notable scholastic work, the *Summa Theologica* (SOOM-uh thee-uh-LOH-jih-kuh), between 1267 and 1273. Although his exposition of Christian belief organized on Aristotelian principles came to be accepted as a masterly demonstration of the reasonableness of Christianity, scholasticism upset many traditional thinkers. Some church authorities tried to ban Aristotle from the curriculum. However, the considerable freedom of medieval universities from both secular and religious authorities enabled the new ideas to prevail over the fears of church administrators.

Humanists and Printers

This period also saw important literary contributions. The Italian Dante Alighieri (DAHN-tay ah-lee-GYEH-ree) (1265–1321) completed a long, elegant poem, the *Divine Comedy*, shortly before his death. This supreme expression of medieval preoccupations tells the allegorical story of Dante's journey through the nine circles of Hell and the seven terraces of Purgatory, followed by his entry into Paradise. The Roman poet Virgil guides him through Hell and Purgatory; Beatrice, a woman he had loved from afar since childhood and whose death inspired the poem, guides him to Paradise.

The *Divine Comedy* foreshadows the literary fashions of the later Italian Renaissance. Like Dante, later Italian writers made use of Greco-Roman classical themes and mythology and sometimes courted a broader audience by writing not in Latin but in their local language (Dante used the vernacular spoken in Tuscany [TUS-kuh-nee]).

The poet Geoffrey Chaucer (ca. 1343–1400), many of whose works show the influence of Dante, wrote in vernacular English. The *Canterbury Tales*, a lengthy poem written in the last dozen years of his life, contains often humorous and earthy tales told by fictional pilgrims on their way to the shrine of Thomas à Becket in Canterbury (see Chapter 11). They present a vivid cross-section of medieval people and attitudes.

humanists (Renaissance)
European scholars, writers, and teachers associated with the study of the humanities (grammar, rhetoric, poetry, history, languages, and moral philosophy), influential in the fifteenth century and later.

Dante influenced a literary movement of the **humanists** that began in his native Florence in the mid-fourteenth century. The term refers to their interest in grammar, rhetoric, poetry, history, and moral philosophy (ethics)—subjects known collectively as the humanities, an ancient discipline. With the brash exaggeration characteristic of new intellectual fashions, humanist writers like the poet Francesco Petrarch (fran-CHES-koh PAY-trahrk) (1304–1374) and the poet and storyteller Giovanni Boccaccio (jo-VAH-nee boh-KAH-chee-oh) (1313–1375) proclaimed a revival of a Greco-Roman tradition they felt had for centuries lain buried under the rubble of post-Roman decay.

This idea of a rebirth of learning dismisses too readily the monastic and university scholars who for centuries had been recovering all sorts of Greco-Roman learning, as well as writers like Dante (whom the humanists revered), who anticipated humanist interests by a generation. Yet the humanists had a great impact as educators, advisers, and reformers. Their greatest influence came in reforming secondary education. They introduced a curriculum centered on the languages and literature of Greco-Roman antiquity, which they felt provided intellectual discipline, moral lessons, and refined tastes. This curriculum dominated European secondary schools well into the twentieth century.

Dante's *Divine Comedy*
This fifteenth-century painting by Domenico di Michelino shows Dante holding a copy of the *Divine Comedy*. Hell is depicted to the poet's right and the terraces of Purgatory behind him, surmounted by the earthly and heavenly Paradise. The city of Florence, with its recently completed cathedral, appears to Dante's left.

akg-images/Rabatti – Domingie

The Art Archive

A French Printshop, 1537 A workman operates the "press," quite literally a screw device that presses the paper to the inked type. Other employees examine the printed sheets, each of which holds four pages. When folded, the sheets make a book. The man on the right is selecting pieces of type from a compartmented box and placing them in a frame for printing.

Many humanists tried to duplicate the elegance of classical Latin and (to a lesser extent) Greek, which they revered as the pinnacle of learning, beauty, and wisdom. Boccaccio gained fame with his vernacular writings, which resemble Dante's, and especially for the *Decameron,* an earthy work that has much in common with Chaucer's boisterous tales. Under Petrarch's influence, however, Boccaccio turned to writing in classical Latin.

As humanist scholars mastered Latin and Greek, they turned their language skills to restoring the original texts of Greco-Roman writers and of the Bible. By comparing different manuscripts, they eliminated errors introduced by generations of copyists. To aid in this task, Pope Nicholas V (r. 1447–1455) created the Vatican Library, buying scrolls of Greco-Roman writings and paying to have accurate copies and translations made. Working independently, the Dutch scholar Erasmus **(uh-RAZ-muhs)** of Rotterdam (ca. 1466–1536) produced a critical edition of the New Testament in Greek. Erasmus corrected many errors and mistranslations in the Latin text that had been in general use throughout the Middle Ages. Later, this humanist priest and theologian wrote—in classical Latin—influential moral guides, including the *Enchiridion militis christiani* (*The Manual of the Christian Knight,* 1503) and *The Education of a Christian Prince* (1515).

The influence of the humanists grew as the new technology of printing made their critical editions of ancient texts, literary works, and moral guides more available. The Chinese and the Arabs used carved woodblocks for printing, and block-printed playing cards circulated in Europe before 1450, but after that date three European improvements revolutionized printing: (1) movable pieces of type consisting of individual letters, independently invented in Korea (see Chapter 12); (2) walnut oil–based ink suitable for printing on paper without smearing; and (3) the **printing press**, a mechanical device that pressed sheets of paper onto inked type.

Johann Gutenberg **(yoh-HAHN GOO-ten-burg)** (ca. 1394–1468) of Mainz led the way. The Gutenberg Bible of 1454, the first book in the West printed from movable type, exhibited a beauty and craftsmanship testifying to the printer's years of experimentation. Humanists worked closely with the printers, who spread the new techniques to Italy and France. Erasmus did editing and proofreading for the Italian scholar-printer Aldo Manuzio (1449–1515) in Venice. Manuzio's press published many critical editions of classical Latin and Greek texts.

By 1500, at least 10 million printed volumes flowed from presses in 238 European towns, launching a revolution that affected students, scholars, and a growing literate population. These readers consumed unorthodox political and religious tracts along with ancient texts.

Renaissance Artists

Although the artists of the fourteenth and fifteenth centuries continued to depict biblical subjects, the Greco-Roman revival led some, especially in Italy, to portray ancient deities and myths. Another popular trend involved scenes of daily life.

printing press A mechanical device for transferring text or graphics from a woodblock or type to paper using ink. Presses using movable type first appeared in Europe in about 1450.

SECTION REVIEW

- Greco-Roman learning returned to Latin Europe through a series of revivals that culminated with the Renaissance.

- An infusion of Greek and Islamic scholarship during the eleventh century helped to prompt the revival of the twelfth and thirteenth centuries.

- Colleges and universities grew, with theology as the preeminent discipline.

- Foreshadowed by Dante, humanism, with its focus on classical languages, literature, ethics, and education, emerged in Italy.

- The influence of the humanists spread through the new print technology.

- Renaissance artists enlarged the thematic and technical resources of painting, sculpture, and architecture.

Scala/Art Resource, NY

Michelangelo's Tomb Statue of Lorenzo de´ Medici   The greatest of the Medici bankers, Lorenzo governed Florence during the height of the Renaissance. At the time of his death in 1492 he had fallen under the influence of Girolamo Savonarola, a stern, moralistic priest who felt that art and morals had departed too far from proper Christianity. Nevertheless, the Roman armor and pensive expression of this statue epitomize the antique revival and dedication to thought associated with the term Renaissance.

Neither theme was entirely new, however. Renaissance art, like Renaissance scholarship, owed a debt to earlier generations. Italian painters of the fifteenth century credited the Florentine painter Giotto (JAW-toh) (ca. 1267–1337) with single-handedly reviving the "lost art of painting." In religious scenes, Giotto replaced the stiff, staring figures of the Byzantine style, which were intended to overawe viewers, with more natural and human portraits with whose depictions of grief and love viewers could identify. Rather than floating on backgrounds of gold leaf, his saints inhabit earthly landscapes.

North of the Alps, the Flemish painter Jan van Eyck (yahn vahn IKE) (ca. 1390–1441) mixed his pigments with linseed oil in place of the egg yolk of earlier centuries. Oil paints dried more slowly and gave pictures a superior luster. Italian painters quickly copied van Eyck's technique, though his own masterfully realistic paintings on religious and domestic themes remained distinctive.

Leonardo da Vinci (lay-own-AHR-doh dah-VIN-chee) (1452–1519) used oil paints for his *Mona Lisa*. Renaissance artists like Leonardo worked in many media, including bronze sculptures and frescos (painting on wet plaster) like *The Last Supper*. Leonardo's notebooks also contain imaginative designs for airplanes, submarines, and tanks. His younger contemporary Michelangelo (my-kuhl-AN-juh-low) (1472–1564) painted frescoes of biblical scenes on the ceiling of the Sistine Chapel in the Vatican, sculpted statues of David and Moses, and designed the dome for a new Saint Peter's Basilica in Rome.

The patronage of wealthy and educated merchants and prelates underlay the artistic blossoming in the cities of northern Italy and Flanders. The Florentine banker Cosimo de' Medici (1389–1464) and his grandson Lorenzo (1449–1492), known as "the Magnificent," spent immense sums on paintings, sculpture, and public buildings. In Rome, the papacy (PAY-puh-see) launched a building program that culminated in the construction of the new Saint Peter's Basilica and a residence for the pope.

These scholarly and artistic achievements exemplify the innovation and striving for excellence of the late Middle Ages. The new literary themes and artistic styles of this period had lasting influence on Western culture. But the innovations in the organization of universities, in printing, and in scientific thought had wider implications, for they were later adopted by cultures all over the world.

POLITICAL AND MILITARY TRANSFORMATIONS

Stronger and more unified states and armies developed in western Europe in parallel with the economic and cultural revivals (see Map 14.3). Crusades against Muslim states brought consolidation to Spain and Portugal. In Italy and Germany, however, political power remained in the hands of small states and loose alliances. Farther to the east, Lithuania, dynastically linked to Poland, became one of Europe's largest states, while Hungary confronted the Ottoman Empire.

Monarchs, Nobles, and the Church

Thirteenth-century states continued early medieval state structures (see Chapter 11). Hereditary monarchs topped the political pyramid, but modest treasuries and the rights of nobles and the church limited their powers. Powerful noblemen who controlled vast estates had an important

The Magna Carta One of four extant copies, this document shows the ravages of time, but the symbolic importance of the charter King John of England signed under duress in 1215 for English constitutional history has not been diminished. Originally a guarantee of the barons' feudal rights, it came to be seen as a limit on the monarch's authority over all subjects. The National Archives, Public Record Office and Historical Manuscripts Commission

voice in matters of state. The church guarded closely its traditional rights and independence. Towns, too, had acquired rights and privileges. Towns in Flanders, the Hanseatic League, and Italy approached independence from royal interference. In theory the ruler's noble vassals owed military service in time of war. In practice, vassals sought to limit the monarch's power.

In the year 1200, knights still formed the backbone of western European armies, but changes in weaponry brought this into question. Improved crossbows could shoot metal-tipped arrows with enough force to pierce helmets and light body armor. Professional crossbowmen, hired for wages, became increasingly common and much feared. Indeed, a church council in 1139 outlawed the crossbow—ineffectively—as being too deadly for use against Christians. The arrival in Europe of firearms based on the Chinese invention of gunpowder (see Chapter 13) further transformed the medieval army, first on the Ottoman frontier and then farther west.

The church also resisted royal control. In 1302, the outraged Pope Boniface VIII (r. 1294–1303) asserted that divine law made the papacy superior to "every human creature," including monarchs. King Philip "the Fair" of France (r. 1285–1314) responded by sending an army to arrest the pope, a chastisement that hastened Pope Boniface's death. Philip then engineered the election of a French pope, who established a new papal residence at Avignon (ah-vee-NYON) in southern France in 1309.

A succession of French-dominated popes residing in Avignon improved church discipline but at the price of compromising their neutrality in the eyes of other rulers. The **Great Western Schism** between 1378 and 1415 saw rival papal claimants at Avignon and Rome vying for Christian loyalties. The papacy eventually regained its independence and returned to Rome, but the long crisis broke the pope's ability to challenge the rising power of monarchs like Philip, who had used the dispute to persuade his nobles to grant him a new tax.

The English monarchy wielded more centralized power as a result of consolidation that took place after the Norman conquest of 1066. Between 1200 and 1400, the Anglo-Norman kings incorporated Wales and reasserted control over most of Ireland. Nevertheless, under King John (r. 1199–1216), royal power suffered a severe setback. Forced to acknowledge the pope as his overlord in 1213, he lost his bid to reassert claims to Aquitaine in southern France the following year and then yielded to his nobles by signing the Magna Carta in 1215. This "Great Charter" affirmed that monarchs were subject to established law, confirmed the independence of the church and the city of London, and guaranteed the nobles' hereditary rights.

Great Western Schism A division in the Latin (Western) Christian Church between 1378 and 1415, when rival claimants to the papacy existed in Rome and Avignon.

Hundred Years' War (1337–1453) Series of campaigns over control of the throne of France, involving English and French royal families and French noble families.

The Hundred Years' War

The conflict between the king of France and his vassals known as the **Hundred Years' War** (1337–1453) grew out of a marriage alliance. Marriage between Princess Isabella of France and King Edward II of England (r. 1307–1327) should have ensured the king's loyalty, as a vassal who had inherited French lands from his Norman ancestors. However, when the French royal line produced no other sons, Isabella's son, King Edward III of England (r. 1327–1377), laid claim to the French throne in 1337.

Early in the war, hired Italian crossbowmen reinforced the French cavalry, but the English longbow proved superior. Adopted from the Welsh, the 6-foot (1.8-meter) longbow could shoot farther and more rapidly than the crossbow. Its arrows could not pierce armor, but concentrated volleys found gaps in the knights' defenses or struck their less-protected horses. Heavier and more encompassing armor provided a defense but limited a knight's movements. Once pulled off his steed by a foot soldier armed with a pike (hooked pole), he could not get up.

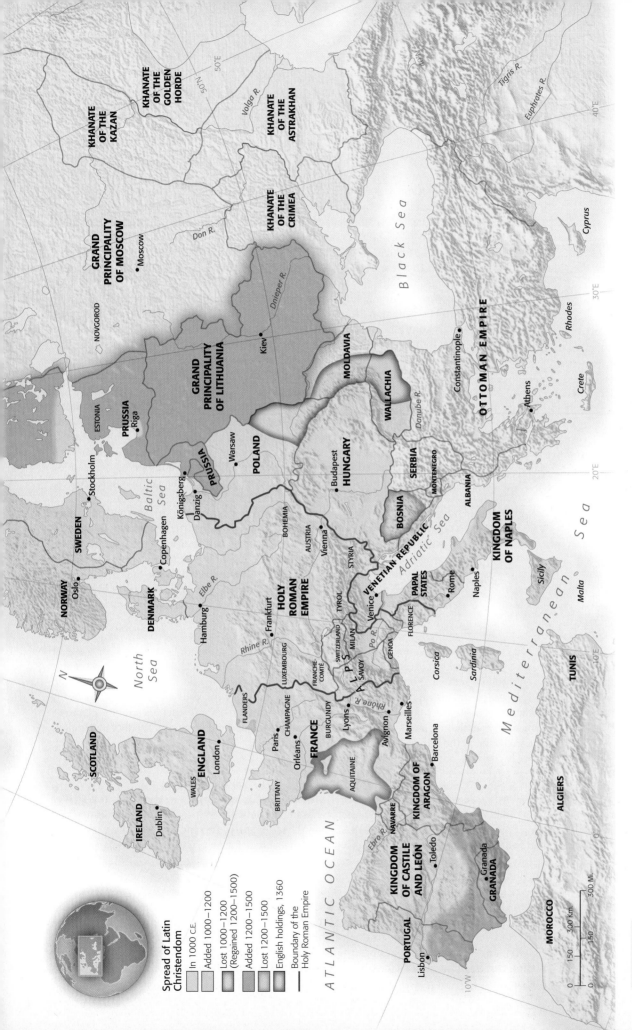

MAP 14.3 **Europe in 1453** This year marked the end of the Hundred Years' War between France and England and the fall of the Byzantine capital city of Constantinople to the Ottoman Turks. Muslim advances into southeastern Europe were offset by the Latin Christian reconquests of Islamic holdings in southern Italy and the Iberian Peninsula and by the conversion of Lithuania. © Cengage Learning

Spread of Latin Christendom

- In 1000 C.E.
- Added 1000–1200
- Lost 1000–1200 (Regained 1200–1500)
- Added 1200–1500
- Lost 1200–1500
- English holdings, 1360
- Boundary of the Holy Roman Empire

KHANATE OF THE KAZAN

KHANATE OF THE GOLDEN HORDE

KHANATE OF THE ASTRAKHAN

GRAND PRINCIPALITY OF MOSCOW

Moscow

NOVGOROD

KHANATE OF THE CRIMEA

Volga R.

Don R.

Dnieper R.

Kiev

GRAND PRINCIPALITY OF LITHUANIA

Black Sea

ESTONIA

PRUSSIA
Riga

Stockholm

SWEDEN

Baltic Sea

Königsberg

Danzig

PRUSSIA

Warsaw

POLAND

Budapest

HUNGARY

MOLDAVIA

WALLACHIA

Danube R.

SERBIA

MONTENEGRO

BOSNIA

ALBANIA

Constantinople

OTTOMAN EMPIRE

Athens

Crete

Rhodes

Cyprus

Tigris R.

Euphrates R.

NORWAY

Oslo

Copenhagen

DENMARK

Hamburg

Elbe R.

BOHEMIA

AUSTRIA

Vienna

STYRIA

TYROL

HOLY ROMAN EMPIRE

Frankfurt

Rhine R.

LUXEMBOURG

FLANDERS

FRANCHE-COMTÉ

SWITZERLAND

MILAN

A L P S

SAVOY

Po R.

GENOA

VENETIAN REPUBLIC

Venice

Adriatic Sea

PAPAL STATES

FLORENCE

Rome

Naples

KINGDOM OF NAPLES

Sicily

Sardinia

Corsica

Malta

Mediterranean Sea

TUNIS

ALGIERS

North Sea

N

SCOTLAND

IRELAND

Dublin

WALES

ENGLAND

London

BRITTANY

Paris

CHAMPAGNE

Orléans

FRANCE

BURGUNDY

Lyons

Rhône R.

AQUITAINE

Avignon

Marseilles

Barcelona

NAVARRE

KINGDOM OF ARAGON

Ebro R.

Toledo

KINGDOM OF CASTILE AND LEÓN

Granada

GRANADA

PORTUGAL

Lisbon

MOROCCO

ATLANTIC OCEAN

0   150   300 Mi.

0   150   300 Km.

Later in the Hundred Years' War, firearms gained prominence. The first cannon scared the horses with smoke and noise but did little damage. As they grew larger, however, they proved effective in battering the walls of castles and towns. The first artillery use against the French, at the Battle of Agincourt (1415), gave the English an important victory.

Faced with a young French peasant woman called Joan of Arc, subsequent English gains stalled. Acting, she believed, on God's instructions, she put on armor and rallied the French troops to defeat the English in 1429. Shortly afterward, she fell into English hands, and in 1431 she was tried by English churchmen and burned at the stake as a witch.

In the final battles, French cannon demolished the walls of once-secure castles held by the English and their allies. Armies now depended less on knights and more on bowmen, pikemen, musketeers, and artillerymen.

New Monarchies in France and England

new monarchies Historians' term for the monarchies in France, England, and Spain from 1450 to 1600. The centralization of royal power was increasing within more or less fixed territorial limits.

The war proved a watershed in the rise of **new monarchies** in France and England, centralized states with fixed "national" boundaries and stronger representative institutions. English monarchs after 1453 consolidated control over territory within the British Isles, though the Scots defended their independence. The French monarchs also turned to consolidating control over powerful noble families in Burgundy and Brittany.

The new monarchies needed a way to finance their full-time armies. Some nobles agreed to money payments in place of military service and to additional taxes in time of war. For example, in 1439 and 1445, Charles VII of France (r. 1422–1461) successfully levied a new tax on his vassals' land. This not only paid the costs of the war with England but also provided the monarchy a financial base for the next 350 years.

Merchants' taxes also provided revenues. Taxes on the English wool trade, begun by King Edward III, paid most of the costs of the Hundred Years' War. Some rulers taxed Jewish merchants or extorted large contributions from wealthy towns. Individual merchants sometimes curried royal favor with loans. The fifteenth-century French merchant Jacques Coeur (cur) gained many social and financial benefits for himself and his family by lending money to French courtiers, but his debtors accused him of murder and had his fortune confiscated.

In the west, the church provided a third source of revenue through voluntary contributions to support a war. English and French monarchs won the right to appoint important church officials in their realms in the fifteenth century. In the east, religion became increasingly a political issue as Catholic Lithuania fought a series of wars with Orthodox Russia with little regard for which faith the common people adhered to.

The shift in power to the monarchs and away from the nobility and the church did not deprive nobles of their social position and roles as government officials and military officers. Moreover, the kings of England and France in 1500 had to deal with representative institutions that had not existed in 1200. The English Parliament proved a permanent check on royal power: the House of Lords contained the great nobles and church officials; and the House of Commons represented the towns and the leading citizens of the counties. In France, the Estates General, a similar but less effective representative body, represented the church, the nobles, and the towns.

Iberian Unification

reconquest of Iberia Beginning in the eleventh century, military campaigns by various Iberian Christian states to recapture territory taken by Muslims. In 1492 the last Muslim ruler was defeated, and Spain and Portugal emerged as united kingdoms.

Spain and Portugal's **reconquest of Iberia** from Muslim rule expanded the boundaries of Latin Christianity. The knights who pushed the borders of their kingdoms southward furthered both Christianity and their own interests. The spoils of victory included irrigated farmland, rich cities, and ports on the Mediterranean Sea and Atlantic Ocean. Serving God, growing rich, and living off the labor of others became a way of life for the Iberian nobility.

The reconquest took several centuries. In 1085 Toledo fell and became a Christian outpost. In 1147 English Crusaders bound for the Holy Land helped take Lisbon, which then displaced the older city of Oporto (meaning "the port"), from which Portugal took its name, as both capital and the kingdom's leading city. After a Christian victory in 1212 broke the back of Muslim power, the reconquest accelerated. Within decades, Portuguese and Castilian forces captured the prosperous cities of Córdova (1236) and Seville (1248) and drove the Muslims from the southwestern region known as Algarve (ahl-GAHRV) ("the west" in Arabic). Only the small kingdom of Granada hugging the Mediterranean coast remained in Muslim hands.

By incorporating Algarve in 1249, Portugal attained its modern territorial limits. After a pause to colonize, forcibly Christianize, and consolidate this land, Portugal took the crusade

Conquest of Granada   A Muslim state since 1238, Granada was conquered in 1492 by the armies of Ferdinand of Aragon and Isabella of Castile. This relief sculpture from the sixteenth century shows the sultan Mohammad XI surrendering the keys of the capital city.

to North Africa. In 1415, Portuguese knights seized the port of Ceuta (say-OO-tuh) in Morocco, where they learned more about the Saharan caravan trade in gold and slaves. During the next few decades, Portuguese mariners sailed down the Atlantic coast of Africa seeking rumored African Christian allies and access to this trade (see Chapter 16).

Elsewhere in Iberia, the reconquest continued. Princess Isabella of Castile married Prince Ferdinand of Aragon in 1469. A decade later, when they inherited their respective thrones, the two kingdoms united to become Spain. Their conquest of Granada in 1492 secured the final piece of Muslim territory for the new kingdom.

Ferdinand and Isabella sponsored the first voyage of Christopher Columbus in 1492 (see Chapter 16). In a third momentous event of that year, the monarchs expelled the Jews from their kingdoms. Attempts to convert or expel the remaining Muslims led to a revolt at the end of 1499 that lasted until 1501, and in 1502 the Spanish rulers expelled the last Muslims. Portugal expelled the Jews in 1496, including 100,000 refugees from Spain. For some time afterward the Spanish Inquisition, a tribunal established by the two monarchs, exerted itself in identifying and punishing Jews, called Marranos, and Muslims, called Moriscos, who had nominally converted to Christianity but secretly retained their old, forbidden faiths.

The Ottoman Frontier

As Islam receded in the west, it advanced in the east as the Ottoman Empire (see Chapter 13) inflicted defeat after defeat on the Christian Balkan kingdoms. The Ottoman military was balanced between cavalry archers, primarily Turks, and slave infantrymen armed with hand-held firearms.

Slave soldiery had a long history in Islamic lands (see Chapter 10), but the conquest of the Balkans in the late fourteenth century gave the Ottomans access to a new military resource: Christian prisoners of war enslaved and converted to Islam. These "new troops," called *yeni cheri* in Turkish and *janissaries* (JAN-i-say-ree) in English, gave the Ottomans unusual military flexibility. Not coming from a nomadic background like the Turks, they readily accepted the idea of fighting on foot and learning to use guns, which at that time were still too heavy and awkward for a horseman to load and fire. The janissaries lived in barracks and trained all year round.

The process of selection for janissary training changed early in the fifteenth century. The new system, called the *devshirme*, imposed a regular levy of male children on Christian villages in the Balkans. Selected children were placed with Turkish families to learn their language and then sent to Istanbul for instruction in Islam, military training, and, for the most talented, opportunities to become senior military commanders and heads of government departments. The Christian European contest between nobles, monarchs, and church authorities scarcely existed in the Ottoman realm.

SECTION REVIEW

- Between 1200 and 1500, monarchs, nobles, and the church struggled over political power.

- Tensions between the French monarchy and the papacy resulted in the Great Western Schism.

- In England, royal power was checked by the papacy and nobility, the latter imposing the Magna Carta on King John.

- The Hundred Years' War between the French monarchy and its vassals introduced new military technologies.

- The war also stimulated the rise of the new centralized monarchies of England and France.

- Spain and Portugal continued the reconquest of Muslim Iberia, a process completed by Ferdinand and Isabella.

- As Muslim territory in Iberia shrank, the rising Ottoman Empire took over much of southeastern Europe.

CONCLUSION

Ecologically, the peoples of Latin Europe harnessed the power of wind and water and mined and refined their mineral wealth at the cost of localized pollution and deforestation. However, inability to improve food production and distribution in response to population growth created a demographic crisis that climaxed with the Black Death that devastated Europe in the mid-fourteenth century.

Politically, basic features of the modern European state began to emerge. Frequent wars caused kingdoms of moderate size to develop exceptional military strength. The ruling class, seeing economic strength as the twin of political power, promoted the activities of commercial cities and taxed their profits.

Culturally, autonomous universities and printing supported the advance of knowledge, while art and architecture reached unsurpassed peaks in the Renaissance. Late medieval society also displayed a fundamental fascination with tools and techniques, many of them acquired from the Muslim world or farther east. European success, however, depended just as much on strong motives for expansion. From the eleventh century onward, population pressure, religious zeal, economic enterprise, and intellectual curiosity drove an expansion of territory and resources that took the Crusaders to the Holy Land, merchants to the eastern Mediterranean and Black Seas, German settlers across the Elbe River, and Iberian Christians into the Muslim south. The early voyages into the Atlantic, discussed in Chapter 16, extended these activities.

KEY TERMS

three-field system p. 340
Black Death p. 341
Hanseatic League p. 345
guild p. 346
Gothic cathedrals p. 347
Renaissance (European) p. 351
universities p. 351
scholasticism p. 351
humanists (Renaissance) p. 352
printing press p. 353
Great Western Schism p. 355
Hundred Years' War p. 355
new monarchies p. 357
reconquest of Iberia p. 357

SUGGESTED READING

Alland, Christopher. *The Hundred Years War: England and France at War, ca. 1300–ca. 1450.* 1988. Key events in the Anglo-French dynastic conflict.

Bartlett, Robert. *The Making of Europe: Conquest, Colonization, and Cultural Change.* 1993. Shows Europe as the product of conquest and colonization before it became a colonizer.

Bechmann, Roland. *Trees and Man: The Forest in the Middle Ages.* 1990. A pioneering work in environmental history.

Cantor, Norman F. *In the Wake of the Plague: The Black Death and the World It Made.* 2001. A thorough introduction.

Gies, Frances, and Joseph Gies. *Women in the Middle Ages.* 1978. A general introduction.

Gimpel, Jean. *The Medieval Machine: The Industrial Revolution of the Middle Ages.* 1977. A general introduction to the technological issues of the period.

Holmes, George. *Europe: Hierarchy and Revolt, 1320–1450,* 2d ed. 2000. A comprehensive overview.

Huizinga, Johan. *The Waning of the Middle Ages.* 1924. A classic account of the "mind" of the fifteenth century.

Jardine, Lisa. *Worldly Goods: A New History of the Renaissance.* 1996. A well-illustrated and balanced survey.

Lopez, Robert S. *The Commercial Revolution of the Middle Ages, 950–1350.* 1976. Surveys the West's economic revival and growth.

McNeill, William H. *The Pursuit of Power: Technology, Armed Force, and Society Since* A.D. *1000.* 1982. An influential interpretation by an eminent world historian.

O'Callaghan, Joseph F. *A History of Medieval Spain.* 1975. Provides the best one-volume coverage.

Oakley, Francis C. *The Western Church in the Later Middle Ages.* 1985. A reliable summary of modern scholarship.

Phillips, J. R. S. *The Medieval Expansion of Europe,* 2d ed. 1998. European adventurism from Greenland to West Africa to China.

Stow, Kenneth R. *Alienated Minority: The Jews of Medieval Latin Europe.* 1992. A fine survey through the fourteenth century.

15

Chapter Outline

Tropical Africa and Asia
➤ *How did environmental differences shape cultural differences in tropical Africa and Asia?*

New Islamic Empires
➤ *Under what circumstances did the first Islamic empires arise in Africa and India?*

Indian Ocean Trade
➤ *How did cultural and ecological differences promote trade, and in turn how did trade and other contacts promote state growth and the spread of Islam?*

Social and Cultural Change
➤ *What social and cultural changes are reflected in the history of peoples living in tropical Africa and Asia during this period?*

The Western Hemisphere
➤ *What were the key differences between societies in Africa and Asia and the empires of the Aztecs and Inkas?*

Conclusion

- **MATERIAL CULTURE** Salt
- **DIVERSITY + DOMINANCE** Personal Styles of Rule in India and Mali
- **ENVIRONMENT + TECHNOLOGY** The Indian Ocean Dhow

East African Pastoralists Herding large and small livestock has long been a way of life in drier parts of the tropics.

Southern Empires, Southern Seas, 1200–1500

Sultan Abu Bakr (a-BOO BAK-uhr) customarily offered hospitality to distinguished visitors to his city of Mogadishu, an Indian Ocean port on the northeast coast of Africa. In 1331, he provided food and lodging for Muhammad ibn Abdullah **Ibn Battuta** (IB-uhn ba-TOO-tuh) (1304–1369), a young Muslim scholar from Morocco who had set out to explore the Islamic world. With a pilgrimage to Mecca and travel throughout the Middle East behind him, Ibn Battuta was touring the trading cities of the Red Sea and East Africa. Subsequent travels took him to Central Asia and India, China and Southeast Asia, Muslim Spain, and sub-Saharan West Africa. Recounting some 75,000 miles (120,000 kilometers) of travel over twenty-nine years, Ibn Battuta's journal provides invaluable information on these lands.

Ibn Battuta Moroccan Muslim scholar, the most widely traveled individual of his time. He wrote a detailed account of his visits to Islamic lands from China to Spain and the western Sudan.

Hospitality being considered a noble virtue among Muslims, regardless of physical and cultural differences, the reception at Mogadishu mirrored that at other cities. Ibn Battuta noted that Sultan Abu Bakr had skin darker than his own and spoke a different native language (Somali), but as brothers in faith, they prayed together at Friday services, where the sultan greeted his foreign guest in Arabic, the common language of the Islamic world: "You are heartily welcome, and you have honored our land and given us pleasure." When Sultan Abu Bakr and his jurists heard and decided cases after the mosque service, they used the religious law familiar in all Muslim lands.

Islam aside, the most basic links among the diverse peoples of Africa and southern Asia derived from the tropical environment itself. A network of overland and maritime routes joined their lands, providing avenues for the spread of beliefs and technologies, as well as goods. Ibn Battuta sailed with merchants down the coast of East Africa and joined trading caravans across the Sahara from Morocco to West Africa. His path to India followed overland trade routes, and a merchant ship carried him on to China.

The tropics of the Western Hemisphere lay beyond even Ibn Battuta's prodigious itinerary. Nevertheless, their environmental features resembled those of tropical Africa and Asia and they witnessed the rise of the impressive empires of the Aztecs and Inkas.

TROPICAL AFRICA AND ASIA

The tropical regions of Africa and Asia shared environmental similarities, but they differed markedly in the extent of their interactions with other parts of the world (see Chapter 9). The western regions of Africa were semi-isolated by the Atlantic Ocean and Sahara Desert, while Africa's east coast was in maritime contact with the lands bordering the Indian Ocean. India had long been affected by overland routes through Afghanistan to the Middle East and Central Asia, and it in turn influenced cultural developments in both mainland and island Southeast Asia.

The Tropical Environment in Africa and Asia

tropics Equatorial region between the Tropic of Cancer and the Tropic of Capricorn. It is characterized by generally warm or hot temperatures year-round, though much variation exists due to altitude and other factors. Temperate zones north and south of the tropics generally have a winter season.

Because of the angle of the earth's axis, the sun's rays warm the **tropics** year-round. The equator marks the center of the tropical zone, and the Tropic of Cancer and Tropic of Capricorn its outer limits. Africa lies almost entirely within the tropics, as do southern Arabia, most of India, and both mainland and island Southeast Asia (see Map 15.1). In the Western Hemisphere the regions that produced the earliest civilizations, Mesoamerica and the Andes and Pacific coast of South America, also lay in the tropics.

Lacking the hot and cold seasons of temperate lands, the rainy and dry seasons of the Afro-Asian tropics derive from atmospheric patterns across the surrounding oceans. Winds flow away from areas of high atmospheric pressure toward areas of low pressure. The earth's rotation causes these winds to move in a clockwise direction (anticyclone) north of the equator and a counter-clockwise direction south of the equator. Thus a permanent high-pressure air mass over the South Atlantic delivers heavy rainfall to the western coast of Africa during much of the year. However, in December and January, large high-pressure zones over northern Africa and Arabia produce a southward movement of dry air that limits the inland penetration of the moist ocean winds.

monsoon Seasonal winds in the Indian Ocean caused by the differences in temperature between the rapidly heating and cooling landmasses of Africa and Asia and the slowly changing ocean waters. These strong and predictable winds have long been ridden across the open sea by sailors, and the large amounts of rainfall that they deposit on parts of India, Southeast Asia, and China allow for the cultivation of several crops a year.

In the lands around the Indian Ocean, the rainy and dry seasons reflect the influence of alternating winds known as **monsoons**. A gigantic high-pressure zone over the Himalaya (him-AH-la-yuh) Mountains that peaks from December to March produces southern Asia's dry season by forcing strong southward and westward air movements (the northeast monsoon) in the western Indian Ocean. Between April and August, a low-pressure zone over India reverses the process by drawing moist oceanic air from the south and west (the southwest monsoon). This brings southern Asia the heavy rains of its wet season, usually called the monsoon season.

Areas with the heaviest rainfall—the broad belt along the equator in coastal West Africa and West-Central Africa, parts of coastal India, and Southeast Asia—have dense rain forests. Lighter rains produce other forest patterns. The English word *jungle* comes from an Indian word for the tangled undergrowth in the forests that once covered most of tropical India.

Some other parts of the tropics rarely see rain at all. The world's largest desert, the Sahara, stretches across northern Africa and continues eastward across Arabia, southern Iran and Pakistan, and northwest India. Another desert occupies southwestern Africa. Tropical India and Africa fall mostly between the deserts and rain forests and experience moderate rainy seasons. These lands range from fairly wet woodlands to the much drier grasslands characteristic of much of East Africa.

Altitude produces other climatic variations. Thin atmospheres at high altitudes hold less heat than atmospheres at lower elevations. Snow covers some of the volcanic peaks of eastern Africa all or part of the year. The snowcapped Himalayas that form India's northern frontier rise so high that they block cold air from moving south and thus give northern India a more tropical climate than its latitude would suggest. The plateaus of inland Africa and the Deccan (DEK-uhn) Plateau of central India also enjoy cooler temperatures than the coastal plains.

Human Ecosystems

A careful observer touring the tropics in 1200 would have noticed many differences in societies deriving from their particular ecosystems—that is, from how human groups used the plants, animals, and other resources of their physical environments. These systems varied greatly in the density of population they could support.

Some peoples continued to rely primarily on hunting, fishing, and gathering and lived in small, mobile groups. For Pygmy (PIG-mee) hunters in the dense forests of Central Africa, small size permitted pursuit of prey through dense undergrowth. Hunting also prevailed among some inland groups in Borneo, New Guinea, and the Philippines. A Portuguese expedition led by Vasco da Gama visited the arid coast of southwestern Africa in 1497 and saw there a healthy group of people feeding themselves on "the flesh of seals, whales, and gazelles, and the roots of wild plants." Fishing, which was common along all the major lakes and rivers as well as in the oceans, could be combined with farming or with ocean trade, particularly in Southeast Asia.

Herding provided sustenance in areas too arid for agriculture. Pastoralists consumed milk and sometimes blood from their herds but did not eat a lot of meat since their animals were of greater value to them alive than dead. The deserts of northern Africa and Arabia had small populations that ranged widely with their camels, goats, and donkeys. Some, like the Tuareg (TWAH-reg) of the western Sahara, proved invaluable as caravan guides because of their

CHRONOLOGY

	Tropical Africa	Tropical Asia	Western Hemisphere
1200	1230s Mali Empire founded 1270 Solomonic dynasty in Ethiopia founded	1206 Delhi Sultanate founded in India 1298 Delhi Sultanate annexes Gujarat	
1300	1324–1325 Mansa Musa's pilgrimage to Mecca	1398 Timur sacks Delhi; Delhi Sultanate declines	1325 Aztec capital Tenochtitlan founded
1400	1400s Great Zimbabwe at its peak 1433 Tuareg retake Timbuktu; Mali declines		1430s Inka expansion begins
1500		1500 Port of Malacca at its peak	1500–1525 Inka conquer Ecuador 1502 Moctezuma II crowned Aztec ruler

intimate knowledge of the desert. Along the Sahara's southern edge the cattle-herding Fulani (foo-LAH-nee) gradually extended their range and by 1500 had spread throughout the western and central Sudan. Other cattle herders lived on either side of the Nile in Sudan and in Somalia.

Pastoral groups in India were less numerous and located mostly in the northwestern deserts. South and Southeast Asia, being generally wetter than tropical Africa outside the rain forest zone, did not favor pastoralism but did allow for intensive cultivation. High yields supported dense populations. In 1200, over 100 million people lived in South and Southeast Asia, more than four-fifths of them on the fertile Indian mainland. Though a little less than the population of China, this was triple the number of people living in all of Africa and nearly double the number in Europe.

Rice cultivation dominated in the fertile Ganges Plain of northeast India, mainland Southeast Asia, and southern China. In drier areas, farmers grew grains—wheat, sorghum, and millet—and legumes such as peas and beans whose ripening cycles matched the pattern of the rainy and dry seasons. Tree crops, such as kola nuts in West Africa, coconuts in Southeast Asia, and bananas everywhere, made major contributions to the diet, as did the root crops characteristic of rain forest clearings.

The spread of farming, including the movement to Africa of Indo-Malayan bananas and root crops like yams and cocoyams, also known as taro, did not necessarily change the natural environment. In most of sub-Saharan Africa and much of Southeast Asia, extensive rather than intensive cultivation prevailed. Instead of enriching fields with manure and vegetable compost so they could be cultivated year after year, farmers abandoned fields when the natural fertility of the soil fell and cleared new fields. Ashes from the brush, grasses, and tree limbs they cut down and burned boosted the new fields' fertility. Shifting to new land every few years made efficient use of labor in areas with comparatively poor soils and abundant space.

Water Systems and Irrigation

Though the inland delta of the Niger River in West Africa received naturally fertilizing annual floods and could grow rice for sale to the trading cities along the Niger bend, many tropical farmers in India and Southeast Asia had to bring water to their crops. Conserving some of the monsoon rainfall for use during the dry season helped in Vietnam, Java, Malaya, and Burma (now Myanmar), which had terraced hillsides with special water-control systems for growing rice. Villagers in southeast India built stone and earthen dams across rivers to store water for gradual release through elaborate irrigation canals. Similar dam and canal systems supplied water farther north.

As had been true since the first river-valley civilizations (see Chapter 2), governments built and controlled the largest irrigation systems. The **Delhi (DEL-ee) Sultanate** (1206–1526) in northern India developed extensive new water-control systems. One large reservoir that supplied Delhi in the first quarter of the thirteenth century had fields of sugar cane, cucumbers, and melons planted along its rim as the water level fell during the dry season. Irrigation canals

Delhi Sultanate Centralized Indian empire of varying extent, created by Muslim invaders.

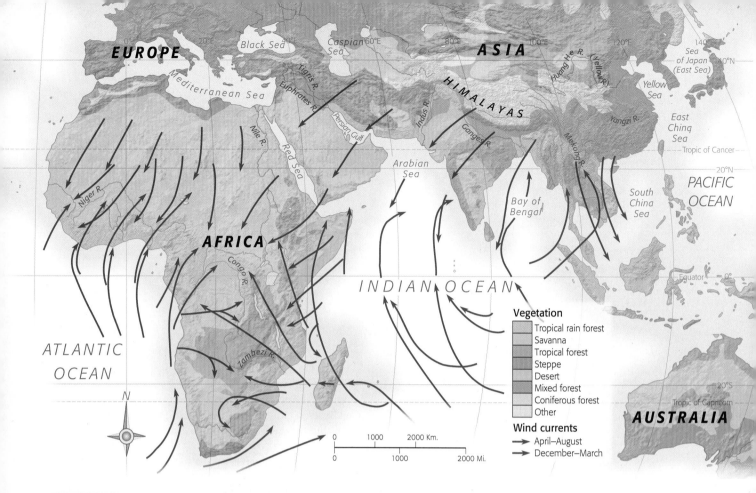

MAP 15.1 **Africa and the Indian Ocean Basin: Physical Characteristics** Seasonal wind patterns control rainfall in the tropics and produce the different tropical vegetation zones to which human societies have adapted over thousands of years. Wind patterns have also dominated sea travel in the Indian Ocean. © Cengage Learning

built in the Ganges Plain in the fourteenth century remained unsurpassed for five hundred years. Such systems made it possible to grow crops throughout the year.

Since the tenth century, the island of Ceylon (ancient Serandip; modern Sri Lanka [sree LAHNG-kuh]) off India's southern tip possessed the world's greatest concentration of irrigation reservoirs and canals. These facilities supported the population of a large Sinhalese-speaking (sin-huh-LEEZ) kingdom in arid northern Ceylon. In Southeast Asia, another impressive system of reservoirs and canals served Cambodia's capital city, Angkor (ANG-kor).

Between 1250 and 1400, however, the irrigation complex in Ceylon fell into ruin when invaders from south India disrupted the Sinhalese government. As a result, malaria spread by mosquitoes breeding in the irrigation canals ravaged the population. In the fifteenth century, the great Cambodian system fell into ruin when the government that maintained it collapsed. Neither system was ever rebuilt.

The vulnerability of complex irrigation systems built by powerful governments contrasts with village-based irrigation systems. Invasion and natural calamity might damage the latter, but they usually bounced back because they depended on local initiative and simpler technologies.

Mineral Resources

Throughout the tropics, ironworking provided the hoes, axes, and knives farmers used to clear and cultivate their fields. Between 1200 and 1500, the rain forests of coastal West Africa and Southeast Asia opened up for farming. Iron also supplied spear and arrow points, needles, and

Salt

Though sodium chloride, or table salt, is one of the world's most abundant chemicals, its abundance in some areas and scarcity in others has frequently given it an important role in economic history. Here are some examples.

Outcroppings of rock salt known as salt licks play a nutritional role in the lives of many wild mammals. Prehistoric human hunters sought game at these natural animal gathering places, and some scholars believe that human provision of salt played an important role in domesticating some species.

Trade in salt from the southern regions of the Sahara Desert is described as early as the ninth century C.E., but it is probably much older because the Saharan deposits formed an important nutritional source for salt-poor sub-Saharan Africa. The legendary exchange of salt for equivalent quantities of gold symbolizes this commercial importance. Bilma, an oasis town in eastern Niger, still produces salt that is distributed by means of camel caravans trekking across the sand dunes of the Ténéré Desert.

In ancient Rome, a strong-smelling sauce known as *garum* became a cooking staple and an important export item. *Garum* was made by crushing cut up fish, with their entrails, in a small amount of brine. The salt prevented the sauce from spoiling. For common people, using *garum* was a way of avoiding the tax on salt.

Early in the fourteenth century C.E. a Flemish fisherman devised a method of preserving herring, a small fish. After the head and certain internal organs were removed, enzymes from the pancreas began to digest the flesh and make it tender. Then the fish were packed with salt in casks. Salted herring and its raw materials, salt and herring, became mainstays of the commerce of Scotland, northern Germany, and in particular the Netherlands. A Dutch proverb maintains that the city of Amsterdam was built on herring casks.

In France, a salt tax known as the *gabelle* became a permanent part of royal revenues in the late fourteenth century C.E. Everyone over the age of eight was forced to buy a minimum amount of salt every week at a price fixed by the government. Most of the salt was produced by evaporating seawater, but inland provinces in the east exploited salt marshes. Popular resentment against the tax contributed to the French Revolution in 1789. A year later the *gabelle* was canceled.

In nineteenth-century China, where the salt tax had been a mainstay of government revenues since the Tang dynasty, brine (saltwater) wells around the western city of Zigong became the basis for one of the country's most prosperous industries. The family-based trusts that extracted the salt from as deep as 3,000 feet were comparable in capital accumulation, management skill, and technological innovation to contemporary European corporations.

In 1930 the British monopoly on salt production in India became the center of a peaceful protest led by Mahatma Gandhi. With seventy-eight followers he marched 240 miles to the seacoast, where the protestors picked up a small lump of salt, thereby breaking the law against private harvesting of salt. Though many were imprisoned, the Salt March became an important model of civil disobedience.

Though salt naturally brings a taste to mind, its historic role relates more to its chemical properties. Salt in water passes

Camel Caravan Carrying Salt in West Africa Natural salt deposits, such as those at Bilma in the southern Sahara Desert in Niger, have time and again become the bases for extensive regional and international trade. Transporting the salt can be a challenge, however. Camel transport made salt trading an integral part of the trade between the Saharan region and the agricultural countries of West Africa. In northern Europe the salt springs at Lüneburg near Hamburg, Germany, fed into a maritime trading network throughout the Baltic and North Sea region. Coastal lands could extract salt from seawater by evaporation, though in colder climates, such as Japan, boiling was needed to supplement the power of natural sunlight and heat.

easily through the membranes that surround the cells of plants and animals. After a period of time, the moisture within the cell acquires the chemical properties of the salty moisture on the outside. Pieces of pork transform into ham, cucumbers and other vegetables become pickles, and sturgeon eggs become caviar. Since high concentrations of salt kill bacteria, salted foods can be transported and stored for long periods without spoiling or becoming dangerous to eat.

Producing salt from seawater and other sources of brine requires evaporation or boiling. But salt is also available in solid form and can be mined. Cities like Salzburg (literally "Salt Town") in Austria have grown up around salt mines. Underground layers of salt, sometimes hundreds of feet thick, are the residue of dried-up prehistoric seas or oceans. In addition to being processed for consumption, rock salt is used on icy roads. Since saltwater freezes at a lower temperature than fresh water, salt deposited on snow or ice causes melting.

QUESTIONS FOR ANALYSIS

1. Why did salt become such an important trade product?

2. Why would a tax on salt be easy to administer?

3. How many uses of salt can you think of?

King and Queen of Ife This copper-alloy work shows the royal couple of the Yoruba kingdom of Ife, the oldest and most sacred of the Yoruba kingdoms of southwestern Nigeria. The casting dates to the period between 1100 and 1500, except for the reconstruction of the male's face, the original of which shattered in 1957 when the road builder who found it accidentally struck it with his pick. Andre Held Collection/akg-image

nails. Indian armorers became known for forging strong and beautiful swords. In Africa, many people attributed magical powers to iron smelters and blacksmiths.

The Copperbelt of southeastern Africa came into prominence during the fourteenth and fifteenth centuries. Smelters cast the metal into large X-shaped ingots (metal castings) that local coppersmiths worked into wire and decorative objects.

A mining town in the western Sudan visited by Ibn Battuta produced two sizes of copper bars that served as currency in place of coins. Coppersmiths in the West African city of Ife (now in southern Nigeria) cast highly realistic copper and brass (an alloy of copper and zinc) statues and heads that now rank as masterpieces of world art. They utilized the "lost-wax" method, in which molten metal melts a thin layer of wax sandwiched between clay forms, replacing the "lost" wax with hard metal.

African gold moved in quantity across the Sahara and into the Indian Ocean and Red Sea trades. Some came from streambeds along the upper Niger River and farther south in modern Ghana (GAH-nuh). Far to the south, beyond the Zambezi (zam-BEE-zee) River (in modern Zimbabwe [zim-BAHB-way]), archaeologists have discovered thousands of mineshafts, dating from 1200, that were sunk up to 100 feet (30 meters) into the ground to get at gold ores. Although panning for gold remained important in the streams descending from the mountains of northern India, the gold and silver mines in India seem to have been exhausted by this period. Thus, Indians imported considerable quantities of gold for jewelry and temple decoration from Iran and the Ottoman Empire as well as from Southeast Asia and Africa.

NEW ISLAMIC EMPIRES

Paradoxically, given the Mongol destruction of the Baghdad caliphate in 1258 (see Chapter 13), the territorial expansion of Islam between 1200 and 1500 exceeded the Arab conquests of the seventh century. The Ottoman conquests in Europe extended Muslim domains in the Mediterranean heartland, but most of the expansion took place in the Muslim south in Africa, South Asia, and Southeast Asia.

The empires of Mali in West Africa and Delhi in northern India formed the largest and richest tropical states during Islam's second period of expansion. Both utilized administrative and military systems introduced from the Islamic heartland. Yet **Mali**, an indigenous African dynasty, grew out of the peaceful influence of Muslim merchants and scholars, while the Delhi Sultanate was founded and ruled by invading Turkish and Afghan Muslims.

Mali Empire created by indigenous Muslims in western Sudan of West Africa from the thirteenth to fifteenth century. It was famous for its role in the trans-Saharan gold trade.

Mali in the Western Sudan

Muslim rule in North Africa beginning in the seventh century (see Chapter 10) greatly stimulated trade across the Sahara. In the centuries that followed, the faith of Muhammad spread slowly to the lands south of the desert, which the Arabs called the *bilad al-sudan* (bih-LAD uhs-soo-DAN), "land of the blacks."

Muslim Berbers invading out of the desert in 1076 caused the collapse of Ghana, the empire that preceded Mali in the western Sudan (see Chapter 10). Takrur (TAHK-roor), a kingdom on the Atlantic coast whose ruler had become the first sub-Saharan ruler to adopt Islam in the 1030s, allied with the invaders but remained a small state when the Berbers' interests in Morocco and Spain drew their attention away from the sub-Saharan region. Farther east, a truce that had endured since 652 between Christian Nubia along the Nile and Muslim Egypt fell apart in the thirteenth century as the Mamluks of Cairo (see Chapter 10) made repeated attacks. The

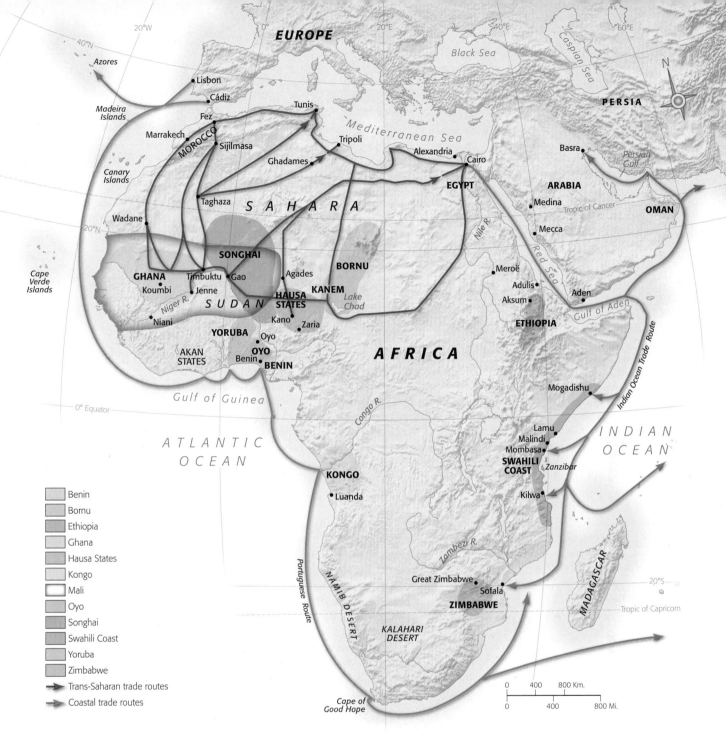

MAP 15.2 **Africa, 1200–1500** Many African states had beneficial links to the trade that crossed the Sahara and the Indian Ocean. Before 1500, sub-Saharan Africa's external ties were primarily with the Islamic world. © Cengage Learning

small Christian kingdoms weakened and fell over the next two centuries, but Christian Ethiopia successfully withstood Muslim advances.

In general, however, Islam's spread south of the Sahara followed a pattern of gradual and peaceful conversion. The expansion of commercial contacts in the western Sudan and on the East African coast greatly promoted the conversion process.

Shortly after 1200, Takrur expanded under King Sumanguru (soo-muhn-GOO-roo), only to suffer a major defeat some thirty years later at the hands of Sundiata (soon-JAH-tuh), the upstart leader of the Malinke (muh-LING-kay) people. Though both leaders professed Islam, Malinke legends recall their battles as clashes between powerful magicians, suggesting how much old and new beliefs mingled. Sumanguru could reportedly appear and disappear at will, assume dozens of shapes, and catch arrows in midflight. Sundiata defeated Sumanguru's much larger forces through superior military maneuvers and by wounding his adversary with a special arrow that robbed him of his magical powers. Other victories followed and the Mali Empire was born (see Map 15.2).

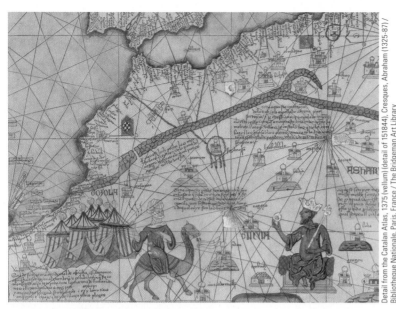

Detail from the Catalan Atlas, 1375 (vellum) (detail of 151844), Cresques, Abraham (1325–87) / Bibliotheque Nationale, Paris, France / The Bridgeman Art Library

Map of the Western Sudan (1375) A Jewish geographer on the Mediterranean island of Majorca drew this lavish map in 1375, incorporating all that was known in Europe about the rest of the world. This portion of the Catalan Atlas shows a North African trader approaching the king of Mali, who holds a gold nugget in one hand and a golden scepter in the other. A caption identifies the black ruler as Mansa Musa, "the richest and noblest king in all the land."

Mansa Kankan Musa Ruler of Mali (r. 1312–1337). His pilgrimage through Egypt to Mecca in 1324–1325 established the empire's reputation for wealth in the Mediterranean world.

Sundiata's empire depended on a well-developed agricultural base and control of the regional and trans-Saharan trade routes, as had Ghana before it. Mali, however, controlled a greater area than Ghana, including not only the core trading area of the upper Niger but also the gold fields of the Niger headwaters to the southwest. Moreover, its rulers fostered the spread of Islam among the empire's political and trading elites. Control of the gold and copper trades and contacts with North African Muslim traders gave Mali unprecedented prosperity.

Under the ruler **Mansa Kankan Musa** (MAHN-suh KAHN-kahn MOO-suh) (r. 1312–1337), the empire's reputation for wealth spread far and wide. Mansa Musa's pilgrimage to Mecca in 1324–1325 fulfilled his personal duty as a Muslim and at the same time put on display his exceptional wealth. He traveled with a large entourage. Besides his senior wife and five hundred of her ladies in waiting and their slaves, one account says there were also sixty thousand porters and a vast caravan of camels carrying supplies and provisions. For purchases and gifts, he brought along eighty packages of gold, each weighing 122 ounces (3.8 kilograms). In addition, five hundred slaves each carried a golden staff. Mansa Musa dispersed so many gifts when he passed through Cairo that the value of gold was depressed for years. Obviously the days were past when caravan merchants could trade gold for an equal weight of salt because the value of the precious metal on north side of the Sahara was not known on the south side (see Material Culture: Salt).

Two centuries after its founding, Mali began to disintegrate. Mansa Suleiman's successors could not prevent rebellions breaking out among the diverse peoples subjected to Malinke rule. Other groups attacked from without. The desert Tuareg retook their city of Timbuktu (tim-buk-TOO) in 1433. By 1500, the rulers of Mali had dominion over little more than the Malinke heartland.

The cities of the upper Niger survived Mali's collapse, but some trade and intellectual life moved east to the central Sudan. Shortly after 1450, the rulers of several Hausa city-states officially adopted Islam. These states took on importance as manufacturing and trading centers, becoming famous for cotton textiles and leatherworking. The central Sudanic state of Kanem-Bornu (KAH-nuhm–BOR-noo) also expanded in the late fifteenth century from the ancient kingdom of Kanem, whose rulers had accepted Islam in about 1085. At its peak around 1250, Kanem had absorbed the state of Bornu south and west of Lake Chad and gained control of routes crossing the central Sahara. As Kanem-Bornu's armies conquered new territories, they also spread the rule of Islam.

The Delhi Sultanate in India

Having long ago lost the defensive unity of the Gupta Empire (see Chapter 7), the divided states of northwest India fell prey to raids by the powerful sultan Mahmud (mah-MOOD) based in Ghazna, Afghanistan, beginning in the early eleventh century. Repeated campaigns by successive rulers led to a series of Afghan and Turkic dynasties ruling from the city of Delhi from 1206 to 1526. One partisan Muslim chronicler wrote: "The city [Delhi] and its vicinity was freed from idols and idol-worship, and in the sanctuaries of the images of the [Hindu] Gods, mosques were raised by the worshippers of one God."[1] Turkish adventurers from Central Asia flocked to join the invading armies, overwhelming the small Indian states, which were often at war with one another.

Between 1206 and 1236, the Muslim invaders extended their rule over the Hindu princes and chiefs in much of northern India. Sultan Iltutmish (il-TOOT-mish) (r. 1211–1236) consolidated the conquest in a series of military expeditions that made his realm the largest in India

---

[1]Hasan Nizami, *Taju-l Ma-asir*, in Henry M. Elliot, *The History of India as Told by Its Own Historians*, ed. John Dowson (London: Trübner and Co., 1869–1871), 2:219.

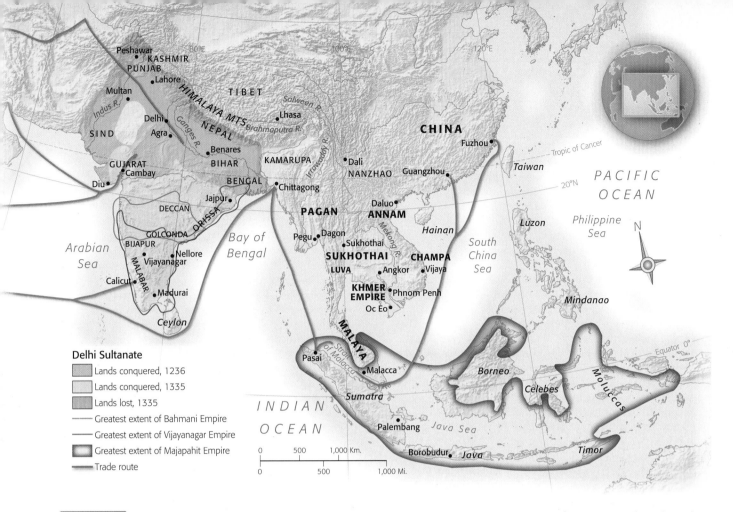

MAP 15.3 **South and Southeast Asia, 1200–1500** The rise of new empires and the expansion of maritime trade reshaped the lives of many tropical Asians. © Cengage Learning

Map legend:

Delhi Sultanate
- Lands conquered, 1236
- Lands conquered, 1335
- Lands lost, 1335
- Greatest extent of Bahmani Empire
- Greatest extent of Vijayanagar Empire
- Greatest extent of Majapahit Empire
- Trade route

(see Map 15.3). The caliph in Baghdad, soon to be killed by the Mongols, officially recognized the Delhi Sultanate as a Muslim realm. Incorporating north India into the Islamic world marked the beginning of the invaders' transformation from brutal conquerors to somewhat more benign rulers. Though doctrinally opposed to idol worship, they granted the Hindus freedom from persecution in return for paying the *jizya*, a tax required of Jews and Christians.

Iltutmish astonished his ministers by passing over his weak and pleasure-seeking sons and designating as his heir his beloved and talented daughter Raziya (**RAH-zee-uh**). He reportedly said, "My sons are devoted to the pleasures of youth: no one of them is qualified to be king. . . . There is no one more competent to guide the State than my daughter." Her brother, who was given to riding his elephant through the bazaar and showering the crowds with coins, ruled ineptly for seven months before the ministers relented and put Raziya on the throne.

A chronicler who knew her explained why this able ruler lasted less than four years (r. 1236–1240):

Dijinguere Ber Mosque in Timbuktu Built almost entirely of earth and organic materials, this fourteenth-century mosque can accommodate 2,000 worshipers. Mansa Kankan Musa, the most famous ruler of the Mali Empire, is said to have paid Abu Ishaq al-Sahili, a native of Granada in Muslim Spain, 200 kilograms of gold for designing this masterful combination of Islamic and African traditions.

Nik Wheeler/Corbis

369

Personal Styles of Rule in India and Mali

Ibn Battuta wrote vivid descriptions of the powerful men who dominated the Muslim states he visited. Although his accounts are explicitly about the rulers, they also raise important issues about rulers' relations with their subjects. The following account of Sultan Muhammad ibn Tughluq of Delhi may be read as a treatise on the rights and duties of rulers and ways in which individual personalities shaped diverse governing styles.

Muhammad is a man who, above all others, is fond of making presents and shedding blood. There may always be seen at his gate some poor person becoming rich, or some living one condemned to death. His generous and brave actions, and his cruel and violent deeds, have obtained notoriety among the people. In spite of this, he is the most humble of men, and the one who exhibits the greatest equity. The ceremonies of religion are dear to his ears, and he is very severe in respect of prayer and the punishment which follows its neglect. . . .

When drought prevailed throughout India and Sind, . . . the Sultan gave orders that provisions for six months should be supplied to all the inhabitants of Delhi from the royal granaries. . . . The officers of justice made registers of the people of the different streets, and these being sent up, each person received sufficient provisions to last him for six months.

The Sultan, notwithstanding all I have said about his humility, his justice, his kindness to the poor, and his boundless generosity, was much given to bloodshed. It rarely happened that the corpse of some one who had been killed was not seen at the gate of his palace. I have often seen men killed and their bodies left there. One day I went to his palace and my horse shied. I looked before me, and I saw a white heap on the ground, and when I asked what it was, one of my companions said it was the trunk of a man cut into three pieces. The sovereign punished little faults like great ones, and spared neither the learned, the religious, nor the noble. Every day hundreds of individuals were brought chained into his hall of audience; their hands tied to their necks and their feet bound together. Some of them were killed, and others were tortured, or well beaten. . . .

The Sultan has a brother named Masud Khan, [who] was one of the handsomest fellows I have ever seen. The king suspected him of intending to rebel, so he questioned him, and, under fear of the torture, Masud confessed the charge. Indeed, every one who denies charges of this nature, which the Sultan brings against him, is put to the torture, and most people prefer death to being tortured. The Sultan had his brother's head cut off in the palace, and the corpse, according to custom, was left neglected for three days in the same place. The mother of Masud had been stoned two years before in the same place on a charge of debauchery or adultery. . . .

One of the most serious charges against this Sultan is that he forced all the inhabitants of Delhi to leave their homes. [After] the people of Delhi wrote letters full of insults and invectives against [him,] the Sultan . . . decided to ruin Delhi, so he purchased all the houses and inns from the inhabitants, paid them the price, and then ordered them to remove to Daulatabad. . . .

The greater part of the inhabitants departed, but [h]is slaves found two men in the streets: one was paralyzed, the other blind. They were brought before the sovereign, who ordered the paralytic to be shot away from a *manjanik* [catapult], and the blind man to be dragged from Delhi to Daulatabad, a journey of forty days' distance. The poor wretch fell to pieces during the journey, and only one of his legs reached Daulatabad. All of the inhabitants of Delhi left; they abandoned their baggage and their merchandize, and the city remained a perfect desert.

A person in whom I felt confidence assured me that the Sultan mounted one evening upon the roof of his palace, and, casting his eyes over the city of Delhi, in which there was neither fire, smoke, nor light, he said, "Now my heart is satisfied, and my feelings are appeased." . . . When we entered this capital, we found it in the state which has been described. It was empty, abandoned, and had but a small population.

Sultan Raziya was a great monarch. She was wise, just, and generous, a benefactor to her kingdom, a dispenser of justice, the protector of her subjects, and the leader of her armies. She was endowed with all the qualities befitting a king, but she was not born of the right sex, and so in the estimation of men all these virtues were worthless. May God have mercy upon her![2]

Doing her best to prove herself a proper king, Raziya dressed like a man and led her troops atop an elephant. In the end, however, the Turkish chiefs imprisoned her; she escaped, but was killed by a robber soon afterward.

After a half century of stagnation and rebellion, the ruthless but efficient policies of Sultan Ala-ud-din Khalji (uh-LAH–uh–DEEN KAL-jee) (r. 1296–1316) increased control over the empire's outlying provinces. Successful frontier raids and high taxes filled his treasury, wage and price controls in Delhi kept down the cost of maintaining a large army, and a network of spies stifled intrigue. When a Mongol threat from Central Asia eased, Ala-ud-din's forces marched southward, capturing the rich trading state of **Gujarat** (goo-juh-RAHT) in 1298 and then briefly seizing the southern tip of the Indian peninsula.

Gujarat Region of western India famous for trade and manufacturing; the inhabitants are called Gujaratis.

[2]Minhaju-s Siraj, Tabakat-i Nasiri, in ibid., 2:332–333.

In his description of Mansa Suleiman of Mali in 1353, Ibn Battuta places less emphasis on personality, a difference that may only be due to the fact that he had little personal contact with him. He stresses the huge social distance between the ruler and the ruled, between the master and the slave, and goes on to tell more of the ways in which Islam had altered life in Mali's cities; he also complains about customs that the introduction of Islam had not changed.

It happened that Mansa Suleiman, the Sultan of Mali, a most avaricious and worthless man, made a feast by way of kindness. I was present at the entertainment with some of our theologians. When the assembly broke up, I saluted him, having been brought to his knowledge by the theologians. When I had left the place he sent me a meal, which he forwarded to the house of the Judge. Upon this occasion the Judge came walking hastily to me, and said: Up, for the Sultan has sent you a present. I hastened, expecting that a dress of honour, some horses, and other valuables, had been sent; but, behold! they were only three crusts of bread, with a piece of fried fish, and a dish of sour milk. I smiled at their simplicity, and the great value they set on such trifles as these. I stayed here, after this meal, two months; but saw nothing from him, although I had often met him in their friendly meetings. I one day, however, rose up in his presence, and said: I have travelled the world over, and have seen its kings; and now, I have been four months in thy territories, but no present, or even provision from thee, has yet reached me. Now, what shall I say of thee, when I shall be interrogated on the subject hereafter? Upon this, he gave me a house for my accommodation, with suitable provisions. After this, the theologians visited me in the month of Ramadan, and, out of their whole number, they gave me three and thirty methkals of gold. Of all people, the blacks debase themselves most in the presence of their king: for when any one of them is called upon to appear before him, he will immediately put off his usual clothing, and put on a worn-out dress, with a dirty cap; he will then enter the presence like a beggar, with his clothes lifted up to the middle of his legs; he will then beat the ground with both his elbows, and remain in the attitude of a person performing a prostration. When the Sultan addresses one of them, he will take up the garment off his back, and throw dust upon his head; and, as long as the Sultan speaks, every one present will remain with his turban taken off. One of the best things in these parts is, the regard they pay to justice; for, in this respect, the Sultan regards neither little nor much. The safety, too, is very great; so that a traveller may proceed alone among them, without the least fear of a thief or robber. Another of their good properties is, that when a merchant happens to die among them, they will make no effort to get possession of his property: but will allow the lawful successors to it to take it. Another is, their constant custom of attending prayers with the congregation; for unless one makes haste, he will find no place left to say his prayers in. Another is, their insisting on the Koran's being committed to memory: for if a man finds his son defective in this, he will confine him till he is quite perfect, nor will he allow him his liberty until he is so. As to their bad practices, they will exhibit their little daughters, as well as their male and female slaves, quite naked. In the same manner will the women enter into the presence of the King, which his own daughters will also do. Nor do the free women ever clothe themselves till after marriage.

QUESTIONS FOR ANALYSIS

1. How would the actions of these rulers have enhanced their authority? To what extent do their actions reflect Islamic influences?

2. Although Ibn Battuta tells what the rulers did, can you imagine how one of their subjects would have described his or her perception of the same events and customs?

3. Which parts of Ibn Battuta's descriptions seem to be objective and believable? Which parts are more reflective of his personal values?

Sources: First selection from Henry M. Elliot, *The History of India as Told by Its Own Historians* (London: Trübner and Co., 1869–1871) 3:611–614. Second selection as seen in *The Travels of Ibn Battuta in the Near East, Asia and Africa, 1325–1354*, translated and edited by Rev. Samuel Lee, 2004, pp. 239–240.

SECTION REVIEW

- Islam spread into western sub-Saharan Africa usually by peaceful conversion through trading contacts.

- Founded by Sundiata, Mali depended on agriculture and control of trade routes, and Islam spread among its elites.

- Mali reached its height under Mansa Kankan Musa but declined after the death of his successor, and power shifted eastward.

- Muslim invaders from Afghanistan conquered much of Hindu northern India to establish the Delhi Sultanate.

- The sultanate grew to encompass most of India; the sultans ruled through force, pillage, and heavy taxation.

- Though efficient, the sultanate suffered from internal struggles and fell under pressure from rival states and invaders.

Sultan Muhammad ibn Tughluq (TOOG-look) (r. 1325–1351) (see Diversity and Dominance: Personal Styles of Rule in India and Mali) enlarged the sultanate to its greatest extent at the expense of the independent Indian states but balanced his aggressive policy with religious toleration. He even attended Hindu religious festivals. However, his successor, Firuz Shah (fuh-ROOZ shah) (r. 1351–1388), alienated powerful Hindus by taxing the Brahmin elite. Muslim chroniclers praised him for constructing forty mosques, thirty colleges, and a hundred hospitals.

A small minority in a giant land, the Delhi sultans relied on force to keep their subjects submissive, on military reprisals to put down rebellion, and on pillage and high taxes to sustain the ruling elite in luxury and power. The sultanate never escaped the disadvantage of foreign origins and alien religious identity, but some sultans did incorporate a few Hindus into their administrations, and

Minakshi Temple, Madurai, India Some 15,000 pilgrims a day visit the large Hindu temple of Minakshi (the fish-eyed goddess) in the ancient holy city of Madurai in India's southeastern province of Tamil Nadu. The temple complex dates from at least 1000 C.E., although the elaborately painted statues of these gopuram (gate towers) have been rebuilt and restored many times. The largest gopura rises 150 feet (46 meters) above the ground.

some members of the Muslim elite married women from prominent Hindu families, though the brides had to convert to Islam.

Personal and religious rivalries within the Muslim elite, along with Hindu discontent, threatened the Delhi Sultanate whenever it showed weakness and finally hastened its end. In the mid-fourteenth century, Muslim nobles challenged the sultan's dominion and established the independent Bahmani **(bah-MAHN-ee)** kingdom (1347–1482) on the Deccan Plateau. Defending against the southward push of Bahmani armies, the Hindu states of south India united to form the Vijayanagar **(vee-JAY-yah-nah-GAR)** Empire (1336–1565), which at its height controlled rich trading ports on both coasts of south India and held Ceylon as a tributary state.

Hindu Vijayanagar and the Muslim Bahmani state turned a blind eye to religious differences when doing so favored their interests. Bahmani rulers sought to balance Muslim domination by incorporating Hindu leaders into the government, marrying Hindu wives, and appointing Brahmins to high offices. Vijayanagar rulers hired Muslim horsemen and archers to strengthen their military forces and formed an alliance with the Muslim-ruled state of Gujarat.

By 1351, when all of south India had cast off Delhi's rule, much of north India rose in rebellion. In the east, Bengal broke away from the sultanate in 1338. In the west, Gujarat regained its independence by 1390. The weakening of Delhi's central authority tempted fresh Mongol interest in the area. In 1398, the Turko-Mongol leader Timur (see Chapter 13) captured the city of Delhi. When his armies withdrew the next year with vast quantities of loot and tens of thousands of captives, the largest city in southern Asia lay empty and in ruins. The Delhi Sultanate never recovered.

For all its shortcomings, the Delhi Sultanate triggered the development of centralized political authority in India. Prime ministers and provincial governors serving under the sultans established a bureaucracy, improved food production, promoted trade, and put in circulation a common coinage. Despite the many conflicts that Muslim conquest and rule provoked, Islam gradually acquired a permanent place in South Asia.

INDIAN OCEAN TRADE

When the collapse of the Mongol Empire in the fourteenth century disrupted overland routes across Central Asia, the Indian Ocean assumed greater strategic importance in tying together the peoples of Eurasia and Africa. Between 1200 and 1500, the volume of trade in the Indian Ocean increased. The Indian Ocean routes also facilitated the spread of Islam.

Monsoon Mariners

The prosperity of Islamic and Mongol empires in Asia, cities in Europe, and new kingdoms in Africa and Southeast Asia stimulated and contributed to the vitality of the Indian Ocean network. The demand for luxuries—precious metals and jewels, rare spices, fine textiles, and other manufactures—rose. Larger ships made shipments of bulk cargoes of ordinary cotton textiles, pepper, food grains (rice, wheat, barley), timber, horses, and other goods profitable. Some goods were transported from one end of this trading network to the other, but few ships or crews made a complete circuit. Instead, the Indian Ocean trade divided into two legs: from the Middle East across the Arabian Sea to India and from India across the Bay of Bengal to Southeast Asia (see Map 15.4).

The Indian Ocean Dhow

The sailing vessels that crossed the Indian Ocean shared the diversity of that trading area. The name by which we know them, *dhow*, comes from the Swahili language of the East African coast. The planks of teak from which their hulls were constructed were hewn from the tropical forests of south India and Southeast Asia. Their pilots, who navigated by stars at night, employed techniques that Arabs had used to find their way across the desert. Some pilots used a magnetic compass, which originated in China.

Dhows came in various sizes and designs, but all had two distinctive features in common. The first was hull construction. The hulls of dhows consisted of planks that were sewn together, not nailed. Cord made of fiber from the husk of coconuts or other materials was passed through rows of holes drilled in the planks. Because cord is weaker than nails, outsiders considered this shipbuilding technique strange. Marco Polo fancifully suggested that it indicated sailors' fear that large ocean magnets would pull any nails out of their ships. Better explanations observe that pliant sewn hulls were cheaper to build than rigid nailed hulls and were less likely to be damaged if the ships ran aground on coral reefs.

The second distinctive feature of dhows was their sails made of palm leaves or cotton. Sails that were either triangular (lateen) or had a very short leading edge were suspended from tall masts and could be turned to catch the wind.

Sewn hulls and lateen sails had appeared centuries earlier, but two innovations appeared between 1200 and 1500. First, a rudder positioned at the stern (rear end) of the ship replaced the large side oar that formerly had controlled steering. Second, shipbuilders increased the size of dhows to accommodate bulkier cargoes.

Dhow This modern model shows the vessel's main features.
SSPL/Getty Images

dhows Characteristic cargo and passenger ships of the Arabian Sea.

Shipyards in ports on the Malabar Coast (southwestern India) and in the Persian Gulf built large numbers of **dhows** (dow), the characteristic cargo and passenger ships of the Arabian Sea. They grew from an average capacity of 100 tons in 1200 to 400 tons in 1500. On a typical expedition, a dhow might sail west from India to Arabia and Africa on the northeast monsoon winds (December to March) and return on the southwest monsoons (April to August). Small dhows kept the coast in sight. Relying on the stars to guide them, skilled pilots steered large vessels by the quicker route straight across the water. A large dhow could sail from the Red Sea to mainland Southeast Asia in two to four months, but few did so. Eastbound cargoes and passengers from dhows reaching India were likely to be transferred to junks, which dominated the eastern half of the Indian Ocean and the South China Sea (see Environment and Technology: The Indian Ocean Dhow).

Junks, the largest, most technologically advanced, and most seaworthy vessels of the time, appeared first in China and spread as a part of Chinese overseas culture. Enormous nails held together hulls of heavy spruce or fir planks, in contrast with dhows, whose planks were sewn together with palm fiber. Below the deck, watertight compartments minimized flooding in case of damage to the ship's hull. The largest junks reportedly had twelve sails made of bamboo strips woven into mats and carried a crew of a thousand men, including four hundred soldiers. A large junk might accommodate a hundred passenger cabins and a cargo of over 1,000 tons. Junks dominated China's foreign shipping to Southeast Asia and India, but the Chinese did not control all of the junks that plied these waters. During the fifteenth century, similar vessels came out of shipyards in Bengal and Southeast Asia to be sailed by local crews.

Swahili Coast East African shores of the Indian Ocean between the Horn of Africa and the Zambezi River; from the Arabic *sawahil*, meaning "shores."

Decentralized and cooperative commercial interests, rather than political authorities, connected the several regions that participated in the Indian Ocean trade. The **Swahili** (swah-HEE-lee) **Coast** supplied ivory, wood, and gold from inland areas of Africa, while ports around

373

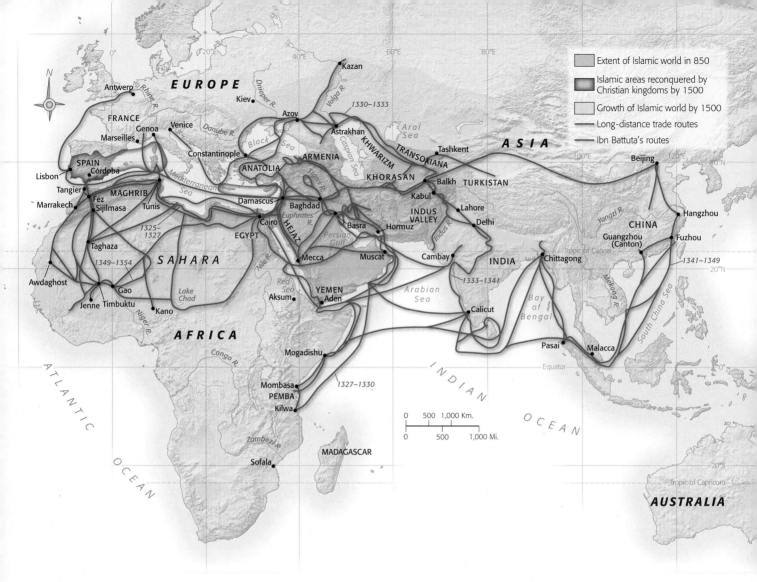

MAP 15.4 **Arteries of Trade and Travel in the Islamic World, to 1500** Ibn Battuta's journeys across Africa and Asia made use of land and sea routes along which Muslim traders and the Islamic faith had long traveled. © Cengage Learning

the Arabian peninsula supplied horses, incense, and manufactured goods from the Mediterranean region. Merchants in the cities of coastal India received goods from east and west, sold some locally, passed others along, and added Indian goods to the trade. The Strait of Malacca (meh-LAK-eh), between the eastern end of the Indian Ocean and the South China Sea, provided a meeting point for trade from Southeast Asia, China, and the Indian Ocean. In each region, certain ports functioned as giant emporia, consolidating goods from smaller ports and inland areas for transport across the seas.

Africa: The Swahili Coast and Zimbabwe

Trade expanded steadily along the East African coast from about 1250, giving rise to between thirty and forty separate city-states by 1500. After 1200, masonry buildings as much as four stories high replaced mud and thatch dwellings, and archaeological findings include Chinese porcelain, imported glass beads, and other exotic goods. Coastal and island peoples shared a common culture and a language built on African grammar and vocabulary but enriched with many Arabic and Persian terms and written in Arabic script. In time, these people became known as "Swahili," from the Arabic word *sawahil* (suh-WAH-hil), meaning "shores."

Great Zimbabwe City, now in ruins (in the modern African country of Zimbabwe), whose many stone structures were built between about 1250 and 1450, when it was a trading center and the capital of a large state.

What attracted the Arab and Iranian merchants whom oral traditions associate with the Swahili Coast's commercial expansion? By the late fifteenth century, the major port of Kilwa, described by Ibn Battuta as "one of the most beautiful and well-constructed towns in the world," was annually exporting a ton of gold mined by inland Africans much farther south. Much of it came from or passed through a powerful state on the plateau south of the Zambezi River. At its peak in about 1400, its capital city, now known as **Great Zimbabwe**, occupied 193 acres (78 hectares) and had some eighteen thousand inhabitants.

Royal Enclosure, Great Zimbabwe Inside these oval stone walls the rulers of the trading state of Great Zimbabwe lived. Forced to enter the enclosure through a narrow corridor between two high walls, visitors were meant to be awestruck.

Between about 1250 and 1450, local African craftsmen built stone structures for Great Zimbabwe's rulers, priests, and wealthy citizens. The largest structure, an enclosure the size and shape of a large football stadium with walls of unmortared stone 17 feet (5 meters) thick and 32 feet (10 meters) high, served as the king's court. A large conical stone tower was among the many buildings inside the walls.

As in Mali, mixed farming and cattle herding provided the economic basis of the Great Zimbabwe state, but long-distance trade brought added wealth. Trade began regionally with copper ingots from the upper Zambezi Valley, salt, and local manufactures. Gold exports to the coast expanded in the fourteenth and fifteenth centuries and brought Zimbabwe to its peak. However, historians suspect that the city's residents depleted nearby forests for firewood while their cattle overgrazed surrounding grasslands. The resulting ecological crisis hastened the empire's decline in the fifteenth century.

Arabia: Aden and the Red Sea

Aden Port city in the modern south Arabian country of Yemen. It has been a major trading center in the Indian Ocean since ancient times.

The city of **Aden** (ADD-en) near the southwestern tip of the Arabian peninsula had a double advantage in the Indian Ocean trade. Monsoon winds brought enough rainfall to supply drinking water to a large population and grow grain for export, and its location made it a convenient stopover for trade with India, the Persian Gulf, East Africa, and Egypt. Aden's merchants dealt in cotton cloth and beads from India; spices from Southeast Asia; horses from Arabia and Ethiopia; pearls from the Red Sea; manufactured luxuries from Cairo; slaves, gold, and ivory from Ethiopia; and grain, opium, and dyes from Aden's own hinterland.

Common commercial interests generally promoted good relations among the different religions and cultures of this region. For example, in the mid-thirteenth century, a wealthy Jew from Aden named Yosef settled in Christian Ethiopia, where he acted as an adviser. South Arabia had been trading with neighboring parts of Africa since before the time of King Solomon of Israel. The dynasty that ruled Ethiopia after 1270 boasted (legendary) descent from Solomon and the Queen of Sheba from across the Red Sea. Ethiopia's Solomonic dynasty greatly increased trade through the Red Sea port of Zeila (ZAY-luh), including slaves, amber, and animal pelts, which went to Aden and on to other destinations.

Friction sometimes arose, however. In the late fifteenth century, Ethiopia's territorial expansion and efforts to increase control over the trade provoked conflicts with Muslims who ruled the coastal states of the Red Sea.

India: Gujarat and the Malabar Coast

The state of Gujarat in western India prospered from the expanding trade of the Arabian Sea and the rise of the Delhi Sultanate. Blessed with a rich agricultural hinterland and a long coastline, Gujarat attracted new trade after the Mongol destruction of Baghdad in 1258 disrupted the northern land routes. Despite the violence of its forced incorporation into the Delhi Sultanate in 1298, Gujarat prospered from increased commercial interaction with Delhi's ruling class. Independent again after 1390, the Muslim rulers of Gujarat extended their control over neighboring Hindu states and regained their preeminent position in the Indian Ocean trade.

Gujaratis exported cotton textiles and indigo to the Middle East and Europe in return for gold and silver. They also shipped cotton cloth, carnelian beads, and foodstuffs to the Swahili Coast in exchange for ebony, slaves, ivory, and gold. During the fifteenth century, Gujarat's trade zone expanded eastward to the Strait of Malacca. There Gujarati merchants helped spread the Islamic faith among East Indian traders, some of whom even imported specially carved gravestones from Gujarat.

Unlike Kilwa and Aden, Gujarat manufactured goods for trade. According to the thirteenth-century Venetian traveler Marco Polo, Gujarat's leatherworkers dressed enough skins in a year to fill several ships to Arabia and other places. They made sleeping mats for export to the Middle East "in red and blue leather, exquisitely inlaid with figures of birds and beasts, and skillfully embroidered with gold and silver wire," as well as leather cushions embroidered in gold.

Later observers compared the Gujarati city of Cambay (modern name Khambhat) with cities in Flanders and northern Italy (see Chapter 14) in the scale, craftsmanship, and diversity of its textile industries. Cotton, linen, and silk cloth, along with carpets and quilts, found a large market in Europe, Africa, the Middle East, and Southeast Asia. Cambay also produced polished gemstones, gold jewelry, carved ivory, stone beads, and both pearls and mother of pearl. At the height of its prosperity in the fifteenth century, its well-laid-out streets and open places boasted fine stone houses with tiled roofs. Although Muslim residents controlled most Gujarati overseas trade, its Hindu merchant caste profited so much from related commercial activities that their wealth and luxurious lives became the envy of other Indians.

More southerly cities on the well-watered western coast of India, called the Malabar Coast, imitated Gujarat's success. Calicut (KAL-ih-cut) (modern name Kozhikode) and other coastal cities prospered from locally woven cotton textiles and locally grown grains and spices. They also served as clearing-houses for the long-distance trade of the Indian Ocean. The Zamorin (ZAH-much-ruhn) (ruler) of Calicut presided over a loose federation of its Hindu rulers that united the coastal region, but steep mountains known as the Western Ghats cut the coast off from the inland areas on the Deccan Plateau. As in eastern Africa and Arabia, rulers generally tolerated religious and ethnic groups who contributed to commercial profits. Most trading activity lay in the hands of Muslims, many originally from Iran and Arabia, who intermarried with local Indian Muslims. Jewish merchants also operated from Malabar's trading cities.

Southeast Asia

At the eastern end of the Indian Ocean, the Strait of Malacca between the Malay Peninsula and the island of Sumatra provided the principal passage into the South China Sea (see Map 15.3). As trade increased in the fourteenth and fifteenth centuries, this commercial choke point became the site of political rivalry.

The mainland kingdom of Siam controlled most of the upper Malay Peninsula, while the Java-based kingdom of Majapahit (mah-jah-PAH-heet) extended its dominion over the lower Malay Peninsula and much of Sumatra. Majapahit, however, could not suppress a nest of Chinese pirates based at the Sumatran city of Palembang (pah-lem-BONG) who preyed on ships sailing through the strait. In 1407, a fleet from China commanded by the admiral Zheng He (see Chapter 13) smashed the pirates' power and took their chief back home for trial.

Majapahit, weakened by internal struggles, could not take advantage of China's intervention, making the chief beneficiary the newer port of **Malacca** (or Melaka), which dominated the narrowest part of the strait. Under a prince from Palembang, Malacca had grown from an obscure fishing village into an important port through a series of astute alliances. Nominally subject to the king of Siam, Malacca also secured an alliance with China that was sealed by the visit of the imperial fleet in 1407. The conversion of an early ruler from Hinduism to Islam helped promote trade with Muslim merchants from Gujarat and elsewhere. Merchants also appreciated Malacca's security and low taxes.

Malacca served not just as a meeting point but also as an emporium for Southeast Asian products: rubies and musk from Burma, tin from Malaya, gold from Sumatra, cloves and nutmeg from the Moluccas (or Spice Islands, as Europeans later dubbed them). Shortly after 1500, when Malacca was at its height, one resident counted eighty-four languages spoken among the merchants gathered there, who came from as far away as Turkey, Ethiopia, and the Swahili Coast. Four officials administered the foreign merchant communities: one for the Gujaratis, one for other Indians and Burmese, one for Southeast Asians, and one for the Chinese and Japanese. Malacca's wealth and its cosmopolitan residents set the standard for luxury in Malaya for centuries to come.

Malacca Port city in the modern Southeast Asian country of Malaysia, founded about 1400 as a trading center on the Strait of Malacca.

SECTION REVIEW

- Traversed by dhows and junks, the maritime trade network of the Indian Ocean tied together peoples of Asia, Africa, and Europe.

- Decentralized commercial interests rose throughout the network, including the Swahili city-states that exported African gold from Great Zimbabwe.

- Aden dealt in a variety of goods from Africa, Arabia, and Southeast Asia and traded with Zeila on the Red Sea.

- Despite political turmoil, the cities of Gujarat and the Malabar Coast prospered through agriculture, manufacture, and trade.

- Through astute alliances, Malacca grew into the predominant emporium of Southeast Asia.

SOCIAL AND CULTURAL CHANGE

State growth, commercial expansion, and the spread of Islam between 1200 and 1500 led to changes in the society and cultural life of numerous peoples. Muslim political and commercial elites grew in numbers and power, and religious agents sought converts both within and beyond the boundaries of Muslim states. Yet Africa and India saw many and diverse instances of local art traditions, rituals, and even theological doctrines being combined with those of Islam to form syncretic religious formations, often in the guise of Sufi brotherhoods, reminiscent of the syncretism of the Hellenistic period (see Chapter 5).

Architecture, Learning, and Religion

Social and cultural changes typically affected cities more than rural areas. As travelers often observed, wealthy merchants and ruling elites spent lavishly on mansions, palaces, and places of worship while the lives of common people were less affected. Most mosques, local pilgrimage sites, and Sufi shrines surviving from this period blend older traditions and new influences. African Muslims produced Middle Eastern mosque designs in local building materials: sun-baked clay reinforced by wooden crossbeams in the western Sudan, masonry using blocks of coral on the Swahili Coast. Hindu temple architecture influenced, and sometimes provided material for, Muslim places of worship not only in newly Islamized regions like Gujarat, but also in older Muslim lands like Afghanistan and Iran that South Asian artisans were free to travel to once their homelands came under Muslim rule.

The congregational mosque at Cambay, built in 1325, utilized pillars, porches, and arches taken from sacked Hindu and Jain **(jine)** temples. The congregational mosque erected at the Gujarati capital of Ahmadabad **(AH-muhd-ah-bahd)** in 1423 had the open courtyard typical of mosques everywhere, but the surrounding verandas incorporated many Gujarati details and architectural conventions.

Mosques, churches, and temples were centers of education as well as prayer and ritual. Muslims promoted literacy among their sons (and sometimes their daughters) so that they could read sacred texts. In some lands south of the Sahara, Ethiopia excepted, Islam provided the first exposure to literate culture. In much of South Asia, literacy in Indo-European languages like Sanskrit and Dravidian languages like Tamil had been established many centuries before. Even there, however, a migration of Arabic and Persian vocabulary into local languages produced significant changes. Scholars adapted the Arabic alphabet to write local languages like Hausa in Mali and numerous tongues in the Malay Peninsula and island Southeast Asia.

Urdu A Persian-influenced literary form of Hindi written in Arabic characters and used as a literary language since the 1300s.

Persian became the court language of the Delhi sultanate, but **Urdu (ER-doo)**, a Persian-influenced form of the local Hindustani tongue of northern India, eventually became an important literary language written in Arabic characters. Muslims also introduced paper into their new lands. Although this was an improvement over palm leaves and other fragile materials, tropical humidity and insect life nevertheless made preservation of written knowledge difficult.

Timbuktu City on the Niger River in the modern country of Mali. It was founded by the Tuareg as a seasonal camp sometime after 1000. As part of the Mali Empire, Timbuktu became a major terminus of the trans-Saharan trade and a center of Islamic learning.

Muslim scholars everywhere studied the Quran along with Islamic law and theology. A few demonstrated a high level of interest in mathematics, medicine, science, and philosophy, partly derived from ancient Greek writings translated into Arabic (see Chapter 10). In sixteenth-century **Timbuktu** (see Map 15.2), over 150 schools taught the Quran while leading clerics taught advanced classes in mosques or homes. Books imported from North Africa brought high prices. Al-Hajj Ahmed, a scholar who died in Timbuktu in 1536, possessed some seven hundred volumes, an unusually large library for that time. In Southeast Asia, Malacca became a center of Islamic learning from which scholars spread Islam throughout the region. Some of the most influential scholars made the pilgrimage to Mecca and studied there before returning home to teach others. Other important centers of learning developed in Muslim India, particularly in Delhi, the capital.

Even in lands seized by conquest, Muslim rulers seldom required conversion. Example and persuasion by merchants and Sufis proved more effective in winning new believers. Muslim domination of long-distance trade assisted the adoption of Islam. Commercial transactions could take place across religious boundaries, but the common code of morality and law that Islam provided encouraged trust and drew many local merchants to Islam. From the major trading centers along the Swahili Coast, in the Sudan, in coastal India, and in Southeast Asia, Islam's influence spread along regional trade routes.

Islam also spread among rural peoples, such as the pastoral Fulani of West Africa and the Somali of northeastern Africa. In Bengal, Muslim religious figures working for state officials oversaw the conversion of jungle into rice paddies and thereby gained converts among the people who came to work the land and inhabit the new villages. At first the new converts melded Islamic beliefs with Hindu traditions, seeing Muhammad, for example, as a manifestation of the god Vishnu. Over time, however, more standard versions of Islam gained headway.

Marriage also played a role. Single Muslim men traveling to and settling in tropical Africa and Asia often married local women. Their children grew up in the paternal faith because Islamic doctrine specified the transmission of religious identity in the male line. Some wealthy men had dozens of children from up to four wives and additional slave concubines. Servants and slaves in such households normally professed Islam.

In India, Muslim invasions eliminated the last strongholds of long-declining Buddhism, including, in 1196, the great Buddhist center of study at Nalanda (nuh-LAN-duh) in Bihar (bee-HAHR). Its manuscripts were burned and thousands of monks killed or driven into exile in Nepal and Tibet. With Buddhism reduced to a minor faith in the land of its birth, Islam emerged as India's second most important religion. Islam displaced Hinduism as the elite religion in most of maritime Southeast Asia and slowly supplanted a variety of local cults. In mainland Southeast Asia, Buddhism and Islam vied for supremacy, with Islam prevailing in the south and Buddhism prevailing farther north in Thailand, Cambodia, and Burma (Myanmar).

Social and Gender Distinctions

A growth in slavery accompanied the rising prosperity of the elites. Military campaigns in India, according to Islamic sources, reduced hundreds of thousands of Hindu "infidels" to slavery. Delhi overflowed with slaves. Sultan Ala-ud-din owned 50,000 and Firuz Shah 180,000, including 12,000 skilled artisans. Sultan Tughluq sent 100 male slaves and 100 female slaves as a gift to the emperor of China in return for a similar gift.

When African awareness of the value of gold in Mediterranean lands cut into the profitability of trans-Saharan trade, Mali and Bornu sent slaves across the Sahara to North Africa. The expanding Ethiopian Empire regularly sent captives for sale to Aden traders at Zeila. Many eunuchs (castrated males) were included in this trade. According to modern estimates, Saharan and Red Sea traders sold about 2.5 million enslaved Africans between 1200 and 1500. African slaves from the Swahili Coast played conspicuous roles in the navies, armies, and administrations of some Indian states, especially in the fifteenth century. A few African slaves even reached China, where a source from about 1225 says rich families preferred gatekeepers with bodies "black as lacquer." Later Chinese paintings show Portuguese ships manned almost entirely by African seamen.

With "free" labor abundant and cheap, few slaves worked as farmers. In some places, hereditary castes of slaves dominated certain trades and military units. Indeed, the rulers of the Delhi Sultanate included a number of mamluks, or Turkic military slaves (see Chapter 10). A slave general in the western Sudan named Askia Muhammad seized control of the Songhai Empire (Mali's successor) in 1493. Less fortunate slaves, like the men and women who mined copper in Mali, did hard menial work.

Wealthy households used many slave servants. Eunuchs guarded the harems of wealthy Muslims, but women predominated as household slaves, serving also as entertainers and concubines. Some rich men aspired to having a concubine from every part of the world. One of Firuz Shah's nobles reportedly had two thousand harem slaves, including women from Turkey and China.

Hindu legal digests and commentaries suggest that the position of Hindu women may have improved somewhat compared to earlier periods. The ancient practice of sati (suh-TEE)—that is, of an upper-caste widow throwing herself on her husband's funeral pyre—remained a meritorious act strongly approved by social custom. But Ibn Battuta makes it clear that sati was strictly optional. Since the Hindu commentaries devote considerable attention to the rights of widows without sons to inherit their husbands' estates, one may even conclude that sati was exceptional.

Indian parents still gave their daughters in marriage before the age of puberty, but consummation of the marriage took place only when the young woman was ready. Wives faced far stricter rules of fidelity and chastity than their husbands and could be abandoned for any serious breach. But other offenses against law and custom usually brought lighter penalties than for men. A woman's male master—father, husband, or owner—determined her status. Women seldom played active roles in commerce, administration, or religion. Differences between Muslims and Hindus on matters relating to gender were not as great as the formal religious texts of the two religious traditions would suggest. South Asian tradition tended to outweigh Muslim practices imported from Arabia and Persia.

African Islam showed similar inclinations in the area of gender. In Mali's capital, Ibn Battuta was appalled that Muslim women both free and slave did not completely cover their bodies and veil their faces when appearing in public. He considered their nakedness an offense to women's (and men's) modesty. Elsewhere in Mali, he berated a Muslim merchant from Morocco for permitting his wife to sit on a couch and chat with her male friend. The husband replied, "The association of women with men is agreeable to us and part of good manners, to which no suspicion attaches." Ibn Battuta refused to visit the merchant again.

Besides child rearing, women involved themselves with food preparation and, when not prohibited by religious restrictions, brewing. In many parts of Africa, women commonly made beer from grains or bananas. These mildly alcoholic beverages played an important part in male rituals of hospitality and relaxation.

Throughout tropical Africa and Asia, women did much of the farm work. They also toted home heavy loads of food, firewood, and water balanced on their heads. Other common female activities included making clay pots for cooking and storage and making clothing. In India, the spinning wheel, possibly a local invention, sped up the process of making thread for weaving and thus reduced the cost. Women typically spun at home, leaving weaving to men. In West Africa, women often sold agricultural products, pottery, and other craftwork in the markets.

SECTION REVIEW

- Social and cultural life changed as a result of state formation, commercial expansion, and the spread of Islam.

- These changes mostly affected cities, where elites financed building programs, fostering hybrid styles of religious architecture.

- Islam spread mainly through peaceful adaptation and promoted education and scholarship.

- With rising prosperity came the expansion of slavery, which was endorsed by Islam.

- The position of Indian women seems to have improved, and the spread of Islam did not mean adoption of Arab gender customs.

THE WESTERN HEMISPHERE

Though isolated from the Eastern Hemisphere by oceans that were not crossed until the end of the fifteenth century, the tropical regions of the Western Hemisphere shared many of the climatic characteristics of the Old World tropics (see Chapter 8). However, the region's two most powerful urbanized empires, the Aztec of Mexico and the Inka of Peru, developed at altitudes above 7,000 feet, thus experiencing lower average rainfall and temperature than is common across the tropics. They also differed in being themselves centers of civilization rather than subsidiary to dominating political and economic powers located in temperate lands to the north or south.

Mesoamerica had witnessed a series of urbanized societies—such as the Olmec, Maya, and Toltecs—from the second millennium B.C.E. onward, and the mountains and coastal deserts of the Andean region had an equally long sequence, including Moche, Tiwanaku, Wari, and Chimu. Apart from these advanced regions, which saw the rise of powerful empires between 1300 and 1500 C.E., most Western Hemisphere societies of the period subsisted at more basic levels as hunters and gatherers or village agriculturists.

Mesoamerica: The Aztecs

The Mexica (meh-SHE-ca) were among the northern peoples who pushed into central Mexico in the wake of the Toltec collapse (see Chapter 8). As their power grew through political alliances and military conquest, they created a Mexica-dominated regional power called the Aztec Empire (see Map 15.5). At the time of their arrival the Mexica were organized as an **altepetl** (al-TEH-peh-tel), an ethnic state led by a tlatoani (tlah-toh-AHN-ee) or ruler. The altepetl, the common political building block across the region, directed the collective religious, social, and political obligations of the ethnic group. A group of **calpolli** (cal-POH-yee), each with up to a hundred families, served as the foundation of the altepetl, controlling land allocation, tax collection, and local religious life.

In their new environment the Mexica began to adopt the political and social practices that they found among the urbanized agriculturalists of the valley. At first, they served their more powerful neighbors as serfs and mercenaries. As their strength grew, they relocated to small islands near the shore of Lake Texcoco, and around 1325 C.E. they began the construction of their

altepetl An ethnic state in ancient Mesoamerica, the common political building block of that region.

calpolli A group of up to a hundred families that served as a social building block of an altepetl in ancient Mesoamerica.

MAP 15.5 **Major Meso-american Civilizations, 1000 B.C.E.–1519 C.E.** The Aztec Empire in 1518 was based on military conquest. The Aztec capital of Tenochtitlan was located near the classic era's largest city, Teotihuacan, and Tula, capital city of the post-classic Toltecs. © Cengage Learning

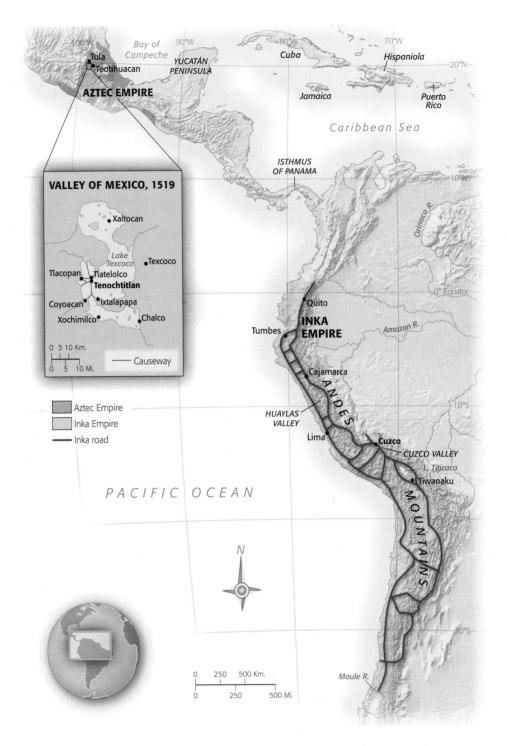

Tenochtitlan Capital of the Aztec Empire, located on an island in Lake Texcoco. Its population was about 125,000 on the eve of Spanish conquest. Mexico City was constructed on its ruins.

Aztecs Also known as Mexica, the Aztecs created a powerful empire in central Mexico (1325–1521 C.E.). They forced defeated peoples to provide goods and labor as a tax.

twin capitals, **Tenochtitlan (teh-noch-TIT-lan)** and Tlatelolco **(tla-teh-LOHL-coh)** (together the foundation for modern Mexico City).

Military successes allowed the Mexica to seize control of additional agricultural land along the lakeshore and to forge military alliances with neighboring altepetl. Once these more complex political and economic arrangements were in place, the Mexica-dominated alliance became the Aztec Empire (see Map 15.5). With increased economic independence, greater political security, and territorial expansion, the **Aztecs** transformed their political organization by introducing a monarchical system similar to that found in more powerful neighboring states and selecting a ruling dynasty with ties to the Toltecs (see Chapter 8). A council of powerful aristocrats selected new rulers from among male members of the ruling lineage. Once selected, the ruler had to renegotiate the submission of tribute dependencies and then demonstrate his divine mandate by undertaking a new round of military conquests. For the Aztecs war was infused with religious meaning, providing the ruler with legitimacy and increasing the prestige of successful warriors.

The Aztecs succeeded in developing a remarkable urban landscape. The population of Tenochtitlan and Tlatelolco combined with that of the cities and towns of the surrounding lakeshore was approximately 500,000 by 1500 C.E. Three causeways connected this island capital to the lakeshore. Planners laid out the urban center as a grid where canals and streets intersected at right angles to facilitate the movement of people and goods.

Although warfare gave increased power and privilege to males, women held substantial power and exercised broad influence in Aztec society. The roles of women and men were clearly distinguished, but women were held in high esteem. Scholars call this "gender complementarity." Following the birth of a boy, his umbilical cord was buried on the battlefield and he was given implements to signal his occupation or his role as a warrior. In the case of a girl, her umbilical cord was buried near the hearth and she was given weaving implements and female clothing. Women dominated the household and the markets, and they also served as teachers and priestesses. They were also seen as the founders of lineages, including the royal line.

Aztec military successes and territorial expansion allowed the warrior elite to seize land and peasant labor as spoils of war. In time, the royal family and highest-ranking members of the aristocracy possessed extensive estates that were cultivated by slaves and landless commoners. The lower classes received some material rewards from imperial expansion but lost most of their ability to influence or control decisions. Some commoners were able to achieve some social mobility through success on the battlefield.

However, by 1500 C.E. great inequalities in wealth and privilege characterized Aztec society. One of the Spaniards who participated in the conquest of the Aztec Empire remembered his first meeting with the Aztec ruler Moctezuma (mock-teh-ZU-ma) II (r. 1502–1520): "Many great lords walked before the great Montezuma [Moctezuma II], sweeping the ground on which he was to tread and laying down cloaks so that his feet should not touch the earth. Not one of these chieftains dared look him in the face."[3] While commoners lived in small dwellings and ate a limited diet of staples, members of the nobility lived in large, well-constructed, two-story houses and consumed a diet rich in animal protein.

A specialized class of merchants controlled long-distance trade. Given the absence of draft animals and wheeled vehicles, lightweight and valuable products like gold, jewels, feathered garments, cacao, and animal skins dominated this commerce. Merchants also provided essential political and military intelligence for the Aztec elite. But although merchants became wealthy and powerful as the Aztecs expanded their empire, they were denied the privileges of the high nobility, which was jealous of its power.

The Aztec state met the challenge of feeding an urban population of approximately 150,000 by efficiently organizing the labor of the calpolli and of additional laborers sent by defeated peoples to expand agricultural land. Aztec chinampas (artificial island gardens) contributed maize, fruits, and vegetables to the markets of Tenochtitlan. The imposition of a **tribute system** on conquered peoples also helped relieve some of the pressure of Tenochtitlan's growing population. Unlike the tribute system of Tang China, where tribute had a more symbolic character (see Chapter 12), one-quarter of the Aztec capital's food requirement was satisfied by tribute payments of maize, beans, and other foods sent by nearby political dependencies.

Like commerce throughout the Mesoamerican world, Aztec commerce was carried on without money and credit. Barter was facilitated by the use of cacao beans, quills filled with gold, and cotton cloth as standard units of value to compensate for differences in the value of bartered goods. Aztec expansion facilitated the integration of producers and consumers in the central Mexican economy. Hernán Cortés (1485–1547), the Spanish adventurer who eventually conquered the Aztecs, expressed his admiration for the abundance of the Aztec marketplace:

> *One square in particular is twice as big as that of Salamanca and completely surrounded by arcades where there are daily more than sixty thousand folk buying and selling. Every kind of merchandise such as may be met with in every land is for sale. . . . There is nothing to be found in all the land which is not sold in these markets, for over and above what I have mentioned there are so many and such various things that on account of their very number . . . I cannot detail them.*[4]

tribute system A system in which defeated peoples were forced to pay a tax in the form of goods and labor. This forced transfer of food, cloth, and other goods subsidized the development of large cities. An important component of the Aztec and Inka economies.

---

[3]Bernal Díaz del Castillo, *The Conquest of New Spain*, trans. J. M. Cohen (London: Penguin Books, 1963), 217.

[4]Hernando Cortés, *Five Letters, 1519–1526*, trans. J. Bayard Morris (New York: Norton, 1991), 87.

Religious rituals dominated public life in Tenochtitlan. Like the other cultures of the Meso-american world, the Aztecs worshiped a large number of gods. Most of these gods had a dual nature—both male and female. The chief god of the Mexica was Huitzilopochtli (**wheat-zeel-oh-POSHT-lee**) or southern hummingbird. Originally associated with war, the Aztecs later identified this god with the Sun. Tenochtitlan was architecturally dominated by a great twin temple devoted to Huitzilopochtli and Tlaloc, the storm-god, symbolizing the two bases of the Aztec economy: war and agriculture.

The Andes: The Inka

Inka Largest and most powerful Andean empire. Controlled the Pacific coast of South America from Ecuador to Chile from its capital of Cuzco.

In little more than a hundred years, the **Inka** developed a vast imperial state, which they called "Land of Four Corners." By 1525 the empire had a population of more than 6 million and stretched from the Maule River in Chile to northern Ecuador, conquered between 1500 and 1525, and from the Pacific coast across the Andes to the upper Amazon and, in the south, into Argentina (see Map 15.5). In the early fifteenth century the Inka were one of many competing military powers in the southern highlands, an area of limited political significance after the collapse of Wari (see Chapter 8). Centered in the valley of Cuzco, the Inka were initially organized as a chiefdom based on reciprocal gift giving and the redistribution of food and textiles. Strong and resourceful leaders consolidated political authority in the 1430s and undertook an ambitious campaign of military expansion.

The Inka state, like earlier highland powers, utilized traditional Andean social customs and economic practices. Tiwanaku had relied in part on the use of colonists to provide supplies of resources from distant, ecologically distinct zones. The Inka built on this legacy by conquering additional distant territories and increasing the scale of forced exchanges. Crucial to this process was the development of a large military. Unlike the peoples of Mesoamerica, who distributed specialized goods through markets and tribute relationships, Andean peoples used state power to broaden and expand the vertical exchange system that had permitted self-governing extended family groups called ayllus to exploit a range of ecological niches (see Chapter 8). Like earlier highland civilizations, the Inka were pastoralists, and their prosperity and military strength depended on vast herds of llamas and alpacas, which provided food and clothing as well as transport for goods. They gained access to corn, cotton, and other goods from the coastal region via forced exchanges.

Collective efforts by mita labor, a system of forced service to the ruler (see Chapter 8), made the Inka Empire possible. Cuzco, the imperial capital, and the provincial cities, the royal court, the imperial armies, and the state's religious cults all rested on this foundation. The mita system also created the material surplus that provided the bare necessities for the old, weak, and ill of Inka society. Each ayllu contributed approximately one-seventh of its adult male population to meet these collective obligations. These draft laborers served as soldiers, construction workers, craftsmen, and runners to carry messages along post roads. They also drained swamps, terraced mountainsides, filled in valley floors, built and maintained irrigation works, and built storage facilities and roads. Inka laborers constructed 13,000 miles (20,930 kilometers) of road, facilitating military troop movements, administration, and trade.

The hereditary chiefs of ayllus, a group that included women, carried out local administrative and judicial functions. As the Inka expanded, they generally left local rulers in place. By doing so they risked rebellion, but they controlled these risks by means of a thinly veiled system of hostage taking and the use of military garrisons. The rulers of defeated regions were required to send their heirs to live at the Inka royal court in Cuzco. Inka leaders even required that defeated peoples send representations of important local gods to Cuzco to be included in the

Werner Forman/Universal Images Group/Getty Images

Inka Tunic Andean weavers produced beautiful textiles from cotton and from the wool of llamas and alpacas. The Inka inherited this rich craft tradition and produced some of the world's most remarkable textiles. The quality and design of each garment indicated the weaver's rank and power in this society. This tunic was an outer garment for a powerful male.

imperial pantheon. These measures promoted imperial integration while at the same time providing hostages to ensure the good behavior of subject peoples.

Conquests magnified the authority of the Inka ruler and led to the creation of an imperial bureaucracy drawn from among his kinsmen. The royal family claimed descent from the Sun, the primary Inka god. Members of the royal family lived in palaces maintained by armies of servants, and their lives were dominated by political and religious rituals that helped legitimize their authority. Among the many obligations associated with kingship was the requirement to extend imperial boundaries by warfare. Thus each new ruler began his reign with conquest.

Tenochtitlan, the Aztec capital, had a population of about 150,000 in 1520. At the height of Inka power in 1530, Cuzco had a population of less than 30,000. Nevertheless, Cuzco was a remarkable place. The Inka were highly skilled stone craftsmen and constructed their most impressive buildings of carefully cut stones fitted together without mortar. Planners laid the city out in the shape of a giant puma (a mountain lion). At the city center were the palaces of rulers as well as the major temples. The richest was the Temple of the Sun, its interior lined with sheets of gold and its patio decorated with golden representations of llamas and corn. The ruler made every effort to awe and intimidate visitors and residents alike with a nearly continuous series of rituals, feasts, and sacrifices. Sacrifices of textiles, animals, and other goods sent as tribute dominated the city's calendar. The destruction of these valuable commodities, and a small number of human sacrifices, helped give the impression of splendor and sumptuous abundance that appeared to demonstrate the ruler's claimed descent from the Sun.

Inka cultural achievement rested on the strong foundation of earlier Andean civilizations. We know that astronomical observation was a central concern of the priestly class, as in Mesoamerica. The collective achievements of Andean peoples were accomplished with a limited record-keeping system adapted from earlier Andean civilizations. Administrators used knotted colored cords, called **khipus** (KEY-pooz), for public administration, population counts, and tribute obligations. Inka weaving and metallurgy, also based on earlier regional development, was more advanced than in Mesoamerica. Inka craftsmen produced utilitarian tools and weapons of copper and bronze as well as decorative objects of gold and silver. Inka women produced textiles of extraordinary beauty from cotton and the wool of llamas and alpacas.

Although the Inka did not introduce new technologies, they increased economic output and added to the region's prosperity. The conquest of large populations in environmentally distinct regions allowed the Inka to multiply the yields produced by the traditional exchanges between distinct ecological niches. This expansion of imperial economic and political power was purchased at the cost of reduced equality and diminished local autonomy. Members of the imperial elite, living in richly decorated palaces in Cuzco and other urban centers, were increasingly distant from the masses of Inka society. Even members of the provincial nobility were held at arm's length from the royal court, while commoners could be executed if they dared to look directly at the ruler's face.

After only a century of regional dominance, the Inka Empire faced a crisis in 1525. The death of the ruler Huayna Capac at the conclusion of the conquest of Ecuador initiated a bloody struggle for the throne. The rivalry of two sons compelled both the professional military and the hereditary Inka elite to choose sides. Civil war was the result. Regionalism and ethnic diversity had always posed a threat to the empire. Now civil war weakened the imperial state and ignited the resentments of conquered peoples on the eve of the arrival of Europeans.

khipus System of knotted colored cords used by preliterate Andean peoples to transmit information.

SECTION REVIEW

- The Western Hemisphere tropics, unlike the temperate zones, were major centers of civilization.

- The Aztecs used conquest, trade, and an extensive irrigation system to build a mighty empire.

- Religion and sacrifice played an important role in Aztec life.

- The Inka relied on forced labor, conquest, and an extensive road system to hold together a diverse empire.

- Vertical exchange of highland products for lowland products benefited everyone in the empire.

CONCLUSION

Tropical Africa and Asia contained 40 percent of the world's population and over a quarter of its habitable land. Between 1200 and 1500, commercial, political, and cultural currents drew the region's peoples closer together. The Indian Ocean became the world's most important and richest trading area; the Delhi Sultanate brought the greatest political unity to India since the decline of the Guptas; and Mali extended the political and trading role pioneered by Ghana in the western Sudan. Trade and empire followed closely the enlargement of Islam's presence and the accompanying diversification of Islamic customs.

Yet many social and cultural practices remained stable. Most tropical Africans and Asians never ventured far outside the rural communities where their families had lived for generations. Their lives followed the patterns of agricultural or pastoral life, the cycle of religious observations, traditional occupational and kinship divisions, and the individual's passage through the stages of life from childhood to elder status. Village communities proved remarkably hardy. They might be ravaged by natural disaster or pillaged by advancing armies, but over time most recovered. Empires and kingdoms rose and fell, but village life endured.

In the Western Hemisphere the powerful empires of the Aztecs and Inka rose in Mesoamerica and the Andean region, respectively. Each was heir to a series of preceding cultures in their area, but they had in common an unprecedented territorial extent. Warfare and religious rituals were hallmarks of both empires, and their success depended on the economic subordination of conquered peoples as well as specialized production in a variety of environmentally distinct regions. The Aztecs excelled at irrigation and trade, the Inka at labor organization and road building.

KEY TERMS

Ibn Battuta p. 361
tropics p. 362
monsoon p. 362
Delhi Sultanate p. 363
Mali p. 366
Mansa Kankan Musa p. 368

Gujarat p. 370
dhows p. 373
Swahili Coast p. 373
Great Zimbabwe p. 374
Aden p. 375
Malacca p. 376

Urdu p. 377
Timbuktu p. 377
altepetl p. 379
calpolli p. 379
Tenochtitlan p. 380
Aztecs p. 380

tribute system p. 381
Inka p. 382
khipus p. 383

SUGGESTED READING

Chaudhuri, K. N. *Asia Before Europe: Economy and Civilization of the Indian Ocean from the Rise of Islam to 1750.* 1991. A broad conceptual approach.

Coedes, G. *The Indianized States of Southeast Asia*, ed. Walter F. Vella. 1968. Remains a basic text in this field.

Connah, Graham. *African Civilizations: Precolonial Cities and States in Tropical Africa: An Archaeological Perspective.* 1987. See especially later chapters.

Davies, Nigel. *The Aztec Empire: The Toltec Resurgence.* 1987. The best summary of Aztec history.

Dunn, Ross E. *The Adventures of Ibn Battuta: A Muslim of the 14th Century.* 1986. Provides a modern retelling of his travels with commentary.

Ehret, Christopher. *The Civilizations of Africa: A History to 1800.* 2002. Chapters 6 and 7 summarize a great deal of new scholarship on Africa in this period.

Lieberman, Victor. *Strange Parallels: Integration on the Mainland, Southeast Asia in Global Context, c. 800–1830.* 2003. Integrates several national histories over a long period.

Lovejoy, Paul E. *Transformations in Slavery: A History of Slavery in Africa*, 2d ed. 2000. See the first two chapters.

Ludden, David. *A Peasant History of South India.* 1985. Presents an intriguing perspective.

Majumdar, R. C., ed. *The History and Culture of the Indian People*, vol. 4, *The Delhi Sultanate*, 2d ed. 1967. A comprehensive coverage of India.

Risso, Patricia. *Merchants and Faith: Muslim Commerce and Culture in the Indian Ocean.* 1995. A fine place to begin.

Rostworoweski de Diez Canseco, María. *History of the Inka Realm*, trans. Harry B. Iceland. 1999. The best modern synthesis of Inka history.

Tarling, Nicholas, ed. *The Cambridge History of Southeast Asia*, vol. 1. 1992. Various authors cover the period from prehistory to 1500 C.E.

Go to the History CourseMate website for primary source links, study tools, and review materials for this chapter.
CourseMate www.cengagebrain.com

Chapter Outline

Global Maritime Expansion Before 1450
➤ *What were the objectives and major accomplishments of the voyages of exploration undertaken by Chinese, Polynesians, and other non-Western peoples?*

European Expansion, 1400–1550
➤ *In this era of long-distance exploration, did Europeans have any special advantages over other cultural regions?*

Encounters with Europe, 1450–1550
➤ *What explains the different nature of Europe's interactions with Africa, India, and the Americas?*

Conclusion

- **ENVIRONMENT + TECHNOLOGY**   Vasco da Gama's Fleet
- **DIVERSITY + DOMINANCE**   Kongo's Christian King

INTERFOTO/Alamy

Ferdinand Magellan Navigating the Straits Connecting the Atlantic and Pacific Oceans   This late-sixteenth-century print uses fanciful representations of native peoples and creatures to embellish Magellan's circumnavigation of the globe.

The Maritime Revolution, to 1550

In 1511 young Ferdinand Magellan sailed from Europe around the southern tip of Africa and eastward across the Indian Ocean as a member of the first Portuguese expedition to explore the East Indies (maritime Southeast Asia). Eight years later, this time in the service of Spain, he led an expedition that sought to reach the East Indies by sailing westward. By the middle of 1521 Magellan's expedition had achieved its goal by sailing across the Atlantic, rounding the southern tip of South America, and crossing the Pacific Ocean—but at a high price.

Of the five ships that had set out from Spain in 1519, only three made the long passage across the vast Pacific. Dozens of sailors died from starvation and disease during the voyage. In the Philippines, Magellan, having survived numerous mutinies during the voyage, died in battle on April 27, 1521, while aiding a local ruler who had promised to become a Christian.

To consolidate their dwindling resources, the expedition's survivors burned the least seaworthy of their remaining three ships and consolidated men and supplies. In the end only the *Victoria* made it home across the Indian Ocean and back to Europe. Nevertheless, the *Victoria*'s return to Spain on September 8, 1522, was a crowning example of Europeans' determination to make themselves masters of the oceans. A century of daring and dangerous voyages backed by the Portuguese crown had opened new routes through the South Atlantic to Africa, Brazil, and the rich trade of the Indian Ocean. Rival voyages sponsored by Spain since 1492 opened new contacts with the American continents. A maritime revolution was under way that would change the course of history.

This new maritime era marked the end of a long period when Asia had initiated most overland and maritime expansion. Asia had been the source of the most useful technologies and the most influential systems of belief. It was also home to the most powerful states and the richest trading networks. The success of Iberian voyages of exploration in the following century would redirect the world's center of power, wealth, and innovation to the West.

This maritime revolution broadened and deepened contacts, alliances, and conflicts across ancient cultural boundaries. Some of these contacts ended tragically for individuals like Magellan. Some proved disastrous for entire populations: Amerindians, for instance, suffered conquest, colonization, and a rapid decline in numbers. And sometimes the results were mixed: Asians and Africans found both risks and opportunities in their new relations with Europe.

GLOBAL MARITIME EXPANSION BEFORE 1450

Since ancient times travel across the world's seas and oceans had been one of the great challenges to technological ingenuity. Ships had to be sturdy enough to survive heavy winds and seas, and pilots had to learn how to cross featureless expanses of water to reach their destinations. In time ships, sails, and navigational techniques perfected in the more protected seas were adapted to open oceans.

However complex the solutions and dangerous the voyages, the rewards of sea travel made them worthwhile. Ships could move goods and people more profitably than any form of overland travel then possible. Crossing unknown waters, finding new lands, developing new markets, and establishing new settlements attracted adventurers from every continent. By 1450 daring mariners had discovered and settled most of the islands of the Pacific, the Atlantic, and the Indian Ocean, but no one had yet crossed the Pacific in either direction. Even the smaller Atlantic remained a barrier to contact between the Americas, Europe, and Africa. The inhabitants of Australia were also nearly cut off from contact with the rest of humanity. All this was about to change.

The Indian Ocean

The archipelagos and coastal regions of Southeast Asia were connected in networks of trade and cultural exchange from an early date. While the region was divided politically, culturally, and religiously, the languages of Malaysia, Indonesia, and the Philippines—as well as coastal regions of Thailand, southern Vietnam, Cambodia, and Hainan, China—all originated from a common Austronesian linguistic root. Scholars often use the term *Malayo Indonesians* or *Malay* to describe the early peoples of this maritime realm.

The region's sailors were highly skilled navigators as well as innovative shipbuilders and sail makers who, in addition to their own achievements, influenced later Chinese and Arab maritime advances. Around 350 they discovered two direct sea routes between Sri Lanka and the South China Sea through the Straits of Malacca and Sunda, thus opening a profitable link to China's silk markets. They were also the first to use the seasonal monsoon winds of the Indian Ocean to extend their voyages for thousands of miles, ultimately reaching East Africa and settling in Madagascar.

By the first century C.E. the mariners and merchants of India and Southeast Asia were trading across the region for spices, gold, and aromatic woods, even sending spices as far west as Rome through Mediterranean intermediaries (see Chapter 7). Their success attracted African, Arab, and Chinese mariners and merchants into the region, creating a large, integrated, and highly profitable market in the centuries that followed. By 1000 the dhows (dow) of Arabs and Africans, as well as Malay *jongs* and Chinese junks, came together in the region's harbors for commerce.

The rise of medieval Islam (see Chapter 10) gave Indian Ocean trade an important boost. The great Muslim cities of the Middle East provided a demand for valuable commodities, and networks of Muslim traders were active across the region. These traders shared a common language, ethic, and law and actively spread their religion to distant trading cities. By 1400 there were Muslim trading communities all around the Indian Ocean. Chinese merchant communities were present as well.

Indian Ocean traders largely operated outside the control of the empires and states they served, but in East Asia imperial China's rulers were growing more and more interested in these wealthy ports of trade. In 1368 the Ming dynasty overthrew Mongol rule and began to reestablish China's predominance and prestige abroad. Having restored Chinese power and influence in East Asia, the Ming moved to establish direct contacts with the peoples around the Indian Ocean, sending out seven imperial fleets between 1405 and 1433 (see Chapter 13). The enormous size of these expeditions, far larger than needed for exploration or promoting trade, indicates that the Ming sought to inspire awe of their power and achievements. While curiosity about this prosperous region may have been a motive, the fact that the ports visited by the fleets were major commercial centers suggests that expanding China's trade was also an objective.

CHRONOLOGY

	Pacific Ocean	Atlantic Ocean	Indian Ocean
1400	300 B.C.E.–1000 C.E. Polynesian settlement of Pacific islands	770–1200 Viking voyages	350–1000 Development and integration of Southeast Asian maritime markets
	By 1000 Sporadic Polynesian contacts with American mainland	1300s Settlement of Madeira, Azores, Canaries	
	1200–1300 Polynesian societies in Hawaii, Tonga, and elsewhere develop clear class structures with hereditary chiefs	Early 1300s Mali voyages	
		1418–1460 Voyages of Henry the Navigator	1405–1433 Voyages of Zheng He
		1440s First slaves from West Africa sent to Europe	
		1482 Portuguese at Gold Coast and Kongo	
		1486 Portuguese at Benin	
		1488 Bartolomeu Dias reaches Indian Ocean	
		1492 Columbus reaches Caribbean	
		1492–1500 Spanish conquer Hispaniola	
		1493 Columbus returns to Caribbean (second voyage)	
		1498 Columbus reaches mainland of South America (third voyage)	1497–1498 Vasco da Gama reaches India
1500		1500 Cabral reaches Brazil	
			1505 Portuguese bombard Swahili Coast cities
			1510 Portuguese take Goa
			1511 Portuguese take Malacca
			1515 Portuguese take Hormuz
	1519–1522 Magellan expedition	1519–1521 Cortés conquers Aztec Empire	
		1531–1533 Pizarro conquers Inka Empire	
		1536 Rebellion of Manco Inka in Peru	1535 Portuguese take Diu
			1538 Portuguese defeat Ottoman fleet
			1539 Portuguese aid Ethiopia

The scale of the Ming expeditions to the Indian Ocean Basin reflects imperial China's resources and importance. The first consisted of sixty-two specially built "treasure ships," large Chinese junks each about 300 feet long by 150 feet wide (90 by 45 meters). There were also at least a hundred smaller vessels. Each treasure ship had nine masts, twelve sails, many decks, and a carrying capacity of 3,000 tons (six times the capacity of Columbus's entire fleet). One expedition carried over 27,000 crew and passengers, including infantry and cavalry troops. The ships were armed with small cannon, but in most Chinese sea battles arrows from highly accurate crossbows dominated the fighting.

Admiral **Zheng He** (jung huh) (1371–1435) commanded the expeditions. A Chinese Muslim with ancestral connections to the Persian Gulf, Zheng was a fitting emissary to the increasingly Muslim-dominated Indian Ocean Basin. The expeditions carried other Arabic-speaking Chinese as interpreters. One of them recorded local customs and beliefs in a journal, observing new flora and fauna and noting exotic animals such as the black panther of Malaya and the tapir of

Zheng He An imperial eunuch and Muslim, entrusted by the Ming emperor Yongle with a series of state voyages that took his gigantic ships through the Indian Ocean, from Southeast Asia to Africa.

Sumatra. In India he described the division of the coastal population into five classes, which correspond to the four Hindu varna and a separate Muslim class. He also recorded that traders in the rich Indian trading port of Calicut (KAL-ih-kut) could perform error-free calculations by counting on their fingers and toes rather than using the Chinese abacus. After his return, the interpreter went on tour in China, telling of these exotic places and "how far the majestic virtue of [China's] imperial dynasty extended."[1]

The Chinese "treasure ships" carried rich silks and other valuable goods intended as gifts for distant rulers. In return those rulers sent back gifts of equal or greater value to the Chinese emperor. Although the main purpose of these exchanges was diplomatic, they also stimulated trade between China and its southern neighbors. Interest in new contacts was not limited to the Chinese.

At least three trading cities on the Swahili (swah-HEE-lee) Coast of East Africa sent delegations to China between 1415 and 1416. The delegates from one of them, Malindi, presented the emperor of China with a giraffe, creating quite a stir among normally reserved imperial officials. These African delegations may have encouraged more contacts because the next three of Zheng's voyages reached the African coast. Unfortunately, no documents record how Africans and Chinese reacted to each other during these historic meetings between 1417 and 1433, but it appears that China's lavish gifts stimulated the Swahili market for silk and porcelain.

Had the Ming court wished to promote trade for the profit of its merchants, Chinese fleets might have come to play a dominant role in Indian Ocean trade. But some high Chinese officials opposed increased contact with peoples whom they regarded as barbarians incapable of making contributions to China. Such opposition caused a suspension in the voyages from 1424 to 1431. The final Chinese expedition sailed between 1432 and 1433.

While later Ming emperors would focus their attention on internal matters, long-established Chinese merchant communities continued as major participants in Indian Ocean trade, contributing to the rapid growth of prosperous commercial entrepôts (ON-truh-pohs) (places

---

[1]Ma Huan, *Ying-yai Sheng-lan: "The Overall Survey of the Ocean's Shores,"* ed. Feng Ch'eng-Chün, trans. J. V. G. Mills (Cambridge, England: Cambridge University Press, 1970), 180.

Chinese Junk This modern drawing shows how much larger one of Zheng He's ships was than one of Vasco da Gama's vessels. Watertight interior bulkheads made junks the most seaworthy large ships of the fifteenth century. Sails made of pleated bamboo matting hung from the junk's masts, and a stern rudder provided steering. European ships of exploration, though smaller, were faster and more maneuverable. Dugald Stermer

where goods are stored or deposited and from which they are distributed) throughout the region. As the sultan of one of the most prosperous trade centers, Melaka (in modern Malaysia), described the era in 1468, "We have learned that to master the blue oceans people must engage in commerce and trade. All the lands within the seas are united in one body. Life has never been so affluent in preceding generations as it is today."[2]

The Pacific Ocean

Around 3000 B.C.E. seafaring peoples from Southeast Asia reached the island of New Guinea. Sustained contact between these Austronesian-speaking migrants and the island's original population accelerated agricultural development and led to population expansion and the settlement of nearby islands. The descendants these peoples eventually forged a new cultural identity, called Lapita by archaeologists, as they colonized the island chains of Melanesia (mel-uh-NEE-zhuh). Lapita settlers reached Tonga, Fiji, and Samoa around 1000 B.C.E.

By 500 B.C.E. a linguistically and culturally distinct Polynesian culture emerged from this Lapita origin. While the dates for Polynesian colonization of the remote islands of the Pacific are still debated, their mastery of long-distance maritime exploration in an era when European sailors still stayed close to shore is undeniable. Pushing east from Tonga, Samoa, and Fiji, Polynesians colonized the Marquesas (mar-KAY-suhs) and the Cook and Society archipelagos by approximately 300 B.C.E. Before 500 C.E. Polynesian colonies were established on the Hawaiian Islands 2,200 miles (3,541 kilometers) away, and Polynesian colonists settled Easter Island, 2,300 miles (3,702 kilometers) to the southeast, by 800 C.E. Finally, they established permanent colonies in New Zealand around 1000 C.E. Polynesian voyagers also made periodic contact with the mainland of South America after 1000 C.E., passing on the domesticated Asian chicken and returning with the sweet potato, an American domesticate that soon became a staple throughout the Pacific region.

Both DNA evidence and linguistic evidence make clear that the Polynesian settlement of the islands of the eastern Pacific was planned and not the result of accident. Following voyages of reconnaissance, Polynesian mariners carried colonizing expeditions in fleets of large double-hulled canoes that relied on scores of paddlers as well as sails. Their largest canoes reached 120 feet (37 meters) in length and carried crews of fifty. A wide platform connected the two hulls of these crafts and permitted the transportation of animals and plants crucial to the success of distant and isolated settlements. Long-range expeditions took pigs, dogs, and chickens with them as well as domesticated plants such as taro, bananas, yams, and breadfruit. Their success depended upon reliably navigating across thousands of miles of ocean using careful observation of the currents and stars as the crews searched for evidence of land (see Map 16.1).

The most hierarchical social structures and political systems developed in the Hawaiian and Tongan archipelagos, where powerful hereditary chiefs controlled the lives of commoners and managed resources. Here, as well as in New Zealand, competition among chiefs led to chronic warfare.

While all Polynesian societies descended from the same originating culture and all began with the same tools and the same farming and fishing technologies, significant differences in the geography and climate led inexorably to the development of unique social, political, and economic systems. Most Polynesian communities depended on farming and fishing, but the intensity of these practices depended on local conditions. In Hawaii, for example, low-lying native forests were converted to farmland using controlled burns, and fishponds were built to increase fish yields. As a result, the Polynesian communities of this archipelago thrived into the era of European expansion. However, on Easter Island, among the most isolated of the Polynesian colonies, population growth led to total deforestation, soil erosion, intense resource competition, and, ultimately, to a brutal cycle of warfare that drastically reduced the population.

---

[2]Quotation in Craig A. Lockard, "'The Sea Common to All': Maritime Frontiers, Port Cities, and Chinese Traders in the Southeast Asian Age of Commerce, ca. 1400–1750," *Journal of World History* 21, no. 2 (2010): 228.

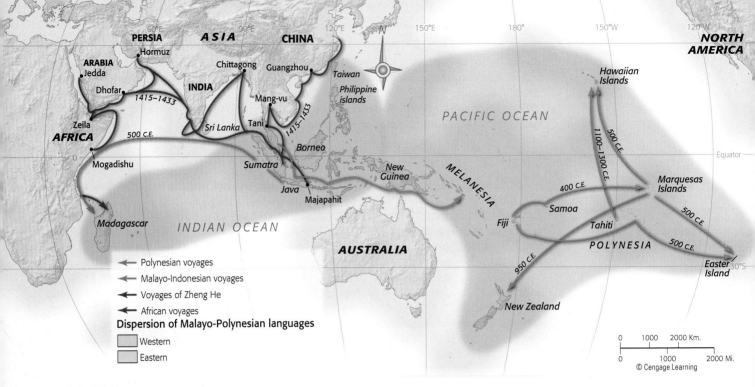

MAP 16.1 **Exploration and Settlement in the Indian and Pacific Oceans Before 1500** Over many centuries, mariners originating in Southeast Asia gradually colonized the islands of the Pacific and Indian Oceans. The Chinese voyages led by Zheng
He in the fifteenth century were lavish official expeditions. © Cengage Learning

The Atlantic Ocean

The Vikings were the greatest mariners of the Atlantic in the early Middle Ages. These northern
European raiders used their small, open ships to attack Europe's coastal settlements for several
centuries. Like the Polynesians, the Vikings used their knowledge of the heavens and the seas
rather than maps and other navigational devices to find their way over long distances.

The Vikings first settled Iceland in 770 and established a colony on Greenland in 982. By
accident one group sighted North America in 986. Fifteen years later Leif Ericsson established a
short-lived Viking settlement on the island of Newfoundland, which he called Vinland. When a
colder climate returned after 1200, the northern settlements in Greenland went into decline and
the Vikings abandoned Vinland.

Some southern Europeans applied maritime skills acquired in the Mediterranean and along
the North Atlantic coast to explore to the south. Genoese and Portuguese expeditions pushed
into the Atlantic in the fourteenth century, eventually exploring and settling the islands of
Madeira (muh-DEER-uh), the Azores (A-zorz), and the Canaries.

There is some evidence of African voyages of exploration in this period. The celebrated
Syrian geographer al-Umari (1301–1349) relates that when Mansa Kankan Musa (MAHN-suh
KAHN-kahn MOO-suh), the ruler of the West African empire of Mali, passed through Egypt on
his lavish pilgrimage to Mecca in 1324, he told of voyages into the Atlantic undertaken by his predecessor, Mansa Muhammad. According to this source, Muhammad had sent out four hundred
vessels with men and supplies, telling them, "Do not return until you have reached the other side
of the ocean or if you have exhausted your food or water." After a long time one canoe returned,
reporting that the others were lost in a "violent current in the middle of the sea." Muhammad
himself then set out at the head of a second, even larger, expedition, from which no one returned.

In the Americas, early Amerindian voyagers from the Caribbean coast of South America
colonized the West Indies. By the year 1000 Amerindians known as the **Arawak** (AR-uh-wahk)
(also called Taino) had followed the small islands of the Lesser Antilles (Barbados, Martinique,
and Guadeloupe) to the Greater Antilles (Cuba, Hispaniola, Jamaica, and Puerto Rico) as well as
to the Bahamas (see Map 16.2). The Carib followed the same route in later centuries, and by the

Arawak Amerindian peoples
who inhabited the Greater
Antilles of the Caribbean at the
time of Columbus.

late fifteenth century they had overrun most Arawak settlements in the Lesser Antilles and were raiding parts of the Greater Antilles. Both Arawak and Carib peoples also made contact with the North American mainland.

The transfer of maize cultivation to South America after its domestication in Mesoamerica is suggestive of an early chain of contacts among Amerindian peoples, including the use of small boats along the Pacific coast. In the centuries after 100 there were significant ongoing maritime contacts between Pacific coast populations in South America and Mesoamerica. Mariners carried pottery, copper, gold and silver alloy jewelry, and textiles from the coast of Ecuador north in two-masted, balsa wood rafts that measured up to 36 feet (11 meters) in length. Rafts of this size could carry more than 20 metric tons of cargo and ten or more crew members. Travel north was facilitated by the favorable winds and currents of the Pacific, but these craft had the capacity to make the return trip carrying cargos of sacred spondylus shells as well. One important result of these contacts was the introduction of metallurgy to Mesoamerica after 500.

SECTION REVIEW

- Polynesians explored and settled the eastern Pacific from the Marquesas to Hawaii and Easter Island.

- The Indian Ocean became a center of commerce and cultural exchange. Between 1405 and 1433 Chinese admiral Zheng He's seven expeditions established contacts with South Asian and African peoples.

- Vikings, Amerindians, and Africans also pursued long-distance explorations and settlements.

MAP 16.2 **Middle America to 1533** Maritime contacts led to the settlement of the islands of the Greater and Lesser Antilles by South American peoples and to the dissemination of important technologies like metallurgy and maize agriculture along the Pacific coast. The arrival of Europeans in 1492 led to conquest and colonization.   © Cengage Learning

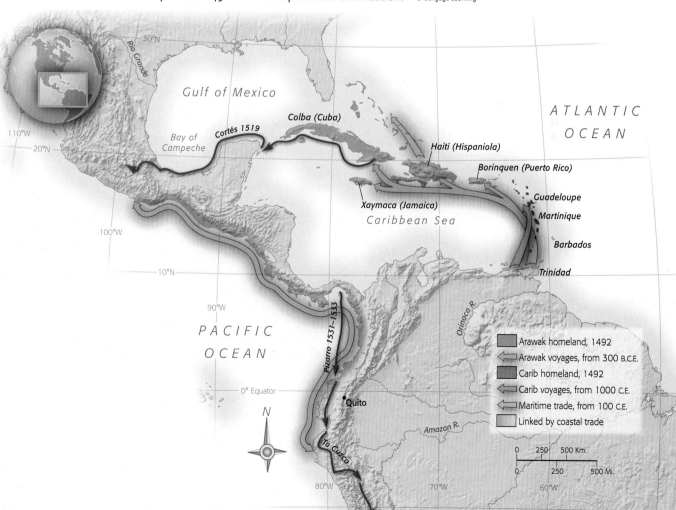

EUROPEAN EXPANSION, 1400–1550

While the pace and intensity of maritime contacts increased in many parts of the world before 1450, the epic sea voyages sponsored by the Iberian kingdoms of Portugal and Spain are of special interest because they began a maritime revolution that profoundly altered the course of world history. The Portuguese and Spanish expeditions ended the isolation of the Americas and increased the volume of global interaction.

Iberian overseas expansion was the product of two related phenomena. First, Iberian rulers had strong economic, religious, and political motives to expand their influence. And second, improvements in maritime and military technologies gave Iberians the means to master treacherous and unfamiliar ocean environments, seize control of existing maritime trade routes, and conquer new lands.

Motives for Exploration

The ambitions and adventurous personalities of the rulers of Portugal and Spain led them to sponsor voyages of exploration in the fifteenth century, but these voyages built upon four trends evident in Latin Europe since about the year 1000: (1) the revival of urban life and trade, (2) the unique alliance between merchants and rulers in Europe, (3) a struggle with Islamic powers for dominance of the Mediterranean that mixed religious motives with the desire for trade, and (4) growing intellectual curiosity about the outside world.

By 1450 the city-states of northern Italy had well-established trade links to northern Europe, the Indian Ocean, and the Black Sea, and their merchant princes had also sponsored an intellectual and artistic Renaissance. The Italian trading states of Venice and Genoa also maintained profitable commercial ties in the Mediterranean that depended on alliances with Muslims and gave their merchants privileged access to lucrative trade from the East. Even after the expansion of the Ottoman Empire disrupted their trade to the East, these cities did not take the lead in exploring the Atlantic. However, many individual Italians played leading roles in the Atlantic explorations.

In contrast, the history and geography of the Iberian kingdoms led them in a different direction. Muslim invaders from North Africa had conquered most of Iberia in the eighth century. Centuries of warfare between Christians and Muslims followed, and by 1250 the Iberian kingdoms of Portugal, Castile, and Aragon had reconquered all of Iberia except the southern Muslim kingdom of Granada (see Chapter 14). The dynastic marriage of Isabel of Castile and Ferdinand of Aragon in 1469 facilitated the conquest of Granada in 1492 and began the creation of Spain, sixteenth-century Europe's most powerful state.

Christian militancy continued to be an important motive for both Portugal and Spain in their overseas ventures. But the Iberian rulers and their adventurous subjects also sought material returns. With only a modest share of the Mediterranean trade, they were much more willing than the Italians to seek new routes to the rich trade of Africa and Asia via the Atlantic. Both kingdoms participated in the shipbuilding and the gunpowder revolutions that were under way in Atlantic Europe, and both were especially open to new geographical knowledge.

Portuguese Voyages

Portugal's decision to invest significant resources in new exploration rested on a well-established Atlantic fishing industry and a history of anti-Muslim warfare. When the Muslim government of Morocco in northwestern Africa showed weakness in the fifteenth century, the Portuguese attacked, conquering the city of Ceuta (say-OO-tuh) in 1415. The capture of this rich North African city gave the Portuguese better intelligence of the caravans bringing gold and slaves to Ceuta from African states south of the Sahara. Militarily unable to push inland and gain direct access to the gold trade, the Portuguese sought contact with the gold producers by sailing down the African coast.

Henry the Navigator Portuguese prince who promoted the study of navigation and directed voyages of exploration down the western coast of Africa in the fifteenth century.

Prince Henry (1394–1460), third son of the king of Portugal, had led the attack on Ceuta. Because he devoted the rest of his life to promoting exploration, he is known as **Henry the Navigator**. His official biographer emphasized Henry's mixed motives for exploration—converting Africans to Christianity, making contact with Christian rulers in Africa, and launching joint crusades with them against the Ottomans. Prince Henry also wished to discover new places and hoped that such new contacts would be profitable. Early explorations

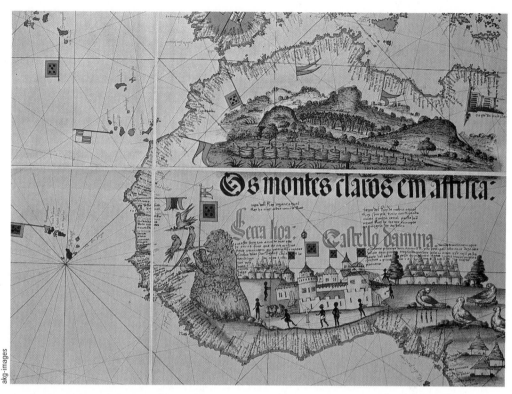

akg-images

Portuguese Map of Western Africa, 1502   This map shows in great detail a section of African coastline that Portuguese explorers charted and named in the fifteenth century. The cartographer illustrated the African interior, which was almost completely unknown to Europeans, with drawings of birds and views of coastal sights: Sierra Leone (Serra lioa), named for a mountain shaped like a lion, and the Portuguese Castle of the Mine (Castello damina) on the Gold Coast.

focused on Africa, but reaching India became the eventual goal of Portuguese explorers. While called "the Navigator," Henry himself never ventured far from home. Instead, he founded a center of research at Sagres (SAH-gresh) to study navigation that built on the pioneering efforts of Italian merchants and fourteenth-century Jewish cartographers. This center collected geographical information from sailors and travelers and sponsored new expeditions to explore the Atlantic. Henry's ships established permanent contact with the islands of Madeira in 1418 and the Azores in 1439.

Henry's staff also improved navigational instruments that had been first developed elsewhere. These instruments included the magnetic compass, first developed in China, and the astrolabe, an instrument of Arab or Greek invention that enabled mariners to determine their location at sea by measuring the position of the sun or the stars in the night sky. Even with such instruments, however, voyages still depended on the skill and experience of navigators.

Portuguese mariners also developed vessels appropriate for voyages of long-distance exploration. Neither the galleys in use in the Mediterranean, powered by large numbers of oarsmen, nor the three-masted ships of northern Europe with their square sails proved adequate for the Atlantic. The large crews of the galleys could not carry enough supplies for long voyages and the square-rigged northern vessels had trouble sailing at an angle to the wind. Instead, the voyages of exploration made use of a new vessel, the **caravel** (KAR-uh-vel), that was much smaller than either the largest European ships or the Chinese junks Zheng used to explore the Indian Ocean. Their size permitted them to enter shallow coastal waters and explore upriver, but they were strong enough to weather ocean storms. They could be equipped with triangular lateen sails that could take the wind on either side for enhanced maneuverability or fitted with square Atlantic sails for greater speed in a following wind. The addition of small cannon made them good fighting ships as well. The caravels' economy, speed, agility, and power justified a contemporary's claim that they were "the best ships that sailed the seas."[3]

caravel A small, highly maneuverable three-masted ship used by the Portuguese and Spanish in the exploration of the Atlantic.

[3]Alvise da Cadamosto in *The Voyages of Cadamosto and Other Documents*, ed. and trans. G. R. Crone (London: Hakluyt Society, 1937), 2.

Pioneering captains had to overcome the common fear that South Atlantic waters were boiling hot or contained ocean currents that would prevent any ship entering them from ever returning home. It took Prince Henry fourteen years—from 1420 to 1434—to coax an expedition to venture beyond southern Morocco (see Map 16.3). It would ultimately take the Portuguese four decades to cover the 1,500 miles (2,400 kilometers) from Lisbon to Sierra Leone (see-ER-uh lee-OWN); it then took only three additional decades to explore the remaining 4,000 miles (6,400 kilometers) to the southern tip of the African continent. With experience, navigators learned how to return home speedily by sailing northwest into the Atlantic to the latitude of the Azores, where they picked up prevailing westerly winds. The knowledge that ocean winds tend to form large circular patterns helped later explorers discover many other ocean routes.

During the 1440s Portuguese raids on the northwest coast of Africa and the Canary Islands began to return with slaves, finding a profitable market in an Iberia still recovering from the population losses of the Black Plague. The total number of Africans captured or purchased on voyages exceeded eighty thousand by the end of the century and rose steadily thereafter. However, the gold trade quickly became more important once the Portuguese contacted the trading networks that flourished in West Africa and reached across the Sahara. By 1457 enough African gold was coming back to Portugal for the kingdom to issue a new gold coin called the *cruzado* (crusader), another reminder of how deeply the Portuguese entwined religious and secular motives.

While the Portuguese crown continued to sponsor voyages, the growing participation of private commercial interests accelerated the pace of exploration. In 1469 a prominent Lisbon merchant named Fernão Gomes purchased from the Crown the privilege of exploring 350 miles (550 kilometers) of African coast in return for a trade monopoly. He discovered the uninhabited island of São Tomé (sow toh-MAY) located on the equator and converted it to a major producer of sugar dependent on slaves imported from the African mainland. In the next century the island would serve as a model for the sugar plantations of Brazil and the Caribbean. Gomes also explored the **Gold Coast**, which became the headquarters of Portugal's West African trade.

The desire to find a passage around Africa to the rich spice trade of the Indian Ocean spurred the final thrust down the African coast. In 1488 **Bartolomeu Dias** became the first Portuguese explorer to round the southern tip of Africa and enter the Indian Ocean. In 1497–1498 **Vasco da Gama** sailed around Africa and reached India (see Environment and Technology: Vasco da Gama's Fleet). Then, in 1500, ships on the way to India under the command of Pedro Alvares Cabral (kah-BRAHL) sailed too far west and reached the South American mainland. This discovery established Portugal's claim to Brazil, which would become one of the Western Hemisphere's richest colonies. The gamble that Prince Henry had begun eight decades earlier was about to pay off handsomely.

Spanish Voyages

In contrast to the persistence and planning behind Portugal's century-long exploration of the South Atlantic, haste and blind luck lay behind Spain's early discoveries. Throughout most of the fifteenth century, the Spanish kingdoms were preoccupied with internal affairs: completion of the reconquest of southern Iberia from the Muslims; consolidation of the territories of Isabel and Ferdinand; and the conversion or expulsion of religious minorities. The Portuguese had already found a new route to the Indian Ocean by the time the Spanish monarchs were ready to turn to overseas exploration.

The leader of the Spanish overseas mission was **Christopher Columbus** (1451–1506), a Genoese mariner. His four voyages between 1492 and 1504 established the existence of a vast new world across the Atlantic, whose existence few in "old world" Eurasia and Africa had ever suspected. But Columbus refused to accept that he had found unknown new continents and peoples, insisting that he had succeeded in finding a shorter route to the Indian Ocean.

As a young man Columbus gained considerable experience of the South Atlantic while participating in Portuguese explorations along the African coast, but he had become convinced there was a shorter way to reach the riches of the East than the route around Africa. By his reckoning (based on a serious misreading of a ninth-century Arab authority), the Canaries were a mere 2,400 nautical miles (4,450 kilometers) from Japan. The actual distance was five times as far.

Columbus proposed to reach Asia by sailing west, but Portuguese authorities twice rejected his plan. Columbus first proposed his expedition to Castile's able ruler Queen Isabel in 1486, but he was rejected. In 1492 his persistence was finally rewarded when the queen and her husband, King Ferdinand of Aragon, agreed to fund a modest expedition.

Gold Coast Region of the Atlantic coast of West Africa occupied by modern Ghana; named for its gold exports to Europe from the 1470s onward.

Bartolomeu Dias Portuguese explorer who in 1488 led the first expedition to sail around the southern tip of Africa from the Atlantic and sight the Indian Ocean.

Vasco da Gama Portuguese explorer. In 1497–1498 he led the first naval expedition from Europe to sail to India, opening an important commercial sea route.

Christopher Columbus Genoese mariner who in the service of Spain led expeditions across the Atlantic, reestablishing contact between the peoples of the Americas and the Old World and opening the way to Spanish conquest and colonization.

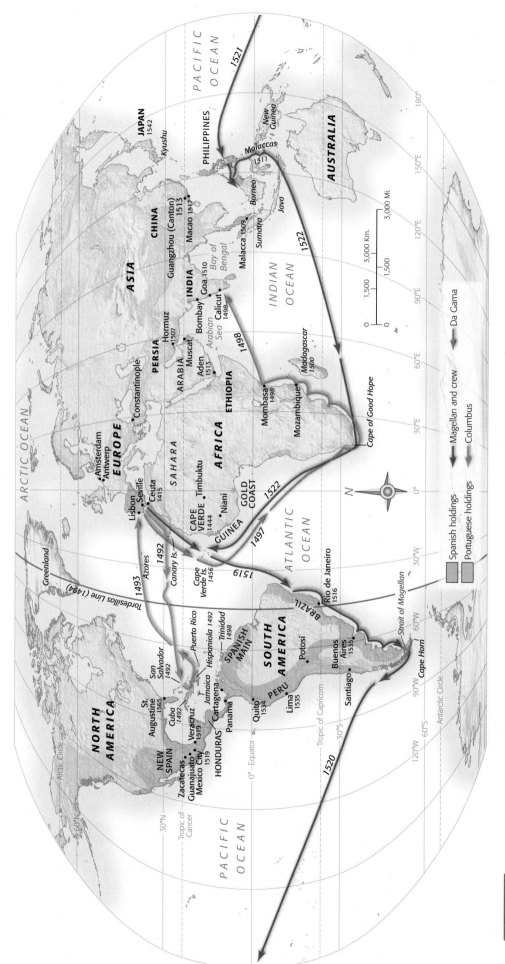

MAP 16.3 **European Exploration, 1420–1542** Portuguese and Spanish explorers showed the possibility and practicality of intercontinental maritime trade. Before 1540 European trade with Africa and Asia was much more important than that with the Americas, but after the Spanish conquest of the Aztec and Inka Empires, transatlantic trade began to increase. Notice the Tordesillas line, which in theory separated the Spanish and Portuguese spheres of activity. © Cengage Learning

Vasco da Gama's Fleet

The four small ships that sailed for India from Lisbon in June 1497 may seem a puny fleet compared to the sixty-two Chinese vessels that Zheng He had led into the Indian Ocean ninety-five years earlier. But given the fact that China had a hundred times as many people as Portugal, Vasco da Gama's fleet represented at least as great a commitment of resources. In any event, the Portuguese expedition had a far greater impact on the course of history. Having achieved its aim of inspiring awe at China's greatness, the Chinese throne sent out no more expeditions after 1433. Although da Gama's ships seemed more odd than awesome to Indian Ocean observers, that modest fleet began a revolution in global relations.

Portugal spared no expense in ensuring that the fleet would make it to India and back. Craftsmen built extra strength into the hulls to withstand the powerful storms that Dias had encountered in 1488 at the tip of Africa. Small enough to be able to navigate any shallow harbors and rivers they might encounter, the ships were crammed with specially strengthened casks and barrels of water, wine, oil, flour, meat, and vegetables far in excess of what was required even on a voyage that would take the better part of a year. Arms and ammunition were also in abundance.

Three of da Gama's ships were rigged with square sails on two masts for speed and a lateen sail on the third mast. The fourth vessel was a caravel with lateen sails. Each ship carried three sets of sails and plenty of extra rigging so as to be able to repair any damages due to storms. The Crusaders' red crosses on the sails signaled one of the expedition's motives.

The captains and crew—Portugal's most talented and experienced—received extra pay and other rewards for their service. Yet there was no expectation that the unprecedented sums spent on this expedition would bring any immediate return. According to a contemporary chronicle, the only

The Pierpont Morgan Library/Art Resource, New York

Vasco da Gama's Flagship This vessel carried the Portuguese captain on his second expedition to India in 1505.

immediate return the Portuguese monarch received was "the knowledge that some part of Ethiopia and the beginning of Lower India had been discovered." However, the scale and care of the preparations suggest that the Portuguese expected the expedition to open up profitable trade to the Indian Ocean. And so it did.

Columbus recorded in his log that he and his crew of ninety men "departed Friday the third day of August of the year 1492" toward "the regions of India." Their mission, the royal contract stated, was "to discover and acquire certain islands and mainland in the Ocean Sea." He carried letters of introduction from the Spanish sovereigns to Eastern rulers, including one to the "Grand Khan" (meaning the Chinese emperor), and brought along an Arabic interpreter to facilitate communication with the peoples of eastern Asia. The expedition traveled in three small ships, the *Santa María*, the *Niña*, and the *Pinta*. The *Niña* and the *Pinta* were caravels.

Unfavorable headwinds had impeded other attempts to explore the Atlantic west of the Azores, but Columbus chose a southern route because he had learned in his service with the Portuguese of west-blowing winds in the latitudes of the Canaries. In October 1492 the expedition reached the islands of the Caribbean. Columbus insisted on calling the inhabitants "Indians" because he believed that the islands were part of the East Indies. His second voyage to the Caribbean in 1493 did nothing to change his mind. Even when, two months after Vasco da Gama reached India in 1498, Columbus first sighted the mainland of South America on his third voyage, he stubbornly insisted it was part of Asia. But by then other Europeans were convinced that he had discovered islands and continents previously unknown to the Old World. Amerigo Vespucci's explorations, first on behalf of Spain and then for Portugal, led mapmakers to name the new continents "America" after him, rather than "Columbia" after Columbus.

To prevent disputes arising from their efforts to exploit their new discoveries and spread Christianity, Spain and Portugal agreed to split the world between them. The Treaty of Tordesillas (tor-duh-SEE-yuhs), negotiated by the pope in 1494, drew an imaginary line down the middle of the North Atlantic Ocean. The treaty allocated lands east of the line in Africa and southern Asia to Portugal; lands to the west in the Americas were reserved for Spain. Cabral's discovery of Brazil, however, gave Portugal a valid claim to the part of South America located east of the line.

Where would Spain's and Portugal's spheres of influence divide in the East? Given Europeans' ignorance of the earth's true size in 1494, it was not clear whether the Moluccas (muh-LOO-kuhz), whose valuable spices had been a goal of the Iberian voyages, were on Portugal's or Spain's side of the Tordesillas line. The size of the Pacific Ocean would determine the boundary. In the end, the Moluccas turned out to lie well within Portugal's sphere, as Spain formally acknowledged in 1529.

Ferdinand Magellan Portuguese navigator who led the Spanish expedition of 1519–1522 that was the first to sail around the world.

In 1519 **Ferdinand Magellan** (ca. 1480–1521) began his expedition to complete Columbus's interrupted westward voyage by sailing around the Americas and across the Pacific. Despite his death during this voyage on behalf of the king of Spain, Magellan was considered the first person to encircle the globe because a decade earlier he had sailed from Europe to the East Indies as part of an expedition sponsored by his native Portugal. His two voyages took him across the Tordesillas line, through the separate spheres claimed by Portugal and Spain, and established the basis for Spanish colonization of the Philippines after 1564.

Although Columbus failed to find a new route to the East, the consequences of his voyages for European expansion were momentous. Those who followed in his wake laid the basis for Spain's large colonial empire in the Americas and for the empires of other European nations. In turn, these empires promoted the growth of a major new trading network whose importance rivaled and eventually surpassed the Indian Ocean network. Both the eastward and the westward voyages of exploration marked a tremendous expansion of Europe's role in world history.

SECTION REVIEW

- Portugal and Spain initiated oversees explorations to expand Christianity and gain new markets.

- Portugal, aided by Prince Henry the Navigator, created a trading empire in Africa and the Indian Ocean.

- Columbus first revealed the Americas to Europe, and other Spanish explorers reached Asia by crossing the Pacific.

ENCOUNTERS WITH EUROPE, 1450–1550

European actions alone did not determine the global consequences of these new contacts. The ways in which Africans, Asians, and Amerindians perceived these visitors and interacted with them influenced developments as well. Everywhere indigenous peoples evaluated the Europeans as potential allies or enemies, and everywhere Europeans attempted to insert themselves into existing commercial and geopolitical arrangements. In general, Europeans made slow progress in establishing colonies and asserting political influence in Africa and Asia, even while profiting from new commercial ties. In the Americas, however, Spain, Portugal, and later other European powers moved rapidly to create colonial empires. In this case the long isolation of the Amerindians from the rest of the world made them more vulnerable to the diseases that these outsiders introduced, limiting their potential for resistance and facilitating European settlement.

Western Africa

Many along the West African coast were eager for trade with the Portuguese, since it offered new markets for exports and access to imports cheaper than those transported overland from the Mediterranean. This was evident along the Gold Coast of West Africa, first visited by the Portuguese in 1471. Miners in the hinterland had long sold their gold to traders, who took it to trading cities along the southern edge of the Sahara, where it was sold to traders who had crossed the desert from North Africa. Recognizing that they might get more favorable terms from the new visitors from the sea, coastal Africans were ready to negotiate with the royal representative of Portugal who arrived in 1482 to seek permission to erect a trading fort.

This Portuguese noble and his officers (likely including the young Christopher Columbus, who had entered Portuguese service in 1476) were eager to make a proper impression. They dressed in their best clothes, erected and decorated a reception platform, celebrated a Catholic Mass, and signaled the start of negotiations with trumpets, tambourines, and drums. The African king, Caramansa, staged his entrance with equal ceremony, arriving with a large retinue of attendants and musicians. Through an African interpreter, the two leaders exchanged flowery

Bronze Figure of Benin Ruler Both this prince and his horse are protected by chain mail introduced in the fifteenth century to Benin by Portuguese merchants. Antenna Gallery
Dakar Senegal/ G.Dagli Orti/The Art Archive

speeches pledging goodwill and mutual benefit. Caramansa then gave permission for a small trading fort, assured, he said, by the appearance of the Portuguese that they were honorable persons, unlike the "few, foul, and vile" Portuguese visitors of the previous decade.

Neither side made a show of force, but the Africans' upper hand was evident in Caramansa's warning that he and his people would move away, depriving their fort of food and trade, if the Portuguese acted aggressively. Trade at the post of Saint George of the Mine (later called Elmina) enriched both sides. The Portuguese crown had soon purchased gold equal to one-tenth of the world's production at the time. In return, Africans received large quantities of goods that Portuguese ships brought from Asia, Europe, and other parts of Africa.

After a century of aggressive expansion, the kingdom of Benin in the Niger Delta was near the peak of its power when it first encountered the Portuguese. Its oba (king) presided over an elaborate bureaucracy from a spacious palace in his large capital city, also known as Benin. In response to a Portuguese visit in 1486, the oba sent an ambassador to Portugal to learn more about these strangers. He then established a royal monopoly on trade with the Portuguese, selling pepper and ivory tusks (for export to Portugal) as well as stone beads, textiles, and prisoners of war (for resale as slaves at Elmina). In return, Portuguese merchants provided Benin with copper and brass, fine textiles, glass beads, and a horse for the king's royal procession. In the early sixteenth century, as the demand for slaves for the Portuguese sugar plantations on the nearby island of São Tomé grew, the oba first raised the price of slaves and then imposed restrictions that limited their sale.

Early contacts generally involved a mix of commercial, military, and religious exchanges. Some African rulers appreciated the advantage of European firearms over spears and arrows in conflicts with their enemies and actively sought them in trade. Because African religions were generally not exclusive, coastal rulers were also willing to test the value of the Christian practices promoted by the Portuguese. The rulers of Benin and Kongo, the two largest coastal kingdoms, accepted both Portuguese missionaries and soldiers as allies in battle to test the efficacy of the Christian religion and European weaponry.

However, Portuguese efforts to persuade the king and nobles of Benin to accept the Catholic faith ultimately failed. Early kings showed some interest, but after 1538 rulers declined to receive more missionaries. They also closed the market in male slaves for the rest of the sixteenth century. We do not know why Benin chose to limit its contacts with the Portuguese, but the result makes clear that these rulers had the power to control their contacts with Europeans.

Farther south, on the lower Congo River, relations between the kingdom of Kongo and the Portuguese began similarly but had a very different outcome. Like the oba of Benin, the manikongo (mah-NEE-KONG-goh) (king of Kongo) sent delegates to Portugal, established a royal monopoly on trade with the Portuguese, and expressed interest in Christian teachings. Deeply impressed with the new religion, the royal family made Catholicism the kingdom's official faith. But Kongo, lacking ivory and pepper, had less to trade than Benin. To acquire the goods brought by Portugal and to pay the costs of the missionaries, it had to sell more and more slaves.

Soon the manikongo began to lose his royal monopoly over the slave trade. In 1526 the Christian manikongo, Afonso I (r. 1506–ca. 1540), wrote to his royal "brother," the king of Portugal, begging for his help in stopping the trade because unauthorized Kongolese were kidnapping and selling people, even members of good families (see Diversity and Dominance: Kongo's Christian King). Alfonso's appeals for help received no reply from Portugal, whose interests were now concentrated in the Indian Ocean. Soon the effects of rebellion and the relocation of the slave trade from his kingdom to the south weakened the manikongo's authority.

Eastern Africa

Different still were the reactions of the Muslim rulers of the coastal trading states of eastern Africa. As Vasco da Gama's fleet sailed up the coast in 1498, most rulers gave the Portuguese a cool reception, suspicious of the intentions of visitors who painted Crusaders' crosses on their sails. But the ruler of one of the ports, Malindi, seeing the Portuguese as potential allies who could help him expand the city's trading position, provided da Gama with a pilot to guide him to India. The initial suspicions of the other rulers were proven correct seven years later when a Portuguese war fleet bombarded and looted most of the coastal cities of eastern Africa in the name of Christianity and commerce, while sparing Malindi.

Christian Ethiopia was another eastern African state that saw potential benefit in an alliance with the Portuguese. In the fourteenth and early fifteenth centuries, Ethiopia faced increasing conflict with Muslim states along the Red Sea. Emboldened by the rise of the Ottoman Turks, who had conquered Egypt in 1517 and launched a major fleet in the Indian Ocean to counter the Portuguese, the talented warlord of the Muslim state of Adal launched a furious assault on Ethiopia. Adal's decisive victory in 1529 reduced the Christian kingdom to a precarious state. At that point Ethiopia's contacts with the Portuguese became crucial.

For decades, delegations from Portugal and Ethiopia had explored a possible alliance based on their mutual adherence to Christianity. A key figure was Queen Helena of Ethiopia, who acted as regent for her young sons after her husband's death in 1478. In 1509 Helena sent a letter to "our very dear and well-beloved brother," the king of Portugal, along with a gift of two tiny crucifixes said to be made of wood from the cross on which Christ had died in Jerusalem. In her letter she proposed an alliance between her army and Portugal's fleet against the Turks; however, Helena's death in 1522 occurred before the alliance could be arranged. Ethiopia's situation then grew more desperate.

Finally, in 1539, when another woman ruler was holding what was left of the empire together, a small Portuguese force commanded by Vasco da Gama's son Christopher arrived to aid Ethiopia. With Portuguese help the Ethiopians renewed their struggle. While Muslim forces captured and tortured to death Christopher da Gama, their attack failed when their own leader was mortally wounded in battle. Portuguese aid helped the Ethiopian kingdom save itself from extinction, but a permanent alliance faltered because Ethiopian rulers refused to transfer their Christian affiliation from the patriarch of Alexandria to the Latin patriarch of Rome (the pope) as the Portuguese insisted.

Kongo's Christian King

The new overseas voyages brought conquest to some and opportunities for fruitful borrowings and exchanges to others. The decision of the ruler of the kingdom of Kongo to adopt Christianity in 1491 added cultural diversity to Kongolese society and in some ways strengthened the hand of the king. From then on Kongolese rulers sought to introduce Christian beliefs and rituals while at the same time Africanizing Christianity to make it more intelligible to their subjects. In addition, the kings of Kongo sought a variety of more secular aid from Portugal, including schools and medicine. But trade with the Portuguese introduced new social and political tensions, especially in the case of the export trade in slaves for the Portuguese sugar plantations on the island of São Tomé to the north.

Two letters sent to King João (zhwao) III of Portugal in 1526 illustrate how King Afonso of Kongo saw his kingdom's new relationship with Portugal and the problems that resulted from it. (Afonso adopted that name when baptized as a young prince.) After the death of his father in 1506, Afonso successfully claimed the throne and ruled until 1542. His son Henrique became the first Catholic bishop of the Kongo in 1521.

These letters were written in Portuguese and penned by the king's secretary, João Teixera (tay-SHER-uh), a Kongo Christian who, like Afonso, had been educated by Portuguese missionaries.

6 July 1526

To the very powerful and excellent prince Dom João, our brother:

On the 20th of June just past, we received word that a trading ship from your highness had just come to our port of Sonyo. We were greatly pleased by that arrival for it had been many days since a ship had come to our kingdom, for by it we would get news of your highness, which many times we had desired to know, . . . and likewise as there was a great and dire need for wine and flour for the holy sacrament; and of this we had had no great hope for we have the same need frequently. And that, sir, arises from the great negligence of your highness's officials toward us and toward shipping us those things. . . .

Sir, your highness should know how our kingdom is being lost in so many ways that we will need to provide the needed cure, since this is caused by the excessive license given by your agents and officials to the men and merchants who come to this kingdom to set up shops with goods and many things which have been prohibited by us, and which they spread throughout our kingdoms and domains in such abundance that many of our vassals, whose submission we could once rely on, now act independently so as to get the things in greater abundance than we ourselves; whom we had formerly held content and submissive and under our vassalage and jurisdiction, so it is doing a great harm not only to the service of God, but also to the security and peace of our kingdoms and state.

And we cannot reckon how great the damage is, since every day the mentioned merchants are taking our people, sons of the land and the sons of our noblemen and vassals and our relatives, because the thieves and men of bad conscience grab them so as to have the things and wares of this kingdom that they crave; they grab them and bring them to be sold. In such a manner, sir, has been the corruption and deprivation that our land is becoming completely depopulated, and your highness should not deem this good nor in your service. And to avoid this we need from these kingdoms [of yours] no more than priests and a few people to teach in schools, and no other goods except wine and flour for the holy sacrament, which is why we beg of your highness to help and assist us in this matter. Order your agents to send here neither merchants nor wares, because it is our will that in these kingdoms there should not be any dealing in slaves nor outlet for them, for the reasons stated above. Again we beg your highness's agreement, since otherwise we cannot cure such manifest harm. May Our Lord in His mercy have your highness always under His protection and may you always do the things of His holy service. I kiss your hands many times.

From our city of Kongo. . . .

The King, Dom Afonso

As these examples illustrate, African encounters with the Portuguese before 1550 varied considerably, as much because of the strategies and leadership of particular African states as because of Portuguese policies. Africans and Portuguese might become royal brothers, bitter opponents, or partners in a mutually profitable trade, but Europeans remained a minor presence in most of Africa in 1550. By then the Portuguese had become far more interested in the Indian Ocean trade.

Indian Ocean States

Vasco da Gama did not make a great impression on the citizens of Calicut when he arrived on the Malabar Coast of India in May 1498. Da Gama's four small ships were far less imposing than

18 October 1526

Very high and very powerful prince King of Portugal, our brother,

Sir, your highness has been so good as to promise us that anything we need we should ask for in our letters, and that everything will be provided. And so that there may be peace and health of our kingdoms, by God's will, in our lifetime. And as there are among us old folks and people who have lived for many days, many and different diseases happen so often that we are pushed to the ultimate extremes. And the same happens to our children, relatives, and people, because this country lacks physicians and surgeons who might know the proper cures for such diseases, as well as pharmacies and drugs to make them better. And for this reason many of those who had been already confirmed and instructed in the things of the holy faith of Our Lord Jesus Christ perish and die. And the rest of the people for the most part cure themselves with herbs and sticks and other ancient methods, so that they live putting all their faith in these herbs and ceremonies, and die believing that they are saved; and this serves God poorly.

And to avoid such a great error, I think, and inconvenience, since it is from God and from your highness that all the good and the drugs and medicines have come to us for our salvation, we ask your merciful highness to send us two physicians and two pharmacists and one surgeon, so that they may come with their pharmacies and necessary things to be in our kingdoms, for we have extreme need of each and every one of them. We will be very good and merciful to them, since sent by your highness, their work and coming should be for good. We ask your highness as a great favor to do this for us, because besides being good in itself it is in the service of God as we have said above.

Moreover, sir, in our kingdoms there is another great inconvenience which is of little service to God, and this is that many of our people, out of great desire for the wares and things of your kingdoms, which are brought here by your people, and in order to satisfy their disordered appetite, seize many of our people, freed and exempt men. And many times noblemen and the sons of noblemen, and our relatives are stolen, and they take them to be sold to the white men who are in our kingdoms and take them hidden or by night, so that they are not recognized. And as soon as they are taken by the white men, they are immediately ironed and branded with fire. And

when they are carried off to be embarked, if they are caught by our guards, the whites allege that they have bought them and cannot say from whom, so that it is our duty to do justice and to restore to the free their freedom. And so they went away offended.

And to avoid such a great evil we passed a law so that every white man living in our kingdoms and wanting to purchase slaves by whatever means should first inform three of our noblemen and officials of our court on whom we rely in this matter, namely Dom Pedro Manipunzo and Dom Manuel Manissaba, our head bailiff, and Gonçalo Pires, our chief supplier, who should investigate if the said slaves are captives or free men, and, if cleared with them, there will be no further doubt nor embargo and they can be taken and embarked. And if they reach the opposite conclusion, they will lose the aforementioned slaves. Whatever favor and license we give them [the white men] for the sake of your highness in this case is because we know that it is in your service too that these slaves are taken from our kingdom; otherwise we should not consent to this for the reasons stated above that we make known completely to your highness so that no one could say the contrary, as they said in many other cases to your highness, so that the care and remembrance that we and this kingdom have should not be withdrawn. . . .

We kiss your hands of your highness many times.

From our city of Kongo, the 18th day of October,

The King, Dom Afonso

QUESTIONS FOR ANALYSIS

1. **What sorts of things does King Afonso desire from the Portuguese?**

2. **What is he willing and unwilling to do in return?**

3. **What problem with his own people has the slave trade created, and what has King Afonso done about it?**

4. **Does King Afonso see himself as an equal to King João or his subordinate? Do you agree with that analysis?**

Source: From António Brásio, ed., *Monumenta Missionaria Africana: Africa Ocidental (1471–1531)* (Lisbon: Agência Geral do Ultramar, 1952), I: 468, 470–471, 488–491. Translated by David Northrup.

the Chinese fleets that had called at Calicut sixty-five years earlier and no larger than many of the dhows that filled the harbor of this rich and important trading city. The samorin (ruler) of Calicut and his Muslim officials showed only mild interest in the Portuguese as new trading partners, since the gifts brought by da Gama had provoked derisive laughter. The twelve pieces of fairly ordinary striped cloth, four scarlet hoods, six hats, and six wash basins he presented had seemed inferior goods to those accustomed to the luxuries of the Indian Ocean trade. When da Gama tried to defend his gifts as those of an explorer, not a rich merchant, the samorin cut him short, asking whether he had come to discover men or stones: "If he had come to discover men, as he said, why had he brought nothing?"

Coastal rulers soon discovered that the Portuguese had no intention of remaining poor competitors in the rich trade of the Indian Ocean. Upon da Gama's return to Portugal in 1499,

Portuguese in India In the sixteenth century Portuguese men moved to the Indian Ocean Basin to work as administrators and traders. This Indo-Portuguese drawing from about 1540 shows a Portuguese man speaking to an Indian woman, perhaps making a proposal of marriage. Album/Art Resource, NY

the jubilant King Manuel styled himself "Lord of the Conquest, Navigation, and Commerce of Ethiopia, Arabia, Persia, and India," thus setting forth the ambitious scope of his plans. Previously the Indian Ocean had been an open sea, used by merchants (and pirates) of all the surrounding coasts. Now the Portuguese crown intended to make it a Portuguese sea, the private property of Portugal alone.

The ability of little Portugal to assert control over the Indian Ocean stemmed from the superiority of its ships and weapons over those of the regional powers, especially the lightly armed merchant dhows. In 1505 a Portuguese fleet of eighty-one ships and some seven thousand men bombarded Swahili Coast cities. Indian ports were the next targets. Goa, on the west coast of India, fell to a well-armed fleet in 1510, becoming the base from which the Portuguese menaced the trading cities of Gujarat (goo-juh-RAHT) to the north and Calicut and other Malabar Coast cities to the south. The Portuguese also took the port of Hormuz, controlling entry to the Persian Gulf, in 1515, but Aden, at the entrance to the Red Sea, successfully resisted. The addition of the Gujarati port of Diu in 1535 consolidated Portuguese dominance of the western Indian Ocean.

Meanwhile, Portuguese explorers had reconnoitered the Bay of Bengal and the waters farther east. The city of Malacca (muh-LAH-kuh) on the strait between the Malay Peninsula and

Sumatra became the focus of their attention. During the fifteenth century Malacca had become the main entrepôt for the trade from China, Japan, India, the Southeast Asian mainland, and the Moluccas. Among the city's more than 100,000 residents an early Portuguese visitor counted eighty-four different languages, including those of merchants from as far west as Cairo, Ethiopia, and the Swahili Coast of East Africa. Many non-Muslim residents of the city supported letting the Portuguese join its cosmopolitan trading community, perhaps hoping to offset the growing power of Muslim traders. In 1511, however, the Portuguese seized this strategic trading center outright with a force of a thousand fighting men, including three hundred recruited in southern India.

Force was not always necessary. On the China coast, local officials and merchants interested in profitable new trade with the Portuguese persuaded the imperial government to allow the Portuguese to establish a trading post at Macao (muh-COW) in 1557. Operating from Macao, Portuguese ships came to nearly monopolize trade between China and Japan.

In the Indian Ocean, the Portuguese used their control of major port cities to enforce an even larger trading monopoly. As their power grew, they required all spices, as well as goods carried between major ports like Goa and Macao, to be carried in Portuguese ships. In addition, the Portuguese tried to control and tax other Indian Ocean trade by requiring all merchant ships entering and leaving one of their ports to carry a Portuguese passport and pay customs duties. Portuguese patrols seized vessels that attempted to avoid these monopolies, confiscated their cargoes, and either killed the captain and crew or sentenced them to forced labor.

Reactions to this power grab varied. Like the emperors of China, the Mughal (MOO-gahl) emperors of India largely ignored Portugal's maritime intrusions, seeing their interests as maintaining control over their vast land possessions. The Ottomans responded more aggressively, supporting Egypt against the Christian intruders with a large fleet and fifteen thousand men between 1501 and 1509. Then, having absorbed Egypt into their empire, the Ottomans sent another large expedition against the Portuguese in 1538. Both expeditions failed because Ottoman galleys were no match for the faster, better-armed Portuguese vessels in the open ocean. However, the Ottomans continued to exercise control over the Red Sea and Persian Gulf.

The smaller trading states of the region were less capable of challenging Portuguese domination head-on, since rivalries among them impeded the formation of a common front. Some chose to cooperate with the Portuguese to maintain their prosperity and security. Others engaged in evasion and resistance. Two examples illustrate the range of responses among Indian Ocean peoples.

The merchants of Calicut put up some of the most sustained resistance. In retaliation, the Portuguese embargoed all trade with Aden, Calicut's principal trading partner, and centered their trade on the port of Cochin, which had once been a dependency of Calicut. Some Calicut merchants became adept at evading Portuguese naval patrols, but the price of resistance was the shrinking of Calicut's commercial importance as Cochin gradually became the major pepper-exporting port on the Malabar Coast.

The traders and rulers of the state of Gujarat farther north had less success in keeping the Portuguese at bay. At first they resisted Portuguese attempts at monopoly and in 1509 joined Egypt's failed effort to sweep the Portuguese from the Arabian Sea. But in 1535, finding his state at a military disadvantage due to Mughal attacks, the ruler of Gujarat made the fateful decision to allow the Portuguese to build a fort at Diu in return for their support. Once established, the Portuguese gradually extended their control, so that by midcentury they were licensing and taxing all Gujarati ships. Even after the Mughals (who were Muslims) took control of Gujarat in 1572, the Mughal emperor Akbar permitted the Portuguese to continue their maritime monopoly in return for allowing one ship a year to carry pilgrims to Mecca without paying the Portuguese any fee.

The Portuguese never gained complete control of the Indian Ocean trade, but their naval supremacy allowed them to dominate key ports and trade routes during the sixteenth century. The resulting profits from spices and other luxury goods had a dramatic effect. The Portuguese were now able to break the pepper monopoly long held by Venice and Genoa, who both depended on Egyptian middlemen, by selling at much lower prices. They were also able to fund a more aggressive colonization of Brazil.

In both Asia and Africa the consequences flowing from these events were startling. Asian and East African traders were now at the mercy of Portuguese warships, but their individual responses affected their fates. Some were devastated. Others prospered by meeting Portuguese demands or evading their patrols. Because the Portuguese sought to control trade routes, not occupy large territories, Portugal had little impact on the Asian and African mainlands, in sharp contrast to what was occurring in the Americas.

The Americas

In contrast to the trading empires the Portuguese created in Africa and Asia, the Spanish established a vast territorial empire in the Americas. This outcome had little to do with differences between the two kingdoms, even though Spain had a much larger population and greater resources. The Spanish and Portuguese monarchies had similar motives for expansion and used identical ships and weapons. Rather, the isolation of the Amerindian peoples made their responses to outside contacts different from those of African and Indian Ocean peoples. Isolation slowed the development of metallurgy and other militarily useful technologies in the Americas and also made these large populations more susceptible to new diseases introduced by Europeans. It was the spread of deadly new diseases, especially smallpox, among Amerindians after 1518 that weakened their ability to resist and facilitated Spanish and Portuguese occupation.

The first Amerindians to encounter Columbus were the Arawak of Hispaniola (modern Haiti and the Dominican Republic) in the Greater Antilles and the Bahamas to the north (see Map 16.2). They cultivated maize (corn), cassava (a tuber), sweet potatoes, and hot peppers, as well as cotton and tobacco. Although the islands did not have large gold deposits, and, unlike West Africans, the Arawak had not previously traded gold over long distances, the natives were skilled at working gold. While the Arawak at first extended a cautious welcome to the Spanish, they soon learned to tell exaggerated stories about gold deposits in other places to persuade them to move on.

When Columbus made his second trip to Hispaniola in 1493, he brought several hundred settlers who hoped to make their fortune, as well as missionaries who were eager to persuade the Amerindians to accept Christianity. The bad behavior of the settlers, including forced labor and sexual assaults on native women, provoked the Arawak to rebel in 1495. In this and later conflicts, steel swords, horses, and body armor led to Spanish victories and the slaughter of thousands. Thousands more were forced to labor for the Spanish. Meanwhile, cattle, pigs, and goats introduced by the settlers devoured the Arawak's food crops, causing deaths from famine and disease. A governor appointed by the Spanish crown in 1502 institutionalized these demands by dividing the surviving Arawak on Hispaniola among his allies as laborers.

The actions of the Spanish in the Antilles imitated Spanish actions and motives during the wars against the Muslims in Spain in previous centuries: they sought to serve God by defeating nonbelievers and placing them under Christian control—and to become rich in the process. Individual **conquistadors** (kon-KEY-stuh-dor) (conquerors) extended that pattern around the Caribbean as gold and indigenous labor became scarce on Hispaniola. New expeditions searched for gold and Amerindian laborers across the Caribbean region, capturing thousands of Amerindians and relocating them to Hispaniola as slaves. The island of Borinquen (Puerto Rico) was conquered in 1508 and Cuba between 1510 and 1511.

Following two failed expeditions to Mexico, Governor Velázquez of Cuba appointed an ambitious and ruthless nobleman, **Hernán Cortés** (kor-TEZ) (1485–1547), to undertake a new effort. Cortés left Cuba in 1519 with six hundred fighting men, including many who had sailed with the earlier expeditions, and most of the island's stock of weapons and horses. After demonstrating his military skills in a series of battles with the Maya, Cortés learned of the rich Aztec Empire in central Mexico.

The Aztecs (also called Mexica) had conquered their vast empire only during the previous century and a half, and many subject peoples were ready to embrace the Spanish as allies. They resented the tribute payments, forced labor, and large-scale human sacrifices demanded by the Aztecs. The Aztecs also had powerful native enemies, including the Tlaxcalans (thlash-KAH-lans), who became crucial allies of Cortés. Like the peoples of Africa and Asia when confronted by Europeans, Amerindian peoples, like the Tlaxcalans of Mexico, calculated as best they could the potential benefit or threat represented by these strange visitors. Individual Amerindians

conquistadors Early-sixteenth-century Spanish adventurers who conquered Mexico, Central America, and Peru.

Hernán Cortés Spanish explorer and conquistador who led the conquest of Aztec Mexico in 1519–1521 for Spain.

Coronation of Emperor Moctezuma   This painting by an unnamed Aztec artist depicts the Aztec ruler's coronation. Moctezuma, his nose pierced by a bone, receives the crown from a prince in the palace at Tenochtitlan.   Montezuma wearing on his back the royal standard of green Quetzal bird feathers, copied from a native artist (colour litho), . / Private Collection / Peter Newark American Pictures / The Bridgeman Art Library

also made these calculations. Malintzin (mah-LEENT-zeen) (also called Malinche), a native woman given to Cortés shortly after his arrival in the Maya region, became his translator, key source of intelligence, and mistress. As peoples and as individuals, native allies were crucial to the Spanish campaign.

Moctezuma II Aztec emperor who died while in custody of the Spanish conquistador Hernán Cortés.

While the emperor **Moctezuma II** (mock-teh-ZOO-ma) (r. 1502–1520) hesitated to use force and attempted diplomacy instead, Cortés pushed toward the Aztec capital of Tenochtitlan (teh-noch-TIT-lan). Spanish forces used firearms, cavalry tactics, and steel swords to great advantage in battles along their route. In the end Moctezuma agreed to welcome the Spaniards. As they approached his island capital, the emperor went out in a great procession, dressed in his finery, to welcome Cortés.

The Execution of Inka Ruler Atahuallpa
Felipe Guaman Poma de Ayala, a native Andean from the area of Huamanga in Peru, drew this representation of the execution. While Pizarro sentenced Atahuallpa to death by strangulation, not beheading, Guaman Poma's illustration forcefully made the point that Spain had imposed an arbitrary and violent government on the Andean people.

Despite Cortés's initial pledge that he came in friendship, Moctezuma was quickly imprisoned. The Spanish looted his treasury, interfered with the city's religious rituals, and eventually massacred hundreds during a festival. These actions provoked a mass rebellion directed against both the Spanish and Moctezuma. During the Spaniards' desperate escape, the Aztecs killed half the Spanish force and four thousand of Cortés's native allies. In the confusion Moctezuma also lost his life, either killed by the Spanish or in the Aztec attack.

The survivors, strengthened by Spanish reinforcements and aided by the Tlaxcalans, renewed their attack and captured Tenochtitlan in 1521. Their victory was aided by a smallpox epidemic that killed more of the city's defenders than did the fighting. One source remembered that the disease "spread over the people as a great destruction." Many Amerindians as well as Europeans blamed the devastating spread of this disease on supernatural forces. Cortés and other Spanish leaders then led expeditions to the north and south accompanied by the Tlaxcalans and other indigenous allies. Everywhere epidemic disease, especially smallpox, helped crush indigenous resistance.

Spanish settlers in Panama had heard tales of rich and powerful civilizations to the south even before the conquest of the Aztecs. During the previous century the Inka had built a vast empire along the Pacific coast of South America (see Chapter 15). As the empire expanded through conquest, the Inka enforced new labor demands and taxes and even exiled rebellious populations from their lands.

Atahuallpa Last ruling Inka emperor of Peru. He was executed by the Spanish.

Francisco Pizarro Spanish explorer who led the conquest of the Inka Empire of Peru in 1531–1533.

About 1525 the Inka ruler Huayna Capac **(WHY-nah KAH-pak)** died in Quito, where he had led a successful military campaign. Two of his sons then fought for the throne. In the end **Atahuallpa (ah-tuh-WAHL-puh)** (r. 1531–1533), the candidate of the northern army, defeated Huascar, the candidate of the royal court at Cuzco. As a result, the Inka military was decimated and the empire's political leadership weakened by the violence; at this critical time **Francisco Pizarro (pih-ZAHR-oh)** (ca. 1478–1541) and his force of 180 men, 37 horses, and two cannon entered the region.

Pizarro had come to the Americas in 1502 at the age of twenty-five to seek his fortune and had participated in the conquest of Hispaniola and in Balboa's expedition across the Isthmus of Panama to the Pacific. In the 1520s he gambled his fortune to finance the exploration of the Pacific south of the equator, where he learned of the riches of the Inka. With a license from the king of Spain, he set out from Panama in 1531 to conquer them.

Having seen signs of the civil war after landing, Pizarro arranged to meet the Inka emperor, Atahuallpa, near the Andean city of Cajamarca (kah-hah-MAHR-kah) in November 1532. With supreme boldness and brutality, Pizarro's small band of armed men attacked Atahuallpa and his followers as they entered an enclosed courtyard. Though surrounded by an Inka army of at least forty thousand, the Spaniards were able to use their cannon to create confusion while their swords brought down thousands of the emperor's lightly armed retainers and servants. Pizarro now replicated in Peru Cortés's strategy by capturing the Inka ruler.

Atahuallpa, seeking to guard his authority, quickly ordered the execution of his imprisoned brother Huascar. He also attempted to purchase his freedom. Having noted the glee with which the Spaniards seized gold and silver, Atahuallpa offered a ransom he thought would satisfy even the greediest among them: rooms filled to shoulder height with gold and silver. The Inka paid the ransom of 13,400 pounds (6,000 kilograms) of gold and 26,000 pounds (12,000 kilograms) of silver, but the Spaniards still executed Atahuallpa. With the unity of the Inka Empire already battered by the civil war and the death of the ruler, the Spanish occupied Cuzco, the capital city.

Nevertheless, Manco Inka, whom the Spanish had placed on the throne following the execution of his brother Atahuallpa, led a massive native rebellion in 1536. Although defeated by the Spanish, Manco Inka and his followers retreated to the interior and created a much-reduced independent kingdom that survived until 1572. The victorious Spaniards, now determined to settle their own rivalries, initiated a bloody civil war fueled by greed and jealousy. Before peace was established, this struggle took the lives of Francisco Pizarro and most of the other prominent conquistadors. Incited by the fabulous wealth of the Aztecs and Inka, conquistadors now extended their exploration and conquest of South and North America, dreaming of new treasures to loot.

SECTION REVIEW

- African kingdoms reacted in various ways to the opportunities and threats created by the arrival of the Portuguese, but only Kongo embraced Christianity and accepted a large Portuguese military presence in the sixteenth century.

- However, the Portuguese used military force to consolidate a trade empire in the Indian Ocean.

- After the Spanish occupied the Caribbean, Cortés led an expedition that conquered the Aztecs, weakened by epidemic.

- The Spanish under Pizarro conquered the Inka Empire, already suffering from civil war, and then fell on each other, but surviving conquistadors continued to explore the Americas.

CONCLUSION

The voyages of exploration undertaken by the Malays, Chinese, and Polynesians pursued diverse objectives. Malay voyagers were crucial participants in the development of the rich and varied commerce of Southeast Asia and initiated connections between these markets and Arabia and Africa. The great voyages of the Chinese in the early fifteenth century were motivated by an interest in trade, curiosity, and the desire to project imperial power. For the Polynesians, exploration opened the opportunity to both project power and demonstrate expertise while at the same time settling satellite populations that would relieve population pressures. The Vikings, Africans, and Amerindians all undertook long-distance explorations as well, although with fewer lasting consequences.

The projection of European influence between 1450 and 1550 was in some ways similar to that of other cultural regions in that it expanded commercial linkages, increased cross-cultural contacts, and served the ambitions of political leaders. But the result of their voyages proved to be a major turning point in world history. During those years European explorers opened new long-distance trade routes across the world's three major oceans, for the first time establishing regular contact among all the continents. As a result, a new balance of power arose in parts of Atlantic Africa, the Indian Ocean, and the Americas.

The rapid expansion of European empires and the projection of European military power around the world would have seemed unlikely in 1492. No European power matched the military and economic strength of China, and few could rival the Ottomans. Spain lacked strong national institutions, and Portugal had a small population; both had limited economic resources. Because of these limitations, the monarchs of Spain and Portugal allowed their subjects greater initiative as they engaged distant cultures.

The pace and character of European expansion in Africa and Asia were different than in the Americas. In Africa local rulers were generally able to limit European military power to coastal outposts and to control European trade. Only in the Kongo were the Portuguese able to project their power inland. In the Indian Ocean there were mature markets and specialized production for distant consumers when Europeans arrived. Here Portuguese (and later Dutch and British) naval power allowed Europeans to harvest large profits and influence regional commercial patterns, but most native populations continued to enjoy effective autonomy for centuries.

In the Americas, however, the terrible effects of epidemic disease and the destructiveness of the conquest led to the rapid creation of European settlements and the subordination of the surviving indigenous population. The Spanish and Portuguese found few long-distance markets and little large-scale production of goods that they could export profitably to Europe. The Americas would eventually produce great amounts of wealth, but this production of gold, silver, and sugar resulted from the introduction of new technologies, the imposition of oppressive new forms of labor, such as slavery, and the development of new roads and ports.

KEY TERMS

Zheng He p. 389
Arawak p. 392
Henry the Navigator p. 394
caravel p. 395

Gold Coast p. 396
Bartolomeu Dias p. 396
Vasco da Gama p. 396
Christopher Columbus p. 396

Ferdinand Magellan p. 399
conquistadors p. 406
Hernán Cortés p. 406
Moctezuma II p. 407

Atahuallpa p. 408
Francisco Pizarro p. 408

SUGGESTED READING

Abu-Lughod, Janet. *Before European Hegemony: The World System, A.D. 1250–1350*. 1989. A speculative reassessment of the Mongols and the Indian Ocean trade in the creation of an economic world system.

Bellwood, Peter, ed. *The Austronesians: Historical and Comparative Perspectives*. 2006. Useful introduction to topic.

Cipolla, Carlo M. *Guns, Sails, and Empires: Technological Innovation and the Early Phases of European Expansion, 1400–1700*. 1965. A simple introduction to the technologies of European expansion.

Cuyvers, Luc. *Into the Rising Sun: The Journey of Vasco da Gama and the Discovery of the Modern World*. 1998. Examines the impact of finding a sea route to India.

Fernandez-Armesto, Felipe. *Before Columbus: Exploration and Colonization from the Mediterranean to the Atlantic, 1229–1492*. 1987. Examines the medieval background to European intercontinental voyages.

Hemming, John. *The Conquest of the Incas*. 2003. The best introduction to these events.

Kamen, Henry. *Spain, 1469–1714: A Society of Conflict*, 2d ed. 1991. A reliable guide to Spain in the age of maritime empire.

Levenson, Joseph R., ed. *European Expansion and the Counter Example of Asia, 1300–1600*. 1967. A collection of essays on the different expansions covered by this chapter.

McNeil, William F. *Visitors to Ancient America: The Evidence for European and Asian Presence in America Prior to Columbus*. 2004. Examines evidence of early voyages and contacts across both the Atlantic and Pacific.

Northrup, David. *Africa's Discovery of Europe, 1450–1850*. 2002. Looks at the perceptions of the peoples European explorers encountered.

Pearson, Michael. *The Indian Ocean*. 2003. A general introduction to regional geography and history.

Phillips, William D., and Carla Rhan Phillips. *The Worlds of Christopher Columbus*. 1992. Examines the mariner and his times in terms of modern concerns.

Reid, Anthony. *Southeast Asia in the Age of Commerce, 1450–1680*, 2 vols. 1988, 1993. Deals with what were known as the East Indies.

Russell-Wood, A. J. R. *The Portuguese Empire: A World on the Move*. 1998. The earliest European maritime empire.

Scammell, G. V. *The World Encompassed: The First European Maritime Empires, c. 800–1650*. 1981. A good general introduction to European expansion.

Thomas, Hugh. *Conquest: Cortés, Montezuma, and the Fall of Old Mexico*. 1995. A reliable and comprehensive survey of the topic.

Thornton, John. *Africa and Africans in the Making of the Atlantic World, 1400–1800*, 2d ed. 1998. Examines Africans' encounters with Europeans and their involvement in the Atlantic economy.

Todorov, Tzvetan. *The Conquest of America*. 1985. Focuses on the shortcomings of Columbus and his Spanish peers.

Vinton, Patrick. *On the Road of the Winds: An Archaeological History of the Pacific Islands Before European Contact*. 2002. Good survey but must be supplemented with recent DNA research.

CourseMate Go to the History CourseMate website for primary source links, study tools, and review materials for this chapter. www.cengagebrain.com

Climate and Population to 1500

During the millennia before 1500, human populations expanded in three momentous surges. The first occurred after 50,000 B.C.E. when humans emigrated from their African homeland to all of the inhabitable continents. After that, the global population remained steady for several millennia. During the second expansion, between about 5000 and 500 B.C.E., population rose from about 5 million to 100 million as agricultural societies spread around the world (see Figure 1). Again population growth then slowed for several centuries before a third surge took world population to over 350 million by 1200 C.E. (Figure 2 shows population in China and Europe).

For a long time historians tended to attribute these population surges to cultural and technological advances. Indeed, a great many changes in culture and technology are associated with adaptation to different climates and food supplies in the first surge and with the domestication of plants and animals in the second. However, historians have not found a cultural or technological change to explain the third surge, nor can they explain why creativity would have stagnated for long periods between the surges. Something else must have been at work.

Recently historians have begun to pay more attention to the impact of long-term variations in global climate. By examining ice cores drilled out of glaciers, scientists have been able to compile records of thousands of years of climate change. The comparative width of tree rings from ancient forests has provided additional data on periods of favorable and unfavorable growth. Such evidence shows that cycles of population growth and stagnation followed changes in global climate.

Historians now believe that global temperatures were above normal for extended periods from the late 1100s to the late 1200s C.E. In the temperate lands where most of the world's people lived, above-normal temperatures meant a longer

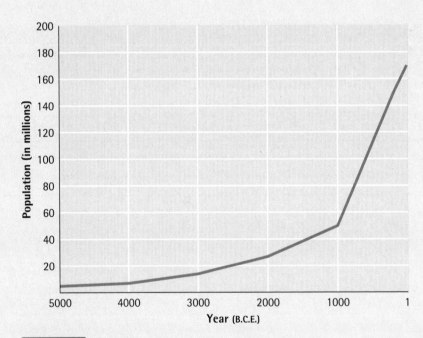

FIGURE 1 World Population, 5000–1 B.C.E. © Cengage Learning

growing season, more bountiful harvests, and thus a more adequate and reliable food supply. The ways in which societies responded to the medieval warm period are as important as the climate change, but it is unlikely that human agency alone would have produced the medieval surge. One notable response was that of the Vikings, who increased the size and range of their settlements in the North Atlantic, although their raids also caused death and destruction.

Some of the complexities involved in the interaction of human agency, climate, and other natural factors are also evident in the demographic changes that followed the medieval warm period. During the 1200s the Mongol invasions caused death and disruption of agriculture across Eurasia. China's population, which had been over 100 million in 1200, declined by a third or more by 1300. The Mongol invasions did not cause harm west of Russia, but climate changes in the 1300s resulted in population losses in Europe. Unusually heavy rains caused crop failures and a prolonged famine in northern Europe from 1315 to 1319.

The freer movement of merchants within the Mongol Empire also facilitated the spread of disease across Eurasia, culminating in the great pandemic known as the Black Death in Europe. The demographic recovery under way in China was reversed. The even larger population losses in Europe may have been affected by the decrease in global temperatures to their lowest point in many millennia between 1350 and 1375. After 1400 improving economic conditions enabled population to recover more rapidly in Europe than in China, where the conditions of rural life remained harsh.

Because many other historical circumstances interact with changing weather patterns, historians have a long way to go in deciphering the role of climate in history. Nevertheless, it is a factor that can no longer be ignored.

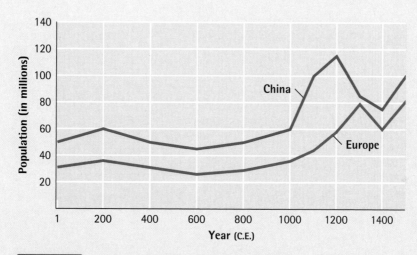

FIGURE 2 Population in China and Europe, 1–1500 C.E. © Cengage Learning

Index

Abbasid Caliphate, 251–252, 253(*map*), 254–255, 256; literature of, 260–261

Abbas (uncle of Muhammad), 251

Abbots, 279, 280. *See also* Monasteries (monks and nuns)

Abd al-Rahman, Caliph, 253

Abraham (Ibrahim), 67–68, 247, 248

Abu Bakr, Caliph, 248, 249

Abu Bakr, Sultan, 361

Academies: in Assyria, 67; Athens, 132; Tamil, in India, 180; Song China, 300

Achaean League, 137

Achaeans, 62. *See also* Greece

Achaemenids, 116, 140. *See also* Persia

Acropolis, 124, 125(*illus.*), 128, 129, 131

Ada, of Bremen, 279

Adal, 401

Adalbert, Archbishop of Hamburg-Bremen, 279

Adam and Eve story, 5

Aden, 375, 378, 404, 405

Administration (administrators). *See also* Bureaucracy; Government; Mesopotamian, 31, 32, 34; Egyptian, 42, 43; Mycenaean Greek, 61, 63; Assyrian Empire, 65; early China, 89, 90; Persian Empire, 117–118, 135, 140; Hellenistic kingdoms, 136, 137; Roman Empire, 148, 153, 166; imperial China, 158, 163, 166; imperial India, 179, 181; Andean peoples, 209; Islamic caliphate, 251; Christian monasteries, 280; Russian clergy and, 283; Japan, 305; Il-khanate, 321; Yuan China, 327

Aedisius, 239–240

Aegean world, 53, 60–62, 123(*map*). *See also* Greece; Minoan Crete, 60, 61(*map*), 62, 63(*illus.*)

Afghanistan (Afghans), 59, 377; Alexander the Great in, 238(*illus.*); Bactrian kingdom in, 179; Kushans in, 180, 227, 238; Timurids in, 322; India and, 368

Afonso I (Kongo), 401, 402–403

Africa (Africans). *See also* East Africa; North Africa; Sub-Saharan Africa; West Africa; *and specific countries and peoples*; human origins in, 5–10, 24; migration out of, 6, 7, 8–10, 9(*map*); agriculture in, 17; pastoralism in, 19; foraging in, 20; Bantu migrations in, 221, 233(*map*), 240; cultural unity in, 235–236; chronology (1230s–1433), 363; ivory trade in, 96, 230; climatic zones of, 233(*map*); Asian food crops in, 230; gold trade, 190, 252, 394, 396, 399; Portuguese exploration of, 395(*illus.*), 396, 397(*map*), 399–400, 401

African slave trade, 368, 378, 394; Portugal and, 396, 400, 401, 402, 403

Afro-Asiatic languages, 22

Afterlife, belief in: Stone Age, 15; Egyptian, 41, 44, 45(*illus.*), 46, 50; Kushite, 96; Celtic, 105; Zoroastrian, 119; Chinese, 87, 159

Agincourt, Battle of (1415), 357

Agriculture. *See also* Farmers; Irrigation; Landowners (landownership); Peasants (peasantry); Plows; Rural societies; *and specific crops*; transition from food gathering, 16–17; Neolithic revolution in, 16–20, 98; Mesopotamian, 29–30; population growth and, 20, 21, 24, 171, 412; Egyptian, 43; Chinese, 84, 87; Nubian, 96; Assyrian Empire, 66; Greek, 123(*map*), 125; Indian, 171, 181; Mesoamerica, 197, 199, 204; Chavín, 198; Roman, 144, 165; imperial China, 160, 165, 301–302, 331; swidden (shifting), 17, 186, 201, 283, 307, 363; Amerindian mound builder, 208; Southwestern desert cultures, 206; Andean civilizations, 209, 211; sub-Saharan Africa, 240; Muslim Spain, 253; Kievan Russia, 283; medieval European, 275, 284, 288, 340; East Asian, 304; Il-khanate,

321; Aztec, 380, 381; Korean, 334; Japanese, 335

Ahhijawa, 62. *See also* Greece

Ahmadabad, 377

Ahmose (Egypt), 57

Ahuramazda, 118, 120

Ain Jalut, Battle of (1260), 256, 316

A'isha (wife of Muhammad), 249, 260

Akbar, Sultan, 405

Akhenaten (Amenhotep IV), 57–58

Akkad, 32

Akkadian language, 30, 54, 56

Aksum, 98, 239–240; Stele of, 239(*illus.*)

Alalakh, 58

Al-Andalus, 253–254, 285

Alaska, Siberian land bridge and, 10

Ala-ud-Din Khalji, Sultan, 370, 378

Alcoholic beverages: beer, 20, 134, 210, 379; wine, 134–135 *and illus.*, 149

Aleppo (Syria), 258

Alexander the Great, 134–136, 137(*map*), 140; in Afghanistan, 238(*illus.*); Aristotle and, 132; death of, 136; in India, 48, 172(*map*), 178, 179, 228; Mausoleum of, 138

Alexandria, 135, 137, 139; Christianity in, 239, 258; patriarch of, 240, 258, 401

Alexius Comnenus (Byzantium), 269, 286

Algarve, 357

Algeria, 232, 253

Al-Hajj Ahmed, 377

Ali (Muhammad's son-in-law), 248, 250, 251; Fatima and, 249, 260

Al-Kashi, Ghiyas al-Din Jamshid, 324

Alliances: Hiram-Solomon, 69, 74; Mesopotamian, 32; Greek polis, 130; of Srivijayan kings, 189; in medieval Europe, 275; Mongol marriage and, 314; Mediterranean trade, 394; Portugal-Ethiopia, 401; Spanish-Amerindian, 406–407, 408

Al-Nadim, Abu al-Faraj Muhammad, 243

Alpacas, 75, 210. *See also* Llamas

Alphabet: cuneiform and, 56; Phoenician, 74; Greek, 122–123, 140, 218; Armenian, 239; Cyrillic, 270, 282; Roman, 270; Viking runes, 273(*illus.*)

Al-Rashid, Harun, Caliph, 251

Altepetl, 379

Al-Umari, 392

Amarna, 57

Americas (New World). *See also* Amerindians; North America; Mesoamerica; burial mounds in, 21; chronology (1325–1502), 363; migrations to, 9(*map*), 10; domesticated plants and animals in, 18(*map*), 19; first civilizations of, 192–217; Spanish conquistadors in, 406–409, 410

Amerindians. *See also* Andean region; Mesoamerica; hunting by, 19, 20; Northern peoples, 195, 206–209, 216; Caribbean region, 392–393 *and map*, 406; disease and, 406, 408

Amon (god), 44, 57, 58, 97 *and illus.*, 98

Amorites, 32, 99

Amos (Israel), 72–73

Amulet, 35, 45, 262(*illus.*)

Anasazi, 206–207, 208(*illus.*)

Anatolia (modern Turkey). *See also* Armenia; Ottoman Empire; Turkic (Turkish) peoples; Indo-Europeans in, 21; Çatal Hüyük, 22–23 *and illus.*; in Late Bronze Age, 79; Assyria and, 55–56, 64; Hittites in, 54(*map*), 56, 58, 62, 237; silver in, 56, 58; Troy in, 62; Celts in, 102; Lydia in, 116, 129, 238; Persia and, 115, 116, 129; Greek settlements in, 122; Seleucids in, 136, 137(*map*); Christianity in, 153, 239; Seljuk conquest of, 254, 286

Ancestor cult: Neolithic, 21; Egyptian, 45; Chinese, 86, 87, 88, 94, 135, 162, 164, 166; Roman, 147(*illus.*), 166; Southeast Asian, 188; Andean, 198; Maya, 202; Korean, 304

Andean region, 209–216; textiles of, 75, 198, 211; Chavín, 194, 196(*map*), 197–198, 209; Chimú (Chimor), 215, 216; chronology (5000 B.C.E.–1470s C.E.), 195; cultural response to environment in, 209–210, 216; Mesoamerica compared to, 216; Moche, 210–211 *and map*, 212 *and illus.*, 215; Tiwanaku and Wari, 211, 213–215; Inka Empire, 380(*map*), 382–383, 408–409 *and illus*; Spanish conquest, 408–409

Andronicus of Cyrrhus, 139(*illus.*)

Angkor (Cambodia), 364

Anglo-Saxons, 272 *and map*

Angra Mainyu, 118

Animals, 389. *See also* Camels; Cattle; Horses; Hunting; Llamas; in cave paintings, 12–13 *and illus.*; domestication of, 18(*map*), 19–20, 29, 43, 98, 108–109; as source of disease, 20; sacrifice of, 35, 70, 88, 89, 109, 126, 383; in ancient Egypt, 43; jaguar-god, 75, 195, 198; slaughter of, 320

An Lushan rebellion, 295, 297

Anna Comnena, 270

Annam, 308. *See also* Vietnam

Antigonids, 136, 137(*map*)

Antioch, 136, 239; crusaders in, 255, 285, 287; patriarch of, 258

Anyang (Shang capital), 87

Apedemak (god), 98

Aphrodite (goddess), 136(*illus.*)

Apiru, 68. *See also* Israel

Apollo (god), 88, 124, 126, 127(*illus.*)

Apologus (Basra), 231

Apostles, of Jesus, 153

Appenine Mountains, 144

Aqueducts, 154, 155(*illus.*)

Aquitaine, 287, 355, 356(*map*)

Arab armies, 250–251, 261, 267, 268; in Spain, 271

Arab caliphate. *See* Caliphates

Arabia (Arabian peninsula). *See also* Yemen (south Arabia); camel domestication in, 233, 234 *and illus.*; before Muhammad, 246–247; chronology (570–1260), 245; origins of Islam in, 246–250; Indian Ocean trade and, 227; pastoralism in, 244, 246; Chinese expeditions to, 329, 330(*map*)

Arabian Nights, 243, 251

Arabian Sea, 184, 373, 375

Arabic language, 243, 251, 254, 323; Islam and, 250, 253, 262, 361; works of Aristotle in, 251, 253, 287, 351

Arabic numerals, 181, 182

Arabic script, 377

Arab merchants, 227, 246, 374

Aragon, 394

Aramaic language, 30, 67, 99

Aramaeans, 71, 99

Arawak, 406; voyages of, 392–393 *and map*

Arcesilas of Cyrene, 112(*illus.*), 113

Archers. *See* Bows and arrows (archers)

Arches: Roman use of, 154, 155(*illus.*); in Gothic cathedrals, 347(*illus.*)

Archilochus, 126–127

Architecture. *See also* Construction materials and techniques; Housing; *and specific types of buildings (e.g., churches, pyramids, temples)*; in Mesopotamia, 34(*illus.*), 35, 39; Egyptian pyramids, 41, 42(*illus.*), 45; Gupta India, 176(*illus.*); Mesoamerican pyramids, 194, 199(*illus.*), 201 *and illus.*; Toltec, 202(*illus.*), 205; Andean, 213, 214; Aksumite, 239(*illus.*); Islamic, 255(*illus.*), 377; Byzantine, 270; Japanese, 306, 308(*illus.*), 335; Timurid, 323(*illus.*); Chinese, 329; mosques, in India, 377

Ardashir (Iran), 244

Ares (war god), 100

Aristarchus, 139

Aristocracy (nobility). *See also* Elite class; Landowners; Egyptian, 43; Mycenean, 61; Israelite, 70, 71; Assyrian, 64; Carthaginian, 77; early Chinese, 90, 95; Persian, 116, 117; Greek, 125–126, 131; Roman, 145, 147, 151, 157; Teotihuacan, 200; Andean peoples, 210, 215; Chinese imperial, 158, 159, 165, 292, 301; Sasanid Empire, 244 *and illus.*; in Byzantine Empire, 269, 270; Crusades and, 285, 286, 287; Japanese, 305, 307; Mongol, 318–319, 321, 328; medieval Europe, 273, 275 *and illus.*, 339–340, 354–355; Aztec, 380, 381; Inka, 383

Aristotle, 132, 139; Arab translations of, 251, 253, 287, 351; European scholars and, 351

Arizona, native peoples of, 206, 207 *and map*

Arjuna, 169, 180

Ark of the Covenant, 69

Armed forces (soldiers). *See also* Cavalry; Military; Navy (warships); War (warfare); Warrior elite; *and specific wars*; Mesopotamian, 32, 39; Egyptian, 43; Israelite, 69; Assyrian Empire, 77; early Chinese, 95; Greek (hoplites), 124, 126, 128, 130; Macedonian, 134; Persian Empire, 130; Roman, 147, 148 *and illus.*, 149, 153, 154, 155, 166; imperial Chinese, 159, 160, 161(*illus.*), 166; Indian, 179, 181; Toltec, 204; Arab Muslim, 250–251, 261, 267, 268, 271; Khitan, 298; Mongol, 315, 326, 334, 335, 341; Delhi Sultanate, 370

Armenia (Armenians), 64; Christianity in, 239; Urartu in, 79, 115

Armillary spheres, 301(*illus.*), 323 *and illus.*

Armor, body: Greek hoplite, 124, 147; of medieval knights, 274, 276, 287(*illus.*); in China, 300; conquistador, 406

Art and artists. *See also* Cave paintings; Painting(s); Wall murals (frescoes); Gandhara, 175(*illus.*), 238(*illus.*); Saharan rock art, 4, 5(*illus.*), 231, 232(*illus.*), 236; Byzantine, 270; Renaissance Europe, 353–354 *and illus.*

Arthashastra, 178–179, 185

Artillery, 357. *See also* Cannon

Artisans (craftspeople). *See also* *specific crafts*; Neolithic, 22, 23; in Mesopotamia, 31, 33; Aegean trade and, 62; Assyrian, 66; Egyptian, 96; Kushite, 96; Scythian, 100(*illus.*); Greek, 126; Indian guilds, 180, 181, 184; Olmec, 196; Silk Road trade and, 224; Anasazi, 206; Andean, 198, 211, 213; medieval Europe, 275, 283; Kievan Russia, 283; printing, 353; in Samarkand, 323(*illus.*); guilds of, in Europe, 342; Venetian, 346

Art of War (Sunzi), 90

Aryas, 171–172, 175, 176

Asceticism, 280. *See also* Monasteries; in India, 174

Ashikaga Shogunate (Japan), 335–336

Ashoka (India), 178; Buddhism and, 174(*illus.*), 179, 238

Ashurbanipal (Assyria), 67

Ashur (city), 55, 64, 65

Ashur (god), 64

Asia. *See also* Central Asia; East Asia; Southeast Asia; Western Asia; early humans in, 6; trade and communication routes in, 226(*map*); as center of power, 387

Askia Muhammad, 378

Assassin sect, 323

Assembly: Mesopotamia, 32; Carthage, 77; Athens, 129, 132; Alexandria, 138; Roman, 144, 145, 149

Assyria (Assyrians), 55–56, 59

Assyrian Empire (Neo-Assyrian Empire), 64–67; conquest and control in, 64–65 *and map*; Egypt and, 64, 79, 97; kingship, 64; mass deportations in, 65, 66, 71, 79, 80; Medes and, 79, 115; Persian Empire and, 118; society and culture, 65–66; trade in, 64; tribute and, 64, 65, 71, 74(*illus.*), 77

Astarte (goddess), 76

Astrolabe, 323, 395

Astrology, horoscopes and, 88

Astronomy: Mesopotamian, 39; Babylonian, 138–139; Olmec, 195; Greek, 138, 139 *and illus.*; Islamic, 258, 327, 337; Il-khanate, 323–324; imperial China, 164, 299, 301(*illus.*), 329; Korean, 333; observatories and, 323–324 *and illus.*, 329; Copernican, 323, 351

Aswan, 40, 96

Atahualpa (Inka), 408 *and illus.*, 409

Aten (sun-god), 57

Athena (goddess), 125(*illus.*), 230(*illus.*)

Athens, 123, 124, 128–129; acropolis in, 125(*illus.*), 128; democracy in, 129, 130, 131, 132; height of power, 130–132; in Hellenistic Age, 137–138; navy of, 130, 131(*illus.*); Peloponnesian War and, 133; slavery in, 129, 132; Tower of the Winds in, 139(*illus.*)

Atlantic Ocean, exploration of: (1450–1550), 395–396, 397(*map*), 398; before 1450, 78, 272, 389, 392–393, 413; chronology (770–1536), 389; winds of, 396, 398

Atman (self), 173, 175

Atomic theory, 127

Auctoritas, of Roman men, 145

Augustus (Octavian), 146(*map*), 154, 167; equites and, 149

Australia: migration to, 9(*map*), 10; extinctions in, 12; foraging peoples in, 20

Australopithecines, 6, 7, 11

Australopithecus africanus, 6

Austria: mining in, 343; salt mines in, 365

Austronesian languages, 388, 391

Authoritarian rule, 86. *See also* Tyrants

Avataras, 178

Averroës (Ibn Rushd), 253–254

Avicenna (Ibn Sina), 287, 351

Avignon, popes in, 349, 355

Ayllu (Andean clan), 210, 211, 213

Azerbaijan, 262

Azores Islands, 392, 395, 396

Aztecs (Aztec Empire), 379–382, 380(*map*). *See also* Mexica; Inka compared to, 384; Toltecs and, 204, 205, 380; Spanish conquest of, 381, 406–408

Baal (Hammon), 71, 78

Babylon (city), 32, 99; New Year's Festival, 35, 36–37; Assyrian conquest of, 79; Cyrus in, 71; Israelites in, 71; protests against ruling class in, 73; renaissance of, 80

Babylonia. *See also* Mesopotamia; Creation Myth, 35, 36–37; Hammurabi's Law Code in, 32, 33; Kassite dynasty in, 54–55; Neo-Babylonian (Chaldaean), 71, 76, 79, 80; Persian Empire and, 116, 117; world map from, 2(*illus.*)

Babylonian language, 55

Bactria, 175, 228

Baghdad: books in, 242(*illus.*), 243; caliphate in, 251, 252, 258; decline of, 255; Mongol sack of, 251, 253(*map*), 256, 315, 320, 375

Bahamas, Columbus in, 406

Bahmani kingdom, 369(*map*), 372

Balboa, Vasco Núñez de, 409

Balkan kingdoms, 326

Balkh, 316, 321

Ball games, in Mesoamerica, 195, 196, 202(*illus.*)

Baltic region: Germans in, 340; trading cities in, 345; trading fairs in, 281

Baluchistan desert, 114

Bananas, 230, 235, 236, 363, 379, 391

Banks, in medieval Europe, 346–347

Bantu migrations, in Africa, 221, 233(*map*), 240; iron working and, 236–237

Ban Zhao, 162

Barbarians: China and, 158, 159, 165, 166, 294, 295, 390; Greeks and, 125, 132; Rome and, 166

Barley, 17, 18(*map*), 23, 24, 29, 48, 108, 122, 331

Barter: in Mesopotamia, 33; in Rome, 157; in medieval Europe, 273; in Byzantium, 269; Aztec, 381

Basra (Apologus), 231, 257, 258

Bathing (purification) rites: in Israel, 71; in India, 173, 177

Batu, Khan, 314, 316(*fig.*), 317(*map*), 320, 324, 325. *See also* Golden Horde

Bayeaux Tapestry, 266(*illus.*), 275, 284

Beer making, 20, 134, 210, 379

Beeswax, for candles, 38

Beijing, 314, 315; Forbidden City in, 327, 329, 330; observatory in, 323

Belgium. *See* Flanders (Flemish)

Benedictine abbey of Cluny, 280

Benedict of Nursia, 279

Bengal, Islam in, 377–378

Benin: bronze of, 400(*illus.*); Portuguese in, 400 *and illus.*, 401

Berbers, 228; revolts by, 252; in Spain, 250, 253, 271; collapse of Ghana and, 366

Berytus, 74

Bhagavad-Gita, 169, 176, 180

Bible, the: Hebrew (Old Testament), 5, 67–69, 71, 74; Islam and, 247, 248; New Testament, 153, 353; Gutenberg, 353

Bilma, salt trade in, 365 *and illus.*

Bindusara (India), 178

Bipedalism, 6, 7, 10(*illus.*)

Birth control, 259

Bisexuality, in ancient Greece, 133

Bishops, 154, 280; appointment (investiture) of, 277; councils of, 245, 275; Ethiopian, 240

Bison (buffalo), 20

Black Death, 338(*illus.*), 339, 341, 342 *and map*, 359, 413; Jews and, 346, 349

Black Sea area, 256; colonies in, 100, 124, 345; Italian city-states and, 394; plague in, 341, 342(*map*)

Blacksmiths, 56, 71, 276, 366. *See also* Iron industry and tools

Blombos Cave (South Africa), 12

Bloodletting rituals, 196, 202, 203. *See also* Sacrifice

Boats. *See also* Canoes; Ships and shipping; Mesopotamian, 32, 37; Norman, 266(*illus.*); in coastal Pacific, 393; Kievan Russia, 281

Boccaccio, Giovanni, 352, 353

Bodhisattvas, 175, 189, 239, 292–293. *See also* Mahayana Buddhism; rulers as, 294, 298

Body armor. *See* Armor, body

Bolivia, Tiwanaku in, 211, 213

Bologna, University of, 351

Boniface, Bishop of Mainz, 278–279

Boniface VIII, Pope, 355

Book of Changes, 90, 91

Book of Documents, 89, 91

Book of Kells, 280(*illus.*)

Book of Songs, 89, 90, 91

Book of the Dead, Egyptian, 45 *and illus.*

Books. *See also* Libraries; Literacy; Printing technology; Maya, 214; in Baghdad, 242(*illus.*), 243; in China, 301

Bordeaux, 274

Borobodur temple (Java), 189(*illus.*), 190, 222(*illus.*)

Bows and arrows (archers): Iceman, 16 *and illus.*; Mesopotamian, 39; Hyksos, 57; Assyrian, 65; Egyptian, 59 *and illus.*; Nubian, 97; crossbows, 164, 355, 389; Indian, 181; Central Asian, 227; flaming arrows, 300, 316, 332 *and illus.*; Mongol, 316; Khitan, 298; in Mali, 367; English longbow, 355

Bo Zhuyi, 295

Brahmanas, 173

Brahmins, 172, 173, 175, 183, 186; oral tradition and, 219; Muslim rule and, 371, 372

Brain size, in early humans, 6, 7, 8(*illus.*), 11, 14

Brazil, 19; Portuguese claim to, 396, 399, 405; sugar and slavery on, 396

Breadfruit, 391

Bridge building: Roman, 154; in China, 300

Britain, 59. *See also* England; Celts in, 102, 103(*map*), 104, 105;

Romans in, 146(*map*), 155; Viking raids in, 272; salt trade monopoly and, 368

Bronze: in Mesopotamia, 37; oil lamp, 38(*illus.*); coins, 125; in early China, 85, 86(*illus.*), 87, 94(*illus.*), 135; iron compared to, 53, 111, 171; in Aegean Sea region, 62; in Southeast Asia, 187; for cannon, 326, 332; Benin, 400(*illus.*)

Bronze Age. *See* Late Bronze Age

Bruges, 285, 345

Brunei, 330

Brutus "the Liberator," 144

Bubonic plague, 269, 326; as Black Death in Europe, 338(*illus.*), 339, 341, 342 *and map*; at Kaffa, 320, 341

Buddha (Siddhartha Gautama), 174, 175(*illus.*)

Buddhism. *See also* Mahayana Buddhism; origins of, in India, 173, 174–175, 178, 179, 180, 183 *and illus.*; cave paintings, 183 *and illus.*, 299(*illus.*); in Central Asia, 227; in China, 164, 181, 291, 292, 298, 300–301; in East Asia, 309; in Japan, 305, 306, 335; in Korea, 304, 305, 333; Mahayana, 175, 178, 239, 292–293, 298, 308; missionaries, 188, 291; pilgrims, 174(*illus.*), 181, 189, 229, 238, 291; in Southeast Asia, 378; spread of, 175, 221, 226(*map*), 238–239; temples, 189(*illus.*), 190, 222(*illus.*), 292, 306; Theravada, 175, 239; Tibetan, 327, 329; Mongols and, 320, 327, 329; Zen (Chan), 301, 333, 335

Buddhist monasteries (monks and nuns), 164, 175, 181, 183, 190, 378; in China, 292, 293, 295–296, 305; gunpowder and, 332; head shaving in, 263

Bukhara, 223; Samanids in, 252, 255(*illus.*)

Bureaucracy (bureaucrats). *See also* Administration; Sumerian, 32; Egyptian, 43; Mycenaean Greek, 60; Israelite, 69; in Hellenistic kingdoms, 137; Roman, 149; Indian, 181; Southeast Asian, 188; Chimú (Peru), 215; imperial Chinese, 163, 291, 301, 304; Inka, 383; Vietnamese, 336; Delhi

Sultanate, 372; West African (Benin), 400

Burials (graves). *See also* Tombs; Stone Age, 15; Neolithic, 21; Egyptian, 58; Mycenaean, 60, 61; Siberian, 101; Celtic, 105; Chinese, 163(*illus.*); Northern Amerindian, 209; Andean, 211, 212 *and illus.*; Maya, 212 *and illus.*; in Kievan Russia, 283; Black Death, 338(*illus.*)

Burma (Myanmar), 376; Buddhism in, 239

Business, in China, 303, 328

Buyid family, 252, 254

Byblos, 74

Byzantine Empire, 158, 287–288; (600–1200), 267–270; beleaguered, 267–268; Crusades and, 285; cultural achievements, 270; Russia and, 267, 281–282 *and map*, 283; Sasanid Iran and, 244, 246; scholars in, 351; Seljuk challenge to, 254, 286; society and urban life, 269–270; Ottoman Empire and, 326, 356(*map*)

Byzantium, 157, 326. *See also* Constantinople

Cabral, Pedro Alvares, 396, 399

Cacao (cocoa), 196, 212

Cadiz (Gades), 76 *and map*

Caesar, 148. See *also* Augustus (Octavian)

Cahokia, mound builders of, 208–209

Cairo (Fustat), 256, 345, 368; Islamic Caliphate and, 253, 254(*illus.*), 258; Mamluks in, 366

Calendars: stone circle, 21; Sumerian, 32; Egyptian, 46, 138; Mesoamerican, 195, 203; Chinese, 299, 301(*illus.*), 329; Yuan China, 327; Il-khanate, 323; Inka, 383; Korean, 331, 333, 334

Calicut (modern Kozhikode), 376, 390; Portuguese and, 402–403, 405

Caliphates (Arab Caliphates, 632–1258 C.E.), 249–256. *See also* Islam; Abbasid, 251–252, 253(*map*), 254–255, 256; rise and fall of, 250–256; assault on, 254–256; bookstores in, 243; cities of, 253, 254, 257–258; Fatimid, 252–253 *and map*, 254; political

fragmentation, 251–254, 261; Umayyad, 249, 251, 253(*map*), 254, 285

Calixtus II, Pope, 277

Calpolli, Aztec, 379, 381

Cambay (modern Khambhat), 376, 377

Cambodia, Angkor, 364

Cambridge University, 351

Cambyses (Persia), 113, 114(*map*), 116

Camel, Battle of the (656), 249, 260

Camels, 30, 98, 246; domestication of, 59, 109, 232; saddles for, 234 *and illus.*; Silk Road trade and, 227(*illus.*); trans-Saharan caravan routes and, 232–233, 234(*illus.*), 365 *and illus.*, 368; used in warfare, 234

Cameroon, 237

Canaan (Canaanites), 74. *See also* Phoenicia; Israel and, 69, 70–71, 80

Canals. *See also* Irrigation; in Mesopotamia, 31; in Egypt, 46; in Persia, 117; in China, 164, 292, 327

Canary Islands, 392, 396, 398

Candles and lamps, 38 *and illus.*

Cannon, 331, 347, 357; bronze for, 326, 332; on ships, 389, 395; conquistador, 408, 409

Canoes: in Southeast Asia, 187; of Africans, 237, 392; of Madagascar colonists, 230; of Polynesian colonists, 391

Canon law, 275

Canterbury: archbishop of, 277, 341; pilgrimage to, 277

Canterbury Tales (Chaucer), 343, 346, 352

Caracalla (Rome), 153

Caracol, 193

Caramansa, 399–400

Caravan trade and routes. *See also* Silk Road; Trans-Saharan trade and caravan routes; Egypt and, 43, 58; Nubia and, 96; in Arabia, 246, 247

Caravel (ship), 395, 398 *and illus.*

Caribbean Sea and region (West Indies): Amerindians of, 392–393 *and map*; Columbus's exploration of, 398, 406; sugar and slavery on, 396

Carib people, voyages of, 392–393 *and map*

Carolingian Empire, 272. *See also* Charlemagne

Carthage (Carthaginians), 52(*illus.*), 77–79; founding of, 53, 77; child sacrifice in, 78, 79(*illus.*); commercial empire of, 77–78; naval power of, 77, 78, 80; war and religion, 78–79; wars with Rome, 148

Castes (varna), in India, 172–173, 183, 390

Castile, 394

Castle of the Mine, 395(*illus.*)

Çatal Hüyük, 22–23 *and illus.*

Catapults, 134, 316, 334

Cathedrals. *See* Churches (cathedrals)

Catholicism (Catholic church), 339; head shaving in, 263; in Lithuania, 325; missionaries, 351, 401; in Africa, 401

Cattle (cattle herders). *See also* Oxen; domestication of, 19, 24, 98, 108, 231; Saharan, 4(*illus.*), 5, 231–232 *and illus.*; Indo-European; Nubian, 96; Celtic, 103; Israelite, 68; Greek, 122; Indian, 171; sub-Saharan Africa, 235, 363; Khitan, 298; in Egypt, 236; Zimbabwe, 375

Caucasus, Golden Horde in, 320

Cavalry (horsemen). *See also* Horses; Knights; Assyrian, 65; Philip II's use of (Macedonia), 134; Chinese, 159, 161, 164; Indian, 181; Scythian, 225; stirrups and, 227, 274, 292, 295(*illus.*); Russian, 283; Inner Asian, 292, 295(*illus.*); Khitan, 298; Tang woman, 297(*illus.*); Korean, 305(*illus.*); Mongol, 316, 327, 334, 335; Benin, 400(*illus.*); conquistador, 406, 407, 408

Cave paintings: Stone Age, 11, 12–13 *and illus.*, 15; Saharan rock art, 4(*illus.*), 5, 231, 232(*illus.*); Buddhist, in India, 183 *and illus.*; Buddhist, in China, 299(*illus.*)

Celtic languages, 102, 272(*map*)

Celts (Celtic Europe), 81, 102–105. *See also* Ireland (Irish); Scotland; Wales (Welsh); belief and knowledge, 104–105; in Britain, 102, 103(*map*), 104; chronology (1000–390 B.C.E.), 85; Druids (priests), 89, 103, 104, 105, 218; legends of, 105, 219; Romans and, 103, 104, 105, 148; society of, 103–104; spread of, 102–103

Census: in Israel, 69; in China, 162, 327, 328

Central Africa. *See* Sub-Saharan Africa

Central Asia (Central Asians). *See also* Il-khanate Empire (Iran); Inner Asia; pastoralism in, 19; horses from, 59; nomadism in, 179, 185, 187, 314; Rome and, 146(*map*); Silk Road and, 185, 223, 226–227; China and, 293, 295(*illus.*); chronology (747–1036), 245; Nestorial Christianity in, 245–246; Turkic peoples of, 252; bubonic plague in, 320; Chagatai khanate in, 315, 317(*map*), 321; chronology (1219–1453), 315; Yuan China and, 327, 328

Centralization. *See also* Monarchy; in Yuan China, 327; in East Asia (1200–1500), 333–336; Delhi Sultanate, 372

Ceramics. *See also* Porcelain; Pottery; Olmec, 198; Hohokam, 206; Andean, 211 *and illus.*, 215; Maya, 192(*illus.*); Chinese, 297(*illus.*), 332

Cernunnos (god), 104, 105(*illus.*)

Ceuta (Morocco), Portuguese in, 394

Ceylon (Sri Lanka), 388; Buddhism in, 238, 239; as Indian tributary state, 372; irrigation in, 364; Sinhalese in, 364

Chaco Canyon, 206–207

Chagatai Khanate, 315, 317(*map*), 321

Chaldaean dynasty (Neo-Babylonian Kingdom), 71, 76, 79, 80, 116

Champa, 308, 330(*map*). *See also* Vietnam; Mongols and, 336

Champagne fairs, 345

Champa rice, 308

Chan Chan, 215

Chandra Gupta (India), 181, 185

Chandragupta Maurya (India), 178

Chang'an, 161, 162–163, 166; Silk Road trade and, 223; as Sui and Tang capital, 292, 298

Charcoal, for ironworking, 276, 343

Chariots: Persian, 116(*illus.*); in Sahara region, 232

Chariot warfare, 39, 61, 65, 69, 169, 179, 227; Egyptian, 56, 57, 59 *and illus.*; in early China, 86, 90

Charlemagne, 267, 276; intellectual revival under, 272, 280, 350

Charles Martel, 272

Charles VII (France), 357

Chaucer, Geoffrey, 343, 346, 352

Chauvet caves (France), 12 *and illus.*, 13

Chavín, 194, 196(*map*), 209; trade of, 197–198

Chavín de Huantar, 196(*map*), 197, 198

Chemistry: Egyptian, 45; Islamic, 262

Cheras, 180

Chess (game), 259(*illus.*)

Chichen Itza, 204(*map*), 205

Chickens, 109, 391

Chieftains (chiefdoms): Northern Amerindian, 206, 207, 208; Arab, 244, 246; Germanic, 274; Japanese, 305; Liao, 298; Aztec, 381; Inka, 382; Polynesian, 391

Childrearing, 14, 75, 104, 162. *See also* Family

Child sacrifice (infanticide): in Carthage, 78, 79(*illus.*); in Greece, 132

Chimú Empire (Chimor), 215, 216

China, early: rice in, 17, 18(*map*), 84, 87(*map*); agriculture, 84, 87; domesticated animals in; ancestor worship, 86, 87, 88, 135; Yellow River Valley in, 27, 28(*map*), 81; bronze in, 85, 86(*illus.*), 87, 94(*illus.*), 135; chronology (8000–338 B.C.E.), 85; Confucianism in, 91–94; Daoism in, 91, 92, 94; divination in, 88, 89(*illus.*), 90; geography and resources, 84; Legalism in, 92, 93, 95; monarchy, 86, 88–89; Shang period, 85–88, 87(*map*); Warring States Period, 92, 95, 101; warrior elite, 86; women and men in, 94; Zhou period, 87(*map*), 88–95

China, imperial. *See also* Han Empire; Song Empire; Tang Empire; Yuan Empire; *and individual emperors*; expansion of, 160(*map*), 161, 166; agriculture in, 160, 165, 301–302, 331; origins of, 158–165; slavery in, 378; Qin, 95, 158–159, 160(*map*), 304; society in, 162–163, 300–304; aristocracy in, 158, 159, 165, 292, 301; Rome compared to, 143, 150–151, 164, 165–167; cities, 161, 162–163, 166, 302, 303, 327–328;

nomadic peoples and, 159, 160(*map*); military of, 159, 161, 163, 165, 292, 302; population of, 162, 302, 340, 413 *and fig.*; family in, 91, 162, 166, 295, 302; chronology (480 B.C.E.–220 C.E.), 145; Funan and, 188; glass industry in, 156; India and, 188; taxation, 159, 295, 327, 328, 365; trade in, 293, 302, 303, 329, 373; Buddhist pilgrims from, 174(*illus.*), 181, 229, 238–239; women, 294–295, 297(*illus.*), 303–304 *and illus.*; chronology (220–1279), 293; copper coinage in, 238, 328; rebellions in, 159, 165, 295, 297, 298; Sui Empire, 291, 292; gentry in, 295, 298, 302, 303; Japan and, 294(*map*), 298, 328; chronology (1234–1433), 315; headcovering in, 263; emperors, 160–161 *and illus.*, 165, 167, 292, 300; Portugal and, 405

Chinampas (floating gardens), 200, 211, 216, 381

Chinese language, 86, 158, 293, 306 *and illus.*, 328

Chinggis Khan, 316(*fig.*), 337; conquests of, 313, 314–315, 317(*map*)

Choe dynasty (Korea), 333

Cholas, 180, 190

Cholula, 205, 216

Choson kingdom (Korea), 333–334

Christianity (Christians). *See also* Christian Orthodoxy; Israel and, 67; rise of, 153–154, 167; in Africa, 394, 401, 402–403; Jesus Christ and, 153; spread of, 221, 239–240; Zoroastrianism and, 119, 245; Constantine and, 157; conversion to, 157; Egyptian, 251; Ethiopian, 239–240, 367, 375, 401; Islam and, 246, 248, 261, 271(*map*); Nestorian, 227, 245; pilgrims, 277, 285; protection for Jews and, 348–349; scholasticism and, 351

Christian militancy, 394. *See also* Conquistadors; Crusades

Christian missionaries, 275; in Africa, 239–240; in Caribbean, 406; Nestorian, 245; Orthodox, 270, 282

Christian monasteries and convents, 278–280; Irish, 263, 280 *and illus.*

Christian Orthodoxy: Byzantine churches, 268(*illus.*), 270, 281, 282 *and illus.*, 283; missionaries, 270, 282; Russian, 270, 281–282, 283, 288, 324, 325; schism with Latin Church, 268–269

Christian patriarchs. *See* Patriarch

Christian (Western) Church, 275–280. *See also* Papacy; monasticism, 278–280; politics and, 276–278; schism in, 355; struggle for morality in, 278–279

Chunkey (Amerindian game), 208–209

Churches (cathedrals): Byzantine, 268(*illus.*), 270, 281, 282 *and illus.*, 283; medieval Europe, 275(*illus.*); Gothic, 347, 349; St. Peter's Basilica, 354

Cimmerians, 100

Circassians, 256

Cities and towns (urban centers). *See also* City-states; Urbanization; *and specific cities and towns*; Neolithic, 22–23; Indus Valley, 47, 48(*illus.*), 49; Israelite, 69, 70; in ancient Egypt, 42, 44; Carthage, 77; in early China, 90; Nubian, 96, 98; Hellenistic Age, 136; in Roman Empire, 150–152 *and illus.*, 166; in imperial China, 161, 162–163, 166; Andean, 197, 213(*illus.*), 215; India, 179, 180; Mesoamerican, 193, 203, 204–205; Northern Amerindian, 208–209; Olmec, 194–195, 196; on Silk Road, 226; Indian Ocean trade and, 229, 404; Islamic caliphate, 253, 254, 257–258; in Kievan Russia, 281, 283; revival of, in medieval Europe, 283, 284–285; Mongol siege of, 316; in imperial China, 302, 303, 327–328; in late medieval Europe, 343–346 *and map*, 355; Aztec, 381; in Andean region, 382, 389, 409

Citizenship (citizens): Greek, 128, 129; Alexandria, 138; Roman, 144, 148, 153, 154

City-states: definition of, 31; Mesopotamian, 31; Phoenician, 53, 71, 74, 76, 80; Greek polis, 122–126 (*See also* Athens; Sparta); Maya, 193, 201; North African, 252–253; East African ports, 374; Italian, 394; Hausa, 367(*map*), 368

Civilization(s): definition of, 23; river valley, 3, 27, 28(*map*), 29, 49; indicators of, 27; Minoan Crete, 53, 60–62, 61(*map*), 63(*illus.*); Mycenean Greece, 60–63 *and map*

Civil service. *See also* Administration; Bureaucracy; Roman, 149, 166; Chinese, 166, 301; examinations for, in East Asia, 161, 163, 300, 301, 305, 331 *and illus.*,336

Civil wars. *See also specific civil wars*; in China, 92, 95, 101, 165; in Roman Republic and Empire, 149, 155; in Islam, 249; in Japan, 307, 336; in Inka Empire, 383, 409

Clans. *See also* Kinship systems; Chinese, 94; Japanese, 307; Andean ayllu, 210, 211, 213; Aztec calpolli, 379, 381

Classes. *See* Social classes; *and specific classes*

Classic of the Way of Virtue, 91

Claudius (Rome), 146(*map*)

Clay, in Mesopotamia, 2(*illus.*)

Cleopatra (Egypt), 137

Clergy. *See* Priests (clergy)

Clermont, Council of (1095), 286

Climate and weather (climate change). *See also* Monsoons; Natural disasters; Rainfall; early humans and, 7; Agricultural Revolution and, 20, 24; in Sahara, 40–41; Indus Valley, 48; East Asia, 84; Southeast Asia, 186; Africa, 233(*map*); in Iran and Iraq, 254, 255, 284; medieval Europe, 283, 340; tropical environments, 302; Korean meteorology, 331, 334; Vikings and, 392; population and, 412–413 *and fig.*

Clocks: in China, 301(*illus.*); in European cities, 350 *and illus.*

Clothing (costume). *See also* Textiles (textile industry); Iceman, 15, 16(*illus.*); Celtic warrior, 103; Roman toga, 153; Mesoamerican, 202 *and illus.*; Indian, 229; head coverings, 263 *and illus.*; Mongol nobles, 318–319

Cluny, Benedictine abbey of, 280

Cnossus, palace complex at, 60

Coal mining, 326; in China, 299

Coca, 198, 210

Cochin, 405

Cocoa (cacao), 196, 212

Coeur, Jacques, 357

Coins (coinage): invention of, 125; devalued Roman, 157; Indian, 179, 180, 181; copper, 238, 328; gold, 125, 251, 252, 253, 285, 396; silver, 125, 251, 285; spread of idea of, 238; Muslim, 251, 252, 253, 258, 285; imperial China, 158, 238, 328; Kievan Russia, 281; Hellenistic, 230(*illus.*); Delhi Sultanate, 372

Coleridge, Samuel Taylor, 327

Colleges and universities: in Athens, 138; in Han China, 161; in India, 183; Islamic madrasas, 262, 351; European Renaissance and, 350–351

Colonies (colonization). *See also* Expansion; Portuguese maritime exploration; *specific colonial powers*; Phoenician, 75, 76 *and map*, 79; Greek, 100, 124, 136; Indonesian, in Madagascar, 222(*illus.*), 230; Andean, 210; Black Sea area, 100, 124, 345; Roman, in North Africa, 234; Pacific Islands, 391, 392(*map*)

Colorado, native peoples of, 206, 207, 208(*illus.*)

Columbus, Christopher, 311, 358, 396, 397(*map*), 399; in Caribbean region, 398, 406

Communes, in medieval Europe, 284

Communication(s). *See also* Language(s); Writing; in ancient Egypt, 42; in Assyrian Empire, 65; exchange networks and, 223; and trade, in Asia, 226(*map*); Chinese canal and, 291–292

Compass, 299, 373, 395

Concordat of Worms (1122), 277

Concrete, invention of, 154

Concubines, 94, 259, 295, 378

Confederacy of Corinth, 134

Conflict of the Orders (Rome), 145

Confucianism, 91–94, 291; Buddhism and, 164, 293–294; Daoism and, 91, 92, 94; family and, 166; scholar-officials and, 94, 158, 161–162, 163; Legalism and, 92, 93, 158; in East Asia (other than China), 304, 305, 307, 308, 309; Neo-Confucianism, 300, 301, 333; revival of, in Song China, 300, 301, 303; in Yuan China, 327, 333; examination system and, 331

Confucius (Kongzi), 89; Analects of, 91, 92–93

Congo River, 401

Conquistadors, in Americas, 406–409

Conscript army, in China, 90, 163, 165

Constantine (Byzantium), 157–158

Constantinople, 239, 254, 288; founding of, 157–158; Crusade against, 285, 286 *and map*, 345; Hagia Sofia cathedral in, 270; patriarch of, 268, 275, 282; pilgrims in, 270; Russia and, 281–282, 324; Ottoman conquest of, 326, 339, 356(*map*)

Construction materials and techniques. *See also* Architecture; Engineering; Housing; Neolithic, 17(*illus.*); Mesopotamia, 34(*illus.*), 39; Egyptian pyramids, 41, 42(*illus.*); Indus Valley, 47; Athens, 125(*illus.*); Andean, 198; medieval Europe, 275(*illus.*); Japanese, 306, 308(*illus.*)

Cooking, invention of, 14

Copernicus, Nicholas, 323, 351

Copper, 23, 47, 56(*illus.*); Andean, 211; for bronze, 59, 62; Chinese coins, 238, 328; African, 236, 252, 366 *and illus.*, 375, 378; Indian, 182(*illus.*); Hungarian, 343, 347

Coptic language, 251

Córdova (Spain), 253, 261, 357

Corinth, Confederacy of, 134

Corn. *See* Maize

Corporations, in Yuan China, 328

Corpus Juris Civilis (Body of Civil Law), 270, 278

Cortés, Hernán, 381, 406–408

Cosmic order (cosmology). *See also* Creation myths; Hindu (Indian), 176, 182; Maya, 202; sub-Saharan Africa, 235; Chinese, 300

Cosmopolitanism: Late Bronze Age (Middle East), 54–59, 80; in Hellenistic Age, 136; in Indian Ocean system, 231; in Tang China, 293; in Yuan China, 327; in Malacca, 376, 405

Cotton (cotton industry). *See also* Textiles (textile industry); for lamp wicking, 38; Indian, 184, 375, 376; Anasazi, 206; Andean, 210; Islamic Iran, 258; Chinese, 328, 331; Aztec, 381; Hausa, 368;

Korean, 334; Italian, 346; Caribbean, 406

Council of Clermont (1095), 286

Councils: in Greek city-states, 125, 129, 138; in Roman towns, 151; of bishops, 245, 275; Mongol, 314

Craftspeople. *See* Artisans; *specific crafts*

Creation myths, 5; Babylonian, 35, 36–37; Egyptian, 40; Indian, 172, 182

Credit (loans): in China, 302; in late medieval Europe, 346, 347

Crete, 286(*map*); Minoan civilization in, 53, 60–62, 61(*map*), 63(*illus.*); as Venetian colony, 345, 346

Crimea: khanate of, 324; plague in, 320

Crossbows, Chinese, 164, 292, 389

Crusades (crusaders), 285–287, 287(*illus.*), 288; Byzantine Empire and, 268; First, 255, 286 *and map*; Muslims and, 255, 256, 339; roots of, 285–286; Second, 286(*map*), 287; impact of, 286–287; Third, 286(*map*), 287; Fourth, 285, 286 *and map*, 345; Mongols and, 320–321, 325–326; Portuguese, 358, 396

Cruzado (coin), 396

Cuba, 406

Culhuacán, 205

Cults. *See also* Ancestor cult; Fertility cults; Gods and goddesses; Shrines; at Çatal Hüyük, 23; Greek, 126; Christianity, 154; Egyptian, 44, 236; Roman emperor, 149

Cultural communities, growth of, 221

Cultural diversity. *See* Diversity

Culture(s). *See also* Art and artists; Civilization(s); Literature; Oral culture (orality); Poets and poetry; defined, 11; Ice Age, 11–16; Neolithic, 21–22; Assyrian, 66–67; Rome and China compared, 166; Hindu-Buddhist in Southeast Asia, 187, 188; Saharan, 231–232; African unity, 235–236; great and small traditions, 235, 240, 256; Byzantine, 270; Kievan Russia, 283; late medieval Europe, 341

Cuneiform writing, 32, 35–36, 54, 56; alphabetic systems and, 122

Currency. *See also* Coins (coinage); bars of metal used as, 366; paper money, in China, 302, 328; paper money, in Mongolian Empire, 321, 324; exchanges, in Europe, 345

Customs and traditions: small *vs.* great traditions, 235, 240, 256; Germanic, 271, 273

Cuzco (Inka capital), 382, 383; Spanish conquest of, 409

Cylinder seals, 33(*illus.*)

Cyprus, 76, 286(*map*), 346; copper from, 58

Cyrene, 112(*illus.*), 113

Cyrillic alphabet, 270, 282

Cyril (missionary), 270

Cyrus (Persia), 71, 114(*map*), 116, 129

Daedalus, 60

Da Gama, Christopher, 401

Da Gama, Vasco, 362, 396, 397(*map*), 401; ships of, 390(*illus.*), 402–403

Dai Viet, 308, 336. *See also* Vietnam; Mongol attack on, 315

Damascus, 345; Arab Caliphate and, 251, 255, 258

Dams, 328, 363

Dante Alighieri, 352 *and illus.*

Danube River, 116, 155

Danube River Valley, 17

Daoism, 91, 92, 94, 294, 300

Darius III (Persia), 134, 136

Darius I (Persia), 101, 130; expansion under, 114(*map*), 116–117; Persepolis and, 118, 119(*illus.*)

Dart, Raymond, 6

Darwin, Charles, 6

Dasas, 171–172, 176

Date palms, 29

David (Israel), 69

Da Vinci, Leonardo, 354

Deborah the Judge, 70

Debt slavery: in Greece, 126, 129; in Mesopotamia, 33

Decameron (Boccaccio), 353

Deccan Plateau, 180, 181, 186

Deforestation (forest clearing). *See also* Forest products; in China, 331; in Europe, 343; in Zimbabwe, 375; in Polynesia, 391

Deir el-Bahri, 57, 58(*illus.*)

Delhi Sultanate (India), 368–372, 375; chronology, 363; expansion of, 368, 369(*map*), 370–371; Gujarat and, 370, 372, 375; Hindu-Muslim relations in, 368–369, 371–372, 375; slavery in, 378; Timur and, 321, 323, 372; water control systems in, 363–364; women rulers of, 369–370

Delian League, 130

Delphi (Greece), oracle at, 88–89, 124, 126

Democracy, Greek, 126, 129, 130, 131; inequality and, 132

Denmark, 272

Deportation: in Assyrian Empire, 65, 66, 71, 79, 80; in Mauryan India, 179

Descent of Man, The (Darwin), 6

Devi (goddess), 176

Devshirme system, 358

Dhows (ships), 222(*illus.*), 373 *and illus.*, 388, 403, 404

Dias, Bartolomeu, 396

Diaspora, Jewish, 71

Dido, 52(*illus.*), 53

Diet. *See* Food (diet)

Diocletian (Rome), 157

Dionysus (god), 135

Diplomacy, Mongol, 314, 326

Disease. *See also* Bubonic plague; Medicine; in Neolithic Age, 20; plague of Justinian, 269; and diet, in Yuan China, 319; Amerindians and, 406, 408; influenza, 320; typhus, 320; in Kongo, 403; malaria, 332, 364; smallpox, 320, 406, 408

Di (sky-god), 86, 88

Diu, Portuguese fort at, 405

Diversity (cultural diversity). *See also* Cosmopolitanism; in India, 172(*map*), 190; in Mesoamerica, 205; in Indian Ocean maritime system, 231; in African traditions, 235

Divination, 88–89, 90; Chinese oracle bones and, 85–86, 88, 89(*illus.*)

Divine Comedy (Dante), 352 *and illus.*

Divine kingship: Egyptian pharoahs, 41, 42–43, 44, 49; Chinese Mandate of Heaven, 88–89, 167

Divorce. *See also* Marriage; in Egypt, 43; in Israel, 70; in Islam, 259; in China, 303

DNA evidence, of evolution, 6, 8

Dnieper River, 281

Doctors. *See* Medicine (physicians)

Dogs, domestication of, 19(*illus.*), 24, 108

Domestication. *See also specific animals*; *food crops*; adrenaline and, 109; of animals, 18(*map*), 19–20, 24, 29, 43, 98, 108–109; of camels, 59, 109, 232; of cattle, 19, 98, 108, 231; of horses, 59, 99, 108; of llamas, 19, 210; of pigs, 18(*map*), 109, 237, 238; of plants, 17, 18(*map*), 19, 24, 29, 108, 194

Dominican order, 351

Donkeys, 19, 30, 37, 43, 68, 81, 96, 109

Dos Pilas, 193

Drama (theater): Greek, 131, 132; Gupta theater-state, 181; Srivijaya theater-state, 189; Japanese, 335(*illus.*)

Dravidian language, 172 *and map*, 377

Drought: in Indus Valley, 48; in Andean region, 209, 211, 213; in Chaco Canyon, 207

Druids, 89, 103, 104, 105, 218

Druzhina, 281, 283

Dubois, Eugene, 6

Duke of Zhou, 89

Dunhuang, cave monasteries at, 297, 299(*illus.*)

Dur Sharrukin fortress, 65

Dushan, Stephen, 326

Dye (Tyrrian purple), 74, 75, 270

Ea (god), 33(*illus.*), 36

Earth Mother, 21, 177(*illus.*)

Earthquake, 164

East Africa: Great Rift Valley of, 11; Mesopotamian trade with, 230; Muslim travelers in, 361; Chinese voyages to, 330(*map*); pastoralism in, 360(*illus.*); Southeast Asians in, 388; Swahili Coast, 367(*map*), 373, 374, 390; Portuguese in, 401–402

East Asia. *See also* Southeast Asia; *and specific countries*; climate zones of, 84; Sui and Tang China and, 291; Jin and Liao challenge in, 298–299, 300(*map*); new kingdoms in, 304–308; writing in (400–1200), 306 *and illus.*; centralization and militarism in

(1200–1500), 333–336; Chinese power in, 388

Easter Island, 391, 392(*map*)

Eastern Europe: chronology (634–1204), 269; migrations in, 281; Mongol conquest of, 325; new states in, 325–326; serfdom in, 339

East Indies (maritime Southeast Asia): Portuguese expeditions to, 387; spice trade of, 388, 399, 400, 405

Ecological crisis, 12. *See also* Environment; in Indus Valley, 49; in Zimbabwe, 375

Ecological zones: in Srivijaya, 189; in Andean region, 197, 382, 383; in Mesoamerica, 194

Economy (economic factors): Egyptian, 42, 137; Mycenaean Greek, 61; Persian Empire, 117; Athenian, 131; Roman Empire, 155, 157; Chinese, 164, 165; barter, 33, 157, 269, 273; Islamic caliphate, 253; Byzantine Empire, 267, 270; medieval Europe, 273–274, 283; Song China, 300, 302–303, 309; Mongolian Empire, 321, 329

Ecuador, trading boats from, 393

Edessa, 255

Edict of Milan, 157

Education. *See also* Academies; Colleges and universities; Literacy; Schools; in Han China, 163; humanist reform of, 352; in Islam, 377

Edward II (England), 355

Edward III (England), 355

Egypt. *See also* Egypt, ancient; Greek-style cities in, 135; Ptolemaic, 136–137 *and map*; camels in, 233; pork taboo in, 238; Fatimid Caliphate in, 252–253, 255; Islamic conquest of, 250, 268, 269; Mamluks in, 256, 317, 321, 322(*map*), 325, 366; monasticism in, 279; plague in, 320; Ottoman Empire and, 401, 405

Egypt, ancient, 39–46; chronology (3100–1070 B.C.E.), 29; "gift of the Nile," 27, 28(*map*), 39–41, 41(*map*); administration and communication, 42–43; agriculture, 43; irrigation, 40, 43; creation myth, 40; ships, 41(*illus.*); Old Kingdom, 40(*map*), 96;

Egypt, ancient (*Continued*)
   Middle Kingdom, 56, 96;
   pyramids, 41, 42(*illus.*), 45;
   hieroglyphics, 42; people
   of, 43–44; women in, 44, 50;
   megaliths in, 21; beermaking in,
   134; belief and knowledge, 44–46;
   divine kingship (pharaoh), 41,
   42–43, 49, 68, 263; Mesopotamia
   compared, 42, 43, 44, 49–50; New
   Kingdom, 40(*map*), 56–58, 68, 97;
   chronology (2040–671 B.C.E.), 55;
   glassmaking in, 156; trade, 42,
   43, 58–59; Hyksos in, 57, 68, 80;
   Assyrian invasion of, 64, 79, 97;
   Israelites in, 68; Nubia and, 40,
   43, 57, 59(*illus.*), 62, 81, 82(*illus.*),
   95–98, 236; in Persian Empire,
   116; treaty with Hittites, 58
Egyptian Book of the Dead, 45 *and
   illus.*
Eightfold Path, in Buddhism, 174
Elam (Elamites), 30; Assyrians and,
   56, 79; Persia and, 118
Eleanor of Aquitaine, 287
Elephants, 11. *See also* Ivory trade
Elite class (ruling class). *See
   also* Aristocracy (nobility);
   Landowners; Warrior elite;
   Egyptian, 44, 45, 46; Mycenaean,
   63; in Israel and Babylon, 72–73;
   Assyrian, 66; Carthaginian,
   77; Chinese, 86, 89, 90; Celtic,
   102; Roman, 144, 145, 147(*illus.*),
   148, 151; Mayan, 193, 202;
   Mesoamerican, 194, 195, 196,
   199, 200; Olmec, 196; Toltec,
   204; Andean, 211, 212 *and illus.*,
   213, 214–215, 383; Cahokian,
   208–209; great traditions and,
   235; Byzantine, 269; Confucian,
   in China, 163, 295, 298; Turkic,
   in China, 292; Annam, 308;
   Chinese women, 303(*illus.*), 304;
   East Asian, 304; Delhi Sultanate,
   371–372, 375
Emmer wheat, 17, 23
Emperors. *See* Monarchy
   (emperors; kingship)
Empires. *See* Colonies
   (colonization); Expansion; *and
   specific empires and emperors*
Encyclopedias, in China, 330, 331
Engineering. *See also* Construction
   materials and techniques;
   Mesopotamian, 39; Assyrian

Empire, 65; Egyptian, 42(*illus.*),
   46; Macedonian, 134; Roman,
   154, 155(*illus.*); Song Chinese,
   300, 301(*illus.*), 302; Il-khanate,
   323(*illus.*); European cathedrals,
   349
England. *See also* Britain; *and
   individual monarchs*; megaliths
   in, 21; tin in, 78, 104; Celtic fort in,
   104(*illus.*); Norman invasion of,
   266(*illus.*), 272, 275, 285; peasants
   of, 273; Viking raids on, 272;
   Ethelbald of Mercia, 278–279;
   Henry II and, 277–278; population
   growth, 283; monarchy in, 355,
   357; peasants of, 341; war with
   France, 355, 357; wool trade in,
   285, 342, 346, 357; watermills in,
   342; revolt in, 341
English language, 105
Enkidu, 27
Enlightenment (Buddhist nirvana),
   175, 178; bodhisattvas and, 189,
   239, 293, 294
Entrepôts (ports), 324, 390–391; in
   Malacca, 405
Environment (environmental
   stress). *See also* Climate and
   weather (climate changes);
   Drought; Natural disasters; in
   Indus Valley civilization, 46, 48,
   171; Andean cultural response to,
   209–210, 216; Mongol conquest
   and, 320
Environment and technology:
   Iceman, 16 *and illus.*; in
   Indus Valley, 48 *and illus.*;
   textiles and dyes, 75 *and illus.*;
   divination, 88–89 *and illus.*;
   astronomy, 138–139 *and illus.*;
   glassmaking, 156 *and illus.*;
   Indian mathematics, 182 *and
   illus.*; Maya writing system, 214
   and illus.; camel saddles, 234 *and
   illus.*; Islamic chemistry, 262 *and
   illus.*; medieval iron production,
   276 *and illus.*; writing in East
   Asia, 306 *and illus.*; gunpowder
   to guns, 332 *and illus.*; clocks, 350
   and illus.; Indian Ocean dhow,
   373 *and illus.*; da Gama's fleet,
   398 *and illus.*
Ephesus, 286
Epic of Gilgamesh, 26(*illus.*), 27
Epidemics. *See also* Bubonic plague;
   Amerindians and, 408

Epona (goddess), 104
Equatorial forests. *See* Tropical rain
   forest
Equites, in Rome, 149
Erasmus of Rotterdam, 353
Eratosthenes, 139
Eretria, 130
Ericsson, Leif, 392
Estates General (France), 357
Ethelbald of Mercia, 278–279
Ethiopia: plant domestication in,
   17; Aksum in, 98; alliance with
   Portugal, 401; Christianity in,
   239–240, 367, 375, 401; expansion
   of, 375, 378
Ethnography, Greek, 127, 128
Etruscans, 144
Eunuchs (castrates), 295, 378
Euphrates River. *See* Tigris and
   Euphrates Valley
Eurasia: culture and science in,
   321–324; Mongol domains in
   (1300), 317(*map*), 413
Eurasian steppes: China and,
   101–102; chronology (1000–300
   B.C.E.), 85; pastoral nomads of,
   98–102, 108(*illus.*); Scythians of,
   75(*illus.*), 99(*map*), 100–101 *and
   illus.*, 226
European expansion (1400–1550),
   394–399, 409–410; motives
   for, 394; Portuguese voyages,
   394–396, 397(*map*), 398 *and illus.*;
   Spanish voyages, 396–399 *and
   map*
Europe (Europeans). *See also*
   Eastern Europe; Latin West;
   Medieval Europe; Roman Empire;
   Western Europe; Neanderthals
   in, 5; spread of farming in,
   17, 21; skin color in, 10; Venus
   statuettes in, 13; Indo-Europeans
   in, 21; Celtic peoples of, 102–105;
   head coverings in, 263; famine
   in (1315–1317), 340; in 1453,
   356(*map*); encounters with
   (1450–1550), 399–409
"Everlasting Remorse" (Bo), 295
Evolution: human, 6–8, 8(*illus.*), 24;
   skin color and, 10
Examinations, for civil servants: in
   China, 161, 163, 300, 301, 331 *and
   illus.*; in Korea, 305; in Vietnam,
   336
Exchange. *See also* Trade
   (commerce); precious metals

as medium of, 66; coinage as medium of, 125 (*See also* Coins); barter, 33, 157, 269, 273, 381; in Gupta India, 181; networks of communication and, 223; Mesoamerican, 194; in Andean region, 210, 382, 383; in Kievan Russia, 281

Expansion (expansionism). *See also* Colonies; European Expansion; Egyptian, 57, 58, 97; Assyrian, 56, 64–65 *and map*; Tyrian, 77; Persian Empire, 114(*map*), 115–117; Roman, 146(*map*), 147–148, 166; Chinese imperial, 160(*map*), 161, 166; Christian, 154; imperial India, 179; Andean peoples, 215; Islamic, 247(*map*), 250–251; Mongolian Empire, 311, 313, 314–318, 317(*map*), 345; Mali, 368; Delhi Sultanate, 368, 369(*map*), 370–371; Aztec, 380, 381; Ethiopian, 375, 378; Inka, 382; Ottoman Empire, 358, 394; Iberian, 357–358, 394; Spanish Empire, 406–409

Exploration (expeditions). *See also* Maritime revolution; Portuguese maritime explorations; *specific explorers*; Phoenician, 76(*map*); Carthaginian, 78; Chinese (Zheng He), 311, 329–330 *and map*, 376, 389–390, 392(*map*), 398; Viking, 392, 413; Malayo-Polynesian, 391, 392(*map*); Spanish maritime, 387, 396–399 *and map*

Explosives, 300, 331, 332, 334. *See also* Gunpowder

Extinction, 12

Ezana (Aksum), 239–240

Family. *See also* Ancestor cult; Childrearing; Clans; Marriage; Women; early human, 14; Neolithic, 21; Mesopotamian, 31; Israelite, 70; Iranian, 116; Greek, 123; Roman, 145, 147(*illus.*), 166; Chinese, 91, 162, 166, 295, 302; Mongol, 314

Famine (food shortage): on Thera, 113; in Europe (1315–1317), 340; in Caribbean, 406

Farmers (farming). *See also* Agriculture; Peasants; Rural societies; Neolithic, 17, 20, 22; Mesopotamian, 29, 31, 33;

Egyptian, 40; Indus Valley, 46; pastoralists (herders) and, 68, 159, 246; Greek, 122, 123(*map*), 125, 138; Roman, 144, 149, 152, 165, 284; Southeast Asian, 186; Mesoamerican, 194, 201; Chinese, 165, 328; Byzantine, 270; Kievan Russian, 281, 283; medieval European, 273, 284, 339, 340; three-field system, 340; Korean, 334; tropical, 363; Zimbabwe, 375; Polynesian, 391

Fathers. *See also* Family; Patriarchy; and Confucianism, in China, 94

Fatima (daughter of Muhammad), 249, 260

Fatimid Caliphate, 252–253 *and map*, 254, 255; Crusaders and, 286(*map*)

Faxian, 181, 238–239

Feng shui, 90

Ferdinand (Aragon), 358 *and illus.*, 394, 396

Fertile Crescent region, 29. *See also* Mesopotamia

Fertility cults (deities): at Çatal Hüyük, 23 *and illus.*; Celtic, 104; Isis, 44, 98, 154; Cretan, 60; Canaanite, 71; Carthage, 78; Cybele, 154; Greek, 126, 132; Hindu, 176; Mesoamerican, 199–200

Festivals: Babylonian, 35, 36–37; Egyptian, 44–45; Celtic holidays, 104; Greek, 129, 132, 135; Hindu, 168(*illus.*); Roman, 152; Chinese, 290(*illus.*)

Feudalism: in China, 89, 90, 160; in India, 186; in medieval Europe, 274

Fibonacci, Leonardo, 182

Fief (land grant), 160, 274

Fihrist (al-Nadim), 243

Fiji, 391, 392(*map*)

Finance. *See also* Monetary system; in late medieval Europe, 346–347

Finland (Finns), 281, 325

Fire, and cooking, 14

Fire altars, 119

Firearms (guns), 332, 355, 357; Ottoman, 358; Spanish, 407; African trade in, 400–401

First Sermon (Buddha), 174

Firuz Shah, Sultan, 371, 378

Fishing (fishermen): Stone Age, 15; Amerindian, 20; in Mesopotamia,

29; in ancient Egypt, 40, 43; in Indus Valley, 47; in Andean region, 197, 210, 213; in Africa, 237; in medieval Europe, 285; Jurchen, 299; in tropics, 362; salt and, 365; in Polynesia, 391

Flanders (Flemish): Black Death in, 338(*illus.*); fisherman of, 365; trading cities in, 283, 285, 345, 355; painters of, 340(*illus.*), 354; weavers in, 345 *and illus.*, 346

Flooding (floods): in Mesopotamia, 29, 50; Nile River, 17, 40, 50, 138; Indus River, 46; Mekong River, 188; Yellow River, 84, 164, 328; Niger River, 363

Florence, Italy: banking in, 346, 347, 354; humanists in, 352 *and illus.*; Medici family of, 347, 354 *and illus.*

Folk customs. *See* Customs and traditions

Food (diet): early humans, 7; Stone Age, 11, 13–14, 15; in ancient Egypt, 43–44; Greek, 123–124; in Roman Empire, 152(*illus.*); Andean, 213; pork taboo, 71, 238; of medieval Europe, 273; Chinese, 319; salt and, 365

Food gathering. *See also* Hunter-gatherer peoples; in Stone Age, 11, 13, 14; transition to food production, 16–17

Food production. *See also* Agriculture; Farmers; transition from food gathering, 16–17, 21; African innovations, 230; Silk Road innovations, 244; in Islamic lands, 258

Food shortage. *See* Famine

Footbinding, of Chinese women, 303–304

Foraging. *See* Food gathering

Forbidden City (Beijing), 327, 329, 330

Foreign policy: in Egypt, 43; in Carthage, 77, 78; in Sparta, 128; mandala theory, in India, 179

Forest products (management): Southeast Asia, 187; Maya, 201; sub-Saharan Africa, 234; Russian, 281, 283; deforestation, 331, 343, 375, 391; medieval European, 273, 343; tropical, 235, 362, 363

Fortifications (walls): Neolithic, 22; Mesopotamian, 31, 32;

Fortifications (walls) (*Continued*)
Indus Valley, 47, 48(*illus.*); early Chinese, 87; Assyrian, 65; Mycenaean, 61; Carthage, 77; Kush, 96; Celtic, 102, 104(*illus.*); Roman, 155, 166; Chinese, 159, 160(*map*), 163, 166; Andean, 215; medieval Europe, 273, 284; Kremlin (Moscow), 325(*illus.*); Japanese, 335; Great Zimbabwe, 375(*illus.*); Portuguese, 405
Forum (Rome), 144, 145
Fossils, of early humans, 5, 6, 7, 8
Four Corners region (North America), 206, 207 *and map*
"Four Noble Truths" (Buddha), 174
France. *See also* Gaul: Carthage and, 78; cave paintings in, 11, 12–13 *and illus.*, 15; Celts in, 102, 104; Muslims in, 272; Viking raids in, 272; cathedrals in, 347(*illus.*); monastic reform in, 280; peasants in, 273, 340(*illus.*); population growth in, 283; plague in, 341; Aquitaine in, 287, 355, 356(*map*); stone quarries in, 343; trading fairs in, 345; Avignon popes and, 349, 355; monarchy in, 355, 357; revolt in, 341; war with England, 355, 357; printshop in, 353(*illus.*); salt tax in, 365
Franciscan order, 318, 351
Frankincense and myrrh, 230, 246
Franks, 272 *and map*
Frederick II (Holy Roman Emperor), 286 *and map*, 325
Frescoes. *See* Wall murals (frescoes)
Frumentius, 239–240
Fuggers of Augsburg, 347
Fujiwara period (Japan), 307
Fulani people, 363; Islam and, 377
Funan, 187(*map*), 188
Fustat. *See* Cairo (Fustat)

Gabriel (Jibra'il), 247, 260
Gades (modern Cadiz), 76 *and map*
Gaius Marius, 149
Galley (ship), 345, 395
Gandhara, 332; art of, 175(*illus.*), 238(*illus.*)
Gandhi, Mohandas K. (Mahatma), 365
Ganges Plain, 171, 181; irrigation in, 364; rice in, 363
Ganges River, 177, 186

Gaozu (China), 159–160
Gathas (hymns), 118
Gaul (modern France): Celts in, 104, 148; Franks of, 272 *and map*
Gebel Barkal, 97 *and illus.*
Gender roles. *See also* Men; Women; in Ice Age, 14, 24; in ancient Egypt, 44; yin/yang, in China, 94; Islam and, 378–379; Aztec, 381
Genetic code, 6
Genghis Khan. *See* Chinggis Khan
Genoa (Genoese), 284, 341, 405; competition with Venice, 344(*map*), 345
Gentry, in China, 295, 298, 302, 303, 328
Gerbert of Aurillac, 182
Germanic peoples (Germany): Celts and, 105; Rome and, 146(*map*), 155; Christian morality in, 279; customs of, 271, 273; iron swords of, 276; kingdoms of, 272(*map*), 288; migrations of, 281; political order, 273; Teutonic Knights, 325–326, 340; mining in, 342
Ghana: Berber conquest of, 366; gold in, 252, 366
Ghazan, Il-khan, 321
Ghent, 285, 345
Gibraltar, Strait of, 76 *and map*, 78
Gilgamesh, 26(*illus.*), 27, 50
Giotto, art of, 354
Gislebertus, carving of, 347(*illus.*)
Giza, pyramids at, 41, 42 *and illus.*
Glaciers, melting of, 236
Glassmaking, 156 *and illus.*, 283; in Islam, 262(*illus.*); stained glass, 347, 349
Goa, Portuguese in, 404
Goats, 19, 23, 24, 29, 98, 122, 235, 236
Go-Daigo (Japan), 335
Gods and goddesses. *See also* Divine kingship; Monotheism; Polytheism; Religion(s); Shrines; Supernatural, the; Temples; *and specific gods and goddesses*; Neolithic, 21; Çatal Hüyük, 23 *and illus.*; Mesopotamian, 32, 33(*illus.*), 34–35, 36–37, 50; Egyptian, 41, 44–45, 50, 57, 58; sun-gods, 33(*illus.*), 44, 57, 154, 382, 383; Assyrian Empire, 64; Israelite (Yahweh), 67, 68–69, 70–71; Chinese, 86, 88; Phoenician, 76; Carthaginian,

78; Celtic, 104, 105(*illus.*); Persian Empire, 118, 120; Greek, 126, 127 *and illus.*, 135; Roman, 147; Vedic religion, 173; Hindu (India), 169, 175–176; Buddhism and, 293; Mesoamerican, 195, 199–200 *and illus.*, 204; Islamic (Allah), 248
Going Upriver at the Qingming Festival, 290(*illus.*)
Gold Coast (Africa), Portuguese in, 395(*illus.*), 396, 399
Gold coinage, 125, 285; Muslim, 251, 252, 253; Portuguese *cruzado*, 396
Golden Horde khanate, 315, 317(*map*), 322(*map*), 324; rivalry with Il-khans, 320–321
Gold (gold trade), 23; Nubian, 43, 59, 82(*illus.*), 95, 97; Aegean region, 60; African, 190, 252, 394, 396, 399; Andean region, 198, 211, 215; Xiongnu, 162(*illus.*); Scythian, 100(*illus.*), 225(*illus.*); Mongolian Empire, 324; salt and, 365, 368; East African, 373, 374, 375; Saharan caravan trade and, 253, 358, 366; Portuguese and, 396, 400; Caribbean, 406; Inka, 383, 409
Gomes, Fernão, 396
Good and evil, in Zoroastrianism, 119, 246
Government. *See also* Administration; Bureaucracy; Monarchy; Political systems and institutions; in ancient Egypt, 42; in early China, 90, 92; in Assyrian Empire, 65, 66; in Carthage, 77, 78; in Persian Empire, 117, 140; in Roman Empire, 148, 149, 153, 155, 157; in India, 178–179; in Russia, 283; in imperial China, 159, 160, 163, 302–303; in Islamic caliphate, 251; in European cities, 284; in Byzantine Empire, 270; in Japan, 307; in Il-khanate, 321; in Vietnam, 336; in Yuan China, 327, 329; tropical water systems and, 363, 364
Granada, reconquest of, 357, 358(*illus.*), 394
Grand Canal (China), 292, 327
Grapes, 122; for wine, 134–135, 149
Great Famine of 1315-1317, 340
Great Ice Age. *See* Ice Age
Great traditions, 235, 240, 256

Great Wall of China, 159, 160(*map*)
Great Western Schism, 355
Great Zimbabwe, 374–375 *and illus.*
Greco-Bactrian kingdom, 137(*map*), 179. *See also* Bactria
Greco-Roman revival, in Renaissance Europe, 352, 353
Greece (Greeks). *See also* Greek language; Hellenistic Age; agriculture in, 17; oracles in, 88–89, 126; war with Carthage, 78; Mycenaean, 53, 60–63 *and map*, 122; Phoenicians and, 122; Archaic period, 122–123; Dark Age in, 63–64, 122; Celts and, 103; chronology (1150–338 B.C.E.), 115; colonies of, 100, 124; Scythians and, 100; democracy in, 126, 129; rise of, 120–136; geography and resources, 121–122; gods, 126, 127(*illus.*), 135; inequality in, 132–133; new intellectual currents, 126–128, 131; rivalry with Persia, 113, 118, 128, 129–130; transition to literacy in, 123, 131–132, 140, 218–219; wine in, 134, 135; Christianity in, 153; Zhou China compared, 140–141; maritime trade of, 125, 129, 131; medicine of, 112(*illus.*), 113
Greek city-states (polis), 116. *See also* Athens; Sparta; emergence of, 122–126; failure of, 133; Hellenistic Age, 137–138
Greek historians. *See* Herodotus
Greek language, 61, 63, 139, 153, 324
Greek Orthodox Church. *See* Orthodox Christianity
Greek philosophy, 127, 131, 287, 351
Greenland, Vikings in, 272, 392
Gregory VII, Pope, 277, 280
Gregory X, Pope, 348–349
Griot, in West Africa, 218
Guangdong, examination cells in, 331(*illus.*)
Guangwu (China), 165
Guatemala, Maya of, 200–203 *and illus.*, 212 *and illus.*
Guilds: in Mesopotamia, 33; in India, 180, 181; in medieval Europe, 342, 346; teaching, 351
Gujarat: mosque in, 377; Muslim rule of, 375, 376; Portuguese and, 404; trade of, 370, 375–376
Gundestrup cauldron, 105(*illus.*)

Gunpowder, 301, 326, 331, 333, 337; flaming arrows and, 300, 316, 332 *and illus.*
Gunpowder revolution, 394
Guns. *See* Firearms (guns)
Gupta India (320–550 C.E.), 172(*map*), 176(*illus.*), 181–186; trade of, 184–185; women in, 182–183
Gutenburg, Johann, 353
Güyük, Great Khan, 315, 316(*fig.*), 317(*map*)

Hadith (sayings of Muhammad), 251, 257, 258; women and, 259, 260
Hagia Sofia cathedral, 270
Hakra (Saraswati) River, 46, 48, 49
Halevi, Judah, 253
Hammurabi, 54; Law Code of, 32, 33, 50
Handwriting. *See* Script
Han Empire (China), 159–165; chronology (221 B.C.E.–220 C.E.), 145; decline of, 164–165; expansion of, 160(*map*); long reign of, 159–162; new forms of thought in, 163–164; nomadic peoples and, 159, 160, 161, 162(*illus.*); Roman Empire compared to, 143, 150–151, 164, 165–167; Silk Road and, 160(*map*), 161; society in, 162–163; Vietnam and, 308
Han Fei, 92, 93
Han'gul (Korean) writing system, 306, 333(*illus.*), 334
Hangzhou, 299, 302
Hanno, 78
Hanoi (Vietnam), 336
Hanseatic League, 345, 355
Han Yu, 294
Harappa, 47, 48
Harem slaves, 378
Harkhuf, 81
Harness, breast-strap, 284
Harold (Norway), 279
Harsha Vardhana, 186
Hatshepsut (Egypt), 57, 58(*illus.*)
Hattusha, 56, 62
Hausa city-states, 367(*map*), 368
Hawaiian Islands, 391, 392(*map*)
Head coverings, 263 *and illus.*
Heaven (deity), 88–89, 314. *See also* Mandate (Son) of Heaven
Hebrew Bible (Old Testament), 5, 67–69, 71, 74. *See also* Israel; Jews; Book of Amos, 72–73

Hebrew language, 30, 67
Helena (Ethiopia), 401
Hellenistic Age (Hellenism), 136–139, 140; Alexandria in, 135, 137, 139; Antigonids, 136, 137(*map*); chronology (323–30 B.C.E.), 115; Ptolemaic Egypt, 136–137 *and map*; Rome and, 148; Seleucids, 136, 137(*map*)
Helots, in Sparta, 128
Henry II (England), 277–278, 287
Henry IV (Holy Roman Emperor), 277
Henry the Navigator, 394–395, 396
Herat, 322
Herders. *See* Cattle (cattle herders); Pastoralism (pastoralists)
Heresy, 276; Nestorian, 245
Herodotus, 39, 113, 128, 227; on Scythians, 100–101, 225; on Xerxes, 119–120
Hesiod, 138
Hieroglyphics, 56; alphabetic systems and, 122; Egyptian, 42, 98; Maya, 203, 214(*illus.*)
Hildebrand. *See* Gregory VII, Pope
Hindu-Buddhist culture, in Southeast Asia, 187, 188
Hindus (Hinduism): evolution of, 175–178, 191; temples, 168(*illus.*), 170, 176(*illus.*), 177, 183, 372(*illus.*); Delhi sultanate and, 368–369, 371–372; Islam and, 376, 377; *sati* (widow burning) in, 183, 378
Hippalus, 227–228, 229
Hiram (Tyre), 69, 74
Hispaniola, 406
Histories (Herodotus), 128
History (historians): Chinese (Sima Qian), 101, 161, 164, 295; Greek, 127–128; Il-khanate, 321–322
Hittites, 54(*map*), 62; ironworking of, 56, 237; treaty with Egypt, 58
Hohokam, 206, 207(*map*)
Holy Land, Crusades to, 285–287 *and map*
Holy Roman Empire, 288, 356(*map*); papacy and, 276–277
Homer, 62, 125, 126
Hominids, 6–8, 24
Homo erectus, 7–8, 11
Homo floresiensis, 10
Homo habilis, 7–8, 11
Homo sapiens, 7, 8, 14
Homosexuality, in Islam, 260–261
Hongwu (China), 329

Hopewell people, 207–208

Hopi people, 5

Hoplites, 126, 130, 133, 140; weaponry of, 124, 134, 147

Hormuz, 329; Portuguese control of, 404

Horse collar, 164, 284

Horses, 30. *See also* Cavalry; Chariots; Central Asian steppes, 90, 101; domestication of, 59, 99, 109; Greek, 122; breast-strap harness for, 284; horseshoes, 284; in medieval Europe, 274, 287(*illus.*), 343; Khitan, 298; Koreans and, 304; plows and, 108, 284, 340

Horus, 44

House of Commons, 357

House of Lords, 357

Housing (dwellings). *See also* Construction materials and techniques; Neolithic, 17(*illus.*), 23; Aztec, 381; Mesopotamian, 31(*illus.*); Carthaginian, 77; Celtic, 103–104; Roman, 151; Andean, 198, 214, 215; Anasazi, 206, 208(*illus.*); Central Asian yurts, 108(*illus.*), 225, 226, 318; in Chinese cities, 302; medieval Europe, 340 *and illus.*

Huang Chao, 298

Huang Dao Po, 328

Huang He (Yellow) River, 27, 29(*map*), 81, 159; flooding of, 84, 164, 328

Huascar (Inka), 409

Huayna Capac (Inka), 383, 408

Hülegü, Il-khan, 316(*fig.*), 317(*map*), 320, 321, 322. *See also* Il-khanate Empire (Iran)

Human communities, emergence of, 3; African genesis, 5–10; brain size and, 6, 7, 8(*illus.*), 11; evolution and, 6–8, 8(*illus.*), 24

Humaneness (*ren*), 91, 92, 93

Humanism, in Renaissance Europe, 352–353

Human sacrifice: early China, 86, 87; Kushite, 96; child, in Carthage, 78, 79(*illus.*); Celtic, 89, 104; Mesoamerica, 196, 200; Andean, 211, 212, 214, 383; Cahokia, 209; Aztec, 406

Hundred Years War (1337–1453), 355, 357

Hunefar, 45(*illus.*)

Hungary: copper mining in, 343, 347; Mongols and, 314

Huns, 185

Hunter-gatherer peoples. *See also* Food gathering; Hunting; cave paintings, 11, 12–13 *and illus.*, 15; dwellings of, 15; Ice Age, 11–13, 14, 15; women in, 14; Northern Amerindian, 20, 207; in sub-Saharan Africa, 235; in tropics, 362

Hunting (hunters): in Stone Age, 11–13; dogs and, 19(*illus.*); Amerindian, 19, 20; at Çatal Hüyük, 23; Egyptian, 40; in ancient China, 86; in Sahara region, 231; Sasanid kings, 244(*illus.*); by Maya, 201; by Mongol khans, 318–319

Husayn (Shi'ite martyr), 249, 250

Hu Szu-hui, 319

Hyksos, 57, 68, 80

Iberian expansion, 394. *See also* Portuguese maritime explorations; Spanish maritime expeditions; and unification, 357–358

Ibn al-Arabi, 254

Ibn al-Haytham, 258

Ibn Battuta, Muhammad ibn Abdullah, 366, 373, 374(*map*); in Delhi, 370, 378; in Mali, 371, 379; in Mogadishu, 361

Ibn Hazm, 253

Ibn Khaldun, 322

Ibn Rushd (Averroës), 253–254

Ibn Sina (Avicenna), 287, 351

Ibn Tufayl, 254

Ibn Tughluq, Muhammad, Sultan, 370, 371

Ice Age, 7, 8, 9(*map*), 10, 24; technology and culture in, 11–16; end of, 236

Iceland, Vikings in, 272, 392

Iceman, 15, 16(*illus.*)

Ideas, spread of, 237–240. *See also* Intellectual life (intellectuals); Philosophy; Buddhism, 238–239; Christianity, 239–240; material evidence and, 237–238

Iliad (Homer), 62, 125, 126

Il-khanate Empire (Iran), 317(*map*), 322(*map*); culture and science in, 321–324; rivalry with Golden

Horde, 320–321; Timurids and, 321

Iltutmish, Sultan, 368–369

Imam, 250, 252

Immigrants. *See* Migration (population movement)

India, religions of, 190. *See also* Hindus; Buddhism, 173, 174–175, 178, 179, 180, 378; Jainism, 173, 174, 180; Parsees, 119; Vedism, 175, 183

India (Indian civilization), 169–186; Indo-Europeans in, 21; Alexander the Great in, 48, 172(*map*), 178, 179, 228; cattle domestication in, 19; rice cultivation in, 17; Arya-Dasa conflict in, 171–172; foundations of, 170–178; agriculture in, 171, 181; as subcontinent, 170–171; castes (varna) in, 172–173, 183, 390; chronology (1500 B.C.E. –647 C.E.), 171; commerce and culture, 179–181; Vedic Age, 171–173; epic literature of, 169, 180–181; Mauryan Empire (324–184 B.C.E.), 172(*map*), 178–179, 238; Southeast Asia and, 187–188, 190; women and marriage in, 182–183, 184–185; Gupta Empire (320–550 C.E.), 172(*map*), 181–186; Chinese silk and, 187; concept of time in, 190; pilgrims in, 174(*illus.*), 181, 229; political fragmentation in, 169, 179–181, 186; widow burning (*sati*) in, 183, 378; Indian Ocean trade and, 228–229; Chinese voyages to, 329, 330(*map*); Delhi sultanate in, 363, 368–372; gold trade of, 366; Malabar Coast, 373, 375, 376, 402–403, 404, 405; Mughals in, 405; Portuguese in, 402–403, 404 *and illus.*, 405; British salt monopoly in, 365

Indian Ocean exploration: by Malays, 187; by Chinese, 388–390, 392(*map*); chronology (350–1539), 389; by Portuguese, 396, 410

Indian Ocean trade (maritime system), 227–231, 388–391; origins of contacts and trade, 229; China and, 388–390; chronology (1st century C.E.), 225; Buddhism and, 226(*map*); Mediterranean trade and, 229–230, 284; Southeast Asia and, 238; travel accounts, 228–229; impact of, 230–231; monsoons and, 228, 230, 231, 362, 372–373, 375; Aden and Red Sea, 375; glass in, 156; Gujarat and Malabar Coast, 375–376; dhows (ships) in, 222(*illus.*), 373 *and illus.*, 388, 403, 404; Swahili Coast and Zimbabwe, 373, 374–375 *and illus.*; China and, 373; pepper and spices in, 230, 375, 376, 400, 405; Portugal and, 398, 402–405

Indigo, 375

Individualism: Greek, 126; Buddhism and, 175

Indo-European languages, 21–22, 99, 113; in India, 171, 172(*map*), 180

Indo-European speakers: migration of, 60, 99, 171, 172 *and map*

Indonesia, 184–185; early humans in, 10; colonists in Madagascar from, 222(*illus.*), 230

Industry. *See also* Iron industry; Silk (silk industry and trade); in Song China, 299–300; in Yuan China, 328

Indus Valley civilization, 27, 28(*map*) 46–49, 136; chronology (2600–1900 B.C.E.), 29; natural environment of, 46–47, 171; urban centers in, 47, 48(*illus.*), 49; material culture of, 47–49; trade, 48–49, 230; transformation of, 49, 50; irrigation in, 48; Persia and, 116; Sind, 250

Inequality. *See also* Social classes (social stratification); in classical Greece, 132–133; in Roman society, 145

Infanticide: in Carthage, 78, 79(*illus.*); in Greece, 132

Inflation. *See also* Price controls; in ancient Rome, 157; in Song China, 302

Inheritance: in Israel, 70; in China, 158; women and, 259; in Islam, 259

Inka (Inka Empire), 380(*map*), 382–383; Aztec compared to, 384; Spanish conquest of, 408–409

Inner Asia. *See also* Central Asia; Buddhism in, 293; chronology (751–1227), 293; Sui China and, 292; Tang China and, 293, 294(*map*); nomadism in, 225–226; Mongols and, 329

Inquisition, in Spain, 358

Intellectual life (intellectuals). *See also* Philosophy; in European Renaissance, 350–351; in Greece, 126–128, 131; in Muslim Spain, 253–254; in imperial China, 163–164, 292; under Charlemagne, 272, 350; humanism, in Europe, 352

Interest (usury), 347

Investiture controversy, 277

Ionia: Greeks in, 122, 123(*map*), 127; rebellion in, 130–131

Iran (Iranians), 113–120. *See also* Persia (Persian Empire); Indo-Europeans in, 21; Assyrian Empire and, 64; Elamites of, 56; Medes, 79; geography and resources, 114–115; rise of Persian Empire in, 115–117; Shakas, 179–180; chronology (224–945), 245; pork taboo in, 238; Silk Road trade and, 226, 227(*illus.*), 244; Sogdiana and, 223; Buyid dynasty in, 252; climate change in, 254, 255; cotton production in, 258; Sasanid Empire, 244–246 *and illus.*, 250, 251, 258, 264; Islam in, 251, 257–258, 377; Samanid dynasty in, 252, 254; scholars from, 262, 287; shah of, 244 *and illus.*, 246, 250, 251, 263; in Tang China, 292; merchants from, 374; Mongol conquest of, 314, 316

Iraq (Iraqis), 264. *See also* Mesopotamia; Tigris-Euphrates Valley in, 27, 29; reed huts in, 31(*illus.*); Buyid dynasty in, 252; Islam in, 250, 257, 258; climate change in, 254, 255, 284; Mongols and, 316

Ireland (Irish): Neolithic tomb in, 22(*illus.*); Celts in, 89, 102, 104, 105; Christian morality in, 278; monks from, 263, 280 *and illus.*; English conquest of, 355

Iron Age, 53

Iron industry: Hittite, 56; Assyrian, 65; Philistine, 74; Chinese, 90; Meroë, 98; bronze compared, 53, 111, 171; charcoal for, 276, 343; Indian, 171; steppe nomads and, 226; stirrups, 292, 295(*illus.*); sub-Saharan Africa, 235, 236–237; medieval Europe, 276 *and illus.*, 343; Song China,

299–300; for cannon balls, 332; horseshoes, 284; tropical regions, 364, 366

Irrigation: Mesopotamia, 29, 31, 34; ancient Egypt, 40, 43; Indus Valley, 48; Iranian, 114; Indian, 179; Funan, 188; Anasazi, 206; Mesoamerica, 200, 201, 204; Andean region, 198, 209, 211, 215; China, 292; Muslim lands, 253, 254, 258; Vietnam, 308; Yuan China, 328; Delhi Sultanate, 363–364

Isaac (Israel), 68

Isabel (Castile), 358 *and illus.*, 394, 396

Ishmael (Isma'il), 247

Ishtar (goddess), 33(*illus.*)

Isis (goddess), 44, 98, 154

Islamic empires. *See* Caliphates

Islam (Islamic civilization), 246–265. *See also* Muhammad (Prophet); Muslims; Shi'ite Islam; Jerusalem and, 70(*illus.*); meaning of word, 238; origins of, 246–250; Byzantine Empire and, 267; headcoverings in, 263; Christianity and, 67, 246, 248, 271(*map*); cities in, 253, 254, 257–258; civil war in, 249; conquests of (634–711), 247(*map*), 250–251; conversion to, 250, 251–252, 253, 257, 258; Five Pillars of, 249; in Spain, 253–254 *and map*, 256(*illus.*), 259(*illus.*); laws of (Shari'a), 257, 259; polygamy in, 259, 378; revolts within, 252; Kharjites, 250, 251, 252; Quran, 249, 251, 257, 259, 262(*illus.*), 377; recentering of, 261–262; mosques, 254(*illus.*), 258, 368, 369(*illus.*), 377; scholars in, 254, 257, 351; slavery and, 259, 261; Sufism, 262, 263, 264, 377; Sunni-Shi'ite rivalry in, 250, 252, 254, 255, 256, 257, 321; umma, 248–249, 252, 254, 257, 261, 264; women in, 34, 259–260 *and illus.*; world map, 220(*illus.*); in Central Asia, 315; trade and travel in, 374(*map*); in sub-Saharan Africa, 366–368; Mongols and, 315, 320–324, 329; Hellenistic technology and, 343; in Southeast Asia, 377, 378; literacy and, 259, 377; spread of, 375

Israel (Israelites), 67–71, 99. *See also* Jews; Judaism; Assyrian power and, 79; bronze lamp from, 38(*illus.*); pork taboo and, 71, 238; origins, exodus and settlement, 67–69; protests against ruling class in, 70, 72–73; rise of monarchy, 69–70 *and illus.*, 80; trade with Sheba, 69; fragmentation and dispersal, 70–71; Christianity in, 153

Italy (Italians): Celts in, 102; Greek colonists in, 124, 127; Roman expansion in, 144, 147; Carolingian Empire and, 272; monasticism in, 279; universities in, 351; plague in, 341; trading cities of, 283, 284, 343, 355, 394 (*See also* Florence; Genoa; Venice); Renaissance art in, 353–354

Ivan III (Russia), 325

Ivory trade, 62, 74(*illus.*), 96, 400; in Indian Ocean trade, 230, 373, 375, 376

Jacob (Israel), 68, 69

Jacquerie revolt (France, 1358), 341

Jaguar-god, 75, 195, 198

Jahiz, 260–261

Jainism, in India, 173, 174, 180, 183

Janissaries, 358

Japan (Japanese), 305–307; migration to, 10; Buddhism in, 305, 306, 335; China and, 294(*map*), 298, 328; chronology (645–1185), 293; Confucianism in, 305; Shotoku's Constitution in, 296–297, 306; writing in, 306; Fujiwara period, 307; Kamakura shogunate, 307, 334–335; Mongol invasion of, 312, 315, 316, 334–335 *and map*, 337; Ashikaga Shogunate, 335–336; chronology (1274–1338), 315; piracy and, 330, 336

Jati (Indian castes), 172–173

Java, 316; human fossils in, 6, 8; early migration from, 10, (*map*); Buddhist temples in, 189(*illus.*), 190, 222(*illus.*); Majapahit kingdom in, 376

Jericho, 21, 22

Jerusalem: Temple in, 67, 69–70 *and illus.*, 71, 74; Jesus in, 153; Christians in, 154, 239, 258; crusaders in, 255, 285, 286, 325

Jesus Christ, 153–154. *See also* Christianity; divinity of, 245, 246, 249

Jewelry: amulets, 35, 45, 262(*illus.*); Indus Valley, 47; Scythian gold, 100(*illus.*), 225(*illus.*); Mycenaean gold, 60; Andean, 211, 212; Anasazi, 206; Indian, 376

Jews. *See also* Israel; Judaism; diaspora of, 71; rules and strictures of, 71; in Alexandria, 138–139; Jesus and, 153–154; Christianity and, 154; in Sasanid Empire, 245; Islam and, 248, 249, 261; in China, 292; in Spain, 253; mapmaking by, 368(*map*), 396; moneylending by, 347; persecution of, in Europe, 348–349; expelled from Spain, 346, 358

Jin Empire, 299, 300(*map*); Mongols and, 314, 327

Jingdezhen, ceramic works at, 332

Joan of Arc, 357

João III (Portugal), 402

John (England), 287, 355 *and illus.*

Jordan River, 67, 69

Joseph (Israel), 68, 69

Joshua (Israel), 69

Judaea, 153, 154

Judah, 70, 71, 79

Judaism, 67. *See also* Israel; Jews; Christianity and, 67, 154; Zoroastrianism and, 119, 140; headcoverings in, 263; Islam and, 248; Khazar Turks and, 281

Julius Caesar, 148

Jungle, 362. *See also* Tropical rain forest

Junks (ships), 299, 373, 390(*illus.*)

Jurchens, 299

Justinian (Byzantine Empire), 150, 270; plague of, 269

Juvaini, 'Ata-Malik, 318–319, 321

Juvenal, 150–151

Ka'ba (shrine), 247, 248, 249

Kadesh, Battle at, 58

Kaffa, plague in, 320, 341, 342(*map*)

Kaifeng (Song capital), 290(*illus.*), 299, 301(*illus.*)

K'ak Tiliw Chan Chaak (Maya), 193

Kali (Durga), 176

Kamakura Shogunate (Japan), 307, 334–335

Kama Sutra (Vatsyayana), 184–185

Kamikaze (divine wind), 335

Kamose (Egypt), 57

Kanishka (Kushan), 238

Karakorum, 315, 317(*map*), 327, 332

Karma, 173

Kassites, 30, 54, 57

Kautilya, 178, 185

Kenya, early humans in, 8

Keraits, 313

Kerma, 81, 96

Khadija (wife of Muhammad), 247, 248, 260

Khadim al-Haramain, 255–256

Khafre, pyramid of, 41, 42 *and illus.*

Khajuraho, Hindu temple at, 176(*illus.*)

Khanates. *See* Golden Horde khanate; Il-khanate Empire (Iran); Jagadai khanate; Yuan Empire

Khans, 316(*fig.*) *See also* Mongolian Empire; *and specific khans*

Kharijite Islam, 250, 251, 252

Khazar Turks, 281

Khipus, 383

Khitan language, 306

Khitan people, 298–299

Khoisan peoples, 235

Khubilai, Great Khan, 315, 316(*fig.*), 317(*map*), 326–327; invasion of Japan and, 330, 334, 335; Marco Polo and, 327; observatory of, 323

Khufu, pyramid of, 41, 42 *and illus.*

Khurusan, Islam in, 251

Khwarezm, 314

Kievan Empire (Russia), 281–283; Byzantium and, 267, 281–282 *and map*, 283, 288; rise of, 281–282; society and culture, 283; Mongol conquest of, 314, 325

Kilwa, 374

Kingship. *See* Monarchy (emperors; kingship)

King's Peace (England), 277

King's Peace (Greece), 133

Kinship systems. *See also* Clans; Lineages; in farming communities, 21; Chinese, 94; Celtic, 103; Greek, 124; Northern Amerindian, 207; Indian, 171, 181; Islam and, 247, 248

Kipchak khanate. *See* Golden Horde khanate

Kivas, of Anasazi people, 206

Knights, 273, 355; armor and horses of, 274, 276, 287(*illus.*); Crusades and, 285, 287(*illus.*); Portuguese, 358

Koguryo (Korea), 305

Kola nuts, 234, 363

Kongo, slave trade in, 401, 402–403

Kongzi. *See* Confucius (Kongzi)

Korea: Buddhism in, 305; China and, 161, 292, 294(*map*), 298, 304, 305; Choson kings in, 333–334; chronology (1258–1392), 315; printing in, 305, 333–334 *and illus.*; *hangul* writing in, 306, 333(*illus.*), 334; Mongol conquest of, 333; technology in, 331, 332

Koryo, 305, 333–334

Kosovo, Battle of (1389), 326

Kra, Isthmus of, 187(*map*), 188

Kremlin, in Moscow, 325(*illus.*)

Krishna (god), 169, 176, 180

Kshatriyas, 172

Kufa, 257, 258

Kush, 40, 96–97. *See also* Nubia

Kushan Empire, 99(*map*), 172(*map*), 180, 227; Buddhism in, 238

Kyoto (Heian), 306, 307, 308(*illus.*), 335, 336

Labor (labor force). *See also* Slaves (slavery); in Mesopotamia, 31; in ancient Egypt, 41; Assyrian, 65, 66(*illus.*); Persian workers, 118; Olmec, 197; Chavín civilization and, 198; in China, 159; Andean (mit'a), 210, 215, 216

Laconia, 128. *See also* Sparta

Lamas (Buddhist priests), 327

Lambeyeque Valley, Peru, 211

Lamps and candles, 38 *and illus.*

Land grants: in Assyrian Empire, 65; in China, 160; in India, 186; in Persian Empire, 117; in Egypt, 137; in Islamic caliphate, 255; in medieval Europe, 274; in Japan, 334

Landowners (landownership): in Mesopotamia, 33; in Assyrian Empire, 64; in early China, 89; English, 342; in Greece, 126; in Persia, 116; in Roman Republic and Empire, 144, 149, 152, 157, 166; in imperial China (gentry), 158, 165, 166, 301, 302; in Byzantine Empire, 269; in medieval Europe, 273, 274–275, 284; in East Asia, 304; in Korea, 305, 333; in Vietnam, 336

Language(s). *See also* Arabic language; Writing; Afro-Asiatic, 22; human larynx and, 7; Semitic, 30; Akkadian, 30, 54, 56; Aramaic, 30, 67, 99; Indo-European, 21–22, 99, 113, 171, 172, 180; Sumerian, 32; Hebrew, 30, 67; Dravidian, 172; Celtic, 102; Meroitic, 98; English, 105; Turkic, 101; Chinese, 86, 158, 293, 306 *and illus.*, 328; Latin, 144, 153, 339, 351, 353; Persian, 140, 252, 262; Greek, 61, 63, 139, 153, 324; Sanskrit, 173, 180, 182, 291, 292, 377; Bantu, 233(*map*), 237; Coptic, 251; Khitan, 306; Tibetan, 293; Austronesian, 388, 391; Malayo-Polynesian, 391, 392(*map*); of Malaccan traders, 376; Slavic, 281, 324; Swahili, 374; vernacular, 352, 353

Laozi, 91. *See also* Daoism

Lapita peoples, 391

Lascaux (France) cave paintings, 11, 12

Late Bronze Age (1600–1000 B.C.E.), 54–64, 80. *See also* Assyrian Empire; China, early; in Aegean region, 60–62, 63(*illus.*); fall of, 62–64, 80; in Middle East, 54–59

Lateen sails, 229, 373 *and illus.*, 395, 398 *and illus.*

Latifundia (estates), 149

Latin Church, 281. *See also* Catholicism; Christian Church

Latin language, 144, 153; in Europe, 339, 353; in universities, 351

Latin West (Europe 1200–1500), 338–359; civic life, 346–347; Gothic cathedrals, 347, 349; humanists and printers, 352–353; Hundred Years War, 355, 357; Iberian unification, 357–358; mills and mines, 342–343; monarchs, nobles and church in, 354–355; monarchy in France and England, 357; Ottoman frontier, 358; peasants, population and plague in, 338(*illus.*), 339–341; persecution of Jews, 348–349; political and military changes in, 354–358; Renaissance, 350–351, 353–354; rural growth and crisis, 339–343; social rebellion, 341–342; trading cities, 344–346 *and map*; universities and scholars, 350–351; urban revival, 343–350

La Venta (Olmec center), 194

Laws (legal codes): of Hammurabi, 32, 33, 50; Israelite, 69; Chinese, 158, 296; Islamic Shari'a, 257, 259; Roman, 145, 149–150, 270, 278; church canons, 275, 278; Germanic, 278; Japanese, 305; Vietnamese, 336; English, 343

Leakey, Louis, 6, 7

Leakey, Mary, 6, 10(*illus.*)

Leakey, Richard, 6, 8

Leatherworking (tanning), 368, 375–376; pollution from, 343

Lebanon, 74. *See also* Phoenicia

Legalism, in China, 95, 159; Confucianism and, 92, 93, 158

"Lessons for Women" (Ban Zhao), 162

Levant, 43, 68(*map*). *See also* Israel; Lebanon; Syria

Liao Empire, 298–299, 300(*map*)

Libraries. *See also* Books; in Assyria, 67; in Alexandria, 138; monastic, 280(*illus.*); in Vatican, 353; in Timbuktu, 377

Libya, 43, 76; Greek colony in, 124; Persians in, 116; Romans in, 236, 284

Li family, 292

Li Qingzhao, 303

Li Shimin (China), 292, 295(*illus.*)

Li Si, 158

Lighthouse of Alexandria, 138

Limbourg brothers, 340(*illus.*)

Lineages. *See also* Clans; Patriarchy; matrilineage, 21, 98; Maya, 193; Aztec, 380

Linear B (clay) tablets, 61, 63

Lisbon, 357

Literacy: in Egypt, 42; Greek transition to, 123, 131–132, 140, 218–219; Islam and, 259, 377; Christian monks and, 280; in Chinese bureaucracy, 301; of Chinese women, 303; in East Asia, 304; Korean, 333(*illus.*), 334

Literature. *See also* Books; Libraries; Poets and poetry; Printing technology; Writing; Chinese, 163, 331–332; Indian epics, 169, 180–181; Maya, 214; Abbasid Caliphate and, 260–261; Japanese women and, 306, 307; European humanist, 352

Lithuania, 325; Poland and, 326, 356(*map*); war with Russia, 357

Liu Bang, 159

Llamas, 19, 198, 209, 213; and alpacas, 75, 210, 382(*illus.*), 383
Loans (credit): in China, 302; in late medieval Europe, 346, 347
Loess (soil), 84
Logographers, Greek, 127, 128
London, peasant revolt in, 341
Longbow, 355
Looms, 345(*illus.*). *See also* Weaving
Lords and vassals, in medieval Europe, 274, 355
Louis IX (France), 286(*map*)
Louis the Pious, 272
Louis VII (France), 287
Lü (China), 160
Lugal ("big man"), 32
Lug (god), 104
Luo Guanzhong, 331–332
Luoyang, 90, 163, 164
Lyceum, of Aristotle, 132
Lydia, 116, 129; coinage in, 125, 238

Ma'at (divine order), 41
Macao, Portuguese in, 405
Macedonia, 133–134 *and illus.*; Antigonids in, 136, 137 *and map*
Madagascar, 228; Indonesian colonists in, 222(*illus.*), 230; migrations to, 388
Madeira Island, 392, 395, 396
Madrasa (Islamic college), 262, 351
Madurai, temple at, 168(*illus.*), 372(*illus.*)
Magadha, 178, 179
Magellan, Ferdinand, 386(*illus.*), 387, 397(*map*), 399
Magic. *See also* Shamans; cave paintings and, 15; in Mesopotamia, 35; in ancient Egypt, 45; in Celtic legends, 105; in China, 164; in Srivijaya, 190; in Africa, 367
Magi (Persia), 116
Magna Carta (England), 355 *and illus.*
Magnetic compass, 299, 373, 395
Mahabharata, 180, 181
Mahavira, 174
Mahayana Buddhism, 178, 298, 308; bodhisattvas, 175, 239, 292–293
Mahmud, Sultan, 368
Maimonides, 253
Maize (corn), 197, 198, 209, 210, 393, 406; beans, squash, and, 24, 194, 206, 208, 216, 381
Majapahit Empire, 369(*map*), 376

Malabar Coast (India), 373, 375, 376; Portuguese and, 402–403, 404, 405
Malacca (Melaka), 391; Islamic scholars in, 377; port of, 376; Portuguese in, 404–405; Strait of, 374, 375, 376, 388
Malaria, 332, 364
Malaya (Malaysia), 302; tin from, 376
Malayo-Polynesian languages, 391, 392(*map*)
Malay Peninsula (Malays), 184; Indian Ocean trade and, 187, 227, 376; maritime exploration by, 187 *and map*; Srivijaya and, 187(*map*), 188–190
Mali, 232, 366–368; Ghana and, 252, 366; griot (storyteller), 218; Ibn Battuta in, 371; mosque in, 369(*illus.*); slave trade in, 378; trans-Saharan trade and, 367(*map*), 368; women and Islam in, 379
Malindi, 390, 401
Malinke people, 367, 368
Malintzin (Malinche), 407
Malta, 76 *and map*
Mamluks (Turks), 254; in Egypt, 256, 317(*map*), 321, 325, 366; as military slaves, 252, 378; Mongols and, 316, 317(*map*)
Mammoths and mastodons, 12, 13
Manchuria, 161
Mandala theory, in India, 179
Mandate (Son) of Heaven: in China, 88–89, 167; in Japan, 306
Manetho, 41
Mani and Manichaeism, 227, 246
Manko Inka, 409
Manors, in medieval Europe, 273
Mansa Kankan Musa (Mali), 368 *and illus.*, 369(*illus.*), 392
Mansa Muhammad (Mali), 392
Mansa Suleiman (Mali), 368
Manuel (Portugal), 404
Manufactured goods (manufacturing). *See also* Pottery; Textiles; *and specific manufactures*; Mesopotamian, 31; Carthaginian, 78; Egyptian, 97; Roman, 152, 156, 234; Indian Ocean trade and, 230; trans-Saharan trade and, 234, 252; caravan trade and, 246; in Kievan Russia, 281; in medieval Europe,

284, 287, 344(*map*), 345; of Ming China, 332; Venetian, 346; Gujarati, 375–376; Hausa, 368
Manuscripts, 280 *and illus.*
Manuzio, Aldo, 353
Manzikert, Battle of (1071), 254, 286
Maodun (Xiongnu), 159
Mapmaking (cartography): Babylonian, 2 (*illus.*); Roman, 110(*illus.*); Islamic, 220(*illus.*); German, 310(*illus.*); Jewish, 368(*map*), 396; naming of America and, 398; Portuguese, 395(*illus.*)
Maragheh, observatory at, 323
Marduk (god), 35, 36–37
Mari, 58
Maritime revolution (to 1550), 386–410; global (before 1450), 388–393; Americas, 406–409; Atlantic Ocean, 389, 392–393; chronology, 389; Indian Ocean, 388–391, 392(*map*); European (1400–1550), 394–399, 397(*map*); Magellan, 386(*illus.*), 387, 397(*map*); Pacific Ocean, 389, 391, 392(*map*); Portuguese in Africa, 395(*illus.*), 396, 399–400, 401; Portuguese voyages, 387, 394–396, 397(*map*), 398 *and illus.*; Spanish voyages, 387, 396–399 *and map*; Africa and, 399–403
Markets. *See also* Merchants (traders); Trade; Greek agora, 124; Chinese, 163; in Kievan Russia, 281; Champagne fairs, 345; West African women and, 379; Aztec, 381
Marquesas Islands, 391, 392(*map*)
Marriage. *See also* Polygamy; of Neolithic farmers, 21; in Mesopotamia, 31, 32, 34; in Egypt, 43; in Israel, 70; in China, 90, 94, 303; in Celtic Europe, 104; Alexander and, 135; in Greece, 132; in Rome, 145, 147; in India, 182–183, 184–185; intermarriage, 139; divorce, 43, 70, 259, 303; Indian Ocean traders and, 231; in Islam, 259; in medieval Europe, 275, 276; Mongol alliances, 314; in Delhi Sultanate, 378
Marv, 250
Mary (mother of Jesus), 245
Mass deportation: in Assyrian Empire, 65, 66, 71, 79, 80; in Mauryan India, 179

Mass production, in China, 300
Mathematics (mathematicians): Mesopotamian, 39, 88; Egyptian, 46; Babylonian, 139; Indian, 181, 182; concept of zero, 181, 182, 203; Chinese, 299, 301(*illus.*); fractions and, 299; Maya, 203; decimals, 324; Il-khanate, 322–323, 324; Korean, 333; value of pi, 324
Matrilineal societies, 21; Nubian, 98; Maya, 193
Mauritania, 252
Mauryan Empire (India), 172(*map*), 178–179; Buddhism in, 179, 238
Maya, 200–203, 200(*map*); ball games of, 202(*illus.*); calendar, 203; elite burials, 212 *and illus.*; pyramids, 201 *and illus.*; Toltecs and, 204(*map*), 205; urban centers, 193; women in, 193, 202–203; writing of, 193(*illus.*), 203, 214 *and illus.*
Mbuti Pygmies, 235
Meat eating: in Stone Age, 11; in Egypt, 43
Mecca: Muhammad in, 247–248, 249, 258; pilgrimage to, 247, 249, 368, 405; shrines in, 247
Mechanization: in Korea, 334; in medieval Europe, 342
Medes, 79, 115–116
Medici family, 347, 354 *and illus.*
Medicine (physicians): Egyptian, 46; Greek, 112(*illus.*), 113; wine as, 135; Indian, 180; Silk Road trade and, 224; Islamic, 287; Chinese, 327; medieval Europe, 341, 351; Kongo, 403
Medieval Europe (600–1200), 271–275; Charlemagne, 267; Christian church, 271(*map*), 275–280; chronology, 269; Crusades, 285–287; Germanic kingdoms, 272 *and map*, 273; Kievan Russia, 281–283, 282(*map*); population of, 413 *and fig.*; revival of (1000–1200), 283–285; self-sufficient economy, 273–274; society, 274–275; technology in, 276 *and illus.*, 283–284; time of insecurity, 271–272; Viking raids in, 272
Medina, 248, 249, 250
Mediterranean Sea and region. *See also specific civilizations, peoples, and countries*; trade

in, 56(*illus.*); chronology (2000–300 B.C.E.), 55; Phoenician expansion into, 74, 75, 76 *and map*, 78, 80; Greeks and, 121, 124; climate, 144; Roman expansion into, 146(*map*), 147–148; wine in, 134–135; glass industry in, 156; Indian Ocean ships compared, 229–230; Fatimid Caliphate power in, 253; medieval Europe and, 273; gold coinage in, 285; northern Italian cities and, 284, 343, 346; galleys in, 395; trading alliances in, 394
Megaliths, 21, 22(*illus.*)
Mehmet II, Sultan, 326
Mekong River Delta, 188, 308
Melaka. *See* Malacca
Melanesia, colonization of, 391, 392(*map*)
Melqart (god), 76
"Memorial on the Bone of Buddha" (Han), 294
Memphis (Egypt), 41, 42, 44, 97
Men. *See also* Family; Gender roles; Marriage; Patriarchy; Ice Age hunters, 14, 16 *and illus.*; early agriculture and, 17, 34; Israelite, 70; and yin/yang concept, 94; fathers, in China, 94; Celtic, 103; Spartan, 128; bisexual, in Greece, 133; Roman, 145; Indian ritual and, 178; Muslim misogyny and, 259; Sufi brotherhoods, 262, 264
Mencius (Mengzi), 91, 162
Menes (Egypt), 41
Menkaure, pyramid of, 42(*illus.*)
Mercenaries: Mycenaean, 61, 62; Carthaginian, 78; Greek, 140
Merchant ships. *See* Ships and shipping (merchant marine)
Merchants (traders). *See also* Markets; Trade; Mesopotamian, 32–33; Indus Valley, 48–49; Assyrian, 55; Carthaginian, 77, 80; Cretan, 62; Egyptian, 81; Phoenician, 76; Greek, 126; Roman, 153; Silk Road, 164; imperial China, 163, 165, 166, 292, 302, 303; Indian, 180, 181, 184, 187; Persian, 227; Arab, 227, 246, 374; Byzantine, 270; Italian, 284; Kievan Russia, 281; European guilds of, 346; Indian Ocean trade and, 227, 374; Chinese, in Southeast Asia,

329; Mongolian Empire, 319, 327–328; taxes on, 357; credit and finance for, 346–347; Korean, 333; Gujarati, 375, 376; Muslim, 368, 376, 377, 379, 388, 405; northern Italian, 345, 347, 394; Aztec, 381; Chinese in Indian Ocean trade, 388, 390; of Calicut, 405; Portuguese, 400; spread of disease and, 413
Meroë, 97–98, 237
Mesa Verde cliff dwelling, 206, 207(*illus.*)
Mesoamerica: Andean civilization compared to, 216; Olmecs, 89, 194–197 *and illus.*, 216; agriculture in, 18(*map*), 19; Aztecs, 406–408; chronology (5000 B.C.E.–1300 C.E.), 195; classic era (200–900), 199–203; divination in, 89; Maya, 193, 200–203, 200(*map*); Northern peoples and, 206, 208; post-classic era (900–1500), 203–205; pyramids, 194, 196, 199(*illus.*), 201(*illus.*), 202; Teotihuacan, 199–200; Toltecs, 202(*illus.*), 204–205 *and map*, 216; trade with South America, 393; Aztecs, 379–382, 380(*map*)
Mesopotamia, 29–39. *See also* Assyrian Empire; Babylonia; Iraq; agriculture in, 29–30; mapmaking, 2(*illus.*); astronomy in, 88; Sumerians in, 30, 32, 34; beermaking in, 134; Tigris and Euphrates Valley, 27, 28(*map*), 29, 56; chronology (3000–1150 B.C.E.), 29; cities, kings and trade in, 31–33; cylinder seal from, 33(*illus.*); divination in, 88; Egypt compared to, 42, 43, 44, 49–50; *Epic of Gilgamesh*, 26(*illus.*), 27; Amorites in, 32, 99; city-states, 31; glassmaking in, 156; gods, priests, and temples in, 34–35; society, 33–34; technology and science, 35–39; irrigation, 29, 31; Kassites in, 54–55; Medes and, 115; Persian Empire and, 116, 118, 140; religious diversity in, 245; Seleucids in, 136, 137(*map*); Silk Road trade and, 244; Alexander the Great in, 135; trade of, 230, 246; decline of, 79, 255
Messenians, 128

Messiah: in Zoroastrianism, 119; Jesus as, 153; in Islam, 252

Metals (metallurgy). *See also* Bronze; Copper; Gold; Iron industry; Mining (minerals); Silver; Steel; Tin; at Çatal Hüyük, 23; in Mesopotamia, 37; in Indus Valley, 47–48; Late Bronze Age trade in, 59; Kushite, 96; Celtic, 104, 105(*illus.*); Iranian, 115; in Southeast Asia, 187; Andean, 198, 211, 383; coinage and, 238; Song China, 300; in tropical regions, 364, 366; Mongol, 326; lost-wax method, 366 *and illus.*; in Mesoamerica, 393

Methodius (missionary), 270

Mexica, 379–382, 380(*map*). *See also* Aztec

Mexico (Mexicans). *See also* Mesoamerica; maize agriculture in, 19; Olmecs in, 89, 194–197; Teotihuacan in, 199–200, 204; Maya in, 200; Mexica people, 379–380, 406; Toltecs in, 202(*illus.*), 204–205 *and map*; Valley of (1519), 380(*map*); Aztec Empire, 379–382; Spanish conquest of, 406–408

Michelangelo, 354 *and illus.*

Michelino, Domenico di, 352(*illus.*)

Middle Ages, in Europe. *See* Medieval Europe (600–1200)

Middle class: Mesopotamian, 34; Egyptian, 42, 43; Greek, 126, 129; Roman, 145, 166

Middle East. *See also* Arabs; Islam (Islamic civilization); Mesopotamia; *and specific countries, cultures, empires, and regions*; Neanderthals in, 5; burial mounds in, 21; domesticated animals in, 19; early towns in, 22–23; Agricultural Revolution in, 17, 20; beermaking in, 20; trade in, 54(*map*); Late Bronze Age cosmopolitanism in, 54–59; glassmaking in, 156; Hellenism in, 140; Chinese trade with, 223, 329; chronology (1219–1453), 315; Yuan China and, 327, 328; Muslim traders of, 388

Migration (population movement). *See also* Colonies; Nomadic peoples; out of Africa, 6, 7, 8–10, 9(*map*); pastoralists and, 19–20; to

ancient Egypt, 41; deportations, in Assyrian Empire, 65, 66, 71, 79, 80; Indo-European, 60, 99, 171, 172(*map*); Israelite, 68; Kassites, 54–55; Celtic, 102–103; within China, 165; Greek, 137 *and map*, 139; in Roman Empire, 157; from China to Southeast Asia, 187; from Southeast Asia to Madagascar, 222(*illus.*), 230; Bantu-speaking peoples, 233(*map*), 236–237, 240; Islam and, 257–258; Turkic peoples, 281; East Asian languages and, 304; from Southeast Asia, 391, 392(*map*)

Militarism, in East Asia, 333–336

Military. *See also* Armed forces; Navy; War; Weapons and military technology; Mesopotamian, 31, 32, 39; in Egypt, 43; Assyrian Empire, 64–65; Carthaginian, 78; in early China, 86, 95; Persian, 117; Spartan, 128; Macedonian, 133–134; Roman, 147, 148 *and illus.*, 154; imperial China, 159, 161, 163, 165, 292, 302; Maya, 202; Teotihuacan, 200; Toltec, 204; Andean region, 211, 213; Mamluk, 252; medieval Europe, 272, 274; Jurchen, 299; Khitan, 298; Crusades and, 285; Delhi Sultanate, 368; Ottoman, 358; Aztec, 380–381

Military conscription, in China, 90, 163, 165

Military slaves, 252, 358, 378

Millet (grain), 17, 18(*map*), 84, 85, 235, 236, 299, 331, 363

Minakshi, temple of (Madurai), 168(*illus.*), 170, 372(*illus.*)

Ming Empire (China): achievements of, 331–332; early (1368–1500), 328–332; Mongol foundation of, 328–329; technology and population, 330–331; Vietnam and, 329, 330(*map*); Zheng He's voyages in, 311, 329–330 *and map*, 376, 389–390 *and illus.*, 392(*map*), 398

Mining (minerals). *See also* Metals (metallurgy); *specific minerals*; of coal, 299, 326; in east-central Europe, 342; tax on, in China, 330; in tropics, 364–366

Minoan Crete, 53, 60–62, 61(*map*), 63(*illus.*)

Minos (Crete), 60

Minotaur, 60

Minyak people, 298

Missionaries, Buddhist, 188, 291

Missionaries, Christian, 275, 406; in Africa, 239–240, 401; Catholic, 351, 401; Nestorian, 245; Orthodox, 270, 282

Mississippian culture, 206, 207, 208–209

Mit'a labor, in Andes, 210

Mitanni, 56

Mithra (sun-god), 154

Mixcoatl (Toltec), 205

Moche, 210–211 *and map*, 215; elite burials, 212 *and illus.*

Mocteczuma II (Aztec), 381, 407–408 *and illus.*

Mogadishu, 361

Mohenjo-Daro, 47 *and illus.*, 48 *and illus.*

Moksha (liberation), 173, 178

Moluccas (Spice Islands), 376, 399

Monarchy (emperors; kingship). *See also* Divine kingship; *and specific monarchs and emperors*; in Mesopotamia, 32, 36, 37, 49; in early China, 86, 88–89; Egyptian (pharoahs), 41, 42–43, 44; Minoan, 60; Hittite, 62; Assyrian Empire, 64; Israelite, 69–70 *and illus.*, 80; Kushite, 96; Nubian queens, 98; Scythian, 100; Buddhism and, 298; Persian Empire, 116, 117, 118, 120–121; Roman, 149, 153, 167; Indian, 179, 181; Srivijaya, 189–190; Chinese, 160–161 *and illus.*, 165, 167, 292, 300; Mesoamerican, 195; Sasanid Iran, 244 *and illus.*; sub-Saharan Africa, 236; Aksumite, 239 *and illus.*; Byzantine, 268, 269; crowns for, 263; Christian church and, 274–275, 355; English, 287, 355 *and illus.*; Germanic kingdoms, 272; Japanese, 306; Chinese, 319; French, 355; Mongol (khans), 314–315, 316(*fig.*), 317(*map*); Korean, 333; Serbian, 326; West African, 366 *and illus.*, 367–368 *and illus.*; women, in Delhi Sultanate, 369–370; Zimbabwe, 375; Aztec, 381, 407–408 *and illus.*; Inka, 408, 409; Kongo, 401, 402–403; Portuguese, 404; Spanish, 396

Monasteries (monks and nuns): Buddhist, 164, 175, 181, 183, 190, 292, 293, 332, 378; Christian,

278–280; headshaving in, 263; Irish, 263, 280 *and illus.*; nuns, 280, 295

Monetary system. *See also* Banks; Coins; Currency; Chinese paper, 302, 328; Mongol paper, 321, 324

Moneylending, 347. *See also* Loans (credit)

Möngke, Great Khan, 316(*fig.*)

Mongolia (Mongols): iron working in, 226; Liao capital in, 299

Mongolian Empire (Mongols), 312–329, 336–337. *See also specific khans*; Khanates; sack of Baghdad by, 251, 253(*map*), 256, 315, 320, 375; in China (*See* Yuan Empire); chronology (1206–1368), 315; conquests of (1215–1283), 311, 313, 314–318, 317(*map*); culture and science in, 321–324; invasion of Japan by, 312(*illus.*), 315, 316, 334–335 *and map*, 337; Islam and (1260–1500), 315, 320–324, 329; Korea and, 333; in Middle East (*See* Il-khanate); Ming China and, 328–329; nomadism and, 314; rise of (1200–1260), 314–320; Russia and, 314, 315, 317(*map*), 324–325, 337; Silk Road trade and, 313, 327; trade and disease in, 318–320; Vietnam and, 315–316, 336; women in, 314

Monks. *See* Monasteries (monks and nuns)

Monophysite theology, 246

Monopolies, trading: Carthage, 78; Egyptian, 137; Chinese, 161, 302; Indian, 179; Byzantine, 270; Portuguese, 396; West African, 400, 401

Monotheism: Egyptian, 57; Israelite, 70, 71; Zoroastrianism, 119; Christianity, 154, 167; Islamic, 248

Monsoons: China and, 84, 87(*map*); India and, 46, 171; Indian Ocean trade and, 228, 230, 231, 362, 372–373, 375, 388; Korea and, 304; Southeast Asia and, 186, 188, 363

Morocco, 76, 253; Portuguese in, 358, 394; travelers from (*See* Ibn Battuta, Muhammad ibn Abdullah)

Mosaics: Northern Amerindian, 206; Roman, 142(*illus.*), 234

Moscow: Kremlin in, 325(*illus.*); Mongol conquest of, 314, 324–325

Moses (Israel), 68–69

Mosques, 258; in Egypt, 254(*illus.*); in India, 368, 377; in Timbuktu, 369(*illus.*)

Mosul, 258

Mother goddess. *See* Fertility cults (deities)

Mound builders, Amerindian, 207–209

Movable type, in printing: in Europe, 353; in Korea, 301, 305, 333–334 *and illus.*; in Song China, 301

Mozambique Channel, 230

Mu'awiya, 249

Mughal Empire (India), 405

Muhammad (Prophet), 221, 264; in Mecca and Medina, 247–248, 258; sayings of (hadith), 251, 257, 258, 259, 260; succession to, 249–250

Mummification, 45, 46, 98

Mural painting. *See* Wall murals (frescoes)

Murasaki Shikibu, 306

Museum of Alexandria, 138

Music: in early China, 94(*illus.*); African, 236; Byzantine, 270; European troubadour, 287; Chinese women and, 303(*illus.*); Japanese drama and, 335(*illus.*)

Muslims. *See also* Islam; pork taboo and, 238; Crusades against, 255, 285–287, 339; meaning of word, 238; in France, 272; in Spain, 253–254 *and map*, 256(*illus.*), 259(*illus.*), 287; head coverings, 263 *and illus.*; in North Africa, 284; in China, 329; driven from Iberian peninsula, 357; hospitality and, 361; Italian cities allied with, 346; and Hindus, in Delhi Sultanate, 368–369, 375; as traders and merchants, 368, 376, 377, 379, 388, 405; in Red Sea region, 375

Mycenaean Greece, 53, 60–63 *and map*, 122

Myrrh, 43, 57, 58(*illus.*), 230, 246

Nabopolassar (Neo-Babylonia), 80

Nabta Playa, 236

Nalanda, Buddhist center at, 183, 376

Nanjing, 329

Napata, 97, 98

Naqsh-i Rustam, 118

Nara (Japan), 306

Naranjo, 193

Nasir al-Din Tusi, 322–323

Nationalism, in Japan, 335

Natural disasters. *See also* Drought; Flooding (floods); Volcanic eruptions; Indus Valley and, 49; Moche decline and, 211

Natural resources. *See* Raw materials (resources)

Natural selection, 6

Nature. *See also* Environment (environmental stress); Daoism and, 94; Chinese deities and, 164

Navigation (navigational tools). *See also* Sailing (seafaring); Ships and shipping; in Southeast Asia, 187; rear-positioned rudders, 373; astrolabe, 395; magnetic compass, 299, 373, 395; Polynesian, 391; Portuguese, 395; Viking, 392

Navy (warships). *See also* Pirates; Egyptian, 57; Minoan, 63(*illus.*); Carthaginian, 77, 78, 80; Athenian, 130, 131(*illus.*), 133; Persian, 130; Chinese, 329; Mongol, 312(*illus.*), 334 *and map*, 335; Portuguese, 401, 404, 405, 406, 410; Ottoman, 405

Neanderthals, 5, 8, 10, 12

Nebuchadnezzar (Neo-Babylonia), 71, 80

Nefertiti (Egypt), 57

Neo-Assyrian Empire. *See* Assyrian Empire

Neo-Babylonian kingdom (Chaldaean dynasty), 71, 76, 79, 80; Persian Empire and, 116, 117

Neo-Confucianism, 300, 301, 333

Neolithic Age (New Stone Age), 11, 16–23; agricultural revolution in, 16–20; life in communities of, 20–23; in China, 85

Nepotism, 276

Nestorian Christianity, 227, 245, 292

Nevskii, Alexander, 324, 325, 326

Nevskii, Daniel, 324

Newfoundland, Vikings in, 272

New Guinea, 10, 391, 392(*map*)

New Mexico, native peoples of, 206–207

New Stone Age. *See* Neolithic Age

New Testament (Bible), 153, 353

New Year's Festivals, 35, 36–37, 119

New Zealand, 391, 392(*map*)

Nicholas IV, Pope, 320

Nicholas V, Pope, 353

Niger, 232; salt trade in, 365 *and illus.*

Niger River, 235; Benin and, 400 *and illus.*; flooding of, 363; gold mining in, 368; inland delta, 363

Niger Valley, copper in, 236

Nile River, 39–41, 236; canal to Red Sea, 117; flooding of, 17, 40, 50, 138; geography of, 40(*map*); in Nubia, 96 *and map*

Nile Valley, 27, 28(*map*). *See also* Egypt, ancient; migration to, 17, 236

Niña (ship), 398

Nineveh, 66(*illus.*)

Nirvana. *See* Enlightenment

Nishapur, 257–258

Nobility. *See* Aristocracy (nobility)

Noh drama, in Japan, 335(*illus.*)

Nomadic peoples (nomadism). *See also specific peoples*; Mesopotamia and, 32; Semites, 30; Egypt and, 43; Israelites and, 67, 71; early China and, 87(*map*), 90; Meroë and, 98; in Eurasian steppes, 98–102, 108(*illus.*); imperial China and, 159, 160(*map*); Silk Road trade and, 185, 187; Central Asian, 179, 225–226; in Saharan region, 232; Arab, 244, 246; Kievan Russia and, 281; Inner Asian, 314

Normans. *See also* Vikings; conquest of England (1066), 266(*illus.*), 272; in Sicily, 272, 285

North Africa. *See also specific peoples and countries*; cattle in, 19; Carthage and, 53; Phoenician settlements in, 76 *and map*, 237; Greek colony in, 112(*illus.*), 113; Greek culture in, 136; Rome and, 155, 234; camels in, 98, 232–233; Arab city-states in, 252–253; Berbers of, 251, 366; trading cities of, 284; Portuguese in, 394; Muslim rule in, 366, 394

North America: Amerindians of, 195, 206–209, 207(*map*), 216; mound builders, 207–209; Southwestern desert cultures, 206–207, 208(*illus.*); Vikings in, 392

North China Plain, 84, 86, 87(*map*), 105, 326

Northeast Asia, chronology (313–1115), 293

North Sea region, 285

Norway, 272. *See also* Vikings; King Harold of, 279

Novgorod, 345; Rus of, 281, 282, 283

Nubia, 95–98; chronology (4500–300 B.C.E.), 85; Egypt and, 40, 43, 57, 59(*illus.*), 62, 83, 95–98, 236; gold of, 43, 59, 82(*illus.*), 95, 97; Christianity in, 240, 366; Meroë and, 97–98; Persian expedition to, 116

Number system. *See also* Mathematics; Mesopotamian, 39; Indian (Arabic), 181, 182; Roman, 182

Nuns, 280, 295. *See also* Monasteries

Nur al-Din ibn Zangi, 255

Observatories: in China, 323, 329; in Persian Il-khanate, 324

Obsidian (stone), 23, 196, 204

Octavian. *See* Augustus (Octavian)

Odyssey (Homer), 125, 126

Ögödei, Great Khan, 314, 315, 317(*map*), 326

Ohio River Valley, Amerindians of, 206, 207–208

Oil lamps, 38 *and illus.*

Old Stone Age (Paleolithic), 11–16, 236

Old Testament. *See* Hebrew Bible

Olduvai Gorge, 7

Oligarchy, in Greece, 126

Olives and olive oil, 122, 128, 129, 234

Olmecs, 89, 194–197, 196(*map*); stone heads, 196, 197(*illus.*); urban centers, 194–195, 196

Oman, Indian Ocean trade and, 230

Omar Khayyam, 323

Onin War (1477, Japan), 336

Oracles: Assyrian, 64; Chinese, 85–86, 88, 89(*illus.*); Greek, 88–89, 126

Oral culture (orality): Israelite, 68; Celtic legends, 102, 219; Greek, 123, 127, 131; Indian Brahmins, 219; literacy and, 123, 131, 218–219; West African griot, 218

Origin of Species (Darwin), 6

Orthodox Christianity: Byzantine churches, 268(*illus.*), 270, 281, 282 *and illus.*, 283; missionaries, 270,

282; schism with Latin Church, 268–269; Russian, 270, 281–282, 283, 288, 324, 325

Osiris (god), 44

Ottoman Empire: royal headdress in, 263; conquest of Constantinople by, 326, 339, 356(*map*); Egypt and, 401, 405; expansion of, 358, 394

Oxen, plows and, 17, 29, 108, 109, 171, 284, 340

Oxford University, 351

Pacific Ocean, 399; Amerindian trade in, 393; chronology, 389; exploration of (before 1450), 187; Magellan's crossing of, 387, 397(*map*), 399; Polynesian migration in, 391, 392(*map*); Balboa and, 409

Paekche kingdom (Korea), 305

Painting(s). *See also* Art and artists; cave, 11, 12–13 *and illus.*; Aegean frescoes, 60, 61, 63(*illus.*); Greek vase, 127(*illus.*), 133(*illus.*); Roman frescoes, 151; Buddhist caves, 183 *and illus.*, 299(*illus.*); Chinese, 290(*illus.*), 303(*illus.*); Iranian miniature, 322; Flemish, 340(*illus.*), 354; Renaissance, 352(*illus.*), 354

Pakistan, 179; Punjab in, 134; Gandhara in, 175(*illus.*), 238(*illus.*), 332; Indus Valley civilization in, 27, 28(*map*) 46–49, 250; Kushans in, 180

Palembang, 187(*map*), 188, 190, 376

Paleolithic (Old Stone Age), 11–16, 236

Palestine, 97. *See also* Syria-Palestine region; Crusaders in, 286

Palm oil trade, 234

Panama, 19; Isthmus of, 409

Pandyas, 180

Papacy (popes), 275–278. *See also specific popes*; schism with Orthodox Church, 268–269; monarchs and, 276–278; excommunication and, 277, 325, 348; Crusades and, 286; Jews protected by, 346, 348–349; Peter's pence and, 346; building program of, 354; schisms and, 355; treaty negotiation by, 398

Papermaking: papyrus for, 40, 42, 74; in China, 164; in Middle East, 243, 251

Paper money: in China, 302, 328; in Mongolian Empire, 321, 324

Papyrus, 40, 42, 74

Paris: watermills in, 342; University of, 351

Parliament, British, 343, 357

Parsees, 119

Parthenon, in Athens, 125(*illus.*), 131

Parthians, 244, 245; Hellenistic kingdoms and, 137(*map*); Rome and, 102, 146(*map*), 155

Passport, in Mongolian Empire, 316(*illus.*), 325

Pastoralism (pastoralists). *See also* Cattle (cattle herders); animal domestication and, 19–20; gods of, 21; Israelite, 67–68; Central Asian, 19; trade with farmers, 68, 159; in Africa, 234, 360(*illus.*); on Eurasian steppes, 98–102, 108(*illus.*); Arab, 244, 246; in tropics, 362–363

Pataliputra (modern Patna), 179, 181

Paterfamilias, in Rome, 145

Patriarchs: of Alexandria, 240, 258, 401; of Antioch, 258; of Constantinople, 268, 275, 282; of Serbia, 326

Patriarchy: in Iran, 116; in Rome, 145; in India, 171

Patrick (Saint), 278

Patrilineage, 21

Patron/client relationship, 145

Paul (apostle), 153–154

Pax deorum (peace of the gods), 147

Pax romana (Roman peace), 152

Peasants (peasantry). *See also* Farmers; Rural societies; Egyptian, 43; Late Bronze Age, 54; Mycenaean, 61; Israelite, 70; Tunisian, 78; Chinese, 90–91, 159, 165; Persian, 116; Greek, 126; Indian, 183; Roman, 149; Mesoamerican, 200; medieval European, 273–274, 339–340 *and illus.*; Russian, 283, 325; revolts by, 339

Pei, W. C., 6

Peking man, 6, 8

Peloponnesian League, 128

Peloponnesian War, 133

People of the Book, 261. *See also* Christians; Jews; Zoroastrians

Pepi II (Egypt), 81

Pepin (Franks), 272, 276

Pepper trade, 400, 405. *See also* Spice trade

Pericles (Greece), 125(*illus.*), 129, 131, 133

Periplus of the Erythraean Sea, 228–229

Persepolis (Parsa), 118, 119(*illus.*)

Persian Gulf region: Medes and, 115–116; Indian Ocean trade and, 227, 230, 231, 373; shipbuilding in, 299; Chinese expeditions to, 329, 330(*map*); Ottoman control of, 405; Hormuz and, 404

Persian language, 140, 252, 262, 377

Persian Wars, 129–130, 134

Persia (Parsa), 30, 227

Persia (Persian Empire), 113–120. *See also* Iran; chronology (1000–30 B.C.E.), 115; ideology and religion, 118–119, 120, 140; kingship in, 120–121; organization of, 117–118; rise of, 115–117; rivalry with Greece, 113, 118, 128, 129–130, 133; Alexander's conquest of, 134–135; Scythians and, 101

Peru. *See also* Inka; textiles of, 75; Chavín of, 196(*map*), 197–198; Chimú Empire in, 215; Moche of, 210–211 *and map*, 212 *and illus.*; Wari of, 214–215

Peter's pence, 346

Petrarch, Francesco, 352, 353

Petronius, 156

Peutinger Table, 110(*illus.*)

Pharaohs, of Egypt, 57–58, 68; crowns of, 41, 263

Philip II (Macedonia), 132, 133–134 *and illus.*

Philippines, Spanish claim to, 387, 399

Philip "the Fair" (France), 355

Philistines, 62; Israel and, 67, 69, 74, 80

Philosophy. *See also* Confucianism; Daoism; *specific philosophers*; Greek, 127, 131, 287, 351; in Islamic Spain, 253–254

Phoenician language, 30

Phoenicia (Phoenicians), 68(*map*), 80; alliance with Israel, 69, 74; city-states, 53, 71, 74, 76; colonies of, 75, 76 *and map*, 78, 79, 237; dyes and textiles of, 74, 75; explorations of, 76(*map*), 227;

trade of, 74, 76 *and map*; writing of, 74, 122, 218

Piccolomini, Aeneas Silvius, 339

Pigs, 23, 85; domestication of, 18(*map*), 109, 237–238; taboo on eating (pork), 238

Pilgrims (pilgrimages): Buddhist, 174(*illus.*), 181, 189, 229, 238, 291; Hindu, 177, 372(*illus.*); Mesoamerican, 200, 205; Mississippian, 208; East Asian, 188; Christian, 277, 285; Islamic (Mecca), 247, 249, 368

Pillow Book (Sei), 307

Pimiko (Himiko, Japan), 305

Pinta (ship), 398

Piraeus, 131, 133

Pirates. *See also* Vikings; Greek, 61; Southeast Asian, 189, 376; Japanese, 330, 336

Pisa, 284

Pisistratus, 125(*illus.*), 129

Pizarro, Francisco, 408–409

Plague of Justinian, 269. *See also* Bubonic plague

Plato, 131, 132, 351

Pleiades (star cluster), 138

Pleistocene epoch, 8

Plows, 19, 270, 283, 301, 335; horses and, 108, 284, 340; oxen and, 17, 29, 108, 109, 171, 284, 340

Plutarch, 78

Poets and poetry: Egyptian, 44; Greek, 62, 125, 126–127; Roman, 147, 150; Arab and Islamic, 251; Chinese, 90, 165, 223, 295, 303; European troubadour, 287; Japanese, 307; Italian, 352

Poland (Poles), 285; Lithuania and, 326; Mongols and, 314

Polis (city-state), in Greece, 122–126. *See also* Athens; Sparta

Political systems and institutions. *See also* Administration; Government; Monarchy; Political thought; *and specific institutions*; Mesopotamian, 32; Athenian, 129; Indian, 169, 179–181, 186; Olmec, 194; Anasazi, 206; imperial China, 291; Japanese, 334–336; Aztec alteptl, 379, 380

Political thought (ideology). *See also* Confucianism; Legalism, in China, 92, 93, 95; democracy, in Greece, 126

Politics. *See also* Political systems and institutions; Sasanid Iran, 244; fragmentation of Arab caliphate and, 251–254; Christian Church and, 276–278; Mongol, 314

Polo, Marco, 319, 373, 375; route of, 317(*map*)

Polygamy: in Mesopotamia, 34; in Egypt, 58; in Israel, 68; of Kushite kings, 96; of Persian kings, 117; of Alexander the Great, 135; in Islam, 259, 378; in Kievan Russia, 283; in China, 303; Mongol, 318

Polynesia, colonization of, 391, 392(*map*)

Polytheism: Olmec, 195; Teotihuacan, 199–200 *and illus.*; Maya, 201–203; Moche, 210–211 *and illus.*; Tiwanaku, 213(*illus.*); Aztec, 382; Inka, 382; Semitic, 246–247; Christian church and, 276; Kievan Russian, 283

Pompeii, destruction of (79 C.E.), 152(*illus.*)

Pontius Pilate, 153

Popes. *See* Papacy (popes)

Population movements. *See* Migration(s)

Population (population growth): agriculture and, 20, 21, 24, 171, 412; Indus Valley, 49; Carthage, 77; climate and, 412–413 *and fig.*; Greece, 123–124, 125; Mesoamerica, 200, 201; Andean, 213; imperial China, 162, 302, 328, 331; late medieval Europe, 283, 340, 341; South Asia, 363; Inka, 382

Porcelain, Chinese, 332, 336, 390. *See also* Pottery

Pork. *See also* Pigs; taboo on eating, 71, 238

Portugal (Portuguese). *See also* Portuguese maritime exploration; African slave trade and, 396, 400, 401, 402–403; in North Africa, 358, 394; claim to Brazil, 396, 399; Iberian unification and, 357; Indian Ocean trade and, 398, 402–405

Portuguese maritime exploration, 387, 394–396, 397(*map*); in Africa, 395(*illus.*), 396, 397(*map*), 399–400, 401; in Atlantic, 392, 397(*map*); da Gama, 396, 397(*map*), 398 *and illus.*, 401, 402–403

Poseidon (god), 126

Postal system, in Arabic Caliphate, 251–252

Potatoes, 198, 209, 210; sweet, 194, 331, 391, 406

Potter's wheel, 39, 48, 85

Pottery. *See also* Ceramics; Porcelain, Chinese; Mesopotamian, 39; Cretan, 60, 62; Greek vases, 62, 127(*illus.*), 133(*illus.*), 135; Southwestern desert cultures, 206; Chinese, 227(*illus.*), 230, 292; Korean, 333

Poverty (the poor). *See also* Peasants (peasantry); in Roman Empire, 149, 151; in medieval Europe, 340, 347

Po Zhuyi, 223

Prakrits (languages), 180

Price controls, in Roman Empire, 157

Priests (clergy). *See also* Bishops; Brahmins; Papacy; Religion(s); Mesopotamian, 35, 36; Egyptian, 44–45; Indus Valley, 47(*illus.*); Assyrian, 64; Israelite, 67, 70; Celtic Druids, 89, 103, 104, 105, 218; Iranian (Magi), 116; Roman, 147; Mesoamerican, 195, 200, 202; Andean peoples, 198; headshaving by, 263; Christian, 154, 276; Zoroastrian, 246; European monks, 279–280; in Kievan Russia, 281, 283; Muslim clerics, 377; Tibetan lamas, 327

Primogeniture, 158

Printing technology. *See also* Books; in China, 301; Korean, 301, 305, 333–334 *and illus.*; woodblock, 262(*illus.*), 301, 305, 333–334; movable type, 301, 305, 333–334 *and illus.*, 353; and humanists in Europe, 353 *and illus.*

Prisoners of war, 87. *See also* Slaves, prisoners of war

Propaganda: Assyrian, 64; Persian kings and, 116, 118, 120

Proper and Essential Things for the Emperor's Food and Drink, 319

Property rights. *See also* Inheritance; Landowners (landownership); in China, 158; of women, 44, 259, 366

Prophets: Israelite, 70, 71, 72–73; Islamic (*See* Muhammad (Prophet))

Prostitution, 27. *See also* Concubines

Prussia, 340, 345; Jews in, 346

Ptolemaic Egypt, 136–137 *and map*, 228

Ptolemy, Claudius, 139, 351

Pueblo peoples, 206–207

Puerto Rico (Borinquen), 406

Puja (service to gods), 177

Punjab, 46, 134, 178

Punt, 43, 57

Purification (bathing) rites: in Israel, 71; in India, 173, 177

Pygmies, of Central Africa, 362

Pyramids: Egyptian, 41, 42(*illus.*), 45; Nubian, 98; Mesoamerican, 194, 196, 199(*illus.*), 201(*illus.*), 202

Qin China, 158–159, 160(*map*); Korea and, 304

Quetzalcoatl, 199(*illus.*), 200, 204, 205

Quinoa (grain), 197, 210

Quran, 249, 251, 257, 262(*illus.*); literacy and, 259, 377

Quraysh, 247, 249

Rainfall. *See also* Drought; Monsoons; in Africa, 17; in Punjab, 47; in Greece, 122; in Korea, 334

Rain forests, in tropics, 235, 362, 363

Ramayana, 180

Ramesses II (Egypt), 58, 59(*illus.*)

Rashid al-Din, 321–322

Raw materials (resources). *See also* Metals (metallurgy); Mining; *and specific raw materials*; Egyptian, 40; Indus Valley, 49; Carthaginian trade in, 77; Phoenician trade in, 74, 76(*map*); Greece and, 120, 122, 123(*map*), 124; Japanese, 336; Chinese, 292

Raziya, Sultan, 369–370

Rebellions (revolts). *See also* Civil wars; in Persian Empire, 129–130; in Roman Judaea, 154; within Islam, 251, 252; Berber, 252; by Spanish Muslims, 358; in China, 159, 165, 295, 297, 298, 328, 329; peasant, 339; in Mali, 368; in France, 341; in Delhi Sultanate, 370; Arawak, 406; Aztec, 408; Inka, 409

"Red Eyebrow" uprising, in China, 165

Red Sea region: Egypt and, 57; canal linking Nile to, 117; Aksum, 239; Muslims in, 401; trade in, 375; Ottoman control of, 405

Reforms: of Akhenaten (Egypt), 57–58; in Roman Empire, 157; in China, 164; of Christian popes, 280; Truce of God, 285; Taika (Japan), 305

Reincarnation: Celtic belief in, 105; in Vedic religion, 173, 175

Religion(s). *See also* Afterlife, belief in; Buddhism; Christianity; Confucianism; Creation myths; Cult(s); Gods and goddesses; Hinduism; Islam; Judaism; Priests (clergy); Sacrifice; Shamans; Shrines; Supernatural, the; Temples; *and specific religions*; Stone Age, 13, 15; Neolithic, 21; Mesopotamia, 32; in Carthage, 78; Egyptian, 44–45, 57; Assyrian, 64; Olmec, 194–195; Chinese, 164 (*See also* Buddhism; Confucianism); Persian (*See* Zoroastrianism); Greek, 126, 127(*illus.*); wine used in, 135; Maya, 202; Teotihuacan, 200; Toltec, 203; pork taboo in, 238; head coverings in, 263; Sasanid Iran, 245–246; Shinto (Japan), 306; Lithuania-Russia war and, 357; Aztec, 382

Religions, of India, 190. *See also* Hindus; Buddhism, 173, 174–175, 179, 180, 183 *and illus.*, 378; Jainism, 173, 174, 180, 183; Parsees, 119; Vedism, 175, 183

Religious orders. *See also* Sufis; Dominicans, 351; Franciscans, 318, 351

Religious toleration, 313, 371, 376

Renaissance: in Babylon, 80; Italian, 351, 394; artists of, 353–354 *and illus*; universities and, 350–351

Renfrew, Colin, 21

Re (sun-god), 44

Revolution(s). *See also* Maritime revolution; Rebellions (revolts); Neolithic, 16–20

Rhetoric, Greek, 131

Rhine River, 154, 155

Rice and rice cultivation: domestication of, 17, 18(*map*), 24; in Java, 189; in China, 84, 87(*map*), 299, 301, 331; in Southeast Asia, 17, 18(*map*), 186, 363; in East Asia, 304; Champa, 308, 336; in Ganges Plain, 363; in Vietnam, 188, 308; in Japan, 306, 335; in tropical lands, 363; in Bengal, 378

Richard I, the Lion-Hearted (England), 286(*map*), 287

Rig Veda, 173

Rituals. *See also* Religion; at Çatal Hüyük, 23; Mesopotamian, 34, 35; Canaanite, 70–71; Chinese, 91, 94; Greek, 127(*illus.*), 132; Indian, 173, 177, 178; Olmec, 195; Maya, 201, 203; Northern Amerindian, 206, 207; of Andean peoples, 213; pork taboo in, 238; Aztec, 382

Rivers. *See also* Flooding; *and specific rivers*; early civilizations and, 28(*map*); of sub-Saharan Africa, 235; in Kievan Russia, 281, 282; in Vietnam, 188, 308; watermills on, 342

River Valley civilizations (3500–1500 B.C.E.), 3, 27, 28(*map*), 29, 49, 105. *See also* Egypt, ancient; Indus Valley civilization; Mesopotamia

Roads: in Mesopotamia, 32; in Persian Empire, 114(*map*), 117; in Roman Empire, 152, 154; in China, 160(*map*), 164; in India, 180

Rock art, in Sahara region, 4(*illus.*), 5, 231, 232(*illus.*), 236

Roman alphabet, 270

Roman Catholicism. *See* Catholicism

Romance of the Three Kingdoms, 331–332

Roman Empire (31–476 C.E.), 146(*map*), 236. *See also* Greco-Roman civilization; *and individual emperors*; army of, 147, 148 *and illus.*, 149, 153, 154, 155, 166; Celts and, 103, 104, 105; China compared to, 143, 150–151, 164, 165–167; Christianity in, 153–154; chronology, 145; Constantine and, 157–158; Germanic peoples and, 146(*map*), 155, 273; glass industry in, 156 *and illus.*; mapmaking in, 110(*illus.*); Parthians and, 102, 146(*map*), 155; Principate in, 149–150; salt tax in, 365; technology, 154–155; third-century crisis in, 155, 157; trans-Saharan trade and, 233, 234; urban empire, 150–153 *and illus.*; medieval Europe and, 273

Romania (Dacia), 146(*map*), 148(*illus.*)

Romanization, 153

Roman law, 145, 149–150; *Corpus Juris Civilis*, 270, 278

Roman numerals, 182

Roman Republic (507–31 B.C.E.), 144–149; Carthage and, 78; chronology, 145; expansion of, 147–148; failure of, 148–149; patron-client relations in, 145; slavery in, 149; women in, 145, 147

Rome (city), 150–151, 166. *See also* Papacy; wine in, 134, 135; founding of, 144; grain importation by, 149; housing in, 151; Constantinople compared to, 270; pilgrimage to, 285; Jews in, 346; St. Peter's Basilica, 354

Romulus (Rome), 144

Rouissillion, Berthe de, 275(*illus.*)

Rule of Benedict, 279, 280

Ruling class. *See* Aristocracy; Elite class

Rural societies (rural areas). *See also* Farmers; Peasants; Villages; in Mesopotamia, 31; in Greece, 124; in Roman Empire, 152, 157; Mesoamerican, 196; late medieval Europe, 339–343; Vietnamese, 336

Russia: Kievan, 281–283; chronology (1221–1505), 315; Mongols and, 314, 315, 317(*map*), 324–325, 337 (*See also* Golden Horde khanate)

Russian language, 324

Russian Orthodox Church, 270, 281–282, 288, 324, 325

Saba (Sheba), 69

Sabbath, 71

Sacrifice. *See also* Human sacrifice; Mesopotamian, 34, 35; animal, 35, 70, 88, 89, 109; Persian, 116; Greek, 126, 127(*illus.*); Indian, 173, 175; Roman, 147

Sagres, 395

Sahara region, 362. *See also* Trans-Saharan trade and caravan routes; rock art in, 4(*illus.*), 5, 231, 232(*illus.*), 236; climate changes in, 40–41, 236; pastoralism in, 19, 231–232, 362; Tuareg of, 232, 234(*illus.*)

Sahel region, in Africa, 233(*map*), 235; herders of, 232(*illus.*); salt trade in, 234, 252

Sailing (seafaring). *See also* Navigation; Ships and shipping; Indian Ocean maritime system and, 372–373 *and illus.*; lateen sails, 229, 373 *and illus.*, 395, 398 *and illus.*; Polynesian, 391

Saint George of the Mine (Elmina), 400

Saint Peter's Basilica, 354

Salah-al-Din (Saladin), 255–256, 287

Salt (salt trade), 196, 365 *and illus.*; trans-Saharan, 234, 252, 365, 368

Salvation, paths to: in Zoroastrianism, 119; in Buddhism, 173, 329

Samanid dynasty (Iran), 252, 254

Samaria, 70

Samarkand, 223, 321, 322; observatory in, 324; tomb of Timur in, 323(*illus.*)

Samarra, 252

Samoa, 391, 392(*map*)

Samurai (Japanese warrior), 307

Sanchi, Great Stupa at, 174(*illus.*)

San Lorenzo, 194, 196

Sanskrit language, 180, 182, 292, 377; writings (texts), 173, 291

Santa Maria (ship), 398

Santiago de Compostela, 285

São Tomé, 396, 400

Saqqara, 41

Sarai (Old Sarai), 320, 324, 325, 327

Sardinia, 76 *and map*, 78, 148

Sargon (Akkad), 32

Sasanid Empire (Iran), 243, 244–246, 258; politics and society, 244; religions and, 245–246, 264; shahs (kings), 244 *and illus.*, 246, 250, 251, 263

Satavahana dynasty (India), 180

Sati (widow burning), 183, 378

Satraps, in Persia, 117

Saul (Israel), 69

Savanna, in sub-Saharan Africa, 235

Scandinavia, 285. *See also* Denmark; Finland; Norway; Sweden; Christian morality in, 279; Vikings, 272, 274

Schism, in Christianity, 269, 355

Schliemann, Heinrich, 60

Scholasticism, 351

Schools and scholars. *See also* Academies; Assyrian, 66–67; Athenian, 132; in Alexandria, 138; Confucian, in China, 94, 158, 161–162, 163; Islamic, 254, 257, 262, 327, 351, 377; Korean, 333, 334; legal, in Italy, 351; Jewish, 351

Science(s). *See also* Astronomy; Mathematics; chemistry, 45, 262; Chinese, 164; Islamic, 258, 262 *and illus.*, 322–324

Scotland (Scots), 105, 355

Scribes, 122; Mesopotamian, 34, 118; ancient Egyptian, 42; Assyrian, 64; Israelite, 71; Phoenician, 74; Maya, 192(*illus.*), 203, 214; in Islam, 260; Christian monks, 280

Script. *See also* Writing (written language); Egyptian, 42; Mycenaean, 61, 63; Phoenician, 67; Japanese women and, 307; Arabic, 377

Scythians, 99(*map*), 116; felt cloth, 75(*illus.*); gold ornaments, 100(*illus.*), 225(*illus.*); Herodotus on, 100–101, 225; ironworking by, 226

Seal stones: Mesopotamian, 33(*illus.*); Indus Valley, 48, 49

Seclusion and veiling, of women, 259 *and illus.*, 260, 269

Seine River, watermills on, 342

Sei Shonagon, 307

Seleucid kingdom, 136, 137(*map*)

Seljuk Turks, 323; Byzantines and, 268, 286; Crusades and, 254, 255

Semites: Hyksos, 57; polytheism of, 246–247; Sumerians and, 30, 34

Senate: Carthage, 77, 78; Rome, 144, 149

Senegal, 252

Sennacherib, palace of, 66(*illus.*)

Serbia, patriarchate of, 326

Serfs (serfdom), 273–274. *See also* Peasants; freedom for, 284, 339, 341–342

Seville (Spain), 253, 357

Sex and sexuality: Stone Age, 14; prostitution, 27; bisexuality, in Greece, 133; male homosexuality, in Islam, 260–261

Shaft graves, at Mycenae, 60, 61

Shahs, Sasanid Iran, 244 *and illus.*, 246, 250, 251, 263

Shaitans and *jinns*, 248

Shakas, 179–180

Shamans (shamanism): Olmec, 195; Maya, 203; Japanese, 305; Korean, 304; Mongol, 314, 320

Shamash (sun-god), 33(*illus.*)

Shams al-Din, Sayyid Ali, 327

Shangdu (Xanadu), 327

Shang period (China), 85–88, 87(*map*); bronze in, 85, 86(*illus.*), 87; oracle bones in, 85–86, 88, 89(*illus.*)

Shang (Qin), 95

Shari'a (Islamic law), 257, 259

Shawabti figurines, 46, 98

Sheba, Israelite trade with, 69, 375

Sheep, 68, 103, 246, 342. *See also* Wool trade; and goats, 19, 23, 24, 29, 98, 108, 109, 122, 236

Shifting cultivation. *See* Swidden agriculture

Shi Huangdi (China), 158–159; tomb of, 159, 161(*illus.*)

Shi'ite Islam, 249–250, 251; Buyid dynasty and, 252, 254; rivalry with Sunnis, 250, 252, 254, 255, 257, 321; Assassin sect of, 322

Shinto, in Japan, 306

Ships and shipping (merchant marine). *See also* Navigation; Navy; Pirates; Sailing; Egyptian, 41(*illus.*); Late Bronze Age, 56(*illus.*); Carthaginian, 77; Celtic, 104; Greek, 122; Indian Ocean trade, 229–230, 372–373 *and illus.*; lateen sails for, 229, 373 *and illus.*, 395, 398 *and illus.*; Viking, 272, 392; Mediterranean, 62, 273; cannon on, 389, 395; Chinese (junks), 299, 373, 388–390 *and illus.*; European trading cities and, 345; galleys, 345, 395; Indian (dhows), 222(*illus.*), 373 *and illus.*, 388, 403, 404; Portuguese (caravels), 395, 398 *and illus.*, 402–403; Portuguese taxation of, 405

Shiva (god), 175–176 *and illus.*

Shotoku (Japan), 296–297, 306

Shrines: at Çatal Hüyük, 23; Mesopotamian, 35; Israelite, 69; in China, 164; Hindu, 177; Buddhist, in India, 174(*illus.*), 183(*illus.*); Islamic, 247; Christian, in Europe, 285, 352

Shudras, 172, 182

Siam. *See* Thailand

Siberia: land bridge from, 10; steppe nomads of, 75(*illus.*), 99(*map*); burial mounds in, 101

Sicily, 76 *and map*, 124, 144, 346, 351; Rome and, 148; Crusades and, 286(*map*); Normans in, 272, 285

Siddhartha Gautama (Buddha), 174, 175(*illus.*)

Sidon, 74

Siege weapons and tactics. *See also* Fortifications; Weapons and military technology; Mesopotamian, 39; Assyrian, 65; Roman, 154; catapults, 134, 316, 334; Khitan, 298; Mongol, 316

Sierra Leone, Portuguese in, 395(*illus.*), 396

Sijilmasa, 252

Silk Road, 160(*map*), 223; origins and operations of, 161; Buddhism and, 164, 226(*map*), 238; chronology (247 B.C.E.–400 C.E.), 225; cities on, 252; nomadic peoples and, 185, 187; impact of, 226–227; Mesopotamia and, 244; Mongol diversion of, 256, 313, 327

Silk (silk industry and trade): Rome-China trade, 142(*illus.*); Chinese, 85, 163(*illus.*), 390; Southeast Asia trade and, 187; Mongol nobles and, 318–319

Silla (Korea), 305

Silphium, 112(*illus.*), 113

Silver, 23; Celtic, 105(*illus.*); from Anatolia, 56, 58; as medium of exchange, 66; Sasanid, 244(*illus.*); coins, 125, 251, 285; in Ming China, 329; in Mongolian Empire, 324, 325; Inka, 409

Sima Qian, 101, 161, 164

Simony, 276

Sind, 250

Sinhalese, in Sri Lanka, 364

Sino-Tibetan languages, 22

Sipán, Peru, Moche tomb at, 212 *and illus.*

Skin color, 10, 43; in India, 171–172

Sky gods, 21, 86, 126, 147, 173, 314

Slash-and-burn agriculture. *See* Swidden (shifting) cultivation

Slave soldiery, 358; Mamluk, 256, 378

Slaves (slavery): in Mesopotamia, 33; Israelite, 68; prisoners of war, 65, 86, 118, 149, 261, 314, 358; in Greece, 126, 129; in

Roman Republic and Empire, 149; Islamic, 259, 261; Aztec, 381; Varangian trade in, 281; Mongol, 314; in India, 378; sugar plantations, 346, 396, 400

Slave trade, African, 368, 378, 394; Portuguese and, 396, 400, 401, 402, 403

Slavic languages, 281, 324

Slavs (Slavic peoples), 268, 288; in Kievan Russia, 281–282 *and map*, 283; Mongols and, 325; Orthodox Christianity and, 270, 281–282, 283

Smallpox, 320, 406, 408

Small traditions, 235, 240; Islam and, 256, 264

Social classes (social hierarchy). *See also* Aristocracy; Elite class; Middle class; Peasants; Slaves (slavery); Mesopotamian, 33, 50; Egyptian, 43; Persian, 116; Athenian, 129; Andean peoples, 211; Indian, 172–173, 183, 390; African, 236; head coverings and, 263

Society (social conditions). *See also* Social classes; *and specific societies and social issues*; Stone Age, 14; Mesopotamian, 33–34; Assyrian, 65–66; Roman, 145, 150–151; imperial China, 91, 162–163, 300–304; Anasazi, 206; Sasanid Iran, 244; medieval Europe, 273–275; Byzantine Empire, 269–270; Kievan Russia, 283; spread of Islam and, 377–379

Socrates, 131, 132

Soga clan (Japan), 305–306, 307

Sogdiana, 223

Soil (loess), 84

Solomon (Israel), 69, 70 *and illus.*, 74; Sheba and, 69, 375

Solon (Athens), 128–129

Somalia (Horn of Africa), 69, 329; Islam in, 377

Song Empire (China), 291, 298–304, 332; cities, 290(*illus.*); economy and society in, 300–304, 309; industries of, 299–300; Korea and, 305; Liao and Jin challenge to, 298–299, 300(*map*); neo-Confucianism in, 300, 301; Southern Song, 299, 300(*map*); Vietnam (Annam) and, 308, 336; women in, 303–304 *and illus.*

Songhai Empire, 378

Soninke people, 252

Son of Heaven. *See* Mandate of Heaven

Sophists, 131

Sorghum (grain), 17, 18(*map*), 235, 236, 363

South America. *See also* Andean region; agriculture in, 18(*map*); Amerindian voyages from, 392, 393(*map*); migration to, 9(*map*), 10; Columbus in, 398; Polynesian voyagers in, 391; trade with Mesoamerica, 393

South Arabia. *See* Yemen (south Arabia)

South Asia, chronology (1206–1500), 363

South Asia, empires in. *See* Delhi Sultanate (India); Gupta India; Mauryan Empire

South China Sea, 227, 373, 376, 388

Southeast Asia, 186–190. *See also* Burma; East Indies; Thailand; Vietnam; migration to, 10; animal domestication in, 18(*map*); rice cultivation in, 17, 18(*map*), 186, 363; early civilizations, 186–188; geography and climate of, 186; Indian Ocean trade and, 227, 231, 376; spice trade in, 187; chronology (2000 B.C.E.–1025 C.E.), 171; Srivijaya, 187(*map*), 188–190; Funan and, 187(*map*), 188; Hindu-Buddhist culture in, 187, 188; pig domestication in, 237, 238; chronology (1283–1500), 315; fishing in, 362; Angkor (Cambodia), 364; migration from, 391, 392(*map*); Islam in, 377, 378; trade networks from, 388

Southern Africa, cave art in, 12

Southern Song (China), 299, 300(*map*); Mongols and, 314, 317(*map*), 327

Southwestern desert cultures, North America, 206–207, 208(*illus.*)

Spain (Spanish Empire): cave paintings in, 12; Celtiberian culture of, 102, 105; Phoenician colonies in, 76 *and map*; Carthage and, 78; Berbers in, 250, 253; Rome and, 148, 155(*illus.*); agriculture in, 253; Jews in, 253; women in, 259(*illus.*);

Spain (Spanish Empire) (*Continued*) Ummayyad Caliphate in, 253 *and map*, 271; Viking raids on, 272; Visigoths in, 271; pilgrimage in, 285; Muslims in, 253–254 *and map*, 256(*illus.*), 259(*illus.*), 287, 323, 394; windmills in, 342; Jews expelled from, 346, 358; Muslims driven from, 357; unification of, 358, 394; Philippines in, 387, 399; Aztecs and, 381, 406–408; conquistadors and, 406–409; Inkas and, 408–409

Spanish maritime expeditions, 387, 396–399 *and map*; Columbus, 396, 397(*map*), 398, 399; Magellan, 386(*illus.*), 387, 397(*map*), 399

Sparta (Spartans), 128, 129, 130; in Hellenistic Age, 137; Peloponnesian War and, 133; women of, 132

Speech, development of, 7, 8. *See also* Language(s)

Spice Islands (Moluccas), 376

Spice trade, 187, 284, 345, 388, 399; Indian Ocean trade and, 230, 375, 376; pepper, 400, 405; Portuguese and, 405

Spinning wheels: in England, 346; in Korea, 334; in India, 379

Spring and Autumn Annals, 90, 91

Sri Lanka (Ceylon), 388; Buddhism in, 238, 239; as Indian tributary state, 372; irrigation in, 364; Sinhalese in, 364

Srivijaya, 187(*map*), 188–190

Standardization, 32, 47; in Qin China, 158

Steel: Chinese, 90, 299; Japanese, 331, 335; for swords, 335, 406, 407

Stele (stone monuments), 193; of Aksum, 239(*illus.*)

Steppes (prairies), 328; Eurasian, 98–102; sub-Saharan, 235

Stirrups, 227, 274, 292, 295(*illus.*)

Stone Age, 11–16. *See also* Ice Age; Neolithic Age; cave paintings, 11, 12–13 *and illus.*, 15; clothing, 15, 16(*illus.*); food gathering and tools, 11–14. 15, 16(*illus.*); gender roles and social life in, 14–15; hearths and culture in, 15

Stone construction: megaliths, 21, 22(*illus.*), 236; Egyptian

pyramids, 41, 42 *and illus.*; Buddhist temples, 189(*illus.*), 190, 222(*illus.*); by Andean peoples, 213 *and illus.*; Maya, 201(*illus.*), 202(*illus.*); stele, 193, 239(*illus.*); in Russia, 325(*illus.*); in France, 343; Gothic cathedrals, 347 *and illus.*, 349; in Great Zimbabwe, 375(*illus.*); Inka, 383

Stone heads, Olmec, 196, 197(*illus.*)

Stonehenge, 21

Stone tools, 11, 14 *and illus.*, 16, 17; at Çatal Hüyük, 23; in Mesopotamia, 37; in ancient Egypt, 41; obsidian, in Mesoamerica, 196, 204

Strabo, 89

Strasbourg, 350; burning of Jews in, 349; cathedral of, 349

Stupas (Buddhist shrines), 174(*illus.*)

Sub-Saharan Africa, 235–237; farming in, 17, 363; Egypt and, 43, 57; Carthage and, 78; Nubia and, 95, 98; cattle in, 235; trans-Saharan trade and, 234; Bantu migrations, 233(*map*), 236–237, 240; cultural unity in, 235–236, 240; geography of, 235; ironworking in, 236–237; Islam and literacy in, 377; Islamic Empires in, 366–368; gold trade and, 394

Sudan, 363; coppersmiths of, 366 *and illus.*; Islamic empires in, 366–368; mosques in, 377

Sufis (Sufism), 262, 263, 264, 377

Sugar cane, 258, 363

Sugar plantations, slave labor on, 346, 396, 400

Sui Empire (China), 291–292

Suiko (Japan), 305–306

Sultan. *See also* Delhi Sultanate; Ottoman Empire; of mamluk Turks, 254

Sumatra, 329; Buddhism in, 239; pirates in, 376; Srivijaya, 187(*map*), 188–190

Sumerian language, 32

Sumerians. *See also* Mesopotamia; gods of, 34; kings of, 32; Semites and, 30, 34

Summa Theologica (Aquinas), 348, 351

Sunda Strait, 388

Sundiata (Mali), 367–368

Sun-gods: Shamash, 33(*illus.*); Re, 44; Aten, 57; Mithra, 154; Aztec (Huitzilopochtli), 382; Inka, 383

Sunni-Shi'ite rivalry, in Islam, 250, 252, 254, 255, 256, 257; Il-khans and, 321

Sunzi, 90

Supernatural, the. *See also* Magic; Religion(s); Shamans; Egyptian belief in, 50; Celtic belief in, 105; in Mesoamerican cultures, 195, 202; Mongol, 314; spread of disease and, 408

Susa, 118

Su Song, clock of, 301(*illus.*)

Swahili Coast, 367(*map*), 377, 390; Indian Ocean trade and, 373, 374, 375; slave trade in, 378; China trade and, 390; Portuguese and, 404

Swahili language, 374

Sweden (Swedes): ironworking in, 276; Varangians, 272, 281

Sweet potatoes, 194, 331, 391, 406. *See also* Yams

Swidden (shifting) cultivation, 17; in Southeast Asia, 186; Maya, 201; in Kievan Russia, 283; in Japan, 307; in tropical lands, 363

Swords: Greek, 124; Germanic, 276; Japanese, 312(*illus.*), 330, 335, 336; Mongol, 316; Indian, 366; conquistador, 406, 409

Sylvester II, Pope, 182

Synposion, in Greece, 135

Synagogue, 71

Syria: Assyria and, 62; early cities in, 31, 56; Seleucids in, 136, 137(*map*); Seljuks in, 254; Islamic conquest of, 249, 250, 255, 268, 269; defeat of Mongols in, 256; Crusaders in, 286; caravan trade and, 246; Umayyad caliph in, 271

Syria-Palestine region, 62, 68(*map*). *See also* Canaan; Israel; Phoenicia (Phoenicians); Aramaeans in, 71, 99; Assyrian invasions of, 64, 77; chronology (1800–515 B.C.E.), 55; Egypt and, 57, 58, 136; Christianity in, 153

Tabriz, 327

Tahert, 252

Taika reform, in Japan, 305

Takrur (Sudan), 367

Talas River, Battle of (751), 292, 294(*map*), 297

The Tale of Genji, 306, 307

The Tale of the Heike, 307

Tamerlane. *See* Timur

Tamil kingdoms, 180–181

Tang Empire (China), 292–298, 305; Buddhism and, 291, 292–293, 294, 295–296, 304; cities in, 292; as cosmopolitan era, 293; East Asia and, 304; end of, 297–298; law code, 296; pottery, 227(*illus.*), 297(*illus.*); powerful women in, 294–295; upheavals and repression in, 293–295; Vietnam and, 307–308, 336

Tanggut, 298; Mongols and, 314, 327

Tanit (goddess), 78

Tanning. *See* Leatherworking

Tanzania, early humans in, 7, 10(*illus.*)

Taro (root vegetable), 363, 391

Tarquinus Superbus (Rome), 144

Tarragona, Roman aqueduct near, 155(*illus.*)

Taxation: ancient Egypt, 42, 57; Assyrian Empire, 64, 65; Israel, 69; early China, 91; Persian Empire, 117; Roman Empire, 148, 153, 155, 157; India, 179; Arab caliphate, 252; imperial China, 159, 295, 327, 328; Russia, 283, 325; English wool, 357; French monarchy, 357; on salt, 365; Delhi Sultanate, 369, 370, 371; Portuguese, 405

Tax farming: in Iran and Iraq, 255; in China, 303, 326, 328; Il-khanate, 321

Technology. *See also* Construction materials and techniques; Environment and technology; Manufactured goods; Metals (metallurgy); Ships and shipping; Weapons and military technology; of early humans, 7; Ice Age culture and, 11–16; defined, 35; in Mesopotamia, 35; in Roman Empire, 154–155; in China, 164, 330–331; Islamic, 258(*illus.*), 262 *and illus.*; in medieval Europe, 276 *and illus.*, 283–284, 341

Temples: Mesopotamian, 32, 34(*illus.*), 35; Egyptian, 44, 57, 58(*illus.*); Phoenician, 76; in

Jerusalem, 67, 69–70 *and illus.*, 71, 74; Nubian, 97 *and illus.*, 98; Greek, 125(*illus.*), 129, 131; Hindu, 168(*illus.*), 170, 176(*illus.*), 177, 183, 372(*illus.*); Buddhist, 189(*illus.*), 190, 222(*illus.*), 292, 306; Mesoamerican, 199 *and illus.*, 200, 202; Zoroastrian, 255(*illus.*); Kievan Russia, 281; Aztec, 382; Inka, 383

Temüjin, 313. *See also* Chinggis Khan

Ten Commandments, 69

Tenochtitlan, 380 *and map*, 381, 382, 383; Spanish conquest of, 407–408

Teotihuacan, 199–200, 204; pyramids in, 199 *and illus.*

Terracing: in Andes, 200, 209; in Mesoamerica, 201, 204

Terror: in Assyrian Empire, 65; Mongols and, 326

Teutonic Knights, 325–326, 340

Textiles (textile industry). *See also* Clothing; Cotton (cotton industry); Silk (silk industry and trade); Weaving; Wool trade; Scythian, 75(*illus.*); Tyrian purple, 74, 75, 270; in Islamic world, 256(*illus.*), 258; Andean, 198, 211, 382(*illus.*), 383; Flemish, 345 *and illus.*; in late medieval Europe, 347(*map*); Gujarati, 376; women's role in, 211, 346, 383

Thailand (Siam), 302, 376; Buddhism in, 239; Stupa in, 188(*illus.*)

Theater (drama): Greek, 131, 132; Gupta theater-state, 181; Srivijaya theater-state, 189; Japanese, 335(*illus.*)

Thebes (Egypt), 42, 44, 57, 58; Assyrian invasion and, 97

Theology, 351, 353. *See also* Religion(s); Monophysite, 246

Thera, 113; fresco from, 63(*illus.*)

Theravada Buddhism, 175, 239

Thesmophoria festival, 132

Third Dynasty of Ur, 32

Third Satire (Juvenal), 150–151

Thomas à Becket, 277–278, 352

Thomas Aquinas, 340; *Summa Theologica*, 348, 351

Thrace, 116–117

Three-field system, 340

Thucydides, 128

Tiamat, 36–37

Tian (Heaven), 88, 90

Tiberius (Rome), 156

Tiber River, 144

Tibet: Buddhism in, 239; China and, 293, 294(*map*)

Tibetan language, 293

Tiglathpileser III (Assyria), 64–65

Tigris and Euphrates Valley, 30(*map*), 48, 255. *See also* Iraq; floods in, 50; Mesopotamia and, 27, 28(*map*), 29, 56

Tikal, Great Plaza at, 201(*illus.*)

Timbuktu, 368; library in, 377; mosque in, 369(*illus.*)

Timekeeping. *See also* Calendars; clocks, 301(*illus.*), 350 *and illus.*; Indian concept of, 190

Timur (Tamerlane), 322, 326; Delhi and, 321, 323, 372; tomb of, 323(*illus.*)

Tin, 47, 56(*illus.*), 78, 104, 376; for bronze, 56, 59, 62

Tiwanaku, 211, 213–214 *and illus.*

Tlatelolco, 380 *and map*, 381

Tlaxcalans of Mexico, 406, 408

Tobacco, 406

Toledo (Spain), 253, 351, 357

Toltecs, 202(*illus.*), 204–205, 380; Maya and, 204(*map*), 205

Tombs. *See also* Burials (burial practices); Neolithic, 22(*illus.*); Egyptian, 41, 42–43, 45–46, 49; Celtic, 104; Chinese, 86, 87, 159, 161(*illus.*); Persian kings, 118; Moche, 212 *and illus.*; Aksumite kings, 239(*illus.*); Samanid, in Bukhara, 255(*illus.*)

Tonga, 391, 392(*map*)

Tools. *See* Iron industry; Stone tools; Technology

Tophets (Carthage), 78, 79(*illus.*)

Topiltzin (Toltec), 205

Tordesillas, Treaty of (1494), 397(*map*), 398–399

Tours, Battle of (732), 272

Towns. *See* Cities and towns (urban centers)

Trade (commerce). *See also* Barter; Merchants (traders); Ships and shipping; Spice trade; Trade routes; *and specific commodities*; Çatal Hüyük, 23; Mesopotamian, 32, 33; beeswax, 38; Egyptian, 42, 43, 58–59; Indus Valley, 47, 48–49; Nubian, 96; Celtic Europe, 104;

Trade (commerce) (*Continued*)
Middle East, 54(*map*); Minoan
and Mycenaean, 53, 60, 62, 63;
Assyrian Empire, 64; Israelite,
67, 69; Phoenician, 74, 76 *and
map*; Carthaginian, 77–78;
coinage and, 125; Greek, 125,
129, 131; Hellenistic Age, 134;
Roman Empire, 152, 157; Indian,
180, 184–185; Islamic world,
258; Srivijaya and, 189, 190; in
Andean region, 197–198, 213;
Mesoamerican, 194, 196, 381;
Northern Amerindian, 208, 209;
Kievan Russia, 281, 282, 283;
spread of ideas and, 240; medieval
Europe, 283, 284–285, 343–346
and map; and communication
routes, in Asia, 226(*map*);
imperial China, 293, 302, 303,
329; Mongolian Empire, 318–319,
327–328; Delhi Sultanate, 372;
Italian city-states, 343, 355, 394;
Japanese, 336; Zimbabwe, 375
Trade monopoly. *See* Monopolies,
trading
Trade routes, 221. *See also* Caravan
trade and routes; Exploration
(expeditions); Indian Ocean
trade (maritime system); Silk
Road; Trade; Trans-Saharan
trade and caravan routes; Aegean
Sea, 62; Late Bronze Age, 58, 59;
Assyrian control of, 55; China
and, 160(*map*), 161; Meroë and,
98; India and, 181; Southeast Asia
and, 187, 188–189, 388; Asian,
226(*map*); Islamic World
(to 1500), 374(*map*)
Trading entrepôts: 324, 390–391, 405
Traditions. *See also* Customs and
traditions; great and small, 235,
240, 256
Trajan (Rome), 146(*map*); column
of, 148(*illus.*)
Tran Hung Dao, 315
Transportation. *See also* Canals;
Roads; Ships and shipping; in
Mesopotamia, 37; in Late Bronze
Age, 59; llamas used for, in
Andean region, 198
Trans-Saharan trade and caravan
routes, 231–234, 233(*map*);
chronology (500 B.C.E.–300 C.E.),
225; African gold in, 253, 358,
366, 396; camels in, 232–233,

234(*illus.*), 365 *and illus.*, 368;
early Saharan cultures and,
231–233 *and illus.*; salt trade, 234,
252, 365 *and illus.*; Tuareg and,
232, 234(*illus.*), 362; Mali and,
367(*map*), 368; slaves in, 358;
Portuguese and, 358, 396
Travel (travelers). *See also*
Exploration (expeditions);
Pilgrimages; Roads; Ships
and shipping; Trade routes;
Transportation; in ancient Egypt,
57; Romans in China, 143; Silk
Road, 223; Mongol passport,
316(*illus.*); Muslim (*See* Ibn
Battuta; Zheng He); Marco Polo,
317(*map*), 319, 373, 375
Tres Zapotes (Olmec center), 194
Tribes. *See also* Clans; Israelite, 69
Tribute systems. Egyptian, 57;
Assyrian Empire, 64, 65, 71,
74(*illus.*), 77; Persian, 117;
Cahokian elite and, 208; Andean
peoples, 215; Chinese, 292,
294(*map*), 299, 329; Vietnam, 308;
Japan, 334; Mongol, 314, 315, 329,
336; South Asian, 372; Aztec, 381
Tripoli, 255
Triremes (ships), 130, 131(*illus.*)
Tropical Africa and Asia, 361–366.
See also Sub-Saharan Africa;
South Asia; Southeast Asia;
environment, 362; human
ecosystems, 362–363; mineral
resources, 364–366; social and
cultural change, 377–379; water
systems and irrigation, 363–364
Tropical rain forest, 362; in sub-
Saharan Africa, 235; in Southeast
Asia, 363
Troubadours (poets), 287
Troy, siege of, 62
Truce of God, 285
Trung sisters (Vietnam), 308
Tsars, of Russia, 325
Tuareg people, 232, 234(*illus.*), 362,
368
Tughluq, Sultan, 378
Tughril Beg (Seljuk), 254
Tula (Toltec capital), 202(*illus.*),
204–205 *and map*, 216
Tunisia, 53, 77, 78. *See also* Carthage
(Carthaginians); Arab conquest
of, 250, 268; camel saddles in,
234; farmers in, 284; Fatimid
Caliphate in, 252, 253, 261

Turkey. *See* Anatolia (modern
Turkey)
Turkic languages, 101
Turkic (Turkish) peoples, 260–261.
See also Xiongnu; ironworking
by, 226; Khazar, 281; Uighurs,
293, 306, 323; of Central Asia,
252; Mamluks, 252, 254, 256;
migration of, 281; Keraits, 313;
Seljuks, 254, 255, 268, 286;
Mongols and, 315, 328–329; in
Delhi Sultanate, 368
Turkmenistan, 250
Turner, M. W., 52(*illus.*)
Turquoise, 206
Tutankhamen (Egypt), 58
Tyler, Wat, 341
Tyrants: in Greece, 126, 129; in
Korea, 333
Tyre, 69, 80; Assyria and, 77, 79;
Carthage and, 53; colonies of, 76
and map; purple cloth of, 74, 75,
270

Ugarit, 56, 58, 62
Uighur language, 293, 306
Uighurs, 323
Ukraine, 281; Scythians in, 100 *and
illus.*, 226; Mongol conquest of,
324, 325
Ulama, 254, 262
Ulugh Beg, 323–324
Umar, Caliph, 250
Umayyad Caliphate, 249, 251,
253(*map*), 271; Al-Andalus and,
253–254, 285
Umma, 252, 254, 257, 261, 264;
formation of, 248–249
Universities and colleges: in
Athens, 138; in Han China, 161; in
India, 183; Islamic madrasas, 262,
351; European Renaissance and,
350–351
Untouchables, in India, 172
Upanishads, 0, 174
Upper class. *See* Aristocracy; Elite
class
Ur, Third Dynasty of, 32
Urartu, 79, 115. *See also* Armenia
Urban II, Pope, 286
Urbanization. *See also* Cities
and towns (urban centers);
in Americas, 199; in Islamic
civilization, 257–258
Urdu language, 377
Uruk, 35

Usury (interest), 347
Uthman, Caliph, 249
Uzbekistan, 180

Vaishyas, 172
Van Eyck, Jan, 354
Varangians (Swedes), 272, 281
Varnas (castes), in India, 172–173, 183, 390
Vassals and lords, in medieval Europe, 274, 355
Vatican. *See also* Papacy (popes); library in, 353; Sistine chapel in, 354
Vatsyayana, 184
Vedic Age, in India, 171–173
Vedism (Vedic religion), 175, 183
Venice (Venetians), 284, 405; colonies of, 345; printing in, 353; sack of Constantinople and, 286, 345; sea power of, 344(*map*), 346
Venus (goddess), 13
Verdun, Treaty of (843), 272
Vertical exchange, in Andes, 210, 382
Vespucci, Amerigo, 310(*illus.*), 398
Vesuvius, eruption of, 152(*illus.*)
Victoria (ship), 387
Vietnam: Annam, 308; China and, 161, 292, 302, 307–308, 329, 330(*map*), 336; Funan, 187(*map*), 188; emergence of (1200–1500), 336; Mongol invasion of, 315–316, 336; women of, 308
Vijayanagar Empire, 369(*map*), 372
Vikings, 274; Atlantic exploration by, 272, 392, 413; runestone, 273(*illus.*)
Villages: Neolithic, 22; Mesopotamian, 31; Egyptian, 40, 43; Chinese, 87, 328; Nubian, 96; Greek, 124; Indian, 181, 183, 363; in Southeast Asia, 187; Bantu, 237; Arab, 246; medieval Europe, 273; in tropics, 384
Vinland, Vikings in, 272, 392
Vishnu (god), 175–176, 177(*illus.*), 182
Visigoths, in Spain, 271
Vladimir I (Russia), 281, 282
Volcanic eruptions, 63(*illus.*), 186; Vesuvius 152(*illus.*); in Mesoamerica, 194, 200
Volga River, 281, 282; Golden Horde and, 314, 320, 324

Wac-Chanil-Ahau (Maya), 193, 203
Waldseemüller, Martin, 310
Wales (Welsh), 355; Celts in, 104, 105
Wall murals (frescoes): Çatal Hüyük, 23; Egyptian, 59(*illus.*); Assyrian relief, 66(*illus.*); Minoan, 60, 63(*illus.*); Mycenaean, 61; Nubian, 82(*illus.*); Roman, 151; Indian cave shrines, 183 *and illus.*; Teotihucan, 200; Moche, 211; Central Asian, 227; Italian Renaissance, 354
Walls, city. *See* Fortifications (walls)
Wang Mang (China), 164–165
Wari, 211, 214–215
War prisoners. *See* Slaves, prisoners of war
Warring States Period (China), 92, 95, 101
Warrior elite: early Chinese, 86; steppe nomads, 99; Celtic, 103, 104, 105(*illus.*); Iranian, 116, 117; Indian, 169, 171, 186; Mesoamerican, 202; Moche, 211 *and illus.*, 212; Arab, 251; Turkic mamluks, 252, 254; Viking, 272; European knights, 273, 274, 285, 287(*illus.*); Japanese, 307, 312(*illus.*), 335 *and illus.*; Mongol, 314, 335; Aztec, 381
Warships. *See* Navy (warships)
War (warfare). *See also* Armed forces; Chariot warfare; Civil wars; Military; Navy; Warriors; Weapons and military technology; *and specific wars*; in early China, 90, 95; Celtic, 103; among Greek city-states, 133; Greek-Persian, 129–130, 134; Roman expansion and, 147–148; Rome-Carthage, 78, 148; Chavín, 198; Maya, 202; Andean, 215; in medieval Europe, 274; Crusades, 255, 256, 285–287; Mongol, 314; Hundred Years', 355–357 *and map*; Aztec, 381; in Polynesia, 391
Water buffalo, domestication of, 19
Water control systems. *See also* Canals; Dams; Irrigation; Water wheels; in Islam, 258(*illus.*); Roman aqueducts, 154, 155(*illus.*); in China, 301(*illus.*), 302; in tropics, 363–364; watermills, 164, 342–343

Water Margin, 331, 332
Waterways. *See* Canals; Rivers
Water wheels: in China, 300, 301(*illus.*), 328; in Japan, 335; in Korea, 334
Wax, for candles, 38
Weapons and military technology. *See also* Armor; Bows and arrows; Cannon; Chariot warfare; Fortifications; Gunpowder; Swords; War (warfare); Assyrian, 65; Greek hoplite, 124, 134, 147; siege, 39, 65, 134, 154, 298; Islamic chemistry and, 262; Silk Road trade and, 227; stirrups, 227, 274, 292, 295(*illus.*); catapults, 134, 316, 334; European crusader, 287, 288; explosives, 300, 331, 332, 334; Chinese, 292, 295(*illus.*), 300, 331, 332 *and illus.*; Japanese, 312(*illus.*), 330, 335; Korean, 331, 333; Mongol, 316, 334; guns (firearms), 332, 355, 357, 358, 400–401, 407; in Hundred Years' War, 355; Portuguese, 404; conquistador, 406, 408, 409
Weather. *See* Climate and weather
Weaving (textiles). *See also* Textiles (textile industry); women and, 75, 203, 211, 346; of Anasazi, 206; of Andean peoples, 211, 383; in China, 331; in medieval Europe, 345(*illus.*), 346; looms, 345(*illus.*)
Wei River Valley, 88, 95, 158; Chang'an in, 162
Wen (China), 88
West Africa. *See also* Mali; *and specific countries*; Yoruba people of, 5, 366(*illus.*); farming in, 17; griot in, 218; Saharan culture patterns in, 232; Islamic Empires in, 366–368; salt trade in, 365(*illus.*); encounters with Europe, 399–401; gold in, 366; ironworking in, 364; coppersmiths of, 366 *and illus.*; market women of, 379; Portuguese in, 395(*illus.*), 396, 399; slave trade in, 396
Western Asia, 57. *See also* Middle East; chronology (2000 B.C.E.– 612 B.C.E.), 55; Late Bronze Age in, 54–59; Persian Empire and, 114(*map*), 116, 140; Greek culture in, 136
Western Eurasia, Mongol Empire and, 324–326

Western Europe. *See also* Latin West (Europe 1200–1500); Medieval Europe (300–1200); Roman Empire; Celts in, 102–105; Byzantium and, 267–268; cities and trade in, 284–285; chronology (711–1095), 269; revival of (1000–1200), 283–285; Crusades and, 285–287; technology in, 283–284

Western Hemisphere. *See* Americas (New World)

Westernization, headcovering and, 263

Western Sudan (Mali), 366–368. *See also* Mali

Whale oil, for lamps, 38

Wheat, 18(*map*), 24, 108, 234, 363; in China, 84, 87(*map*), 299, 331; emmer, 17, 23

White Horde (khanate), 324

Widow-burning (*sati*), in India, 183, 378

William of Rubruck, 318

William the Conquerer, 266(*illus.*), 272, 275

William the Pious, 280

Windmills, in Europe, 342–343

Winds. *See also* Monsoons; *kamikaze*, in Japan, 335; in Indian Ocean, 364(*map*); westerlies, in Atlantic, 396, 398

Wine, 134–135 *and illus.*, 149

Women. *See also* Family; Fertility cults; Gender roles; Marriage; Men; Polygamy; Ice Age, 14; Neolithic Age, 17; at Çatal Hüyük, 21; Mesopotamian, 34; Egyptian, 44, 50; Cretan, 60; Nubian queens, 98; Celtic, 104; Israelite, 70; Persian, 117, 118; Greek, 132–133 *and illus.*, 135; Roman, 145, 147; imperial China, 160, 162; Indian, 173, 176; widow burning (*sati*), 183, 378; Maya elite, 193, 202–203; Anasazi, 206; Central Asian nomads, 225; Indian Ocean trade and, 231; Iranian dancing girls, 223; as concubines, 94, 259, 295, 378; as nuns, 280, 295; seclusion and veiling of, 259 *and illus.*, 260, 263;

weaving by, 75, 203, 211, 346; in medieval Europe, 275 *and illus.*, 340 *and illus.*, 345(*illus.*), 346; Islamic, 34, 259–260 *and illus.*, 378; in Byzantine Empire, 269; headcoverings for, 263; in Kievan Russia, 283; property rights of, 44, 259, 336; Vietnamese, 308, 336; Japanese, 305–306, 307; imperial China, 294–295, 297(*illus.*), 303–304 *and illus.*; Mongol, 314; as rulers, in Delhi Sultanate, 369–370

Wonhyo (Buddhist monk), 305

Woodblock printing: in Islamic lands, 262(*illus.*); in China, 301; in Korea, 305, 333–334; movable type, 301, 305, 353

Wool trade: Mycenaean Greek, 61; Andean peoples, 75, 198, 210, 382(*illus.*), 383; English, 285, 342, 346, 357; Flemish, 345

Workers. *See also* Labor; Peasants; Slaves; Persian Empire, 118

Works and Days (Hesiod), 138

Worldmaps. *See* Mapmaking (cartography)

Worms, Concordat of (1122), 277

Writing (written language). *See also* Literacy; Scribes; Mesopotamian (cuneiform), 2(*illus.*), 32, 35–36, 56; Egyptian (hieroglyphics), 42, 56, 98; Linear B tablets (Mycenaean), 61, 63; in Indus Valley, 48; Phoenician, 74, 122, 218; Sanskrit, 173, 291; Greek, 122–123; Chinese, 86, 158, 293, 306 *and illus.*; Maya, 193(*illus.*), 203, 214 *and illus.*; Olmec, 195; oral societies and, 218–219; in East Asia (400–1200), 306 *and illus.*; Cyrillic, 270, 282; Japanese, 306, 307; Korean (han'gul), 306, 334(*illus.*), 335

Wu (China), 88, 156, 160–161; Sima Qian and, 101, 161, 164

Wu Zhao (China), 294–295

"Xanadu" (Coleridge), 327

Xenophanes, 127

Xerxes (Persia), 114(*map*), 120–121, 130; Persepolis and, 118, 119(*illus.*)

Xia dynasty (China), 85

Xiongnu, 99(*map*), 101, 102, 160; Confederacy of, 159, 161, 162(*illus.*); gold belt buckle, 162(*illus.*)

Xuanzang, 229

Xunzi, 91

Yahweh (god), 67, 68–69, 70–71

Yam, 83. *See also* Nubia

Yamatai (Japan), 3–5

Yams (vegetable), 17, 18(*map*), 230, 235, 363, 391. *See also* Sweet potatoes

Yang Guifei, 295, 297

Yangzi River, 84, 291, 328

Yangzi River Valley, 84, 165, 292

Yazdigird III, Shah, 250

Yazid, 249

Yellow River, 27, 29(*map*), 81, 159; flooding of, 84, 164, 328

Yemen (south Arabia), 59, 69; camel saddles in, 234 *and illus.*; coins from, 230(*illus.*); Ethiopia and, 239, 240; myrrh from, 230; Aden in, 375, 378, 404, 405

Yin/yang concept, 94

Yi Songgye, 333

Yongle (China), 329, 330

Yoruba people, 5, 366(*illus.*)

Yosef (Jew), 375

Ypres, 285; weavers of, 345(*illus.*)

Yuan Empire (China), 315, 326–329. *See also* Khubilai, Great Khan; diet and illness in, 319; early Ming and, 328–329; fall of, 328–329; Korea and, 333; Vietnam and, 336

Yucatán, Maya of, 204(*map*), 205

Yuezhi, 101

Yurts (felt huts), 108(*illus.*), 225, 226

Zacharias, Pope, 278

Zagros Mountains, 54, 59, 114

Zaire River, 235

Zambezi River, 235; gold mines on, 366, 374

Zamorin of Calicut, 376

Zamzam, 247

Zarathushtra, 118. *See also* Zoroastrianism

Zebu cattle, 19

Zeila, 375, 378

Zen (Chan) Buddhism, 301, 333, 335

Zero, concept of, 181, 182, 203

Zeus (god), 126

Zhang Jian, 228

Zhang Zeduan, 290(*illus.*)

Zheng (China), 158

Zheng He, voyages of, 311, 329–330 *and map*, 376, 389–390 *and illus.*, 392(*map*), 398

Zhou period (China), 87(*map*), 88–95; Confucianism and Daoism in, 91–94; Greece compared, 140–141; Warring States Period, 92, 95, 101

Zhu Xi, 300

Zhu Yuanzhang, 328, 329

Ziggurat, 34(*illus.*), 35, 39

Zimbabwe, 374–375 *and illus.*; gold in, 374, 375

Zoroastrianism, 118–119, 140, 227, 239; Christianity and, 119, 245, 261; fire temple, 119, 255(*illus.*); good and evil in, 119, 246